CRIMINOLOGY
Power, crime, and criminal law

THE DORSEY SERIES IN SOCIOLOGY

Editor ROBIN M. WILLIAMS, JR. *Cornell University*

CRIMINOLOGY

Power, crime, and criminal law

JOHN F. GALLIHER, Ph.D.

and

JAMES L. McCARTNEY, Ph.D.

both of the
Department of Sociology
University of Missouri—Columbia

1977

THE DORSEY PRESS   Homewood, Illinois   60430
Irwin-Dorsey Limited   Georgetown, Ontario   L7G 4B3

First Printing, February 1977

ISBN 0-256-01942-8
Library of Congress Catalog Card No. 76–47733

Printed in the United States of America

To Jeanne
—J.F.G.

To Jean, Brian, and Carrie
—J.L.McC.

Preface

This text provides an alternative approach to the study of crime found in most criminology textbooks by developing an explicit ethical orientation. This ethical orientation lists what are taken to be fundamental human rights, to be used as a guide in the study of crime and criminal law. Most criminology textbooks give considerable coverage to description and analysis of various types of criminal behavior together with a largely unrelated section dealing with the various elements of the criminal justice system such as the police and courts. This textbook, in contrast, is mainly devoted to an analysis of the criminal justice system and discusses criminal behavior mainly as a political and cultural product created by powerful interest groups and their representatives: legislators, police, and judges.

The first chapter develops the ethical orientation and indicates how this influences the text's intellectual assumptions. The moral philosophy of this book hinges upon both the discussion of the Nuremberg trials and the lives and works of Mahatma Gandhi and Dr. Martin Luther King, Jr. The second chapter also includes the historical development of a series of what were initially new criminal laws including vagrancy laws, drug laws, national prohibition, and embezzlement laws. Chapter 3 reflects the historical development of criminology. The current theoretical state of criminology is assessed and important new directions for growth are explored emphasizing the study of the social bases of law and its administration.

Chapter 4 demonstrates how the American police are used by powerful interest groups and elites to control the behavior of other citizens, especially economic and racial minorities. Chapter 5 deals with U.S. courts including the bail system, American juries, defense attorneys including public defenders, psychiatrists, judges, and the trial process itself to demonstrate the specific ways in which all of these operate to the disadvantage of economic and racial minorities. Chapter 6 argues that if laws are written and administered to serve the interests of powerful groups, then obviously groups without power will appear most often in government arrest statistics. Other less class-biased methods of crime measurement are suggested.

Chapter 7 intentionally focuses on selected types of crime to illustrate the political and cultural process involved in creating a type of crime and how the interests of powerful groups are served by these definitions which they usually control. As a case in point, the usual definition of "violent crime" includes armed robbery but not conspiracy to design and manufacture automobiles that kill and maim occupants in low-speed crashes. Chapter 8 discusses alternative models for crime control including punishment and rehabilitation. Research indicating that the most severe punishment is usually reserved for economic and racial minorities will be reviewed. The seldom recognized coercive potential of rehabilitation then is discussed. This chapter criticizes from a humanist perspective our society's efforts at crime control. Each chapter is followed by two selections which support and elaborate the argument contained in the chapter.

The authors are very grateful for the help of Jeanne Zuk Galliher in typing and editing several versions of each chapter and for the intelligent guidance of Robin Williams. David Peterson, Stephen Norland, Drew Humphries, and Paul Friday also contributed many useful suggestions in their reviews of the manuscript.

January 1977   JOHN F. GALLIHER
                                  JAMES L. McCARTNEY

Contents

xi

Assumptions regarding the nature of people. Criminological research methods: *Data sources.*

Chapter 4   The administration of justice: The police   175

The delivery of police services. Explanations of police behavior: *Psychological perspective. Demands of the immediate situation. Role conflict. Subcultural approach. Departmental characteristics approach. Sociocultural approach.* Empirical evidence for the various conceptual models: *Dirty work at home and abroad.*

Chapter 5   The administration of justice: The courts   233

Court processes. Social roles in the administration of justice: *Operation of the bailbondsman. Regulation and corruption of bailbondsmen. The courts and the bail system. Alternatives to the bail system.* Criminal lawyers: *Social class background. Legal counsel for indigent defendants. Private defense attorneys.* Judges. Juries. Psychiatrists: *Pretrial psychiatric examination (fitness to stand trial). Criminal responsibility.* Juvenile justice: *Goals of the juvenile court. Constitutional rights of juveniles.*

Chapter 6   The measurement of crime   319

Political and technical problems in crime recording: *Police records. Other official crime statistics. Interpretation of official crime records and the mass media. Other crime measurement techniques.* The meaning and construction of crime rates.

Chapter 7 Real crime, other crime, and juvenile delinquency 369

Real crime: *Violent crime. Drugs and drug abuse. Organized crime. Summary.* Other crime: *Witchcraft. The crime of communism. Crimes of businessmen. Black marketing. Embezzlement and price fixing. Ghetto merchants. Assigning blame. Rape. Female crime. Summary.* Juvenile delinquency: *Definitions of delinquency—Old and new, at home and abroad. The invention of delinquency. Summary.*

Chapter 8 The control and prevention of crime 459

The control of crime through punishment. Control of crime through rehabilitation: *The incompatibility between rehabilitation and criminal justice. The myth of rehabilitation. Social science knowledge. Types of rehabilitation programs. Uses of the rehabilitation myth. Traditional versus democratic treatment alternatives. Setting up the rehabilitation program.* Constitutional change to control crime. Legalization and decriminalization. Crime prevention.

Chapter 1

Introduction

Recently Gresham Sykes (1974) has suggested that dramatic changes are currently emerging in academic criminology. These changes run along four lines: (1) a belief that criminal justice agencies serve the interests of the repression of one social class by a ruling social class; (2) a belief that the statutes as written are also the work of the ruling class and also reflect repressive class interests; (3) a belief that official crime statistics are a product of these repressive interests; and therefore (4) a total rejection of theories which attempt to explain the causes of criminal behavior as irrelevant once we recognize the arbitrary and imposed nature of what is called crime. This book mirrors these changes.

In our view one can best understand crime in a class-structured society such as the United States as the end product of a chain of interactions involving powerful groups that use their power to establish criminal laws and sanctions against less powerful persons and groups that may pose a threat to the groups in power. Most important, we view the United States as a relatively class-structured society in which such designations as "upper class," "middle class," and "working class" or "lower class" are essential in accounting for how persons will be affected by the criminal justice system. Despite a mythology of egalitarianism in the United States, such as that expressed in the phrase "all men are created equal," it seems clear that one's position in the social class structure is associated with great differences in the control of money, property, and political power.

Def.

1

Since income and property are highly unequally distributed among the social classes in the United States, and since defending oneself in the criminal justice system can be fairly expensive, it is not surprising that crime statistics usually seem to establish that crime is most prevalent among the lower class. We suggest that the criminal behavior of the lower class may not be markedly different from that of the more affluent classes and that the latter have more resources with which to defend themselves and to elude the consequences of being stigmatized as "criminals."

CRIME AND THE POLITICAL PROCESS

The most obvious fact about crime is that political entities—nations, states—define it by creating and then enforcing criminal laws. The critical question is, which persons or groups in the body politic have most influence or power in the creation and, eventually, in the selective enforcement of criminal laws?

Political sociologists have proposed three different models to account for the distribution and exercise of power in society (Goertzel, 1976) (the passing of criminal laws is just one manifestation of political power):

The *class model* asserts that people's economic circumstances determine their political life. Those with wealth dominate the political life of those without wealth. In the Marxist conception, those who own and control the means of production (capitalists) control the political life of the workers (proletarians).

In the *elitist model,* power is also viewed as unequally distributed, and some few persons or groups monopolize political power because of their special qualities of intelligence, expertise, or strength, but not necessarily wealth. This elite creates laws affecting the masses.

Finally, the *pressure group* (or interest group) *model* proposes a pluralist conception of the political process. In this view, society is composed of a multiplicity of groups with different interests which try to maintain themselves in a favored position relative to that of other groups. Not infrequently, groups with opposing interests come into conflict. They compete politically by trying to have laws passed that favor their interests, or that restrict or limit the interests of other groups.

Given the present state of our knowledge about the dynamics

and interrelations of power, law, and crime, it is difficult to accept any one of these three models as wholly convincing or adequate. In Chapter 2 we will examine some specific instances of how criminal laws have originated, and we will find examples that support all three models. On the other hand, each model has some serious weaknesses as a complete explanation of all the cases. As we will demonstrate, some laws have their origins in the interests of wealthy corporations, some reflect the views of the middle- and upper-class citizens independent of corporate needs, and some reflect religious interests.

Since none of these models seems comprehensive, some borrowing from their varied assumptions is necessary to understand crime. Yet we are sympathetic to the class model, for as we shall see in later chapters, there is much evidence that persons without wealth and political power are most likely to be defined as criminals. The upper and middle classes are most often able to control the political process by controlling party nominations through financial support to candidates and officeholders so that criminal laws preserve wealth and property and punish those who might threaten the existing distribution of wealth and property. If upper- and upper middle-class persons are apprehended for a crime, they are better able to afford expensive and sophisticated legal counsel, either to avoid conviction or to gain leniency in sentencing. In some instances, as we shall see in the discussion of marijuana laws in Chapter 2, persons with wealth and power may be able to change the laws they have violated so that their actions are punished less severely.

ETHICAL ORIENTATION

Unlike many social science textbooks dealing with crime, this text openly acknowledges a specific ethical orientation toward social life. Its position is that an ethical social ordering within any society, or among societies, requires that all men, women, and children have equal chances for personal freedom and physical survival. Such an ethical stance seems required to avoid an unreflective acceptance of the criminal justice system, official crime statistics, and criminal statutes as they are, and it mirrors the Charter of the United Nations, which begins as follows (United Nations Conference, 1945: 1):

WE THE PEOPLES OF THE UNITED NATIONS
DETERMINED

> to save succeeding generations from the scourge of war, which twice in our lifetime has brought untold sorrow to mankind, and
> *to reaffirm faith in fundamental human rights, in the dignity and worth of the human person, in the equal rights of men and women and of nations large and small* . . . (emphasis ours)

The statement of purpose of the United Nations reads in part (United Nations Conference, 1945: 3):

> To develop friendly relations among nations based on respect for the principle of *equal rights and self-determination of peoples* . . . (emphasis ours)

Indeed, the U.S. Declaration of Independence reads:

> We hold these Truths to be self-evident, that all Men are created equal, that they are endowed by their Creator with certain unalienable Rights.

Our ethical orientation is also reflected in the first ten amendments to the U.S. Constitution—the Bill of Rights—which guarantee all American citizens protection from self-incrimination, excessive bail, cruel and unusual punishment, and unreasonable search and seizure, as well as the right to speedy trials and trial by jury—all, of course, directly related to crime and its control (U.S. Constitution, Amendments 1–10). This ethical orientation obviously has implications for numerous social and economic issues, such as the distribution of food, petroleum, and other resources, but it will only be developed here in relation to the issue of crime and its control.[1] The orientation has important consequences for the initial assumptions which inform the study of crime and its control.

An excellent test of the morality and justice of such an ethical position has been proposed by John Rawls (1971). Rawls suggests that in order to determine what is indeed a just society, people must return to what he calls the "original position," a position in which they are without information on their social or economic status in society. Only when in this position behind what Rawls calls the "veil of ignorance" can people make just or fair decisions on how society should be organized. Since people in the original position are deprived of knowledge of their position in society,

---

[1] For another statement of human rights as related to criminology, see Schwendinger (1970).

their predictable and rational decision for ordering social life would be true equality. For people in such a position to select a highly stratified society modeled after, say, czarist Russia would be very risky since their chances of being powerless peasants would be much greater than their chances of being members of the nobility. However, once people occupy a position of privilege in an established society, a social leveling is not attractive to them. In a society with great inequality in the distribution of resources, the poor would most readily accept equality for all.

TRADITIONAL ASSUMPTIONS

1) The traditional assumptions of social science in general and of criminology in particular include the position usually referred to as *cultural relativism.* This position argues that, though there are observable differences in cultural practices and beliefs across various societies, including differences in legal codes and their enforcement, it is impossible to assess these different practices and beliefs in terms of moral superiority or inferiority. Cultural relativism suggests that societies are only different from one another, not better or worse. Because it is impossible to develop any scientific measures for use in comparing values and cultures, cultural relativism views all societies as having equal merit. It is sometimes claimed that such an orientation, which assumes equality of differing value patterns, should generate tolerance and understanding among the various cultures of the world (Bidney, 1968: 545). Cultural relativism seeks to avoid ethnocentrism, which is the belief that one's own values and way of life are superior to all others. To avoid this possibility, cultural relativists make no judgments of others' cultures (Bidney, 1968: 546). As practiced in much of traditional criminology, cultural relativism leads scholars to accept the legal codes of a society as givens, without fundamental moral examination of those codes.

2)
MORAL
NSENSIS

A second traditional assumption often made in U.S. criminology, which is not explicitly rejected in most of the professional literature, is that written statutes more or less represent the will of most of the people in a society, at least in a democracy such as the United States. Some discussions of crime and criminal law mention how elites and powerful interest groups create the criminal law and then proceed to ignore this issue, implicitly treating crime as having an existence independent of the will of elites or interest groups. Sutherland and Cressey (1970), for example, mention the elitist theory regarding the nature of crime and criminal law as one of many possible orientations and then proceed largely to ignore this perspective in favor of a focus on criminal behavior, devoting chapters to such topics as the relationship between race and crime and between home life and crime. According to Newman (1966), such concern with the causes of criminal behavior has been the major thrust of the work of sociologists, and this emphasis is clearly reflected in criminology texts. In any event, by not emphasizing the role of power and elites, the impression is maintained that in states with elected governments the majority rules in all major political issues, including the structuring of the criminal code. This majority rule orientation is seen in the following statement: "The only common characteristic of all crimes is that they consist . . . in acts universally disapproved of by all members of each society" (Durkheim, 1933: 73).

3)   Another traditional assumption of criminology is the *discriminatory nature of the criminal justice process,* including both the systems of arrest and trial. As will be shown in the following chapters, criminologists have demonstrated that police and the courts often discriminate against racial and economic minorities. In the United States, blacks are more likely than whites to be arrested, convicted, and sentenced for the same offense. Therefore, official records of arrests or convictions for crimes reflect not only the law-violating behavior in the community but also the biases of the criminal justice system (Matza, 1969: 96–98).

4)   Another traditional assumption is that criminal behavior and criminals are *objects* amenable to scientific study. That is, the unit of analysis is the individual, called a criminal, and it is assumed that something about the individual can be isolated as the cause of the criminal behavior. Also, crime and criminals are assumed to be *morally inferior* to noncrime and noncriminals (Matza, 1969: 17 ff.; Vold, 1958). It is taken for granted that the people and behavior in question should be controlled. Naturally, if it is assumed that crime and criminals are morally inferior, then it follows that crime must be prevented or, failing that, that crime and criminals must at least be controlled within limits.

The assumptions of traditional criminology suffer from several internal inconsistencies. The social scientists working in this tradition are supposedly dispassionately studying commonsense assumptions, but in fact accept them as their own because traditional criminology accepts the commonsense position that crime is a moral problem. A nondiscriminating cultural relativism which holds that all cultural practices are of equal ethical merit is inconsistent with the proposition that certain behavior within a society, namely crime, is inferior to other behavior and should be controlled. All the nonjudgmental social scientist should logically claim is that criminals and criminal behavior are differently defined from other people and behavior. Moreover, if criminal codes, the police, the courts, and official crime records are recognized as often discriminatory, then it is inconsistent to view those behaviors officially termed crime and those people labeled criminals as necessarily morally different from other behaviors and people. By not assuming any necessary moral reality to crime and criminals, and by recognizing the role of power in society, one avoids the inconsistencies found in the assumptions of traditional criminology.

DIVERGENT ASSUMPTIONS OF THIS APPROACH

This new approach to the study of crime and its control does not challenge traditional criminology's assertions regarding observable differences in cultural practices and beliefs. Unlike traditional criminology, however, this approach does not concede that it is impossible to make moral distinctions among such beliefs and practices. In other words, it is not necessarily true that one culture's legal practices are as just and fair as another's. The mass execution of Jews by the Third Reich in wartime Germany is not merely different from other cultural practices but represents one moral low point in any cross-cultural comparison.

Indeed, we even assume that some crime may be morally superior to some noncrime. For example, obeying the law and carrying out orders to exterminate Jews in Nazi Germany certainly would be judged as morally inferior to disobeying the law and fighting the organized state. Nor is conformity to southern state statutes which require the segregation of races by definition morally superior to open and consistent violation of those statutes. According to Mouledous (1967: 229): "What is critical is that the behaviors which we are encouraging or discouraging should not be determined by existing social norms nor by administrative judgment. Sociologists cannot abdicate the responsibility of judgment and accept the state's criteria of crime. A superior referent must be sought."

One measure of the morality of specific criminal statutes has been proposed by Mouledous (1967), who suggests that *exclusive* criminal statutes which apply only to specific groups of people (such as laws restricting the voting or residential location of a specific racial group) are morally inferior to statutes which apply to all persons living in a society, irrespective of racial or class characteristics. We hope this provides a beginning for the development of a general set of principles against which we can judge written law, remembering that equality has been established as our moral referent.

NB

Our orientation, unlike that of traditional criminology, assumes that many written statutes are the will, not of all the people or even of a majority, but rather usually represent the orientation of organized interest groups with the political power to make legislation reflect their will. Laws prohibiting embezzlement represent mainly and most directly the interests of employers who desire protection from employees. Yet at times sample surveys of Americans' attitudes on social issues show something approaching a consensus on various issues relating to crime and its control. Much of this consensus can be explained as follows. Contrary to the myth of an independent and constitutionally free press in the United States, the media are a part of the larger corporate structure and generally represent that structure's definitions of reality, including what is and what is not defined as crime and how crime can be controlled. This media orientation manufactures much of the consensus on crime and crime control (Cohen and Young, 1973). Even though there is seldom any government censorship, wealthy corporations nonetheless largely control the mass media indirectly through advertising and directly through actual ownership of the media. These corporations effectively use the media to set the limits within which public debate on issues is confined (Sallach, 1974). In some instances, such as the laws governing rape and homicide, it can be convincingly argued that class or corporate interests are not reflected in the written law and that all classes derive the same benefits from the protection provided by the law. However, in laws involving personal assault and some offenses against property, class interests are reflected not in the terms of the law itself but in its differential enforcement, for one of the chief complaints among economic and racial minorities is that they do not receive adequate police protection (Hahn, 1971). Many blacks feel, for example, that the police consider offenses against their homes or assaults against their persons to be less serious than similar incidents occurring in the white community (Ennis, 1967). In this sense, even laws protecting persons and property do not serve all classes. In other words, even if the written law represents a broad range of class interests, it often becomes discriminatory in its administration.

This approach agrees with the assumption of traditional criminology that the criminal justice process is often discriminatory and arbitrary, making official records distorted reflections of crime. A system of law enforcement that gives special privileges to the affluent is a critical moral problem in a society which claims to afford equal rights under law to all people, as does the United States. Finally, this approach, unlike that of traditional criminology, does not assume a reality to crime and criminals independent of the application of culturally specific social definitions (Becker, 1963). It claims that there are no universally valid statutory distinctions separating crime from noncrime or criminals from noncriminals. Specific crimes and criminals may be legally condemned only within a particular society, and this should sensitize the social analyst to make moral judgments independent of any particular social order. Indeed, the social analyst can arrive at some moral conclusions about many of a given culture's practices in the definition and control of crime rather than assume, as does traditional criminology, that behavior defined as criminal in a society should necessarily be studied, controlled, and implicitly considered immoral.

LAW AND MORALITY

Most sociologists studying the law feel, as do most criminologists, that morality has no place in what they feel should be a scientific pursuit (Schur, 1968: 51–58; Quinney, 1973: 1–16). However, the early criminologist Beccaria (1775) made the moral value judgment that all people should be equal before the law. That proposal is also reflected in the teachings of Dr. Martin

Luther King, Jr., and it is accepted here. Certainly not all writers have accepted this premise. Plato (Taylor, 1934) and Aristotle (Barker, 1946) rejected such equality as unjust. For example, both accepted slavery and the inequality of slaves and masters as morally legitimate.

If sociology makes no moral judgments independent of criminal statutes, it becomes sterile and inhumane—the work of moral eunuchs or legal technicians. Recognizing that cultural definitions of crime are a product only of powerful interest groups in government, the analyst of crime should not necessarily be tied to the moral judgments reflected in those statutes. If moral judgments above and beyond criminal law were not made, the laws of Nazi Germany would be indistinguishable from the laws of many other nations. Yet the Nuremberg trials after World War II advanced the position that numerous officials of the Nazi government, although admittedly acting in accord with German laws, were behaving in such a grossly immoral fashion as to be criminally responsible. Some obedience to law was held by the Nuremberg tribunal to be morally reprehensible and therefore criminal.

As might be expected, the advocates of a higher morality than that embodied in written law have often been those outside government who were rebelling against governmental authority, as did Martin Luther King (1963; also see Gandhi, 1951). However, in the Nuremberg trials, representatives of the Allied governments—France, England, the Soviet Union, and the United States—explicitly and publicly supported the idea of a moral order and moral judgments independent of written law. No claim was made by the Allied prosecutors that those on trial had violated German statutes; rather, the claim was that, by enforcing those statutes, the defendants had committed atrocities against humanity. At Nuremberg four major world powers endorsed the idea of a higher moral order than that necessarily found in written laws, which perhaps lends a credibility to this position that it might otherwise not enjoy. The example of Nuremberg shows that moral judgments by students of crime can be made independently of particular cultural definitions of crime.

On October 7, 1942, President Roosevelt released the following statement:

It is our intention that just and sure punishment shall be meted out to [those] responsible for the organized murder of thousands of innocent persons and the commission of atrocities which *have violated every tenet of the Christian faith* (emphasis ours) (Jackson, 1949: 9).

And on March 24, 1944, President Roosevelt declared:

In one of the blackest crimes of all history—begun by the Nazis in the day of peace and multiplied by them a hundred times in time of war—the wholesale systematic murder of the Jews of Europe goes on unabated every hour. . . . It is therefore fitting that we should again proclaim our determination that *none who participate in these acts of savagery shall go unpunished.* The United Nations have made it clear that they will pursue the guilty and deliver them up in order that Justice be done. *That warning applies not only to the leaders but also to their functionaries and subordinates* in Germany and in the satellite countries. All who knowingly take part in the deportation of Jews to their death in Poland or Norwegians and French to their death in Germany are equally guilty with the executioner. All who share the guilt shall share the punishment (emphasis ours) (Jackson, 1949: 12–13).

Bereft of moral judgment, the social analyst can provide only a description of the development or administration of the laws and must at least pretend not to make any critical judgments. Yet the social analyst does make moral judgments, even if only in picking topics for study (Black, 1973: 48), and even if unaware of making those moral judgments. For example, the selection for study of the effects of social stratification on the administration of the law, which Skolnick (1965: 4) says is typical of the sociology of law, often reflects the view that nothing is fundamentally wrong with the basic assumptions of the criminal justice system. The argument continues that the system requires only a few minor modifications to operate with proper equality for all, such as the provision of legal counsel for the indigent and the use of better-educated, less-prejudiced police. (This argument is criticized in Chapter 4.) In any case, to be completely honest, rather than claim an objectivity that is impossible, perhaps it is best to recognize and be explicit about our moral biases so that the observer can take these into account in considering our work.

The alternative assumptions of the orientation in the chapters that follow stress (1) the unjust and class-based nature of what is usually called crime; (2) the law as a defining mechanism of crime; and (3) the failure of law enforcement agencies to produce data suited for the scientific study of people or their behavior. Therefore, before considering the behavior defined as criminal in a particular society, it is important to discuss what is known about the nature and origins of law (Chapter 2). Next, the traditional assumptions of criminology will be presented in a survey of its historical development (Chapter 3). The administration of the law, an important part of this framework, will be covered in Chapters 4 and 5, which deal with the police and the courts, respectively. The measurement of crime, which determines conclusions regarding the amount and patterns of crime, will be considered in Chapter 6. Like other discussions of crime, our orientation lends itself to distinctions among types of crime (Chapter 7) and analysis of various strategies of crime control (Chapter 8).

Finally, it seems appropriate to observe that not all of those who place morality above the written law arrive at the conclusions embodied in this text. Those who oppose equality for women, blacks, and other minorities, even in opposition to statutory provisions, are able to find moral justifications for their positions. Therefore, resolution of the issue of the relation between law and morality requires the activation of individual conscience, and this may well usher in an increased professional awareness of the role of conflict and lack of consensus which will in turn be reflected in a new direction of theory and research in criminology. No longer can the thoughtful student of law, crime, and morality claim that "it must be immoral or it would not be illegal." Duly constituted laws can command the segregation of educational facilities along racial lines, and violation of such laws is not necessarily immoral.

REFERENCES

Barker, Ernest, trans.
  1946   *The Politics of Aristotle*. Book 1. London: Oxford University Press.

Beccaria, Cesare B.
  1775   *An Essay on Crimes and Punishments*. 4th ed. London: E. Newbery.

Becker, Howard S.
  1963   *Outsiders*. New York: Free Press of Glencoe.

Bidney, David
  1968   "Cultural Relativism," pp. 543–547 in *International Encyclopedia of the Social Sciences*, vol. 3. New York: Macmillan Co. and Free Press.

Black, Donald
    1973   "The Boundaries of Legal Sociology," pp. 41–56 in Donald Black and Maureen Mileski, eds., *The Social Organization of Law.* New York: Seminar Press.

Cohen, Stanley and Jock Young, eds.
    1973   *The Manufacture of News.* Beverly Hills, Calif.: Sage Publications.

Durkheim, Emile
    1933   *The Division of Labor in Society.* George Simpson, trans. New York: Free Press of Glencoe.

Ennis, Philip H.
    1967   *Criminal Victimization in the United States: A Report of a National Survey.* National Opinion Research Center, University of Chicago. Washington, D.C.: U.S. Government Printing Office.

Gandhi, Mahatma K.
    1951   *Non-violent Resistance.* New York: Schocken Books.

Goertzel, Ted George
    1976   *Political Society.* Chicago: Rand McNally College Publishing Co.

Hahn, Harlan
    1971   "Ghetto Assessments of Police Protection and Authority," *Law and Society Review* 6(November): 183–194.

Jackson, Robert H.
    1949   *International Conference on Military Trials.* Department of State Publication 3080, International Organization and Conference Series 2. Washington, D.C.: U.S. Government Printing Office.

King, Martin Luther, Jr.
    1963   "Letter from Birmingham Jail," *Why We Can't Wait* (April 16). New York: Harper & Row, Publishers, Inc.

Matza, David
    1969   *Becoming Deviant.* Englewood Cliffs, N.J.: Prentice-Hall.

Mouledous, Joseph C.
    1967   "Political Crime and the Negro Revolution," pp. 217–231 in Marshall B. Clinard and Richard Quinney, eds., *Criminal Behavior Systems: A Typology.* New York: Holt, Rinehart and Winston.

Newman, Donald J.
    1966   "Sociologists and the Administration of Criminal Justice," pp. 177–187 in Arthur B. Shostak, ed., *Sociology in Action.* Homewood, Ill.: Dorsey Press.

Quinney, Richard
   1973   *Critique of Legal Order: Crime Control in Capitalist Society.* Boston:
           Little, Brown and Co.

Rawls, John
   1971   *A Theory of Justice.* Cambridge, Mass.: Belknap Press of Har-
           vard University Press.

Sallach, David L.
   1974   "Class Domination and Ideological Hegemony," *Sociological
           Quarterly* 15(Winter): 38–50.

Schur, Edwin M.
   1968   *Law and Society: A Sociological View.* New York: Random House.

Schwendinger, Herman and Julia
   1970   "Defenders of Order or Guardians of Human Rights?" *Issues
           in Criminology* 5(Summer): 123–157.

Skolnick, Jerome H.
   1965   "The Sociology of Law in America: Overview and Trends,"
           Law and Society (a supplement to *Social Problems*) (Summer):
           4–39.

Sutherland, Edwin H. and Donald R. Cressey
   1970   *Criminology.* 8th ed. Philadelphia: J. B. Lippincott Co.

Sykes, Gresham M.
   1974   "The Rise of Critical Criminology," *Journal of Criminal Law and
           Criminology* 65(June): 206–213.

Taylor, A. E., trans.
   1934   *The Laws of Plato.* Section 757. London: J. M. Dent and Sons.

United Nations Conference on International Organization
   1945   *Charter of the United Nations Together with the Statute of the Interna-
           tional Court of Justice.* Department of State Publication 2353,
           Conference Series 74. Washington, D.C.: U.S. Government
           Printing Office.

U.S. Constitution Amendments 1–10.

U.S. Declaration of Independence
   1776

Vold, George B.
   1958   *Theoretical Criminology.* New York: Oxford University Press.

1

*Letter from Birmingham Jail**

Martin Luther King, Jr.

My Dear Fellow Clergymen:

While confined here in the Birmingham city jail I came across your recent statement calling my present activities "unwise and untimely." Seldom do I pause to answer criticism of my work and ideas. If I sought to answer all the criticisms that cross my desk, my secretaries would have little time for anything other than such correspondence in the course of the day, and I would have no time for constructive work. But since I feel that you are men of genuine good will and that your criticisms are sincerely set forth, I want to try to answer your statement in what I hope will be patient and reasonable terms.

I think I should indicate why I am here in Birmingham, since you have been influenced by the view which argues against "outsiders coming in." I have the honor of serving as President of the Southern Christian Leadership Conference, an organization operating in every southern state, with headquarters in Atlanta, Georgia. We have some 85 affiliate organizations across the south, and one of them is the Alabama Christian Movement for Human Rights. Frequently we share staff, educational and financial resources with our affiliates. Several months ago the affiliate here in Birmingham asked us to be on call to engage in a nonviolent direct action program if such were deemed necessary. We readily consented, and when the hour came we lived up to our promise. So I, along with several members of my staff, am here because I was invited here. I am here because I have organizational ties here.

---

* Reprinted from *Why We Can't Wait* (1963).

I

But more basically, I am in Birmingham because injustice exists here. Just as the prophets of the eight century B.C. left their villages and carried their "thus saith the Lord" far afield and just as the Apostle Paul left his village of Tarsus and carried the gospel of Jesus Christ to the far corners of the Greco-Roman world, so am I compelled to carry the gospel of freedom beyond my own home town. Like Paul, I must constantly respond to the Macedonian call for aid.

Moreover, I am cognizant of the interrelatedness of all communities and states. I cannot sit idly by in Atlanta and not be concerned about what happens in Birmingham. Injustice anywhere is a threat to justice everywhere. We are caught in an inescapable network of mutuality, tied in a single garment of destiny. Whatever affects one directly affects all indirectly. Never again can we afford to live with the narrow, provincial "outside agitator" idea. Anyone who lives inside the United States can never be considered an outsider anywhere within its bounds.

You deplore the demonstrations taking place in Birmingham. But your statement, I am sorry to say, fails to express a similar concern for the conditions that brought about the demonstrations. I am sure that none of you would want to rest content with the superficial kind of social analysis that deals merely with effects and does not grapple with underlying causes. It is unfortunate that demonstrations are taking place in Birmingham, but it is even more unfortunate that the city's white power structure left the Negro community with no alternative.

II

In any nonviolent campaign there are four basic steps: collection of the facts to determine whether injustices exist, negotiation, self-purification and direct action. We have gone through all these steps in Birmingham. There can be no gainsaying the fact that racial injustice engulfs this community. Birmingham is probably the most thoroughly segregated city in the United States. Its ugly record of police brutality is widely known. Its unjust treatment of Negroes in the courts is a notorious reality. There have been more unsolved bombings of Negro homes and churches in Birmingham than in any other city in the nation. These are the hard, brutal facts of the case. On the basis of these conditions Negro leaders sought to negotiate with the city fathers. But the latter consistently refused to engage in good-faith negotiation.

Then last September came the opportunity to talk with leaders of Birmingham's economic community. In the course of the negotiations certain promises were made by the merchants—for example, the promise to remove the stores' humiliating racial signs. On the basis of these promises the Rev. Fred Shuttlesworth and the leaders of the Alabama Christian Movement for Human Rights agreed to a moratorium on all demonstrations. As the weeks and months went by we realized that we were the victims of a broken promise. The signs remained.

As in so many past experiences, our hopes had been blasted, and our disappointment was keenly felt. We had no alternative except to prepare for direct action, whereby we would present our very bodies as a means of laying our case before the conscience of the local and the national community. Mindful of the difficulties involved, we decided to undertake a process of self-purification. We began a series of workshops on nonviolence, and we repeatedly asked ourselves: "Are you able to accept blows without retaliating?" "Are you able to endure the ordeal of jail?" We decided to schedule our direct action program for the Easter season, realizing that except for Christmas this is the main shopping period of the year. Knowing that a strong economic withdrawal program would be the by-product of direct action, we felt that this would be the best time to bring pressure to bear on the merchants.

But Birmingham's mayoral election was coming up in March, and when we discovered that Commissioner of Public Safety Eugene "Bull" Connor was to be in the run-off, we decided to postpone our demonstrations until the day after the run-off so that they could not be used to cloud the issues. It is evident, then, that we did not move irresponsibly into direct action. Like many others, we wanted to see Mr. Connor defeated, and to this end we endured postponement after postponement. Having aided in this community need, we felt that our direct action program could be delayed no longer.

III

You may well ask, "Why direct action? Why sit-ins, marches, etc.? Isn't negotiation a better path?" You are quite right in calling for negotiation. Indeed, this is the very purpose of direct action. Nonviolent direct action seeks to foster such a tension that a community which has constantly refused to negotiate is forced to confront the issue. It seeks so to dramatize the issue that it can no longer be ignored. My citing the creation of tension as part of the work of the nonviolent resister may sound rather shocking. But I readily acknowledge that I am not afraid of the word "tension." I have earnestly opposed violent tension, but there is a type of constructive, nonviolent tension which is necessary for growth. Just as Socrates felt that it was necessary to create a tension in the mind so that individuals could shake off the bondage of myths and half-truths and rise to the realm of creative analysis and objective appraisal, so must we see the need for nonviolent gadflies to create the kind of tension in society that will help men rise from the dark depths of prejudice and racism to the majestic heights of understanding and brotherhood.

The purpose of our direct action program is to create a situation so crisis-packed that it will inevitably open the door to negotiation. I therefore concur with you in your call for negotiation. Too long has our beloved southland been bogged down in a tragic effort to live in monologue rather than dialogue.

One of the basic points in your statement is that the action that I and my associates have taken in Birmingham is untimely. Some have asked, "Why didn't you give the new city administration time to act?" The only answer that I can give to this query is that the new Birmingham administration must be prodded about as much as the outgoing one before it will act. We are sadly mistaken if we feel that the election of Albert Boutwell as mayor will bring the millennium to Birmingham. While Mr. Boutwell is a much more gentle person than Mr. Connor, they are both segregationists, dedicated to maintenance of the status quo. I have hope that Mr. Boutwell will be reasonable enough to see the futility of massive resistance to desegregation. But he will not see this without pressure from devotees of civil rights. My friends, I must say to you that we have not made a single gain in civil rights without determined legal and nonviolent pressure. Lamentably, it is a historical fact that privileged groups seldom give up their privileges voluntarily. Individuals may see the moral light and voluntarily give up their unjust posture; but, as Reinhold Niebuhr has reminded us, groups tend to be more immoral than individuals.

We know through painful experience that freedom is never voluntarily given by the oppressor; it must be demanded by the oppressed. Frankly, I have yet to engage in a direct action campaign that was "well timed" in the view of those who have not suffered unduly from the disease of segregation. For years now I have heard the word "Wait!" It rings in the ear of every Negro with piercing familiarity. This "Wait" has almost always meant "Never." As one of our distinguished jurists once said, "Justice too long delayed is justice denied."

IV

We have waited for more than 340 years for our constitutional and God-given rights. The nations of Asia and Africa are moving with jetlike speed toward gaining political independence, but we still creep at horse-and-buggy pace toward gaining a cup of coffee at a lunch counter. Perhaps it is easy for those who have never felt the stinging darts of segregation to say "Wait." But when you have seen vicious mobs lynch your mothers and fathers at will and drown your sisters and brothers at whim; when you have seen hate-filled policemen curse, kick and even kill your black brothers and sisters with impunity, when you see the vast majority of your 20 million Negro brothers smothering in an air-tight cage of poverty in the midst of an affluent society; when you suddenly find your tongue twisted as you seek to explain to your six-year-old daughter why she can't go to the public amusement park that has just been advertised on television, and see tears welling up when she is told that Funtown is closed to colored children, and see ominous clouds of inferiority beginning to form in her little mental sky, and see her beginning to distort her personality by unconsciously developing a bitterness toward white people; when you have to concoct an answer for a five-year-old son asking, "Daddy, why do white people treat colored people so mean?"; when you take a cross-country drive and find it necessary to sleep night after night in the uncomfortable corners of your automobile because no motel will accept you; when you are humiliated day in and day out by nagging signs reading "white" and "colored"; when your first name becomes "nigger," your middle name becomes "boy" (however old you are) and your last name becomes "John," and your wife and mother are never given the respected title "Mrs.";

when you are harried by day and haunted by night by the fact that you are a Negro, never quite knowing what to expect next, and are plagued with inner fears and outer resentments; when you are forever fighting a degenerating sense of "nobodiness"—then you will understand why we find it difficult to wait. There comes a time when the cup of endurance runs over, and men are no longer willing to be plunged into an abyss of injustice where they experience the bleakness of corroding despair. I hope, sirs, you can understand our legitimate and unavoidable impatience.

V

You express a great deal of anxiety over our willingness to break laws. This is certainly a legitimate concern. Since we so diligently urge people to obey the Supreme Court's decision of 1954 outlawing segregation in the public schools, at first glance it may seem rather paradoxical for us consciously to break laws. One may well ask, "How can you advocate breaking some laws and obeying others?" The answer lies in the fact that there are two types of laws: just and unjust. I agree with St. Augustine that "an unjust law is no law at all."

Now what is the difference between the two? How does one determine whether a law is just or unjust? A just law is a man-made code that squares with the moral law or the law of God. An unjust law is a code that is out of harmony with the moral law. To put it in the terms of St. Thomas Aquinas, an unjust law is a human law that is not rooted in eternal law and natural law. Any law that uplifts human personality is just. Any law that degrades human personality is unjust. All segregation statutes are unjust because segregation distorts the soul and damages the personality. It gives the segregator a false sense of superiority and the segregated a false sense of inferiority. Segregation, to use the terminology of the Jewish philosopher Martin Buber, substitutes an "I-it" relationship for an "I-thou" relationship and ends up relegating persons to the status of things. Hence segregation is not only politically, economically and sociologically unsound, it is sinful. Paul Tillich has said that sin is separation. Is not segregation an existential expression of man's tragic separation, his awful estrangement, his terrible sinfulness? Thus it is that

I can urge men to disobey segregation ordinances, for such ordinances are morally wrong.

Let us consider some of the ways in which a law can be unjust. A law is unjust, for example, if the majority group compels a minority group to obey the statute but does not make it binding on itself. By the same token a law in all probability is just if the majority is itself willing to obey it. Also, a law is unjust if it is inflicted on a minority that, as a result of being denied the right to vote, had no part in enacting or devising the law. Who can say that the legislature of Alabama which set up that state's segregation laws was democratically elected? Throughout Alabama all sorts of devious methods are used to prevent Negroes from becoming registered voters, and there are some counties in which, even though Negroes constitute a majority of the population, not a single Negro is registered. Can any law enacted under such circumstances be considered democratically structured?

Sometimes a law is just on its face and unjust in its application. For instance, I have been arrested on a charge of parading without a permit. Now there is nothing wrong in having an ordinance which requires a permit for a parade. But such an ordinance becomes unjust when it is used to maintain segregation and to deny citizens the First-amendment privilege of peaceful assembly and protest.

I hope you are able to see the distinction I am trying to point out. In no sense do I advocate evading the law, as would the rabid segregationist. That would lead to anarchy. One who breaks an unjust law must do so *openly, lovingly,* and with a willingness to accept the penalty. I submit that an individual who breaks a law that conscience tells him is unjust and who willingly accepts the penalty of imprisonment in order to arouse the conscience of the community over its injustice is in reality expressing the highest respect for law.

Of course, there is nothing new about this kind of civil disobedience. It was evidenced sublimely in the refusal of Shadrach, Meshach and Abednego to obey the laws of Nebuchadnezzar, on the ground that a higher moral law was at stake. It was practiced superbly by the early Christians who were willing to face hungry lions rather than submit to certain unjust laws of the Roman empire. To a degree, academic freedom is a reality today because

Socrates practiced civil disobedience. We should never forget that everything Adolf Hitler did in Germany was "legal" and everything the Hungarian freedom fighters did in Hungary was "illegal." It was "illegal" to aid and comfort a Jew in Hitler's Germany. Even so, I am sure that had I lived in Germany at the time I would have aided and comforted my Jewish brothers. If today I lived in a communist country where certain principles dear to the Christian faith are suppressed, I would openly advocate disobeying that country's antireligious laws.

VI

I must make two honest confessions to you, my Christian and Jewish brothers. First, I must confess that over the past few years I have been gravely disappointed with the white moderate. I have almost reached the regrettable conclusion that the Negro's great stumbling block in his stride toward freedom is not the White Citizen's Counciler or the Klu Klux Klanner but the white moderate who is more devoted to "order" than to justice; who prefers a negative peace which is the absence of tension to a positive peace which is the presence of justice; who constantly says "I agree with you in the goal you seek, but I cannot agree with your methods"; who paternalistically believes he can set the timetable for another man's freedom; who lives by a mythical concept of time and who constantly advises the Negro to wait for a "more convenient season." Shallow understanding from people of good will is more frustrating than absolute misunderstanding from people of ill will. Lukewarm acceptance is much more bewildering than outright rejection.

I had hoped that the white moderate would understand that law and order exist for the purpose of establishing justice and that when they fail in this purpose they block social progress. I had hoped that the white moderate would understand that the present tension in the south is a necessary phase of the transition from an obnoxious negative peace, in which the Negro passively accepted his unjust plight, to a substantive and positive peace, in which all men will respect the dignity and worth of human personality. Actually, we who engage in nonviolent direct action are not the creators of tension. We merely bring to the surface the hidden tension that is already alive. We bring it out in the open where it can be seen and dealt with. Like a boil that can never be cured so long as it is covered up but must be opened with all its pus-flowing ugliness to the natural medicines of air and light, injustice must be exposed, with all the tension its exposure creates, to the light of human conscience and the air of national opinion before it can be cured.

In your statement you assert that our actions, even though peaceful, must be condemned because they precipitate violence. But is this a logical assertion? Isn't this like condemning a robbed man because his possession of money precipitated an act of robbery? Isn't this like condemning Socrates because his unswerving commitment to truth and his philosophical inquiries precipitated the act by the misguided populace in which they made him drink hemlock? Isn't this like condemning Jesus because his unique God-consciousness and never-ceasing devotion to God's will precipitated the evil act of crucifixion? We must come to see that, as the federal courts have consistently affirmed, it is wrong to urge an individual to cease his efforts to gain his basic constitutional rights because the quest may precipitate violence. Society must protect the robbed and punish the robber.

I had also hoped that the white moderate would reject the myth concerning time in relation to the struggle for freedom. I have just received a letter from a white brother in Texas. He writes: "All Christians know that the colored people will receive equal rights eventually, but it is possible that you are in too great a religious hurry. It has taken Christianity almost 2,000 years to accomplish what it has. The teachings of Christ take time to come to earth." Such an attitude stems from a tragic misconception of time, from the strangely irrational notion that there is something in the very flow of time that will inevitably cure all ills. Actually, time itself is neutral; it can be used either destructively or constructively. More and more I feel that the people of ill will have used time much more effectively than have the people of good will. We will have to repent in this generation not merely for the hateful words and actions of the bad people but for the appalling silence of the good people. Human progress never rolls in on wheels of inevitability; it comes through the tireless efforts of men willing to be co-workers with God, and without this hard work time itself becomes an ally of the forces of social stagnation. We must use time creatively, in the knowledge that the time is always ripe to do right. Now is the time to make real the promise of democracy and transform our pending national elegy into a creative psalm of brotherhood. Now is the time to lift our national policy from the quicksand of racial injustice to the solid rock of human dignity.

VII

You speak of our activity in Birmingham as extreme. At first I was rather disappointed that fellow clergymen would see my nonviolent efforts as those of an extremist. I began thinking about the fact that I stand in the middle of two opposing forces in the Negro community. One is a force of complacency made up of Negroes who, as a result of long years of oppression, are so completely drained of self-respect and a sense of "somebodiness" that they have adjusted to segregation, and of a few middle class Negroes who, because of a degree of academic and economic security and because in some way they profit by segregation, have unconsciously become insensitive to the problems of the masses. The other force is one of bitterness and hatred, and it comes perilously close to advocating violence. It is expressed in the various black nationalist groups that are springing up across the nation, the largest and best-known being Elijah Muhammad's Muslim movement. Nourished by the Negro's frustration over the continued existence of racial discrimination, this movement is made up of people who have lost faith in America, who have absolutely repudiated Christianity, and who have concluded that the white man is an incorrigible "devil."

I have tried to stand between these two forces, saying that we need emulate neither the "do-nothingism" of the complacent nor the hatred of the black nationalist. For there is the more excellent way of love and nonviolent protest. I am grateful to God that, through the influence of the Negro church, the way of nonviolence became an integral part of our struggle.

If this philosophy had not emerged, by now many streets of the south would, I am convinced, be flowing with blood. And I am further convinced that if our white brothers dismiss as "rabble-rousers" and "outside agitators" those of us who employ nonviolent direct action and if they refuse to support our nonviolent efforts, millions of Negroes will, out of frustration and despair, seek solace and security in black nationalist ideologies—a development that would inevitably lead to a frightening racial nightmare.

VIII

Oppressed people cannot remain oppressed forever. The yearning for freedom eventually manifests itself, and that is what has happened to the American Negro. Something within has reminded him of his birthright of freedom, and something without has reminded him that it can be gained. Consciously or unconsciously, he has been caught up by the *Zeitgeist,* and with his black brothers of Africa and his brown and yellow brothers of Asia, South America and the Caribbean, the U.S. Negro is moving with a sense of great urgency toward the promised land of racial justice. If one recognizes this vital urge that has engulfed the Negro community, he should readily understand why public demonstrations are taking place. The Negro has many pent-up resentments and latent frustrations, and he must release them. So let him march; let him make prayer pilgrimages to the city hall; let him go on freedom rides—and try to understand why he must do so. If his repressed emotions are not released in nonviolent ways, they will seek expression through violence; this is not a threat but a fact of history. I have not said to my people, "Get rid of your discontent." Rather I have tried to say that this normal and healthy discontent can be channeled into the creative outlet of nonviolent direct action. And now this approach is being termed extremist.

But though I was initially disappointed at being categorized as an extremist, as I continued to think about the matter I gradually gained a measure of satisfaction from the label. Was not Jesus an extremist for love: "Love your enemies, bless them that curse you, do good to them that hate you, and pray for them which despitefully use you, and persecute you." Was not Amos an extremist for justice: "Let justice roll down like waters and righteousness like an everflowing stream." Was not Paul an extremist for the Christian gospel: "I bear in my body the marks of the Lord Jesus." Was not Martin Luther an extremist: "Here I stand; I can do no other so help me God." And John Bunyan: "I will stay in jail to the end of my days before I make a butchery of my conscience." And Abraham Lincoln: "This nation cannot survive half slave and half free." And Thomas Jefferson: "We hold these truths to be self-evident, that all men are created equal . . ." So the question is not whether we will be extremists but what kind of extremists we will be. Will we be extremists for hate or for love? Will we be extremists for the preservation of injustice or for the extension of justice? Perhaps the south, the nation and the world are in dire need of creative extremists.

I had hoped that the white moderate would see this need. Perhaps I was too optimistic; perhaps I expected too much. I suppose I should have realized that few members of the oppressor race can understand the deep groans and passionate yearnings of the oppressed race, and still fewer have the vision to see that injustice must be rooted out by strong, persistent and determined action. I am thankful, however, that some of our white brothers have grasped the meaning of this social revolution and committed themselves to it. They are still all too few in quantity, but they are big in quality. Some—such as Ralph McGill, Lillian Smith, Harry Golden and James McBride Dabbs—have written about our struggle in eloquent and prophetic terms. Others have marched with us down nameless streets of the south. They have languished in filthy, roach-infested jails, suffering the abuse and brutality of policemen who view them as "dirty nigger lovers." Unlike so many of their moderate brothers and sisters, they have recognized the urgency of the moment and sensed the need for powerful "action" antidotes to combat the disease of segregation.

IX

Let me take note of my other major disappointment. Though there are some notable exceptions, I have also been disappointed with the white church and its leadership. I do not say this as one of those negative critics who can always find something wrong with the church. I say this as a minister of the gospel, who loves the church; who was nurtured in its bosom; who has been sustained by its spiritual blessings and who will remain true to it as long as the cord of life shall lengthen.

When I was suddenly catapulted into the leadership of the bus protest in Montgomery, Alabama, a few years ago I felt we would be supported by the white church. I felt that the white ministers, priests and rabbis of the south would be among our strongest allies. Instead, some have been outright opponents, refusing to understand the freedom movement and misrepresenting its leaders; all too many others have been more cautious than courageous and have remained silent and secure behind stained-glass windows.

In spite of my shattered dreams I came to Birmingham with the hope that the white religious leadership of this community would see the justice of our cause and with deep moral concern would serve as the channel through which our just grievances could reach the power structure. But again I have been disappointed.

I have heard numerous southern religious leaders admonish their worshipers to comply with a desegregation decision because it is the *law*, but I have longed to hear white ministers declare, "Follow this decree because integration is morally *right* and because the Negro is your brother." In the midst of blatant injustices inflicted upon the Negro I have watched white churchmen stand on the sideline and mouth pious irrelevancies and sanctimonious trivialities. In the midst of a mighty struggle to rid our nation of racial and economic injustice I have heard many ministers say, "Those are social issues with which the gospel has no real concern," and I have watched many churches commit themselves to a completely otherworldly religion which makes a strange, unbiblical distinction between body and soul, between the sacred and the secular.

We are moving toward the close of the 20th century with a religious community largely adjusted to the status quo—a taillight behind other community agencies rather than a headlight leading men to higher levels of justice.

X

I have traveled the length and breadth of Alabama, Mississippi and all the other southern states. On sweltering summer days and crisp autumn mornings I have looked at the south's beautiful churches with their lofty spires pointing heavenward, and at her impressive religious education buildings. Over and over I have found myself asking: "What kind of people worship here? Who is their God? Where were their voices when the lips of Governor Barnett dripped with words of interposition and nullification? Where were they when Governor Wallace gave a clarion call for defiance and hatred? Where were their voices of support when bruised and weary Negro men and women decided to rise from the dark dungeons of complacency to the bright hills of creative protest?"

Yes, these questions are still in my mind. In deep disappointment I have wept over the laxity of the church. But be assured that my tears have been tears of love. There can be no deep disappointment where there is not deep love. Yes, I love the church. How could I do otherwise? I am in the rather unique position of being the son, the grandson and the great-grandson of preachers. Yes, I see the church as the body of Christ. But, oh! How we have blemished and scarred that body through social neglect and through fear of being nonconformists.

There was a time when the church was very powerful—in the time when the early Christians rejoiced at being deemed worthy to suffer for what they believed. In those days the church was not merely a thermometer that recorded the ideas and principles of popular opinion; it was a thermostat that transformed the mores of society. Whenever the early Christians entered a town the power structure immediately sought to convict them for being "disturbers of the peace" and "outside agitators." But the Christians pressed on, in the conviction that they were "a colony of heaven," called to obey God rather than man. Small in number, they were big in commitment. By their effort and example they brought an end to such ancient evils as infanticide and gladiatorial contest.

XI

Things are different now. So often the contemporary church is a weak, ineffectual voice with an uncertain sound. So often it is an archdefender of the status quo. Far from being disturbed by the presence of the church, the power structure of the average community is consoled by the church's silent—and often even vocal—sanction of things as they are.

But the judgment of God is upon the church as never before. If today's church does not recapture the sacrificial spirit of the early church, it will lose its authenticity, forfeit the loyalty of millions, and be dismissed as an irrelevant social club with no meaning for the 20th century. Every day I meet young people whose disappointment with the church has turned into outright disgust.

Perhaps I have once again been too optimistic. Is organized

religion too inextricably bound to the status quo to save our nation and the world? Perhaps I must turn my faith to the inner spiritual church, the church within the church, as the true *ecclesia* and the hope of the world. But again I am thankful to God that some noble souls from the ranks of organized religion have broken loose from the paralyzing chains of conformity and joined us as active partners in the struggle for freedom. They have left their secure congregations and walked the streets of Albany, Georgia, with us. They have gone down the highways of the south on torturous rides for freedom. Yes, they have gone to jail with us. Some have been kicked out of their churches, have lost the support of their bishops and fellow ministers. But they have acted in the faith that right defeated is stronger than evil triumphant. Their witness has been the spiritual salt that has preserved the true meaning of the gospel in these troubled times. They have carved a tunnel of hope through the dark mountain of disappointment.

I hope the church as a whole will meet the challenge of this decisive hour. But even if the church does not come to the aid of justice, I have no despair about the future. I have no fear about the outcome of our struggle in Birmingham, even if our motives are at present misunderstood. We will reach the goal of freedom in Birmingham and all over the nation, because the goal of America is freedom. Abused and scorned though we may be, our destiny is tied up with America's destiny. Before the pilgrims landed at Plymouth we were here. Before the pen of Jefferson etched across the pages of history the mighty words of the Declaration of Independence, we were here. For more than two centuries our forebears labored in this country without wages; they made cotton king; they built the homes of their masters while suffering gross injustice and shameful humiliation—and yet out of a bottomless vitality they continued to thrive and develop. If the inexpressible cruelties of slavery could not stop us, the opposition we now face will surely fail. We will win our freedom because the sacred heritage of our nation and the eternal will of God are embodied in our echoing demands.

XII

Before closing I feel impelled to mention one other point in your statement that has troubled me profoundly. You warmly commended the Birmingham police force for keeping "order" and "preventing violence." I doubt that you would have so warmly commended the police force if you had seen its angry dogs sinking their teeth into six unarmed, nonviolent Negroes. I doubt that you would so quickly commend the policemen if you were to observe their ugly and inhuman treatment of Negroes here in the city jail; if you were to watch them push and curse old Negro women and young Negro girls; if you were to see them slap and kick old Negro men and young boys; if you were to observe them, as they did on two occasions, refuse to give us food because we wanted to sing our grace together. I cannot join you in your praise of the Birmingham police department.

It is true that the police have exercised discipline in handling the demonstrators. In this sense they have conducted themselves rather "nonviolently" in public. But for what purpose? To preserve the evil system of segregation. Over the past few years I have consistently preached that nonviolence demands that the means we use must be as pure as the ends we seek. I have tried to make clear that it is wrong to use immoral means to attain moral ends. But now I must affirm that it is just as wrong, or perhaps even more so, to use moral means to preserve immoral ends. Perhaps Mr. Connor and his policemen have been rather nonviolent in public, as was Chief Pritchett in Albany, Georgia, but they have used the moral means of nonviolence to maintain the immoral end of racial injustice. As T. S. Eliot has said, there is no greater treason than to do the right deed for the wrong reason.

XIII

I wish you had commended the Negro sit-inners and demonstrators of Birmingham for their sublime courage, their willingness to suffer and their amazing discipline in the midst of great provocation. One day the south will recognize its real heroes. They will be the James Merediths, with a noble sense of purpose facing jeering and hostile mobs and the agonizing loneliness that characterizes the life of the pioneer. They will be old, oppressed, battered Negro women, symbolized in a 72-year-old woman in Montgomery, Alabama, who rose up with a sense of dignity and with her people decided not to ride segregated buses, and who responded with ungrammatical profundity to one who inquired about her: "My feet is tired, but my soul is rested." They will be the young high school and college students, the young ministers of the gospel and a host of their elders courageously and nonviolently sitting in at lunch counters and willingly going to jail for conscience' sake. One day the south will know that when these disinherited children of God sat down at lunch counters they were in reality standing up for what is best in the American dream and for the most sacred values in our Judeo-Christian heritage, thereby bringing our nation back to those great wells of democracy which were dug deep by the founding fathers in their formulation of the Constitution and the Declaration of Independence.

Never before have I written so long a letter. I can assure you that it would have been much shorter if I had been writing from a comfortable desk, but what else can one do when he is alone for days in a narrow jail cell, other than write long letters, think long thoughts and pray long prayers?

If I have said anything in this letter that overstates the truth and indicates an unreasonable impatience, I beg you to forgive me. If I have said anything that *under*states the truth and indicates my having a patience that allows me to settle for anything less than brotherhood, I beg God to forgive me.

I hope this letter finds you strong in the faith. I also hope that circumstances will soon make it possible for me to meet each of you, not as an integrationist or a civil rights leader but as a fellow clergyman and a Christian brother. Let us all hope that the dark clouds of racial prejudice will soon pass away and the deep fog of misunderstanding will be lifted from our fear-drenched communities and in some not too distant tomorrow the radiant stars of love and brotherhood will shine over our great nation with all their scintillating beauty.

2

*The rise of critical criminology**

Gresham M. Sykes

I

In the last ten to fifteen years, criminology in the United States has witnessed a transformation of one of its most fundamental paradigms for interpreting criminal behavior. The theory, methods and applications of criminology have all been exposed to a new scrutiny, and there seems to be little doubt that the field will be involved in an intricate controversy for many years to come. It is the nature of that controversy, its sources and possible consequences with which this paper is concerned.

In the social turbulence of the 1960s, institutions of higher education were at the center of the storm. Students supplied much of the motive force, and the university frequently served as a stage for, as well as a target of, conflict. The university, however, is more than a place or a social organization. It is also a collection of academic disciplines, and these too felt the tremors of the time. Sociology, in particular, was subjected to a barrage of criticism from a variety of sources, and it is within that framework that we need to examine the change that has overtaken criminology.

It was the special claim of sociology—as almost every introductory textbook in the field was quick to point out—that the discipline had largely freed itself from social philosophy. If the status of sociology as a science was not exactly clear, there was no doubt about its dedication to scientific methods and objectivity.[1] Sociology, it was said, was value-free.

---

* Reprinted by special permission of the *Journal of Criminal Law and Criminology,* vol. 65, no. 2 (June 1974), Northwestern University School of Law, pp. 206–213.

[1] See, e.g., Mazur, "The Littlest Science," 3 *Am. Sociologist* 195 (1968).

It was precisely this point, however, that served as the focus of attack for a number of students and teachers.[2] Sociology, they argued, was still contaminated by the bias and subjectivity of particular interest groups in society. The claim to the cool neutrality of science was a sham. This was especially evident in the area of sociological theory. Social structure, it was said, had been interpreted in terms of consensus, but it was really conflict that lay at the heart of social organization. People in positions of power had traditionally been analyzed in terms of bureaucratic roles aimed at the rational accomplishment of organizational objectives. In reality, people in positions of power were motivated largely by their own selfish interests. A great variety of social problems had been viewed by sociology as flowing from individual pathologies. In fact, however, this approach merely disguised the extent to which the existing social system was at fault, and thus helped to buttress the status quo. Sociology had long been wedded to an evolutionary model of social change, whereas the truth of the matter was that real social change came about not through small increments but through far more radical leaps.

This debate, which broke out into the open in the sixties, involved a great many of the intellectual specialties of sociology, but it was particularly evident in the field of criminology. The study of crime, its causes and its cure had long been regarded as a borrower rather than a lender when it came to the intellectual substance of the social sciences. It had seemed a bit marginal to the major concerns of a science of society, from the viewpoint of many sociologists—perhaps because of its connections with the study of social problems, which many sociologists had viewed as being too deeply enmeshed in value judgments. Now, however, the growing argument about the objectivity of sociology suddenly found many of its crucial themes exemplified in how academic criminology had handled the subject of crime.

II

As a special field of knowledge, criminology had its origins in the attempt to reform the criminal law of the eighteenth century.

---

[2] See, e.g., Gouldner, "Anti-Minotaur: The Myth of a Value-Free Sociology," 9 *Social Problems* 199 (1962).

Bentham, Romilly and Beccaria were all children of the En-
lightenment, and they shared the objective of making the law a
more just, humane and rational instrument of the state. With the
rise of the Positivist School in the nineteenth century, however,
with its optimistic faith in science, criminology began to move
away from the domain of legal thinkers—a movement that became particularly marked in the United States after 1900.[3] In
some parts of Europe, and in Latin America, criminology maintained its links with jurisprudence, but in the United States we
witnessed a peculiar split. Criminal law became a subject matter
for lawyers and law schools; criminology, on the other hand,
turned up in the liberal arts curriculum of almost every college
and university, largely a creature of the social sciences and particularly sociology.

In some ways, this might have seemed to be a reasonable division of labor. A knowledge of the criminal law was, after all, a part
of the lawyer's professional training, even if, until fairly recently, it
tended to lack the éclat that attached to areas of law that were
potentially more financially productive. The lawyer's interest in
the criminal law was apt to center on the nature of the legal rules
and their interpretation by the courts; and his concern with why
people break the rules and what happens to them after they leave
the courtroom was likely to be rather fleeting. These were questions, however, that fell naturally into the theoretical and conceptual framework of the sociologist. Often enough, he had neither
the training nor the inclination to enter the thoughtways of the
legal scholar to pursue the law's meaning of *mens rea*, search and
seizure and conspiracy.[4]

It is possible that this matter of thoughtways was as important as
any special taste in subject matter in the mutual neglect exhibited
by criminologists and scholars of criminal law. The study of the
law, it has been said, is organized for action, while the social sciences are organized for the accumulation of knowledge; and this
aphorism points to a fundamental conflict between the intellectual
discipline of law and sociology that helped to keep their practitioners apart. As Robert Merton has indicated, sociologists are
guided in their work by the scientific ethos, not in terms of an

---

[3] See H. Mannheim, *Comparative Criminology* (1965).

[4] See R. Quinney, *The Problem of Crime* (1970).

individual ethical choice, but as a matter of institutionalized professional norms. The search for knowledge is to be undertaken in a spirit of neutrality, and the scientist must have the same passion for proving his hypotheses wrong as for proving them right. The validity of ideas is to be established by impersonal standards of proof; and learned authority must stand on an equal footing with the brashest newcomer when it comes to the empirical testings of facts. Scientific knowledge must be shared with one's colleagues, and no information is to be kept secret because it might bring an advantage or because it might be disturbing. Finally, the scientist is supposed to be under the sway of an organized skepticism that accepts no conclusion as final, no fact as forever proven. Every issue can be reopened and reexamined.[5]

These norms may not always be followed by social scientists as they go about their work, but in a rough way they do guide much scientific behavior, including the behavior of sociologists. The settling of legal disputes, however, is cut on a very different pattern. Lawyers are typically involved as partisans with a far from disinterested concern in the outcome of a case. At law, much is made of the weight of authority, and the discrediting of arguments on an *ad hominem* basis is a familiar occurrence. Information may be withheld on the grounds of privileged communication or with the idea that it would distort the reasoning of the triers of fact. There is a strong impulse to settle cases quickly and not to reopen old disputes.

These differences in the intellectual styles of professional work in sociology and in law appear to have greatly increased the difficulty of exchanging ideas between the two fields, and reinforced their separate development. In any event, the fact that criminal law and criminology tended to remain in separate academic compartments over much of the recent past led to a number of unfortunate consequences. First, many aspects of the criminal law's operation, such as arrest procedures, the activities of the grand jury, trials, and the statutory revision of the criminal law, often remained outside the purview of criminologists. Some attention was given to these matters, it is true, but the bulk of the attention of academic criminology was devoted to questions of crime causation and corrections. One need but review textbooks in criminology of

---

[5] See R. Merton, *Social Theory and Social Structure* (1949).

ten or twenty years ago to be struck by the short shrift frequently accorded the criminal law and other issues that loom large in the eyes of the legal scholar and that are, in fact, vital to understanding the relationship between crime and society. Second, the concept of crime was apt to remain singularly crude as the social scientist pursued his goal of building an explanatory schema for criminal behavior. A great variety of acts were frequently lumped together under headings such as "norm violation" and "delinquency," and the careful refinements of legal thought were shoved to one side. Many of the distinctions were quite irrelevant, it is true, from the viewpoint of the social sciences, for they were based on the needs of prosecution, an outmoded concept of man as a hedonistic calculator, and arbitrary, inconsistent categories such as felonies and misdemeanors. But the law at least recognized that "crime" was far from a homogeneous form of behavior, while criminology exhibited a disquieting tendency to speak of crime and the criminal in general. A greater interplay between the two fields might have stimulated efforts to build useful typologies.[6] Third, the fact that the two fields had so little to do with one another meant that many of the findings emerging from criminology received a less than sympathetic ear from those more closely tied to the criminal law. Serious doubts about the effectiveness of juvenile services, prisons, probation and so on were expressed by criminologists, but their voices seldom seemed to carry beyond the groves of academe.

III

In the late fifties and early sixties, a distinct change began to make its appearance. Topics that had long received relatively little attention in criminology (such as the day-to-day operations of the police) began to be examined by increasing numbers of sociologists. The crude classifications of earlier years began to give way to the empirical study of relatively specific types of criminal activity. The criminal law, which had been taken as a fixed parameter for so long by so many criminologists, began to be examined with a much more inquiring turn of mind. In short, the rather narrow viewpoint of criminology in the United States began to be

---

[6] Extended efforts to construct typologies of crime are fairly recent. See Clinard and Quinney, *Criminal Behavior Systems: A Typology* (1973).

enlarged and much of its proper subject matter—long left to others—began to be addressed at a serious and systematic level. The change, however, was not mainly because the criminal law and criminology had somehow found a way to end their long estrangement, although this played some part. Rather, a major reason for the shift appears to have been rooted in the same social forces that were modifying sociology as an academic discipline. By the beginning of the 1970s, it was evident that a new strain of thought had entered American criminology, challenging many of its basic assumptions.

Some have spoken of a "radical criminology," but the term is misleading since it suggests a particular ideological underpinning that probably does not exist. I think "critical criminology" is a somewhat better term, at least for the purposes of this discussion, keeping in mind that all such summary phrases can obscure as well as illuminate.

The themes involved in this new orientation can be roughly summarized as follows:

First, there is a profound skepticism accorded any individualistic theory of crime causation. It is not merely biological theories and psychological theories of personality maladjustment that have been abandoned. Sociological theories, dependent on notions of the individual's "defects" due to inadequate socialization or peer group pressures, are also viewed with a wary eye. The problem has become not one of identifying the objectively determined characteristics that separate the criminal and non-criminal, but of why some persons and not others are stigmatized with the label of "criminal" in a social process. "If preconceptions are to be avoided," writes Austin Turk, "a criminal is most accurately defined as any individual who is identified as such. . . ."[7] The roots of this idea in labeling theory are clear enough.[8] A number of writers in criminology today, however, have pushed the idea within a hairline of the claim that the only important reality is the act of labeling—and not because labeling ignores who is a criminal and who is not, but because we are all criminals.

Second, what I have called "critical criminology" is marked by a profound shift in the interpretation of motives behind the actions

---

[7] A. Turk, *Criminality and the Legal Order* 18 (1969).

[8] See E. Schur, *Labeling Deviant Behavior* (1971).

of the agencies that deal with crime. Many writers, of course, had long been pointing out that the "criminal-processing system" was often harsh and unfair, and, more specifically, that the poor and members of minority groups suffered from an acute disadvantage. Few criminologists, however, were willing to go so far as to claim that the system was inherently unjust. Rather, the usual argument was that our legal agencies were frequently defective due to lack of funds, unenlightened policies, and individual stupidity, prejudice and corruption. Now, however, among a large number of writers, the imputation of motives is of a different order: The operation of legal agencies is commonly interpreted as (1) the self-conscious use of the law to maintain the status quo for those who hold the power in society; or (2) activity aimed at maintaining organization self-interests, with "careerism" as both the carrot and the stick. If the system is unjust, then, we are not to look for relatively minor structural defects or random individual faults. Rather, the criminal law and its enforcement are largely instruments deliberately designed for the control of one social class by another.[9]

Third, the rightfulness of the criminal law had been questioned infrequently in the work of American criminologists, even if they were willing to admit that its application sometimes left something to be desired. The insanity plea, the definition of juvenile delinquency, the death sentence, the prohibition of gambling—these areas and a few others were open to vigorous critical scrutiny. By and large, however, the great bulk of the criminal law was taken as expressing a widely shared set of values. In any event, the question of "rightfulness" was not a suitable topic for the social sciences. In the last decade or so, however, there was a growing number of criminologists who found that assumption unrealistic. We could no longer accept the idea presented by Michael and Adler some forty years ago, said Richard Quinney, that "most of the people in any community would probably agree that most of the behavior which

---

[9] See, e.g., J. Douglas, *Crime and Justice in American Society* xviii (J. Douglas ed. 1971): "If there were no groups trying to control the activities of other groups, and capable of exercising sufficient power to try to enforce their wills upon those other groups through the legislative processes, there would be no laws making some activities 'crimes' and there could, consequently, be no 'criminals'. . . .

"[C]riminal laws are specifically enacted by the middle and upper classes to place the poorer classes under the more direct control of the police. . . ."

is proscribed by their criminal law is socially undesirable."[10] According to the emerging "critical criminology," the criminal law should not be viewed as the collective moral judgments of society promulgated by a government that was defined as legitimate by almost all people. Instead, our society was best seen as a *Gebeitsverband*, a territorial group living under a regime imposed by a ruling few in the manner of a conquered province.[11] The argument was not that murder, rape and robbery had suddenly become respectable but that popular attitudes toward the sanctity of property, the sanctity of the physical person, and the rather puritanical morality embedded in the law were far less uniform than American criminology had been willing to admit.

Fourth, American criminologists had long been skeptical of the accuracy of official crime statistics which they nonetheless accepted, reluctantly, as a major source of data for their field. The Uniform Crime Reports of the Federal Bureau of Investigation were, after all, "the only game in town," as far as national figures on criminal behavior were concerned. If the use of other official statistics derived from cities, states and particular legal agencies were almost always coupled with disclaimers, still, they were used.

The problem with these statistics, as criminologists were quick to point out, was that they could lead to either overestimation or an underestimation of the total amount of crime in any given year, but no one could be sure which was the case. Furthermore, the components of the total crime rate might be in error, and some of the components might be too high while others were too low. The data were based on thousands of local police jurisdictions throughout the country, and even the FBI refused to vouch for their accuracy.

It was clear that a part of the difficulty was the fact that the police had a stake in the amount of crime recorded in official records: if the crime rate went down, the police could win public acclaim for their efficiency in dealing with the crime problem; if the crime rate went up, the police could demand greater financial and political support as they fought their battle with the underworld. This issue, however, was apt to be treated in a rather desultory fashion, in terms of developing a theory about the relation-

---

[10] R. Quinney, *The Problem of Crime* 29 (1970).

[11] See M. Weber, *The Theory of Social and Economic Organization* 337 (T. Parsons ed. 1947).

ship between crime and society, or simply noted as one more
difficulty placed in the path of securing precise data for the construction of a theory of crime causation. The essential task was to
find ways to get "better" data, either by seeing to it that official statistics became more accurate, or by finding alternative ways to
gather information about the true incidence of criminal behavior,
such as self-reporting methods or sociological surveys using the reports of victims to uncover the amount of crime. Since the sixties,
however, another view of the matter has become increasingly popular in criminological thought. Rather than dismissing the interest
of law enforcement agencies in crime statistics as an unfortunate
source of error, the collection and dissemination of information
about the incidence of crime has become, for many, an important
theoretical variable in its own right. The crime rate, writes Peter
Manning, is "simply a construction of police activities," and the actual amount of crime is unknown and probably unknowable.[12]
Whether there is more or less "actual" criminality, notes Richard
Quinney, is not the issue. "The crucial question is why societies
and their agencies report, manufacture, or produce the volume of
crime that they do."[13]

The legitimacy of the rules embedded in the criminal law could
no longer be taken for granted, then, and neither could the credibility of the government that reported on their violation. The most
fruitful line of inquiry with regard to the causes of inaccuracy is
not chance error or simple bias. Instead, we must look for a systematic distortion that is part of the machinery for social control.[14]

IV

"Critical criminology" cannot, I think, be viewed as merely a
matter of emphasis, with its major themes no more than bits and
pieces of the conventional wisdom of the field. The set of ideas do

---

[12] Manning, "The Police: Mandate, Strategies, and Appearances," in *Crime and Justice in
American Society* 169 (J. Douglas ed. 1971).

[13] R. Quinney, *supra* note 4, at 122.

[14] See Biderman and Reiss, Jr., "On Exploring the 'Dark Figure' of Crime," 374 *Annals*
15 (1967): "Any set of crime statistics, including those of the survey, involves some evaluative, institutional processing of people's reports. Concepts, definitions, quantitative models,
and theories must be adjusted to the fact that the data are not some objectively observable
universe of 'criminal acts,' but rather those events defined, captured and processed as such
by some institutional mechanism."

form a coherent whole that is sufficiently different from much of American criminology of the period immediately before and after World War II to warrant the label "new." At the heart of this orientation lies the perspective of a stratified society in which the operation of the criminal law is a means of controlling the poor (and members of minority groups) by those in power who use the legal apparatus to (1) impose their particular morality and standards of good behavior on the entire society; (2) protect their property and physical safety from the depredations of the have-nots, even though the cost may be high in terms of the legal rights of those it perceives as a threat; and (3) extend the definition of illegal or criminal behavior to encompass those who might threaten the status quo. The middle classes or the lower-middle classes are drawn into this pattern of domination either because (1) they are led to believe they too have a stake in maintaining the status quo; or (2) they are made a part of agencies of social control and the rewards of organizational careers provide inducements for keeping the poor in their place.

The coercive aspects of this arrangement are hidden—at least in part—by labeling those who challenge the system as "deviants" or "criminals" when such labels carry connotations of social pathology, psychiatric illness and so on. If these interpretative schemes are insufficient to arouse widespread distaste for the rule-breaker as "bad" or "tainted," official statistics can serve to create a sense of a more direct and personal danger in the form of a crime wave that will convince many people (including many of the people in the lower classes) that draconian measures are justified.

The poor, according to this viewpoint, may or may not break the legal rules more often than others, although they will certainly be arrested more often and treated more harshly in order to prevent more extensive nonconformity. In a sense, they are expendable in the interest of general deterrence. In any event, they are probably driven in the direction of illegal behavior, even if they do not actually engage in it, because (1) the rules imposed on them from above have little relationship to the normative prescriptions of their own subculture; (2) the material frustrations of the lower classes in a consumer society where the fruits of affluence are publicized for all, but available only to some, prove almost unbearable; and (3) there is generated among the lower classes a deep hostility to a social order in which they are not allowed to participate and had little hand in the making.

The perspective sketched in above would seem to fit well with a radical view of American society, or at least with an ideological position on the left side of the political spectrum. While this might possibly account for the attention the perspective has received from some writers in the field of criminology (and some students with a very jaundiced view of the capitalist-industrial social order), I would very much doubt that critical criminology can be neatly linked to any special political position.[15]

At the same time, it does not appear that this new viewpoint in criminology simply grew out of the existing ideas in the field in some sort of automatic process where pure logic breeds uncontaminated by the concerns and passions of the times. Nor does it appear that a flood of new data burst upon the field, requiring a new theoretical synthesis. Instead, as I have suggested at the beginning of this article, it seems likely that the emergence of critical criminology is a part of the intellectual ferment taking place in sociology in general, and both have much of their source in the socio-historical forces at work in the 1960s.

Among the many elements that have been involved, there are at least three social-historical changes that appear to have played a major role. First, the impact of the Vietnam war on American society has yet to be thoroughly analyzed and assessed, but it is clear that it has had an influential part in the rise of a widespread cynicism concerning the institutions of government, the motives of those in power, and the credibility of official pronouncements. The authority of the state has been called into question, including the authority of the state made manifest in the law as its instrument. The good intentions—indeed, the good sense—of those running the apparatus of the state have, for many, become suspect. The truth of official statements, whether it be body counts or crime counts, is no longer easily accepted among many segments of the population. The notion of a Social Contract as the basis of government may have been long recognized as a fiction in Ameri-

---

[15] In the current intellectual climate, there are a great many pressures to identify particular scientific ideas with particular ideological positions. Ideas and ideology, however, still exhibit a peculiar independence despite strident claims that they must go together; and if some criminologists believe that the viewpoint of critical criminology is something that must be considered, there is no iron necessity that ties them to either a liberal or a conservative stance. For an illuminating examination of the issue in another field, see Herrnstein, "On Challenging an Orthodoxy," 55 *Commentary* 52 (1973).

can life, but it was also widely accepted as a metaphor expressing a belief in government by consent. In the 1960s, there were many people (including many in the social sciences) who felt that the metaphor was coming apart. Government was far more apt to be seen as manipulation and coercion, and the legal rules could be more easily interpreted, at least by some, as part of a social order imposed by a ruling elite. "Property is theft," said Proudhon in 1840. In the 1960s, his curt saying had taken on a new bite.

Second, the growth of a counter-culture in the United States in the last decade admittedly remains within the realm of those ideas that are far from precise. Yet, there seems no question that a shift in values and ideas did take place and that the use of drugs— particularly marijuana—was a major theme. The arguments about drugs have been repeated so often, the facts and theories elaborated upon in such familiar detail, that discussion of the subject has taken on the appearance of a litany. Nonetheless, for present purposes, it is important to point out that millions of people engaged in behavior they regarded as harmless, but that was defined by society as a crime—not a minor or relatively harmless breach of the law, according to the authorities, but a serious, dangerous offense. Whatever may have been the consequences in terms of popular attitudes toward the law and law-enforcement agencies, another reaction was let loose, namely, a long skeptical look at traditional ideas about the nature of the criminal and the causes of criminal behavior.

In addition, as a consumer-oriented middle class wedded to establishment values emerged as a favorite whipping boy in the analysis of what was wrong with American life, evidence of white-collar crime took on a new prominence.[16] Far from being a form of behavior largely confined to those at the bottom of the social heap, crime was everywhere. "If you are a typical American citizen," says Erik Olin Wright, "chances are that in your life you have committed some crime for which you could have been sent to jail or prison."[17] If this were true, and if the people caught up and punished by the system of criminal justice were so largely drawn from the lower classes, then the machinery of the criminal law

---

[16] It should be pointed out, to underline the idea that these ideas were not the sole property of a particular ideological position, that attacks on the middle class style of life often came from the Right as well as the Left, with much discussion of the perils of a lower middle class moving into affluence.

[17] E. Wright, *The Politics of Punishment* 3 (1973).

must be far from fair or impartial. If you were labeled a criminal, something more than criminal behavior must be involved.

Third, the rise of political protest in the 1960s took on a variety of forms, ranging from heated discussions to bloody confrontations in the streets. It became clear that even the most dispassionate of observers would have to agree that in a number of instances the police power of the state had been used illegally to suppress political dissent. Some accounts, such as those dealing with the deliberate elimination of the Black Panther leadership, might be shown to have been slipshod in their facts; other accounts might be hopelessly confusing when it came to pinning down precisely the illegality of police actions. Enough evidence remained, however, to show that the police had been used in many instances beyond the limits of the law to silence political opposition. In addition, there were a large number of cases (more murky, perhaps, in terms of being able to disentangle the facts) in which it was believed that the law had acted legally to apprehend and punish a law breaker, but in which the law's actions were due to the individual's social and political beliefs rather than to his criminal behavior. The criminal law, in short, was seen by many as becoming more than a device for controlling run-of-the-mill criminality. It was becoming an arm of Leviathan, not as a matter of abstract theory, but as something directly experienced or immediately observed.[18]

It was the intellectual climate produced by these and similar social-historical events, I would argue, that played a major part in the rise of critical criminology, as much as any forces at work within the field of traditional criminology itself. The new perspective is touched by ideology, but not determined by it; incorporates points made before, but builds something different; and offers a new interpretation or point of view rather than a vast quantity of new data. All of this, of course, leaves untouched the issue of the potential contribution of this perspective to the study of crime and society.

V

Is critical criminology valid? The question is really an unanswerable one, I believe, because what we are confronted with is not

---

[18] See T. Becker, *Political Trials* (1971).

so much a body of precise, systematic theoretical propositions as a viewpoint, a perspective or an orientation—terms that I have deliberately used throughout the discussion. A theory states the relationships among a number of variables that are well defined; a viewpoint, on the other hand, urges us to look in one direction rather than another, points to promising lines of inquiry, singles out one interpretation from a set of possible interpretations dealing with the same set of facts. In this sense, the viewpoint of critical criminology as it stands today probably cannot be said to be true or false. Rather, it is a bet on what empirical research and theoretical development in the field will reveal in the future. In many ways, I think the bet is not a bad one.

However, before examining what some of the contributions of critical criminology might be, let us look briefly, at its more obvious defects. In the first place, criminologists writing from this perspective have a tendency to uncover the latent functions of the criminal law and its operation and then convert these latent functions into manifest ones—unfortunately, all too easily.[19] That is to say, the administration of the criminal law frequently works to the disadvantage of the poor, members of minority groups and the uneducated. It is then assumed, often with little concrete evidence, that this, in fact, is the intended and recognized goal of those administering the criminal law. The task of sociological analysis, however, requires a good deal more than this rather superficial imputation of motive which is apt to degenerate into glib cynicism.

In the second place, a number of writers who are exploring the ideas we have presented under the heading of "critical criminology" often use a model of social stratification that is either overly simplified or ambiguous. We are frequently presented with the poor on the one hand, and the Establishment or those in power on the other, with a vaguely defined middle class being portrayed sometimes as another victim of injustice and sometimes as a co-opted agent of those on the top of the socio-economic scale. In reality, however, there is probably a great deal of variation in different socioeconomic groups in attitudes toward the criminal law and its administration (such as lower class support of the police

---

[19] I am here following the usage provided by Robert Merton, who defines manifest functions as the objective consequences of social action intended and recognized by the actors involved, whereas latent functions are consequences that are neither intended nor recognized. See R. Merton, supra note 5, at ch. 1.

and upper class use of drugs); and, if this is true, the idea that the criminal law is predominantly something imposed from above has need to be substantially modified.

In the third place, we may all indeed be criminals, in the sense that most adults have committed an act at one time or another that would be called a crime by the criminal law. This does not mean, however, that we are all murderers, rapists, robbers, burglars and auto thieves. Persistent criminals or criminals considered serious may be singled out for the law's attention without reducing a criminal conviction to a mere label that has no connection with an objective reality. Labeling theory in sociology has never quite come to grips with the relationship between the dynamics of the labeling process and the realities of the behavior being categorized; its tendency toward solipsism has been noted by others.[20] If critical criminology is to make a significant contribution to a sociology of crime, it will need to avoid the error of believing that because the legal stigma of crimes does not match the occurrence of crime-in-general in the population, the stigma is necessarily based on irrelevant factors such as income and race. Certain patterns of criminal behavior may still have much to do with the matter.

While recognizing these strictures, I think it can be argued that "critical criminology" holds out the promise of having a profound impact on our thinking about crime and society. It forces an inquiry into precisely how the normative content of the criminal law is internalized in different segments of society, and how norm-holding is actually related to behavior. It makes us examine how the legal apparatus designed for the control of crime takes on a life of its own, and begins to pursue objectives that may have little to do with modifying the crime rate. It directs needed attention to the relationship between the political order and nonconformity, thus revitalizing one of sociology's most profound themes, the relationship between the individual and the state. And it impels us, once again, to analyze equality before the law as a basic element of a democratic society. As T. H. Marshall has pointed out, much of the history of the last 250 years or so in Western societies can be seen as an attempt to achieve citizenship for all, which he defines as a kind of basic human equality associated with the concept of

---

[20] See, e.g., E. Schur, supra note 8.

full membership in a community.[21] The concept of legal equality emerged in the eighteenth century, the concept of political equality in the nineteenth, and the concept of social equality in the twentieth. But none of the gains can be taken for granted, for they can be lost as well as won. In the administration of the criminal law in our society today, there is ample evidence that our ideals of equality before the law are being compromised by the facts of income and race in an industrial, highly bureaucratized social order. If a "critical criminology" can help us solve that issue, while still confronting the need to control crime, it will contribute a great deal.

---

[21] T. H. Marshall, *Citizenship and Social Class* (1950).

Chapter 2

The social basis of law

IS LAW NECESSARY?

A discussion of the social or political basis of criminal law should initially address the question of whether society really needs written laws in order to exist. The evidence suggests that written laws are not always necessary since not all societies have had a codified body of rules comparable to a modern criminal code. In smaller, less complex societies than our own we find that traditions serving a function similar to that of modern laws exist but that these are often not codified, written statutes (Mair, 1962; MacIver and Page, 1964: 166–188). Such traditions cover all aspects of communal life, including prescribed sexual and family arrangements and rules for sharing goods, protecting property, and settling disputes. However, as societies grow, at some point a written criminal code seems to be required. As Murdock (1950: 715) observes, small groups of any type can rely solely on unwritten or informal understandings; however, in larger groups such understandings must be reduced to writing to insure the necessary coordination of activities:

[When] human beings found themselves for the first time living in local aggregations of appreciably more than a thousand people, they discovered that informal mechanisms of control no longer sufficed to maintain social order. Face-to-face relationships could not now be maintained with everyone, and tended to be limited to smaller groups of relatives or close neighbors. Individual deviants were presented for the first time with an alternative to conformity. They could sever old relationships and cultivate new ones among persons ignorant or tolerant of their lapses. Thus was born the possibility of escape from the "tyranny" of social control which is exemplified at its maximum today in the anonymity of the individual in a large city.

Suggesting, as this book does, that criminal laws in a given society often reflect the interests of elites and powerful interest groups is quite another thing than claiming that criminal laws of some type are not necessary for organized social life. In a heterogeneous mass society such as our own, where a variety of people are thrown together in often anonymous relationships, laws are useful and necessary for the organization and coordination of activities. However, since ours is a society with very powerful interest groups and wealthy elites, the particular laws that come into existence will not usually conflict with the interests of those groups.

Nevertheless, anarchists and some Marxist theorists contend that law is not necessary for society. One Marxist argument is that the state, including its laws and its police, is not required by mass society but rather is required by the bourgeoisie to control the mass of workers in a capitalist economy but would not be required in a true communist society, regardless of size. According to this reasoning, after the revolution of the proletariat, citizens will voluntarily cooperate with one another, and coercion by the state will no longer be required. Therefore, the state including the laws and the police, will "wither away" (Schlesinger, 1945; Berman, 1963). Unfortunately, using either China or the Soviet Union as examples of societies which have had such revolutions, we see no evidence that the state is withering away. In both the Soviet Union and China we observe a large and powerful central government. It does not appear that the revolutions in these two countries have produced such a degree of commitment to the social norms that the force of law is no longer necessary.

Indeed, it appears that a formal written criminal law only comes into existence when commitment to the social norms of a society becomes too weak to restrain widespread violations of those norms. Before such violations occur on any large scale, it is obviously unnecessary to write laws prescribing penalties to cover such behavior. Joseph Eaton (1952: 334) observes:

New rules . . . are usually proposed . . . to combat a specific innovation in personal behavior of some members, which some . . . regard as a violation of the unwritten mores. The new practice must be more than an isolated deviation of the sort which is controlled effectively through the normal processes of community discipline—punishment of the offender by admonition. . . . Only when a deviation becomes widespread . . . are the leaders likely to appeal for a formal statement of the unwritten community code.

Thus a written criminal code is necessary in a mass society, and especially in a highly stratified society such as our own, in which there is a marked lack of consensus about the social norms.

Originally no written law existed in what is today the nation of Great Britain. Initially a set of principles emerged which derived "their authority solely from usages and customs of immemorial antiquity, or from the judgments and decrees of the courts recognizing, affirming, and enforcing such usages and customs" (Black, 1951: 345–346). It is from these principles, called *common law,* that a good deal of American criminal law has been borrowed.

LAW IN SMALL NONLITERATE SOCIETIES

In small nonliterate societies that do not have a complex division of labor, it is exceedingly difficult to distinguish law from other norms or customs. Perhaps this is why some anthropologists say that primitive society has no law and therefore, of course, no crime. Some observers of primitive life have claimed that "custom is king." They argue that the rule of custom is so strong and pervasive in primitive social groups that no law is required and none emerges. Hoebel (1954) says that this is untrue and that custom can and should be distinguished from law. He uses the example of an Indian warrior whose horse was taken by another warrior of his tribe. The aggrieved warrior submitted his complaint to the tribal chiefs. They had the other warrior brought in from a distant camp. The accused warrior offered restitution as well as a suitable explanation for his conduct. After settling the dispute as a court, the chiefs went on to act as a legislature and made a new rule against "borrowing" horses without permission. The chiefs also assumed the responsibility for retrieving goods borrowed without permission and established the rule that henceforth the punishment for borrowers who resisted would be a whipping.

On an even less complex level of social organization, such as that of the Eskimo, the opinion of all adult males may be polled before a given punishment is meted out by a citizen who the others agree can act as an agent of the tribe in this one case. All the men help make what is both a legislative and a judicial decision—namely that a given act must be punished in a specific way and that a certain person may administer the punishment on behalf of the group. No citizen has a permanent specialized legislative, judicial, or police role. So it seems that the fundamental or most basic quality of law in any society is not a permanent set of law enforcement officials but the legitimate application of physical coercion by some socially authorized agent.

The development of a formal legal system with specialized occupational roles, however, is not an all-or-nothing matter, as this discussion might suggest. In a study of 51 societies, Schwartz and Miller found that some societies have only partially developed legal systems in this sense. The elements which Schwartz and Miller (1964: 161) identified as the parts of a formal legal system were:

counsel: regular use of specialized non-kin advocates in the settlement of disputes

mediation: regular use of non-kin third party intervention in dispute settlement

police: specialized armed force used partially or wholly for norm enforcement.

The least complex societies had none of these elements. Typically, if societies have any elements of a legal system, it is mediation, or the use of nonkin in dispute settlements. In somewhat more complex societies police are typically found as well. In the most complex societies legal counsel is also present. As will become clear in the next chapter, it is not until permanent and specialized law enforcement agencies develop, such as legislatures, police, and courts, that people begin to reflect on the nature of crime and criminal law.

LEGAL CHANGE AND HUMAN VALUES

When contemporary laws are compared with those of less complex societies, a massive change in legal structure is evident. It is apparent that written laws change, as do the values of people in society. In modern America this does not imply a democratic leveling of power, however, for there is some indication, as discussed in Chapter 1, that business-owned and -controlled mass media manipulate the attitudes of the mass of citizens (Sallach, 1974; Cohen and Young, 1973). In any event, however, attitudes do change, and one need only look to assorted laws covering a variety of behaviors ranging blasphemy and abortion to the use of alcohol and marijuana to recognize that as attitudes change, laws also change, though sometimes only very haltingly and slowly and often lagging behind the changes in attitudes. There is less agreement, however, on the issue of whether a change in the law can help bring about a later change in people's attitudes and behaviors. Some supporters of the civil rights legislation of the 1960s argued that laws requiring equal treatment for blacks—covering voting rights, open public accommodations, and equal employment opportunities—would create a social environment that would make for later positive attitude change (Civil Rights Act of 1964). Those opposed to such laws argued that "you can't legislate morality" or even force people to obey laws with which they do not agree. Duster (1970) observes, however, that among those who argue that morality in racial relations cannot be legislated, many oppose the legalization of prostitution on the ground that state approval of sexual immorality would corrupt and weaken the moral foundations of society. In other words, the typical position is that the state cannot legislate morality but that it can legitimate immorality. As might be expected, citizens often argue that the law is only effective in supporting what in fact is their preexisting moral persuasion. So the claim that morality in race relations cannot be legislated often suggests that the person who advances it does not want a new morality to be enforced under law.

Duster (1970) observes that, as a matter of fact, in some instances legal change has been followed by changes in behavior as well as changes in values and attitudes. The Harrison Tax Act of 1914 is given major credit for transforming the typically tolerant view of drug addiction that existed prior to 1900 into our current intolerance. Although we have in this century become more tolerant of physical and mental illness, we have become less tolerant of addiction because, along with the legal change, the social characteristics of addicts have also changed. Unlike the typically middle-class addicts around the turn of the century, today's addicts are typically poor. In light of the Harrison Tax Act it seems that new morality can be legislated only when the poor are the targets and not the beneficiaries of legal change, and when the legal change does not conflict with the moral concerns of more affluent citizens. This would help explain why alcohol prohibition did not work— too many powerful citizens enjoyed drinking.

LEGAL CHANGE AND DISOBEDIENCE

Whether or not legal change alters or only reflects other social change, it is apparent that laws do change over time. Because this is so, some argue that in a democracy which is also a mass society, complete obedience to the law should not be encouraged. Disobedience to the law may be a good thing because it tests and pushes the limits of the law. Resistance to written laws runs the gamut from covert individual violations, such as the frequent use of marijuana in the United States, to massive violent rebellion, such as the Bolshevik revolution in Russia. Nonviolent civil disobedience falls somewhere between these extremes and will be explored more fully, since it dramatizes ideally the relationship between law and morality. Mahatma Gandhi (1869–1948), the political and moral leader of India during its fight for independence from Britain, advocated such techniques of nonviolent civil disobedience as nonpayment of fines and taxes, boycott of courts, fasting, picketing, and strikes (Gandhi, 1951). One of the few ways in which citizens in a democratic mass society like our own can have an impact upon the law is through direct nonviolent civil disobedience. In his letter from Birmingham Jail, Martin Luther King, Jr. (1963: 769), wrote:

One may well ask, "How can you advocate breaking some laws and obeying others?" The answer lies in the fact that there are two types of laws: just and unjust. I agree with St. Augustine that "an unjust law is no law at all."

Now what is the difference between the two? How does one determine whether a law is just or unjust? A just law is a man-made code that squares with the moral law or the law of God. An unjust law is a code that is out of harmony with the moral law. To put it in the terms of St. Thomas Aquinas, an unjust law is a human law that is not rooted in eternal law and natural law. Any law that uplifts human personality is just. Any law that degrades human personality is unjust. All segregation statutes are unjust because segregation distorts the soul and damages the personality.

. . . . .

I hope you are able to see the distinction I am trying to point out. In no sense do I advocate evading the law, as would the rabid segregationist. That would lead to anarchy. One who breaks an unjust law must do so *openly, lovingly,* and with a willingness to accept the penalty. I submit that an individual who breaks a law that conscience tells him is unjust and who willingly accepts the penalty of imprisonment in order to arouse the conscience of the community over its injustice is in reality expressing the highest respect for law.[1]

In our mass society of more than 200 million people, town meetings where everyone can have a direct and personal voice in government are not feasible. Since laws do change over time, part of this change can be brought about by nonviolent civil disobedience. Regardless of how one feels about civil disobedience, it is clear that the civil disobedience of Dr. King and his followers in the South was responsible for some legal change, including the ending of legal racial segregation of public accommodations. Moreover, the philosophy of Martin Luther King and the results he achieved are not as unique as they appear to be at first glance. In the remaining sections of this chapter we will see through several examples how specific powerful interest groups had a similarly direct impact on written laws. The argument that society, government, and the law are structured to benefit most those in positions of power is reflected in these illustrations. If powerful groups have a direct impact on the law, the question can be raised about the legitimacy of others also directly influencing the law. Although sociologists have typically described how inequality has influenced the administration of the law, a prior question which will be addressed later in this chapter involves the effect of inequality on the creation of the written law.

ASSUMPTIONS REGARDING THE ROLE OF LAW IN SOCIETY

From the rhetoric of political leaders we are led to believe that law and order are always associated in fact. The idea is that the

---

[1] See also *The City of God by St. Augustine* (Healey, 1903); and *Aquinas Ethicus: or The moral teaching of St. Thomas* [St. Thomas Aquinas] (Rickaby, 1896): "A tyrannical law, not being according to reason, is not, absolutely speaking, a law, but rather, a perversion of law" (p. 272). "A law that is not just, goes for no law at all (p. 292)."

rule of law or obedience to law and social orderliness are necessarily bound together (Skolnick, 1966: 1–22). Former President
Richard Nixon always stressed this point in his political campaigns.
Yet his administration provides a dramatic demonstration that law
and order are not in fact complementary. During his administration the United States appeared to become increasingly orderly
after the tumult of the 1960s, which included urban ghetto riots
and campus antiwar demonstrations. This orderliness, however,
was not a result of the rule of law, for the evidence presented at
the Watergate investigation shows that the Nixon Administration
was systematically and routinely violating criminal laws. This
example suggests that social order can be maintained in a number
of ways and that use of the law is just one such mechanism. Police
states which have existed in Greece and Chile are ruled not so
much by laws as by guns, and "a concentration camp is more
orderly than a town meeting" (Gaylin and Rothman, 1976: xxviii).
Although ruling military juntas have no constitutional authority,
they are able to maintain order by the threat of personal injury. In
fact, the threat of violence seems to be the most efficient means of
maintaining order, for before their military coups Greece and
Chile had much more political disorder. The rule of law implies
some restriction on governmental efforts at social control, such as
allowing citizens constitutional rights of due process against government prosecution. However, the commonsense association of
law violation and disorder is hard to destroy. Most citizens, and
perhaps police especially, are suspicious of anything that seems
out of order or out of place (Skolnick, 1966).

Perhaps part of the confusion over the relationship between law
and order can be cleared up when it is recognized that what is
defined as order is heavily dependent on human perceptions of
the symbolic properties of events rather than the events themselves. For example, college students disrupting traffic and damaging some property to celebrate a football victory are often tolerated by the local citizens and police. Similar student actions to
protest the war in Vietnam were occasionally met with massive
arrests, beatings, tear gas, and sometimes even shootings. In both
types of activity, students conducted themselves similarly, but their
actions symbolized vastly different things, and this explains the
differential response. The point is that the relationship between
the rule of law and maintenance of order is confusing because of
changing definitions of social order.

Aside from the commonsense view that the role of law is to achieve order in society, three recognizable intellectual traditions may be found in the criminological literature. These are (1) that law is a product of democratic compromise among competing interest groups, (2) that law is a product of political domination by either an elite or a dominant class, and (3) that law serves mainly the symbolic or public relations function of convincing the masses of the legitimacy of government.

One view, then, is that through law people in social groups compromise on their interests and ultimately achieve some *consensus* as to what is best for society.

Looked at functionally, the law is an attempt to satisfy, to reconcile, to harmonize, to adjust these overlapping and often conflicting claims and demands, either through securing them directly and immediately, or through securing certain individual interests, or through delimitations or compromises of individual interests, so as to give effect to the greatest total of interests that weigh most in our civilization, with the least sacrifice of the scheme of interests as a whole (Pound, 1943: 39).

Assuming such consensus, Durkheim (1933: 73) defines crime as follows:

The only common characteristic of all crimes is that they consist . . . in acts universally disapproved of by members of each society. . . . crime shocks sentiments which, for a given social system, are found in all healthy consciences.

Indeed, as indicated in Chapter 1, even when consensus does exist, this may reflect the influence of largely corporate-owned and -controlled mass media. Yet in spite of corporate controls on the flow of ideas in the mass media, currently many Americans probably recognize the role of power, interest groups, and elites in government, including the lawmaking process.

An alternative view is that law is the result of the *dominance* of one group over another. Through law the interests of more powerful groups are enforced by the state, and opposing groups are controlled (Vold, 1958; Quinney, 1970). Vold (1958: 208) observes: "As political groups line up against one another, they seek the assistance of the organized state to help them defend their 'rights' and protect their interests. . . . Whichever group interest can marshal the greatest number of votes will determine whether or not there is to be a new law to hamper and curb the interests of some opposition group."

One service provided by the criminal justice system is the prosecution of charges involving checks written on insufficient funds. Citizens are prosecuted, convicted, and incarcerated for writing bad checks, not so much because this threatens the whole community, but rather because "bad check" writers are mainly an annoyance to merchants, and the criminal justice system gives merchants help in collecting on such checks.

In reflecting on contemporary political domination, Reich (1970: 110) suggests that during this century a situation has developed in the United States which has

produced law that fell into line with the requirements of organization and technology, and that supported the demands of administration rather than protecting the individual. Once law had assumed this role, there began a vast proliferation of laws, statutes, regulations, and decisions. For the law began to be employed to aid all of the work of the Corporate State by compelling obedience to the State's constantly increasing demands.

And (Reich, 1970: 115):

The greater the quantity of legal rules, the greater the amount of discretionary power is generated. If a licensed pharmacist is subject to fifty separate regulations, he can be harassed by one after another, as soon as he proves himself to have complied with the first.

In addition, the state dominates some citizens more than others (Reich, 1970: 114):

It can be seen that for each status, class, and position in society, there is a different set of laws. There is one set of laws for the welfare recipient, one for the businessman. . . . for example, the constitutional right of privacy is treated differently for a businessman or farmer than for a welfare recipient. A person receiving Medicare is required to take a loyalty oath; others are not. If "law" means a general rule to govern a community of people, then in the most literal and precise sense we have *no* law; we are a lawless society.

Moreover, Rich (1970: 110) observes that despite the proliferation of corporate power over citizens, corporations have largely not been held subject to the Bill of Rights by the courts and can, for example, fire employees who exercise their "freedom" of speech. Reich (1970: 116) concludes:

The point is this: there can be no rule of law in an administrative state. The ideal of the rule of law can be realized only in a political-conflict state which places limits upon official power and permits diversity to exist.

This perspective, which stresses political domination, undoubtedly gives a more convincing picture of the role of criminal law, at least in modern states. Yet it might be argued that though some criminal laws, such as those involving bad checks, serve mainly and most directly the interests of the powerful, many laws appear to protect the poor and powerless as well as the more influential members of society. It might seem, for example, that murder and rape laws offer the same protection to all groups. In such cases, however, class interests are usually reflected in the administration or application of laws, a topic that will be covered in Chapters 4 and 5, which deal with the police and the courts, respectively. Indeed, a continuing complaint of the black community is that offenses against black people are taken less seriously by the police and are responded to with less official action than are identical offenses committed in the white community (for example, see Ennis, 1967: 55; and Hahn, 1971).

Both the consensus and the conflict orientations assume that people typically make rational decisions to maximize their material gains. However, Edelman (1964) suggests that this assumption may be incorrect, and that citizens often base their political behavior not on their real or material interests, but on whether or not a given piece of legislation *symbolically reassures* them. Edelman suggests that the masses are often reassured by the mere passage of legislation which conflicts with the interests of organized pressure groups. Yet such legislation is typically not enforced, which in turn satisfies the needs of organized groups. The history of antitrust laws and national prohibition can be interpreted in this way. Antitrust laws were passed at a time when great public hostility was directed against large trusts. The laws satisfied the public that "something was being done," and yet the corporations could continue largely as before. Similarly, national prohibition was forced through by largely rural Protestant interests; yet since the interests of many powerful consumers' and producers groups conflicted with the new law, it was enforced only episodically and was widely disregarded or evaded. Both direct political domination and symbolism as vehicles for the control exercised by powerful groups seem apparent in the following review of the origins of various kinds of criminal legislation.

LEGAL CHANGE AND SOCIAL POWER

In this section we will examine case studies to determine how various powerful groups in England and the United States have exercised their power to forge new legislation suited to their unique interests.

Chambliss (1964) convincingly demonstrates that the historical origins of vagrancy laws in England can be traced to the needs of the changing power structure. He suggests that the earliest forerunners of modern vagrancy laws originated in the 13th century. In a strict sense these were not vagrancy laws since they did not seek to prevent the movement of citizens from one place to another. Rather, their aim was to relieve churches of their traditional responsibility for providing free food and shelter to travelers. These laws merely prohibited people from sleeping and eating at any place other than their own homes, including churches, unless they were invited.

The first real vagrancy statutes were enacted in the 14th century. At that time it became a crime to give alms to anyone who was able to work yet unemployed, and it also became a crime to refuse work or leave a job without permission. These new laws were a product of the Black Death, which decimated the labor force in 14th century England. Since few workers were available, the landowners required such legislation to force laborers to accept employment at low wages.

However, even with this help, the landowners were losing power, and by the 16th century there was yet another shift in the vagrancy laws. They were no longer designed to force laborers to work but to control individuals who looked "suspicious"—the type of people who might be robbers or thieves. Now the punishments for vagrancy convictions became very severe. The new vagrancy laws served the interests of the merchant groups. These groups were gaining in power and influence in England at the time and desired to have their goods in transit protected under law. Thus three powerful interest groups—the church, the landowners, and the merchants—were served at different periods by the changing vagrancy legislation.

Hall's (1952: 3–40) study of embezzlement also vividly demonstrates the role of power in the development of written criminal laws in England. Under early English common law it was not considered criminal for a person to convert to his own use property that an employer had given him to use in working for the employer. In other words, there was no known crime of embezzlement. Apparently, it was thought that the owner should have protected himself by selecting a more trustworthy person to use his property while in his service. Such common-law practices seem to have been satisfactory during the Middle Ages when the economy was dominated by employers who owned feudal estates, and their employees were serfs who were tied to the land. At that time the essential means of trade was barter—trading one commodity for another. In such a situation, an embezzlement law was not required.

At the end of the Middle Ages, however, several changes occurred that forced the emergence of some government control of what we today call embezzlement. Merchant trading companies were growing rapidly, and the feudal estates were breaking up. Therefore, employees were no longer bound to the land. Moreover, barter was being replaced by the widespread use of paper money. The new mobility of employees, plus the increased use of paper money, made embezzlement much easier, and the growing power of commercial groups forced the required legislation through Parliament. This illustrates that new legislation is not generated merely because a group has a specific need for such legislation; it is also necessary that the group be powerful enough to have its needs protected by law.

The rise to power of the merchant class had another interesting effect on the law. Nineteenth century merchants objected to the capital penalty which was prescribed for many nonviolent crimes involving property, such as theft. The merchants argued that the severity of the prescribed punishment discouraged the prosecution of property crimes. Because of their reluctance to inflict the prescribed punishments, judges and juries used any pretext to render a verdict of not guilty even in the face of convincing contrary evidence. Thus, theft and other property crimes went unpunished, and the severity of the laws actually encouraged criminality. Ironically, the merchants' support for less severe legal penalties was motivated by a desire for more, not less, punishment (Hall, 1952: 110–152).

The American Colonies also provide support for the contention that the interests of powerful groups are protected by the laws. Originally there was a close association between sin and crime in the Colonies because the Puritan leaders looked to the Bible in drafting criminal statutes (Nelson, 1967: 450–482). Therefore, court records up until the Revolution indicate that most prosecutions were for sin-crimes, such as fornication, violation of the Sabbath, and adultery. Since crime, like sin, could strike anywhere, offenders were found in all social classes. However, by the early 1800s the basic use of the law had shifted from the preservation of morality to the protection of property. By the early 1800s, probably as a consequence of an economic depression and widespread unemployment, most people were being convicted of property offenses. Predictably, the records show that the typical offenders were now the urban poor, as is currently true. This example clearly shows that the function of the law had shifted to protect the interests of the more affluent, the property owners, against the less affluent. Economic distress and consequent increases in property violations seem to have caused concern with sin-crimes to be forgotten.

Sinclair (1962) demonstrates how rural Protestant interests organized to push through the national prohibition of alcohol in the United States. According to Becker (1963: 135–146), the influence of the Protestant ethic was also responsible for the repressive governmental policy toward the use of some addictive drugs. Musto (1973) points out that the narcotics laws in the United States are also a product of the fear that certain drugs make specific minorities more difficult to control. White Southerners alleged that cocaine enabled blacks to withstand bullets which would kill normal persons and stimulated sexual assault among blacks. Such fears are reflected in the 1914 Harrison Act, which legally controlled opium and coca products, including cocaine. Fear among whites in California that smoking opium encouraged sexual contacts between Chinese and white Americans was a factor in its prohibition.

According to Musto (1973), there was little fear of marijuana until the 1930s, and for this reason it was not prohibited under federal law until 1937. Mexican nationals came into the United States in great numbers during the 1920s and brought with them traditions of marijuana use. Although Anglos in the Southwest may have disliked the habit, it was usually tolerated because the

Mexicans provided an inexpensive source of labor during this period of economic boom. However, during the depression of the 1930s, Mexicans were seen as competitors for scarce jobs, and their habits began to seem more threatening. This was especially true in the Southwest, where the Mexican immigrants were concentrated.

Physicians recognize that barbiturates, like heroin, are addictive (Smith and Wesson, 1973), and that barbiturates are undoubtedly more widely used than heroin (Brecher, 1972). Yet barbiturates, unlike heroin, are easily available from physicians by prescription. One explanation for the differential handling of heroin and barbiturates is the different social status and power of the users of these drugs. The users of heroin are predominantly poor, whereas barbiturate addicts are generally more affluent (Smith and Wesson, 1973). The addiction of the poor is legally proscribed and subject to police harassment, whereas the addiction of the more affluent is not. Similarly, the prohibition of alcohol was ultimately defeated not because it is safe to use alcohol but because of the power of its users.

The pressure of powerful groups also helps to explain the recent massive change in attempts to control marijuana use in the United States. Earlier, the accepted model of controlling drug use had been one of increasing the prescribed penalties (see Lindesmith, 1965: 80–82; Clausen, 1961: 215–217). However, since late 1968, all 50 states in the United States have reduced first-offense possession of a limited amount of marijuana from a felony, usually punishable by more than a year in prison, to at most a misdemeanor, usually punishable by a fine and/or less than one year in confinement. The new awareness that marijuana use is no more hazardous than the use of other drugs, such as tobacco and alcohol, and should not be treated any more seriously, is undoubtedly tied to the recent widespread use of marijuana among affluent citizens (Clausen, 1961: 181–221; Goode, 1970: 35–40, 1972: 36–37).

The demand for leniency in marijuana offenses can be clearly shown to result in part from class interests in the case of Nebraska, which in April 1969 became the second state to make the possession of marijuana a misdemeanor. This radical departure was hardly expected from such a conservative state. The explanation was, in part, that a prosecutor's son had been arrested for the possession of marijuana six months prior to the bill's passage (Galliher et al., 1974). The prosecutor expressed outrage at the state's felony law for possession and publicly vowed to fight the law, which he did. The prosecutor's son and another young man who had been arrested in the same case were represented by a past Republican governor and by a Democrat who was to become the president of the Nebraska Bar Association. A more politically powerful defense team could not have been found in the state. Since the case against their clients was airtight, the defense attorneys decided to fight the existing law, and the ex-governor drafted the proposed legislation. It was presented to the legislature and passed, retroactive to the date of the young men's arrest. It would be hard to make a stronger case for the role of power in legal change.

The influence of elites has also been reflected in other drug legislation. Graham (1972) observes that eight to ten billion amphetamine pills are produced and consumed in the United States each year. According to expert medical testimony presented to Congress, only a small percentage of these drugs are actually needed for legitimate medical purposes. The remainder of this massive overproduction, Graham indicates, is improperly used by students, housewives, and truckers as pep or diet pills, causing widespread physical addiction as well as auto accidents that result from the drug's hallucinatory effects. Although Congress was also told of a widespread diversion of these pills to illegal channels, it failed to control the production of amphetamines in the misnamed "Comprehensive Drug Abuse Prevention and Control Act of 1970." This failure to control amphetamines, Graham demonstrates, was due to the powerful lobbying efforts of drug manufacturers who were reaping a bonanza of profits from the sale of these drugs. So intense were the manufacturers' efforts that the staff of the president of the American Pharmaceutical Association actually helped the Justice Department draft the bill to insure its safety to the drug industry.

Antitrust laws, unlike these criminal statutes which serve societal elites, appear to control large corporations and serve the private citizen (Quinney, 1970: 73–77; Chambliss and Seidman, 1971: 65–66). However, on closer examination, one can recognize that antitrust laws have seldom been enforced and have served to placate a public previously enraged about the abuses of power by large trusts since when such laws are passed the public believes itself to be protected against these abuses. Yet, as Edelman (1964) suggests, often legislation that is passed to mollify an outraged citizenry is ignored and unenforced if it is out of line with the interests of powerful, organized interest groups.

This is not to say that the mass of citizens never react success-fully against societal elites or powerful interest groups. Martin Luther King's nonviolent civil disobedience is usually credited with having had some impact on the passage of the new civil rights legislation of the 1960s, and the campus war protests are believed to have helped deter the United States from waging further war in Southeast Asia and also to have helped end the draft. Even if we ignore the fact that these influences have not been thoroughly documented, the alleged changes pale into insignificance when compared to the changes in the law that have been documented as the work of elites and powerful interest groups.

CONCLUSION

In this chapter we have demonstrated that in a mass society such as the United States, a written criminal code has understand-ably developed, and that this code helps coordinate activities among a heterogeneous people who lack consensus on the societal norms. In a highly stratified society such as the United States, the law predictably reflects the interests of powerful interest groups, and even when it appears to protect the interests of less powerful groups, as in antitrust legislation, it is only an effort to pacify and contain those groups. The operation of various elites and power-ful interest groups is reflected in the laws discussed in this chapter. At first, vagrancy laws reflected the interests of the church, then the interests of landowners, and finally the interests of merchants. In all instances, the transient poor were the objects of control. Severe penalties for property offenses were altered on behalf of business interests to insure more likely punishment of the "dangerous classes." Owners of businesses obtained embezzlement legislation to protect their property against their clerks. In the United States at the beginning of the 19th century, the criminal code began to reflect less concern with sin and more concern with the protection of property owners' interests. Many drug laws show the influence of another influential group. There is some evidence that fundamentalist Protestant interests lie behind national prohibition as well as other narcotics legislation. Yet even here some section of the nation's poor is the object of control—blacks, Mexicans, or Chinese. It has also been shown that the power of economic elites is sometimes reflected not only in the drug-related legislative activities they sponsor but in the drug-related legislation they oppose or help repeal. Having discussed the moral and political foundations of criminal law as an important basis for an alternative criminology, we can now turn to the historical development of traditional criminology.

REFERENCES

Becker, Howard S.
1963   *Outsiders.* New York: Free Press of Glencoe.

Berman, Harold J.
1963   *Justice in the U.S.S.R.* Rev. ed. New York: Vintage Books.

Black, Henry C.
1951   *Black's Law Dictionary.* 4th ed. St. Paul, Minn.: West Publishing Co.

Brecher, Edward M. and *Consumer Reports* Editors
1972   *Licit and Illicit Drugs.* Mount Vernon, N.Y.: Consumers Union.

Chambliss, William J.
1964   "A Sociological Analysis of the Law of Vagrancy," *Social Problems* 12(Summer): 67–77.

Chambliss, William J. and Robert B. Seidman
1971   *Law, Order, and Power.* Reading, Mass.: Addison-Wesley Publishing Co.

Civil Rights Act of 1964
1964   Public Law 88-352, 88th Congress, 2d Session (July 2, 1964): 241–268.

Clausen, J. A.
1961   "Drug Addiction," pp. 181–221 in Robert K. Merton and Robert A. Nisbet, eds., *Contemporary Social Problems.* New York: Harcourt, Brace and World.

Cohen, Stanley and Jock Young, eds.
1973   *The Manufacture of News.* Beverly Hills, Calif.: Sage Publications.

Durkheim, Emile
1933   *The Division of Labor in Society.* George Simpson, trans. Glencoe, Ill.: Free Press.

Duster, Troy
  1970   *The Legislation of Morality: Law, Drugs, and Moral Judgment.* New York: Free Press.

Eaton, Joseph W.
  1952   "Controlled Acculturation: A Survival Technique of the Hutterites," *American Sociological Review* 17(June): 331–340.

Edelman, Murray
  1964   *The Symbolic Uses of Politics.* Urbana: University of Illinois Press.

Ennis, Philip H.
  1967   *Criminal Victimization in the United States: A Report of a National Survey.* National Opinion Research Center, University of Chicago. Washington, D.C.: U.S. Government Printing Office.

Galliher, John F., James L. McCartney, and Barbara Baum
  1974   "Nebraska's Marijuana Law: A Case of Unexpected Legislative Innovation," *Law and Society Review* 8(Spring): 441–455.

Gandhi, Mahatma K.
  1951   *Non-violent Resistance.* New York: Schocken Books.

Gaylin, Willard and David J. Rothman
  1976   "Introduction," pp. xxi–xli in Andrew von Hirsch, *Doing Justice: The Choice of Punishments.* New York: Hill and Wang.

Goode, Erich
  1970   *The Marihuana Smokers.* New York: Basic Books.
  1972   *Drugs in American Society.* New York: Alfred A. Knopf.

Graham, James M.
  1972   "Amphetamine Politics on Capitol Hill," *Transaction* 9(January): 14–22, 53.

Hahn, Harlan
  1971   "Ghetto Assessments of Police Protection and Authority," *Law and Society Review* 6(November): 183–194.

Hall, Jerome
  1952   *Theft, Law, and Society.* 2d ed. Indianapolis: Bobbs-Merrill Co.

Healey, John, trans.
  1903   *The City of God by St. Augustine.* 3 vols. London: J. M. Dent and Co.

Hoebel, E. Adamson
  1954   *The Law of Primitive Man.* Cambridge, Mass.: Harvard University Press.

King, Martin Luther, Jr.
  1963   "Letter from Birmingham Jail," *Why We Can't Wait* (April 16). New York: Harper & Row, Publishers, Inc.

Lindesmith, Alfred R.
  1965   *The Addict and the Law.* Bloomington: Indiana University Press.

MacIver, Robert M. and Charles H. Page
  1964   *Society: An Introductory Analysis.* London: Macmillan and Co.

Mair, Lucy
  1962   *Primitive Government.* Baltimore: Penguin Books.

Murdock, George P.
  1950   "Feasibility and Implementation of Comparative Community
          Research," *American Sociological Review* 15(December): 713–
          720.

Musto, David F.
  1973   *The American Disease: Origins of Narcotic Control.* New Haven:
          Yale University Press.

Nelson, William E.
  1967   "Emerging Notions of Modern Criminal Law in the Revolu-
          tionary Era: An Historical Perspective," *New York University
          Law Review* 42(May): 450–482.

Pound, Roscoe
  1943   "A Survey of Social Interests," *Harvard Law Review* 57(Oc-
          tober): 1–39.

Quinney, Richard
  1970   *The Social Reality of Crime.* Boston: Little, Brown and Co.

Reich, Charles A.
  1970   *The Greening of America.* New York: Random House.

Rickaby, Joseph, S.J., trans.
  1896   *Aquinas Ethicus: or the moral teaching of St. Thomas.* [St. Thomas
          Aquinas]. Part 1, questions 90–97. London: Burns and Oates.

Sallach, David L.
  1974   "Class Domination and Ideological Hegemony, *Sociological
          Quarterly* 15(Winter): 38–50.

Schlesinger, Rudolph
  1945   *Soviet Legal Theory.* London: Kegan Paul, Trench, Trubner
          and Co.

Schwartz, Richard D. and James C. Miller
  1964   "Legal Evolution and Societal Complexity," *American Journal of
          Sociology* 70(September): 159–169.

Sinclair, Andrew
  1962   *Prohibition: The Era of Excess.* Boston: Little, Brown and Co.

Skolnick, Jerome H.
  1966   *Justice without Trial: Law Enforcement in Democratic Society.* New York: John Wiley and Sons.

Smith, David E. and Donald R. Wesson, eds.
  1973   *Uppers and Downers.* Englewood Cliffs, N.J.: Prentice-Hall.

Vold, George B.
  1958   *Theoretical Criminology.* New York: Oxford University Press.

3

Nebraska's marijuana law: A case of unexpected legislative innovation*

John F. Galliher, James L. McCartney, and
Barbara E. Baum

The social processes involved in the development of criminal laws have been studied by several scholars (Jeffery, 1957; Hall, 1952; Chambliss, 1964; Lindesmith, 1965; Sutherland, 1950; Becker, 1963). Generally, two major perspectives have guided these studies. One orientation has been the functionalist perspective (Pound, 1922, 1942; Durkheim, 1964) which stresses the emergence of moral consensus and the functional interdependence of the law with other institutions. Dicey (1920) suggests that public consensus is preceded by the origination of such ideas among elites, and is only later accepted by the mass of citizens. Such consensus, he claims, supplies the foundation for eventual legal change. An alternative view is the conflict orientation (Quinney, 1970; Vold, 1958: 203–219; Engels, 1972; Laski, 1935) which views law as the instrument through which one interest group dominates another. In the development of workman's compensa-

* Reprinted from *Law & Society Review*, vol. 8 (Spring 1974), pp. 441–455.

Authors' note: This investigation was supported by Biomedical Sciences Support Grant FR-07053 from the General Research Support Branch, Division of Research Resources, Bureau of Health Professions Education and Manpower Training, National Institutes of Health. We are grateful for the helpful criticism and guidance of Alfred R. Lindesmith, Nicholas Babchuk, Malcolm Spector, and Edward Hunvald. An earlier version of this paper was presented at the annual meetings of the American Sociological Association, New York City, 1973. Readers will note that the anonymity of sources has been preserved throughout the article.

tion laws, Friedman and Ladinsky (1967) trace the history of conflict and eventual accommodation between workers and factory owners.

Both the functionalist and conflict orientations either explicitly or implicitly assume that people typically make rational decisions to maximize what they imagine will be their material gains. However, Edelman (1964) suggests that this assumption may not be correct, and that the political behavior of citizens often is determined not on the basis of their real or material interests, but on whether or not a given piece of legislation symbolically reassures them.

Within the sociology of law there have been more studies directed to the development of radically new legislation than to adjustments in existing statues. Perhaps these latter instances are less dramatic, or it may be that they seem to be less clearly instances supporting the major theoretical perspectives. We have chosen to focus on the process of legal change as represented by the widespread phenomenon of alteration of drug laws controlling the possession of marijuana.

Becker (1963: 121–146) and Dickson (1968: 143–156) have written about the early history of marijuana control legislation, and have shown how the Federal Bureau of Narcotics successfully lobbied during the 1930s for the passage of legislation that would eliminate what it claimed to be the marijuana "drug problem." Although drug use appears to have been viewed earlier as an evil affecting the lower classes (Clausen, 1961: 189–196), by the late 1960s, marijuana use had become fashionable among many middle and upper class college youths (Goode, 1970: 35–40; 1972: 36–37). With this new class of law violators, including the children of senators, judges, and other prominent citizens, the conditions were set for a reconsideration of the existing laws.

Late in 1968 and early in 1969, ten states changed their narcotics control laws to make the maximum penalty for possession of marijuana a misdemeanor, punishable by less than one year of confinement.[1] Nebraska was one of these first states to pass such

---

[1] The first states to pass such drug legislation were Alaska, August 4, 1968; Wyoming, March 7, 1969; New Mexico, April 2, 1969; Utah, May 13, 1969; Washington, May 23, 1969; North Carolina, June 23, 1969; Connecticut, July 1, 1969; Iowa, July 1, 1969; and Illinois, July 18, 1969 (see Rosenthal, 1969; Arnold, 1969: 1, 60). The date of Nebraska's legislation, April 11, 1969, is missing from both of the above accounts.

legislation and, moreover, it established the lowest maximum penalty among these states. In fact, the maximum penalty of seven days, which was prescribed in Nebraska's law, was much lower than that stipulated in the bills of most other states which later passed similar legislation (National Organization for the Reform of Marijuana Laws, 1971).

Earlier, the accepted model for controlling drug usage had been one of increasing prescribed penalties (see Lindesmith, 1965: 80–82; Clausen, 1961: 215–217). Becker (1963: 136) suggests that these attempts to suppress drug use are legitimized by the Protestant Ethic which proscribes loss of self-control, by traditional American values that disapprove of any action taken solely to produce a state of ecstasy, and by the humanitarian belief that all drugs enslave the user. The question that stimulated our research was why a traditionally conservative state such as Nebraska, which, we suspected, might reflect the values discussed by Becker, would be a leader in passing legislation reducing penalities for vice such as marijuana use. Using either the consensus model, which views law as the product of compromise and shared values, or the conflict models, which sees law as the outcome of struggles between the interests of differing groups, one would not predict this development in Nebraska. We would not have predicted early consensus on such a radical departure in social control in this tradition-oriented state, nor would we have predicted that the proponents of reduced penalties would be strong enough to overcome a more conservative orientation in the control of drugs.

PRELUDE TO THE NEW LAW

Before 1969, the penalties in Nebraska for possession or sale of marijuana consisted of a two- to five-year sentence in prison and a fine. Marijuana was classed along with opium derivatives and other narcotic drugs in legislation, modeled after the federal Harrison Act of 1914 (38 Stat. 785 *as amended*), and passed in 1943 (Rev. Stat. of Neb. ch. 28, §§451–470).[2] Drug abuse was a minor problem in Nebraska prior to the late 1960s. Newspaper reports in the state capital, a city of more than 100,000 population, list one case per year between 1950 and 1967 (*Lincoln Star*, 1950–1967).

---

[2] The penalty prescribed under the 1943 Nebraska drug legislation was a fine of up to $3,000 and two to five years in prison.

The Nebraska State Patrol (1970: 3) recorded an average of 15 cases per year for the entire state between 1960 and 1967.

Late in 1967, numerous incidents of marijuana possession were recorded in the press, many of them involving college students. One prominent state senator (hereafter referred to as Senator C) spoke out publicly on the topic. His district, although primarily rural, had the third highest number of cases reported in the late 1960s (Nebraska State Patrol, 1970: 14). He spoke at the state university in November 1967 and was rebuked by a group of students when he proposed spending money for undercover agents to deal with the "definite problem" of marijuana use on campus (DeFrain, 1967: 5). Earlier in 1967, Senator C had been the sponsor of a law which expanded the 1943 drug laws to include depressant, stimulant, and hallucinogenic drugs, and established a narcotics control division in the state highway patrol (Legislative Bill 876, Ch. 161 at 460, June 7, 1967; henceforth LB 876).

In 1968, drug arrests in Nebraska increased sevenfold over the number in 1967 (Nebraska State Patrol, 1970: 3). Many of the arrests involved students; but in the western, more rural part of the state, several out-of-state persons were arrested with substantial harvests of marijuana in the hundreds of pounds. Marijuana had grown abundantly in the state since World War I, when it was commercially harvested to produce rope fiber. One knowledgeable official at the Nebraska State Patrol estimated that there were 115,000 acres of marijuana growing wild in the state as late as 1969 (Thomas, 1969).

Response to the increasing number of arrests consisted primarily of statements of concern by some public officials and occasional newspaper editorials. Senator C felt that administrators at the state university were not taking the problem seriously (Senate Debate on LB 876, May 2, 1967). There was also mention of legislation to declare marijuana a noxious weed and to provide penalties for farmers who did not eradicate it on their property. Farmers vigorously opposed this, maintaining that such weed control was costly, time-consuming, and ultimately impossible (Wall, 1968: 14). The issue was not raised again.

In 1969, Senator C introduced legislation (LB 8, 1969) that would permanently expel from college any student convicted of marijuana possession. It was amended to provide for a 30-day suspension from college, but, although it passed the legislature, it was vetoed by the governor. The veto prompted a public expression of outrage by the senator and an unsuccessful attempt to overturn the veto (*Lincoln Journal,* February 25, 1969).

One day after introducing the suspension bill, Senator C had introduced another bill (LB 2, April 11, 1969) which would have reduced the penalty for possession of marijuana to a misdemeanor; and as amended, it provided for a maximum sevenday sentence for first possession, and a mandatory drug education course. It is this innovative bill that we focus on this paper.

PUBLIC RESPONSE TO LB 2

LB 2 was assigned to the Committee on Public Health and Welfare and the first hearings were held on January 28, 1969. We reviewed newspapers from the two urban areas of the state, Omaha and Lincoln, the state capital, from January 1969 to June 1969. This included the period immediately preceding the bill's introduction, during its consideration by the legislature, and after its passage. We wanted to see what publicly identifiable groups were lobbying for or against the legislation and what the public reaction was to its passage. We expected that most of the interest in drugs and related legislation would be concentrated in these two cities since they had recorded the greatest increase in drug arrests, and since both had several colleges in addition to a university.

We found no debate about the bill in the press either by politicians or citizens. The newspapers merely noted that the bill was being considered. It quickly passed the unicameral legislature without a dissenting vote, and was signed into law by the governor with little commentary thereafter. A total of three short articles appeared within six months of the bill's passage, all supporting the educational provision of the legislation. We also reviewed the newspaper from January to June 1969 in the small town where Senator C lived, to see the reaction of his constituents. As with the urban newspapers, the local paper simply noted the bill, but made no editorial comment.

LEGISLATIVE HEARINGS

Another reflection of lack of concern with this legislation is that only one witness came to the public hearings. A county attorney argued in favor of the new law as more reasonable and humane than treating "experimenting" with drugs by young people as a felony (Public Hearings on LB 2, January 28, 1969: 4).[3]

The sponsor of the bill, Senator C, was from a rural area of the state and was well-known for being one of the most conservative members of a very conservative legislature. Considering his previous record for introducing tough drug bills (LB 876 and LB 8), he hardly seemed the type of person to introduce such lenient legislation. Nevertheless, the records of public hearings, legislative debate, and our personal interviews with Senator C revealed quite clearly that his motivation for introducing the bill was punitive and not humanitarian. His argument to the senate, supported indirectly by the prosecutor at the public hearings, was that too many people had been getting away without being punished for possession of marijuana. Prosecutors and judges did not favor convicting young people under a law requiring what these officials considered to be much too severe a punishment.

We have found the penalties were too severe . . . to the point where we nullified what we are trying to do because the courts in many cases would not enforce the penalties (Public Hearings on LB 2, January 28, 1969: 1).

The County Attorneys of this state and the courts that would hear these charges feel that the felony charge in the case of possession for the first time is too strong and irregardless [*sic*] of the evidence, generally speaking, they will not enforce it (Senate Debate on LB 8, February 21, 1969: 350).

The penalty of a felony was so great, it was the belief of the County Attorneys that they wasted their time trying to enforce it, because the judges would not apply the felony penalty (Senate Debate on LB 2, March 18, 1969: 744).

To ensure that those found in possession of marijuana would receive some punishment, Senator C advocated a reduction in the penalty to a point that he felt would seem reasonable to those enforcing the law.

With the 7 day penalty for the possession of a nominal amount, the courts will rather promiscuously [*sic*] based on the evidence, apply these penalties (Senate Debate on LB 2, March 18, 1969: 744).

While the sponsor's motivation was clear, it still was not evident why Nebraska was one of the first states to pass this type of legisla-

---

[3] Prosecuting attorneys are called county attorneys in Nebraska.

tion, why it was supported by other legislators, and why no public opposition emerged to this legislation.

CRITICAL EVENTS

To further our understanding of the events involved in the bill's passage, the two senior authors interviewed key informants, including several other members of Nebraska's unicameral legislature, newsmen covering the legislature for both local newspapers, and a legislative reporter for a local radio station. Selected civil servants were also interviewed, including several county attorneys, the head of the state police narcotics division, and the head of the legislative drafting group, an agency of the state legislature which assists elected representatives in writing bills. A professor from the University of Nebraska Law School who specializes in criminal law and two defense attorneys in narcotics cases were also interviewed, as well as the ex-governor under whose administration the bill was passed. We also interviewed several of the former administrative aides to the ex-governor.[4]

The law professor recalled that a few months before the legislation had passed, a county attorney's son had been arrested for possession of marijuana. He felt this might have had some influence on the bill's success. Checking out his lead through back issues of the newspapers in the state capital, we found that, indeed, in August 1968, six months before the new marijuana control bill passed, the son of an outstate county attorney was arrested in the state capital where he was a student at the state university, and charged with possession of marijuana. The county attorney resigned his office to serve as his son's defense attorney, and in a press release he vowed to fight to change what he considered a harmful and unjust law (*Lincoln Journal*, August 13, 1968). Another university student arrested with the county attorney's boy was the son of a university professor. The county attorney's son was represented at first by his father, but soon his father hired a prominent Democratic lawyer who was later to become president

---

[4] Perhaps because of pride in their state's trend-setting legislation, all respondents seemed eager to be interviewed and readily made their files available. Moreover, we found that each respondent volunteered the names of other people who might have some information relevant to our questions, and these other respondents volunteered yet another set of names. In this serial sample selection, we eventually found that no new names were being mentioned and felt we had contacted all knowledgeable respondents.

of the Nebraska Bar Association. The university professor's son was represented by a popular Republic ex-governor who had declined to run for re-election. According to the outstate county attorney, these lawyers were intentionally selected as the most politically powerful bipartisan team of attorneys in the state. With regard to using this influence, the ex-governor said, "We recognized the case on our clients was air-tight so [we] figured it was best to attack the law." He wrote a draft of a first-offense marijuana possession misdemeanor law, and, after discussing the issue with the county attorney who was prosecuting the two boys, sent him the proposal.

This county attorney said that during the fall of 1968 he felt compelled to prosecute his colleague's son in part because, in his judgment, the boys had quite a large amount (one ounce) of marijuana in their possession. He claimed to have had no enthusiasm for his task, yet he indicated that he never considered not enforcing the law. Undoubtedly, the unusual publicity created by this case narrowed his options. The notion of a marijuana misdemeanor law provided him with an option in handling his colleague's son's case, and he said that, more importantly, it provided an avenue for getting more convictions in other drug cases. He said that, in enforcing the felony law, "We felt compelled to reduce charges to all sorts of ridiculous things such as disturbing the peace." Reducing the penalty to a misdemeanor would result in more convictions on appropriate charges since judges and juries would be more willing to convict if penalties were lowered. He said that the County Attorneys Association unofficially endorsed the idea because the prosecutors from Lincoln and Omaha had experienced special difficulties in getting convictions in drug cases. Since large quantities of drugs had not yet penetrated the other areas of the state, the other county attorneys were not as concerned. The Association, therefore, did not go on record in favor of such legislation for fear of appearing to take a promarijuana position. Nevertheless, the county attorney said, they were all concerned about the potential of a felony conviction for "college kids just experimenting with marijuana"—a concern reflected in the testimony of the county attorney who testified at the public hearings. In short, the county attorneys wanted a more nearly just and enforceable law, one that both should be and could be enforced. The county attorney in Lincoln sent a tentative version of the bill to the state legislative drafting group and contacted a friend in the legislature, Senator C, asking him to sponsor the bill. In making this request, he argued that, if penalties were reduced, it would help get more convictions. Senator C agreed to sponsor the bill.

Just prior to introducing the misdemeanor marijuana bill, Senator C introduced another bill (Public Hearings on LB 8, January 27, 1969) which would have suspended college students for life from any Nebraska college or university, state or private, upon conviction of possession of marijuana.[5] The day after the school suspension bill was introduced, Senator C introduced the county attorney's misdemeanor bill. No one except a TV newsman (Terry, 1969) characterized this legislator's proposal as being soft on drug offenses; certainly none of his colleagues in the legislature did. To think of this man introducing a permissive piece of drug legislation was beyond credibility, given his general conservatism and longstanding and well-known hostility toward drug use. Not only had he introduced anti-LSD legislation and the punitive college suspension bill, but he also had argued that the misdemeanor legislation would make it harder on drug users.[6] With these strong credentials, he hardly could be accused of being permissive on the drug issue.

Yet, even the punishment-oriented sponsor of the bill recognized the wisdom of leniency for at least some of the middle and upper classes. During the public hearings on the college suspension bill, a member of the firm of the ex-governor representing the

---

[5] The suspension period was amended to 30 days (Public Hearings LB 8, January 27, 1969: 12), and was passed, aided by what was often characterized as Senator C's aggressive, overwhelming style (Senate Debate LB 8, February 4, 1969: 105–08; February 21, 1969: 345–51). The bill, however, was vetoed by the governor, and the outraged sponsor was only a few votes short of overriding the veto (Senate Debate LB 8, February 27, 1969: 454–66).

[6] Two years before, in 1967, this legislator had introduced a bill creating penalties for possession of LSD and establishing a narcotics control division in the state highway patrol (LB 876, effective June 7, 1967). He justified this legislation in punitive and control terms (Public Hearings on LB 876, April 18, 1967; Senate Debate on LB 876, May 2, 1967).

"As far as I am concerned, nothing can be too harsh for those people who pervade [*sic*] this step, because I can think of nothing more horrible, than to have a son or daughter of mine become afflicted with this habit . . . [and] . . . be unable to break themselves or himself of the habit" (Public Hearings on LB 876, April 18, 1967: 3).

"Are you going to wait until it happens in your family, to your son or daughter becomes contaminated [*sic*] or maybe your grandchild or the kid next door. [*sic*] Are you going to wait till you have to have a vivid explanation of this thing or are you going to do something about it? I think drugs is [*sic*] the most terrible thing that can happen to the human mind. And I am not willing to sit still and not attempt to do something about it" (Senate Debate on LB 876, May 2, 1967: 1913).

professor's son spoke against the suspension bill and in support of the misdemeanor bill which the legislator had publicly promised to introduce. Senator C was unusually courteous and respectful of him and publicly volunteered to make the misdemeanor bill retroactive to cover the ex-governor's client (Public Hearings on LB 8, January 27, 1969: 12), which he later did (Senate Debate on LB 2, March 18, 1969: 745).

CONCLUSION

Nebraska was one of the first states to reduce first-offense possession of marijuana to a misdemeanor, and several events and conditions seem to explain its early lead. The timing of the county attorney's son's arrest was important, of course, as a triggering event. This case assumed special significance because of the prestige of the defense attorneys. The speed with which the unicameral legislature can respond to such incidents is also an essential element in this explanation. A unicameral legislature avoids the usual conflict between the two houses, which often delays and sometimes kills prospective legislation. Moreover, several informants mentioned that in Nebraska there was perhaps special reluctance to punish young people for using marijuana because it commonly grows wild in the state. Reflecting this attitude was an editorial in one of the Lincoln newspapers (Dobler, 1968: 4), appearing approximately two months after the arrest of the outstate prosecutor's son, which discussed the long history of marijuana in the state. The editorial observed that the state had long endured the presence of large amounts of marijuana without serious disruption.

One of the most striking features in Nebraska's early lead, paradoxically, was the absence of any organized support for or opposition to this legislation. The only organization known to have supported this bill was the County Attorneys Association, and this support was unofficial, or at least not publicly announced. From newspaper reports it was clear that at least some students favored reducing or eliminating penalties for marijuana use, but we could find no evidence of any active support by students.[7] The bill

---

[7] Because of his strong position on drugs and from other university-baiting positions, Senator C was not a popular figure on the state university campus. Perhaps this accounts for lack of student enthusiasm for his bill, or perhaps more likely, students might have viewed it as still too punitive to merit active support.

quickly passed with *no* opposition. It could not have been predicted that a radically different and apparently lenient piece of drug legislation would go unnoticed in a state supposed to be very much influenced by the fundamentalist sentiments which justify punitive reactions to drug use (cf. Becker, 1963: 136).

One explanation for both the absence of organized support as well as the unexpected lack of opposition may be that the felony marijuana law which had previously been used only on the lower classes was threatening to middle class families. Whether or not middle class parents continued to perceive marijuana as a harmful drug, the threat of a felony charge and a prison term for their children clearly was perceived as more harmful—a theme that emerged often in our interviews. This threat is clearly illustrated in the case of the prosecutor's son. In the search for support for the bill this type of interest is not visible as are organized groups, yet its influence in forestalling opposition may be no less real.

Both moral conservatives and liberals, for different reasons of course, supported the bill. The more liberal members of the state government, including the governor, backed the legislation as a remedy against sending "decent" college kids to the penitentiary for a "minor mistake." This opposition to severe punishment for marijuana possession reflects a widespread feeling, according to Lindesmith (letter in possession of authors), that victimless crime or morality legislation arbitrarily creates "criminals" who not only do not view themselves as such; but, more importantly, are not so viewed by much of the public because of the absence of external social harm.

Apparently the moral conservatives in the state legislature did not oppose this bill because its sponsor justified it as a vehicle for insuring a greater likelihood of punishment since the felony possession law was not being enforced. Hall (1952) suggests that in a similar fashion at the end of the Middle Ages in England, merchants lobbied for the elimination of the death penalty for property crimes since severe penalties, out of line with public sentiment, allowed property offenders to escape any punishment under the law. In drug cases, Lindesmith (1965: 80–82) has also observed that, since felony convictions take more time in courts than do misdemeanors and are more difficult to get because of "technicalities," police will make fewer felony arrests and instead reduce charges to loitering or vagrancy. Also, with high minimum penalties, judges and prosecutors are likely to collaborate in avoiding imposition of the severe penalties by accepting guilty pleas to lesser charges. All of these things, apparently, were happening in Nebraska.

The issue of the seriousness of marijuana possession laws only developed with visible and seemingly widespread marijuana use among the middle and upper classes. As long as marijuana use appeared only among the poor, the problem of drug convictions didn't emerge for either conservatives or liberals. Only when confronting an increasing number of cases of middle class defendants did judges and juries begin to balk. While conservatives became angry with the leniency of the courts toward affluent defendants, liberals became worried and disgusted by the law's potential results, which included sending middle class defendants to prison.

Both moral conservatives and liberals recognized, for differing reasons, that severe penalties for possession of marijuana were not appropriate when the defendants were the children of middle class, affluent parents. Borrowing from the *consensus* and *conflict* models of legal change, we see that both conservatives and liberals *agreed* on the specific law although they fundamentally *disagreed* on the basic issue covered by the law. Perhaps most significantly, this consensus among diverse groups may offer some clues to understanding why a number of states in rapid succession passed similar legislation even though these laws represented a radical departure in controlling marijuana use.[8] Yet, contrary to the conflict orientation, no organized interest groups are in evidence in this case; and, unlike the functionalist perspective, there is no evidence of a massive opinion shift involved in this legislative change. For a com-

---

[8] It is interesting to observe that most of the states that were in the initial group making a first offense of marijuana possession punishable only as a misdemeanor or at least giving this option to the court were in the west or western plains. Besides Nebraska, these states include Alaska, California, Iowa, Montana, New Mexico, North Dakota, South Dakota, Utah, Washington, and Wyoming. Only Connecticut, Illinois, and North Carolina are early passage states clearly not in this region. Aside from mere geographical proximity which makes the spread of ideas easily understandable, the agricultural and cultural characteristics of Nebraska undoubtedly exist to a degree in many of these other western states. Large quantities of open land where marijuana grows wild is one similarity. Since many of these states are predominantly rural in character, the concern with sending local (often country) boys to the penitentiary may have been widespread. Finally, many of these states are also predominantly rural Protestant so that punitive and repressive arguments in favor of reduction of penalties were likely to have been used.

plete understanding of these events, we must turn, as Edelman (1964) advises, to the symbolic properties of political events.

We see some parallels in our data with the argument by Warriner (1958) about the symbolic functions of preserving official morality. In a small Kansas community he found inconsistencies between citizens' public expressions and private behavior regarding alcohol consumption. Publicly, they were uniformly opposed to drinking, yet most drank within the privacy of their homes. Irrespective of their behavior, citizens felt that it was important to give symbolic support to the community's normative structure. Public support for national prohibition, according to Gusfield (1963: 1967), was also mainly a result of an effort to give symbolic support to the values prescribing total abstinence. Gusfield distinguishes this *symbolic* function of the law from its *instrumental* or actual enforcement or control function. Edelman (1964) observes that often citizens are satisfied that their interests are being protected once relevant legislation is passed, even if it is not enforced. The mere passage of the law symbolizes to them that their values are being supported. This, apparently, was the case with national prohibition (Gusfield, 1963).

This distinction between the instrumental and symbolic functions of law seems ideally suited for an analysis of Nebraska's marijuana law. Using this distinction, it becomes clear that the senate sponsor of the misdemeanor marijuana bill essentially argued that it would be an improvement because of its instrumental features, i.e., its ability to control. One unspoken, but no less real cost of this legislation was a certain loss of symbolic support for norms prohibiting drug use. Marijuana possession was still punishable under criminal law but the punishment was so light as to imply the offense was trivial. Those less condemning of marijuana use, on the other hand, gained some symbolic support for their position, and in fact made some instrumental gains as well because, while the probability of conviction might increase, the punishment was minimal. The basis for consensus on the legislation becomes clear: both moral conservatives and liberals gained something from this legal change.

Ironically, the pressure to enforce the law rather than to ignore it, as Edelman says so often occurs, was the result of the dramatic opposition to the law by the county attorney whose son was arrested. Because he was a prosecutor, he was in a special position to call public attention to his son's arrest. Moreover, his son was arrested in the state capital where state government and the mass media were centralized, which further served to publicize the case. Therefore, the other county attorney could not use the technique of ignoring the law to suit these specific interests. His options seemed limited by the publicity. The only course of action seemed to be a direct effort to change the relevant law.

It would appear that Senator C was taking a considerable chance of being labeled permissive regarding drug usage by introducing such legislation. He might have been protected from such criticism, however, by introducing the college suspension bill the day before. This emphasized his position on drugs, and, given the suspension bill's extreme provisions, absorbed most of the public and media attention. Like the county prosecutors, the senator made no statements to the press on behalf of the misdemeanor bill. Perhaps both the prosecutors and the senator were afraid of or at least uncertain of possible public reaction. However, the senator did have considerable commentary regarding the suspension bill and its ultimate veto. (See footnote 5.)

One possible interpretation of these events is that the senator intentionally introduced the suspension bill immediately prior to the misdemeanor bill in an attempt to distract the public and the media. Indeed, several respondents mentioned that the senator typically supports both extremes on an issue in an effort to protect himself from criticism. Another (not mutually exclusive) possibility is that those in the mass media felt that the bill was reasonable and they did not wish to arouse public indignation. Cooperation between the media and political officials is not uncommon, as Ross and Staines (1972) have concluded.

While the full impact of this legislation is not possible to assess so soon after its passage, some subsequent developments relevant to the legal change are apparent. In Omaha, which accounts for almost 50 percent of all drug offenses in Nebraska (Nebraska State Patrol, 1970: 14), a city ordinance allowed cases involving possession of marijuana to be prosecuted in city courts as misdemeanors or, alternatively, under state law as felonies. Under the new state law county attorneys now have no option and must handle possession of marijuana as a misdemeanor. In Lincoln, where nearly one-fourth of all state narcotics cases are processed (Nebraska State Patrol, 1970: 14), the prosecutor claimed that all marijuana possession cases are now prosecuted as such, while under the previous felony law guilty pleas were often accepted to lesser non-narcotic offenses such as peace disturbance.

During the first full year this law was in effect, arrests involving marijuana possession nearly doubled (Nebraska State Patrol, 1970: 9). Even though arrests have rapidly escalated, a review of Omaha and Lincoln newspapers since the bill's passage indicates that neither student nor other groups have publicly protested, and there is no public argument that the law is oppressive. A maximum sentence of seven days is apparently acceptable, or at least tolerable. On the other hand, the bill's senate sponsor feels that most law-abiding citizens recognize that the increased arrests vividly demonstrate that the legislation which he introduced was badly needed. The lack of conflict regarding the consequences of the bill offers testimony to the symbolic and instrumental utility of the law. Moral conservatives may indeed feel, as Senator C speculates, that the new law offers more control as evidenced by increased convictions; those more tolerant of marijuana use may well regard the law as an instrumental and certainly a symbolic victory.

REFERENCES

Arnold, Martin
  1969   "Varied Drug Laws Raising U.S. Fears," *New York Times* (August 17).

Becker, Howard S.
  1963   *Outsiders.* New York: Free Press of Glencoe.

Chambliss, William J.
  1964   "A Sociological Analysis of the Law of Vagrancy," 12 *Social Problems* 67.

Clausen, J. A.
  1961   "Drug Addiction," in Robert K. Merton and Robert A. Nisbet (eds.), *Contemporary Social Problems.* New York: Harcourt, Brace and World.

De Frain, John
  1967   "Students Clash over Narcotics," *Lincoln Journal* (November 21).

Dicey, A. V.
  1920   *Lectures on the Relation between Law and Public Opinion in England during the Nineteenth Century.* London: Macmillan.

Dickson, Donald T.
   1968   "Bureaucracy and Morality: An Organizational Perspective on a Moral Crusade," 16 *Social Problems* 143.

Dobler, William O.
   1968   "In Perspective," *Lincoln Star* (October 9).

Durkheim, Emile
   1964   *The Division of Labor in Society.* New York: Free Press of Glencoe.

Edelman, Murray
   1964   *The Symbolic Uses of Politics.* Urbana: University of Illinois Press.

Engels, Frederick
   1972   *The Origin of the Family, Private Property, and the State.* New York: International Publishers.

Friedman, Lawrence M. and Jack Ladinsky
   1967   "Social Change and the Law of Industrial Accidents," 67 *Columbia Law Review* 50.

Goode, Erich
   1970   *The Marijuana Smokers.* New York: Basic Books.
   1972   *Drugs in American Society.* New York: Alfred A. Knopf.

Gusfield, J. R.
   1963   *Symbolic Crusade: Status Politics and the American Temperance Movement.* Urbana: University of Illinois Press.
   1967   "Moral Passage: The Symbolic Process in Public Designations of Deviance," 15 *Social Problems* 175.

Hall, Jerome
   1952   *Theft, Law, and Society.* Indianapolis: Bobbs-Merrill.

Jeffery, C. R.
   1957   "The Development of Crime in Early English Society," 47 *Journal of Criminal Law, Criminology, and Police Science* 647.

Laski, Harold J.
   1935   *The State in Theory and Practice.* New York: Viking Press.

Lindesmith, Alfred R.
   1965   *The Addict and the Law.* Bloomington: Indiana University Press.

National Organization for the Reform of Marijuana Laws
   1971   "The Criminal Penalties under the Current Marijuana Laws." Washington: National Organization for the Reform of Marijuana Laws.

Nebraska State Patrol, Division of Drug Control
   1970   *Activity Summary: Drug and Narcotic Cases.* Lincoln: Nebraska State Patrol.

Pound, Roscoe
  1922   *An Introduction to the Philosophy of Law.* New Haven: Yale University Press.
  1942   *Social Control through Law.* New Haven: Yale University Press.

Quinney, Richard
  1970   *The Social Reality of Crime.* Boston: Little, Brown and Co.

Rosenthal, M. P.
  1969   "A Plea for Amelioration of the Marijuana Laws," 47 *Texas Law Review* 1359.

Ross, Robert and Graham L. Staines
  1972   "The Politics of Social Problems," 20 *Social Problems* 18.

Sutherland, E. H.
  1950   "The Diffusion of Sexual Psychopath Laws," 56 *American Journal of Sociology* 142.

Terry, Lee
  1969   KETV, Channel 7 News Observation, Omaha (February 27).

Thomas, Fred
  1969   "Puffers Find Pot of Gold under Nebraska Rainbow," *Omaha World Herald* (August 31).

Vold, George B.
  1958   *Theoretical Criminology.* New York: Oxford University Press.

Wall, Millan
  1968   "Farmers Oppose Declaring Marijuana a Noxious Weed," *Lincoln Star* (February 15).

Warriner, C. K.
  1958   "The Nature and Functions of Official Morality," 64 *American Journal of Sociology* 165.

4

Amphetamine politics on Capitol Hill*

James M. Graham

The American pharmaceutical industry annually manufactures enough amphetamines to provide a month's supply to every man, woman and child in the country. Eight, perhaps ten, billion pills are lawfully produced, packaged, retailed and consumed each year. Precise figures are unavailable. We must be content with estimates because until 1970, no law required an exact accounting of total amphetamine production.

Amphetamines are the drug of the white American with money to spend. Street use, contrary to the popular myths, accounts for a small percentage of the total consumption. Most of the pills are eaten by housewives, businessmen, students, physicians, truck drivers and athletes. Those who inject large doses of "speed" intravenously are but a tiny fragment of the total. Aside from the needle and the dose, the "speed freak" is distinguishable because his use has been branded as illegal. A doctor's signature supplies the ordinary user with lawful pills.

All regular amphetamine users expose themselves to varying degrees of potential harm. Speed doesn't kill, but high sustained dosages can and do result in serious mental and physical injury, depending on how the drug is taken. The weight-conscious housewife, misled by the opinion-makers into believing that amphetamines can control weight, eventually may rely on the drug to alter her mood in order to face her monotonous tasks. Too fre-

* Reprinted from *Transaction*, vol. 9, no. 3 (January 1972), pp. 14–22, 53.

quently an amphetamine prescription amounts to a synthetic substitute for attention to emotional and institutional problems.

Despite their differences, all amphetamine users, whether on the street or in the kitchen, share one important thing in common—the initial source of supply. For both, it is largely the American pharmaceutical industry. That industry has skillfully managed to convert a chemical, with meager medical justification and considerable potential for harm, into multihundred-million-dollar profits in less than 40 years. High profits, reaped from such vulnerable products, require extensive, sustained political efforts for their continued existence. The lawmakers who have declared that possession of marijuana is a serious crime have simultaneously defended and protected the profits of the amphetamine pill-makers. The Comprehensive Drug Abuse Prevention and Control Act of 1970 in its final form constitutes a victory for that alliance over compelling, contrary evidence on the issue of amphetamines. The victory could not have been secured without the firm support of the Nixon Administration. The end result is a national policy which declares an all-out war on drugs which are *not* a source of corporate income. Meanwhile, under the protection of the law, billions of amphetamines are overproduced without medical justification.

HEARINGS IN THE SENATE

The Senate was the first house to hold hearings on the administration's bill to curb drug abuse, The Controlled Dangerous Substances Act (S-3246). Beginning on September 15, 1969 and consuming most of that month, the hearings before Senator Thomas Dodd's Subcommittee to Investigate Juvenile Delinquency of the Committee on the Judiciary would finally conclude on October 20, 1969.

The first witness was John Mitchell, attorney general of the United States, who recalled President Nixon's ten-point program to combat drug abuse announced on July 14, 1969. Although that program advocated tighter controls on imports and exports of dangerous drugs and promised new efforts to encourage foreign governments to crack down on production of illicit drugs, there was not a single reference to the control of domestic manufacture of dangerous drugs. The president's bill when it first reached the Senate placed the entire "amphetamine family" in Schedule III, where they were exempt from any quotas and had the benefit of lesser penalties and controls. Hoffman-LaRoche, Inc. had already been at work; their depressants, Librium and Valium, were completely exempt from any control whatsoever.

In his opening statement, Attorney General Mitchell set the tone of administrative policy related to amphetamines. Certainly, these drugs were "subject to increasing abuse"; however, they have "widespread medical uses" and therefore are appropriately classed under the administration guidelines in Schedule III. Tight-mouthed John Ingersoll, director of the Bureau of Narcotics and Dangerous Drugs (BNDD), reaffirmed the policy, even though a Bureau study over the last year (which showed that 92 percent of the amphetamines and barbiturates in the illicit market were legitimately manufactured) led him to conclude that drug companies have "lax security and recordkeeping."

Senator Dodd was no novice at dealing with the pharmaceutical interests. In 1965 he had steered a drug abuse bill through the Senate with the drug industry fighting every step of the way. Early in the hearings he recalled that the industry "vigorously opposed the passage of [the 1965] act. I know very well because I lived with it, and they gave me fits and they gave all of us fits in trying to get it through."

The medical position on amphetamine use was first presented by the National Institute of Mental Health's Dr. Sidney Cohen, a widely recognized authority on drug use and abuse. He advised the subcommittee that 50 percent of the lawfully manufactured pep pills were diverted at some point to illicit channels. Some of the pills, though, were the result of unlawful manufacture as evidenced by the fact that 33 clandestine laboratories had been seized in the last 18 months.

Dr. Cohen recognized three categories of amphetamine abuse, all of which deserved the attention of the government. First was their "infrequent ingestion" by students, businessmen, truck drivers and athletes. Second were those people who swallowed 50–75 milligrams daily without medical supervision. Finally, there were the speed freaks who injected the drug intravenously over long periods of time. Physical addiction truly occurs, said Dr.

Cohen, when there is prolonged use in high doses. Such use, he continued, may result in malnutrition, prolonged psychotic states, heart irregularities, convulsions, hepatitis and with an even chance of sustained brain damage.

As the hearings progressed, the first two classes of abusers described by Dr. Cohen would receive less and less attention, while the third category—the speed freaks—would receive increasing emphasis. The amphetamine industry was not at all unhappy with this emphasis. In fact, they would encourage it.

Ingersoll had already said that BNDD statistics indicated that only 8 percent of illicit speed was illegally manufactured. Thomas Lynch, attorney general of California, testified that his agents had in 1967 successfully negotiated a deal for one-half million amphetamine tablets with a "Tijuana café man." Actual delivery was taken from a California warehouse. All of the tablets seized originated with a Chicago company which had not bothered to question the authenticity of the retailer or the pharmacy. Prior to the 1965 hearings, the Food and Drug Administration completed a ten-year study involving 1,658 criminal cases for the illegal sale of amphetamines and barbiturates. Seventy-eight percent of all convictions involved pharmacists, and of these convictions 60 percent were for illicit traffic in amphetamines.

The pharmacists were not the source of illicit diversion, according to the National Association of Retail Druggists (NARD) and the National Association of Chain Drug Stores. Indeed, NARD had conducted an extensive educational program combating drug abuse for years, and, as proof of it, introduced its booklet, "Never Abuse—Respect Drugs," into the record. Annual inventories were acceptable for Schedule I and II drugs, NARD continued, but were unwarranted for the remaining two schedules which coincidently included most of their wares—unwarranted because diversion resulted from forged prescriptions, theft and placebo (false) inventories.

The amphetamine wholesalers were not questioned in any detail about diversion. Brief statements by the National Wholesale Druggists Association and McKesson Robbins Drug Co. opposed separate inventories for dangerous drugs because they were currently commingled with other drugs. Finally, the massive volume of the drugs involved—primarily in Schedule III—was just too great for records to be filed with the attorney general.

DODGING THE DIVERSION ISSUE

The representative of the prescription drug developers was also not pressed on the question of illicit diversion. Instead, the Pharmaceutical Manufacturers' Association requested clarifications on the definitional sections, argued for formal administrative hearings on control decisions and on any action revoking or suspending registration, and endorsed a complete exemption for over-the-counter non-narcotic drugs.

With some misgivings, Carter-Wallace Inc. endorsed the administration bill providing, of course, the Senate would accept the president's recommendation that meprobamate not be subjected to any control pending a decision of the Fourth Circuit as to whether the drug had a dangerously depressant effect on the central nervous system. On a similar special mission, Hoffman-LaRoche, Inc. sent two of its vice-presidents to urge the committee to agree with the president's recommendation that their "minor tranquilizers" (Librium and Valium) remain uncontrolled. Senator Dodd was convinced that both required inclusion in one of the schedules. The Senator referred to a BNDD investigation which had shown that from January 1968 to February 1969, three drug stores were on the average over 30,000 dosage units short. In addition, five inspected New York City pharmacies had unexplained shortages ranging from 12 to 50 percent of their total stock in Librium and Valium. Not only were the drugs being diverted, but Bureau of Narcotics information revealed that Librium and Valium, alone or in combination with other drugs, were involved in 36 suicides and 750 attempted suicides.

The drug company representatives persisted in dodging or contradicting Dodd's inquiries. Angry and impatient, Senator Dodd squarely asked the vice-presidents, "Why do you worry about putting this drug under control?" The response was as evasive as the question was direct: There are hearings pending in HEW, and Congress should await the outcome when the two drugs might be placed in Schedule III. (The hearings had begun in 1966; no final administrative decision had been reached and Hoffman-LaRoche had yet to exercise its right to judicial review.)

In the middle of the hearings, BNDD Director Ingersoll returned to the subcommittee to discuss issues raised chiefly by drug industry spokesmen. He provided the industry with several comforting administrative interpretations. The fact that he did not even mention amphetamines is indicative of the low level of controversy that the hearings had aroused on the issue. Ingersoll did frankly admit that his staff had met informally with industry representatives in the interim. Of course, this had been true from the very beginning.

The president of the American Pharmaceutical Association, the professional society for pharmacists, confirmed this fact: His staff participated in "several" Justice Department conferences when the bill was being drafted. (Subsequent testimony in the House would reveal that industry participation was extensive and widespread.) All the same, the inventory, registration and inspection (primarily "no-knock") provisions were still "unreasonable, unnecessary and costly administrative burden[s]" which would result in an even greater "paper work explosion."

For the most part, however, the administration bill had industry support. It was acceptable for the simple reason that, to an unknown degree, the "administration bill" was a "drug company bill" and was doubtless the final product of considerable compromise. Illustrative of that give-and-take process is the comparative absence of industry opposition to the transfer of drug-classification decision and research [from] HEW to Justice. The industry had already swallowed this and other provisions in exchange for the many things the bill could have but did not cover. Moreover, the subsequent windy opposition of the pill-makers allowed the administration to boast of a bill the companies objected to.

When the bill was reported out of the Committee on the Judiciary, the amphetamine family, some 6,000 strong, remained in Schedule III. Senator Dodd apparently had done some strong convincing because Librium, Valium and meprobamate were now controlled in Schedule III. A commission on marijuana and a declining penalty structure (based on what schedule the drug is in and whether or not the offense concerned trafficking or possession) were added.

DEBATE IN THE SENATE—ROUND I

The Senate began consideration of the bill on January 23, 1970. This time around, the amphetamine issue would inspire neither debate nor amendment. The energies of the Senate liberals were consumed instead by unsuccessful attempts to alter the declared law enforcement nature of the administration bill.

Senator Dodd's opening remarks, however, were squarely directed at the prescription pill industry. Dodd declared that the present federal laws had failed to control the illicit diversion of lawfully manufactured dangerous drugs. The senator also recognized the ways in which all Americans had become increasingly involved in drug use and that the people's fascination with pills was by no means an "accidental development": "Multihundred million dollar advertising budgets, frequently the most costly ingredient in the price of a pill, have, pill by pill, led, coaxed and seduced post–World War II generations into the 'freaked-out' drug culture. . . . Detail men employed by drug companies propagandize harried and harassed doctors into pushing their special brand of palliative. Free samples in the doctor's office are as common nowadays as inflated fees." In the version adopted by the Senate, Valium, Librium and meprobamate joined the amphetamines in Schedule III.

HEARINGS IN THE HOUSE

On February 3, 1970, within a week of the Senate's passage of S-3246, the House began its hearings. The testimony would continue for a month. Although the Senate would prove in the end to be less vulnerable to the drug lobby, the issue of amphetamines—their danger and medical justification—would be aired primarily in the hearings of the Subcommittee on Public Health of the Committee on Interstate and Foreign Commerce. The administration bill (HR 13743), introduced by the chairman of the parent committee, made no mention of Librium or Valium and classified amphetamines in Schedule III.

As in the Senate, the attorney general was scheduled to be the first witness, but instead John Ingersoll of the BNDD was the administration's representative. On the question of amphetamine diversion, Ingersoll gave the administration's response: "Registration is . . . the most effective and least cumbersome way" to prevent the unlawful traffic. This coupled with biennial inventories of all stocks of controlled dangerous drugs and the attorney general's authority to suspend, revoke or deny registration would go a long way in solving the problem. In addition, the administration was proposing stronger controls on imports and exports. For Schedules I and II, but not III or IV, a permit from the attorney general would be required for exportation. Quotas for Schedules I and II, but not III or IV, would "maximize" government control. For Schedules III and IV, no approval is required, but a supplier must send an advance notice on triple invoice to the attorney general in order to export drugs such as amphetamines. A prescription could be filled only five times in a six-month period and thereafter a new prescription would be required, whereas previously such prescriptions could be refilled as long as a pharmacist would honor them.

The deputy chief counsel for the BNDD, Michael R. Sonnenreich, was asked on what basis the attorney general would decide to control a particular drug. Sonnenreich replied that the bill provides one of two ways: Either the attorney general "finds *actual street abuse* or an interested party (such as HEW) feels that a drug should be controlled." (Speed freaks out on the street are the trigger, according to Sonnenreich; lawful abuse is not an apparent criterion.)

The registration fee schedule would be reasonable ($10.00—physician or pharmacist; $25.00—wholesalers; $50.00—manufacturers). However, the administration did not want a formal administrative hearing on questions of registration and classification, and a less formal rule-making procedure was provided for in the bill.

Returning to the matter of diversion, Sonnenreich disclosed that from July 1, 1968 to June 30, 1969 the BNDD had conducted full-scale compliance investigations of 908 "establishments." Of this total, 329 (or about 36 percent) required further action, which included surrender of order forms (162), admonition letters (38), seizures (36) and hearings (31). In addition to these full-scale investigations, the Bureau made 930 "visits." (It later came to light that when the BNDD had information that a large supply of drugs was unlawfully being sold, the Bureau's policy was to warn those involved and "90 percent of them do take care of this matter.") Furthermore, 574 robberies involving dangerous drugs had been reported to the Bureau.

Eight billion amphetamine tablets are produced annually, according to Dr. Stanley Yolles, director of the National Institute of Mental Health, and although the worst abuse is by intravenous injection, an NIMH study found that 21 percent of all college students had taken amphetamines with the family medicine cabinet acting as the primary source—not surprising in light of the estimate that 1.1 billion prescriptions were issued in 1967 at a consumer cost of $3.9 billion. Of this total, 178 million prescriptions for amphetamines were filled at a retail cost of $692 million. No one knew the statistics better than the drug industry.

Representing the prescription-writers, the American Medical Association also recognized that amphetamines were among those drugs "used daily in practically every physician's armamentarium." This casual admission of massive lawful distribution was immediately followed by a flat denial that physicians were the source of "any significant diversion."

The next witness was Donald Fletcher, manager of distribution protection, Smith Kline & French Laboratories, one of the leading producers of amphetamines. Fletcher, who was formerly with the Texas state police, said his company favored "comprehensive controls" to fight diversion and stressed the company's "educational effort." Smith Kline & French favored federal registration and tighter controls over exports (by licensing the exporter, *not* the shipment). However, no change in present record-keeping requirements on distribution, production or inventory should be made, and full hearings on the decisions by the attorney general should be guaranteed.

The committee did not ask the leading producer of amphetamines a single question about illicit diversion. Upon conclusion of the testimony, Subcommittee Chairman John Jarman of Oklahoma commented, "Certainly, Smith Kline & French is to be commended for the constructive and vigorous and hard-hitting role that you have played in the fight against drug abuse."

Dr. William Apple, executive director of the American Pharmaceutical Association (APhA), was the subject of lengthy questioning and his responses were largely typical. Like the entire industry, the APhA was engaged in a massive public education program. Apple opposed the inventory provisions, warning that the cost would be ultimately passed to the consumer. He was worried about the attorney general's power to revoke registrations ("without advance notice") because it could result in cutting off necessary drugs to patients.

Apple admitted organizational involvement "in the draft stage of the bill," but all the same, the APhA had a "very good and constructive working relationship" with HEW. Apple argued that if the functions are transferred to Justice, "We have a whole new ball game in terms of people. While some of the experienced people were transferred from HEW to Justice, there are many new people, and they are law-enforcement oriented. We are health-care oriented." Surely the entire industry shared this sentiment, but few opposed the transfer as strongly as did the APhA.

Apple reasoned that since the pharmacists were not the source of diversion, why should they be "penalized by costly overburdensome administrative requirements." The source of the drugs, Apple said, were either clandestine laboratories or burglaries. The 1965 Act, which required only those "records maintained in the ordinary course of business" be kept, was sufficient. Anyway, diversion at the pharmacy level was the responsibility of the pharmacists—a responsibility which the APhA takes "seriously and [is] going to do a better job [with] in the future."

Congress should instead ban the 60 mail-order houses which are not presently included in the bill. (One subcommittee member said this was a "loophole big enough to drive a truck through.") The corner druggist simply was not involved in "large-scale diversionary efforts."

The Pharmaceutical Manufacturers' Association (PMA) was questioned a bit more carefully in the House than in the Senate. PMA talked at length about its "long and honorable history" in fighting drug abuse. Its representative echoed the concern of the membership over the lack of formal hearings and requested that a representative of the manufacturing interests be appointed to the Scientific Advisory Committee. Significantly, the PMA declined to take a position on the issue of transfer from HEW to Justice. The PMA endorsed the administration bill. PMA Vice-President Brennan was asked whether the federal government should initiate a campaign, similar to the one against cigarettes, "to warn people that perhaps they should be careful not to use drugs excessively." Brennan's response to this cautious suggestion is worth quoting in full:

I think this is probably not warranted because it would have the additional effect of giving concern to people over very useful commodities. . . . There is a very useful side to any medicant and to give people pause as to whether or not they should take that medication, particularly those we are talking about which are only given by prescription, I think the negative effect would outweigh any sociological benefit on keeping people from using drugs.

"LIMITED MEDICAL USE"

There was universal agreement that amphetamines are medically justified for the treatment of two very rare diseases, hyperkinesis and narcolepsy. Dr. John D. Griffith of the Vanderbilt University School of Medicine testified that amphetamine production should be limited to the needs created by those conditions: "A few thousand tablets [of amphetamines] would supply the whole medical needs of the country. In fact, it would be possible for the government to make and distribute the tablets at very little cost. This way there would be no outside commercial interests involved." Like a previous suggestion that Congress impose a one cent per tablet tax on drugs subject to abuse, no action was taken on the proposal.

The very next day, Dr. John Jennings, acting director of the Food and Drug Administration (FDA), testified that amphetamines had a "limited medical use" and their usefulness in control of obesity was of "doubtful value." Dr. Dorothy Dobbs, director of the Marketed Drug Division of the FDA, further stated that there was now no warning on the prescriptions to patients, but that the FDA was proposing that amphetamines be labeled indicating among other things that a user subjects himself to "extreme psychological dependence" and the possibility of "extreme personality changes . . . [and] the most severe manifestation of amphetamine intoxication is a psychosis." Dr. Dobbs thought that psychological dependence even under a physician's prescription was "quite possible."

Congressman Claude Pepper of Florida, who from this point on would be the recognized leader of the anti-amphetamine forces, testified concerning a series of hearings which his Select Committee on Crime had held in the fall of 1969 on the question of stimulant use.

Pepper's committee had surveyed medical deans and health organizations on the medical use of amphetamines. Of 53 responses, only one suggested that the drug was useful "for *early* stages of a diet program." (Dr. Sidney Cohen of NIMH estimated that 99 percent of the total legal prescriptions for amphetamines were ostensibly for dietary control.) Pepper's investigation also confirmed a high degree of laxness by the drug companies. A special agent for the BNDD testified that by impersonating a physician, he was able to get large quantities of amphetamines from two mail-order houses in New York. One company, upon receiving an order for 25,000 units, asked for further verification of medical practice. Two days after the agent declined to reply, the units arrived. Before Pepper's committee, Dr. Cohen of NIMH testified that amphetamines were a factor in trucking accidents due to their hallucinatory effects.

Dr. John D. Griffith from Vanderbilt Medical School, in his carefully documented statement on the toxicity of amphetamines, concluded "amphetamine addiction is more widespread, more incapacitating, more dangerous and socially disrupting than narcotic addiction." Considering that 8 percent of all prescriptions are for amphetamines and that the drug companies make only one-tenth of one cent a tablet, Dr. Griffith was not surprised that there was so little scrutiny by manufacturers. Only a large output would produce a large profit.

Treatment for stimulant abuse was no easier than for heroin addiction and was limited to mild tranquilization, total abstinence and psychiatric therapy. But, heroin has not been the subject of years of positive public "education" programs nor has it been widely prescribed by physicians or lawfully produced. A health specialist from the University of Utah pointed out that the industry's propaganda had made amphetamines: "One of the major ironies of the whole field of drug abuse. We continue to insist that they are good drugs when used under medical supervision, but their greatest use turns out to be frivolous, illegal and highly destructive to the user. People who are working in the field of drug abuse are finding it most difficult to control the problem, partly because they have the reputation of being legal and good drugs."

The thrust of Pepper's presentation was not obvious from the questioning that followed, because the subcommittee discussions skirted the issue. Pepper's impact could be felt in the subsequent testimony of the executive director of the National Association of Boards of Pharmacy. The NABP objected to the use of the word "dangerous" in the bill's title because it "does little to enhance the legal acts of the physician and pharmacist in diagnosing and dispensing this type of medication." (The Controlled Dangerous Substances Act would later become the Comprehensive Drug Abuse Prevention and Control Act of 1970.)

As in the Senate hearings, Ingersoll of the BNDD returned for a second appearance and, this time, he was the last witness. Ingersoll stated that he wished "to place . . . in their proper perspective" some "of the apparent controversies" which arose in the course of testimony. A substantial controversy had arisen over amphetamines, but there was not a single word on that subject in Ingersoll's prepared statement. Later, he did admit that there was an "overproduction" of amphetamines and estimated that 75 percent to 90 percent of the amphetamines found in illicit traffic came from the American drug companies.

Several drug companies chose to append written statements rather than testifying.

Abbott Laboratories stated that it "basically" supported the administration bills and argued that because fat people had higher mortality rates than others, amphetamines were important to the public welfare, ignoring the charge that amphetamines were not useful in controlling weight. Abbott then argued that because their products were in a sustained-release tablet, they were "of little interest to abusers," suggesting that "meth" tablets per se cannot be abused and ignoring the fact that they can be easily diluted.

Eli Lilly & Co. also endorsed "many of the concepts" in the president's proposals. They as well had "participated in a number of conferences sponsored by the [BNDD] and . . . joined in both formal and informal discussions with the Bureau personnel regarding" the bill. Hoffman-LaRoche had surely watched, with alarm, the Senate's inclusion of Librium and Valium in Schedule III. They were now willing to accept all the controls applying to Schedule III drugs, including the requirements of record-keeping, inventory, prescription limits and registration as long as their "minor tranquilizers" were not grouped with amphetamines. Perhaps, the company suggested, a separate schedule between III and IV was the answer. The crucial point was that they did not want the negative association with speed and they quoted a physician to clarify this: "If in the minds of my patients a drug which I prescribe for them has been listed or branded by the government in the same category as 'goofballs' and 'pep pills' it would interfere with my ability to prescribe . . . and could create a mental obstacle to their . . . taking the drug at all."

When the bill was reported out of committee to the House, the amphetamine family was in Schedule III, and Hoffman-LaRoche's "minor tranquilizers" remained free from control.

DEBATE IN THE HOUSE—ROUND I

On September 23, 1970, the House moved into Committee of the Whole for opening speeches on the administration bill now known as HR 18583. The following day, the anti-amphetamine forces led by Congressman Pepper carried their arguments onto the floor of the House by way of an amendment transfering the amphetamine family from Schedule III into Schedule II. If successful, amphetamines would be subject to stricter import and export controls, higher penalties for illegal sale and possession and the possibility that the attorney general could impose quotas on production and distribution. (In Schedule III, amphetamines were exempt from quotas entirely.) Also, if placed in Schedule II, the prescriptions could be filled only once. Pepper was convinced from previous experience that until quotas were established by law the drug industry would not voluntarily restrict production.

Now the lines were clearly drawn. The House hearings had provided considerable testimony to the effect that massive amphetamine production coupled with illegal diversion posed a major threat to the public health. No congressman would argue that this was not the case. The House would instead divide between those who faithfully served the administration and the drug industry and those who argued that Congress must act or no action could be expected. The industry representatives dodged the merits of the opposition's arguments, contending that a floor amendment was inappropriate for such "far reaching" decisions.

"Legislating on the floor . . . concerning very technical and scientific matters," said subcommittee member Tim Lee Carter of Kentucky, "can cause a great deal of trouble. It can open a Pandora's Box" and the amendment which affected 6,100 drugs "would be disastrous to many companies throughout the land."

Paul G. Rogers of Florida (another subcommittee member) stated that the bill's provisions were based on expert scientific and law enforcement advice, and that the "whole process of manufacture and distribution had been tightened up." Robert McClory of Illinois, though not a member of the subcommittee, revealed the source of his opposition to the amendment:

Frankly . . . there are large pharmaceutical manufacturing interests centered in my congressional district. . . . I am proud to say that the well-known firms of Abbott Laboratories and Baxter Laboratories have large plants in my [district]. It is my expectation that C. D. Searl & Co. may soon establish a large part of its organization [there]. Last Saturday, the American Hospital Supply Co. dedicated its new building complex in Lake County . . . where its principal research and related operations will be conducted.

Control of drug abuse, continued McClory, should not be accomplished at the cost of imposing "undue burdens or [by taking] punitive or economically unfair steps adversely affecting the highly successful and extremely valuable pharmaceutical industries which contribute so much to the health and welfare of mankind."

Not everyone was as honest as McClory. A parent committee member, William L. Springer of Illinois, thought the dispute was basically between Pepper's special committee on crime and the subcommittee on health and medicine chaired by John Jarman of Oklahoma. Thus phrased, the latter was simply more credible than the former. "There is no problem here of economics having to do with any drug industry."

But economics had everything to do with the issue according to Representative Jerome R. Waldie of California: "[T]he only opposition to this amendment that has come across my desk has come from the manufacturers of amphetamines." He reasoned that since the House was always ready to combat crime in the streets, a "crime that involved a corporation and its profits" logically merits equal attention. Waldie concluded that the administration's decision "to favor the profits [of the industry] over the children is a cruel decision, the consequences of which will be suffered by thousands of our young people." Pepper and his supporters had compiled and introduced considerable evidence on scientific and medical opinions on the use and abuse of amphetamines. It was now fully apparent that the evidence would be ignored because of purely economic and political considerations. In the closing minutes of debate, Congressman Robert Giaimo of Connecticut, who

sat on neither committee, recognized the real issue: "Why should
we allow the legitimate drug manufacturers to indirectly supply
the [*sic*] organized crime and pushers by producing more drugs
than are necessary? When profits are made while people suffer,
what difference does it make where the profits go?"

Pepper's amendment was then defeated by a voice vote. The bill
passed by a vote of 341 to 6. The amphetamine industry had won
in the House. In two days of debate, Librium and Valium went
unmentioned and remained uncontrolled.

DEBATE IN THE SENATE—ROUND II

Two weeks after the House passed HR 18583, the Senate began
consideration of the House bill. (The Senate bill, passed eight
months before, continued to languish in a House committee.) On
October 7, 1970, Senator Thomas Eagleton of Missouri moved to
amend HR 18583 to place amphetamines in Schedule II. Although he reiterated the arguments used by Pepper in the House,
Eagleton stated that his interest in the amendment was not solely
motivated by the abuse by speed freaks. If the amendment carried, it would "also cut back on abuse by the weight-conscious
housewife, the weary long-haul truck driver and the young student trying to study all night for his exams."

The industry strategy from the beginning was to center congressional outrage on the small minority of persons who injected
large doses of diluted amphetamines into their veins. By encouraging this emphasis, the drug companies had to face questioning about illicit diversion to the "speed community," but they were
able to successfully avoid any rigorous scrutiny of the much larger
problem of lawful abuse. The effort had its success. Senator
Thomas J. McIntyre of New Hampshire, while noting the general
abuse of the drugs, stated that the real abuse resulted from large
doses either being swallowed, snorted or injected.

Senator Roman Hruska of Nebraska was not surprisingly the
administration and industry spokesman. He echoed the arguments that had been used successfully in the House: The amendment seeks to transfer between 4,000 and 6,000 products of the
amphetamine family; "some of them are very dangerous" but the
bill provides a mechanism for administrative reclassification; administration and "HEW experts" support the present classification

and oppose the amendment; and, finally, the Senate should defer to the executive where a complete study is promised.

It would take three to five years to move a drug into Schedule II by administrative action, responded Eagleton. Meanwhile amphetamines would continue to be "sold with reckless abandon to the public detriment." Rather than placing the burden on the government, Eagleton argued that amphetamines should be classed in Schedule II and those who "are making money out of the misery of many individuals" should carry the burden to downgrade the classification.

Following Eagleton's statement, an unexpected endorsement came from the man who had steered two drug control bills through the Senate in five years. Senator Dodd stated that Eagleton had made "a good case for the amendment." Senator John Pastore was sufficiently astonished to ask Dodd pointedly whether he favored the amendment. Dodd unequivocally affirmed his support. Dodd's endorsement was clearly a turning point in the Senate debate. Hruska's plea that the Senate should defer to the "superior knowledge" of the attorney general, HEW and BNDD was met with Dodd's response that, if amphetamines were found not to be harmful, the attorney general could easily move them back into Schedule III. In Schedule II, Dodd continued, "only the big powerful manufacturers of these pills may find a reduction in their profits. The people will not be harmed." With that, the debate was over and the amendment carried by a vote of 40 in favor, 16 against and 44 not voting.

Dodd may have been roused by the House's failure, without debate, to subject Librium and Valium to controls which he had supported from the beginning. Prior to Eagleton's amendment, Dodd had moved to place these depressants in Schedule IV. In that dispute, Dodd knew that economics was the source of the opposition: "It is clearly evident . . . that [the industry] objections to the inclusion of Librium and Valium are not so much based on sound medical practice as they are on the slippery surface of unethical profits." Hoffman-LaRoche annually reaped 40 million dollars in profits—"a tidy sum which [they have] done a great deal to protect." Senator Dodd went on to say that Hoffman-LaRoche reportedly paid a Washington law firm three times the annual budget of the Senate subcommittee staff to assure that their drugs would remain uncontrolled. "No wonder," exclaimed Dodd, "that the Senate first, and then the House, was overrun by Hoffman-LaRoche lobbyists," despite convincing evidence that they were connected with suicides and attempted suicides and were diverted in large amounts into illicit channels.

By voice vote Hoffman-LaRoche's "minor tranquilizers" were brought within the control provisions of Schedule IV. Even Senator Hruska stated that he did not oppose this amendment, and that it was "very appropriate" that it be adopted so that a "discussion of it and decision upon it [be] made in the conference."

The fate of the minor tranquilizers and the amphetamine family would now be decided by the conferees of the two houses.

IN CONFERENCE

The conferees from the Senate were fairly equally divided on the issue of amphetamine classification. Of the eleven Senate managers, at least six were in favor of the transfer to Schedule II. The remaining five supported the administration position. Although Eagleton was not appointed, Dodd and Harold Hughes would represent his position. Hruska and Strom Thurmond, both of whom had spoken against the amendment, would act as administration spokesmen.

On October 8, 1970, before the House appointed its conferees, Pepper rose to remind his colleagues that the Senate had reclassified amphetamines. Although he stated that he favored an instruction to the conferees to support the amendment, he inexplicably declined to so move. Instead, Pepper asked the conferees "to view this matter as sympathetically as they think the facts and the evidence they have before them will permit." Congressman Rogers, an outspoken opponent of the Pepper amendment, promised "sympathetic understanding" for the position of the minority.

Indeed, the minority would have to be content with that and little else. All seven House managers were members of the parent committee, and four were members of the originating subcommittee. Of the seven, only one would match support with "sympathetic understanding." The other six were not only against Schedule II classification, but they had led the opposition to it in floor debate: Jarman, Rogers, Carter, Staggers and Nelsen. Congressman Springer, who had declared in debate that economics had nothing to do with this issue, completed the House representation. Not a single member of Pepper's Select Committee on Crime was appointed as a conferee. On the question of reclassification, the pharmaceutical industry would be well represented.

Hoffman-LaRoche, as well, was undoubtedly comforted by the presence of the four House subcommittee conferees: The subcommittee had never made any attempt to include Valium and Librium in the bill. On that question, it is fair to say that the Senate managers were divided. The administration continued to support no controls for these depressants.

At dispute were six substantive Senate amendments to the House bill: Three concerned amphetamines, Librium and Valium; one required an annual report to Congress on advisory councils; the fifth lessened the penalty for persons who gratuitously distributed a small amount of marijuana; and the sixth, introduced by Senator Hughes, altered the thrust of the bill and placed greater emphasis on drug education, research, rehabilitation and training. To support these new programs, the Senate had appropriated $26 million more than the House.

The House, officially, opposed all of the Senate amendments.

From the final compromises, it is apparent that the Senate liberals expended much of their energy on behalf of the Hughes amendment. Although the Senate's proposed educational effort was largely gutted in favor of the original House version, an additional 25 million dollars was appropriated. The bill would also now require the inclusion in state public health plans of "comprehensive programs" to combat drug abuse and the scope of grants for addicts and drug-dependent persons was increased. The House then accepted the amendments on annual reports and the possession charge for gratuitous marijuana distributors.

The administration and industry representative gave but an inch on the amphetamine amendment: Only the liquid injectible methamphetamines, speed, would be transferred to Schedule II. All the pills would remain in Schedule III. In the end, amphetamine abuse was restricted to the mainlining speed freak. The conference report reiterated the notion that further administrative action on amphetamines by the attorney general would be initiated. Finally, Librium and Valium would not be included in the bill. The report noted that "final administrative action" (begun

in 1966) was expected "in a matter of weeks." Congress was con-
tented to await the outcome of those proceedings.

ADOPTION OF THE CONFERENCE REPORT

Pepper and his supporters were on their feet when the agreement on amphetamines was reported to the House on October 14,
1970. Conferee Springer, faithful to the industry's tactical line,
declared that the compromise is a good one because it "singles out
the worst of these substances, which are the liquid, injectible
methamphetamines and puts them in Schedule II." If amphetamine injection warranted such attention, why, asked Congressman Charles Wiggins, were the easily diluted amphetamine
and methamphetamine pills left in Schedule III? Springer responded that there had been "much discussion," yes and "some
argument" over that issue, but the conferees felt it was best to
leave the rest of the amphetamine family to administrative action.

Few could have been fooled by the conference agreement. The
managers claimed to have taken the most dangerous and abused
member of the family and subjected it to more rigorous controls.
In fact, as the minority pointed out, the compromise affected the
least abused amphetamine: Lawfully manufactured "liquid meth"
was sold strictly to hospitals, not in the streets, and there was no
evidence of any illicit diversion. More importantly, from the perspective of the drug manufacturers, only five of the 6,000 member
amphetamine family fell into this category. Indeed, liquid meth
was but an insignificant part of the total methamphetamine, not to
mention amphetamine, production. Pepper characterized the new
provision as "virtually meaningless." It was an easy pill for the
industry to swallow. The Senate accepted the report on the same
day as the House.

Only Eagleton, the sponsor of the successful Senate reclassification amendment, would address the amphetamine issue. To him,
the new amendment "accomplish[ed] next to nothing." The reason for the timid, limpid compromise was also obvious to Eagleton: "When the chips were down, the power of the drug companies was simply more compelling" than any appeal to the public
welfare.

A week before, when Dodd had successfully classified Librium
and Valium in the bill, he had remarked (in reference to the

House's inaction): "Hoffman-LaRoche, at least for the moment, have reason to celebrate a singular triumph, the triumph of money over conscience. It is a triumph . . . which I hope will be shortlived."

THE BILL BECOMES LAW

Richard Nixon appropriately chose the Bureau of Narcotics and Dangerous Drugs offices for the signing of the bill on November 2, 1970. Flanked by Mitchell and Ingersoll, the president had before him substantially the same measure that had been introduced 15 months earlier. Nixon declared that America faced a major crisis of drug abuse, reaching even into the junior high schools, which constituted a "major cause of street crime." To combat this alarming rise, the president now had 300 new agents. Also, the federal government's jurisdiction was expanded: "The jurisdiction of the attorney general will go far beyond, for example, heroin. It will cover the new types of drugs, the barbiturates and amphetamines that have become so common *and are even more dangerous because of their use*" (author emphasis).

The president recognized amphetamines were "even more dangerous" than heroin, although he carefully attached the qualifier that this was a result "of their use." The implication is clear: The president viewed only the large dosage user of amphetamines as an abuser. The fact that his full statement refers only to abuse by "young people" (and not physicians, truck drivers, housewives or businessmen) affirms the implication. The president's remarks contained no mention of the pharmaceutical industry, nor did they refer to any future review of amphetamine classification. After a final reference to the destruction that drug abuse was causing, the president signed the bill into law.

Chapter 3

Criminological theories of the nature of crime and the nature of people

SOME HISTORICAL ORIGINS OF MODERN CRIMINOLOGY

In this chapter the historical development of contemporary criminology will be traced, and the various theoretical assumptions and research strategies which have emerged will be discussed. It will be demonstrated that certain theoretical assumptions are related to the choice of specific research strategies as well as to specific proposals for the control of crime.

Classical and other early criminology

The earliest scholarship which can be called criminology or the study of crime-related issues was the work of Cesare Beccaria (1738–94), who is usually referred to as an advocate of the Classical school of criminology (Vold, 1958: 18–24; Monachesi, 1973: 36–50). Unlike most of the later criminologists, Beccaria was not concerned with explaining the causes of criminal behavior but dealt with what he considered to be injustices in the administration of the law, which gave special privileges to the clergy and the nobility. Beccaria observed that laws typically represented only the interests of a few powerful members of a society. He also complained that the same crimes were often punished in a different manner at different times in the same courts. He recommended a literal enforcement of all laws, irrespective of the mental condition or social status of the accused or the social status of the victim. He deliberately ignored questions regarding the individual's motives and in any event considered them unimportant since he believed that all people have a free will and in this sense are alike (Beccaria, 1775).

The problem with completely ignoring the characteristics of the individuals accused is that in no society has the criminal law been administered without considering who is being accused. Moreover, in strict form, Classical criminology would have treated minors and the obviously insane in the same way as any other accused. Also, classical criminology would treat first offenders like repeated offenders since it considers the crime committed and not the characteristics of the accused to be the proper basis for the legal response (Vold, 1958: 24). Yet Beccaria's ideas were of lasting importance because they served as a starting point for a recurrent theme in criminology, namely, demands for legal reforms.

Somewhat later, Jeremy Bentham (1748–1832) also produced a treatise on criminal behavior, criminal law, and legal reform (Bentham, 1823). How Bentham's works can best be categorized is a disputed question (Vold, 1958: 14–26; Mannheim, 1973: 24). Bentham was concerned with the development of a just legal structure, as was Beccaria, and like Beccaria, Bentham viewed people as possessing a free will. However, compared to Beccaria, Bentham is more remembered for his concern with criminal behavior and its control. He is often remembered for recommending that a set of penalties be developed to control criminal behavior. His idea, which he called the *principle of utility,* though it is often referred to as the *hedonistic calculus,* is that the criminal laws should prescribe punishment just severe enough to offset the pleasure people receive from committing a given criminal act. Any more severe punishment is unnecessarily brutal and therefore unjust.

However, the central pleasure-pain thesis of the hedonistic calculus is questionable from two perspectives. First, there is no evidence that all people derive the same amount of pleasure from the same criminal act. Moreover, there is no evidence that all people suffer the same amount of pain from the imposition of identical criminal sanctions. For example, some prison inmates adjust well to prison life and serve "easy time," whereas for other inmates each day in prison is a nightmare. Despite these considerable shortcomings, Bentham's general orientation is still often used by public officials and laymen alike to justify extreme penalties for what they consider serious crimes.

Positivism in criminology

Next to develop were the ideas of a heterogeneous group of scholars who are known collectively as positivists. Although differences abound in this group, the positivist writers share several central premises. They all assume that people are controlled in some specifiable manner by their biological, psychological, or social characteristics, that these controlling characteristics can be isolated through the use of scientific measurements and of official crime records and that in this way criminal behavior can in turn be more effectively predicted and controlled. Historical accounts of positivism in criminology always mention Cesare Lombroso (1835–1909) as having stressed the role of biological factors in criminal behavior. Lombroso's early research convinced him that convicted criminals in disproportionately high numbers evidenced physical characteristics of man's less evolved apelike ancestors. This suggested to Lombroso, in line with the then new notion of evolution, that criminals were throwbacks to earlier stages in the evolutionary process. For this reason he believed that criminals were unable to adjust to civilized society. In short, according to Lombroso's reasoning, many convicted criminals are literally forced by their physical characteristics to commit crimes.

A sampling of the apelike characteristics which Lombroso found among convicted criminals are:

Unusually large ears, or occasionally very small, or standing out from the head as in the chimpanzee;
Fleshy, swollen, and protruding lips;
Pouches in the cheek like those of lower animals;
Receding chin, or excessively long, or short, or flat, as in apes;
Excessively long arms (Lombroso-Ferrero, 1911: 14–19).

Although Lombroso (1911) later discarded this biological determinism when he found similar biological characteristics among a noncriminal group of Italian soldiers (Vold, 1958: 50–52), his early research is of lasting importance since its general assumptions are reflected in contemporary biological positivism. One contemporary variant of biological positivism is the considerable popular attention that has been directed to genetic, chromosomal linkages with crime. Scores of studies have pointed to a causal link between the presence in some males of an extra Y or male-producing chromosome (XY is normal), designated the XYY or Klinefelter syndrome. The evidence from these studies purports to show that XYY males characterized as subnormal in intelligence and hyperaggressive, appear with greater frequency in institutionalized populations (prisons and mental hospitals) than in the general population (Report on XYY Chromosomal Abnormality, 1970). Even so, a conference of experts convened by the National Institute of Mental Health was reluctant to conclude that the XYY abnormality was definitely or invariably associated with behavioral abnormalities (Report on XYY Chromosomal Abnormality, 1970: 33). One major problem in Lombroso's work and the more recent chromosome research is that at best it grounds the relationship between the alleged biological pathologies and criminal behavior in statistical associations, but has established no causal linkages.

Another biologically based approach to criminality is found in psychiatric theories—primarily those emanating from the work of Sigmund Freud. These theories emphasize the overcoming of the learned aspects of a person's personality by biological drives, with criminal behavior as a consequence (Alexander and Staub, 1931; Abrahamsen, 1964). Although these psychiatric theories regard all people as born criminals, they state that most people learn after birth to control their criminal biological impulses. According to this psychiatric orientation, humans are innately aggressive, and though the veneer of civilization has prevented total chaos, it has not changed fundamental human nature. This reasoning holds that people do not choose to commit crime but are literally driven to it by a combination of physical drives and relatively weak learned inhibitions.

Mental deficiency or feeblemindedness has also been used as a causal explanation for criminal behavior, the notion being that mental defectives have more difficulty than others in adjusting to society. Early works using this approach appeared in the 19th century, but not until Henry Goddard (1914, 1921) translated the

Binet-Simon intelligence scale for American use did the approach become widespread in this country (Fink, 1962: 211 ff.). After an initial surge of popularity in 1910 and shortly thereafter, its use diminished when, after appropriate comparison groups were established, it was shown that incarcerated populations showed approximately the same range of intelligence as so-called normals (Vold, 1958: 75–89).

Sociological positivism

The latest development in criminological positivism is that of 20th century sociology. Émile Durkheim (1858–1917) is often cited as an early sociological positivist with a professional interest in criminal behavior. His position was that social phenomena are just as real as the behavior of individuals or physical objects and that the external characteristics of "social facts" can therefore be studied by objective means (Durkheim, 1938). Durkheim felt that these external characteristics were adequately reflected in official records, which permitted the calculation of such things as suicide and crime rates, and ultimately made possible the analysis and explanation of such rates.

Within sociological positivism in criminology, several major theoretical traditions have developed. The earliest is found in the works of Shaw (1929) and Shaw and McKay (1942). Rather than focus on characteristics of individuals as causal agents in crime, Shaw and McKay looked to the social disorganization or lack of community control found in specific intercity neighborhood districts as responsible for generating high official rates of law violation. High rates of adult crime are found in these areas, along with similarly high rates of juvenile delinquency, mental illness, and poverty. Shaw and McKay found that the high rates of law violation are remarkably consistent in such neighborhoods, irrespective of the particular ethnic group living in them. This suggests that the deteriorating character of neighborhoods characterized by impersonality and transiency gives rise to those rates.

Within sociological positivism, two other theoretical traditions developed in the late 1930s. One orientation is that of anomie theory as developed by Robert K. Merton (1938), and the other is the differential association theory of Edwin Sutherland (1939: 1–9). Anomie theory attempts, as did Shaw and McKay, to explain the high rates of crime among the poor, and maintains that crime is a consequence of discrepancies between culturally prescribed goals and the socially approved means available to achieve those goals. According to anomie theory, in the United States all people are subject to strong social pressures to achieve economic success, yet some people are in relatively unfavorable competitive positions for attaining that goal legitimately. Consequently, people in such positions experience frustration and strain. Since American society stresses economic success rather than the means used to achieve it, these people are strongly motivated to resort to deviant or illegitimate means. This theory, Merton.claims, explains the high rate of officially recorded crime among the poor.

Differential association theory, on the other hand, suggests that people engage in criminal behavior because their predominant intimate contacts have been with criminal behavior patterns. Both criminal techniques and values are learned through such associations. Sutherland claims that a high ratio or "differential" of criminal to noncriminal associations makes it more likely that a person will commit a crime, for such associations shape and control the person's world view. In short, "the principles of the process of association by which criminal behavior develops are the same as the principles of the process by which lawful behavior develops" (Sutherland, 1939: 5).

All positivists, then, see people as essentially compelled to commit crimes because of their biological, psychological, or social conditions. For example, Lobroso claimed that many convicted criminals were impelled to commit misdeeds by their relatively less highly evolved biological capacities; Goddard considered feeble-mindedness to be the main controlling agent; and Sutherland focused on group pressures. Moreover, it is such conditions that make criminals essentially different from noncriminals. These twin assumptions of constraint and differentiation, Matza (1964: 1–32) observes, leave unexplained the consistent features of the lives of criminals and delinquents. If criminals are forced to commit criminal acts, and if they are indeed so different from other people, then how can patterns of occasional law violations separated by long periods of conformity be explained? Matza's point is that if persons are forced to commit crime because of their unique characteristics, logically they should be forced to do so all the time.

The heavy emphasis on the study of criminal *individuals* is expected of biological positivists, but it is somewhat surprising to find sociologists who should be more attuned to group processes and social forces also emphasizing individual characteristics. Moreover, as indicated above, these sociologists rely heavily on the scientific measurement of individual characteristics and on official crime statistics as appropriate sources of information on criminal individuals. This is reflected in a review of the social science research on juvenile delinquency published over the past 30 years. The review indicates a heavy use of official records, of statistical tests and hypothesis testing, both of which are part of the traditional scientific model, and of individual variables, such as respondents' attitudes and values as measured through interviews and questionnaires (Galliher and McCartney, 1973).

Social control and societal reactions

As indicated earlier, Durkheim is usually cited as an early sociological positivist. He was also the first social analyst to suggest that, contrary to the traditional view that crime is only a burden to society, it may serve a positive function in social life. His notion is that if a society is so rigid and binding that no crime occurs, then no other creativity will occur either, and no change or progress will be possible.

To make progress, individual originality must be able to express itself. In order that the originality of the idealist whose dreams transcend his century may find expression, it is necessary that the originality of the criminal, who is below the level of his time, shall also be possible. One does not occur without the other (Durkheim, 1938: 71).

Crime implies not only that the way remains open to necessary changes but that in certain cases it directly prepares these changes (Durkheim, 1938: 71).

Moreover, Durkheim suggests that society's very act of punishing crime mobilizes support for the social norm which has been violated. In this sense as well, crime serves a positive function in society, for the violation and consequent punishment symbolize to everyone the importance of the social norm (Durkheim, 1933:

70–110). Durkheim's concern with the social reactions of a citizenry toward criminal behavior represented a significant departure in the literature dealing with crime, for previous to his work, attention was focused mainly on the criminal.

Another step toward a thorough analysis of citizen reactions and definitions of crime and criminals is seen in Frank Tannenbaum's (1938: 19–21) discussion of what he called the "dramatization of evil." The idea is that once a person has been arrested and taken into court, a process of public redefining and labeling begins which serves to emphasize to the public and to the arrested person that he is indeed a criminal. Not only does the public become convinced of the person's new identity, but the arrestee himself becomes convinced as well and changes his behavior to bring it into line with this new self-image. Very often, children who have been sent to a reformatory emerge from the correctional institution with a clear view of themselves as bad, and they behave accordingly. Thus the very behavior which the community complains of is reinforced by the community's reaction.

The distinction between "primary and secondary deviation," first discussed by Edwin Lemert (1951: 75–78), also deals with the effects of citizen reaction to crime. Some law violation occurs before the actor is publicly labeled a criminal or delinquent. Lemert referred to this as primary deviation. However, once the actor's deviance has been identified, this new public knowledge can alter how he is perceived by himself and others. The new deviant role thus created for the actor encourages further law violation—called secondary deviation. In other words, secondary deviation is a result of the dramatization of evil. In the works of Tannenbaum and Lemert, at least a slight shift of emphasis has been made away from the exclusive study of the behavior of criminals and toward some analysis of the impact of broader social events on the actor once he is identified as a criminal. Public definitions of crime and criminals become objects worthy of study in their own right.

A somewhat more extreme position is the labeling theory perspective of Howard Becker. Becker (1963) maintains that the *audience reaction* to deviance should be of primary interest to social analysts since one cannot determine whether acts are criminal or delinquent independent of that reaction. The definition of "what happened" is recognized as not inherent in the behavior itself (cf. Douglas, 1967).

From this point of view, deviance is *not* a quality of the act the person commits, but rather a consequence of the application by others of rules and sanctions to an "offender." The deviant is one to whom that label has successfully been applied; deviant behavior is behavior that people so label (Becker, 1963: 9).

Whether an act is deviant, then, depends on how other people react to it (Becker, 1963: 11).

Just because one has committed an infraction of a rule does not mean that others will respond as though this had happened. (Conversely, just because one has not violated a rule does not mean that he may not be treated, in some circumstances, as though he had.) (Becker, 1963: 12).

Some people may be labeled deviant who in fact have not broken a rule (Becker, 1963: 9).

Jumping around while shouting and frothing at the mouth can be defined as a glorious religious experience deserving respect and awe, as evidence of mental illness requiring hospitalization, or as an indication that the actor is a witch and merits burning at the stake. The meaning of the act can only be determined by observing the act's significance for the participants. Prostitution, gambling, drunkenness, and begging, which are crimes in our society, are not so defined in all cultures (Vold, 1958: 141–146), but may be seen as behaviors which are appropriate and even honorable on special occasions or when committed by special persons, as in ritual drunkenness at athletic events or ritualized prostitution in temples. What killing a person with an ax is called is a matter of variable human definition. It can be seen as murder, self-defense, battlefield valor, or routine performance of one's job as an executioner. The labeling perspective is useful in demonstrating social and legal variability across cultures, but though we make use of some of its observations, we do not try to avoid making moral judgments about certain cultural practices.

If one uses the labeling perspective, then official crime records become suspect as reflections of actual behavior and tend to be seen as a measure of the reactions to various types of behavior by the organizations which compile those records (Kitsuse and Cicourel, 1963). Within this context, crime rates become useful as a reflection of police activity and decision making and irrelevant as indicators of the amount of criminal behavior taking place in a community. For example, a high rate of narcotics arrests may not mean that an area is being flooded with drugs as compared to neighboring areas but rather that the police are less tolerant of and more vigilant in dealing with such offenses. Not only do labeling theorists reject official records as measures of deviance, but they criticize and abandon scientific methodologies which use such data. The labeling perspective claims that there is a dynamic or processual aspect to human existence which is not adequately described in official records and is retrievable only through field observation. Yet the labeling theorists, like the positivists, continue to study the isolated individual deviant and continue to view this actor as essentially controlled or dominated by his or her environment (Schervish, 1973). Their usual argument is that the actor labeled as a lawbreaker is forced into a life of crime.

In the late 1960s and early 1970s, the labeling perspective enjoyed considerable popularity. The labeling perspective's consideration of the social process involved in defining crime and criminals and its insistence on the arbitrary nature of consequent definitions proved convincing in an era when government was increasingly distrusted. During such an era, official definitions of reality, including official definitions of crime, are less likely to be accepted without question. When the government and its law enforcement agencies are widely suspected of bias and corruption, the official records and official definitions of crime and criminals come to be seen as questionable and come to be regarded as subjects suitable for study in their own right. As Jerome Hall (1945: 345–346) has observed, the positivist orientation toward the study of crime only develops when governments are trusted and above question. Various developments have contributed to the credibility of the labeling position. In the southeastern United States during the various civil rights demonstrations and other related racial clashes of the 1960s, the police and courts often failed to enforce the law when whites assaulted or even killed local blacks. Indeed, the southern police often assumed a leadership role in physical brutality toward black demonstrators, including women and children. With the aid of national television networks, all Americans could easily learn about racist segregation statutes and the racist administration of other criminal laws, at least in the South. More recently, the deceitful actions of a former U.S. president and his attorney general, the chief law enforcement officer of the nation, have insured the continued credibility of the labeling position.

Applications of the societal reaction perspective

Once the social processes involved in defining crime and criminals are recognized, new topics which seem especially relevant to contemporary society can be better understood. Objects, behaviors, and events not usually associated with crime and criminals can be presented in a new light outside the protective shield of commonsense opinion.

Goode has argued convincingly that what is usually considered a "drug" or "narcotic," and therefore what is considered drug abuse, has no basis as a chemical or pharmacological fact, but is merely a cultural fabrication. *"A drug is something that has been arbitrarily defined by certain segments of society as a drug"* (Goode, 1972: 18). Marijuana is routinely classified as a drug, whereas coffee, cigarettes, and alcohol are not. "What this means is that the effects of different drugs have relatively little to do with the way they are conceptualized, defined, and classified" (Goode, 1972: 18).

Ralph Nader's book *Unsafe at Any Speed* (1965) shows that auto manufacturers have collaborated to manufacture cheaply produced autos, but have disregarded the safety of the occupants. The manufacturers' knowledge of engineering must indicate that such autos will kill and maim auto occupants at low-speed crashes. Yet no claims have been made by the public, the press, or prosecutors that auto manufacturers are guilty of conspiracy to commit highway genocide. When a family is slaughtered on the highways, the disaster is blamed on fatigue, drinking, poor visibility, crowded highways, on anything, in fact, but Henry Ford or other corporate executives, even though the elements of a conspiracy resulting in unnecessary deaths seem to be present. The cultural image we have of the responsibility for auto accidents comes from the National Safety Council (NSC), an agency supported in large part with funds from the auto industry (Gusfield, 1975). The NSC does not call attention to the design characteristics of the specific automobiles associated with auto accidents and deaths. The clear implication is that if anyone is to be blamed for auto accidents, it is the driver. Furthermore, there is no evidence that such acts as illegal price fixing by businessmen create public moral indignation, even though such behavior violates criminal statutes and annually costs the American public millions of dollars.

As another case in point, one can observe that much of the

American public was not aroused by the endless bombings of civilians in Southeast Asia, by the presidential decrees of Richard Nixon, in a conflict seldom now justified in military or political terms. Yet many citizens were outraged when the same leader was implicated in what would seem to be the relatively minor crime of conspiracy to obstruct justice in a burglary case. Curiously, the destruction of human life seems to have been considered less serious than was burglary.

Finally, in contrast to dictionary definitions of violence, most American men interviewed in a nationwide survey (Blumenthal et al., 1972) did not see war as violent, nor did a majority see shooting looters as violent, even though the vast majority of the respondents saw looting itself as violent. The point is that even though a behavior is destructive of life or property, this does not insure that the public will define it as violent or as crime. Public definitions of violence, crime, criminals, and immorality are not based on objective measures of physical destruction and human suffering, or even on gross and open violation of criminal statutes. Violence is typically seen by laymen and social scientists solely as a product of the behavior of those outside government even when it is recognized that the representatives of government kill and injure.

Once consensus is achieved regarding what acts have occurred, then the matter of responsibility for those acts must be addressed. The judgments in answer to such questions also have no basis independent of cultural designations. One issue is whether an individual or a gang is responsible for a criminal act. In fact, only a part of an individual's body is held responsible for some crimes in some Arabic societies, as reflected in their practice of cutting off the hands of thieves. In the Western world, on the other hand, we routinely hold people responsible for crimes they have commissioned, including killings, even though they did not participate in the criminal act. This example shows how unimportant objective physical behaviors may be in human definitions. One can be 2,000 miles away from a murder and still be held legally and socially responsible for it. At times, the individual attacked may even be blamed for the assault, as is often true of rape victims. It is frequently alleged that rape victims, by their seductive dress or manner, have created the conditions resulting in their own victimization (Brownmiller, 1975).

The problem of assessing responsibility for actions was addressed in trials conducted by the Allied powers in Nuremberg, Germany, after World War II, which established a principle quite unusual in the history of war among modern nations. Historically, after a war individual operatives of the defeated nation have not been held legally or morally responsible for its acts. The Nuremberg trials, however, abandoned this principle and held various government officials and army officers criminally responsible for the atrocities of the Third Reich. Also, what many regard as a crime crisis in America is alternatively blamed on a communist conspirarcy, the Mafia, or liberal, permissive parents. Indeed, some juvenile court judges have suggested punishment for the parents of youths found to be delinquent. As in definitions of crime, designations of responsibility are totally dependent on varying cultural judgments. By using this labeling perspective, we will explore in Chapter 7 the created nature of a variety of criminals and criminal behaviors.

Conflict theory

In the late 1960s there reemerged in the United States what is usually called the conflict perspective in the study of crime and deviance. More than the labeling perspective, this orientation stresses the role of *power* in winning control over government operations, including the law enforcement (crime-defining) machinery (Quinney, 1970; Turk, 1969).

A recent and well-known conflict approach developed by Quinney has been embodied in a series of theoretical propositions which include the following:

PROPOSITION 1 (DEFINITION OF CRIME): *Crime is a definition of human conduct that is created by authorized agents in a politically organized society* (Quinney, 1970: 15).

PROPOSITION 2 (FORMULATION OF CRIMINAL DEFINITIONS): *Criminal definitions describe behaviors that conflict with the interests of the segments of society that have the power to shape public policy* (Quinney, 1970: 16).

PROPOSITION 3 (APPLICATIONS OF CRIMINAL DEFINITIONS): *Criminal definitions are applied by the segments of society that have the power to shape the enforcement and administration of criminal law* (Quinney, 1970: 18).

The conflict approach to the study of crime can be summarized as follows:

[Crime emerges when] individuals or loosely organized small groups with little power are strongly feared by a well-organized, sizable minority or majority who have a large amount of power (Lofland, 1969: 14).

Then, the existence of state rulings and corresponding enforcement mechanisms . . . provide for the possibility of forceably removing actors from civil society, either by banishment, annihilation or incarceration. Again, it is precisely those actors who have little power and who are not organized toward whom such actions can most successfully be undertaken (Lofland, 1969: 18).

The conflict position takes as its primary article of faith the view that crime is first and foremost a political topic. Black radicals' claims of being political prisoners and the trials of Vietnam war protesters have undoubtedly contributed to the visibility if not the credibility of this position in contemporary America. The evidence in Chapter 2 regarding the role of elites in shaping most criminal statutes would also seem to support this theoretical orientation. The conflict perspective is not new, however, having European origins in the work of the Marxist socialist Willem Bonger (1876–1940), whose *Criminality and Economic Conditions* was published in this country in 1916. Somewhat later the conflict perspective emerged in the United States (Sellin, 1938; Taft, 1942; Vold, 1958). Most recently, in the 1970s, some proponents of the conflict perspective have placed more emphasis on the work of Karl Marx in their explorations of the nature of class conflict and domination, crime, and crime control (Quinney, 1973; Taylor et al., 1975). Like labeling theory, the conflict perspective usually gives some recognition to the notion that definitions of crime and criminals are arbitrary. Yet, as with positivists and to some degree labeling theorists, the conflict perspective's view of humankind is still usually that of actors who are subject to the dictates of social and economic conditions. This view is undoubtedly a result of the perspective's historical roots in Marxism.

Assumptions regarding the nature of people

Assumptions about the nature of people and the nature of crime may be found in all theoretical orientations. People may be seen either as free or as totally or partially constrained, and crime may be seen as real or contrived.

Most study of crime has uncritically accepted the official definitions of the nature of crime and criminals, and in this sense has not differed much from the commonsense explanations of the general public (Phillipson, 1974: 2–3). "Moreover, most of this work has been done within a positivistic frame of reference which typically dehumanizes man by reducing him to an *object* of study; in doing this the work covers its own value commitments by laying spurious claims to scientific status" (Phillipson, 1974: 3).

Our orientation supports the view expounded by labeling and conflict theorists regarding the constructed, arbitrary nature of crime, and therefore challenges the positivists' implicit assumption that crime has some reality independent of human interpretation. However, we disagree with the positivists as well as the labeling and conflict theorists when they picture people as necessarily constrained beings. As the Classical criminologist Beccaria would have claimed, we suggest that even relatively powerless individuals can and do make decisions, that is, choose among alternatives, at least some of the time. Therefore, even such people help create to some degree the environment to which they in turn react. This orientation is true to the dynamic nature of human existence as seen by the actors themselves. It views people not as puppets to be manipulated at government whim but as creatures with inner direction, that is, to some degree independent of immediate controls. It is important to affirm what people everywhere believe—that they are *capable* of self-direction even if a given society does not encourage this freedom. Perhaps the wide consensus that criminals are controlled and without reason has developed because the individuals who commit most traditional crimes are recruited from the poorest strata of society and, indeed, have fewer choices than do other, more affluent citizens. Also, as Matza (1964: 7) has observed, it is relatively easy to accept the notion that those called criminals do not possess free will or the capacity for reason. In other words, it is easy to define criminals as crazy.

This historical discussion of criminological theories is of significance in understanding the development of contemporary conceptions of crime causation. Equally important, however, is the recognition that only when one understands what theories people hold regarding the causes of crime, will one be able to understand

and even predict what social policy measures such people will advocate in the control of crime. Those accepting Bentham's ideas of a hedonistic calculus will undoubtedly argue for more severe penalties to deal with rising crime rates. Legislators at the state and federal level frequently argue for crime control along these lines. Biological positivists have predictably been proponents of both execution and the sterilization of convicted offenders, given the impossibility of reforming what they consider to be inferior biological types. On the other hand, social scientists who support Merton's anomie theory have argued for vocational training programs in both high-crime areas and prisons to open up new legitimate opportunities for economic achievement (Galliher, 1971). And those who locate the source of crime in the individual's mind often suggest some type of psychological treatment or therapy as a solution to the problem of crime.

CRIMINOLOGICAL RESEARCH METHODS

Historically, positivism in criminology has relied very heavily on science. The heart of this scientific method has usually been to contrast exact measurements of biological, psychological, or social traits of criminals with comparable measurements of noncriminals. The assumptions of this method have been challenged, for example in the works of Herbert Marcuse (1964). Marcuse contends that people are increasingly dictated to by science and technology. In the name of rationality, the demands of "scientific progress" have become a form of political domination that is all the more effective because it is not recognized as such (Habermas, 1969: 81–122).

Social scientists, and especially criminologists, have not typically recognized that the development of science is responsive to the governmental and private agencies which pay the research bills (Olson, 1964; McCartney, 1970; Copp, 1972). Given what is now known about funding agencies, the policies of these agencies can usually be expected to represent the interests and biases of the elites which have the greatest political and economic power. Although there has recently been a growing criticism of science, it is still sacrosanct to many, and its very hallowed nature allows it to create and maintain unchallenged a rich folklore about the nature of reality, including the reality of crime. As a case in point, observations of the types of research on juvenile delinquency supported by funding agencies indicate that these agencies have furthered the notion that juvenile delinquency and crime are problems of *individuals,* since individuals and not institutions or organizations are usually the unit of analysis in such funded research. Moreover, funding agencies support research which defines juvenile delinquency as a problem adequately reflected by official statistics, and this in turn makes it seem that delinquency is a proclivity of urban black youths (Galliher and McCartney, 1973). Those studying crime have given most attention to the illegal behavior of the powerless and poor and have largely ignored the "illegal, and destructive actions of powerful individuals, groups, and institutions in our society" (Liazos, 1972: 111; also see Thio, 1973). Marcuse's observations about the enslaving quality of science are accurate, except that we would emphasize that where there are slaves, there are also masters. The interests of government leaders are furthered by the picture of crime created by the criminologist, which describes it as an *individual* as opposed to a *structural* problem and one in which official statistics and therefore arrest practices go essentially unchallenged. Most governments and their funding agencies can be expected to find favor in this positivism, relying as it does on science and official records. Positivists claiming that humankind is controlled strive through science to isolate the specific mechanisms for controlling behavior, including criminal behavior. Marcuse's challenge to scientific technology is in contrast to the approach of most students of crime and deviance. Even the conflict theorist Bonger, who was a Marxist socialist, used official statistics and the scientific method. More recently, Jack Douglas (1967), whose research on suicide questioned the use of official statistics as part of the baggage of science, elsewhere disputed Marcuse's total pessimism about the contributions of science to human freedom (1970: 27): "The growing importance of science in our society, with its fundamental emphasis on free inquiry and free communication, has increased the demands for free speech." Awareness of the implicit assumptions of the scientific method seems largely absent in the study of crime. An alternative to this concern with science, and its emphasis on exacting measurements of individual characteristics, is an attempt to be conscious of a society's historical traditions and of the influence that a society's changing patterns of power has on the passage and enforcement of criminal law or the administration of the law by the police and the courts.

Data sources

A final question regarding the means of studying crime, which criminologists seldom ask yet always, at least implicitly, answer, concerns what the data of criminology are taken to be. Most criminologists implicitly assume that their appropriate data center on the criminal behavior of individuals. This is, of course, true of positivists, but perhaps more surprising, it is also often true of labeling and conflict theorists (Schervish, 1973; Bonger, 1916). In contrast, C. Ray Jeffery (1956) contends that criminal law alone can provide the data for criminology. He argues that one must begin with the study of criminal law, for only the law and its administration can create the environment in which behavior can take on the meaning of crime.

It is also possible, of course, to study criminal behavior within the guidelines presented by Jeffery by considering how the law and the criminal justice system affect people labeled as criminals. It must be recognized, however, that studying behavior as opposed to legal institutions is as much a political as an academic decision. If the problem for criminology is defined as dealing with the individual's behavior to the exclusion of a study of the development and administration of the law, one's research indirectly lends credibility to those with the power to control the legislatures, the police, and the courts, and opposes the interests of those against whom the law is usually enforced. If one studies only the individuals and groups officially defined as the problem rather than the groups which do the defining, such as the police, the courts, and the legislatures, one is actively, even if unwittingly, taking a position in support of the status quo. It is important for criminologists to be self-conscious about criminology's historical development and the forces involved in that development, including funding agencies, as well as to be aware of the historical development and administration of the criminal law which provide the definitional boundaries for what is called crime.

Looking at the whole of the criminal justice process, one sees quite clearly that not all people are as completely constrained as criminologists so often picture them. We will attempt to demonstrate that lawmakers, and those whose interests they represent, are least constrained and most supported by the whole criminal justice system; and that those people called criminals are by definition of the label the most constrained by the law, although far from being totally controlled, as police and prison guards will testify. The revival of the issue of equality before the law raised by Beccaria two centuries ago seems appropriate in an economically stratified and racist society like our own, where—as this book will demonstrate—despite the prevailing myth of democracy and equality before the law, lawmakers and their coteries are largely affluent whites, and those against whom the law is enforced are disproportionately poor and black. As Matza (1969: 94–100) has observed, despite frequent criticism of official records of crime by criminologists, since those records are usually seen as the only information available, they are used anyway in conducting empirical research and generating theories. Science and official records must be recognized as serving the interests of some people while compromising the interests of others, and the substantive and theoretical boundaries of criminology must be provided by a thorough knowledge of the social bases of criminal law and its administration.

CONCLUSION

In this chapter we have briefly traced the historical development of modern criminology, beginning with the "radical" ideas of the Classical criminologist Beccaria, who demanded equal justice for all. Next, we discussed Bentham's notion of using the hedonistic calculus to control rewards and penalties. Both Beccaria and Bentham believed that people possess reason and free will. Following this, we covered several varieties of criminological positivism, including biological positivism, psychological and psychiatric positivism, and the most recent development—sociological positivism. All criminological positivism involves a concentration on the study of criminal individuals through the scientific measurement of their individual characteristics and the use of official records. These records reveal what appears to be a great amount of crime among the poor. The positivist perspective also assumes that criminals are forced to commit crimes because of some unique biological, psychological, or social condition. More recently there has emerged in criminology some recognition of the arbitrary nature of the definitions of crime and criminals, and therefore some recognition of the importance of audience reactions. A critical look was also taken at criminological research methods and the types of data that these methods produce. Finally, it was argued that the boundaries of criminology, that is, what is and what is not an appropriate subject of study for those interested in crime and criminals, can only be provided by a thorough knowledge of the social and historical origins of criminal law. Whatever the origins of specific criminal laws, the social analyst should feel free to make moral judgments of those laws on the basis of their consequences. Moreover, since both traditional criminology and this alternative stress the importance of the administration of criminal justice as an arbitrary and discriminatory defining agent, an analysis of the police and the courts is essential.

REFERENCES

Abrahamsen, David
   1964   *The Psychology of Crime.* New York: John Wiley and Sons.

Alexander, Franz and Hugo Staub
   1931   *The Criminal, the Judge, and the Public: A Psychological Analysis.* New York: Macmillan Co.

Beccaria, Cesare B.
   1775   *An Essay on Crimes and Punishments.* 4th ed. London: E. Newbery.

Becker, Howard S.
   1963   *Outsiders.* New York: Free Press of Glencoe.

Bentham, Jeremy
   1823   *An Introduction to the Principles of Morals and Legislation.* Reprinted 1948. New York: Hafner Publishing Co.

Blumenthal, Monica D., Robert L. Kahn, Frank M. Andrews, and Kendra B. Head
   1972   *Justifying Violence: Attitudes of American Men.* Ann Arbor: Institute for Social Research, University of Michigan.

Bonger, Willem
1916 *Criminality and Economic Conditions.* Henry P. Horton, trans. Boston: Little, Brown and Co.

Brownmiller, Susan
1975 *Against Our Will: Men, Women, and Rape.* New York: Simon and Schuster.

Copp, James H.
1972 "Rural Sociology and Rural Development," *Rural Sociology* 37(December): 515–533.

Douglas, Jack D.
1967 *The Social Meanings of Suicide.* Princeton: Princeton University Press.
1970 *Deviance and Respectability: The Social Construction of Moral Meanings.* New York: Basic Books

Durkheim, Emile
1933 *The Division of Labor in Society.* George Simpson, trans. Free Press of Glencoe.
1938 *The Rules of Sociological Method.* Sarah A. Solovay and John H. Mueller, trans. George E. G. Catlin, ed. Free Press of Glencoe.

Fink, Arthur E.
1962 *Causes of Crime: Biological Theories in the United States 1800–1915.* New York: A.S. Barnes and Co.

Galliher, John F.
1971 "Training in Social Manipulation as a Rehabilitative Technique," *Crime and Delinquency* 17(October): 431–436.

Galliher, John F. and James L. McCartney
1973 "The Influence of Funding Agencies on Juvenile Delinquency Research," *Social Problems* 21(Summer): 77–90.

Goddard, Henry H.
1914 *Feeble-Mindedness: Its Causes and Consequences.* New York: Macmillan Co.
1921 *Juvenile Delinquency.* New York: Dodd, Mead and Co.

Goode, Erich
1972 *Drugs in American Society.* New York: Alfred A. Knopf.

Gusfield, Joseph R.
1975 "Categories of Ownership and Responsibility in Social Issues: Alcohol Abuse and Automobile Use," *Journal of Drug Issues* 5(Fall): 285–303.

Habermas, Jürgen
1969 *Toward a Rational Society: Student Protest, Science, and Politics.* Jeremy J. Shapiro, trans. Boston: Beacon Press.

Hall, Jerome
  1945   "Criminology," pp. 342–365 in Georges Gurvitch and Wilbert
         E. Moore, eds. *Twentieth Century Sociology*. New York: Philo-
         sophical Library.

Jeffery, Clarence R.
  1956   "Crime, Law, and Social Structure," *Journal of Criminal Law,
         Criminology, and Police Science* 47(November–December):
         423–435.

Kitsuse, John I. and Aaron V. Cicourel
  1963   "A note on the Uses of Official Statistics," *Social Problems*
         11(Fall): 131–139.

Lemert, Edwin M.
  1951   *Social Pathology*. New York: McGraw-Hill Book Co.

Liazos, Alexander
  1972   "The Poverty of the Sociology of Deviance: Nuts, Sluts, and
         Preverts," *Social Problems* 20(Summer): 103–120.

Lofland, John
  1969   *Deviance and Identity*. Englewood Cliffs, N.J.: Prentice-Hall.

Lombroso, Cesare
  1911   *Crime: Its Causes and Remedies*. Henry P. Horton, trans. Boston:
         Little, Brown and Co.

Lombroso-Ferrero, Gina
  1911   *Criminal Man, according to the Classification of Cesare Lombroso*.
         New York: G. P. Putnam's Sons.

Mannheim, Hermann, ed.
  1973   *Pioneers in Criminology*. 2nd ed., enlarged. Montclair, N.J.:
         Patterson Smith.

Marcuse, Herbert
  1964   *One-Dimensional Man*. Boston: Beacon Press.

Matza, David
  1964   *Delinquency and Drift*. New York: John Wiley and Sons.
  1969   *Becoming Deviant*. Englewood Cliffs, N.J.: Prentice-Hall.

McCartney, James L.
  1970   "On Being Scientific: Changing Styles of Presentation of
         Sociological Research." *American Sociologist* 5(February):
         30–35.

Merton, Robert K.
  1938   "Social Structure and Anomie," *American Sociological Review*
         3(October): 672–682.

Monachesi, Elio
   1973   "Cesare Beccaria," in Hermann Mannheim, ed., *Pioneers in Criminology*. 2nd ed., enlarged. Montclair, N.J.: Patterson Smith.

Nader, Ralph
   1965   *Unsafe at Any Speed*. New York: Grossman Publishers.

Olson, Philip
   1964   "Rural American Community Studies: The Survival of Public Ideology," *Human Organization* 23(Winter): 342–350.

Phillipson, Michael
   1974   *Understanding Crime and Delinquency*. Chicago: Aldine Publishing Co.

Quinney, Richard
   1970   *The Social Reality of Crime*. Boston: Little, Brown and Co.
   1973   *Critique of Legal Order: Crime Control in Capitalist Society*. Boston: Little, Brown and Co.

Report on the XYY Chromosomal Abnormality
   1970   National Institute of Mental Health, Center for Studies of Crime and Delinquency. Public Health Service Publication 2103 Washington, D.C.: U.S. Government Printing Office.

Schervish, Paul G.
   1973   "The Labeling Perspective: Its Bias and Potential in the Study of Political Deviance," *American Sociologist* 8(May): 47–57.

Sellin, Thorsten
   1938   *Culture Conflict and Crime*. New York: Social Science Research Council.

Shaw, Clifford R.
   1929   *Delinquency Areas*. Chicago: University of Chicago Press.

Shaw, Clifford R. and Henry D. McKay
   1942   *Juvenile Delinquency and Urban Areas*. Chicago: University of Chicago Press.

Sutherland, Edwin H.
   1939   *Principles of Criminology*. 3rd ed. Philadelphia: J. B. Lippincott Co.

Taft, Donald R.
   1942   *Criminology*. New York: Macmillan Co.

Tannenbaum, Frank
   1938   *Crime and the Community*. Boston: Ginn and Co.

Taylor, Ian, Paul Walton, and Jock Young, eds.
    1975   *Critical Criminology.* London: Routledge and Kegan Paul.
Thio, Alex
    1973   "Class Bias in the Sociology of Deviance," *American Sociologist*
            8(February): 1–12.
Turk, Austin T.
    1969   *Criminality and Legal Order.* Chicago: Rand McNally and Co.
Vold, George B.
    1958   *Theoretical Criminology.* New York: Oxford University Press.

5

The poverty of the sociology of deviance: Nuts, sluts, and preverts* †

Alexander Liazos

C. Wright Mills left a rich legacy to sociology. One of his earliest, and best, contributions was "The Professional Ideology of Social Pathologists" (1943). In it, Mills argues that the small-town, middle-class background of writers of social problems textbooks blinded them to basic problems of social structure and power, and led them to emphasize melioristic, patchwork types of solutions to America's "problems." They assumed as natural and orderly the structure of small-town America; anything else was pathology and disorganization. Moreover, these "problems," "ranging from rape in rural districts to public housing," were not explored systematically and theoretically; they were not placed in some larger political, historical, and social context. They were merely listed and decried.[1]

Since Mills wrote his paper, however, the field of social prob-

* The subtitle of this paper came from two sources. (a) A Yale undergraduate once told me that the deviance course was known among Yale students as "nuts and sluts." (b) A former colleague of mine at Quinnipiac College, John Bancroft, often told me that the deviance course was "all about those preverts." When I came to write this paper, I discovered that these descriptions were correct, and concise summaries of my argument. I thank both of them. I also want to thank Gordon Fellman for a very careful reading of the first draft of the manuscript, and for discussing with me the general and specific issues I raise here.

† Reprinted from *Social Problems*, vol. 20, no. 4 (Summer 1972), pp. 103–120.

[1] Bend and Vogenfanger (1964) examined social problems textbooks of the early 1960s; they found there was little theory or emphasis on social structure in them.

lems, social disorganization, and social pathology has undergone considerable changes. Beginning in the late 1940s and the 1950s, and culminating in the 1960s, the field of "deviance" has largely replaced the social problems orientation. This new field is characterized by a number of features which distinguish it from the older approach.[2]

First, there is some theoretical framework, even though it is often absent in edited collections (the Rubington and Weinberg (1968) edited book is an outstanding exception). Second, the small-town morality is largely gone. Writers claim they will examine the phenomena at hand—prostitution, juvenile delinquency, mental illness, crime, and others—objectively, not considering them as necessarily harmful and immoral. Third, the statements and theories of the field are based on much more extensive, detailed, and theoretically-oriented research than were those of the 1920s and 1930s. Fourth, writers attempt to fit their theories to some central theories, concerns, and problems found in the general field of sociology; they try to transcend mere moralizing.

The "deviant" has been humanized; the moralistic tone is no longer ever-present (although it still lurks underneath the explicit disavowals); and theoretical perspectives have been developed. Nevertheless, all is not well with the field of "deviance." Close examination reveals that writers of this field still do not try to relate the phenomena of "deviance" to larger social, historical, political, and economic contexts. The emphasis is still on the "deviant" and the "problems" *he* presents to himself and others, not on the society within which he emerges and operates.

I examined 16 textbooks in the field of "deviance," eight of them readers, to determine the state of the field. (They are preceded by an asterisk in the bibliography.) Theoretically, eight take the labelling-interactionist approach; three more tend to lean to that approach; four others argue for other orientations (anomie, structural-functional, etc.) or, among the readers, have an "eclectic" approach; and one (McCaghy et al., 1968) is a collection of biographical and other statements by "deviants" themselves, and thus may not be said to have a theoretical approach (although, as we shall see, the selection of the types of statements and "deviants"

---

[2] What I say below applies to the "labelling-interactionist" school of deviance of Becker, Lemert, Erikson, Matza, and others: to a large degree, however, most of my comments also apply to the other schools.

still implies an orientation and viewpoint). A careful examination of these textbooks revealed a number of ideological biases. These biases became apparent as much from what these books leave unsaid and unexamined, as from what they do say. The field of the sociology of deviance, as exemplified in these books, contains three important theoretical and political biases.

1. All writers, especially those of the labelling school, either state explicitly or imply that one of their main concerns is to *humanize* and *normalize* the "deviant," to show that he is essentially no different from us. But by the very emphasis on the "deviant" and his identity problems and subculture, the opposite effect may have been achieved. The persisting use of the label "deviant" to refer to the people we are considering is an indication of the feeling that these people are indeed different.

2. By the overwhelming emphasis on the "dramatic" nature of the usual types of "deviance"—prostitution, homosexuality, juvenile delinquency, and others—we have neglected to examine other, more serious and harmful forms of "deviance." I refer to *covert institutional violence* (defined and discussed below) which leads to such things as poverty and exploitation, the war in Vietnam, unjust tax laws, racism and sexism, and so on, which cause psychic and material suffering for many Americans, black and white, men and women.

3. Despite explicit statements by these authors of the importance of *power* in the designation of what is "deviant," in their substantive analyses they show a profound unconcern with power and its implications. The really powerful, the upper classes and the power elite, those Gouldner (1968) calls the "top dogs," are left essentially unexamined by these sociologists of deviance.

I

Always implicit, and frequently explicit, is the aim of the labelling school to humanize and normalize the "deviant." Two statements by Becker and Matza are representative of this sentiment.

In the course of our work and for who knows what private reasons, we fall into deep sympathy with the people we are studying, so that while the rest of society views them as unfit in one or another respect for the deference ordinarily accorded a fellow citizen, we believe that they are at least as good as anyone else, more sinned against than sinning (Becker, 1967: 100–101).

The growth of the sociological view of deviant phenomena involved, as major phases, the replacement of a correctional stance by an *appreciation* of the deviant subject, the tacit purging of a conception of pathology by a new stress on human *diversity,* and the erosion of a simple distinction between deviant and conventional phenomena, resulting from intimate familiarity of the world as it is, which yielded a more sophisticated view stressing *complexity* (Matza, 1969: 10).

For a number of reasons, however, the opposite effect may have been achieved; and "deviants" still seem different. I began to suspect this reverse effect from the many essays and papers I read while teaching the "deviance" course. The clearest example is the repeated use of the word "tolerate." Students would write that we must not persecute homosexuals, prostitutes, mental patients, and others, that we must be "tolerant" of them. But one tolerates only those one considers less than equal, morally inferior, and weak; those equal to oneself, one accepts and respects; one does not merely allow them to exist, one does not "tolerate" them.

The repeated assertion that "deviants" are "at least as good as anyone else" may raise doubts that this is in fact the case, or that we believe it. A young woman who grew up in the South in the 1940s and 1950s told Quinn (1954: 146): " 'You know, I think from the fact that I was told so often that I must treat colored people with consideration, I got the feeling that I could mistreat them if I wanted to.' " Thus with "deviants"; if in fact they are as good as we are, we would not need to remind everyone of this fact; we would take it for granted and proceed from there. But our assertions that "deviants" are not different may raise the very doubts we want to dispel. Moreover, why would we create a separate field of sociology for "deviants" if there were not something different about them? May it be that even we do not believe our statements and protestations?

The continued use of the word "deviant" (and its variants), despite its invidious distinctions and connotations, also belies our explicit statements on the equality of the people under consideration. To be sure, some of the authors express uneasiness over the term. For example, we are told,

In our use of this term for the purpose of sociological investigation, we emphasize that we do not attach any value judgement, explicitly or implicitly, either to the word "deviance" or to those describing their behavior or beliefs in this book (McCaghy et al., 1968: v).

Lofland (1969: 2, 9–10) expresses even stronger reservations about the use of the term, and sees clearly the sociological, ethical, and political problems raised by its continued use. Yet, the title of his book is *Deviance and Identity.*

Szasz (1970: xxv–xxvi) has urged that we abandon use of the term:

Words have lives of their own. However much sociologists insist that the term "deviant" does not diminish the worth of the person or group so categorized, the implication of inferiority adheres to the word. Indeed, sociologists are not wholly exempt from blame: they describe addicts and homosexuals as deviants, but never Olympic champions or Nobel Prize winners. In fact, the term is rarely applied to people with admired characteristics, such as great wealth, superior skills, or fame—whereas it is often applied to those with despised characteristics, such as poverty, lack of marketable skills, or infamy.

The term "social deviants" . . . does not make sufficiently explicit—as the terms "scapegoat" or "victim" do—that majorities usually categorize persons or groups as "deviant" in order to set them apart as inferior beings and to justify their social control, oppression, persecution, or even complete destruction.

Terms like victimization, persecution, and oppression are more accurate descriptions of what is really happening. But even Gouldner (1968), in a masterful critique of the labelling school, while describing social conflict, calls civil-rights and anti-war protesters "political deviants." He points out clearly that these protesters are resisting openly, not slyly, conditions they abhor. Gouldner is discussing political struggles; oppression and resistance to oppression; conflicts over values, morals, interests, and power; and victimization. Naming such protesters "deviants," even if *political* deviants, is an indication of the deep penetration within our minds of certain prejudices and orientations.

Given the use of the term, the definition and examples of "deviant" reveal underlying sentiments and views. Therefore, it is important that we redefine drastically the entire field, especially since it is a flourishing one: "Because younger sociologists have found deviance such a fertile and exciting field for their own work, and because students share these feelings, deviance promises to become an even more important area of sociological research and theory in the coming years" (Douglas, 1970a: 3).

The lists and discussions of "deviant" acts and persons reveal the writers' biases and sentiments. These are acts which, "like robbery, burglary or rape [are] of a simple and dramatic predatory nature . . ." (The President's Commission on Law Enforcement and the Administration of Justice, in Dinitz et al., 1969: 105). All 16 texts, without exception, concentrate on actions and persons of a "dramatic predatory nature," on "preverts." This is true of both the labelling and other schools. The following are examples from the latter:

Ten different types of deviant behavior are considered: juvenile delinquency, adult crime, prison sub-cultures, homosexuality, prostitution, suicide, homicide, alcoholism, drug addiction and mental illness (Rushing, 1969: preface).

Traditionally, in American sociology the study of deviance has focused on criminals, juvenile delinquents, prostitutes, suicides, the mentally ill, drug users and drug addicts, homosexuals, and political and religious radicals (Lefton et al., 1968: v).

Deviant behavior is essentially violation of certain types of group norms; a deviant act is behavior which is proscribed in a certain way. [It must be] in a disapproved direction, and of sufficient degree to exceed the tolerance limit of the community . . . [such as] delinquency and crime, prostitution, homosexual behavior, drug addiction, alcoholism, mental disorders, suicide, marital and family maladjustment, discrimination against minority groups, and, to a lesser degree, role problems of old age (Clinard, 1968: 28).

Finally, we are told that these are some examples of deviance every society must deal with: ". . . mental illness, violence, theft, and sexual misconduct, as well as . . . other similarly difficult behavior" (Dinitz et al., 1969: 3).

The list stays unchanged with the authors of the labelling school.

. . . in Part I, "The Deviant Act," I draw rather heavily on certain studies of homicide, embezzlement, "naive" check forgery, suicide and a few other acts . . . in discussing the assumption of deviant identity (Part II) and the assumption of normal identity (Part III), there is heavy reference to certain studies of paranoia, "mental illness" more generally, and Alcoholics Anonymous and Synanon (Lofland, 1969: 34).

Homicide, suicide, alcoholism, mental illness, prostitution, and homosexuality are among the forms of behavior typically called deviant, and they are among the kinds of behavior that will be analyzed (Lofland, 1969: 1).

Included among my respondents were political radicals of the far left and the far right, homosexuals, militant blacks, convicts and mental hospital patients, mystics, narcotic addicts, LSD and Marijuana users, illicit drug dealers, delinquent boys, racially mixed couples, hippies, health-food users, and bohemian artists and village eccentrics (Simmons, 1969: 10).

Simmons (1969: 27, 29, 31) also informs us that in his study of stereotypes of "deviants" held by the public, these are the types he gave to people: homosexuals, beatniks, adulterers, marijuana smokers, political radicals, alcoholics, prostitutes, lesbians, ex–mental patients, atheists, ex-convicts, intellectuals, and gamblers. In Lemert (1967) we find that except for the three introductory (theoretical) chapters, the substantive chapters cover the following topics: alcohol drinking, four; check forgers, three; stuttering, two; and mental illness, two. Matza (1969) offers the following list of "deviants" and their actions that "must be appreciated if one adheres to a naturalistic perspective": paupers, robbers, motorcycle gangs, prostitutes, drug addicts, promiscuous homosexuals, thieving Gypsies, and "free love" Bohemians (1969: 16). Finally, Douglas' collection (1970a) covers these forms of "deviance": abortion, nudism, topless barmaids, prostitutes, homosexuals, violence (motorcycle and juvenile gangs), shoplifting, and drugs.

The omissions from these lists are staggering. The covert, institutional forms of "deviance" (part II, below) are nowhere to be found. Reading these authors, one would not know that the most destructive use of violence in the last decade has been the war in Vietnam, in which the U.S. has heaped unprecedented suffering on the people and their land; more bombs have been dropped in Vietnam than in the entire World War II. Moreover, the robbery of the corporate world—through tax breaks, fixed prices, low wages, pollution of the environment, shoddy goods, etc.—is passed over in our fascination with "dramatic and predatory" actions. Therefore, we are told that "while they certainly are of no greater social importance to us than such subjects as banking and accounting [or military violence], subjects such as marijuana use and motorcycle gangs are of far greater interest to most of us. While it is only a coincidence that our scientific interests correspond with the emotional interest in deviants, it is a happy coincidence and, I believe, one that should be encouraged" (Douglas, 1970a: 5). And Matza (1969: 17), in commenting on the "appreciative sentiments" of the "naturalistic spirit," elaborates on the same theme: "We do not for a moment wish that we could rid ourselves of deviant phenomena. We are intrigued by them. They are an intrinsic, ineradicable, and vital part of human society."

An effort is made to transcend this limited view and substantive concern with dramatic and predatory forms of "deviance." Becker (1964: 3) claims that the new (labelling) deviance no longer studies only "delinquents and drug addicts, though these classical kinds of deviance are still kept under observation." It increases its knowledge "of the processes of deviance by studying physicians, people with physical handicaps, the mentally deficient, and others whose doings were formerly not included in the area." The powerful "deviants" are still left untouched, however. This is still true with another aspect of the new deviance. Becker (1964: 4) claims that in the labelling perspective "we focus attention on the other people involved in the process. We pay attention to the role of the non-deviant as well as that of the deviant." But we see that it is the ordinary non-deviants and the low-level agents of social control who receive attention, not the powerful ones (Gouldner, 1968).

In fact, the emphasis is more on the *subculture* and *identity* of the "deviants" themselves rather than on their oppressors and persecutors. To be sure, in varying degrees all authors discuss the agents of social control, but the fascination and emphasis are on the "deviant" himself. Studies of prisons and prisoners, for example, focus on prison subcultures and prisoner rehabilitation; there is little or no consideration of the social, political, economic, and power conditions which consign people to prisons. Only now are we beginning to realize that most prisoners are *political prisoners*— that their "criminal" actions (whether against individuals, such as robbery, or conscious political acts against the state) result largely from current social and political conditions, and are not the work of "disturbed" and "psychopathic" personalities. This realization came about largely because of the writings of political prisoners themselves: Malcolm X (1965), Eldridge Cleaver (1968), and George Jackson (1970), among others.[3]

---

[3] The first draft of this paper was completed in July, 1971. The killing of George Jackson at San Quentin on August 21, 1971, which many people see as a political murder, and the Attica prisoner rebellion of early September, 1971, only strengthen the argument about political prisoners. Two things became clear: (*a*) Not only a few "radicals," but many prisoners (if not a majority) see their fate as the outcome of political forces and decisions, and themselves as political prisoners (see Fraser, 1971). Robert Chrisman's argument (in

In all these books, notably those of the labelling school, the concern is with the "deviant's" subculture and identity: his problems, motives, fellow victims, etc. The collection of memoirs and apologies of "deviants" in their own words (McCaghy et al., 1968) covers the lives and identities of "prevert deviants": prostitutes, nudists, abortionists, criminals, drug users, homosexuals, the mentally ill, alcoholics, and suicides. For good measure, some "militant deviants" are thrown in: Black Muslims, the SDS, and a conscientious objector. But one wonders about other types of "deviants": how do those who perpetrate the covert institutional violence in our society view themselves? Do they have identity problems? How do they justify their actions? How did the robber barons of the late 19th century steal, fix laws, and buy politicians six days of the week and go to church on Sunday? By what process can people speak of body counts and kill ratios with cool objectivity? On these and similar questions, this book (and all others)[4] provides no answers; indeed, the editors seem unaware that such questions should or could be raised.

Becker (1964), Rubington and Weinberg (1968), Matza (1969), and Bell (1971) also focus on the identity and subculture of "prevert deviants." Matza, in discussing the assumption of "deviant identity," uses as examples, and elaborates upon, thieves and marijuana users. In all these books, there are occasional references to and questions about the larger social and political structure, but these are not explored in any depth; and the emphasis remains on the behavior, identity, and rehabilitation of the "deviant" himself. This bias continues in the latest book which, following the fashions of the times, has chapters on hippies and militant protesters (Bell, 1971).

Fraser, 1971) points to such a conclusion clearly: "To maintain that all black offenders are, by their actions, politically correct, is dangerous romanticism. Black antisocial behavior must be seen in and of its own terms and corrected for enhancement of the black community." But there is a political aspect, for black prisoners' condition "derives from the political inequity of black people in America. A black prisoner's crime may or may not have been a political action against the state, but the state's action against him is always political." I would stress that the same is true of most white prisoners, for they come mostly from the exploited poorer classes and groups. (*b*) The state authorities, the political rulers, by their deeds if not their words, see such prisoners as political men and threats. The death of George Jackson, and the brutal crushing of the Attica rebellion, attest to the authorities' realization, and fear, that here were no mere riots with prisoners letting off steam, but authentic political actions, involving groups and individuals conscious of their social position and exploitation.

[4] With the exception of E. C. Hughes, in Becker (1964).

Even the best of these books, Simmons' *Deviants* (1969), is not free of the overwhelming concentration of the "deviant" and his identity. It is the most sympathetic and balanced presentation of the lives of "deviants": their joys, sorrows, and problems with the straight world and fellow victims. Simmons demystifies the processes of becoming "deviant" and overcoming "deviance." He shows, as well as anyone does, that these victims *are* just like us; and the differences they possess and the suffering they endure are imposed upon them. Ultimately, however, Simmons too falls prey to the three biases shown in the work of others: (*a*) the "deviants" he considers are only of the "prevert" type; (*b*) he focuses mostly on the victim and his identity, not on the persecutors; and (*c*) the persecutors he does discuss are of the middle-level variety, the agents of more powerful others and institutions.

Because of these biases, there is an implicit, but very clear, acceptance by these authors of the current definitions of "deviance." It comes about because they concentrate their attention on those who have been *successfully labelled as "deviant,"* and not on those who break laws, fix laws, violate ethical and moral standards, harm individuals and groups, etc., but who either are able to hide their actions, or, when known, can deflect criticism, labelling, and punishment. The following are typical statements which reveal this bias.

". . . no act committed by members of occupational groups [such as white-collar crimes], however unethical, should be considered as crime unless it is punishable by the state in some way" (Clinard, 1968: 269). Thus, if some people can manipulate laws so that their unethical and destructive acts are not "crimes," we should cater to their power and agree that they are not criminals.

Furthermore, the essence of the labelling school encourages this bias, despite Becker's (1963: 14) assertion that ". . . insofar as a scientist uses 'deviant' to refer to any rule-breaking behavior and takes as his subjects of study only those who have been *labelled* deviant, he will be hampered by the disparities between the two categories." But as the following statements from Becker and others show, this is in fact what the labelling school does do.

Deviance is "created by society. . . . *social groups create deviance by making the rules whose infraction constitutes deviance,* and by applying those rules to particular people and labelling them as outsiders" (Becker, 1963: 8–9). Clearly, according to this view, in cases where no group has labelled another, no matter what the other group or individuals have done, there is nothing for the sociologist to study and dissect.

Rules are not made automatically. Even though a practice may be harmful in an objective sense to the group in which it occurs, the harm needs to be discovered and pointed out. People must be made to feel that something ought to be done about it (Becker, 1963: 162).

What is important for the social analyst is not what people are by his lights or by his standards, but what it is that people construe one another and themselves to be for what reasons and with what consequences (Lofland, 1969: 35).

. . . deviance is in the eyes of the beholder. For deviance to become a social fact, somebody must perceive an act, person, situation, or event as a departure from social norms, must categorize that perception, must report the perception to others, must get them to accept this definition of the situation, and must obtain a response that conforms to this definition. Unless all these requirements are met, deviance as a social fact does not come into being (Rubington and Weinberg, 1968: v).

The implication of these statements is that the sociologist accepts current, successful definitions of what is "deviant" as the only ones worthy of his attention. To be sure, he may argue that those labelled "deviant" are not really different from the rest of us, or that there is no act intrinsically "deviant," etc. By concentrating on cases of successful labelling, however, he will not penetrate beneath the surface to look for other forms of "deviance"— undetected stealing, violence, and destruction. When people are not powerful enough to make the "deviant" label stick on others, we overlook these cases. But is it not as much a *social fact,* even though few of us pay much attention to it, that the corporate economy kills and maims more, is more violent, than any violence committed by the poor (the usual subjects of studies of violence)? By what reasoning and necessity is the "violence" of the poor in the ghettoes more worthy of our attention than the military boot-camps which numb recruits from the horrors of killing the "enemy" ("Oriental human beings," as we learned during the Calley trial)? But because these acts are not labelled "deviant," because they are covert, institutional, and normal, their "deviant" qualities are overlooked and they do not become part of the province of the sociology of deviance. Despite their best liberal intentions, these sociologists seem to perpetuate the very notions they think they debunk, and others of which they are unaware.

II

As a result of the fascination with "nuts, sluts, and preverts," and their identities and subcultures, little attention has been paid to the unethical, illegal, and destructive actions of powerful individuals, groups, and institutions in our society. Because these actions are carried out quietly in the normal course of events, the sociology of deviance does not consider them as part of its subject matter. This bias is rooted in the very conception and definition of the field. It is obvious when one examines the treatment, or, just as often, lack of it, of the issues of violence, crime, and white-collar crime.

Discussions of violence treat only one type: the "dramatic and predatory" violence committed by individuals (usually the poor and minorities) against persons and property. For example, we read, "crimes involving violence, such as criminal homicide, assault, and forcible rape, are concentrated in the slums" (Clinard, 1968: 123). Wolfgang, an expert on violence, has developed a whole theory on the "subculture of violence" found among the lower classes (e.g., in Rushing, 1969: 233–40). And Douglas (1970a: part 4, on violence) includes readings on street gangs and the Hell's Angels. Thompson (1966), in his book on the Hell's Angels, devotes many pages to an exploration of the Angels' social background. In addition, throughout the book, and especially in his concluding chapter, he places the Angels' violence in the perspective of a violent, raping, and destructive society, which refuses to confront the reality of the Angels by distorting, exaggerating, and romanticizing their actions. But Douglas reprints none of these pages; rather, he offers us the chapter where, during a July 4 weekend, the Angels were restricted by the police within a lakeside area, had a drunken weekend, and became a tourist sideshow and circus.

In short, violence is presented as the exclusive property of the poor in the slums, the minorities, street gangs, and motorcycle beasts. But if we take the concept *violence* seriously, we see that much of our political and economic system thrives on it. In violence, a person is *violated*—there is harm done to his person, his psyche, his body, his dignity, his ability to govern himself (Garver, in Rose, 1969: 6). Seen in this way, a person can be violated in many ways; physical force is only one of them. As the readings in Rose (1969) show, a person can be violated by a system that denies him a decent job, or consigns him to a slum, or causes him brain damage by near-starvation during childhood, or manipulates him through the mass media, and so on endlessly.

Moreover, we must see that *covert institutional violence* is much more destructive than overt individual violence. We must recognize that people's lives are violated by the very normal and everyday workings of institutions. We do not see such events and situations as violent because they are not dramatic and predatory; they do not make for fascinating reading on the lives of preverts; but they kill, maim, and destroy many more lives than do violent individuals.

Here are some examples. Carmichael and Hamilton (1967: 4), in distinguishing between *individual* and *institutional* racism, offer examples of each:

When white terrorists bomb a black church and kill five black children, that is an act of individual racism, widely deplored by most segments of the society. But when in that same city—Birmingham, Alabama—five hundred black babies die each year because of lack of proper food, shelter, and medical facilities, and thousands more are destroyed and maimed physically, emotionally, and intellectually because of conditions of poverty and discrimination in the black community, that is a function of institutional racism.

Surely this is violence; it is caused by the normal, quiet workings of institutions run by respectable members of the community. Many whites also suffer from the institutional workings of a profit-oriented society and economy; poor health, dead-end jobs, slum housing, hunger in rural areas, and so on, are daily realities in their lives. This is surely much worse violence than any committed by the Hell's Angels or street gangs. Only these groups get stigmatized and analyzed by sociologists of deviance, however, while those good people who live in luxurious homes (fixing tax laws for their benefit) off profits derived from an exploitative economic system—they are the pillars of their community.

Violence is committed daily by the government, very often by lack of action. The same system that enriches businessmen farmers with billions of dollars through farm subsidies cannot be bothered to appropriate a few millions to deal with lead poisoning in the slums. Young children

. . . get it by eating the sweet-tasting chips of peeling tenement walls, painted a generation ago with leaded paint.

According to the Department of Health, Education, and Welfare, 400,000 children are poisoned each year, about 30,000 in New York City alone. About 3,200 suffer permanent brain damage, 800 go blind or become so mentally retarded that they require hospitalization for the rest of their lives, and approximately 200 die.

The tragedy is that lead poisoning is totally man-made and totally preventable. It is caused by slum housing. And there are now blood tests that can detect the disease, and medicines to cure it. Only a lack of purpose sentences 200 black children to die each year (Newfield, 1971).[5]

Newfield goes on to report that on May 20, 1971, a Senate-House conference eliminated $5 million from an appropriations budget. In fact, 200 children had been sentenced to death and thousands more to maiming and suffering.

Similar actions of violence are committed daily by the government and corporations; but in these days of misplaced emphasis, ignorance, and manipulation we do not see the destruction inherent in these actions. Instead, we get fascinated, angry, and misled by the violence of the poor and the powerless. We see the violence committed during political rebellions in the ghettoes (called "riots" in order to dismiss them), but all along we ignored the daily violence committed against the ghetto residents by the institutions of the society: schools, hospitals, corporations, the government. Check any of these books on deviance, and see how much of this type of violence is even mentioned, much less explored and described.

It may be argued that some of this violence is (implicitly) recognized in discussions of "white-collar" crime. This is not the case, however. Of the 16 books under consideration, only three pay some attention to white-collar crime (Cohen, 1966; Clinard, 1968; Dinitz et al., 1969); and of these, only the last covers the issue at some length. Even in these few discussions, however, the focus remains on the *individuals* who commit the actions (on their greediness, lack of morality, etc.), not on the economic and political institutions within which they operate. The selection in Dinitz et al.

---

[5] As Gittlin and Hollander (1970) show, the children of poor whites also suffer from lead poisoning.

(1969: 99–109), from the President's Commission on Law Enforcement and the Administration of Justice, at least three times (pp. 101, 103, 108) argues that white-collar crime is "pervasive," causes "financial burdens" ("probably far greater than those produced by traditional common law theft offenses"), and is generally harmful. At least in these pages, however, there is no investigation of the social, political, and economic conditions which make the pervasiveness, and lenient treatment, of white-collar crime possible.

The bias against examining the structural conditions behind white-collar crime is further revealed in Clinard's suggestions on how to deal with it (in his chapter on "The Prevention of Deviant Behavior"). The only recommendation in three pages of discussion (704–7) is to teach everyone more "respect" for the law. This is a purely moralistic device; it pays no attention to the structural aspects of the problem, to the fact that even deeper than white-collar crime is ingrained a whole network of laws, especially tax laws, administrative policies, and institutions which systematically favor a small minority. More generally, discussions on the prevention of "deviance" and crime do not deal with institutional violence, and what we need to do to stop it.[6]

But there is an obvious explanation for this oversight. The people commiting serious white-collar crimes and executing the policies of violent institutions are respectable and responsible individuals, not "deviants"; this is the view of the President's Commission on Law Enforcement and the Administration of Justice.

Significantly, the Antitrust Division does not feel that lengthy prison sentences are ordinarily called for [for white-collar crimes]. It "rarely recommends jail sentences greater than 6 months—recommendations of 30-day imprisonment are most frequent." (Dinitz et al., 1969: 105.)

Persons who have standing and roots in a community, and are prepared for and engaged in legitimate occupations, can be expected to be particularly susceptible to the threat of criminal prosecution. Criminal

---

[6] Investigation of the causes and prevention of institutional violence would probably be biting the hand that feeds the sociologist, for we read that the government and foundations (whose money comes from corporate profits) have supported research on "deviant behavior," especially its prevention. "This has meant particularly that the application of sociological theory to research has increased markedly in such areas as delinquency, crime, mental disorder, alcoholism, drug addiction, and discrimination" (Clinard, 1968: 742). That's where the action is, not on white-collar crime, nor on the covert institutional violence of the government and economy.

proceedings and the imposition of sanctions have a much sharper impact upon those who have not been hardened by previous contact with the criminal justice system (in Dinitz et al., 1969: 104).

At the same time, we are told elsewhere by the Commission that white-collar crime is pervasive and widespread; "criminal proceedings and the imposition of sanctions" do not appear to deter it much.

The executives convicted in the Electrical Equipment case were respectable citizens. "Several were deacons or vestrymen of their churches." The rest also held prestigious positions: president of the Chamber of Commerce, bank director, little-league organizer, and so on (Dinitz et al., 1969: 107). Moreover, "generally . . . in cases of white-collar crime, neither the corporations as entities nor their responsible officers are invested with deviant characters . . ." (Cohen, 1966: 30). Once more, there is quiet acquiescence to this state of affairs. There is no attempt to find out why those who steal millions and whose actions violate lives are not "invested with deviant characters." There is no consideration given to the possibility that, as responsible intellectuals, it is our duty to explore and expose the structural causes for corporate and other serious crimes, which make for much more suffering than does armed robbery. We seem satisfied merely to observe what is, and leave the causes unexamined.

In conclusion, let us look at another form of institutional "deviance." The partial publication of the Pentagon papers (June 1971) made public the conscious lying and manipulation by the government to quiet opposition to the Vietnam war. But lying pervades both government and economy. Deceptions and outright lies abound in advertising (see Henry, 1963). During the 1968 campaign, Presidential candidate Nixon blessed us with an ingenious form of deception. McGinniss (1969: 149–50)[7] is recording a discussion that took place before Nixon was to appear on live TV (to show spontaneity) the day before the election and answer, unrehearsed, questions phoned in by the viewing audience.

"I understand Paul Keyes has been sitting up for two days writing questions," Roger Ailes said.

"Well, not quite," Jack Rourke said. He seemed a little embarrassed.

"What is going to happen?"

"Oh . . ."

---

[7] *The Selling of the President 1968,* copyright © 1969 by Joemac, Inc. Reprinted by permission of Simon & Shuster, Inc.

"It's sort of semiforgery, isn't it?" Ailes said. "Keyes has a bunch of questions Nixon wants to answer. He's written them in advance to make sure they're properly worded. When someone calls in with something similar, they'll use Keyes' question and attribute it to the person who called. Isn't that it?"

"More or less," Jack Rourke said.

In short, despite the supposedly central position of *social structure* in the sociological enterprise, there is general neglect of it in the field of "deviance." Larger questions, especially if they deal with political and economic issues, are either passed over briefly or overlooked completely. The focus on the actions of "nuts, sluts, and preverts" and the related slight of the criminal and destructive actions of the powerful, are instances of this avoidance.

III

Most of the authors under discussion mention the importance of *power* in labelling people "deviant." They state that those who label (the victimizers) are more powerful than those they label (the victims). Writers of the labelling school make this point explicitly. According to Becker (1963: 17), "who can . . . force others to accept their rules and what are the causes of their success? This is, of course, a question of political and economic power." Simmons (1969: 131) comments that historically, "those in power have used their positions largely to perpetuate and enhance their own advantages through coercing and manipulating the rest of the populace." And Lofland (1969: 19) makes the same observation in his opening pages:

It is in the situation of a very powerful party opposing a very weak one that the powerful party sponsors the *idea* that the weak party is breaking the rules of society. The very concepts of "society" and its "rules" are appropriated by powerful parties and made synonymous with their interests (and, of course, believed in by the naive, e.g., the undergraduate penchant for the phrases "society says . . . ," "society expects . . . ," "society does . . ."').

But this insight is not developed. In none of the 16 books is there an extensive discussion of how power operates in the designation of deviance. Instead of a study of power, of its concrete uses in modern, corporate America, we are offered rather fascinating explorations into the identities and subcultures of "deviants," and misplaced emphasis on the middle-level agents of social control.

Only Szasz (1961, 1963, and notably 1970) has shown consistently the role of power in one area of "deviance," "mental illness." Through historical and contemporary studies, he has shown that those labelled "mentally ill" (crazy, insane, mad, lunatic) and institutionalized have always been the powerless: women, the poor, peasants, the aged, and others. Moreover, he has exposed repeatedly the means used by powerful individuals and institutions in employing the "mental illness" label to discredit, persecute, and eliminate opponents. In short, he has shown the political element in the "mental illness" game.

In addition, except for Szasz, none of the authors seems to realize that the stigma of prostitution, abortion, and other "deviant" acts unique to women comes about in large part from the powerlessness of women and their status in society. Moreover, to my knowledge, no one has bothered to ask why there have always been women prostitutes for men to satisfy their sexual desires, but very few men prostitutes for women to patronize. The very word "prostitute" we associate with women only, not men. Both men and women have been involved in this "immoral" act, but the stigma has been carried by the women alone.

All 16 books, some more extensively than others, discuss the ideology, modes of operation, and views of *agents of social control,* the people who designate what is to be "deviant" and those who handle the people so designated. As Gouldner (1968) has shown, however, these are the lower and middle level officials, not those who make basic policy and decisions. This bias becomes obvious when we look at the specific agents discussed.

For example, Simmons (1969: 18) tells us that some of "those in charge at every level" are the following: "university administrators, patrolmen, schoolmasters, and similar public employees. . . ." Do university administrators and teachers run the schools alone? Are they teaching and enforcing their own unique values? Do teachers alone create the horrible schools in the slums? Are the uniformity, punctuality, and conformity teachers inculcate their own psychological hang-ups, or do they represent the interests of an industrial-technological-corporate order? In another sphere, do the police enforce their own laws?

Becker (1963: 14) has shown consistent interest in agents of social control. However, a close examination reveals limitations. He discusses "moral crusaders" like those who passed the laws against marijuana. The moral crusader, "the prototype of the rule creator," finds that "the existing rules do not satisfy him because there is some evil which profoundly disturbs him." But the only type of rule creator Becker discusses is the moral crusader, no other. The political manipulators who pass laws to defend their interests and persecute dissenters are not studied. The "unconventional sentimentality," the debunking motif Becker (1964: 4–5) sees in the "new deviance" is directed toward the police, the prison officials, the mental hospital personnel, the "average" person and his prejudices. The basic social, political, and economic structure, and those commanding it who guide the labelling and persecution, are left untouched. We have become so accustomed to debunking these low-level agents that we do not even know how to begin to direct our attention to the ruling institutions and groups (for an attempt at such an analysis, see Liazos, 1970).

In a later paper, Becker (1967) poses an apparently insoluble dilemma. He argues that, in studying agents of social control, we are always forced to study subordinates. We can never really get to the top, to those who "really" run the show, for if we study X's superior Y, we find Z above him, and so on endlessly. Everyone has somebody over him, so there is no one at the top. But this is a clever point without substance. In this hierarchy some have more power than others and some are at the top; they may disclaim their position, of course, but it is our job to show otherwise. Some people in this society do have more power than others: parents over children, men over women; some have considerable power over others: top administrators of institutions, for one; and some have a great deal of power, those Domhoff (1967) and others have shown to be the ruling class. It should be our task to explore and describe this hierarchy, its bases of strength, its uses of the "deviant" label to discredit its opponents in order to silence them, and to find ways to eliminate this hierarchy.

Discussions of the police reveal the same misplaced emphasis on lower and middle level agents of social control. In three of the books (Matza, 1969: 182–95; Rubington and Weinberg, 1968: ch. 7; Dinitz et al., 1969: 40–47), we are presented with the biases and prejudices of policemen; their modes of operation in confronting delinquents and others; the pressures on them from various quarters; etc. In short, the focus is on the role and psychology of the policeman.

All these issues about the policeman's situation need to be discussed, of course; but there is an even more important issue which these authors avoid. We must ask, who passes the laws the police enforce? Whose agents are they? Why do the police exist? Three excellent papers (Cook, 1968; A. Silver, in Bordua, 1967; T. Hayden, in Rose, 1969) offer some answers to these questions. They show, through a historical description of the origins of police forces, that they have always been used to defend the status quo, the interests of the ruling powers. When the police force was created in England in the early 1800s, it was meant to defend the propertied classes from the "dangerous classes" and the "mob."[8] With the rise of capitalism and industrialism, there was much unrest from the suffering underclass; the professional police were meant to act as a buffer zone for the capitalist elite. Similarly, in America during the early part of this century, especially in the 1930s, police were used repeatedly to attack striking workers and break their strikes. During the Chicago "police riot" of 1968, the police were not merely acting out their aggressions and frustrations; as Hayden shows, they acted with the consent, direction, and blessing of Mayor Daley and the Democratic party (which party represents the "liberal" wing of the American upper class).

It must be stressed that the police, like all agents of social control, are doing someone else's work. Sometimes they enforce laws and prejudices of "society," the much maligned middle class (on sex, marijuana, etc.); but at other times it is not "society" which gives them their directives, but specific interested groups, even though, often, "society" is manipulated to express its approval of such actions. Above all, we must remember that *"in a fundamentally unjust society, even the most impartial, professional, efficient enforcement of the laws by the police cannot result in justice"* (Cook, 1968: 2). More generally, in an unjust and exploitative society, no matter how "humane" agents of social control are, their actions necessarily result in repression.

Broad generalization is another device used by some of these authors to avoid concrete examination of the uses of power in the creation and labelling of "deviance." Clairborne (1971) has called such generalization *"schlock."* The following are some of the tactics

---

[8] See Rude (1966) on the role of mobs of poor workers and peasants in 18th and 19th century England and France.

he thinks are commonly used in writing popular *schlock* sociology (some sociologists of deviance use similar tactics, as we shall see).

The Plausible Passive:
"New scientific discoveries are being made every day. . . . These new ideas are being put to work more quickly. . . ." [Toffler, in *Future Shock*, is] thereby rather neatly obscuring the fact that scientists and engineers (mostly paid by industry) are making the discoveries and industrialists (often with the aid of public funds) are putting them to work. An alternative to the Plausible Passive is the Elusive Impersonal: "Buildings in New York literally disappear overnight." What Toffler is trying to avoid saying is that contractors and real estate speculators *destroy* buildings overnight (Clairborne, 1971: 118).

Rampant Reification, by which "conceptual abstractions are transformed into causal realities," also abounds. Toffler

speaks of the "roaring current of change" as "an elemental force" and of "that great, growling engine of change—technology." Which of course completely begs the question of what fuels the engine and whose hand is on the throttle. One does not cross-examine an elemental force, let alone suggest that it may have been engendered by monopoly profits (especially in defense and aerospace) or accelerated by government incentives (e.g., open or concealed subsidies, low capital gains tax, accelerated depreciation—which Nixon is now seeking to reinstitute) (Clairborne, 1971: 118).

There are parallels in the sociology of deviance. Clinard (1968: ch. 4) argues that urbanization and the slum are breeding grounds for "deviant behavior." But these conditions are reified, not examined concretely. He says about urbanization and social change:

Rapid social and cultural change, disregard for the importance of stability of generations, and untempered loyalties also generally characterize urban life. New ideas are generally welcome, inventions and mechanical gadgets are encouraged, and new styles in such arts as painting, literature, and music are often approved (1968: 90).

But the slum, urbanization, and change are not reified entities working out their independent wills. For example, competition, capitalism, and the profit motive—all encouraged by a government controlled by the upper classes—have had something to do with the rise of slums. There is a general process of urbanization, but at given points in history it is fed by, and gives profits to, specific groups. The following are a few historical examples: the land enclosure policies and practices of the English ruling classes in the 17th and 18th centuries; the building of cheap housing in the 19th century by the owners of factory towns; and the profits derived from "urban renewal" (which has destroyed neighborhoods, created even more crowded slums, etc.) by the building of highways, luxury apartments, and stores.

Another favorite theme of *schlock* sociology is that "All Men Are Guilty." That means nothing can be done to change things. There is a variation of this theme in the sociology of deviance when we are told that (*a*) all of us are deviant in some way, (*b*) all of us label some others deviant, and (*c*) "society" labels. Such statements preclude asking concrete questions: does the "deviance" of each of us have equal consequences for others? Does the labeling of each of us stick, and with what results?

For example, Simmons (1969: 124) says:

. . . I strongly suspect that officials now further alienate more culprits than they recruit back into conventional society, and I think they imprison at least as many people in deviance as they rehabilitate. We must remember that, with a sprinkling of exceptions, officials come from, are hired by, and belong to the dominant majority.

Who is that dominant majority? Are they always the numerical majority? Do they control the labelling and correctional process all by themselves? These questions are not raised.

Another case of *schlock* is found in Matza's discussion (lack of it, really) of "Leviathan" (1969, especially ch. 7). It is mentioned as a potent force in the labelling and handling of "deviance." But, vainly, one keeps looking for some exploration into the workings of "Leviathan." It remains a reified, aloof creature. What is it? Who controls it? How does it label? Why? Matza seems content to try to mesmerize us by mentioning it constantly (Leviathan is capitalized throughout); but we are never shown how it operates. It hovers in the background, it punishes, and its presence somehow cowers us into submission. But it remains a reified force whose presence is accepted without close examination.

The preceding examples typify much of what is wrong with the sociology of deviance: the lack of specific analysis of the role of power in the labelling process; the generalizations which, even when true, explain little; the fascination with "deviants"; the reluctance to study the "deviance" of the powerful.

IV

I want to start my concluding comments with two disclaimers.

(*a*) I have tried to provide some balance and perspective in the field of "deviance," and in doing so I have argued against the exclusive emphasis on *nuts, sluts,* and *preverts* and their identities and subcultures. I do not mean, however, that the usually considered forms of "deviance" are unworthy of our attention. Suicide, prostitution, madness, juvenile delinquency, and others *are* with us; we cannot ignore them. People do suffer when labelled and treated as "deviant" (in *this* sense, "deviants" *are* different from conformists). Rather, I want to draw attention to phenomena which also belong to the field of "deviance."[9]

(*b*) It is because the sociology of deviance, especially the labelling approach, contains important, exciting, and revealing insights, because it tries to humanize the "deviant," and because it is popular, that it is easy to overlook some of the basic ideological biases still pervading the field. For this reason, I have tried to explore and detail some of these biases. At the same time, however, I do not mean to dismiss the contributions of the field as totally negative and useless. In fact, in my teaching I have been using two of the books discussed here, Simmons (1969) and Rubington and Weinberg (1968).

The argument can be summarized briefly. (1) We should not study only, or predominantly, the popular and dramatic forms of "deviance." Indeed, we should banish the concept of "deviance" and speak of oppression, conflict, persecution, and suffering. By focusing on the dramatic forms, as we do now, we perpetuate most people's beliefs and impressions that such "deviance" is the basic cause of many of our troubles, that these people (criminals, drug addicts, political dissenters, and others) are the real "troublemakers"; and, necessarily, we neglect conditions of inequality, powerlessness, institutional violence, and so on, which lie at the bases of our tortured society. (2) Even when we do study the popular forms of "deviance," we do not avoid blaming the victim for his fate; the continued use of the term "deviant" is one clue to this blame. Nor

---

[9] The question of "what deviance is to the deviant" (Gordon Fellman, private communication), not what the labelling, anomie, and other schools, or the present radical viewpoint say *about* such a person, is not dealt with here. I avoid this issue not because I think it unimportant, rather because I want to concentrate on the political, moral, and social issues raised by the biases of those presently writing about the "deviant."

have we succeeded in normalizing him; the focus on the "deviant" himself, on his identity and subculture, has tended to confirm the popular prejudice that he is different.

REFERENCES

Becker, Howard S.
*1963   *Outsiders.* New York: Free Press
*1964   (ed.) *The Other Side.* New York: Free Press.
1967   "Whose side are we on?" *Social Problems* 14: 239–247 (reprinted in Douglas, 1970a, 99–111; references to this reprint).

Bell, Robert R.
*1971   *Social Deviance: A Substantive Analysis.* Homewood, Ill.: Dorsey.

Bend, Emil and Martin Vogenfanger
1964   "A new look at Mills' critique," in *Mass Society in Crisis.* Bernard Rosenberg, Israel Gerver, F. William Howton (eds.). New York: Macmillan, 1964, 111–122.

Bordua, David (ed.)
1967   *The Police.* New York: Wiley.

Carmichael, Stokeley and Charles V. Hamilton
1967   *Black Power.* New York: Random House.

Clairborne, Robert
1971   "Future schlock." *The Nation,* Jan. 25, 117–120.

Cleaver, Eldridge
1968   *Soul on Ice.* New York: McGraw-Hill.

Clinard, Marshall B.
*1968   *Sociology of Deviant Behavior,* (3rd ed.) New York: Holt, Rinehart, and Winston.

Cohen, Albert K.
* 1966   *Deviance and Control.* Englewood Cliffs, N.J.: Prentice-Hall.

Cook, Robert M.
1968   "The police." *The Bulletin of the American Independent Movement* (New Haven, Conn.), 3: 6, 1–6.

Dinitz, Simon, Russell R. Dynes, and Alfred C. Clarke (eds.)
*1969   *Deviance.* New York: Oxford University Press.

Domhoff, William G.
1967   *Who Rules America?* Englewood Cliffs, N.J.: Prentice-Hall.

Douglas, Jack D.
*1970a   (ed.) *Observations of Deviance.* New York: Random House.

*1970b   (ed.) *Deviance and Respectability: The Social Construction of Moral Meanings.* New York: Basic Books.

Fraser, C. Gerald
1971   "Black prisoners finding new view of themselves as political prisoners." *New York Times,* Sept. 16.

Gittlin, Todd and Nanci Hollander
1970   *Uptown: Poor Whites in Chicago.* New York: Harper and Row.

Gouldner, Alvin W.
1968   "The sociologist as partisan: Sociology and the welfare state." *American Sociologist* 3: 2, 103–116.

Henry, Jules
1963   *Culture against Man.* New York: Random House.

Jackson, George
1970   *Soledad Brother.* New York: Bantam Books.

Lefton, Mark, J. K. Skipper, and C. H. McCaghy (eds.)
*1968   *Approaches to Deviance.* Englewood Cliffs, N.J.: Prentice-Hall.

Lemert, Edwin M.
*1967   *Human Deviance, Social Problems, and Social Control.* Englewood Cliffs, N.J.: Prentice-Hall.

Liazos, Alexander
1970   "Processing for unfitness: Socialization of 'emotionally disturbed' lower-class boys into the mass society." Ph.D. dissertation, Brandeis University.

Lofland, John
*1969   *Deviance and Identity.* Englewood Cliffs, N.J.: Prentice-Hall.

McCaghy, Charles H., J. K. Skipper, and M. Lefton (eds.)
*1968   *In Their Own Behalf: Voices from the Margin* © 1968, p.v. Reprinted by permission of Prentice-Hall, Inc., Englewood Cliffs, New Jersey.

McGinniss, Joe
1969   *The Selling of the President, 1968.* New York: Simon & Shuster, Inc.

Malcolm X
1965   *The Autobiography of Malcolm X.* New York: Grove.

Matza, David
*1969   *Becoming Deviant.* Englewood Cliffs, N.J.: Prentice-Hall.

Mills, C. Wright
1943   "The professional ideology of social pathologists." *American Journal of Sociology* 49: 165–180.

Newfield, Jack
  1971   "Let them eat lead." *New York Times,* June 16, p. 45.

Quinn, Olive W.
  1954   "The transmission of racial attitudes among white souther-
          ners." *Social Forces* 33: 1, 41–47 (reprinted in E. Schuler et al.,
          eds., *Readings in Sociology,* 2nd ed., New York: Crowell, 1960,
          140–150).

Rose, Thomas (ed.)
  1969   *Violence in America.* New York: Random House.

Rubington, Earl and M. S. Weinberg (eds.)
  *1968   *Deviance: The Interactionist Perspective.* New York: Macmillan.

Rude, George
  1966   *The Crowd in History.* New York: Wiley.

Rushing, William A. (ed.)
  *1969   *Deviant Behavior and Social Processes.* Chicago: Rand McNally.

Simmons, J. L.
  *1969   *Deviants.* Berkeley, Cal.: Glendessary.

Szasz, Thomas S.
  1961   *The Myth of Mental Illness.* New York: Harper and Row.
  1963   *Law, Liberty, and Psychiatry.* New York: Macmillan.
  1970   *The Manufacture of Madness.* New York: Harper and Row.

Thompson, Hunter S.
  1966   *Hell's Angels.* New York: Ballantine.

6

Criminal behavior as theoretical praxis*

Neal Shover

INTRODUCTION

The "success" and stability of the criminal justice system, at every step, are dependent upon the active cooperation of its clientele: those who are oppressed by it. The police must cultivate and maintain "contacts" with working offenders—many of whom continue their criminal work while assisting the police; the criminal courts must be able to assume in advance—and experience shows they can safely do so—that 90 percent of their defendants will cooperate in their own prosecution by "copping" pleas; and prisons apparently owe their stability in part to the existence of a conservative inmate élite and a fractionated inmate population. It is in this sense, then, that one can say that the stability of the criminal justice system, and the very livelihood of those who are employed in it, require the support of the oppressed.

The support of the oppressed is lent in less tangible ways as well, for in addition to what has already been pointed out, the clients of the system sometimes come to be living testimonials of the ideological supports of the system itself. They often employ the same "theories" currently popular among the system's employees to interpret and "explain" their own criminality. Thus they lend support to the system in the ideological realm as well. The objective in this paper is to suggest how this process occurs.

*Issues In Criminology, vol. 10, no. 1 (Spring, 1975), pp. 95–108.

THEORIES OF CRIMINALITY AND DEVIANCE

Those who produce or promote ideas intended to make sense of the phenomenon of criminal and deviant behavior are generally ignorant of the various ways in which their ideas are shaped by social contexts. They are even more often ignorant of the fact that, once produced, their "theories" do not remain neutral forces in the social world. Instead, these entrepreneurs—usually criminologists of the positivist persuasion—promote their ideas in the theory marketplace as "objective" reflections or explanations of criminal behavior. (For this reason, their theories can be viewed as *ideologies*, and they will be alternatively designated as such at various places in this paper.) Further, criminological theorists typically ignore the fact that in time their theories can influence the objectively- and subjectively-perceived parameters of the very "problems" they are said, originally, to explain. Again, it is the purpose of this paper to suggest some of the reasons why this may be so.

A few preliminary observations are in order concerning a point on which sociologists should require little reminding: the ideologies which persons produce to make sense of crime and deviance are, at the least, culturally and historically relative. Abundant evidence exists to document this claim (cf. Draguns and Phillips, 1972). Taylor and Taylor (1972) have examined changes in the motives ascribed to criminals and deviants during three different periods in the past two centuries. They argue that these changing interpretations of deviant behavior are consistent with "the central features of the culture of the society during each of these three periods" (Ibid.: 80). A little more than a century ago the problem of crime in England, as Tobias (1967) and Silver (1967) have pointed out, was seen almost exclusively as a problem with the so-called dangerous class. Such explanations have, however, fallen into disrepute in our more enlightened contemporary times—though, to be sure, we do have "delinquent subcultures." Further, Erikson (1966) has pointed out that there were sharp contrasts in the American colonies between the images of deviance held by Quakers and the Puritans, differences which were reflected in their respective approaches to the matter of how best to treat those who had transgressed. More recently, Scott (1969) has drawn attention to the considerable differences which exist in Europe and the United States in prevailing ideas about blindness and the appropriate treatments for it. And elsewhere, Scott (1970) has contrasted American and Soviet criminological theories.

The principal reason for calling attention to these examples is simply to emphasize both the existence of relativism in deviance ideologies and to set the stage for an examination of the consequences of this. For just as these dominant ideologies vary, so too do the accounts for criminal and deviant acts which offenders proffer. Moreover, the accounts which offenders advance to "explain" their acts tend to show sufficient congruence with these dominant ideologies as to be generally taken as evidence of their theoretical validity. Or, as Berger and Luckmann (1967: 178) have suggested with respect to psychological theories, they "produce a reality which in turn serves as the basis for their verification."

One example of this is evident in the way in which American Indians came to behave when intoxicated after prolonged contact with Europeans (MacAndrew and Edgerton, 1969). Prior to contact with the white man, Indians generally were no more likely to act unruly or deviant while drunk than they were while sober. However, after observations of the behavior of whites while drunk, and exposure to "white theories" on the relationship between drunkenness and "wild" behavior, the drunken comportment of the Indians changed. An analogous process occurs today in the experiences of "blind" persons with agencies whose mission is to train them to live as normally as possible despite their handicap (Scott, 1969). After a period of "training" the clients come to exhibit the very kinds of behaviors which confirm the agencies' operating theories.

The foregoing supports the argument stated previously, that in time, theories of criminality and deviance can influence the objective and subjective parameters of the very problems they are said, originally, to explain. "Objective parameters" of deviance refers to the volume and type of deviance; and "subjective parameters" of deviance refers to the meanings and identities which deviants ascribe to themselves and their activities. More specifically, following Dinitz and Beran (1971), we could argue that every theory of crime and deviance must provide answers to two questions: (1) who shall be defined as deviant and in need of official attention?

and (2) how can deviance in individual cases be interpreted? The answers to these two questions provided by a particular theory constitute the parameters of the theory. It can be seen that these parameters are embedded in, and vary with, particular criminological theories.

The first of these parameters serves to locate and/or tell us how much deviance there is in time and place. The second parameter deals with how we can recognize deviance when it occurs in individuals. The second of these questions is fundamentally the more important one in producing support for a theory. For once the answer which a theory provides to this question has become legitimated, the answer it provides to the other is easily accepted. Perhaps the most critical evidence supporters of a theory can produce to buttress their claims is individuals whose experiences and interpretations of their *own misbehavior* are consistent with what the theory contends to be true.

Before turning to a discussion of how individuals—and especially the oppressed—can be induced to come forward with such testimonials, it is important to point out that theories of criminality and deviance do not vary in some random fashion across social settings. Lichtman's comments (1970: 78–79) are applicable in this discussion of theories of crime and deviance. He asks:

How many true descriptions of a social act are available? An indefinitely larger number. What is it that I do when I lecture? Amuse students, undermine the university, rationalize the pretended liberality of American society, satisfy parental expections, earn a living, remove my efforts from an indefinitely large number of alternatives, etc.? The list is endless. The same situation holds for any action. When does one conception come to dominate the social perspective of the agents in a given community? How is the meaningful interpretation of action constituted? Democratically? Hardly. *The channelling of interpreted meaning is class structured. It is formed through lived engagement in the predominant class-controlled institutions of the society* (emphasis in the original).

In other words, the content of criminological theories, and the variation in the degree to which they are uncritically accepted, are to some extent determined by political economic variables (Quinney, 1973: 137–63). In this respect, they are not unlike political ideologies—indeed, they are like language categories themselves (Mueller, 1973).

THEORETICAL ACCOUNTS OF CRIMINALITY

There are at least three different avenues through which members of a culture are exposed to ideologies of criminality so that they may come to employ them in making sense of their own or another person's experiences: (1) the mass media; (2) personal experience with control agents who espouse some particular ideology; and (3) by means of the exemplary interpretations of criminality provided by "properly credentialed experts" (e.g., psychiatrists), and apprehended or reformed deviants. These are now considered in turn.

A number of writers (e.g., Scheff, 1966a) have pointed out that from childhood on we are exposed to stereotypic—often false (Gerbner, 1972)—images of criminals and deviants via the mass media (cf. Thornton, 1974). Thus we are presented with examples of persons, and behavior, designated as "crazy," "weird," "nuts" or characteristic of the "hardened criminal" or "psychopath." In this process of exposure we acquire a set of verbalizations for organizing and making sense of our own behavior and the behavior of others. This very process provides us with a typical vocabulary of motives (Mills, 1967b) and simultaneously canalizes our thought (Mills, 1967a). It has been suggested that we are especially likely to bring these verbalizations to bear in organizing our own identities in those situations not already organized from a ready repertoire of identities, thereby aiding us in the construction of lines of action (cf. Foote, 1951). Cressey, for example, has applied this line of analysis to so-called compulsive crimes, maintaining that a learning process precedes a person's definition of himself or herself as a "kleptomaniac":

In order to play a social role, one must anticipate the reactions of others by taking the role implicitly before it is taken overtly. He must look at himself from another's point of view. By hypothesizing the reactions of others, the person looks upon himself as an object and, consequently, identifies himself as a particular kind of object. He then performs the role which is appropriate to the kind of social object with which he has identified himself. The vocabulary of motives employed in the performance of the role also is a corollary of this self-identification. . . . The motives employed in the performance of each role will reflect his particular identification. A similar phenomenon may exist in respect to so-called compulsive crime. For example, a person might in some situation identify himself as a kleptomaniac, since that construct is now popular in our culture, and a full commitment to such an identification includes the use of motives which, in turn, release the energy to perform a so-called compulsive act (1962: 459–60).

Becker (1968) was led to a similar interpretation of the phenomenon of psychotic episodes among users of LSD. He noted that the use of the drug can indeed produce psychic aberrations, but that interpretations of these experiences are potentially variable. Nevertheless,

In any society whose culture contains notions of sanity and insanity, the person who finds his subjective state altered in the way described may think he has become insane. We learn at a young age that a person who "acts funny," "sees things," "hears things," or has other bizarre and unusual experiences may have become "crazy," "nuts," "loony," or a host of other synonyms. When a drug user identifies some of these untoward events occurring in his own experience, he may decide that he merits one of those titles—that he has lost his grip on reality, his control of himself, and has in fact "gone crazy" (Ibid.: 278).

It should not be supposed that this relationship between culturally relative ideologies and subjective experiences is mere speculation, because there has been substantial research supporting it (Zola, 1966). It is a well-documented fact, for example, that persons with different social backgrounds define their personal problems in different ways (Bart, 1968) and subsequently develop different types of symptoms and seek different types of professional assistance (Scheff, 1966b).

This, then, is one of the mechanisms by which prevailing or dominant ideologies of criminality and deviance can indirectly produce a behavioral phenomenon which verifies the assumptions embedded in the ideology. It is but another way of saying that, subjectively, we know or understand criminal behavior, and construct our own criminal or non-criminal lines of action only in terms of the verbalizations and imagery which are presented to us in these dominant ideologies. In light of this argument, then, Bourque and Back (1971) have only partially grasped the *causal* significance of learned verbalizations for behavior in remarking that "the type of language which is available to the individual within the social context helps to determine the way(s) in which the individual will interpret, describe, and utilize his emotional experiences" (Ibid.: 2).

But the direct effects of the mass media are not the only avenue by which we are exposed to deviance ideologies, and learn, therefore, how to make sense of criminal offenders and deviants. We also learn as a result of confrontations with authorized agents of social control. The interaction which takes place during such times is not a neutral process. Typically, what happens, especially in the more serious cases of suspected misconduct, is that deviants are confronted by a representative of the agency who is seen as having great power, and are asked to give an account of themselves. Offenders are concerned with giving accounts (Scott and Lyman, 1968) which either extricate them from the situation altogether or else, while acknowledging that they committed the untoward act, either excuse or justify it. In searching around for an account, suspected deviants may take their cues from the apparent desires of the more powerful agency representative. Indeed, if one examines the interactional process which takes place on such occasions, it is obvious that a learning process is taking place (cf. Scheff, 1968). There is a strong probability that deviants will verbalize and use those accounts which seem to be satisfactory to the agency representative since they can, by doing so, solve their most immediate problem.

The existence of this learning process, and the dynamics of it, have been conceptualized in at least two different ways. Among the first to call attention to it were learning theorists, who viewed the process as one in which punishments and rewards are meted out to alleged deviants by the more powerful of the two participants (cf. Greenspoon, 1962). For example, those who have had occasion to conduct research in mental hospitals have noted how quickly patients learn to act "like mental patients are supposed to act," i.e., to play the sick role (e.g., Erikson, 1968). It is important to note here that one need not make any assumptions about the likelihood of the verbalizations and other behaviors which suspected deviants learn, altering the probabilities of their engaging in future deviance. All that is of interest here is that suspected deviants have, in fact, learned to conduct themselves "properly" and to use certain verbalizations as accounts (Taylor, 1972).

Besides psychological learning theory, however, the principles of symbolic interactionism have been applied to this learning process (e.g., Scheff, 1968). Such an approach permits the assumption that accounts,[1] once learned, become a significant new variable which may influence future behavior of suspected deviants. An interactionist would insist that while techniques of neutralization might in fact be learned *after* engaging in deviant or criminal behavior, they can come in time to "precede deviant behavior and make deviant behavior possible" (Sykes and Matza, 1957: 666). In other words, techniques of neutralization, once learned, modify the probability of the suspected deviant engaging in future deviance; they can influence future behavior whenever they can be used to rationalize some line of action *prior to the act.*

At this point we should note that "ideologies of criminality and deviance" refers primarily to the ideas promoted by alleged behavioral "experts," such as psychiatrists or psychologists. While groups such as these and their explanations for deviance are the principal focus, it would be a mistake to think that it is only they who educate their clients to accept dominant deviance ideologies. There are other social control agents who are sometimes responsible, perhaps even unwittingly, for advancing some particular ideology. Even the police, for example, whom one would ordinarily think of as espousing a rationalistic, free-will orientation toward the explanation of crime, seem to do their share in promoting a quite opposite set of ideas about crime. A review of two standard handbooks in police interrogation techniques revealed a number of examples of this, as is indicated in the following pieces of advice for questioning certain kinds of suspected offenders:

[In cases of rape] If the forcible rape occurred in the suspect's car or in his or the victim's residence, she can be blamed for behaving in such a way as to arouse the subject sexually to a point where he just had to have an outlet for his feelings. For instance: "Joe, this girl was having a lot of fun for herself by letting you kiss her and feel her breasts. For her that would have been sufficient. But men aren't built the same way. There's a limit to the teasing and excitement they can take; then something's got to give" (Inbau and Reid, 1967: 50).

In assault cases, the victim may be referred to as someone who was always "pushing other people around," that perhaps he finally got what was coming to him (Ibid.).

---

[1] "Accounts," as used here, is similar to Sykes and Matza's "techniques of neutralization," i.e., acceptable excuses for deviance.

In embezzlement cases . . . it is well to condemn the employer for paying inadequate and insufficient salaries, or for some unethical or careless practice which may have created a temptation to steal (Ibid.: 51).

Similar techniques are discussed in the other handbook under such headings as "Shifting the Blame," "Too Great a Temptation," and "The Only Human Way to Act" (Aubry and Caputo, 1965: 79–83).

The question might well arise at this stage whether suspected offenders or deviants who are processed by a social control agency "really" buy the agency-proffered accounts of their deviance or merely give the appearance of doing so in order to ease their plight. Even if one were to raise the question, however, it would be necessary to separate analytically the *special effects* of an *apparent* acceptance from the *general effects* of same. The distinction here is borrowed from the literature on deterrence (cf. Andenaes, 1966). The "special effects" of verbalized acceptance of agency accounts refers to the subsequent effects of those accounts on individuals who have already been processed by control agencies; "general effects," on the other hand, refers to the effects of the same public verbalizations on those who have not been processed by control agencies. The significance of this distinction is this: even if one were to argue that deviants who have publicly espoused agency-proffered verbalizations do not "really" believe them, and that they have no subsequent effects on them for that reason, it is still possible that the effects of this process on those who have merely observed them from afar may be considerable.

This brings us to a final mechanism by which deviance ideologies may influence the public's understanding of the nature of deviation and, in time, the very forms that deviance assumes. Reference will be made first to the effects of pronouncements and interpretations of deviance—usually on a case-by-case basis—by persons who are alleged to be experts in such matters; and second, to the impact of pronouncements by apprehended deviants in which they attempt to interpret and make sense of their own involvement in deviance. The impact of such publicly-disseminated "inside" and "expert" information may possibly be the most important single source of knowledge the public has on the problems of deviance. For example, commenting upon the importance of confessions in witchcraft cases in Renaissance Europe, Currie (1968: 14) observes that

. . . confessions were publicly read at executions, and distributed to the populace at large, which reinforced the legitimacy of the trials themselves and recreated in the public mind the reality of witchcraft itself. If people *said* they flew by night to dance with the devil, then surely there was evil in the land . . . (emphasis in the original).

Does not the publication, in our own times, of the autobiographies of former mental patients in which they recount their experiences when "ill" have the same effect? From their observations made after their historical and cross-cultural analysis of the behavioral effects of drunkenness, MacAndrew and Edgerton (1969) suggested:

[We propose] as an alternative to the disinhibition theory of alcohol's workings, that in the course of socialization persons learn about drunkenness whatever their society presumes to be the case; and that, comporting themselves in consonance with what is thus imparted to them, they become the living confirmation of their society's presumptions (Ibid.: 136).

Although the tendency here has been to assume that at any one time there was only one prevailing ideology of deviance within a society, this is obviously an oversimplification. Typically instead, in the modern industrialized country, there are competing ideologies of deviance. Obviously one problem worthy of sociological attention is that of explaining just why some deviance ideologies win out in this contest and gain wide credibility while others fall into disrepute. The process of marketing deviance theories surely is not unlike the process by which social problems become recognized as such (cf. Blumer, 1971). The logical adequacy of the syllogism probably has much less to do with the outcome of this process than does the ability to marshal resources, especially the rhetoric of "science." But for purposes of this analysis, greater unanimity on these matters than probably exists was assumed. It is possible, however, that the mechanisms by which deviance theories come to verify themselves in the world may not be significantly different in either case (i.e., where there is unanimity on one theory, as opposed to where there is theoretical pluralism).

It was suggested earlier that every deviance theory must provide an answer to two questions; and further, that in the process of providing an answer to the second of these questions, the first question is answered. The first question, it might be recalled, was: Who shall be defined as deviant and in need of official attention? In answering this question every deviance ideology will, by definition, provide us with a distributive "picture" of the deviance problem.

Since alternative deviance theories will give different answers to this question, the deviance net which they cast will be of varying size. Moreover, alternative theories will vary in the precision of the answer they give to this question; this is another way of saying that their empirical referents may be more or less precise. Some theories, then, will contain the potential for much greater invention than will others (cf. Currie, 1968). In a recent paper discussing the community mental health movement Dinitz and Beran suggest that, as compared to the legal and traditional mental health approaches to deviance, the community mental health approach amounts to a "boundaryless and boundary-busting system":

. . . the community mental health system offers an all-inclusive response to the question of who shall be defined as deviant in community mental health terms. Moving well beyond traditional mental health's focus on psychopathology, the community mental health system displays concern with the definition and management of any behavior that appears to threaten the quality of human existence. Increasing attention is being directed toward every conceivable form of failure and maladjustment . . . (1971: 100).

So one of the keys to understanding how claims about the amount and nature of deviance in the world get accepted can be found in the fact that those who believe in a particular deviance ideology, who are committed to it, are eventually able to present "evidence" in the form of case examples. In other words, those who are themselves sold on a deviance theory are able to muster deviants who give every appearance of being living proof of the validity of the theory. A theory must be able to marshal supporters among the more powerful and prestigious social control professions, and among the dirty workers of the society, before it can hope to succeed to this extent.

IMPLICATIONS OF CRIMINAL BEHAVIOR AS THEORETICAL PRAXIS

It is by now generally accepted that what comes to be seen as deviant in a society involves a process of definition (cf. Becker, 1963). In this connection, Blumer has taken issue with the position that social problems exist "basically in the form of an identifiable objective condition in a society," arguing instead that a "social problem exists in terms of how it is defined and conceived in a society . . ." (Ibid.: 300). However, the aim in this analysis has been to show that any distinction between objective social conditions and subjective perceptions of problems may be false (Kitsuse and Spector, 1973). It was argued that, at the most general level, the "objective" parameters of our understanding of problems of deviance (or social problems) are influenced by our deviance theories. In a very real sense, then, this suggests that societies produce, experientially, the kinds of criminals (and crime) they have theories to deal with.

During the past century the dominant deviance ideology in Western countries has undergone gradual and definite change. There has been a marked growth of the tendency to medicalize these theories (cf. Zola, 1972). This movement has generally gone forward accompanied by assurances that our understanding of deviance, and our ability to deal with it, would for that very reason become more "scientific" and valid. The "therapeutic" programs spawned by this movement have received critical comments because of the threats they pose to legal and ethical values (cf. Kittrie, 1971). But it seems to us that there has been too little attention paid to the implications of these programs and ideologies for the empirical manifestations of deviance generally. There is a very real possibility that as our deviance theories increasingly stress the deterministic role of emotional or non-rational forces we may create that very kind of offender.

The wide and successful dissemination of such "theories of irrational behavior" results in the simultaneous dissemination of a whole panoply of "irrational" vocabularies of motives. It is, of course, with these that people must interpret the events of everyday life, and construct their own lines of behavior, whether deviant or conforming. Irwin and Yablonsky (1965) have argued that over the past few decades,

. . . the basic personality of the majority of criminals has shifted from the well-trained, resourceful, "ethical" offender of the past to a new, unskilled and reckless deviant type. . . .

The new criminal's crimes tend to be more violent and "senseless." He lacks the skill in his profession that older criminals had. He is more apt to be involved with "kicks" or "thrills" and emotional gratification, and less with the material profit of his crimes (Ibid.: 183).

In their efforts to account for this shift the authors have little to say about shifts in the dominant ideological explanations of deviance which could, indirectly, be partially responsible for it. More attention needs to be paid to such a possibility.

REFERENCES

Andenaes, Johannes
1966   "The General Preventive Effects of Punishment." U. of Pennsylvania Law Review 114(May): 949–83.

Aubry, Arthur S. and Rudolph R. Caputo
1965   *Criminal Interrogation.* Springfield, Ill.: Chas. C Thomas.

Bart, Pauline B.
1968   "Social Structure and Vocabularies of Discomfort: What Happened to Female Hysteria?" *Journal of Health and Social Behavior* 9(September): 188–93.

Becker, Howard S.
1963   *Outsiders.* New York: The Free Press.
1968   "History, Culture, and Subjective Experience: An Exploration of the Social Bases of Drug-Induced Experiences." *Institutions and the Person.* Edited by Howard S. Becker, Blanche Geer, David Reisman, and Robert S. Weiss. Chicago: Aldine: 272–92.

Berger, Peter L. and Thomas Luckmann
1967   *The Social Construction of Reality.* Garden City, N.Y.: Anchor Books.

Blumer, Herbert
1971   "Social Problems as Collective Behavior." *Social Problems* 18(Winter): 298–305.

Bourque, Linda Brookover and Kurt W. Back
1971   "Language, Society, and Subjective Experience." *Sociometry* 34: 1–24.

Cressey, Donald R.
  1962   "Role Theory, Differential Association, and Compulsive Crimes." *Human Behavior and Social Processes.* Edited by Arnold M. Rose. Boston: Houghton Mifflin: 443–65.

Currie, Elliott P.
  1968   "Crimes without Criminals: Witchcraft and Its Control in Renaissance Europe." Law and Society Review 3(August): 7–32.

Dinitz, Simon and Nancy Beran
  1971   "Community Mental Health as a Boundaryless and Boundary-Busting System." *Journal of Health and Social Behavior* 12(June): 99–107.

Draguns, Juris G. and Leslie Phillips
  1972   "Culture and Psychopathology: The Quest for a Relationship." Morristown, N.J.: General Learning Corporation.

Erikson, Kai T.
  1966   *Wayward Puritans.* New York: John Wiley and Sons.
  1968   "Patient Role and Social Uncertainty." *Deviance: The Interactionist Perspective.* Edited by Earl Rubington and Martin S. Weinberg, New York: Macmillan: 337–42.

Foote, Nelson N.
  1951   "Identification as the Basis for a Theory of Motivation." *American Sociological Review* 16(February): 14–21.

Gerbner, George
  1972   "Violence in Television Drama: Trends and Symbolic Functions." *Television and Social Behavior* (volume 1 *Media Content and Control*). A Technical Report to the Surgeon General's Scientific Advisory Committee on Television and Social Behavior. Edited by George A. Comstock and Eli A. Rubenstein. Washington, D.C.: U.S. Government Printing Office: 28–187.

Greenspoon, Joel
  1962   "Verbal Conditioning and Clinical Psychology." *Experimental Foundations of Clinical Psychology.* Edited by Arthur J. Bachrach. New York: Basic Books: 510–53.

Inbau, Fred E. and John E. Reid
  1967   *Criminal Interrogation and Confessions* (Second edition). Baltimore: Williams and Wilkins.

Irwin, John and Lewis Yablonsky
  1965   The New Criminal: A View of the Contemporary Offender. *British Journal of Criminology* 5(April): 183–90.

Kitsuse, John I. and Malcolm Spector
   1973   "Toward a Sociology of Social Problems: Social Conditions, Value-Judgments, and Social Problems." *Social Problems* 20(Spring): 407–18.

Kittrie, Nicholas N.
   1971   *The Right to Be Different: Deviance and Enforced Therapy.* Baltimore: Johns Hopkins Press.

Lichtman, Richard
   1970   "Symbolic Interactionism and Social Reality: Some Marxist Queries." *Berkeley Journal of Sociology* 15: 75–94.

MacAndrew, Craig and Robert B. Edgerton
   1969   Reprinted by permission from Craig MacAndrew and Robert B. Edgerton, *Drunken Comportment* (Chicago: Aldine Publishing Company); Copyright © 1969 by Craig MacAndrew and Robert B. Edgerton.

Mills, C. Wright
   1967a   "Language, Logic, and Culture." *Power, Politics, and People.* Edited by Irving Louis Horowitz. New York: Oxford University Press: 423–38.
   1967b   "Situated Actions and Vocabularies of Motives." *Power, Politics, and People.* Edited by Irving Louis Horowitz. New York: Oxford University Press: 439–53.

Mueller, Claus
   1973   *The Politics of Communication.* New York: Oxford University Press.

Quinney, Richard
   1973   *Critique of Legal Order.* Boston: Little, Brown.

Scheff, Thomas J.
   1966a   *Being Mentally Ill.* Chicago: Aldine.
   1966b   "Users and Non-Users of a Student Psychiatric Clinic." *Journal of Health and Human Behavior* 7(Summer): 114–21.
   1968   "Negotiating Reality: Notes on Power in the Assessment of Responsibility." *Social Problems* 16(Summer): 3–17.

Scott, Marvin B. and Stanford Lyman
   1968   "Accounts." *American Sociological Review* 33(February): 46–61.

Scott, Robert A.
   1969   *The Making of Blind Men.* New York: Russell Sage Foundation.
   1970   "The Construction of Conceptions of Stigma by Professional Experts." *Deviance and Respectability.* Edited by Jack D. Douglas. New York: Basic Books: 255–90.

Silver, Allan
    1967   "The Demand for Order in Civil Society: A Review of Some
            Themes in the History of Urban Crime, Police, and Riot." *The
            Police: Six Sociological Essays*. Edited by David J. Bordua. New
            York: John Wiley and Sons: 1–24.

Sykes, Gresham and David Matza
    1957   "Techniques of Neutralization: A Theory of Delinquency."
            American Sociological Review 22(December): 664–80.

Taylor, Laurie
    1972   "The Significance and Interpretation of Replies to Motiva-
            tional Questions: The Case of Sex Offenders." *Sociology*
            6(January): 23–39.

Taylor, Laurie and Ian Taylor
    1972   "Changes in the Motivational Construction of Deviance."
            Catalyst (Fall): 76–99.

Thornton, William
    1974   "The Mass Media and Public Conceptions of Crime." Unpub-
            lished paper. Department of Sociology, University of
            Tennessee.

Tobias, John J.
    1967   *Crime and Industrial Society in the 19th Century*. New York:
            Schocken Books.

Zola, Irving Kenneth
    1966   "Culture and Symptoms: An Analysis of Patients' Presenting
            Complaints." *American Sociological Review* 31(October): 615–31.
    1972   "Medicine as an Institution of Social Control." *Sociological Re-
            view* 20(November): 487–504.

Chapter 4

The administration of justice: The police

This chapter is based on our assumption that the most important data in the study of crime are information related to the development of laws and their administration rather than information on the behavior of those designated as criminals. Showing that, as written, criminal laws reflect the interests of powerful groups points to only a small portion of the total argument. Perhaps the most consistent complaints from economic and racial minorities concern the administration of laws rather than the laws themselves; and the first steps in the process of administering the criminal laws are, of course, taken by the police. Here we will explore police activities and behavior in modern America.

THE DELIVERY OF POLICE SERVICES

In the American Colonies law enforcement was initially the responsibility of all able-bodied men. These men periodically assumed this responsibility as volunteers. Parks (1970) argues, however, that a specialized modern police department became necessary in the United States as it became more and more difficult to control the increasing numbers of the poor. In referring to the police, Bordua and Reiss (1967: 277) observe: "Increasing social differentiation, heterogeneity, and stratification of the population led to lowered consensus on major values and the necessity to develop formal controls if a heterogeneous community was to have at least a minimum of order."

Historically, in England all adults had some responsibility for making arrests in certain situations. For example, every citizen had the responsibility of raising the "hue and cry"—to assist in the capture of a thief or other person absconding after committing a crime (Puttkammer, 1953: 29–31). Failure to arrest a felon when in a position to do so was, in fact, a separate crime in itself. Today this is no longer recognized as a real civilian responsibility. Such obligations are neither socially nor legally recognized. In 1964 in New York City, a woman named Kitty Genovese was attacked and stabbed to death. This assault did not occur in a lonely alley but in front a large apartment building and in full view of at least 38 adults. The assault lasted about 30 minutes, yet none of the observers intervened or even called the police during that period (Rosenthal, 1964). What has developed has been called "that attitude of an age of specialization: let the cop do the dirty work; what else are we paying him for?"[1]

However much we might condemn this lack of willingness to help the police, it is true that there are some convincing arguments against direct citizen intervention to stop the commission of a crime. Whereas in many jurisdictions police officers injured in the line of duty are covered by hospitalization and life insurance for such injuries, as well as by false arrest insurance, the civilian who encounters problems while trying to help enforce the law is not similarly covered (Ratcliffe, 1966). The legal and social situation of reliance on police officers for crime control is just one example of a broader societal trend toward greater and greater occupational specialization. Two hundred years ago, most American men performed the tasks of farmers, carpenters, and butchers, whereas today a leaking faucet or roof generally prompts us to consult the Yellow Pages for assistance.

Although today the police are expected to do the job of law enforcement alone, they are not efficiently organized to accomplish this task. In the United States, there are thousands of federal, state, and local police departments. These usually do not cooperate completely with one another and sometimes work at direct cross-purposes. In every state in the United States, there are

---

[1] Quotation attributed to Karl Llewellyn (Mayer, 1967: 179).

a myriad of municipal and county police departments, most of which have only a handful of men, usually far too few to offer adequate police coverage. Even at the federal level, there are a host of police agencies, including the FBI, the Secret Service, narcotics agents, border patrols, and postal inspectors, sometimes working on the same case without a fully coordinated effort. A narcotics case can lead several federal police agencies along parallel lines while working independently of one another. This excessive decentralization of police departments is sometimes held to be necessary to avoid a police takeover of our government, yet Great Britain, which had only 158 forces in 1962, has not been taken over by a police junta (Banton, 1964: 88). Assuming that the goal is efficient police operations, consolidation of police departments is required.

Another organizational problem is found in large metropolitan areas, where the chief of police is typically a political appointee, whereas all the other officers on the force have civil service positions. The chief can be replaced as the political winds shift, whereas the other officers' jobs are much more permanent (Puttkammer, 1953: 34). Those who report directly to the chief know that a given incumbent will not last long and that if they attach themselves too closely to any one chief and give him complete support, they may be punished later due to their identification with an ex-chief. So the chief is handicapped by both his own inexperience and a lack of wholehearted support from his men. Yet a police chief is greatly dependent on the cooperation of his men because, unlike most other organizations, where information flows mainly from the top down, in police departments information about events in the community, which the chief needs in order to perform his duties, comes into the organization from the police officers at the bottom, the patrolmen (Banton, 1964: 107–118).

However, despite these organizational problems, most of the complaints about the police do not concern their inefficiency but rather their brutality, prejudice, and cynicism in performing their job. Also, opinion surveys have repeatedly shown blacks to be more negative than whites in their evaluations of the police (Bayley and Mendelsohn, 1969; Ennis, 1967). Only by exploring the combined impact of racial and class conflict on police behavior can a complete understanding of these findings be achieved.

EXPLANATIONS OF POLICE BEHAVIOR[2]

Perhaps because of these recurrent complaints about police activities, in recent years many social scientists have attempted to explain why police behave the way they do in performing their duties. What follows is a review of some dominant themes running through the myriad of articles and books which have appeared on this subject. This survey does not purport to offer an exhaustive coverage of all the relevant literature but is intentionally selective to highlight some observable patterns. In this chapter we will illustrate how social scientists have persistently ignored the effects of social structure on police behavior. By this we mean that they have ignored the influence of community heterogeneity on the behavior of the local police, especially the impact of economic disparity and racial differences.

Psychological perspective

Several sociologists have focused on the personality of the individual police officer as important in determining how he performs his role. Skolnick (1966: 42–70) suggests that policemen have a "working personality," by which he means a set of cognitive tendencies which influence their work. By virtue of enforcing the law, the police become very supportive of the status quo. Skolnick argues that to believe in their task and appear consistent to themselves, police become extremely conservative politically. Moreover, because of their job, police officers are highly sensitive to signs of danger. Due to the constant threat of violence and their job of preventing crime, police often become sensitized to things of which civilians are unaware. In the course of their work, police become suspicious of certain kinds of people whose gestures, language, or clothing they associate with violence or crime. Skolnick (1966: 45–48) refers to people who are viewed in such a manner as "symbolic assailants"—those with long hair or wearing black leather motorcycle jackets, those strutting, or showing insolence, black men in all-white suburbs, and well-dressed or poorly dressed blacks. In fact, almost everything is suspicious in the black ghetto (Schwartz, 1967). "A young man may suggest the threat of violence to the policeman by his manner of walking or 'strutting,' the

---

[2] The remaining sections of this chapter are largely taken from Galliher (1971).

insolence in the demeanor being registered by the policeman as a possible preamble to later attack" (Skolnick, 1966: 46). This helps explain police willingness to act against some citizens which might otherwise be interpreted merely as harassment.

Niederhoffer (1967: 103–151, especially 118–119) speculates that police officers are transformed into authoritarian personalities by virtue of the police role. Included in this authoritarianism is a love of power and toughness and a hatred for weakness. Niederhoffer (1967: 90–102) also suggests that police officers develop a cynicism toward the public which is a consequence of performing their job. Because their job throws them into contact with so many dishonest people, police officers begin to see everyone as corrupt. Niederhoffer (1967: 95) quotes a detective as follows: "I am convinced that we are turning into a nation of thieves. I have sadly concluded that nine out of ten persons are dishonest."

McNamara (1967: 211–212) found an increase in authoritarianism after recruit police training and a further increase after one year on the job. Police with two years of experience were found to be more authoritarian than either of the other groups. This supports the notion that police apparently become more authoritarian as a result of their experience as police officers. McNamara suggests that this increased authoritarianism is likely to lead to disagreement with the courts' emphasis on individual rights.

It should be noted that the significance of McNamara's research is somewhat blunted by Bayley and Mendelsohn's (1969: 17–18) finding that police are, in fact, *less* authoritarian than other citizens. Moreover, even if police are made more authoritarian by their occupational role, this says nothing about the structural determinants of this influence or about why the environment is structured to give officers experiences that increase their authoritarianism.

Demands of the immediate situation

Recently a number of articles have emphasized the great amount of discretion police may use in deciding to make arrests. It has been found that police rely heavily on the characteristics of the immediate situation in making these decisions.

For example, Bittner (1967) found that police on skid row make their decision to arrest an individual mainly on the basis of the perceived risk that the person will create a disorder rather than on the basis of degree of guilt. Black (1970) and Black and Reiss (1970) found that a major component in the decision to arrest is the preference of the complainant. Police usually arrest a suspect if that is the desire of the person making the complaint but release the suspect if that is requested by the complainant. Some studies have also found that the deference displayed by the suspect has a bearing on the use of discretion by the officer (Westley, 1953; Piliavin and Briar, 1964). Piliavin and Briar (1964: 210) suggest that "in the opinion of juvenile patrolmen themselves the demeanor of apprehended juveniles was a major determinant of their decisions for 50–60 percent of the juvenile cases they processed."

However, police use of discretion as well as suspects' behavior are not random occurrences. All occur within a *social structural context*. Unfortunately, some sociologists are mainly concerned with the demands of the immediate situation and neglect the broader social structure within which this interaction occurs. A social structural analysis would require some interpretation of the observation that black Americans, more frequently than other citizens, seem loath to show respect for the police.

Role conflict

Some studies of police behavior locate explanations in a social psychological, role conflict model. The basic idea is that officers perceive conflicting expectations from others regarding how they should carry out their job. Skolnick (1966: 1–22) discusses the policeman's "dilemma" of enforcing the law while at the same time maintaining order. The police believe that they are expected to do both, but maintaining order may at times require the officer to work outside the law, ignoring a suspect's constitutional rights. Wilson (1963: 199) suggests that this conflict between achieving order or catching a suspect and operating within the limits imposed by the law, is especially intense when a "crusade" is launched by a department to solve an important case. The rules of law require respect for civil liberties, but during times of crisis, police feel compelled to forget this and to consider only the efficiency of the means used in catching a suspect.

Wilson (1963: 198–199) observes another source of conflicting expectations. In a heterogeneous society, one part of the public may want different kinds of enforcement from the police than do other parts. For example, urban liberals and blacks feel differently about the police use of force than do other citizens.

Preiss and Ehrlich (1966: 94–121) also report on police officers' perceptions of conflicting expectations among the various audience groups with which they are involved. One example of these conflicting expectations is the discrepancies perceived between the views of police officers' wives and the views of police officers' supervisors regarding the appropriate limitations in the demands of the police officer's job (Preiss and Ehrlich, 1966: 99–101). That is, police officers perceive their wives as believing that their obligations to the job should end after 8 hours, whereas their supervisors see the police officer's obligations as continuing 24 hours a day.

The implication in all of this literature is that because of such role conflicts, officers may be forced to make certain compromises, accommodations, and choices. Unfortunately, no theoretical models are offered to help predict the specific choices made. Perhaps this is true because insufficient attention has been given to the structural bases of the role conflict.

Subcultural approach

Other studies have sought to explain police behavior by using what is essentially a subcultural approach. The argument is that police officers are a unique group. As such, they are subjected to special strains and make collective rather than individual adjustments to these problems.

In an early police study, Westley (1953: 39) found evidence of a police subculture in a code justifying the use of violence to coerce respect.

The most significant finding is that at least 37 percent of the men believed that it was legitimate to use violence to coerce respect. This suggests that policemen use the resource of violence to persuade their audience (the public) to respect their occupational status. In terms of the policeman's definition of the situation, the individual who lacks respect for the police, the "wise guy" who talks back, or any individual who acts or talks in a disrespectful way, deserves brutality.

Westley (1956) also found that this code forbids police from informing against fellow officers. Typically, officers indicated that they would adhere to this rule of secrecy which functions to protect the police against attacks from the community.

However, policemen cannot and do not employ sanctions against their colleagues for using violence, and individual men who personally condemn the use of violence and avoid it whenever possible refuse openly to condemn acts of violence by other men on the force (Westley, 1953: 40).

More recent research by Stoddard (1968), Savitz (1970), and Reiss (1968) supports the notion of a code of secrecy.

Skolnick (1966: 53–58) suggests that the dangerousness of the police mission as well as the requirement that officers use authority against civilians contributes to solidarity. The reasoning is that the more hostility the police receive from the public, the more isolated they become and consequently the more dependent they become on one another.[3]

Although these studies have used sociocultural variables in their analyses of police behavior, they have erred in defining the environment of the police as a given, as constant across all communities. One problem with such an approach is that it is impossible to use it to explain the variations in police attitudes and behavior that are found in different communities. If differences in law enforcement practices exist in various communities, then it seems reasonable to expect differences in the nature of the subculture and related structural strains.

Departmental characteristics approach

The problem of explaining differences in policing styles has received some attention from those focusing on departmental characteristics as independent determinants of police behavior and attitudes. The argument is that police behavior is a result of the particular situation found in each department.[4]

Wilson (1968a: 9–30) compared the handling of juveniles in an efficient, highly trained professional department and in a nonprofessional department. He found that the former was much more likely to process juvenile law violators officially than was the

---

[3] A similar point is made in Fogelson (1968) and Westley (1956: 254–255).

[4] I am indebted to Patrick Donovan for suggesting this type of explanation.

latter. The nonprofessional department relied much more heavily on informal alternatives, such as issuing warnings.

In *Varieties of Police Behavior,* Wilson (1968b) isolates three types of law enforcement style displayed by various departments. One style emphasizes service to the community, another emphasizes strict enforcement of all laws; and the third is mainly oriented toward the maintenance of order. Most important for this discussion is that Wilson pictures police departments as having some independence, as not being directly controlled by the community. One reflection of this independence is that it is not always possible to predict the style of law enforcement from the characteristics of the community (Wilson, 1968b: 227–277).

Gardiner (1969: 72) attributes much of the difference in traffic law enforcement in two communities to the differences in the desires of their respective police chiefs. One problem with this type of analysis is that it implicitly assumes that the recruitment of police chiefs is random, or at least not significantly affected by the desires of the local community.

Neither Gardiner nor Wilson claims that the law enforcement style is completely independent of the community, but they are, nonetheless, unable to develop a conceptual model to handle these social structural relationships.

Sociocultural approach

A few attempts have been made to describe how societies or communities seem to determine the characteristics of local police.

In comparing European police with those in the United States, Berkley (1969: 197) found the latter much more prone to violence. This, he claims, is a direct reflection of American values: "If the American police are prone to use violent and repressive tactics, American society offers them the means and the climate to do so. No other democratic nation compares to the United States in the acceptance and even glorification of violence as a way to solve problems."

Banton (1964: 86–126) attributes many of the differences he found between British and American police officers to the greater social integration that exists in Great Britain. Since Britain is a more homogeneous society, with citizens holding more consistent values, it is predictable that British police would be exposed to less violence. This allows the police to operate differently. There is less reason to smother all internal strains within a department and less reason for departmental solidarity (Banton, 1964: 118–119).

Stinchcombe (1963) compares urban and rural differences in the structural conditions which affect policing. In cities, large numbers of people are concentrated into relatively small amounts of public space. This makes police control of public places more economical. Moreover, in the cities informal controls are weakest and patrol is most necessary. According to Stinchcombe, this makes sense of the fact that police in the cities can and do frequently act on their own initiative in making arrests. Since it is both less economical and less necessary to patrol public places in rural areas, rural police initiate fewer arrests and rely more on citizen complaints to attract their attention to a problem (Stinchcombe, 1963: 152).

Although the sociocultural approaches take greater account of social structural influences than do any of the approaches discussed earlier, on the whole they still offer an incomplete conceptual framework. *The fundamental problem in many of the social science explanations of police behavior is that they take no systematic account of the influence of class conflict on law enforcement.*

EMPIRICAL EVIDENCE FOR THE VARIOUS CONCEPTUAL MODELS

We have just seen that if the psychological characteristics of officers are studied, the implication is that this is important in understanding police behavior. It is also sometimes assumed that by studying the demands of the immediate situation which officers face or their role conflicts, we can better understand their method of operation. Some point to a police subculture or police department leadership to explain officers' behavior. However, only studies that emphasize the social structural environment of policing have the potential of directing attention to social class as a determinant of law enforcement style. All others, of necessity, would miss the importance of class conflict since they direct attention away from the social structure toward a low-level description of the action in immediate law enforcement situations.

Much of police behavior seems most easily explained if one considers that whenever there is a conflict of interests between the dominant classes in a society and less powerful groups, the police protect the interests of the former and regulate the behavior of the latter. If the police role attracts authoritarian individuals, and their authoritarianism increases once they are on the job, perhaps this happens because of the demands made on the police to suppress economic and racial minorities. Such tasks are most attractive to the authoritarian personality, and undoubtedly any of an officer's initial doubts about those tasks are lessened by an increasingly authoritarian orientation. The literature indicating that police are free to follow the demands of the immediate situation in making arrests also shows that this discretion is used to the disadvantage of minority groups (Skolnick, 1966: 85; Goldman, 1963; Wald, 1967: 139–151; Wilson, 1968a). Wilson's (1963: 198–199) observations regarding the differing demands of blacks and urban liberals compared to other citizens as a source of role conflict for the police can be interpreted in class conflict terms. Officers can be seen as experiencing role conflict in part because of different and conflicting demands from various social classes in the community. There is some evidence that police subcultures develop in a department both to legitimate and keep secret brutality toward economic and racial minorities (Reiss, 1968; Westley, 1970). Department leadership and methods of operation can be interpreted as a response to the demands of powerful interest groups (Walker, 1968: especially 13–14). Simple descriptions of police personalities or specific situations faced by the police take no account of class interests and class conflict. Many social scientists have been busy collecting disparate "facts" about policing and have been either unable or unwilling to develop related conceptual frameworks which take account of the social structure, including a consideration of social class. Newman (1966: 181–182) claims that sociological treatment of the criminal justice system, including the police, lacks a theoretical framework, and that the theoretical concern of most criminologists has been the social psychological issue of the causation of criminal behavior. As a consequence of this theoretical naïveté, the sociological study of the criminal justice process is empirically naïve, for without an integrated theoretical framework even intelligent fact-gathering is impossible.

Without considering class and class conflict, one cannot accurately interpret the arrest patterns in the United States. It is well established that in most areas of the United States, the majority of those people arrested are poor and/or black. As indicated earlier, some observers of arrest practices who emphasize that police can exercise great discretion show that in those cases where this discretion can be most easily exercised, the bulk of those arrested are poor and black (Skolnick, 1966: 85; Goldman, 1963; Wald, 1967: 139–151; Wilson, 1968a). There is also an awareness of other discriminatory treatment given to economic and racial minorities by the police, such as verbal and physical harassment (Reiss, 1968; Schwartz, 1967: 446–447). Kitsuse and Cicourel (1963: 136–137) maintain that since official rates of deviant behavior are compiled by specific organizations, these rates reflect organizational methods of operation. Using this reasoning, one readily available pool of information regarding police behavior is arrest data.

Curiously, these patterns found in arrest practices and other police treatment of minorities have not influenced the theoretical models used in explaining police behavior. If they were used, social class and class conflict would necessarily be incorporated into explanations of police behavior. Cook (1967: 120) observes that "there is no recognition that the processes of law enforcement serve the interests of dominant groups in the society and either ignore or oppose the interests of those in lower social strata." Perhaps the reason for this is that social scientists have been misusing arrest data. They have been using it as a basis for generating theories of criminal behavior and have been neglecting its uses as a reflection of police behavior.

Occasionally some cursory recognition of class does appear. Quite early in *Behind the Shield,* Niederhoffer (1967) introduces the notion of class and its effects on law enforcement. He quotes Joseph Lohman, the late dean of the School of Criminology of the University of California at Berkeley, who was himself a police officer at one time. "The police function [is] to support and enforce the interests of the dominant political, social, and economic interests of the town, and only incidentally to enforce the law" (Niederhoffer, 1967: 12). But if Niederhoffer mentions class quickly, he drops it even more quickly in favor of "the principle of equilibrium," meaning that police are mainly concerned with protecting themselves from all criticism from whatever source (Niederhoffer, 1967: 13–15).

Wilson (1963: 213) suggests in passing that a professional police force which applies the law equally to all citizens is impossible in a highly stratified community. Elsewhere in the same paper, he says:

Property owners, for example, may want maximum protection of their property and of their privacy; slum dwellers, however, may not like the amount of police activity necessary to attain the property owners' ends. Negroes and urban liberals may unite in seeking to end "police brutality"; lower-middle-class homeowners whose neighborhoods are "threatened" with Negro invasion may want the police to deal harshly with Negroes or to look the other way while the homeowners themselves deal harshly with them (Wilson, 1963: 198–199).

Even though class is introduced, Wilson either cannot or will not follow through with any analysis. All he can bring himself to say is that this presents the police with an inconsistency. He says nothing about how this inconsistency is resolved.

Westley (1970) cites statements indicating that police respond differently to different social classes. One policeman is quoted as saying that "in the better districts the purpose is to make friends out of the people and get them to like you. If you react rough to them, naturally they will hate you" (Westley, 1970: 98). On the other hand, it seems just as obvious to the police that they can only elicit respect and obedience from slum dwellers by resorting to force (Westley, 1970: 99). Westley (1970: 96–99) suggests that part of the difference in the police perception of the affluent and the poor is due to the differences in the political power of these groups—police are afraid to brutalize the wealthy because of their political influence. Moreover, the poor are seen as more disposed to law violation and conflict with the police because of their great economic need. Just as it appears that Westley is on the verge of a thorough structural analysis of police behavior, he tells the reader that police attitudes and behavior have subcultural roots, and surprisingly, he ignores the effects of class conflict on this subculture.

Dirty work at home and abroad

In any society there are certain thankless, dirty jobs which nonetheless must be done. Handling household trash and the excrement of hospital patients are two examples. Such tasks are extremely unpleasant, and are therefore performed by certain low-status individuals in a way that will not violate the delicate senses of the citizens being served. The garbage collector is usually instructed not to litter middle-class neighborhoods with trash from the truck, and in collecting human waste the hospital orderly must be similarly circumspect so as to avoid upsetting patients or their relatives. There are also elements of dirty work in policing. Police officers are required to work undesirable hours in the most deteriorated parts of communities, and they may have to intervene in vicious family quarrels, inspect corpses, arrest skid row drunks who reek with various odors and sometimes vomit when moved, and keep masses of the unemployed poor from disturbing the peace of the more affluent.

The fact that social scientists have not recognized the dirty nature of police work is perhaps in some ways similar to the German citizens' unfamiliarity with the operation of the SS (Schutzstaffel), the Nazi party's elite military arm, which was responsible for the execution of Jews. Hughes (1962) describes the apparent ignorance of Germans regarding the systematic extermination of the Jews. He contends that the SS was used by the German people to solve their Jewish problem. Most Germans felt that a Jewish problem did exist, but once the SS was created, it not only took care of the problem but allowed most German citizens to remain uninvolved in the solution. Since the SS was sworn to secrecy, German citizens could claim ignorance of what this group was doing. One of Hughes' major assumptions is that the public does not accurately perceive the morally outrageous nature of some dirty work and that keeping unpleasant facts from the public is indeed a function of dirty work.

Some immediate similarities appear between the SS role in wartime Germany and the police role in the United States. Many Americans would doubtlessly agree that we have a "Negro problem." The police, like the SS, are highly secretive (Westley, 1956; Reiss, 1968; Savitz, 1970; Stoddard, 1968), which keeps their morally questionable acts shielded from most Americans. This functions to control poor and black Americans in any way necessary while other citizens can continue to believe that this is a free democratic society and yet have their property protected. In fact, the dirty work of policing American slums is so well hidden from the middle classes that even middle-class sociologists fail to understand that its function is to maintain a highly economically stratified and racist society.[5]

The police are not a part of the dominant classes of American society, usually being recruited from the lower class or lower mid-

---

[5] For a similar analysis, see Rainwater (1967).

dle class (Preiss and Ehrlich, 1966: 12; Niederhoffer, 1967: 36–38; McNamara, 1967: 193; Bayley and Mendelsohn, 1969: 6). It is predictable, however, that largely lower-class individuals would perform the "dirty" police tasks since middle-class and upper-class citizens probably could not comfortably shoot a looter or harass black youngsters but are apparently not bothered by hiring people who cannot afford to be so choosy to do the job.

Social scientists studying the police have typically assumed that individual police officers or departments are free to implement social policy much as they see fit, even though America is recognized as a highly stratified society and the police are known to be lower class or marginally middle class at best. As we observed earlier, in our society some people have considerably more power than others and in this sense are less dominated than others. The police are near the bottom of the stratification system, and are only free to resign their positions if they do not wish to do the bidding of powerful citizen and interest groups. Yet the assumption of police freedom to use great discretion is reflected in much of the literature reviewed here, which stresses the importance of police personalities, subcultures, or police chiefs as determinants of law enforcement style.[6] If social scientists are unable to understand the place of law enforcement in class conflict, then it should not be surprising that other well-educated political liberals, radical students, and many black Americans see the police as a main source of trouble. Their criticism lends public credence to the social science research which implies that the police are somehow individually or collectively responsible for the way in which laws are enforced. To the degree that the police are seen as independent, they will, of course, be held responsible for the manner in which they operate.

CONCLUSION

The absence of references to class conflict in the literature dealing with police behavior is surprising, since both the origins of modern police as well as the paramilitary form of modern police bureaucracies have been explained in class conflict terms.

---

[6] Skolnick's *The Politics of Protest* (1969) is an especially clear illustration of this emphasis on the independence of the police.

Bordua and Reiss (1967: 282) suggest that

the paramilitary form of early police bureaucracy was a response not only, or even primarily, to crime per se, but to the possibility of riotous disorder. Not crime and danger but the "criminal" and "dangerous classes" as part of the urban social structure led to the formation of uniformed and militarily organized police. Such organizations intervened between the propertied elites and the propertyless masses who were regarded as politically dangerous as a class.

It is sometimes said that if the police were better organized, this would help them do a better job and would reduce police-community tensions (Wilson, 1968b; Berkley, 1969). The suggestion is also made that better-trained police would solve many of the problems they encounter (Berkley, 1969: 87; Skolnick, 1969: 290–291; *Task Force Report: The Police,* 1967: 36–37). However, as Terris (1967: 63–64) has shown, some cities with very well-trained police still have major police-minority problems. One explanation is that as long as police are used for the purpose of containing economic and racial minorities, police-minority conflict will not subside. If police are better educated and better organized, they could just as well become more efficient oppressors.

Since there are obvious differences in law enforcement styles across communities and countries, students of police behavior can profit by directing their research toward an analysis of the effect that the presence of large economic and racial minorities has on the style of law enforcement in a given jurisdiction. This question involves the relationship between the scope of class conflict and the behavior of the police. The answer would include a description of the structural linkages between the community and local police departments and of the theoretical model or models which would allow us to predict these linkages.

If it is assumed "that the processes of law enforcement serve the interests of dominant groups in the society and either ignore or oppose the interests of those in lower social strata" (Cook, 1967: 120), one might make certain predictions for police behavior. Taking such a perspective, one might predict, for example, that in heterogeneous communities with large economic and racial minorities, police would behave in an oppressive fashion toward minorities because of the threat they symbolize to the rest of the community. Following this reasoning, such police behavior seems less likely to occur in more homogeneous communities.

REFERENCES

Banton, Michael
1964   *The Policeman in the Community.* New York: Basic Books.

Bayley, David H. and Harold Mendelsohn
1969   *Minorities and the Police.* New York: Free Press.

Berkley, George E.
1969   *The Democratic Policeman.* Boston: Beacon Press.

Bittner, E.
1967   "The Police on Skid-row: A Study of Peace Keeping," *American Sociological Review* 32(October): 699–715.

Black, D. J.
1970   "Production of Crime Rates," *American Sociological Review* 35(August): 733–748.

Black, D. J. and A. J. Reiss, Jr.
1970   "Police Control of Juveniles," *American Sociological Review* 35(February): 63–77.

Bordua, David J. and Albert J. Reiss, Jr.
1967   "Law Enforcement," pp. 275–303 from *The Uses of Sociology* edited by Paul F. Lazarsfeld, William H. Sewell, and Harold L. Wilensky, © 1967 by Basic Books, Inc., Publishers, New York.

Cook, W.
1967   "Policemen in Society: Which Side Are They On?" *Berkeley Journal of Sociology* 12(Summer): 117–129.

Ennis, Philip H.
1967   *Criminal Victimization in the United States: A Report of a National Survey.* National Opinion Research Center, University of Chicago. Washington, D.C.: U.S. Government Printing Office.

Fogelson, R.M.
1968   "From Resentment to Confrontation: The Police, the Negroes, and the Outbreak of the Nineteen-sixties Riots," *Political Science Quarterly* 83(June): 217–247.

Galliher, J. F.
1971   "Explanations of Police Behavior: A Critical Review and Analysis," *Sociological Quarterly* 12(Summer): 308–318.

Gardiner, John A.
1969   *Traffic and the Police: Variations in Law-Enforcement Policy.* Cambridge, Mass.: Harvard University Press.

Goldman, Nathan
1963   *The Differential Selection of Juvenile Offenders for Court Appear-*

ance. New York: National Research and Information Center, National Council on Crime and Delinquency.

Hughes, E. C.
1962   "Good People and Dirty Work," *Social Problems* 10(Summer): 3–11.

Kitsuse, J. I. and A. V. Cicourel
1963   "A Note on the Uses of Official Statistics," *Social Problems* 11(Fall): 131–139.

Mayer, Martin
1967   *The Lawyers.* New York: Harper and Row, Publishers.

McNamara, John H.
1967   "Uncertainties in Police Work: The Relevance of Police Recruits' Backgrounds and Training," pp. 163–252 in David J. Bordua, ed., *The Police: Six Sociological Essays.* New York: John Wiley and Sons.

Newman, Donald J.
1966   "Sociologists and the Administration of Criminal Justice," pp. 177–187 in Arthur B. Shostak, ed., *Sociology in Action.* Homewood, Ill.: Dorsey Press.

Niederhoffer, Arthur
1967   *Behind the Shield: The Police in Urban Society.* Garden City, N.Y.: Doubleday and Co.

Parks, Evelyn L.
1970   "From Constabulary to Police Society: Implications for Social Control," *Catalyst* 5(Summer): 76–97.

Piliavin, I. and S. Briar
1964   "Police Encounters with Juveniles," *American Journal of Sociology* 70(September): 206–214.

Preiss, Jack J. and Howard J. Ehrlich
1966   *An Examination of Role Theory: The Case of the State Police.* Lincoln: University of Nebraska Press.

Puttkammer, Ernst W.
1953   *Administration of Criminal Law.* Chicago: University of Chicago Press.

Rainwater, L.
1967   "Revolt of the Dirty-Workers," *Transaction* 5(November): 2, 64.

Ratcliffe, James M., ed.
1966   *The Good Samaritan and the Law.* Garden City, N.Y.: Anchor Books.

Reiss, A. J., Jr.
  1968   "Police Brutality—Answers to Key Questions," *Transaction* 5(July–August): 10–19.

Rosenthal, A. M.
  1964   *Thirty-eight Witnesses.* New York: McGraw-Hill Book Co.

Savitz, L.
  1970   "The Dimensions of Police Loyalty," *American Behavioral Scientist* (May–June, July–August): 693–704.

Schwartz, H.
  1967   "Stop and Frisk (A Case Study in Judicial Control of the Police)," *Criminal Law, Criminology, and Police Science* 58(December): 433–464.

Skolnick, Jerome H.
  1966   *Justice without Trial.* New York: John Wiley and Sons.
  1969   *The Politics of Protest.* New York: Simon and Schuster.

Stinchcombe, A. L.
  1963   "Institutions of Privacy in the Determination of Police Administrative Practice," *American Journal of Sociology* 69(September): 150–160.

Stoddard, E. R.
  1968   "The Informal 'Code' of Police Deviancy: A Group Approach to 'Blue-coat Crime,' " *Criminal Law, Criminology, and Police Science* 59(June): 201–213.

Task Force Report: The Police
  1967   *Washington, D.C.: U.S. Government Printing Office.*

Terris, B. J.
  1967   "The Role of the Police," *Annals of the American Academy of Political and Social Science* 374(November): 58–69.

Wald, Patricia M.
  1967   "Poverty and Criminal Justice," pp. 139–151 in *Task Force Report: The Courts.* Washington, D.C.: U.S. Government Printing Office.

Walker, Daniel
  1968   *Rights in Conflict.* New York: Bantam Books.

Westley, William A.
  1953   "Violence and the Police," *American Journal of Sociology* 59(July): 34–41.
  1956   "Secrecy and the Police," *Social Forces* 34(March): 254–257.
  1970   *Violence and the Police: A Sociological Study of Law, Custom, and Morality.* Cambridge, Mass.: MIT Press.

Wilson, James Q.
  1963   "The Police and Their Problems: A Theory," pp. 189–216 in
         *Public Policy: A Yearbook of the Graduate School of Public Adminis-
         tration, Harvard University*, vol. 12.
  1968a "The Police and the Delinquent in Two Cities," pp. 9–30 in
         Stanton Wheeler, ed., *Controlling Delinquents*. New York: John
         Wiley and Sons.
  1968b *Varieties of Police Behavior*. Cambridge, Mass.: Harvard Univer-
         sity Press.

7

*From constabulary to police society: Implications for social control**

Evelyn L. Parks

The history of social control in the United States is the history of transition from "constabulary" to "police society" in which the proliferation of criminal laws, enforcement officials, criminal courts, and prisons was not essentially for protection of the "general welfare" of society but was for the protection of the interests and lifestyles of but one segment of society—those holding positions of wealth, "respectability," and power.

The establishment of a police society in the United Sates made possible a new conception of law and order in which more effective control of the population was feasible. Central to this conception were laws governing the private behavior of citizens where no self-defined victims are involved—the vice laws. Thus, the growth of the police was necessary for the growth of both law and crime.

TRANSITION FROM A CONSTABULARY TO A POLICE SOCIETY

The first official responsible for the enforcement of law and order in the New World was the constable. The law as written was oppressive—outlawing swearing, lying, sabbath breaking, and night walking—and gave to the constable almost totalitarian pow-

* Reprinted from *Catalyst,* no. 5 (Summer 1970), special issue: "Crime, Law, and the State," pp. 76–97.

ers to enforce the laws.[1] However, the constable did not use his power to discover and punish deviation from the established laws. Rather, he assisted complaining citizens if and when they sought his help. This reflected the conception of law during colonial times: the written law was regarded as an ideal, rather than as prescriptions actually to be enforced.

Initially, the constableship was a collective responsibility which all able-bodied men were expected to assume. It was not a specialized occupation or an income-producing job, but a service to the community. The constableship was so thankless a task, however, that as early as 1653, fines were sometimes levied against anyone refusing to serve.[2]

The constable served only during the day. At night, the towns formed a citizens' watch or night watch. Supposedly, each adult male took his turn, but as with the constable those who could hired substitutes. In contrast to our present police the concerns of the night watch were more closely related to the general welfare. They included looking out for fires, reporting the time, and describing the weather.

Thus, there was no *one* specialized agency responsible for social control. Not only was the power divided between the constable and the night watch, but initially, both were volunteer services rotated among the citizens. This lack of specialization of enforcement of law and order extended to a comparative lack of specialization in the punishment of offenders. Although prisons were constructed as early as 1637, they were almost never kept in good enough condition to prevent jailbreaks. The financial costs of jails were considered prohibitive; corporal punishments, such as whippings, were preferred.[3] Thus, there was no specialized penal system, staffed and available.

Early police

The constabulary was not able to survive the growth of urban society and the concomitant economic specialization. Charles

---

[1] Carl Bridenbaugh, *Cities in the Wilderness: The First Century of Urban Life in America* (New York: A. A. Knopf, [1938] 1955), p. 64.

[2] Ibid., p. 65.

[3] Carl Bridenbaugh, *Cities in Revolt: Urban Life in America, 1743–1776* (New York: A. A. Knopf, 1955), p. 119.

Reith writes that voluntary observance of the laws

can be seen to have never survived in effective form the advent of community prosperity, as this brings into being, inevitably, differences in wealth and social status, and creates, on this basis, classes and parties and factions with or without wealth and power and privileges. In the presence of these divisions, community unanimity in voluntary law observance disappears and some other means of securing law observance and the maintenance of authority and order must be found.[4]

By 1800 in the larger cities the constabulary had changed from a voluntary position to a quasi-professional one, being either appointed or elected and providing an income. Some people resisted this step, claiming that such police were threats to civil liberty, and that they performed duties each citizen should perform himself. However, in the 1840s and 1850s, the night watch was gradually incorporated into an increasingly professionalized police, establishing twenty-four responsibility and in other ways beginning to institute the type of law enforcement that we have today.[5]

In the 1850s, cities began to employ detectives. The earliest detectives represented an attempt to apply the conception of the constableship to urban society. That is, the duties of the detective were to assist in recovering stolen property, not to prevent crime. However, this application of the constableship to the emerging urban society proved ineffective. For one thing, to recover stolen property effectively, familiarity with criminals was a necessary qualification and quite naturally ex-criminals were often hired. For another, detectives became corrupted through taking advantage of a system known as compromises. Under this system, it was legal for a thief to negotiate with the robbed owner and agree to return part of the stolen goods, if the thief could remain free. Detectives, however, would often supplement their salaries by accepting thieves' offers of a portion of the stolen goods in exchange of their immunity.[6]

---

[4] Charles Reith, *The Blind Eye of History: A Study of the Origins of the Present Police Era* (London: Farber and Farber, 1952), p. 210.

[5] David Bordua and Albert Reiss, Jr., "Law Enforcement," in Paul F. Lazarsfeld and others, *The Uses of Sociology* (New York: Basic Books, Inc., 1967), p. 276.

[6] Edward Crapsey, *The Nether Side of New York* (New York: Sheldon and Co., 1872), pp. 15–16. Today, "compromises" sometimes occur in civil rather than criminal court cases, or as "out of court" settlements, available only in white-collar criminality. See Edwin H. Sutherland, "White Collar Criminality," in *Radical Perspectives on Social Problems*, ed. by Frank Lindenfeld (New York: Macmillan Co., 1968), pp. 149–159.

Understandably, detectives were reluctant to devote their time to anything other than large-scale robbery. Murder, an amateur crime at this time, went uninvestigated. Detectives essentially served the private interests of big business at the expense of the general public.

By 1880, the detective forces as such had acquired such adverse publicity that in most places they were formally abolished. Their functions and services however were incorporated into the regular police. Compromises were no longer legally acceptable.

Historical sources of the change from constabulary to police

Central to the development of the professional police is the development of economic inequality. Seldon Bacon in his study of the development of the municipal police sees the increasing economic specialization and the resulting "class stratification" as the primary cause for the development of police.[7] He argues that specialists could exploit the increasing dependence of the populace on their services. Cities responded by creating specialized offices of independent inspectors who attempted to prevent exploitation or cheating of the populace. For example, the necessity in New Amsterdam to rely on specialized suppliers of firewood led as early as 1658 to the employment of firewood inspectors. Regulation of butchers, bakers, and hack drivers showed the same consequences of the inability of the citizen to rely on his own resources in a period of increasing specialization.[8]

By the time of the emergence of the professional police, the list of regulatory or inspectorial officials had grown quite long. Bacon describes the development of "the night police, the market police, street police, animal police, liquor police, the vagabond and stranger police, vehicle police, fire police, election police, Sunday police and so on."[9] Gradually, many of these special police or inspectors were removed from the professional police to other municipal agencies. "Only slowly did regulaton for the public

---

[7] Seldon Bacon, *The Early Development of American Municipal Police* (unpublished Ph.D. dissertation, Yale University, 1939), vol. 1 and 2.

[8] Bacon, op. cit., vol. 1, cited in Bordua and Reiss, op. cit., p. 277.

[9] Ibid., pp. 279–80.

good and the maintenance of order become themselves specializations and the full-time career police develop."[10]

The other central element in the development of the professional police was rioting, which is closely related to economic inequality. Usually, riots are an attempt by the have-nots to seek a redress of grievances from those with power and wealth. The solid citizens, on the other hand, wanted to prevent riots, to stop the disturbances in the streets. An official history of the Buffalo police states that in March of 1834 complaints of riot and disorder continued to pour in upon the mayor. "Rowdies paraded the streets at night, unmolested, and taxpayers became alarmed regarding both life and property."[11] Roger Lane writes of Boston, that "The problem of mob violence . . . soon compelled the municipality to take a more significant step, to create a new class of permanent professional officers with new standards of performance."[12]

David Bordua and Albert Reiss write:

The paramilitary form of early police bureaucracy was a response not only, or even primarily, to crime *per se,* but to the possibility of riotous disorder. Not crime and danger but the "criminal" and "dangerous classes" as part of the urban social structure led to the formation of uniformed and military organized police. Such organizations intervened between the propertied elites and the propertyless masses who were regarded as politically dangerous as a class.[13]

Riots became so frequent that the traditional method of controlling them by use of military forces became less and less effective. Military forces were unable to arrive at the scene of trouble before rioting had already reached uncontrollable proportions. This illustrates how the military may be able temporarily to enforce laws but are ineffective for sustained law enforcement.[14] The police, not the military, represent the continued presence of the central political authority.

Furthermore, in a riot situation, the direct use of social and

---

[10] Bordua and Reiss, op. cit., p. 280.

[11] Mark S. Hubbell, *Our Police and Our City: A Study of the Official History of the Buffalo Police Department* (Buffalo: Bensler and Wesley, 1893), pp. 57–58.

[12] Roger Lane, *Policing the City—Boston, 1822–1885* (Cambridge: Harvard University Press, 1967), p. 26.

[13] Bordua and Reiss, op. cit., p. 282.

[14] Reith, op cit., p. 19.

economic superiors as the agents of suppression increases class violence.

If the power structure armed itself and fought a riot or a rebellious people, this created more trouble and tension than the original problem. But, if one can have an independent police which fights the mob, then antagonism is directed toward police, not the power structure. A paid professional police seems to separate "constitutional" authority from social and economic dominance.[15]

These trends towards the establishment of a paramilitary police were given further impetus by the Civil War. It was the glory of the Army uniform that helped the public accept a uniformed police. Previously, the police themselves, as well as the public, had objected to uniforms as implying a police state with the men as agents of a king or ruler. A uniformed police was seen as contradictory to the ideals of the American Revolution, to a republic of free men.[16] But after 1860 the police began to carry guns, although at first unofficially. Within twenty years, however, most cities were furnishing guns along with badges.

The professional police and the new concept of law

As the cities changed from a constabulary to a professional police, so was there a change in the conception of law. Whereas the constable had only investigated crimes in which a citizen had complained, the new professional police were expected to *prevent* crime. A preventive conception of law requires that the police take the initiative and seek out those engaged in violating the law—those engaged in specific behaviors that are designated as illegal. Once an individual has been arrested for breaking a law, he is then identified, labeled, and treated as a criminal. The whole person then becomes a criminal—not just an individual who has broken a law. Since now too, professional police were responsible for maintaining public order—seen as preventing crime—they came to respond to individuals who committed unlawful acts as criminal persons—as wholly illegitimate.

---

[15] Allan Silver, "The Demand for Order in Civil Society: A Review of Some Themes in the History of Urban Crime, Police, and Riot," in David J. Bordua, *The Police: Six Sociological Essays* (New York: Wiley, 1967), pp. 11–12.

[16] Raymond Fosdick, *American Police Systems* (New York: The Century Co., 1921), p. 70.

Processing people through this machinery stigmatizes people—i.e., publicly identifies the whole person in terms of only certain of his behavior patterns. At the same time, this often leads to acceptance by such persons of the identity. In this and other ways the transition to police society *created* the underworld. A professional police creates a professional underworld.[17]

The "yellow press," which had emerged by the middle of the nineteenth century, focused on crime and violence. This helped confirm the new definition and stigmatization of the criminal person. Reporters obtained their stories by attending police courts. Police court reportage became so popular that even the conservative press eventually came to adopt it. And the police became guides to the newly discovered underworld.[18]

The establishment of a professional police concerned with prevention increases the power of the state. Roger Lane writes:

> Before the 1830s the law in many matters was regarded as the expression of an ideal. The creation of a strong police raised the exciting possibility that the ideal might be realized, that morality could be enforced and the state made an instrument of social regeneration.[19]

With the idea of prevention, then, law loses its status as only an ideal and becomes a real prescription actually to be enforced.

Those involved in the reform movements of the 1830s were quick to demand the services of the new police. Although they had originally objected to hiring paid, daytime police, they soon began to welcome the police as part of the reform movement, seeing the police as "moral missionaries" eventually eliminating crime and vice.[20] As Howard Becker writes, "The final outcome of a moral crusade is a police force."[21]

During the first half of the nineteenth century, the professional police increasingly took over and expanded the duties of the constableship. This led to the police themselves becoming specialists in the maintenance of public order, which involved a transition to

[17] See Lane, op. cit., p. 54.

[18] Ibid., p. 50.

[19] Ibid., p. 222.

[20] Ibid., p. 49.

[21] Howard S. Becker, *Outsiders: Studies in the Sociology of Deviance* (Glencoe: The Free Press, 1963), p. 156.

emphasizing the prevention of crime, and the role of law as ideal became an attempt to enforce laws as real prescriptions governing conduct. In this way the police, as an agency of the state, took over the function of social control from the members of the local community. The historical sources of the change were economic inequality and increasing riots. Thus, the police became an agency of those with wealth and power, for suppressing the attempts by the have-nots to re-distribute the wealth and power.

Thus, the professional police gave the upper classes an extremely useful and powerful mechanism for maintaining the unequal distribution of wealth and power: Law, which is proclaimed to be for the general welfare, is in fact an instrument in class warfare. This is most clearly demonstrated by looking at the history of the vice laws. Social control is at its greatest when the state has the power to govern the private behavior of citizens—when the state can declare illegal and punish acts in which all parties are willing participants.

THE VICE LAWS AS SOCIAL CONTROL: THE CASE OF ALCOHOL

The most celebrated vice problem in America is the use of alcohol. The use of alcohol dates back to early colonial times, during which nearly everybody drank: men, women, and children—it was an indispensable part of living. Drinking was usually family-centered and family-controlled, or part of community events.[22]

In early colonial times, mostly wine and beer were imbibed, with hard liquor (distilled spirits) in third place. However, hard liquor was much easier to transport as well as less subject to spoilage than wine and beer or the grains from which they were derived. As the colonies developed a market economy, this pushed the manufacturing and selling of hard liquors rather than beer and wine. The manufacturing and selling of hard liquor became an important part of the developing colonial commerce. "During the years immediately preceding the Revolution, more than 600,000 gallons were shipped abroad annually."[23]

---

[22] Robert Straus, "Alcohol," in Robert K. Merton and Robert A. Nisbet, eds., *Contemporary Social Problems* (New York: Harcourt, Brace, and World, Inc., Second ed. 1966), p. 244.

[23] Herbert Asbury, *The Great Illusion: An Informal History of Prohibition* (Garden City, N.Y.: Doubleday and Co., Inc. 1950), p. 7.

As the manufacturing changed from wine and beer to hard liquor, so did the drinking habits of the colonists. By the end of the eighteenth century about 90 percent of the alcohol consumed in this country was in the form of hard liquor. "By 1807, it is recorded that Boston had one distillery for every forty inhabitants—but only two breweries."[24]

Just as the drinking began to change from beer and wine to hard liquor, so also, around 1750, the context began to change from a family activity to an individual one. Men, especially young, unattached men, and other "peripheral segments" of society, began to do most of the drinking.[25] Saloons and taverns, instead of the home, became the place to drink.

These changes brought about a great increase in the amount and frequency of intoxication. Spirits are more intoxicating than either wine or beer, and the context of the saloon places no restrictions on consumption. The thirty years preceding and the fifty years following the American Revolution were an era of extremely heavy drinking.[26]

The Temperance/Prohibition Movement

As the amount and frequency of drunkenness increased, so did social concern about drinking. Drunkenness was often accompanied by destructive behavior. Intoxication came to be seen "as a threat to the personal well-being and property of peaceful citizens."[27] In this way, the call to moderation was an attempt to control those who were seen as a threat by the "solid" citizens. And so the Temperance Movement began in the last half of the eighteenth century.

In the 1830s the Temperance Movement altered its goal from moderation to abstinence. Why did abstinence, rather than moderation, become the symbol of respectability? Joseph R. Gusfield, who has interpreted the Temperance/Prohibition Movement in terms of its symbolic meanings and status conflicts, considers the Temperance Movement and ultimately Prohibition as a quest for

---

[24] Straus, op. cit., p. 245.

[25] Asbury, op. cit., pp. 13–14; Straus, op cit., p. 246.

[26] Asbury, op. cit., p. 13.

[27] Straus, op. cit., p. 246.

honor and power. Gusfield argues that coercive reform, or the change from temperance to abstinence, became necessary with the decline of the pre–Civil War Federalist aristocracy and the rise to social and political importance of the "common man," that which is symbolized by Andrew Jackson's election to the presidency.[28]

To make the new common man respond to the moral ideals of the old order, was both a way of maintaining the prestige of the old aristocracy and an attempt to control the character of the political electorate.[29]

Lyman Beecher, a leading Temperance leader, puts it more forcefully.

When the laboring classes are contaminated, the right to suffrage becomes the engine of destruction. . . . As intemperance increases, the power of taxation will come more and more into the hands of men of intemperate habits and desperate fortunes; of course, the laws will gradually become subservient to the debtor and less efficacious in protecting the rights of property.[30]

The insistence on total abstinence came just when the country's drinking habits were becoming more moderate and changing from hard liquors back again to wine and beer. In 1800, when most drinking was of hard liquor, 90 percent of the white population was from Britain. By 1840, the immigration of ethnic groups from southern, central, and eastern Europe (where drinking habits were of wine and beer) acted as a moderating influence on the drinking habits of the nation.[31] Only total abstinence, then, would be a symbol of power and respectability—moderation was not enough to indicate superiority.

The change from moderation to abstinence was reflected in the laws of Massachusetts. In 1835, a Massachusetts statute revision made single incidences of drunkenness a punishable offense. Prior to this only the habitually drunk were usually arrested. In Boston, the number of drunk arrests jumped from the few hundred annually during the 1830s to several thousand in the 1840s and 1850s. Even before the middle of the century, Theodore Parker

---

[28] Joseph R. Gusfield, *Symbolic Crusade: Status Politics and the American Temperance Movement* (Urbana: University of Illinois Press, 1966).

[29] Ibid., p. 21.

[30] Lyman Beecher, *Six Sermons on Intemperance* (New York: American Trust Society, 1843), pp. 57–58, quoted in Gusfield, ibid., p. 43.

[31] Straus, op. cit., p. 249.

believed that "the 'rude tuition' of courts and constables was improving the drinking habits of the Irish immigrants."[32] In 1841, the Boston Society for the Suppression of Intoxication petitioned for a doubling of the police force.[33]

Thus, the Temperance/Prohibition Movement was an effort to control the "dangerous classes," to make them conform to middle class standards of respectability. As is so often the case, the stated goals of improving society or helping the unfortunates muted the fact that this "help" came in the form of control—the police power of the state. Not only did alcohol use come to be universally defined as a social problem, but criminal law and police enforcement were commonly seen as the solution to the problem.

The thought and research of seemingly all fields could be used to support the claims of the prohibitionists. Based on research done in the last half of the nineteenth century, scientists began to describe the negative effects alcohol has on the human body, and for the first time, claimed that even moderate drinking might cause liver, kidney, and heart diseases.[34]

In 1914, psychiatrists and neurologists meeting in Chicago adopted a resolution concluding that the availability of alcoholic beverages caused a large amount of mental, moral, and physical degeneracy and urged the medical profession "to take the lead in securing prohibitory legislation."[35]

Temperance groups were even able to utilize mortality studies done by insurance companies. A study drawing on the experience of two million policy holders between 1885 and 1908, concluded that those who drank the equivalent of only two glasses of beer each day showed a mortality rate of 18 percent higher than average. Furthermore, those who drank two ounces or more of alcohol each day were found to have a mortality rate of 86 percent higher than insured lives in general.[36]

Social workers, lawyers, and judges began to claim that alcohol

---

[32] Lane, op. cit., p. 49.

[33] Ibid.

[34] J. H. Timberlake, *Prohibition and the Progressive Movement, 1900–1920* (Cambridge: Harvard University Press, 1963), p. 41.

[35] *Anti-Saloon League, Proceedings*, 1919, pp. 45–46, quoted in ibid., p. 47.

[36] Edward B. Phelps, "The Mortality from Alcohol in the United States—The Results of a Recent Investigation of the Contributory Relation with Each of the Assigned Causes of Adult Mortality," International Congress of Hygiene and Demography, *Transactions*, 1912 (6 vols., Washington, 1913), vol. 1, pp. 813–822, quoted in Timberlake, op. cit., pp. 54–55.

played an important role in crime. On the basis of a study of 13,402 convicts in twelve different states, the community leaders of one city concluded that "intemperance had been the sole cause of crime in 16 percent of the cases, the primary cause in 31 percent, and one of the causes in nearly 50 percent."[37] Alcohol was also claimed to be an important factor in prostitution and venereal disease. (One physician reported that 70 percent of all venereal infection in men under 25 was contracted while under the influence of alcohol.)[38]

In addition, Prohibitionists claimed the use of alcoholic beverages was an important factor in domestic unhappiness and broken homes. "According to a study by the U.S. Bureau of the Census, for the years 1887–1906, nearly 20 percent of all divorces were granted for reasons of intemperance."[39]

Even notable academicians argued that alcohol was one of the chief factors creating crime and that the state ought to abolish it.[40] A noted sociologist felt that instituting national prohibition would reduce crime and poverty, improve the position of women and children, benefit the home, purify politics, and elevate the status of the wage earner.[41]

The Volstead Act and enforcement

The Prohibitionists were successful, and in 1918 the Volstead Act was passed. As is well known, the attempt to enforce the Volstead Act resulted in corruption unparalleled in American history. Stories of dry agents and other governmental personnel responsible for enforcement conniving with smugglers or accepting bribes appeared in the newspapers day after day. For example, in Philadelphia, a grand jury investigation in 1928 showed that one police "inspector had $193,533.22 in his bank account, another

---

[37] John Koren, *Economic Aspects of the Liquor Problem* (Boston, 1899), p. 30, quoted in Timberlake, op. cit., p. 57.

[38] John B. Huber "The Effects of Alcohol," *Collier's Weekly*, vol. 57, June 3, 1916, p. 32, quoted in Timberlake, op. cit., p. 58.

[39] George Elliot Howard, "Alcohol and Crime: A Study in Social Causation," *The American Journal of Sociology*, vol. 24, July 1918, p. 79, quoted in Timberlake, op. cit., p. 58.

[40] Howard, op. cit., pp. 61–64, and 80, quoted in Timberlake, op. cit., p. 60.

[41] Edward A. Ross, "Prohibition as a Sociologist Sees It," *Harper's Monthly Magazine*, vol. 142, January 1921, p. 188; this article was reprinted in Ross' *The Social Trend* (New York, 1922), pp. 137–160, and quoted in Timberlake, op. cit., pp. 60–61.

had \$102,829.45, and a third had \$40,412.75. One police captain had accumulated a nest egg of \$133,845.86, and nine had bank accounts ranging from \$14,607.44 to \$68,905.89.″[42]

By the fall of 1923 in Philadelphia, things were so bad that the mayor requested President Harding to lend the city the services of Brigadier General Smedley D. Butler of the Marine Corps, a famous soldier of World War I. General Butler arrived and began a whirlwind round of raids and arrests. At first it appeared he would succeed in enforcing the Volstead Act, but then: places were found empty when raids were attempted (they had been warned); the courts would dismiss cases brought before them. General Butler stuck it out for two years before returning to the Marine Corps declaring the job had been a waste of time: "trying to enforce the law in Philadelphia," he said, "was worse than any battle I was ever in."[43]

When the Volstead Act was passed, the Justice Department made no special preparation to handle extra violators. The result is that within a few months federal courts throughout the country were overwhelmed by the number of dry cases, and Emory R. Buckner, United States Attorney from New York, told a congressional committee in 1926 that

violators of the Volstead Act were being brought into the Federal Building in New York City at the rate of about fifty thousand a year, and the United States Attorney's office was five months behind in the preliminary steps of preparing cases.[44]

The volume of law-breakers was so tremendous that those who could pay the fines and/or bribe the officials, went free. A jury trial was impossible.[45]

And so goes the story of the attempt to enforce Prohibition. It is generally thought of as such a fiasco, such an aberration of American justice, that those who study it feel a need for an explanation of its existence. This need for explanation, however, usually does not extend to our other vice laws, such as drug laws, which are still seen as supporting democracy and justice for all.

---

[42] Asbury, op. cit., p. 185
[43] Ibid., p. 186.
[44] Ibid., p. 169.
[45] Ibid., pp. 169–170.

THE VICE LAWS AS SOCIAL CONTROL: THE CASE OF NARCOTIC DRUGS

The scientific condemnation of the dangers involved in the use of alcohol did not extend even to warnings about the dangers in the use of opium and its derivatives. Indeed, the use of such drugs was systematically encouraged in the nineteenth century. Opium constituted the main therapeutic agent of medical men for more than two thousand years—through the nineteenth century. A physician writes:

Even in the last half of the 19th century, there was little recognition of and less attention paid to overindulgence in or abuse of opium. It was a panacea for all ills. When a person became dependent upon it so that abstinence symptoms developed if a dose or two were missed, more was taken for the aches and pains and other discomforts of abstinence, just as it was taken for similar symptoms from any other cause.[46]

In 1804 a German chemist isolated morphine. In this country, morphine began to be applied hypodermically in the 1850s. At first, it was declared that administration through the skin, as opposed to through the mouth, was *not* habit forming. Although there were soon isolated warnings that the hypodermic habit was even harder to break than the oral habit, the great majority of textbooks on the practice of medicine failed to issue any warning of the dangers of the hypodermic use of morphine until 1900.[47]

In 1898 heroin was isolated. Heroin is approximately three times as powerful as morphine and morphine is more potent than opium. Opium is generally smoked while its derivatives are taken orally or with hypodermic needles.[48] At first, it was also claimed that heroin was free from addiction-forming properties, possessing many of the virtues and none of the dangers of morphine and codeine. Heroin was even recommended as a treatment for those addicted to morphine and codeine. For the next few years, doctors continued to report in medical journals, on the curative and therapeutic value of heroin, either omitting any reference to ad-

---

[46] Nathan E. Eddy, "The History of the Development of Narcotics." Reprinted, with permission, from a symposium on Narcotics appearing in *Law and Contemporary Problems* (Vol. 22, No. 1, Winter, 1957) published by the Duke University School of Law, Durham, North Carolina. Copyright, 1957, by Duke University.

[47] Charles E. Terry and Mildred Pellens, *The Opium Problem* (New York: Haddon Craftsmen, 1928), p. 72.

[48] Alfred R. Lindesmith, *Addiction and Opiates* (Chicago: Aldine, 1968 ed. [first published 1947]), p. 208.

diction, or assuming any addiction to be very mild and much less bothersome than morphine addiction. It was 1910 before the medical profession began to warn of the addictive dangers of heroin.[49]

Throughout the nineteenth century, if overindulgence was necessary, many preferred addiction to narcotics than alcohol. In 1889 a doctor observed:

> The only grounds on which opium in lieu of alcohol can be claimed as reformatory are that it is less inimical to healthy life than alcohol, that it calms in place of exciting the baser passions, and hence is less productive of acts of violence and crime; in short, that as a whole the use of morphine in place of alcohol is but a choice of evils, and by far the lesser. . . .
>
> I might, had I time and space, enlarge by statistics to prove the law-abiding qualities of opium-eating peoples, but of this anyone can perceive somewhat for himself, if he carefully watches and reflects on the quiet, introspective gaze of the morphine habitué and compares it with the riotous devil-may-care leer of the drunkard.[50]

During the nineteenth century it was primarily the respectable rather than the criminal classes who used the drug. It has been suggested that part of the reason the use of opium became so popular at this time was that the respectable people "crave the effect of a stimulant but will not risk their reputation for temperance by taking alcoholic beverages."[51]

Drugs could be purchased openly and cheaply from the drugstores. Not only could the narcotics themselves be bought, but many kinds of opiate-containing patent medicines were advertised. Anyone interested could buy paregoric, laudanum, tincture of opium, morphine, Womslow's Soothing Syrup, Godfrey's Cordial, McMunn's Elixir of Opium, or others.[52] "The more you drink," one tonic advertised, "the more you want." Mothers fed their babies 750,000 bottles of opium-laced syrup a year.[53]

Whereas white Americans previously had used opium in all other derivative forms, the smoking of opium was introduced by

[49] Terry and Pellens, op. cit., pp. 78–85.

[50] J. R. Black, "Advantages for Substituting the Morphia Habit for the Incurably Alcoholic," *Cincinnati Lancet-Clinic*, vol. 22, 1889, pp. 537–541, quoted in Lindesmith, op. cit., pp. 211–212.

[51] Rufus King, "Narcotic Drug Laws and Enforcement Policies," *Law and Contemporary Problems*, vol. 22, Winter 1957, p. 113.

[52] Lindesmith, op. cit., p. 210.

[53] Stanley Meisler, "Federal Narcotics Czar," *The Nation*, February 20, 1960, p. 159.

Chinese immigrants in California, and was outlawed in San Francisco in 1875.[54] This is the first time opium or any of its derivatives were outlawed in the United States. It appears that the legislation outlawing opium was an attempt to control the Chinese immigrants, to make them conform to the "American Way of Life," much as the drinking laws in Boston in the 1830s and 1840s were used to control the Irish immigrants.

THE HARRISON ACT AND ENFORCEMENT

In 1914 Congress passed the Harrison Act. While with the Volstead Act it is clear that total abstinence was the goal and intent of the law, it is unclear as to the actual intentions of Congress when the Harrison Act was passed. Some authors contend that the Harrison Act was intended only as a revenue measure, attempting to tax drugs. The desire was to regulate the use of drugs, not to impose abstinence. The careful wording of the Harrison Act which allows for medical doctors to treat or prescribe drugs for addict-patients is referred to as evidence. Whatever the original intentions of Congress, through a series of Supreme Court rulings, by 1922 the Harrison Act came to mean total abstinence for all.[55]

As with the Volstead Act, legislation of the Harrison Act was easier than enforcement. It is difficult to enforce laws preventing activities in which all parties are willing participants. This is especially true when the contraband object is very small in size. In this way, the existence of laws prohibiting crimes without victims increases the power of the police as it necessitates and legitimates a close surveillance of the population.

In order to enforce laws preventing activities in which there is no citizen-complainant, police must develop an information system and much of police energy is devoted to finding lawbreakers.[56] "The informer system has become such an intrinsic component of police work that the abilities of a professional detective have come to be defined in terms of his capacity to utilize this

---

[54] Terry and Pellens, op. cit., p. 73.

[55] See Lindesmith, op. cit., p. 6; and King, op. cit., p. 121.

[56] See Jerome Skolnick and J. Richard Woodworth, "Bureaucracy, Information, and Social Control: A Study of a Morals Detail," in Bordua (ed.), *The Police: Six Sociological Essays,* op. cit., pp. 99–136.

system."[57] Or as Westley puts it: "a detective is as good as his stool pigeon." Westley adds further that the solutions to crimes are largely the result of bargains detectives make with underworld figures.[58]

The relation of detective to informer is illustrated by the following newspaper report on the retirement of Mr. Dean J. Gavin, detective sergeant of the Buffalo police, after thirty-four years of police work, seventeen of them as a member of the Narcotics Squad.

His contacts in the underworld are legion. And when he sends out a message seeking information on anything from a burglary to a narcotics delivery, the tenants in crime's jungle make certain that Dean Gavin gets the answers.

The criminals who maintain the information-gathering network for Detective Sgt. Gavin have a universal contempt for the police . . . but they respect him.[59]

Police, then, need informers to enforce the vice laws. The existence of vice laws assures the police of a sizeable group who are in need of the favors and generosity of the police, and thus are willing to serve as informers for those favors. Police can reward the cooperative informer by reduced sentences or failure to prosecute. The stiffer and more severe the penalty, the greater the amount of bargaining power or discretion in the hands of the police—the greater the penalty, the greater the power of the police.

The police-informer system rests on the ability of the police to withhold prosecution if they desire. This means the cooperation of the district attorney and even the courts is necessary. An informer system assumes the absence of an injured party, and of a citizen complainant.

The difficulty of enforcing laws without a complainant is clearly shown in the enforcement of the narcotic laws. The addict-informer becomes the chief source of information for violation of the narcotic laws. Police attempt to arrest the big-time operator

---

[57] Jerome H. Skolnick, *Justice without Trial: Law Enforcement in Democratic Society* (New York: Wiley), p. 238.

[58] William A. Westley, *The Police: A Sociological Study of Law, Custom, and Morality* (unpublished Ph.D. dissertation, University of Chicago, 1951), pp. 70–71.

[59] Ray Hill, "Even the Crooks He Pursues Respect Gavin," *Buffalo Evening News,* February 3, 1968, Sunday edition.

through the addict-informer. "The Bureau of Narcotics is authorized to pay the 'operating expenses' of informants whose information leads to seizure of drugs in illicit traffic."[60] Narcotic agents will supply informants with drugs, money to purchase drugs, or allow them to steal for money to purchase drugs. Thus, the law permits narcotic agents to do precisely what it forbids the doctor—supply the addicted with drugs.

Some lawyers have been disturbed at the Federal Bureau's dependence on informers. In a 1960 decision, Judge David Bazelon of the U.S. Court of Appeals for the District of Columbia Circuit criticized the Narcotics Bureau:

> It is notorious that the narcotics informer is often himself involved in the narcotics traffic and is often paid for his information in cash, narcotics, immunity from prosecution, or lenient punishment. . . . Under such stipulation it is to be expected that the informer will not infrequently reach for shadowy leads, or even seek to incriminate the innocent.[61]

In March 1959, in New York, a district judge acquitted a defendant who had been enticed into addiction by an informer for the Bureau of Narcotics. The judge said the defendant's participation in the crime "was a creation of the productivity of law-enforcement officers."[62]

Once an individual is labeled an addict by the police, there is no restraint on their power. Police can break into a known addict's residence. If they find narcotics in his possession or marks on his arm, they can demand that he "rat" on his source or spend ninety days in jail and face the "cold turkey" treatment. Once an individual has had "narcotic" dealings with the police, he can expect further dealings. If he should object to strong-arm methods or lack of "due process," the police can threaten to punish him with the full force of the laws.

It appears, then, that the enforcement of laws against activities in which there is no citizen complainant does not occur along legal lines. Establishing laws which proscribe such activities and establishing a police force to discover and prosecute persons who en-

---

[60] Edwin M. Schur, *Crime without Victims: Deviant Behavior and Public Policy* (Englewood Cliffs, N.J.: Prentice-Hall, Inc., 1965), p. 135.

[61] Stanley Meisler, "Federal Narcotics Czar," *The Nation*, February 20, 1960, p. 160.

[62] Ibid.

gage in such activities maximizes the possibilities of social control, in that it necessitates and legitimates a close surveillance of the population.

SELECTIVE ENFORCEMENT OF THE VICE LAWS: THE IMMUNITY OF THE POWERFUL

It has been argued that the police and the legal system serve the interests of the powerful. This has been shown previously in that the powerful are able to get their own moral values passed as laws of the land—this is part of the definition of power. Also, however, they appear to be immune from the application or enforcement of the law. This can be substantiated by looking at the mechanics of enforcement. The police tend to divide the populace into two groups—the criminal and the non-criminal—and treat each accordingly. In police academies the recruits are told: "There are two kinds of people you arrest: those who pay the fine and those who don't."[63]

William Westley asked the policemen in his study to describe the section of the general public that likes the police. Replies included:

"The law-abiding element likes the police. Well the people that are settled down are polite to policemen, but the floater—people who move around—are entirely different. They think we are after them."[64]

Westley concludes that "the better class of people," those from better residential neighborhoods and skilled workers, are treated with politeness and friendliness, because "that is the way to make them like you." In the policeman's relation to the middle class, "The commission of a crime by an individual is not enough to classify him a criminal."[65]

He sees these people [middle class] as within the law, that is, as being within the protection of the law, and as a group he has to observe the letter of the law in his treatment of them. Their power forces him to do so. No distinction is gained from the apprehension of such a person. Essentially, they do not fall into the category of potential criminals.[66]

---

[63] Westley, op. cit., p. 95.

[64] Ibid., p. 161.

[65] Ibid., p. 166.

[66] Ibid., p. 167.

Whereas, for people in the slums, the patrolman feels that roughness is necessary, both to make them respect the policeman and to maintain order and conformity. Patrolmen are aware that it is slum dwellers' lack of power which enables them to use roughness and ignore "due process."

Skolnick writes that the police wish that "civil liberties people" would recognize the differences that police follow in applying search and seizure laws to respectable citizens and to criminals.[67]

The immunity of those with power and wealth to having the law apply to them is so traditional that the police in one city were able to apply the normally withheld law enforcement to political officials as a measure of collective bargaining. The report of the activities of the Police Locust Club (police union), of Rochester, New York on the front page of the local newspaper is remarkable.

The first move was to ticket cars owned by public officials for violations of the state Motor Vehicle Law.

According to the club president, Ralph Boryszewski, other steps will include:

Refusal to "comply with requests from politicians for favors for themselves and their friends . . ."

Cracking down on after-hours spots and gambling establishments "which have been protected through the silent consent of public officials."

"These evils have existed as long as the police department has, and the public should know what's going on." Boryszewski said today. The slowdown is "really a speedup in enforcement of the law," he said. "The public won't be hurt, we're after the men who think they're above the law."[68]

A Vermont urologist was charged with failure to file an income tax return for the years 1962, 1963, and 1964. However, he entered a plea of nolo on the 1964 charge only. "The judge said he accepted the lesser plea solely because it might jeopardize the doctor's standing in the medical profession."[69]

Drug users who fail to fit the "dope fiend" image, that is, drug users who are from the "respectable" or upper classes, are not regarded as narcotic criminals and do not become part of the

---

[67] Skolnick, *Justice without Trial*, op. cit., p. 147.

[68] Everson Moran, "Officials' Cars Tagged in Police 'Slowdown,' " *The Times Union*, Greater Rochester Edition, July 2, 1968, p. 1.

[69] *Rutland Daily Herald*, April 19, 1969, p. 7.

official reports. When the addict is a well-to-do professional man, such as a physician or lawyer, and is well spoken and well educated, then prosecutors, policemen, and judges alike seem to agree that "the harsh penalties of the law . . . were surely not intended for a person like this, and, by an unspoken agreement, arrangements are quietly made to exempt him from such penalties."[70] The justification usually offered for not arresting addicted doctors and nurses is that they do not resort to crime to obtain drugs and are productive members of the community. "The only reason that users in the medical profession do not commit the crimes against property which other addicts do, is, of course, that drugs are available to them from medical sources."[71]

The more laws a nation passes, the greater the possible size of the criminal population. In 1912, Roscoe Pound pointed out "of one hundred thousand persons arrested in Chicago in 1912, more than one-half were held for violations of legal precepts which did not exist twenty-five years before."[72] Ten years ago, it was established that "the number of crimes for which one may be prosecuted has at least doubled since the turn of the century."[73]

The increase has been in misdemeanors, not felonies. Sutherland and Gehlke, studying trends from 1900–1930, found little increase in laws dealing with murder or robbery. "The increase came in areas where there was no general agreement: public morals, business ethics, and standards of health and safety,"[74]

The prevention of felonies, and the protection of the community from acts of violence, is usually given as the *raison d'être* of criminal law and the justification for a police system and penal sanctions. Yet, most police activity is concerned with misdemeanors, not felonies. Seldon Bacon writes:

> What are the crimes which hurt society so often and so intensely that the society must react to such disorder and must react in an effective way (i.e., with organization, equipment, and specialization)? The answer of the modern criminologist to this question is felonies. The case studies,

---

[70] Lindsmith, *The Addict and the Law,* op. cit., p. 90.

[71] Ibid.

[72] Quoted in Frances A. Allen, "The Borderland of Criminal Law: Problems of 'Socializing' Justice," *The Social Service Review,* vol. 32, June 1958, p. 108.

[73] Ibid.

[74] Cited in Richard C. Fuller, "Morals and the Criminal Law," *Journal of Criminal Law, Criminology, and Police Science,* vol. 32, March–April 1942, pp. 625–626.

however, clearly indicate that society does not react in these ways to felonies nearly as much as to misdemeanors. Indeed, the adjustment to felonious activity is a secondary if not a tertiary sphere of action. Moreover, judicial studies of the present day point to the same findings, misdemeanor cases outnumber felony cases 100 to 1. Yet the criminologists without exception have labored almost exclusively in the sphere of felonies.[75]

One writer noted that "in the three years from 1954 through 1956 arrests for drunkenness in Los Angeles constituted between 43 and 46 percent of all arrest bookings."[76] The importance of this is not in the prevalence of drunkenness as much as it is in the easy rationale afforded the police for maintaining order and conformity, for "keeping the peace."[77] Now that marijuana smoking is apparently so widespread, laws preventing its use give police an excuse to arrest anyone they see as a threat to "order."

Becker writes, "In America, only about six out of every hundred major crimes known to police result in jail sentences."[78] In addition, only about 20 percent of original reports find their way into criminal statistics.[79] It appears, then, that the police have considerable discretion in deciding which violators to punish, or in deciding when an individual has committed a violation.

The greater the number of punitive laws, and the stiffer the penalities, the easier it is to attempt enforcement of any *one* law. Police threaten prostitutes with arrest, using the threat to get a lead on narcotic arrests; if the prostitute informs, then there is no arrest or reduced charges.[80] Liquor laws can be used to regulate or control "homosexual" bars.[81] Burglary informants as well as narcotic informants are usually addicts. Skolnick writes, "In general, burglary detectives permit informants to commit narcotic offenses, while narcotic detectives allow informants to steal."[82]

---

[75] Bacon, vol. 2, op. cit., p. 784.

[76] Allen, op. cit., p. 111.

[77] Egon Bittner notes that "patrolmen do not really enforce the law, even when they do invoke it, but merely use it as a resource to solve certain pressing problems in keeping the peace." Egon Bittner, "The Police on Skid Row: A Study of Peace Keeping," *The American Sociological Review*, vol. 32, October 1967, p. 710.

[78] Becker, op. cit., p. 171.

[79] Skolnick, *Justice without Trial*, op. cit., p. 173.

[80] Ibid., p. 125.

[81] Schur, op. cit., p. 81.

[82] Skolnick, op. cit., p. 129.

As early as 1906, Professor Ernst Freund commented upon the range of criminal legislation. "Living under free institutions we submit to public regulation and control in ways that appear inconceivable to the spirit of oriental despotism."[83]

As the laws increase in range and number, the population is criminalized, especially the population from low-economic background, minority racial groups, or non-conformists in other ways. John I. Kitsuse writes about those labeled as deviant.

For in modern society, the socially significant differentiation of deviants from the nondeviant population is increasingly contingent upon circumstances of situation, place, social and personal biography, and the bureaucratically organized activities of agencies of control.[84]

CONCLUSION

The attempt to enforce vice laws, as laws prohibiting activities in which there is no self-defined victim, is frequently referred to as the attempt to enforce "conventional morality." The implication is that other laws, like laws proscribing murder, have something like a metaphysical transcultural base. Today, however, many conventional sociologists and criminologists have come to the conclusion that *all* activities of police and criminal courts, not just those concerned with vice laws, enforce the moral order—enforce conformity—rather than enforce the law. Bordua and Reiss write, "police above all link daily life to central authority; moral consensus is extended through the police as an instrument of legitimate coercion."[85] Allan Silver sees the extension of moral consensus and the development of the professional police as aspects of the same historical development—the "police are official representatives of the moral order."[86]

This appears to be an apparent conclusion when one realizes that "nothing is a crime which the law does not so regard and punish."[87] As Durkheim suggests, yesterday's bad taste is today's

---

[83] Quoted in Allen, op. cit., p. 108.

[84] John I. Kitsuse, "Societal Reaction to Deviant Behavior: Problems of Theory and Method." *Social Problems,* vol. 9, Winter 1962, p. 256.

[85] Bordua and Reiss, op. cit., p. 282.

[86] Silver, op. cit., in Bordua (ed.), *The Police: Six Sociological Essays,* op. cit., p. 14.

[87] F. H. Wines, *Punishment and Reformation: An Historical Sketch of the Rise of the Penitentiary Systems* (New York: Crowell and Co., 1895), p. 13.

criminal law.[88] Or, as Becker writes, "Deviance is not a quality of the act the person commits, but rather a consequence of the application by others of rules and sanctions to an 'offender.' "[89] F. H. Wines writes:

> Crime is not a character which attaches to an act. . . .
> It is a complex relation which the law created between itself and the law breaker. The law creates crime. It therefore creates the criminal, because crime cannot be said to exist apart from the criminal.[90]

As Saint Paul said, "Without the law, sin is dead."

Instituting prohibitive laws against any activity establishes the "language of punishment." The existence of "the autocratic criminal law . . . compels and accustoms men to control their fellows without their consent and against their wills. It conveys to them the idea that such must be and is inevitable."[91]

For purposes of social control, then, the effects of laws prohibiting murder and beer drinking are the same. The enforcement of both serves to maintain the unequal distribution of power and wealth.

It appears, therefore, that there are no substantive distinctions among the ideas of enforcing the moral order, enforcing conventional morality, enforcing conformity, enforcing the law, and maintaining the unequal distribution of power. Crimes are violations of those moral values that the nation-state enforces through punitive law. The morality enforced is always the morality of those in power and it is primarily enforced upon those without power. That a group's morality and value system is enforced is part of the definition of its having power. To put it thus, the unequal distribution of power and wealth is maintained in part by police enforcement of the morality and value system of those with power and wealth.

The vast number of our laws provides the means for selective enforcement, and selective enforcement means the immunity of

---

[88] Emile Durkheim, *The Rules of Sociological Method,* 8th ed. (Glencoe: The Free Press, 1966).

[89] Becker, op. cit., p. 9.

[90] Wines, op. cit., p. 24.

[91] Paul Reiwald, *Society and Its Criminals,* tr. by T. E. James (London: William Heinemann, 1949), p. 302.

the rich and powerful. The greater the number of laws, the easier it is to control those without power and wealth. The content of the laws is not crucial for purposes of social control. What is crucial is the power to establish the "language of punishment" (or conversely, "the language of legitimacy"), the power to institute both the enforcers of law—the police—and the violators of law—the criminals.

8

*Good people and dirty work**

Everett C. Hughes

". . . une secte est le *noyan* et le *levain* de toute foule. . . . Etudier la foule c'est juger un drame d'après ce qu'on voit sur la scène; étudier la secte c'est le juger d'après ce qu'on voit dans les coulisses."
Sighele, S. *Psychologie des sectes*. Paris, 1898. Pp. 62, 63, 65.[1]

The National Socialist Government of Germany, with the arm of its fanatical inner sect, the SS, commonly known as the Black Shirts or Elite Guard, perpetrated and boasted of the most colossal and dramatic piece of social dirty work the world has ever known. Perhaps there are other claimants to the title, but they could not match this one's combination of mass, speed and perverse pride in the deed. Nearly all peoples have plenty of cruelty and death to account for. How many Negro Americans have died by the hands of lynching mobs? How many more from unnecessary disease and lack of food or of knowledge of nutrition? How many Russians died to bring about collectivization of land? And who is to blame if there be starving millions in some parts of the world while wheat molds in the fields of other parts?

I do not revive the case of the Nazi *Endlösung* (final solution) of

* Reprinted from *Social Problems*, vol. 10, no. 1 (Summer, 1962), pp. 3–11.

[1] ". . . a sect is the nucleus and the yeast of every crowd. . . . To study a crowd is to judge by what one sees on the stage; to study the sect is to judge by what one sees backstage." These are among the many passages underlined by Robert E. Park in his copy, now in my possession, of Sighele's classic work on political sects. There are a number of references to this work in the Park and Burgess *Introduction to the Science of Sociology*, Chicago, 1921. In fact, there is more attention paid to fanatical political and religious behavior in Park and Burgess than in any later sociological work in this country. Sighele's discussion relates chiefly to the anarchist movement of his time. There have been fanatical movements since. The Secret Army Organization in Algeria is but the latest.

the Jewish problem in order to condemn the Germans, or make them look worse than other peoples, but to recall to our attention dangers which lurk in our midst always. Most of what follows was written after my first postwar visit to Germany in 1948. The impressions were vivid. The facts have not diminished and disappeared with time, as did the stories of alleged German atrocities in Belgium in the first World War. The fuller the record, the worse it gets.[2]

Several millions of people were delivered to the concentration camps, operated under the leadership of Heinrich Himmler with the help of Adolf Eichmann. A few hundred thousand survived in some fashion. Still fewer came out sound of mind and body. A pair of examples, well attested, will show the extreme of perverse cruelty reached by the SS guards in charge of the camps. Prisoners were ordered to climb trees; guards whipped them to make them climb faster. Once they were out of reach, other prisoners, also urged by the whip, were put to shaking the trees. When the victims fell, they were kicked to see whether they could rise to their feet. Those too badly injured to get up were shot to death, as useless for work. A not inconsiderable number of prisoners were drowned in pits full of human excrement. These examples are so horrible that your minds will run away from them. You will not, as when you read a slightly salacious novel, imagine the rest. I therefore thrust these examples upon you and insist that the people who thought them up could, and did, improvise others like them, and even worse, from day to day over several years. Many of the victims of the camps gave up the ghost (this Biblical phrase is the most apt) from a combination of humiliation, starvation, fatigue and physical abuse. In due time, a policy of mass liquidation in the gas chamber was added to individual virtuosity in cruelty.

This program—for it was a program—of cruelty and murder was carried out in the name of racial superiority and racial purity.

---

[2] The best source easily available at that time was Eugen Kogon's *Der Ss-Staat: Das System der Deutschen Konzentrationslager*, Berlin, 1946. Many of my data are from his book. Some years later H. G. Adler, after several years of research, wrote *Thereisanstadt, 1941–1945. Das Antlitz einer Zwangsgenmeinschaft* (Tübingen, 1955), and still later published *Die Verheimlichte Wahrheit, Theresienstädter Dokuments* (Tübingen, 1958), a book of documents concerning that camp in which Czech and other Jews were concentrated, demoralized and destroyed. Kogon, a Catholic intellectual, and Adler, a Bohemian Jew, both wrote out of personal experience in the concentration camps. Both considered it their duty to present the phenomenon objectively to the public. None of their statements has ever been challenged.

It was directed mainly, although by no means exclusively, against Jews, Slavs and Gypsies. It was thorough. There are few Jews in the territories which were under the control of the Third German Reich—the two Germanies, Holland, Czechoslovakia, Poland, Austria, Hungary. Many Jewish Frenchmen were destroyed. There were concentration camps even in Tunisia and Algiers under the German occupation.

When, during my 1948 visit to Germany, I became more aware of the reactions of ordinary Germans to the horrors of the concentration camps, I found myself asking not the usual question, "How did racial hatred rise to such a high level?", but this one, "How could such dirty work be done among and, in a sense, *by* the millions of ordinary, civilized German people?" Along with this came related questions. How could these millions of ordinary people live in the midst of such cruelty and murder without a general uprising against it and against the people who did it? How, once freed from the regime that did it, could they be apparently so little concerned about it, so toughly silent about it, not only in talking with outsiders—which is easy to understand—but among themselves? How and where could there be found in a modern civilized country the several hundred thousand men and women capable of such work? How were these people so far released from the inhibitions of civilized life as to be able to imagine, let alone perform, the ferocious, obscene and perverse actions which they did imagine and perform? How could they be kept at such a height of fury through years of having to see daily at close range the human wrecks they made and being often literally spattered with the filth produced and accumulated by their own actions?

You will see that there are here two orders of questions. One set concerns the good people who did not themselves do this work. The other concerns those who did do it. But the two sets are not really separate; for the crucial question concerning the good people is their relation to the people who did the dirty work, with a related one which asks under what circumstances good people let the others get away with such actions.

An easy answer concerning the Germans is that they were not so good after all. We can attribute to them some special inborn or ingrained race consciousness, combined with a penchant for sadistic cruelty and unquestioning acceptance of whatever is done by those who happen to be in authority. Pushed to its extreme, this answer simply makes us, rather than the Germans, the superior race. It is the Nazi tune, put to words of our own.

Now there are deep and stubborn differences between peoples. Their history and culture may make the Germans especially susceptible to the doctrine of their own racial superiority and especially acquiescent to the actions of whoever is in power over them. These are matters deserving of the best study that can be given them. But to say that these things could happen in Germany simply because Germans are different—from us—buttresses their own excuses and lets us off too easily from blame for what happened there and from the question whether it could happen here.

Certainly in their daily practice and expression before the Hitler regime, the Germans showed no more, if as much, hatred of other racial or cultural groups than we did and do. Residential segregation was not marked. Intermarriage was common, and the families of such marriages had an easier social existence than they generally have in America. The racially exclusive club, school and hotel were much less in evidence than here. And I well remember an evening in 1933 when a Montreal businessman—a very nice man, too—said in our living room, "Why don't we admit that Hitler is doing to the Jews just what we ought to be doing?" That was not an uncommon sentiment, although it may be said in defense of the people who expressed it, that they probably did not know and would not have believed the full truth about the Nazi program of destroying Jews. The essential underlying sentiments on racial matters in Germany were not different in kind from those prevailing throughout the western, and especially the Anglo-Saxon, countries. But I do not wish to over-emphasize this point. I only want to close one easy way out of serious consideration of the problem of good people and dirty work, by demonstrating that the Germans were and are about as good and about as bad as the rest of us on this matter of racial sentiments and, let us add, their notions of decent human behavior.

But what was the reaction of ordinary Germans to the persecution of the Jews and to the concentration camp mass torture and murder? A conversation between a German school-teacher, a German architect and myself gives the essentials in a vivid form. It was in the studio of the architect, and the occasion was a rather casual visit, in Frankfurt am Main in 1948.

The architect: "I am ashamed for my people whenever I think of it. But we didn't know about it. We only learned about all that later. You must remember the pressure we were under; we had to join the party. We had to keep our mouths shut and do as we were told. It was a terrible pressure. Still, I am ashamed. But you see, we had lost our colonies, and our national honour was hurt. And these Nazis exploited that feeling. And the Jews, they *were* a problem. They came from the east. You should see them in Poland; the lowest class of people, full of lice, dirty and poor, running about in their ghettos in filthy caftans. They came here, and got rich by unbelievable methods after the first war. They occupied all the good places. Why, they were in the proportion of ten to one in medicine and law and government posts!"

At this point the architect hesitated and looked confused. He continued: "Where was I? It is the poor food. You see what misery we are in here, Herr Professor. It often happens that I forget what I was talking about. Where was I now? I have completely forgotten."

(His confusion was, I believe, not at all feigned. Many Germans said they suffered losses of memory such as this, and laid it to their lack of food.)

I said firmly: "You were talking about loss of national honor and how the Jews had got hold of everything."

The architect: "Oh, yes! That was it! Well, of course that was no way to settle the Jewish problem. But there *was* a problem and it had to be settled some way."

The school-teacher: "Of course, they have Palestine now."

I protested that Palestine would hardly hold them.

The architect: "The professor is right. Palestine can't hold all the Jews. And it was a terrible thing to murder people. But we didn't know it at the time. But I am glad I am alive now. It is an interesting time in men's history. You know, when the Americans came it was like a great release. I really want to see a new ideal in Germany. I like the freedom that lets me talk to you like this. But, unfortunately that is not the general opinion. Most of my friends really hang on to the old ideas. They can't see any hope, so they hang on to the old ideas."

This scrap of talk gives, I believe, the essential elements as well as the flavor of the German reaction. It checks well with formal studies which have been made, and it varies only in detail from other conversations which I myself recorded in 1948.

One of the most obvious points in it is unwillingness to think about the dirty work done. In this case—perhaps by chance, perhaps not—the good man suffered an actual lapse of memory in the middle of this statement. This seems a simple point. But the psychiatrists have shown that it is less simple than it looks. They have done a good deal of work on the complicated mechanisms by which the individual mind keeps unpleasant or intolerable knowledge from consciousness, and have shown how great may, in some cases, be the consequent loss of effectiveness of the personality. But we have taken collective unwillingness to know unpleasant facts more or less for granted. That people can and do keep a silence about things whose open discussion would threaten the group's conception of itself, and hence its solidarity, is common knowledge. It is a mechanism that operates in every family and in every group which has a sense of group reputation. To break such a silence is considered an attack against the group; a sort of treason, if it be a member of the group who breaks the silence. This common silence allows group fictions to grow up; such as, that grandpa was less a scoundrel and more romantic than he really was. And I think it demonstrable that it operates especially against any expression, except in ritual, of collective guilt. The remarkable thing in present-day Germany is not that there is so little reference to something about which people do feel deeply guilty, but that it is talked about at all.

In order to understand this phenomenon we would have to find out who talks about the concentration camp atrocities, in what situations, in what mood, and with what stimulus. On these points I know only my own limited experiences. One of the most moving of these was my first postwar meeting with an elderly professor whom I had known before the Nazi time; he is an heroic soul who did not bow his head during the Nazi time and who keeps it erect now. His first words, spoken with tears in his eyes, were:

"How hard it is to believe that men will be as bad as they say they will. Hitler and his people said: 'Heads will roll,' but how many of us—even of his bitterest opponents—could really believe that they would do it."

This man could and did speak, in 1948, not only to the likes of me, but to his students, his colleagues and to the public which read his articles, in the most natural way about the Nazi atrocities whenever there was occasion to do it in the course of his tireless effort to reorganize and to bring new life into the German universities. He had neither the compulsion to speak, so that he might excuse and defend himself, nor a conscious or unconscious need to keep silent. Such people were rare; how many there were in Germany I do not know.

Occasions of another kind in which the silence was broken were those where, in class, public lecture or in informal meetings with students, I myself had talked frankly of race relations in other parts of the world, including the lynchings which sometimes occur in my own country and the terrible cruelty visited upon natives in South Africa. This took off the lid of defensiveness, so that a few people would talk quite easily of what happened under the Nazi regime. More common were situations like that with the architect, where I threw in some remark about the atrocities in response to Germans' complaint that the world is abusing them. In such cases, there was usually an expression of shame, accompanied by a variety of excuses (including that of having been kept in ignorance), and followed by a quick turning away from the subject.

Somewhere in consideration of this problem of discussion versus silence we must ask what the good (that is, ordinary) people in Germany did know about these things. It is clear that the SS kept the more gory details of the concentration camps a close secret. Even high officials of the government, the army and the Nazi party itself were in some measure held in ignorance, although of course they kept the camps supplied with victims. The common people of Germany knew that the camps existed; most knew people who had disappeared into them; some saw the victims, walking skeletons in rags, being transported in trucks or trains, or being herded on the road from station to camp or to work in fields or factories near the camps. Many knew people who had been released from concentration camps; such released persons kept their counsel on pain of death. But secrecy was cultivated and supported by fear and terror. In the absence of a determined and heroic will to know and publish the truth, and in the absence of all the instruments of opposition, the degree of knowledge was undoubtedly low, in spite of the fact that all knew that something both stupendous and horrible was going on; and in spite of the fact that Hitler's *Mein Kampf* and the utterances of his aides said that no fate was too horrible for the Jews and other wrong-headed or inferior people. This must make us ask under what conditions the will to know and to discuss is strong, determined and effective; this, like most of the important questions I have raised, I leave unanswered except as answers may be contained in the statement of the case.

But to return to our moderately good man, the architect. He insisted over and over again that he did not know, and we may suppose that he knew as much and as little as most Germans. But he also made it quite clear that he wanted something done to the Jews. I have similar statements from people of whom I knew that they had had close Jewish friends before the Nazi time. This raises the whole problem of the extent to which those pariahs who do the dirty work of society are really acting as agents for the rest of us. To talk of this question one must note that, in building up his case, the architect pushed the Jews firmly into an out-group: they were dirty, lousy and unscrupulous (an odd statement from a resident of Frankfurt, the home of old Jewish merchants and intellectual families long identified with those aspects of culture of which Germans are most proud). Having dissociated himself clearly from these people, and having declared them a problem, he apparently was willing to let someone else do to them the dirty work which he himself would not do, and for which he expressed shame. The case is perhaps analogous to our attitude toward those convicted of crime. From time to time, we get wind of cruelty practiced upon the prisoners in penitentiaries or jails; or, it may be, merely a report that they are ill-fed or that hygienic conditions are not good. Perhaps we do not wish that the prisoners should be cruelly treated or badly fed, but our reaction is probably tempered by a notion that they deserve something, because of some dissociation of them from the in-group of good people. If what they get is worse than what we like to think about, it is a little bit too bad. It is a point on which we are ambivalent. Campaigns for reform of prisons are often followed by counter-campaigns against a too high standard of living for prisoners and against having prisons run by softies. Now the people who run prisons are our agents. Just how far they do or could carry out our wishes is hard to say. The minor prison guard, in boastful justification of some of his more questionable practices, says, in effect: "If those reformers and those big shots upstairs had to live with these birds as I do, they would soon change their fool notions about running a prison." He is suggesting that the good people are either naive or hypocritical. Furthermore, he knows quite well that the wishes of his employers, the public, are by no means unmixed. They are quite as likely to put upon him for being too nice as for being too harsh. And if, as sometimes happens, he is a man disposed to cruelty, there may be some justice in his feeling that he is only doing what others would like to do, if they but dared; and what they would do, if they were in his place.

There are plenty of examples in our own world which I might

have picked for comparison with the German attitude toward the concentration camps. For instance, a newspaper in Denver made a great scandal out of the allegation that our Japanese compatriots were too well fed in the camps where they were concentrated during the war. I might have mentioned some feature of the sorry history of the people of Japanese background in Canada. Or it might have been lynching, or some aspect of racial discrimination. But I purposely chose prisoners convicted of crime. For convicts are formally set aside for special handling. They constitute an out-group in all countries. This brings the issue clearly before us, since few people cherish the illusion that the problem of treating criminals can be settled by propaganda designed to prove that there aren't any criminals. Almost everyone agrees that something has to be done about them. The question concerns what is done, who does it, and the nature of the mandate given by the rest of us to those who do it. Perhaps we give them an unconscious mandate to go beyond anything we ourselves would care to do or even to acknowledge. I venture to suggest that the higher and more expert functionaries who act in our behalf represent something of a distillation of what we may consider our public wishes, while some of the others show a sort of concentrate of those impulses of which we are or wish to be less aware.

Now the choice of convicted prisoners brings up another crucial point in inter-group relations. All societies of any great size have in-groups and out-groups; in fact, one of the best ways of describing a society is to consider it a network of smaller and larger in-groups and out-groups. And an in-group is one only because there are out-groups. When I refer to *my* children I obviously imply that they are closer to me than other people's children and that I will make greater efforts to buy oranges and cod-liver oil for them than for others' children. In fact, it may mean that I will give them cod-liver oil if I have to choke them to get it down. We do our own dirty work on those closest to us. The very injunction that I love my neighbor as myself starts with me; if I don't love myself and my nearest, the phrase has a very sour meaning.

Each of us is a center of a network of in and out-groups. Now the distinctions between *in* and *out* may be drawn in various ways, and nothing is more important for both the student of society and the educator than to discover how these lines are made and how they may be redrawn in more just and sensible ways. But to believe that we can do away with the distinction between *in* and *out*, *us* and *them* in social life is complete nonsense. On the positive side, we generally feel a greater obligation to in-groups; hence less obligation to out-groups; and in the case of such groups as convicted criminals, the out-group is definitely given over to the hands of our agents for punishment. That is the extreme case. But there are other out-groups toward which we may have aggressive feelings and dislike, although we give no formal mandate to anyone to deal with them on our behalf, and although we profess to believe that they should not suffer restrictions or disadvantages. The greater their social distance from us, the more we leave in the hands of others a sort of mandate by default to deal with them on our behalf. Whatever effort we put on reconstructing the lines which divide in and out-groups, there remains the eternal problem of our treatment, direct or delegated, of whatever groups are considered somewhat outside. And here it is that the whole matter of our professed and possibly deeper unprofessed wishes comes up for consideration; and the related problem of what we know, can know and want to know about it. In Germany, the agents got out of hand and created such terror that it was best not to know. It is also clear that it was and is easier to the conscience of many Germans not to know. It is, finally, not unjust to say that the agents were at least working in the direction of the wishes of many people, although they may have gone beyond the wishes of most. The same questions can be asked about our own society, and with reference not only to prisoners but also to many other groups upon whom there is no legal or moral stigma. Again I have not the answers. I leave you to search for them.

In considering the question of dirty work we have eventually to think about the people who do it. In Germany, these were the members of the SS and of that inner group of the SS who operated the concentration camps. Many reports have been made on the social backgrounds and the personalities of these cruel fanatics. Those who have studied them say that a large proportion were "gescheiterte Existenzen," men or women with a history of failure, of poor adaptation to the demands of work and of the classes of society in which they had been bred. Germany between wars had large numbers of such people. Their adherence to a movement which proclaimed a doctrine of hatred was natural enough. The movement offered something more. It created an inner group which was to be superior to all others, even Germans, in their emancipation from the usual bourgeois morality; people above and beyond the ordinary morality. I dwell on this, not as a doctrine, but as an organizational device. For, as Eugen Kogon, author of the most penetrating analysis of the SS and their camps, has said, the Nazis came to power by creating a state within a state; a body with its own counter-morality, and its own counter-law, its courts and its own execution of sentence upon those who did not live up to its orders and standards. Even as a movement, it had inner circles within inner circles; each sworn to secrecy as against the next outer one. The struggle between these inner circles continued after Hitler came to power; Himmler eventually won the day. His SS became a state within the Nazi state, just as the Nazi movement had become a state within the Weimar state. One is reminded of the oft-quoted but neglected statement of Sighele: "At the center of a crowd look for the sect." He referred, of course, to the political sect; the fanatical inner group of a movement seeking power by revolutionary methods. Once the Nazis were in power, this inner sect, while becoming now the recognized agent of the state and, hence, of the masses of the people, could at the same time dissociate itself more completely from them in action, because of the very fact of having a mandate. It was now beyond all danger of interference and investigation. For it had the instruments of interference and investigation in its own hands. These are also the instruments of secrecy. So the SS could and did build up a powerful system in which they had the resources of the state and of the economy of Germany and the conquered countries from which to steal all that was needed to carry out their orgy of cruelty luxuriously as well as with impunity.

Now let us ask, concerning the dirty workers, questions similar to those concerning the good people. Is there a supply of candidates for such work in other societies? It would be easy to say that only Germany could produce such a crop. The question is answered by being put. The problem of people who have run aground (gescheiterte Existenzen) is one of the most serious in our modern societies. Any psychiatrist will, I believe, testify that we have a sufficient pool or fund of personalities warped toward perverse punishment and cruelty to do any amount of dirty work that the good people may be inclined to countenance. It would not take a very great turn of events to increase the number of such people, and to bring their discontents to the surface. This is not to suggest that every movement based on discontent with the present state of things will be led by such people. That is obviously untrue; and I emphasize the point lest my remarks give comfort to those who would damn all who express militant discontent. But I think study of militant social movements does show that these warped people seek a place in them. Specifically, they are likely to become the plotting, secret police of the group. It is one of the problems of militant social movements to keep such people out. It is of course easier to do this if the spirit of the movement is positive, its conception of humanity high and inclusive, and its aims sound. This was not the case of the Nazi movement. As Kogon puts it: "The SS were but the arch-type of the Nazis in general."[3] But such people are sometimes attracted for want of something better, to movements whose aims are contrary to the spirit of cruelty and punishment. I would suggest that all of us look well at the leadership and entourage of movements to which we attach ourselves for signs of a negativistic, punishing attitude. For once such a spirit develops in a movement, punishment of the nearest and easiest victim is likely to become more attractive than striving for the essential goals. And, if the Nazi movement teaches us anything at all, it is that if any shadow of a mandate be given to such people, they will—having compromised us—make it larger and larger. The processes by which they do so are the development of the power and inward discipline of their own group, a progressive dissociation of themselves from the rules of human decency prevalent in their culture, and an ever-growing contempt for the welfare of the masses of people.

The power and inward discipline of the SS became such that those who once became members could get out only by death; by suicide, murder or mental breakdown. Orders from the central offices of the SS were couched in equivocal terms as a hedge against a possible day of judgment. When it became clear that such a day of judgment would come, the hedging and intrigue became greater; the urge to murder also became greater, because every prisoner became a potential witness.

Again we are dealing with a phenomenon common in all societies. Almost every group which has a specialized social func-

---

[3] Op. cit. p. 316.

tion to perform is in some measure a secret society, with a body of rules developed and enforced by the members and with some power to save its members from outside punishment. And here is one of the paradoxes of social order. A society without smaller, rule-making and disciplining powers would be no society at all. There would be nothing but law and police; and this is what the Nazis strove for, at the expense of family, church, professional groups, parties and other such nuclei of spontaneous control. But apparently the only way to do this, for good as well as for evil ends, is to give power into the hands of some fanatical small group which will have a far greater power of self-discipline and a far greater immunity from outside control than the traditional groups. The problem is, then, not of trying to get rid of all the self-disciplining, protecting groups within society, but one of keeping them integrated with one another and as sensitive as can be to a public opinion which transcends them all. It is a matter of checks and balances, of what we might call the social and moral constitution of society.

Those who are especially devoted to efforts to eradicate from good people, as individuals, all those sentiments which seem to bring about the great and small dirty work of the world, may think that my remarks are something of an attack on their methods. They are right to this extent; that I am insisting that we give a share of our effort to the social mechanisms involved as well as to the individual and those of his sentiments which concern people of other kinds.

Chapter 5

The administration of justice: The courts

As Americans, we are told that we enjoy a court system unique among modern nations, its hallmarks being the equality of all citizens appearing before the courts and explicit constitutional rights that all citizens may use in defending themselves against government prosecution. These rights include the constitutional guarantee of a speedy public trial; protection against excessive bail; the right to trained defense counsel; protection against compulsory self-incrimination; and the right to a trail by a jury of our peers. Clearly, dictatorships have never bothered with such formalities. The question is, how does this description of the ideal functioning of the system square with what is known about the actual operation of American courts?

COURT PROCESSES

Shortly after a person is arrested, he is brought before a lower or magistrate court either for a trial in the case of lesser crimes—misdemeanors punishable by less than one year in the local jail—or, in the case of felonies, for a hearing to determine whether the suspect should be released or held for a preliminary hearing. If the suspect is held,

the case then is turned over to a prosecuting attorney who charges the defendant with a specific statutory crime. This charge is subject to review

233

by a judge [the same or another magistrate judge] at a preliminary hearing of the evidence and in many places if the offense charged is a felony, by a grand jury that can dismiss the charge, or affirm it by delivering it to a judge in the form of an indictment (President's Commission, 1967: 7).

The preliminary hearing is somewhat similar to actual criminal trial proceedings in that the defendant can be represented by legal counsel and call witnesses on his or her behalf. However, at the preliminary hearing it is only necessary for the magistrate judge to be convinced that there is *probable cause* to suppose that the person may be guilty, not to be convinced of guilt *beyond a reasonable doubt*, as in criminal trials. Also, at preliminary hearings, unlike criminal trials, the defendant has no right to be heard by a jury. If the defendant is held for trial, the magistrate sets the amount of the bail.

[The magistrate] is entitled to inquire into the facts of the case, into whether there are grounds for holding the accused. He seldom does. He seldom can. The more promptly an arrested suspect is brought into magistrate's court, the less likelihood there is that much information about the arrest other than the arresting officer's statement will be available to the magistrate. Moreover, many magistrates, especially in big cities, have such congested calendars that it is almost impossible for them to subject any case but an extraordinary one to prolonged scrutiny (President's Commission, 1967: 10).

After an individual is arrested on a felony charge, the prosecutor must decide whether the person is to be prosecuted and, if so, what the charges are to be. If the person is prosecuted, a document called the information is drafted by the prosecutor. In some jurisdictions the grand jury is also involved in criminal prosecutions. The grand jury is a group of citizens who for a specific period of time are required to investigate, in closed sessions, charges coming from preliminary hearings in magistrate courts and to initiate proceedings if the facts the grand jury uncovers warrant such action. Since the grand jury merely determines whether there is probable cause to believe that the accused is guilty, only the prosecution's evidence is heard. An indictment drafted by the prosecutor outlines the charges against the defendant. After hearing the evidence, the grand jury must decide whether probable cause has been shown to support the charges in the indictment.

Originally the secrecy of the grand jury in England was intended to exclude representatives of the Crown so as to protect private citizens from unfounded government charges and to enable the grand jury to look into misconduct among government officials (Katz et al., 1972: 11–17). However, the grand jury no longer serves this function, and it is now essentially limited to reviewing whether a prosecutor has presented sufficient evidence and testimony to warrant a trial. Usually the grand jury is merely a rubber stamp for the prosecutor and seldom investigates cases on its own. Even when the grand jury does not return an indictment, this may be at the prosecutor's request, as a means of protecting him from losing a marginal case in court or from looking cowardly by dropping charges on his own. In fact, prosecutors sometimes delay a preliminary hearing on a case to wait for a grand jury action in order to avoid disclosing evidence in open court which might allow the defense to develop some answer by the time of trial (Katz et al., 1972: 119). Because of these problems a question that is being asked increasingly is whether the grand jury system is really necessary if the preliminary hearing accomplishes the same general purpose of establishing probable cause.

Whether an individual is prosecuted by information or by indictment, if he is to be tried for a felony, the first step prior to the trial is the arraignment in the trial court. At this step in the proceedings there are generally three things a defendant can do: (1) he can seek a delay before trial for such reasons as obtaining legal counsel or consulting further with his legal counsel; (2) he can plead guilty, not guilty, or *nolo contendere* (no contest); or (3) he can attempt to have the entire case thrown out of court and the trial process stopped by claiming improper procedure in the arrest or preliminary hearing or insufficient evidence. If the case is not delayed, and if the judge does not throw it out, the trial process begins.

The State has the first and the last word in the trial. The prosecution makes the opening statement, outlining its case. The opening statement by the defense follows; then the State submits its evidence and calls its witnesses. The defense then presents its witnesses and contrary evidence; thereupon defense and prosecution may take turns in offering rebuttals, in cross-examining opposing witnesses, and in re-examining its own witnesses. At the end of this rebuttal period, the State summarizes its case and is answered by the *closing argument* of the defense. The State then presents its closing arguments (Korn and McCorkle, 1963: 111–112).

This typical order of events normally gives the State four opportunities to address the court, compared with three provided for the defense. The State not only has *more* opportunities to present its case, but since it has the first and last word, it has the advantage of what are called the primacy and recency effects. Social scientists have documented that the *first* argument and the most *recent* argument that a person hears have a greater impact on beliefs than do other arguments (Miller and Campbell, 1959).

After receiving instructions from the judge on what facts they must believe to find the defendant guilty as charged, the jury retires to attempt to reach a verdict. This usually requires complete consensus of the jurors. If the jurors do find the defendant guilty, usually the judge then begins to consider a sentence, though in some states the jury participates to varying degrees in the sentencing. If the jurors cannot agree, this results in a hung jury, and the prosecutor must decide whether the case is worth a second trial.

SOCIAL ROLES IN THE ADMINISTRATION OF JUSTICE

Having outlined the events leading up to and including the criminal trial, we will describe the roles of the various actors and organizations in this process.

Operation of the bailbondsman

Traditionally the bail system in the United States has allowed the accused to be released before trial after he has posted with the court funds that the court considers sufficient to insure his or her appearance for trial. Perhaps the most outrageous feature of the U.S. bail system is that in most cases the ultimate decision about a defendant's freedom while awaiting trial is not made by the judge or the prosecutor but by a businessman—the bailbondsman. The bailbondsman decides whether the suspect is a good enough risk to do business with, and also decides how much, if any, collateral is required to protect his investment. At times, the bondsman demands collateral in the amount of the bond. This forces the accused to act as his own surety. Here the bondsman merely converts the value of the collateral into ready cash which the court will accept (Ryan, 1967). Bail is easily available for those involved in large-scale racketeering who have organizational backing, or for those who know or are known by bailbondsmen, such as professional thieves. It is the amateurs who are more often likely to be innocent, and especially the poor, who must wait in jail until trial (Goldfarb, 1965: 4).

One abuse of the bondsman's role occurs when he changes his mind about a client after learning something new and discrediting about him. In such instances, the bondsman may no longer be willing to risk his investment and may force a client's return to jail and fail to return the client's initial payment (Wice, 1974: 40–41). From the bondsman's point of view, the best risks include professional gamblers. The bad risks are first offenders who might panic and run away. Indeed, bondsmen turn down many defendants whom they consider poor risks (Wice, 1974: 38–41).

The bondsman's concern is understandable because the defendant who jumps bail and fails to appear for trial loses nothing, since the bondsman charges the defendant a nonreturnable premium (Ryan, 1967). Although insurance companies provide much of the money that bailbondsmen work with, if a bondsman's customer forfeits his bond, then the bondsman must pay the insurance company and absorb the loss (Goldfarb, 1965: 97).

Regulation and corruption of bailbondsmen

In most jurisdictions bondsmen are governed by formal regulations, but these regulations are not effectively enforced. Rates of interest are formally regulated in most areas, but these rates are often circumvented by charging extra fees for night service or minimum fees (Goldfarb, 1965: 100).

In 1961 a grand jury in Kansas City, Missouri, found that most bondsmen were business partners of certain policemen (Goldfarb, 1965: 109–115). Some police making an arrest would refer defendants to specific bondsmen, who would in return kick back a percentage of their fees to the policemen. In St. Louis in 1973 bondsmen were operating in the city courts even though the judges did not require them to forfeit the bonds, and it was alleged that here too some fee splitting was involved, in this instance between bondsmen and judges (*St. Louis Post Dispatch,* 1973: 9A). "In St. Louis, for example, records of the circuit court reveal that of the 318 forfeitures in felony cases in 1970, 304 were set aside" (Wice, 1974: 40). Bondsmen are also at times in collusion with defense attorneys. The bondsman may insist that the defendant use a specific lawyer, who in turn splits the fees with the bondsman. In such cases, the quality and character of the defendant's legal aid are determined by the bondsman. Finally, the bond system in America has at times resulted in kidnappings and beatings of defendants who jump bail and do not show up for their trial. Bondsmen have been known to hire goons to kidnap, drug, and beat up persons who have jumped bail, and then return them to the state court with jurisdiction in the case, notwithstanding the existence of legal processes providing extradition (Katz et al., 1972: 162).

The courts and the bail system

The magistrate judge's power to set the amount of bail is an awesome one. Although these decisions are subject to appellate review and reversal by higher courts, they are seldom overturned (Katz et al., 1972: 158). Bail is usually set on the basis of the severity of the offense with which the suspect is charged. Nevertheless, there is only a slight relationship between the severity of the offense and either the probability of flight to avoid prosecution or the commission of later crimes (Ryan, 1967).

The theory of the bail system is that the accused person has given over enough money to the court to satisfy the judge that he will attend his trial rather than forfeit the money. If so, then the amount of bail set should be based in part on the wealth of the accused, since this will determine how much money is required to deter him from fleeing (Ryan, 1967). In fact, as we have already noted, if the suspect deals with a bondsman, only the bondsman, and not the suspect, stands to lose any money by the suspect's nonappearance. Since wealth is usually not considered by judges in setting bail, obviously the poor are the ones who suffer. They typically go to jail to await trial and usually lose whatever employment they have—often forcing their families to go on relief. All this happens before the trial and the determination, if any, of guilt.

Moreover, the bail system can intentionally be used as a political weapon to punish, in advance of trial, certain groups of people. A defendant can be arrested frivolously in a manner sure not to bring conviction but which nonetheless forces the person to raise the bail money or remain in jail (Goldfarb, 1965). During the civil rights demonstrations in the South in the 1960s, bail was often set very high so that demonstrators were forced to await trial in jail. Sometimes people are arrested and charged with a number of crimes, and the separate bail set for each charge is so high that even nonindigent defendants cannot raise the full amount. Nevertheless, the bail system was never intended as a denial of justice and, in fact, a sentence before trial. It was merely intended as a means to insure that a person charged with a crime would be available for trial—and at this it fails.

Being a prisoner before and during a trial seems to prejudice a jury and judge against the defendant. If the defendant is in jail before and during the trial, he comes to the court in the custody of a guard, and it may appear that he is guilty. Therefore, it is not hard to convince the jury that this is indeed so. Those in jail during a trail experience a higher conviction rate than do those free on bail at that time (Goldfarb, 1965: 38–40). Those in jail while awaiting trial are more often convicted irrespective of the seriousness of the charge, the magnitude of the evidence, and their prior record (New York Legal Aid Society, 1972; also see Rankin, 1964). Aside from the stigma of being a prisoner during the trial, which may prejudice the judge and jury, there are other possible explanations for these results. For one thing, a person released on bail can claim a good work and family record while awaiting trial, which may influence the judge and jury favorably. The jailed defendant does not have this opportunity (Katz et al., 1972: 151–152).

Alternatives to the bail system

Other countries.   In England bail can be provided only by the accused person or by some friend or relative who will post bail for him. There are no professional bondsmen and, in fact, furnishing bonds for profit is a criminal offense (Goldfarb, 1965: 215). Bail is set lower in England than in the United States so that in only 1 percent of the cases in which bail is set are people detained for being unable to raise the money.

In Sweden those freed before trial are ordinarily released on their word that they will return for trial (Goldfarb, 1965: 218–222). In Denmark the same practice is used. Both countries also rely heavily on the summons instead of arrests and bail. The use of summons to appear in court for misdemeanor and felony cases has the advantage of freeing the defendant awaiting trial from the stigma of arrest.

U.S. programs.   In 1961 the New York University Law School started the Manhattan Bail project (Katz et al., 1972: 164). Law students interviewed people in jail, focusing on their residential stability, occupational history, and prior criminal record. The more stable and permanent members of the community were recommended to the judge for release on their own recognizance, that is, on their own promise to return for trial. Under this program, judges tended to release four times as many of the accused, and 98.4 percent of those released showed up for trial.

Another idea to circumvent the problem of bail was first developed in Illinois (Goldfarb, 1965: 198–203). Under this system the defendant can post directly with the court an amount equal to the interest for the bond set (for example, $10 interest on a $100 bond). If the defendant shows up for trial, he gets back the money minus only a small administrative fee (1 percent of the bond). If the defendant does not appear for the trial, the total bond set, and not just the premium, is forfeited. Although this cuts out the bailbondsman, some defendants are so poor that they cannot even post the premium for the bond with the court. Also, it may be impossible to collect the full bail amount from poor defendants who do not appear for trial.

There is some evidence that the Illinois system was pushed through the legislature by defense attorneys (Katz et al., 1972: 169). Everyone who had anything to do with the bail system was getting paid off, and in order to increase the bail fee available for the payoffs, bail was being set at exorbitant rates, leaving the defendants with no money for attorneys. As a convenience and a guarantee for defense attorneys, the Illinois statute now permits a defendant to sign over to his attorney 90 percent of the sum to be returned to him by the court when he appears for trial. This feature, of course, reflects the influence of defense attorneys on the legislation. It shows how some apparently humane and progressive innovations can have exploitative origins.

The question is, why have the courts made no effort to abolish or control the corrupt and unjust bail system? The reason is that bondsmen help manage defendants during the time between arrest and sentencing (Dill, 1975). Bondsmen remind customers of future court dates and help them find courtrooms. Moreover, bondsmen have an interest in guilty pleas which, as we will see, is also true of other court officials. The bondsman's liability for each bond he posts only ends when the case is cleared from the docket, and therefore the bondsman often counsels customers to plead guilty. Most bail forfeitures are set aside by judges, and in return bondsmen deny bail to defendants at the judge's request. Finally, the bondsman has broader legal powers in retrieving defendants who have absconded than does any criminal justice official. He needs no warrants for arrest, and, unlike the police, he is not restricted by interstate extradition laws (Dill, 1975).

CRIMINAL LAWYERS

Social class background

To understand the routine practice of criminal law in America, it is important to recognize that criminal lawyers have lower social class backgrounds than do lawyers in civil practice (Wood, 1967). Moreover, criminal lawyers as a group have attended less prestigious law schools than did those in civil practice, and criminal lawyers generally make less money than do those in civil practice. Most criminal lawyers did not set out to have this kind of practice—rather, this was the only alternative available to them. The apparent lack of enthusiasm of attorneys for the practice of criminal law is understandable. Contrary to the mass media stereotype of the highly paid, brilliant criminal defense counsel, criminal lawyers earn less and have less attrative working conditions and clients than do most attorneys in civil practice. It is from this group of second-class citizens of the legal profession, who may also have received something less than a first-rate education, that most defendants must select counsel.

The criminal lawyer must be able to work with the prosecuting attorney to arrange agreements on reduced charges in exchange for guilty pleas, and must also be able to work with the police to keep the number of charges down and to help arrange speedy bail at the police station. In dealing with police, the similarity between the criminal lawyer's social class background and that of the police may be an important asset.

Legal counsel for indigent defendants

Until recently most jurisdictions in the United States made no allowance, or at best only a small allowance, for the compensation of court-appointed lawyers representing indigents (Tappan, 1960: 368). In areas in which indigent defendants were provided with some legal aid, one traditional method of doing so was for the court to use some type of *rotation* system for assigning indigent cases to members of the local bar. The problems with such a system are all too obvious. Most members of the bar do not practice criminal law and are not really qualified for the task. Also, the typically inadequate compensation places pressure on the court appointed lawyer to persuade a client to plead guilty, thus saving the lawyer time which could be spent on paying clients.

Two Supreme Court decisions made this method of providing legal aid to indigents unworkable. One was the decision in *Gideon* v. *Wainwright* (1963), which required that all indigent defendants accused of a felony must be provided with legal counsel. More recently, this was expanded (*Argersinger* v. *Hamlin,* 1972) to include the requirement of legal aid for any crime for which an accused could be imprisoned.[1] Since legal aid in all parts of the United States was now to be routinely offered to indigent defendants, some more systematic method of offering this service became necessary. It seemed desirable to vest this responsibility in a full-time office—that of the public defender.

As a result of working daily with the judge and prosecutor, the public defender may begin to share their definition of the trial and courtroom situation, especially since both the judge and the prosecutor as elected officials, unlike the public defender, are much more powerful politically than is the public defender. Sudnow

---

[1] Yet the Supreme Court has recently held that indigent defendants have no constitutional right to defense counsel for appeals (*Ross et al.* v. *Moffitt,* 1974). As is well known from the experience of trials of civil rights demonstrators, fairness may not be had at the trial level even with counsel. Therefore, if justice is to be achieved, some provision for counsel on appeal seems required.

(1965) studied the operation of the public defender's office and observed that the main job of the public defender is to convince a client that the chances of acquittal are too slight to warrant the risk of pleading not guilty. The public defender tries to convince a client to see the reasonableness of pleading guilty to a reduced offense. This standard operating procedure is engaged in with the full cooperation of the prosecuting attorney. Both the public defender and the prosecuting attorney are permanent employees in the court, and both realize that the only way they can prevent a great backlog of cases is to have most defendants plead guilty. They share the same assembly-line orientation toward the court system, in which efficiency and speed rather than full justice is seen as the measure of success. The prosecutor and the public defender usually determine the nature of the reduced charge on the basis of what they feel the judge and influential community interest groups desire (Rosett and Cressey, 1976: 85–92) as well as what they see as a reasonable difference between the punishments likely for the two charges (Sudnow, 1965). Their common orientation is to reduce the charge so that the defendant will not get off too easily but to give the defendant enough to insure his or her cooperation. Therefore, the public defender's activity is seldom geared to securing acquittals for clients. The public defender and the prosecuting attorney take it for granted that the persons who come before the court are guilty of crimes and treat them accordingly. The public defender assumes that every client is going to lose the case even if he or she does not plead guilty. So if a defendant will not agree to plead guilty, when the public defender prepares for the trial, this is done in a way that is insufficient to win. The public defender often just glances at the defendant's file immediately before the trial begins (Sudnow, 1965). Indeed, the public defender helps speed the indigent defendant through the court system and, as the defendant's attorney, offers advice which helps control the defendant and helps keep the court system operating as smoothly as possible (Barak, 1975).

Unlike the prosecutor's office, which can merely drop the charges on cases when it gets too far behind, the public defender must accept all cases. Therefore, being typically overworked, the public defender recognizes that his office does not provide a high-quality service to clients. As might be expected, clients are often hostile toward public defenders and may view the public defender as a government agent. For their part, public defenders usually do not believe in their clients' innocence, have mixed emotions about securing acquittals for clients, and have difficulty in identifying with poor, unattractive clients accused of crimes. It is easier for them to identify with fellow lawyers, including prosecutors and judges (Rosett and Cressey, 1976: 122–126).

In our courts, due process requires among other things a presumption of innocence and a truly adversary proceeding in which a person receives a full, fair, and open judicial hearing or trial. The hearing must be a real one, not a contrived pretense. The proceedings must be free from any taint of coercion. Nevertheless, the courts, in fact, now have an overriding goal of assembly-line efficiency and therefore require a high percentage of guilty pleas. This assembly-line system of criminal justice is incompatible with traditional due process. Due process no longer influences the determination of guilt, which is now arrived at through bargained-for guilty pleas (Blumberg, 1967a: 4–5). All the recent discussions of Supreme Court decisions regarding the rights of due process against wiretapping, unlawful search, police coercion, and right to legal counsel have led attention away from the actual operation of the courts. Due process protection for the defendant is meaningless in a system in which defendants are presumed guilty and pressured to plead guilty. If the defendant pleads guilty, the question of whether the police used constitutionally correct means in collecting their evidence is never raised in court. Moreover the right to legal counsel is meaningless if this legal counsel helps pressure the defendant to plead guilty as the prosecution desires.

Private defense attorneys

Even defendants who have sufficient finances to retain private legal counsel get something quite different from the public images of defense attorneys, epitomized by F. Lee Bailey or Clarence Darrow. A few major felony cases drawing great public attention often follow a true adversay model. This also supports the fiction of an adversary system, which we are told distinguishes U.S. courts from those of totalitarian regimes.

The larger the attorney's fee, the more impressive the attorney's performance must be in terms not of a real attack but of generating a stage-managed image as a person of great influence and power in the courtroom. The judge and prosecutor are aware of the extent to which a lawyer's stock-in-trade involves this stage-managed impression, and for this reason alone the lawyer is bound to the court's authority (Blumberg, 1967b). Therefore, if the attorney is well liked and considered reasonable, to some degree the court personnel will aid him or her in maintaining this impression. The judge and prosecutor will not object to having such an attorney use the courtroom to stage-manage an impression of an all-out performance for the accused to help justify the legal fee. The point is that even if a defendant can afford the financial costs of a not guilty plea, something far different from an adversary, combative proceeding is often purchased.

In most areas there is a cadre of lawyers who handle the bulk of all nonindigent criminal cases. These attorneys have greater professional and economic ties to the court system than to their own clients. Criminal lawyers know that they will have a continuing relationship with the other members of the court and that they are expected to be reasonable rather than abrasive (Blumberg, 1967b).

The legal profession is responsible in part for one of the major chronic problems of the modern court system in America—the long delays in bringing a case to trial. Defendants have waited months and even years to be brought to trial, and one reason for the delays in criminal trials is that defense attorneys request such delays until they have been paid in full. Very often the client may be free on bail working to get sufficient money to pay the lawyer. Although it is true that in such cases fees from clients are often hard to collect, it is obvious that in granting delays, with knowledge of the reason, the court becomes a collection agency. This need for court assistance in fee collection also serves to make the defense attorney dependent on the authority of the court (Katz et al., 1972: 77). Another reason for delays which involves attorneys is that in most areas only a few lawyers handle the bulk of all nonindigent criminal cases. These lawyers are simply too busy to handle all cases promptly. For example, one study reported that in Cleveland 12 lawyers were the attorneys of record in one half of all pending felony cases (Katz et al., 1972: 76).

At times the local jail is used to encourage defendants to plead guilty. Blumberg (1967a: 59, 68–69) observes that crowded conditions become extremely useful to the courts. If bail is set at a level which the defendant cannot meet, and he remains in jail, the worse the jail conditions, such as extreme filth and sexual assaults by other prisoners, the greater the pressure felt by the defendant.

Some believe that defense attorneys consider prosecutors' overcharging beneficial because getting a charge reduced enables defense attorneys to show their clients that they are effective. Prosecutors overcharge to bargain down to charges they really want (Katz et al., 1972: 74). Since both the prosecutor and the judge are primarily concerned with maximum production in the court, defense attorneys, whether public defenders or privately retained, must go along with this because they depend on a continuing relationship with court officials (Blumberg, 1967a: 47).

JUDGES

From time to time judges speak of the importance of the jury trial as a central element of American criminal justice, but they nonetheless routinely deny probation to defendants whom juries convict of crimes who might otherwise merit probation. The data indicate that the possibility of probation for a defendant is far greater if he has pleaded guilty to a lesser offense rather than having been convicted at a jury trial. Therefore, a defendant's usual fears of harsh treatment if he does not plead guilty are not groundless (Blumberg, 1967a: 58, 129).

Once the defendant pleads guilty, the judge can presume that he is now a repentant individual who has learned a lesson and deserves lenient treatment.

[The guilty plea is, in fact, an act,] during which an accused must project an appropriate and acceptable degree of guilt, penitence, and remorse. If he adequately feigns the role of the "guilty person," his hearers will engage in the fantasy that he is contrite and thereby merits a lesser plea. One of the essential functions of the criminal lawyer is that he coach his accused-client in this performance (Blumberg, 1967: 89).

Judges can be elected or appointed, and in either case there is no sure protection from corruption and incompetence. The assumption seems to be that merely by virtue of being an attorney, a person is competent for any judgeship. Among the obvious problems in selecting judges in partisan political elections are the favors owed to political backers. The appointment of judges, whether by governors or presidents, risks the same general problems.

There have been attempts, however, to withdraw judges from the traditional pressures of partisan politics. One such scheme is called the Missouri Plan for selecting judges (Watson and Downing, 1969). A list of possible judge candidates is nominated by a commission made up of prominent citizens, including lawyers. Three names selected by the commission are submitted to the state governor, who selects one of them. After serving one year, the person's name appears on the ballot with the question "Shall Judge _____ be retained in office?" If the judge receives a majority of yes votes, he or she remains in office a full term, however long that is for the particular judicial position. This process purportedly takes the selection of judges out of partisan politics, at least to a degree, and insures at least a minimal competence, which the commission, if not the voters, would presumably insist on. The plan was adopted by the Missouri electorate in 1940, and several other states have initiated similar programs since then.

Collectively, however, judges are perhaps best known by the nature of their decisions, and it is to the sentencing decisions of judges that we now turn. Several studies have found that the courts deal more severely with blacks than with whites. For the same offenses, blacks are more likely than whites to be sentenced, and of those sentenced, blacks are often given longer terms (Axelrad, 1952; Bullock, 1961). For those skeptical of these claims of discrimination, the racial distribution of executions provides a dramatic demonstration. Of persons convicted of criminal homicide and sentenced to execution, a significantly higher proportion of blacks than whites were actually executed, whereas a higher proportion of whites had their sentences commuted to life in prison (Wolfgang et al., 1962). Since 1930, 55 percent of the approximately 4,000 people executed, and an astonishing 90 percent of the 455 men executed for rape, were blacks (Greenberg and Himmelstein, 1969; also see Bowers, 1974, for evidence of racial discrimination in executions). One could expect that a racist and class-biased society such as the United States would produce a similar criminal justice system and that discrimination would be reflected in the sentences handed down by judges.

JURIES

If a defendant does not plead guilty, a trial jury must be selected unless the defendant waives the right to a jury trial and accepts trial by a judge. In such cases, the judge not only rules on matters of law but also fills the jury's role in deciding on the facts of the case. Some states restrict the right to waive a jury trial to exclude cases with a possible capital penalty or permit that right to be exercised only with the consent of the court. Some defendants feel that waiving a jury trial may help them because they fear the prejudice of local laymen due to their race, religion, or type of crime.

Picking jurors is much more time consuming in the United States than in England. In England there is less pretrial newspaper publicity to bias jurors. Also, jurors tend to be more alike in England's relatively homogeneous culture. Moreover, judges are not elected in England, and so they are not afraid to antagonize lawyers by refusing to release a juror. Reviewing courts in England do not usually reverse decisions on the basis of a judge's refusal to release a juror, whereas there are reversals for this reason in the United States (Puttkammer, 1953: 180–181).

In selecting a jury, the lawyers generally ask each prospective juror whether he or she has already read about and formed an opinion about the case. Those who admit to having already made up their minds are excused from the jury by the judge. Some critics feel that only citizens who do not read newspapers will not have read about and formed some opinion about most major felony cases, and that juries in such cases are therefore made up primarily of nonreading, nonthinking, marginally intelligent people (Barnes and Tetters, 1959: 272).

However, in a criminal trial, many defense attorneys seek well-educated jurors because these are felt to be harder for the prosecution to convince beyond a reasonable doubt and because it is usually believed that such jurors are more likely to be opposed to criminal punishment of any kind. For the same reasons, the prosecution often wants less highly educated jurors and seeks to eliminate jurors with a good deal of formal education. Of course, both the prosecution and the defense are sensitive to how the social characteristics of the defendant, such as race, ethnicity of name, and social class, mesh with those of prospective jurors.

Generally, professionals are excused by the court from jury service because of the pressure of their occupational responsibilities. Lawyers do not serve on juries, and it is uncommon for other professionals, such as physicians, college professors, or ministers, to serve. Business executives are usually also excused because of their occupational obligations.

It is interesting to note what types of persons escape jury service. Equally interesting are the methods used to select potential jurors. In various areas, names of potential jurors are obtained from voting records and property tax rolls. These means of drawing up lists of potential jurors systematically exclude the poor, who more often than others do not vote or own property. Since most defendants in criminal trials have the common characteristic of poverty, it appears that they are systematically deprived of the constitutional guarantee of a jury of their peers.

Thus the composite picture one gets of the typical American jury is that it includes individuals who are not terribly poor, but who are not professionals or wealthy, and who in any case are not highly educated. This is not to suggest, however, that there is no variation in social class among American jurors, for Strodtbeck et al. (1957) found that during jury deliberations it is the high-status people who do most of the talking and ultimately become opinion leaders for the other jurors. So the biggest impact on juror decisions is made by the jury members who are most unlike the defendants in social class characteristics.

PSYCHIATRISTS

Psychiatrists become involved in two separate phases of the court process and in two separate questions about accused persons. One question deals with whether or not the accused is psychologically fit to stand trial. The other question involves whether or not the alleged act was the product of an intellectually or psychologically diseased mind.

Pretrial psychiatric examination (fitness to stand trial)

It sometimes happens that an individual is judged by psychiatrists to be psychologically unfit to stand trial. Competence to stand trial generally means that the defendant understands the charges and the nature of the trial proceedings, and can assist the legal counsel in the defense. In other words, the law requires that no one should be put on trial who cannot perform the role of defendant (Szasz, 1965). It requires the ability to help defend oneself, but it does not require good physical or mental health. Individuals who are unwilling to cooperate with the defense attorneys will not competently defend themselves, according to the court rules, but they are not necessarily mentally ill—they just choose not to perform the defendant's role properly. If competence to stand trial is not a medical question, then medical experts should not make the decision. Rather, the decision could be made by a judge or a panel of judges, a lawyer or a panel of lawyers, or a jury of laymen. In fact, as human beings, we all evaluate the performance of actors in the various roles they play.

Even though competence to stand trial is not necessarily a medical-psychiatric question, if individuals are found incompetent to stand trial for the crime or crimes they are accused of, they are committed to a mental hospital until such time as they are judged by psychiatrists to be well enough to stand trial. If and when they are certified to have recovered, they are subject to trial and penal commitment. If they are subsequently convicted and sentenced to a penal institution, time spent in the mental hospital is usually not credited on the penal commitment. In such cases we deal more harshly with those thought to be mentally incompetent than with others accused of crime. Many observers suggest that there should be no prosecution following release after commitment for incompetence (Rubin, 1965). Also, civil commitment results in long-term institutional stays. Civil commitment is open-ended and therefore potentially a life sentence, for there is no mandatory release date, as with most prison sentences.

Some constitutional questions can be raised about the determination by psychiatrists of a defendant's compentence to stand trial. Szasz (1963) claims that the Sixth Amendment to the Constitution guarantees the right to a speedy and public trial, and that this right is not contingent on a defendant's capacity to prove his sanity to government psychiatrists. In addition, the Fifth Amendment guarantees that persons cannot be made to testify against themselves. Wiretap evidence is often inadmissible for this reason and because it violates the guarantees against unreasonable searches and seizures provided by the Fourth Amendment. This being true, the logic of the Fifth and Fourth Amendments would seem to extend to "mindtapping" by psychiatrists, who are experts at digging information out of people, but the courts have not accepted this inference.

The Fifth Amendment also guarantees defendants against being tried twice on the same charge. This constitutional protection against double jeopardy appears to be violated when a person is found unfit to stand trial and is committed to a mental hospital, yet is tried later and sentenced to a period of imprisonment. In such cases incarceration in a hospital is a punishment directly attributable to the offense with which the defendant is charged. Incarceration in excess of the prison term that the defendant would have had to serve had he originally been tried, sentenced, and not hospitalized, is clearly a case of double punishment. Usually it is indigent persons who are denied the right to trial by being forced to undergo a pretrial psychiatric examination (Szasz, 1963). The defendants' court-appointed lawyers typically do not care, since if no trial is held, their time is not consumed, which is an even more expedient outcome than they could hope to obtain from a guilty plea.

Criminal responsibility

Although an individual may be judged competent to stand trial, psychiatrists testifying before the court may argue that because of some mental disease or defect the defendant should not be held criminally responsible for the act of which he has been accused. Sometimes the defendant is urged by his attorney to enter a plea of not guilty by reason of insanity or mental defect. Such a plea does not contest the facts of the case but claims that the defendant should not be held criminally responsible and punished. Those found not guilty under such pleas are typically not released but are judged to be still dangerous, and confined for an indeterminate period in a mental hospital. Defendants so processed are burdened with the double stigma of of being labeled both criminal and insane—both bad and mad.

Two central models are used to assess criminal responsibility in the United States. Over a hundred years ago, an important precedent set in England became a guide that is still widely used in assessing criminal responsibility. This was the M'Naghten Case (1843: 719). It states that "to establish a defence on the ground of insanity, it must be clearly proved that at the time of committing the act the party accused was labouring under such a defect of reason, from disease of the mind, as not to know the nature and quality of the act he was doing, or as not to know that what he was doing was wrong." This rule is often simply called the right-wrong test of criminal responsibility.

A different rule was established in a precedent set by the U.S. Court of Appeals in Washington, D.C., in which the defendant, Monte Durham (*Durham* v. *United States,* 1954), was convicted of housebreaking. A psychiatrist testified that the defendant heard voices, suffered from psychoses, and had a psychopathic personality. The Appeals Court rejected the right-wrong test and held instead "that an accused is not criminally responsible if his unlawful act was the product of mental disease or mental defect" (*Durham* v. *United States,* 1954: 874–875). In other words, even if a defendant knew that what he did was wrong, he is not held responsible if his act was caused by mental defect or disease.

One central difference in the effect of the two rules is that more defendants are covered by the Durham rule than by the M'Naghten precedent (Rubin, 1965). It is argued that the Durham rule is more humane and moral because it excludes more people from criminal prosecution than does the M'Naghten rule, and it is also argued that the Durham rule is scientifically sounder because it relies more heavily on the advice of psychiatrists. Psychiatrists usually do have a larger role in jurisdictions where the Durham rule is used. But according to Rubin (1965), it is untrue that excluding people from criminal punishment under the Durham rule is more humanitarian. Whether a person is sentenced to a prison or committed to a mental hospital, that person is still deprived of freedom. More often than not, the conditions and daily routine in the mental hospital are very similar to those in a prison. All that has been changed is the name of the institution, which camouflages the true nature of the situation. Court-appointed psychiatrists offer one more way of short-circuiting the trial process and one more way to deny poor and powerless defendants the rights guaranteed them in the Constitution of the United States.

There is yet another way in which psychiatrists, and sometimes social workers, are used in the criminal justice process. This occurs if the judge requests a presentence investigation of a convicted defendant supposedly as a help in determining an appropriate sentence. However, in reality, judges typically pick over the report selectively to justify the sentence they have already decided on. Since these reports are not taken seriously by judges, it is not surprising to discover that the very busy persons who prepare such reports take various shortcuts, such as the use of stereotypes to describe defendants. Moreover, the reports describe defendants in a way which is consistent with their new status. The defendents' positive characteristics are rarely mentioned, the descriptions consisting mainly of negative and unsupported clichés. A further problem with such reports is that they follow an individual from the court to a correctional institution if the person is incarcerated, and may later be used to influence the prisoner's future (Blumberg, 1967: 157–161).

JUVENILE JUSTICE

Goals of the juvenile court

The alleged goals of the juvenile court unlike those of the criminal court are not to punish or control but to diagnose and treat the problems of the young people who are brought to its attention. A new vocabulary is used in the juvenile court to symbolize the difference between its proceedings and criminal proceedings. Examples of this new terminology include the following: *petition* instead of *complaint, summons* instead of *warrant, initial hearing* instead of *arraignment, finding of involvement* instead of *conviction,* and *disposition* instead of *sentence.* The goals are presumably to investigate, diagnose, and prescribe treatment—not to fix guilt or blame, as in criminal courts. It is merely assumed that the child committed the act being considered (Haskell and Yablonsky, 1974: 30–31); therefore, his or her background becomes more important than the facts of a given incident. In this setting, lawyers are unnecessary since the proceeding is not adversarial—everyone is supposedly trying to help the child. The hearing is informal and private, including only the immediately involved parties. Since the hearing is allegedly not an adversary proceeding, no juries are used.

Constitutional rights of juveniles

In spite of all the fine prose about the juvenile courts' goals of caring for and treating young people, it gradually became clear that in the name of treatment these courts in fact had a highly coercive potential. For one thing, since those brought before juvenile courts were allegedly there for help and not punishment, they were not accorded any of the constitutional rights accorded citizens in criminal courts.

The U.S. Supreme Court's first attempt to specify the constitutional rights of juveniles is embodied in the 1967 *Gault* decision. This case involved a 15-year-old Arizona youth, Gerald Gault, who was taken into custody by a county sheriff because a neighbor complained that she had recieved a "lewd and indecent" phone call from him. No notice of the specific charges to be made in court was given to the boy's parents, nor was notice given of any right to counsel or of privilege against self-incrimination. The hearing was held in juvenile court one week after the boy was apprehended, and the boy's accuser was not required to be present. Gault was sentenced to a state juvenile institution. In 1967 the Supreme Court ruled that the handling of this case was unconstitutional and that juveniles are guaranteed the following rights under the constitution:

1. The right to notice of the charges.
2. The right to counsel.
3. The right to face prosecution witnesses and cross-examine them.
4. The right to refuse to answer questions that might tend to be incriminating.

The Court, however, did not rule in this case that juveniles have the right to bail pending disposition of their case, the right to trial by jury, the right to a public trial, the right to a transcript of the proceedings, or the right to appellate review—all of which are rights that are accorded to adults.

Defense attorneys in the juvenile court are often confused about what role they can play in the proceedings. This confusion arises because the rights of juveniles are unclear and in a state of flux as a result of the combination of constitutional and treatment concerns. The vagueness of delinquency laws also contributes to the confusion (Platt, 1969: 168, 173). One of the confusing aspects of the court process is that the rules of evidence in the juvenile court are unclear. There is much reliance on such information as reports which are the result of interviews with a child's teacher or neighbors, which are legally only hearsay, or secondhand evidence, and inadmissable in criminal trials of adults. Because of this confusion, attorneys in juvenile courts often do nothing (Lemert, 1967). Their inactivity causes juvenile court judges to look down on them for contributing nothing to the process.

The offense alleged does not allow a prediction of the kind of court response. The juvenile court considers not only the offense but also the youth's overall behavior, personality, family, and social circumstances (Emerson, 1969: 89). Essentially, the court wants to know what type of youth is being processed, and this is in turn essentially a question of moral character (Emerson, 1969: 90). Three types of moral character are distinguished by the court: normal, hard-core or criminallike, and disturbed (Emerson, 1969: 91). But the disposition depends on more than judgment of moral character; family background is also important. A hard-core boy from a stable family may be released to his parents, whereas a hard-core boy with a different home situation may go to reform school (Emerson, 1969: 97).

The court presentation by the lawyer or probation officer can depict the youth's character in a favorable light and keep a youth with a long record out of an institution. That is, a *pitch* can be made for the youth. On the other hand, a more severe disposition than usual may be sought by presenting an argument to discredit the youth's character—in other words, a *denunciation* of the youth (Emerson, 1969: 102–106). A denunciation will show that the act is part of a hopelessly criminal career, whereas a pitch will claim that the act is part of growing up into a normal life. Both presentations claim a general pattern of behavior, and both relate the actor to wider social factors, the most important of which is the delinquent's family situation. A pitch can use a bad home life as an *excuse,* whereas a denunciation may cite the family situation as the *cause* of this and other potentially serious delinquency.

Defense strategies include claims of innocence, justification, excuse, or counterdenunciation. A justification advances some higher or competing value against that violated by the act, such as an "appeal to higher loyalties." A youngster might claim, "I had to rob the liquor store because my brother asked me to help him, and I had to help my brother even if it was against the law." An excuse does not challenge the values violated by the act, but merely mitigates the actor's responsibility for misconduct, as, for example, youths who claim that they were forced to commit crimes by older and bigger boys. Complete defenses, such as claims of innocence, are not usually accepted by the court. Counterdenunciations, especially of court officials, are also usually unacceptable (Emerson, 1969: 142–143).

The courtroom ceremony is structured to intimidate the delinquent and saddle him with the role of wrongdoer, denying him an opportunity to express a lack of commitment to that role. Sometimes the court dramatizes the delinquent's powerlessness by announcing a disposition and then at the last minute suspending it and placing the youth on probation (Emerson, 1969: 172–215).

Demeanor regarded as meriting leniency from the court includes expressions of remorse, deference, and appreciation to the court. This involves displaying verbal as well as nonverbal signs of respect, such as facial signs of remorse. The youth, in short, must fully submit to the role of wrongdoer. Normal rules of social interaction do not apply to court personnel, for the judge can stare at the youth, ridicule the youth's appearance, and ask intimate and embarrassing questions. Poise and coolness on the part of a youth, which are normally rewarded in other social situations, are punished in the court. The judge may not be harsh but more matter of fact with a youth if he feels that the youth is not responsible for the delinquent behavior, or if he feels that a youth is hopeless and that a routine commitment is the only alternative. However, once a judge commits a youth, the court's potential sanction has actually been used, and control of the youth's demeanor may become more difficult (Emerson, 1969: 172–215).

CONCLUSION

Shortly after a suspect is arrested for a felony, the case is brought before a judge for a preliminary hearing in a magistrate court and/or is presented to a grand jury for action. If probable cause is found to believe that the accused is guilty, the accused is bound over for a criminal trial in a higher, circuit court. For lesser crimes—misdemeanors—the magistrate court can try the case. While awaiting trial, and during the trial itself, the accused may be released on bail if he can negotiate his release with a bail-bondsman. The bailbondsman has frequently been found to be a corrupting influence on the judicial process. Alternatives to the traditional bail system were and should be explored. Criminal lawyers as a social type are powerless, relatively low in status within their profession, and frequently coopted by the court organization. This applies to public defenders as well as to most privately retained criminal lawyers. Psychiatry plays a coercive role in the court process, in part because it is not recognized by defendants and others as potentially destructive of human dignity and freedom. The methods used to select judges and juries, although alleged to be democratic, are not in fact representative of every class interest. Finally, despite all the inequities in the criminal justice process routinely suffered by adults, the juvenile justice system possesses even fewer qualities of decency and democracy.

The court process seems to work to the disadvantage of the poor and powerless, and this is also true of criminal laws and police operations. The protection against excessive bail, and the right to defense counsel and trial by jury, are so distorted in actual practice as to make a mockery of these constitutional guarantees. Yet there seems to be no movement for radical reform of these processes, since those affected are largely the poor and racial and ethnic minorities. Considering that the operation of the court system is class biased and that police behavior is similarly discriminatory, the data the police and courts produce—official arrest and conviction records—must be suspected of reflecting class interests rather than be regarded as a barometer of criminal behavior. It is to the consequent problems in the measurement of crime or criminal behavior that we now turn.

REFERENCES

Argersinger v. *Hamlin*
  1972 407 U.S. 25

Axelrad, Sydney
  1952 "Negro and White Male Institutionalized Delinquents," *American Journal of Sociology* 57(March): 569–574.

Barak, Gregg
  1975 "In Defense of the Rich: The Emergence of the Public Defender," *Crime and Social Justice* 3(Summer): 2–14.

Barnes, Harry E. and Negley K. Tetters
  1959 *New Horizons in Criminology.* 3d ed. Englewood Cliffs, N.J.: Prentice-Hall.

Blumberg, Abraham S.
  1967a   *Criminal Justice.* Chicago: Quadrangle Books.
  1967b   "The Practice of Law as Confidence Game: Organizational
           Cooptation of a Profession," *Law and Society Review* 1(June):
           15–39.

Bowers, William J.
  1974   *Executions in America.* Lexington, Mass.: Lexington Books.

Bullock, Henry A.
  1961   "Significance of the Racial Factor in the Length of Prison Sen-
          tences," *Journal of Criminal Law, Criminology, and Police Science*
          52(November–December): 411–417.

Dill, Forrest
  1975   "Discretion, Exchange, and Social Control: Bail Bondsmen in
          Criminal Courts," *Law and Society Review* 9(Summer):
          639–674.

Durham v. *United States*
  1954   C.A.D.C. 214 F 2d 862–876 *Federal Reporter.*

Emerson, Robert M.
  1969   *Judging Delinquents: Context and Process in Juvenile Court.*
          Chicago: Aldine Publishing Co.

Gault, In re
  1967   387, U.S. 1

Gideon v. *Wainwright*
  1963   372 U.S. 335

Goldfarb, Ronald
  1965   *Ransom.* New York: John Wiley and Sons.

Greenberg, Jack and Jack Himmelstein
  1969   "Varieties of Attack on the Death Penalty," *Crime and Delin-
          quency* 15(January): 112–120.

Haskell, Martin R. and Lewis Yablonsky
  1974   *Juvenile Delinquency.* Chicago: Rand McNally College Publish-
          ing Co.

Katz, Lewis, Lawrence Litwin, and Richard Bamberger
  1972   *Justice Is the Crime: Pretrial Delay in Felony Cases.* Cleveland:
          Press of Case Western Reserve University.

Korn, Richard R. and Lloyd W. McCorkle
  1963   *Criminology and Penology.* New York: Holt, Rinehart and
          Winston.

Lemert, Edwin M.
  1967   "Legislating Change in the Juvenile Court," *Wisconsin Law Review* 1967(Spring): 421–448.

Miller, Norman and Donald T. Campbell
  1959   "Recency and Primacy in Persuasion as a Function of the Timing of Speeches and Measurements," *Journal of Abnormal and Social Psychology* 59(July): 1–9.

M'Naghten's Case, Daniel
  1843   8 *English Reports* 718–724.

New York Legal Aid Society
  1972   "The Unconstitutional Administration of Bail: *Bellamy* v. *The Judges of New York City*," *Criminal Law Bulletin* 8(July–August): 459–506.

Platt, Anthony M.
  1969   *The Child Savers: The Invention of Delinquency*. Chicago: University of Chicago Press.

President's Commission on Law Enforcement and Administration of Justice
  1967   *The Challenge of Crime in a Free Society*. Washington, D.C.: U.S. Government Printing Office.

Puttkammer, Ernst W.
  1953   *Administration of Criminal Law*. Chicago: University of Chicago Press.

Rankin, Anne
  1964   "The Effect of Pretrial Detention," *New York University Law Review* 39(June): 641–655.

Rosett, Arthur and Donald R. Cressey
  1976   *Justice by Consent: Plea Bargains in the American Courthouse*. Philadelphia: J. B. Lippincott Co.

Ross et al. v. *Moffitt*
  1974   U.S. Supreme Court Bulletin. 1973–74 term. Vol. 2. B 3750. No. 73–786.

Rubin, Sol
  1965   *Psychiatry and Criminal Law*. Dobbs Ferry, N.Y.: Oceana Publications.

Ryan, John V.
  1967   "The Last Days of Bail," *Journal of Criminal Law, Criminology, and Police Science* 58(December): 542–550.

St. Louis Post Dispatch
  1973   "Judge Brown Said to Have Faced Move for Contempt Cita-
          tion," June 7: 9A.

Strodtbeck, Fred L., Rita M. James, and Charles Hawkins
  1957   "Social Status in Jury Deliberations," *American Sociological Re-
          view* 22(December): 713–719.

Sudnow, David
  1965   "Normal Crimes: Sociological Features of the Penal Code in a
          Public Defender Office," *Social Problems* 12(Winter): 255–276.

Szasz, Thomas S.
  1963   *Law, Liberty, and Psychiatry.* New York: Collier Books.
  1965   *Psychiatric Justice.* New York: Collier Books.

Tappan, Paul W.
  1960   *Crime, Justice, and Correction.* New York: McGraw-Hill Book
          Co.

Watson, Richard A. and Rondal G. Downing
  1969   *The Politics of the Bench and the Bar: Judicial Selection under the
          Missouri Nonpartisan Plan.* New York: John Wiley and Sons.

Wice, Paul B.
  1974   "Purveyors of Freedom: The Professional Bondsmen," *Society*
          11 (July–August): 34–41.

Wolfgang, Marvin E., Arlene Kelley, and Hans C. Nolde
  1962   "Comparison of the Executed and the Commuted among
          Admissions to Death Row," *Journal of Criminal Law, Criminol-
          ogy, and Police Science* 53(September): 301–311.

Wood, Arthur L.
  1967   *Criminal Lawyer.* New Haven: College and University Press.

9

Discretion, exchange, and social control: Bail bondsmen in criminal courts*

Forrest Dill

INTRODUCTION

An impression widely held has it that American criminal courts are caught in a crisis. The manifestations of this presumably critical condition are well-known: ever-expanding workloads; indigent defendants held for weeks, months, and sometimes years of pre-trial confinement; officials and attorneys preoccupied with the mechanics of "plea bargains" instead of the intricacies of trials; protracted delays in settling some cases; disposition of other cases by means of arbitrary and prejudicial techniques; pervasive inequalities in sentencing decisions, and so on.

During the last five years, these symptoms have received attention from a number of respected journalists (James, 1971; Downie, 1972; Jackson, 1974). Criminal courts and their ailments have come under extensive study by several recent government commissions (President's Commission, 1967; Skolnick, 1969; National Advisory Commission, 1973). Social scientists have also shown increasing interest in these problems (Skolnick, 1967; Blumberg, 1970; Mileski, 1971; Levin, 1972; Mather, 1974).

Author's note: This work was made possible by financial support from the Russell Sage Foundation and the Water E. Meyer Research Institute of Law and organizational support from the Center for the Study of Law and Society, University of California, Berkeley. I am most grateful to Marc Galanter, Sheldon L. Messinger, Philippe Nonet, Jerome H. Skolnick, and Gerald D. Suttles for helpful comments and criticisms on earlier drafts of this paper.

* Reprinted from *Law & Society Review*, vol. 9, no. 4 (Summer 1975), pp. 639–674.

What has given birth to the apparently mounting concern over criminal courts? Their general state of health may in fact be poor, but there is nothing about the underlying condition that deserves to be called new. Consider, for example, the comments of Raymond Moley (1930: xi–xii), a perceptive observer of American criminal courts fifty years ago:

A large majority of persons whose guilt is established in our criminal courts plead guilty. The proportion varies from state to state and from city to city but it is a fair guess that approximately 80 percent of those who are found guilty in felony prosecutions plead guilty. The tendency is just as marked in the rural districts as in the cities. It is almost universal. The most reliable data show that the percentage in Chicago was in 1926 as high as 90 percent. In New York in 1926 it was about the same. In Detroit in 1928 it was 70 percent. In a number of Michigan counties outside of Detroit 90 percent. In Indianapolis in the same year 60 percent. In rural districts in Indiana over 90 percent. In Los Angeles 75 percent. In a dozen California counties in the same year 85 percent. In Connecticut in 1928, 90 percent. In Iowa in 1928, 93 percent. The practice is becoming standard.

Striking similarities with the contemporary situation are apparent, not only in the magnitudes of the figures presented, but also in the fact that the heavy dependence of criminal courts on guilty pleas was regarded then, as it is now, as the most prominent symptom of institutional breakdown. Thus, Moley wrote that the "tremendous importance of the plea of guilty in the administration of criminal justice" could quite clearly be seen as "a measure of the extent to which jury trial is supplanted by the process of administrative discretion" (1930: xii). Moley also estimated that the proportion of cases settled through guilty pleas in New York had risen from 20 percent in 1850 to 80 percent in the time he was writing, which suggests that treatment of defendants between arrest and disposition may have begun to deteriorate long before the start of this century. It does not appear that the situation of defendant in criminal courts has changed dramatically since Moley wrote (see Pound, 1945; Virtue, 1962: 79–135; Heumann, 1975).

But there has been one development of very great moment for criminal courts during this period. After the Second World War, the pace of civil liberties litigation quickened, partly in response to the shifting policy emphases of the U.S. Supreme Court. Among the cases that began to be heard with accelerating frequency were a number of novel claims to fair procedure by state and federal criminal defendants (Schubert, 1970: 49–50, 62–65). Over the next twenty years, the Court decided a long and complicated series of cases involving virtually the complete range of procedural problems in criminal law. By the middle of the 1960s what started as a trickle of appellate court rulings on criminal procedure had taken on the proportions of a flood (Cox, 1968).

It is common knowledge that many of these cases have resulted in decisions strengthening the rights of criminal defendants. That it has become more difficult to convict accused persons in court is also generally understood. Somewhat less appreciated is the true lineage of these decisions. In fact, they are continuous with what Egon Bittner (1970: 22) has termed "the progressive legalization of the criminal process." This trend has been evident in American society for at least a century and a half. Bittner claims that in recent decades the trend has accelerated "to the point where the rapidity of change bewilders even seasoned jurists"—an accurate perception, indeed, as shown by Leonard Levy's detailed study (1974) of the mixture of genuine bewilderment and intense political resistance that has dealt a serious setback to the legalization movement over the last several years. But without radical change in the American system of government, the possibility that this trend will be reversed is, as Bittner argues, "imponderable" (1970: 22–23).

This movement toward legalization has sent shock waves through the entire system of criminal justice during the last two decades. For example, it has prompted organizational changes in law enforcement (Milner, 1971) and has stimulated the adoption of new practices in corrections (Ohlin, ed. 1973). The movement for procedural reform has hastened the erosion of traditional boundaries between the two formerly separate systems of criminal and juvenile justice (Lefstein et al., 1969; Lemert, 1970). Also, it has undoubtedly contributed to the declining rate of admissions noted by observers of American prisons over the past decade (Rothman, 1972).

Another place where signs of change have appeared within the criminal justice system is the procedural interstice occupied by the institution of bail. Numerous attempts to reform the bail system have been launched over the last fifteen years (Paulsen, 1966; Wice and Simon, 1970). Perhaps surprisingly, appellate courts have had no direct influence on this development. As Caleb Foote (1965: 959) observed ten years ago, bail reform has been "the only major reform of recent decades in which the courts have played a wholly passive role." If this observation seems less puzzling now than it might have a decade ago, it may be that in the intervening years we have come to rely less upon the appellate courts to direct policy and shape reform. Yet it is curious that the last two decades produced no "landmark" U.S. Supreme Court decision about the rights of criminal defendants to release on bail.

This paper supplies part of the explanation for this puzzle. It reports on a study of the role of bail bondsmen in criminal courts. The paper also suggests why the financial bail system has retained its historic importance in the scheme of American criminal justice, despite more than a decade of effort to replace it with more rational and equitable arrangements.

THE STUDY

The legal purpose of bail is to enable persons accused of crime to remain at liberty while preparing for trial, and the only lawful reason for requiring defendants to post bail is to insure their presence for required court appearances. Nevertheless, bail can be and in fact is routinely used by court officials for other purposes not recognized by law—to detain some defendants who are believed dangerous or likely to flee, to punish other defendants who are regarded as disrespectful or troublesome, and to elicit information or confession from still others. In other words, the bail system serves as the key instrument by which officials maintain control over persons arrested for crime.

The perspective that I wish to develop concerns the assistance that bail bondsmen lend to criminal justice officials who are responsible for managing defendants in the period between arrest and disposition. Usually, officials can insure post-arrest confinement of particular defendants without difficulty, because the law allows wide latitude for setting bail amounts (as well as for making initial charging decisions upon which bail determinations are based). In any court system, however, there are customary limits to official discretion in bail setting and physical limits to the facilities available for pre-trial detention of defendants. Court officials therefore turn to bail bondsmen for informal cooperation in managing the population of arrested persons.

In the workings of the bail system, it is possible to discern a pattern of reciprocal sharing of discretionary powers between criminal court officials and bail bondsmen which facilitates the control of defendants in the pre-trial period. Through legitimate discretionary actions of their own, bail bondsmen can help officials to overcome constraints set by resource limitations and to avoid the legal guarantees which are supposed to protect the rights of defendants to bail; officials reciprocate by exercising their discretionary powers in ways that benefit bondsmen. Naturally, this exchange has consequences for both parties. For bondsmen, the consequence is that many defendants who might otherwise represent poor business risks can be welcomed as customers, although other defendants whom the bondsmen view as good business risks must be turned down. The manifest contributions that bondsmen make to the management of arrestees lead court officials to develop a stake in neutralizing the regulatory structure designed by the legislature to govern the activities of bail bondsmen.

The bail bondsman has never been regarded as playing a substantial enough part in the criminal justice process to merit careful analysis. Most observers view the presence of this figure in the courts as an anomaly. A species of private businessman, the bondsman has long been associated in American legal folklore with corruption of officials and exploitation of defendants; recent efforts to reform the bail system have sharpened this image. One contemporary critic has bluntly described the bondsman as "an unappealing and useless member of the society who lives on the law's inadequacy and his fellowman's troubles," and argues that the bondsman "gives nothing in return, or so little as to serve no overriding utilitarian purpose" (Goldfarb, 1965: 102). Thus, although the bondsman's powers are lawful, his very existence strikes some observers as parasitical.

What little is known about the role of the bail bondsman has been strongly biased by the findings of reform oriented investigators. Grand jury studies, legislative investigations, and journalistic exposés have portrayed bondsmen as "fixers" of cases, corrupters of police and judges, and peddlers of illegitimate influence (see Goldfarb, 1965: 102–115; Wice, 1974). In short, bail bondsmen typically have been viewed as essential links in chains of official corruption. Such findings contain an element of truth, of course, but it is hardly surprising that bail bondsmen in corrupt jurisdictions participate in corrupting practices.

The following report is based mainly on direct observation of the activities of bail bondsmen in the criminal courts of two cities which gave no evidence of systematic corruption at the time the study was being done. Two months of field research were carried out by the author in Mountain City and Westville, both located in the same western state. An initial introduction to a Westville bondsman was arranged through a local criminal lawyer. A chain of subsequent introductions led to contacts with six other bondsmen in Westville and five in Mountain City. Periods of observation with individual bondsmen ranged from one to seven days. Bondsmen were observed in various settings, including business offices, restaurants, taverns, courts, and jails.

Although no attempt was made to spend time with all bondsmen working in the two cities (approximately ten in Westville and twenty in Mountain City), data gathered by observing contacted bondsmen were carefully checked against information obtained by interviewing lawyers and court personnel. In addition, available documentary materials on bail bondsmen were consulted. These included historical accounts of the development of the institution of financial bail (Beeley, 1927; Yale Law Journal, 1961), empirical studies of bail administration (Foote, 1954, 1958; Silverstein, 1966), and legal critiques of the bail system (Foote, 1965; Goldfarb, 1965). This examination of the literature suggests that the findings reported in the study represent general patterns.

BUSINESS IMPERATIVES AND ILLEGITIMATE PRACTICES IN BAIL BONDING

The bail system is at once an important legal procedure and a lucrative business enterprise. By allowing commercial intermediaries to post bail for the release of arrested persons prior to trial, the state has created a business operation within the criminal courts. The bondsman's role cannot be neatly catalogued. Freed and Wald (1964: 30) assigned the institution of bail "a hybrid status, somewhere between a free enterprise and a public utility." Bail bondsmen are private businessmen who render a sevice to individuals in return for remuneration at levels fixed by the state. In one sense, then, bondsmen are government sub-contractors. But their work injects them into direct participation in the business of criminal courts, where their actions can and do affect the outcomes of criminal cases. Their behavior must be examined from two different and somewhat conflicting perspectives, the first emphasizing business concerns and the second stressing legal responsibilities.

The business setting

Bail may be looked upon as a specialized insurance system. It is designed to reconcile the conflicting interests between defendants, who desire to be at liberty before trial, and the state, which insists that defendants be present for court proceedings. Bail bondsmen are the visible commercial operatives of this system.[1] In principle, these conflicting interests will be held in balance by the operation of a set of positive and negative incentives. There must be, on the one hand, sufficient financial gain to induce bondsmen to invest in defendants to relieve pressures on custodial facilities. Bondsmen, then, are legally permitted to collect non-refundable premiums or interest charges (usually 10 percent of the amount of bail) from defendants for whom they post bail. Bondsmen regain the bail amounts posted when they have satisfied their promises that defendants will appear in court as required. On the other hand, the state needs to protect itself against the inconvenience and public outrage likely to arise when bailed defendants fail to appear for trial. Thus, the law requires that amounts pledged as security for defendants released on bail will be forfeited to the state in the event of non-appearance.

At one time, bondsmen were marginal, independent entrepreneurs operating with scant resources (Beeley, 1927). Today, major insurance companies stand behind the individual bondsmen who operate the bail bonding business. A dozen companies are said (Sutherland and Cressey, 1970: 404) to control nearly all the corporate bail bonds written in this country. The policies of these companies affect the activities of bondsmen and may thus indirectly affect the administration of criminal law. Bail bondsmen are

---

[1] As one student of the bail system (Hoskins, 1968: 1136) has commented: "In essence, the bail bondsman acts as a broker to accommodate the conflicting interests of the state and arrestee by quickly bailing him out of jail—for a price. The bondsman performs a service for the state by promising to return the arrestee to the court at a specified time, thereby relieving the state of the expense of incarcerating large numbers of persons prior to their trials."

located at the bottom of this business described by Goldfarb (1965: 95–96) as:

a straight line beginning with the large national insurance companies and running down through the regional subadministrators and eventually to local agents (the bondsmen) who camp around the local court houses and actually hustle the business. . . . there is little real business interplay between these three levels. The business functions begin at the top; and the responsibilities and risks increase on the way down, while inversely the profit risks also increase on the way down. The insurance company on top sets the public image of a respectable business and within the working scheme of its bail setup takes no risk with its agents. The agents go about their business in their own fashion, and for this privilege agree to retain only a small percentage of the profit.

This surety-company dominance of the bail bond business is found in most states and in all large metropolitan areas—wherever criminal court activity is sizeable enough to attract and support corporate investment.

A key feature of the business is the low degree of risk for the surety companies. To protect themselves against loss, companies which sell bail bonds require bondsmen to deposit with the companies reserve funds, built up through assessments on fees or premiums bondsmen collect from customers. For each corporate bond used, the bondsman must contribute 10 percent of the premium he collects from the customer to reserve funds. In addition, the surety company levies a 20 percent charge on each premium the bondsman collects for posting a corporate bond. This leaves the bondsman with a gross profit of 70 percent of each premium collected on a corporate surety bond. In theory, the amount of bonds that the bondsman can write is determined by the amount in his reserve fund. Any forfeitures declared against bonds he has written are paid with the reserve fund. If forfeitures exceed the total amount of reserves, the company may take the remaining amount from future premiums the bondsman receives.

The sale of bail bonds is thus an immensely profitable, low-risk arena of enterprise within the insurance industry. Individual bondsmen supply nearly all the labor necessary for corporate profit from the sale of bail bonds and are sometimes said to work for the companies. Bondsmen in fact are not employees of these companies; they are independent businessmen who, by serving as agents of the surety companies, obtain financial backing necessary to satisfy solvency standards set by the state. Bondsmen are not salaried; rather, they receive their earnings on something nearer to a sales-commission basis. They pay their own business expenses, set their own hours, and work out their own local arrangements for conducting their affairs. For example, a bondsman who has developed a large business may employ additional persons on various terms—hourly wages, salaries, or commissions. Moreover, instead of using corporate bonds, they may post their own assets (e.g., treasury bonds or cash) as bail and reap a higher rate of profit. In this respect, their business arrangement is quite different from that of other insurance salesmen.

Surety companies have little direct control over the activities of individual bondsmen despite—or possibly because of—the pattern of corporate authority. Corporate policy may make itself felt in a very general way by placing broad limits on the amount of bonds that particular bondsmen may write at any period of time. Where bondsmen represent several surety companies, corporate influence is weakened.[2] The ability of surety companies to insure themselves against loss reduces their need to exercise continuous supervision and control over bondsmen.

Competition for business

Within the local court system, the bondsman's interactions with defendants, attorneys, [and] law enforcement and court officials are permeated by a multitude of legal and illegal commercial possibilities. For this reason the bondsman's business affairs are subject to comprehensive legal regulation, and his work therefore has some unusual restraints. He must maintain detailed accounts of all his transactions and submit them to state insurance commission officials as matters of public record. He may not legally enter into any special agreements with government officials about when or

---

[2] The relationship between bondsman and surety companies is marked by competition between the companies to increase their shares of the market. In some areas where a company insists on conditions which a bondsman regards as unreasonable, he may elect to write bonds for a competitor company. Bondsmen may be associated with several companies at once. For the individual bondsman, this may be a matter of self-protection, since if one company loses its standing as a qualified surety—perhaps because of the improper actions of other bondsmen using bonds it guarantees—the bondsman can continue to write bonds issued by other companies. (See National Conference on Bail and Criminal Justice, 1965: 228–232.)

on what terms he is to supply his services. Moreover, he is forbidden to offer as incentives to potential clients or as advantages to actual customers any extra services such as legal advice, attorney referral information, or assistance with court cases. Finally, he may bargain with potential clients over fees, but must sell his services at rates set by the state.

The bondsman's primary occupational difficulties stem from the fact that legal restrictions compel him to meet business imperatives without the use of many standard business techniques. Like many small businessmen, the bondsman operates in an environment offering neither steady demand for his services nor reliable means for guarding against incursions by competitors. In other business settings such conditions foster highly competitive modes of behavior. Legal regulations drastically narrow the initiative the bondsman can legitimately exercise, theoretically closing off all but a few forms of competition as illegal practices. Beyond rendering "prompt, courteous service twenty-four hours a day," the only legitimate business technique that the bondsman can use is advertising. In practice, however, only marginal returns are expected from this source.

The principal competitive devices employed by bondsmen are illegal. Reciprocal referrals are a common business arrangement among bondsmen and criminal lawyers. All the bondsmen I talked to have client-sharing agreements with lawyers and assume that the practice is universal. Many bondsmen seek to develop illegal ways of gaining access to potential clients and transforming them into paying customers. They also attempt to cultivate informal exchange relationships with police, judges, and other officials for the information, protection, and administrative influence—in short, the business advantages—that such relationships can provide.

Bondsmen devote considerable effort to developing and expanding illegitimate sources of business within the legal system. One means of illegal recruitment of customers is the "jail-house lawyer." Typically this role is filled by a person who spends a great deal of time in jail on minor charges like intoxication, begging, or loitering. His job is to steer defendants from inside the jail to a particular bondsman on the outside. These services may come quite cheaply, and the relationship is likely to be very casual. The arrangement is not capable of much formalization owing to the irregular habits of the destitute alcoholics available as personnel; for the same reason it is not very productive for bondsmen. Only a few customers are likely to be recruited in this way and they tend to be first offenders facing minor charges. Experienced defendants are more likely to know bondsmen from past encounters with the law or by reputation, and defendants arrested on serious charges are likely to make contact with bondsmen through other channels, usually lawyers.

Practicing attorneys offer a much more important opportunity through which the bondsman recruits business. The bondsman can count on criminal lawyers for a certain proportion of his clientele, since even attorneys not wishing to deal with bondsmen must occasionally enlist their services for defendants.[3] Attorneys may legitimately refer cases to bondsmen, but reciprocal client-referral agreements between lawyers and bondsmen are forbidden. When questioned during field observations, some bondsmen expressed apprehension about this subject and offered insistent denials that any such arrangements existed. In several instances, the subject of bondsmen-attorney arrangements had not even arisen in conversation before bondsmen began making unsolicited denials. The phenomenon is so widespread and so much a part of bail bonding and criminal law practice, however, that it is impossible to conceal for long.[4]

The following event[5] occurred after one week of steady observation with a bondsman in Mountain City. The case was instruc-

---

[3] However, attorneys and bondsmen are both interested in the same question—the defendant's ability to pay (see Wood, 1967; Blumberg, 1967). This means that attorneys may seek to avoid referring cases to bondsmen, and vice versa.

[4] Such relationships are considerably more important to lawyers than to bondsmen. Bail bondsmen have direct access to persons who may need legal representation and thus they occupy an ideal position from which to steer such persons to attorneys. Furthermore, defendants facing minor charges may decide to forego the services of a private lawyer, even if they can pay a bondsman's fee for posting bond. On the other hand, most attorneys handle so few criminal matters that they cannot expect any advantages from offering to exchange business with bondsmen on a client-sharing basis. Even those attorneys specializing in criminal practice may find that clients typically arrive having already enlisted the aid of a bondsman. Accordingly, reciprocation by attorneys may often take the form of direct payment to bondsmen for referrals. Rates of payment vary over time and from bondsman to bondsman, and it is quite likely that local political conditions determine the power of bondsmen to set rates and conditions. For example, a 1960 investigation of bail practices in New York City revealed the influence of bondsmen to be so great that attorneys refusing to pay rates demanded by bondsmen for referral of clients could get no business (Goldfarb, 1965: 114).

[5] All names used in this and other incidents described in this paper are pseudonyms.

tive because the relationship between the bondsman and the attorney was still being defined at the time of the meeting:

Late one morning, Walt told me that he would be meeting a young lawyer named Dave Redding for lunch. Walt explained that he had sent some cases to this attorney in the past. Opening his desk drawer to show me the business cards of several attorneys, he said, "It's against the law to refer attorneys, so I usually show the people these cards and allow them to choose which lawyer they want."

When Redding arrived, Walt suggested that I join them for lunch, but qualified his invitation by saying to Redding, "If you have any private business to talk over, then we of course won't consider this." Redding's immediate reply was: "What do you mean, private business? We have nothing to hide. Our contacts are well regulated by the state insurance commission. Sure he can come along."

On the way to the restaurant, Walt asked: "Well, Dave, what's the purpose of today's meeting, and what can I do for you?" Redding responded: "Oh, there's no special purpose. I just wanted to thank you for the business. This is a courtesy lunch, a social visit, if you will."

After lunch, the two kidded each other about the $200 fee that Redding had collected from Martinez, a young Mexican-American whom Walt had bailed out two weeks earlier on charges of narcotics possession and suspicion of burglary. They also discussed another case involving a defendant's hit-and-run accident. Walt had referred this case to Redding, who had taken it without hesitation. Now some question had arisen about the defendant's ability or willingness to pay Redding's fee. Walt assured him that the defendant had money and counseled Redding to "work on him."

Then Redding said, "I certainly appreciate the business you've sent me. I'm trying to build up a practice and this helps a great deal. I knew this wasn't a get-rich-quick business, but I had no idea it would be this hard." Walt assured him that the future held great promise for a fine young attorney like himself, and then added: "Sure, I'll send you some more cases. And let me ask that in return you refer your cases to me. Now if you ever have anybody who needs to get out and you know he's a good risk, just call me and tell me that he's good as gold and I'll take him right out without collateral. Understand?"

As this case illustrates, the bondsman may have vital knowledge of the defendant's financial situation. First-time defendants in particular may unwittingly reveal financial information to the bondsman during "routine" questioning. Such defendants frequently do not understand the nature of the bondsman's role and may see him as yet another official whose powers must be respected. Inexperienced defendants are more vulnerable to the attorney-referral arrangement. Bondsmen in some other cities are said to exploit defendants by requiring them to take their cases to certain attorneys as a condition of posting bail for their release (Goldfarb, 1965: 114). No evidence of this practice could be found in Westville or Mountain City, where the bondsman-attorney referral system may have been working in favor of defendants. One lawyer speculated that attorneys needed to exercise caution with cases referred from bondsmen. "They have to give these clients a fair deal," he said, "or the defendants might resent the attorney and mess up the system. It's too risky for the attorney working with a bondsman not to give good representation."

Collusion with jail personnel may be another valuable means of customer recruitment for the bondsman. During the period of field observation, it became apparent to me that certain jail police in Mountain City were assisting certain bondsmen in getting customers. The simplest and most reliable method was one that required only a moment's effort by an individual jail staff member. "All he has to do," an attorney explained, "is find out if the defendant has a bondsman lined up. If not, he points to a particular bondsman's number in the telephone directory and pushes a dime into the guy's hand." Even this simple arrangement can result in unexpected complications, as the following account reveals:

I was present with Walt in his office when he received a call from a woman requesting that bail be posted for one of her employees. The defendant had been arrested the night before for driving on a suspended license. Walt told the woman that he would call the jail to determine the amount of bail and then call her back. Bail had been set at $296, making the premium charge $39.60—10 percent of the amount of bail plus an additional $10 charge which bondsmen are allowed to collect on all bails under $500. Walt called the woman back, advising her that she would need to submit the premium as well as her signature to a deed promising to pay the full amount of bail if the defendant failed to appear in court. The woman said that she would send another of her employees with the money to Walt's office.

When the second employee arrived, Walt and I went to jail across the street "to get the body." At the jail another bondsman was waiting to post bail for the defendant Walt had come to get. Walt immediately sensed what was happening and informed one of the jailors that he wanted to talk to the defendant. A jail policeman stepped forward and said, "No, Alvarez wants to go with the other guy." There was some discussion, and eventually it was decided that the defendant would determine which bondsman would "get the bail."

Alvarez (a black) was brought out, and he turned to the other bondsman (also a black). The two spoke briefly in hushed tones. Then Walt (not black) approached Alvarez and said, "Mrs. McGee called me to help you. Your friend Smith is over in my office right now waiting for you." Alvarez turned to the other bondsman, shrugged apologetically, and said, "I guess I'll have to go with him," indicating Walt. As we rode down in the elevator, the other bondsman mumbled that he had also received a telephone call. Walt remained silent. Alvarez said, "Well, that's the way it goes."

After Alvarez and Smith left, I asked Walt how the other bondsman had become involved. Walt speculated that someone in the jail had persuaded Alvarez to call the other bondsman. Smith, Alvarez's co-worker, knew nothing about the other bondsman. I asked whether one of the jail police we had just seen had been responsible for the other bondsman's appearance. Walt replied, "Well, you saw the way he wanted Alvarez to be taken out by the other guy, didn't you?"

The same bondsman related an incident illustrating another variation of this method:

A man entered Walt's office and presented a slip of paper on which had been written the name of the defendant, the charge in exact penal code section terminology, the date of the next court appearance, and the amount of bail. The man was a supervisor in a public utility company where the defendant, a woman, was employed. The slip of paper, Walt was convinced, was *prima facie* evidence that one of the police had recommended a bondsman. Apparently the man had come to the wrong address.

Walt gladly cooperated with the man, however, and immediately went to the jail to take the woman out. When one of the jailors asked about the slip of paper, Walt "played dumb," saying that he never got any slips of paper from the jail. With great reluctance, the jailor released the defendant to Walt, who patiently explained several times that the woman's supervisor was waiting over in his office. "That guy was pretty unhappy, because he'd lost some sure money in the mix-up."

Other methods requiring collective efforts by jail police may sometimes be employed. These are more complicated and carry greater risks of discovery and failure. A Westville bondsman recounted an experience of his at the Mountain City jail:

"I got a call from the relative of a guy who had been put in jail over there. It was a pretty good bail, so I decided to drive over and take him out myself. When I got there I found a police hold on him. Now that hold wasn't on him when I left Westville only a half an hour before, so whoever put it on him should have still been around. But I couldn't find anybody who knew anything about it. They passed the buck and I went from one office to another trying to find out whose hold it was. Nobody knew, and finally they said they were going to let him go. Next thing I knew another bondsman came walking out with the defendant. Then they told me that they had taken the hold off him, but actually they were keeping him for this other bondsman."

In general, collective agreements among jail officials appear necessary to protect the system of collusion. Since this system functions as a means of restricting competition, its value depends on excluding some bondsmen so that business can be channeled to other bondsmen. But competition among bondsmen may result in some degree of participation in the system by nearly all local bondsmen.

There was no evidence to indicate the existence of collusion between jail police and bondsmen in Westville at the time of my study. With a smaller population, a more professionally disciplined police force, and a different political complexion, Westville presented relatively poor opportunities for collusive relations to develop between police and bondsmen. All of my informants claimed that defendants selected bondsmen on their own from inside the jail. If the Westville police were collaborating with particular bondsmen, the arrangement was either very well concealed or quite minor in scale.

In some cities, bondsmen reportedly refuse to extend services to defendants accused of minor offenses which require "nominal"— i.e., low—bail, because they view the modest premiums in such cases as not worth the trouble and risk of posting bond (Freed and Wald, 1964: 33). It seems likely that this practice would be found only where bail bonding had fallen under monopoly control by a small number of bondsmen. By assuring privileged bondsmen a guaranteed share of the profits, monopoly conditions would make it possible for bondsmen to neglect defendants in minor cases.

.Aside from some petty collusion in Mountain City bail practices, bail bonding in the two cities seemed to offer relatively undisturbed market conditions. For most bondsmen operating there, defendants in minor cases appeared to constitute the bulk of business and the most reliable source of income. Such cases were especially attractive because the bondsman could post his own assets and thereby avoid the costs of using corporate surety bonds. Although minor cases yield small premiums, they may be attractive to bondsmen as business opportunities precisely because of the low bail amounts on which the premiums are based. Also, by permitting bondsmen to charge defendants an extra $10 for posting bail in amounts less than $500—as done in the state where this research was carried out—the legal system increases the attractiveness of such cases.

PROFIT MAXIMIZATION AND CASE MANAGEMENT BY BONDSMEN

Shortly after bondsmen enter the criminal justice process, some defendants are granted pre-trial liberty and others are ordered held in detention to await further action in their cases. The timing of these events has created the impression that bondsmen are "purveyors of freedom" who play a key role in determining whether defendants will obtain release before trial (Wice, 1974). This view greatly exaggerates the influence that bondsmen have in such determinations, however.

Although bail procedures in different parts of the country are far from uniform (Silverstein, 1966), it is clear that bail administration everywhere belongs primarily to law enforcement and court officials. The most critical decisions—the bail amounts set in particular cases—are entirely controlled by local criminal justice officials, with prosecuting attorneys taking the dominant role. Bondsmen do not participate at all in these decisions for cases making up the largest volume of criminal court business. This is because of the widespread use of the bail schedule, a form approved by local judges listing uniform bail amounts for the most common misdemeanor violations (e.g., disorderly conduct, petty theft, simple assault, and certain vehicle offenses). It is true that bondsmen can and sometimes do refuse to post bail for defendants in such cases, but decisions as to the amounts required in particular cases are determined more or less automatically as a matter of clerical routine, usually by station-house police.

For cases involving charges of serious misdemeanor and felony offenses, bail setting typically takes place in court at the time of arraignment. This process involves negotiation between the judge, prosecutor, and defense attorney; the prosecutor's recommendations usually determine the final decision (Suffet, 1966). The bondsman plays no formal part in this process, either. In many cases of this kind, the defendant or his attorney may contact a bondsman before the bail hearing, and the bondsman may supply informal advice to the judge or the prosecutor concerning his willingness to post bail for the defendant. This may help the defendant by inducing the judge to set bail at a level which the defendant can afford. It can hardly work to the defendant's disadvantage.

Unlike the standardized bail amounts required in the most common misdemeanor cases, amounts set in cases involving serious offenses often vary a good deal, even when the charges are identical. Defendants who are unable to secure release at amounts initially set may request that bail be lowered. The frequency of bail reduction probably provides a rough measure of the extent of excessive bail in various jurisdictions, although in general bail reduction does not occur with much frequency in most places (Silverstein, 1966: 634–637). Both the bail schedule and the bail hearing lead to decisions that discriminate against sizeable proportions of the defendant population (Foote, 1954, 1958; Ares and Sturz, 1962; Silverstein, 1966). But it is mistaken to attribute these discriminatory results to bail bondsmen, given the economics of the situation in general and the bondsmen's inclinations to seek profits in particular.

The bondsman's interest in court efficiency

If bondsmen play only a minor role in determining defendants' chances for release, the same cannot be said of their role in handling defendants who are released on bail. Bondsmen actively employ a number of different techniques of case management. These practices are aimed at protecting investments and maximizing profits, but they also have positive functions for the court system. Nominally, bondsmen are private businessmen situated outside the criminal courts. Examination of their routine activities, however, indicates that they serve as agents of the court system responding to many of the problems that concern those who occupy official positions within it.

The strategies bondsmen use in managing cases reveal many generic similarities to the practices of lawyers, probation officers, and other agent-mediators within the court system (Blumberg, 1970). An important first step is often to establish a good relationship with the defendant. The bondsman usually extends a cordial, businesslike manner to each customer, seeking to convey a willingness to separate the defendant's specific dereliction from his or her general moral character. He therefore treats in a routine or "professional" way matters that his customers may regard as emergencies, but his mode of dealing with particular customers may vary depending on his perception of situational demands. A bondsman explained, "Each one of these people is different, and you've gotta handle them in different ways." Thus when the customer is a first-time defendant charged with a relatively minor offense, the bondsman's strategy may be to play down the seriousness of the defendant's plight by reciting such homilies as, "We get cases like this every day. Don't worry, it'll come out all right." In other minor cases where the customer is an experienced defendant and perhaps an old customer behind in payments for previous bail bond services, the bondsman may act in a slightly patronizing and officious manner, counseling the defendant to "be a good boy, don't get into any more trouble, and bring that money in next Friday." In cases involving more serious charges, the bondsman may deal calmly and quietly with the customer, emphasizing his neutrality by carefully avoiding any mention of the alleged offense.

Another and more important element of case management involves giving various forms of legal assistance and advice. Bondsmen always remind their customers of future court dates and instruct them about how to find the room in the court building where their cases will be heard, what time to show up, and what to expect during the proceeding. An indirect form of advice is sometimes employed if the defendant has already retained an attorney or has a particular attorney in mind. In this situation, the bondsman may issue a reassuring comment to the defendant, as, for example, "Oh, I know Bart will give you all the help he can. He's a fine lawyer." In another instance, I observed a bondsman attempting vigorously to persuade a defendant whom he had just bailed out to call an attorney whose name the defendant had mentioned as we walked from the jail to the bondsman's nearby office. The defendant was allowed to leave the office only after promising that he would go directly to look up the attorney. Bondsmen may also refer unrepresented defendants to attorneys.

Here, the practice of recommending attorneys appears in a different light, for it has the same purpose as is intended by congratulating the legally sophisticated defendant on his choice of attorney. Both of these techniques serve to increase the customer's feeling of personal competence and to reinforce his self-definition as a "defendant"—a person who is going through the court process and who will accept its judgment. The chances of panic and flight are thereby reduced.

In other cases, the bondsman gives direct legal advice. The following observed instances, both involving the same bondsman, suggest typical possibilities. In the first case, the bondsman counseled against retaining an attorney:

At about one o'clock one afternoon, one of Al's customers came into his office. The man had been arrested for drunk driving many weeks before. His court date was for two o'clock that day. Al told him that he had two alternatives: either he could demand a jury trial and hope that the complaint would be withdrawn, or he could plead guilty and ask the judge for probation and some time "to put a few beans aside and pay the fine."

Al explained: "If you ask for a jury trial, you'll need a lawyer and that can run into money. It might easily run you $250, and then you have no guarantee that you'll be acquitted. Of course, if you get a jury trial and an attorney, you will have a better judge. But with no priors the fine's only $296, so you might as well plead guilty, ask the judge for probation, and then get the money together over a period of time."

The customer contemplated Al's advice, then gave a resigned shrug and said, "Well, I guess I'll plead guilty. See you later."

The second case also involved a motor vehicle code violation:

Shortly after lunch on another afternoon, a young man who had been charged with littering and possessing open containers of beer in his car stopped by to see Al about his case. He was apprehensive about the outcome because the girl who had been arrested with him had already "copped out as charged." He asked: "What will happen if I change my earlier plea to guilty?"

Al answered: "It won't make any difference. They got the girl and all they want are guilty pleas. The judge will fine you $25, and that will be the end of it."

Al was correct. Later that afternoon the client returned and jubilantly told Al, "It's all over. I got out for $29."

Two features of these incidents deserve attention. First, each involved a minor offense. The bondsman's ability to offer sound legal advice depends on the degree to which court processing of the kind of case involved is routinized and therefore predictable. His legal expertise thus seems to be confined to traffic violations, public order offenses such as drunkenness and disturbing the peace, and minor property crimes. For the bondsman this may be a happy coincidence, since the typically small penalties facing defendants in such cases may take much of the risk out of the prospect of confronting the court without legal representation.

Second, the examples suggest that bondsmen share the interests of court officials in guilty pleas. More generally, both groups are interested in efficiency. The bondsman's liability for each bond he posts does not end until the defendant's case is cleared from the court docket. Every new customer represents a case that will remain open and a bond that will remain "out" for an indeterminate but roughly predictable amount of time. For example, after posting bail for a woman charged with welfare fraud, a Westville bondsman explained why this had been a good business decision: "She'll plead guilty and be put on probation. The case will be over in about two and a half months." The strength of the bondsman's business position depends on the volume of cases he handles: the amount of bonds in use is inversely related to the amount of new bonds that he can post. Therefore, his interests lie in efficient, routinized court procedures and compliant defendants. Anything that lengthens the duration of criminal cases—disorderly judicial administration, militant defense attorneys, non-appearance by defendants, new and unfamiliar legal procedures—weakens the bondsman's position.

The quasi-bureaucratic role of the bondsman

An important consideration for understanding the bondsman's activities is that cooperation from defendants may be contingent on the administrative practices of courts. Some defendants may fail to make required court appearances because they get lost in the system. For example, they may have separate appearances scheduled in two different court departments at exactly the same time, or they may be uninformed or confused about the court dates. In other cases, defendants may be unable to comply with required court appearances because of employment obligations or family emergencies.

Such problems are less likely to arise for defendants who have private legal representation. One of the key functions performed by attorneys in the criminal process is to direct the passage of cases through the procedural and bureaucratic mazes of the court system (Blumberg, 1967). For unrepresented defendants, however, the bondsman may perform the crucial institutional task of helping to negotiate court routines. In order to protect his investment, the bondsman may find it not merely desirable but necessary to guide defendants through the court process. By providing legal advice to his customers, arranging more convenient court dates for them, and negotiating their passage through the court process, the bondsman increases his chances of collecting fees and reduces the amount of time that his assets are encumbered. At the same time, these methods of case management promote orderly and efficient court administration. They also implicate bondsmen in unauthorized practice of law.

Efforts by bondsmen to organize the actions of individual customers in relation to the actions of court officials deepen the involvement of bondsmen in the criminal justice process. Not only do these efforts require frequent visits to court rooms, but they may also require informal assistance from court personnel. The experienced bondsman knows each of the bailiffs, court clerks, and accounting office members on a first-name basis and how much and what kinds of assistance each is willing to provide. The bondsman typically takes advantage of mutualized exchange opportunities at Christmas and New Year to reciprocate favors received through court "connections." If it is consistent with his personal style, he may seek to improve his relations with court clerks, bailiffs, and other court participants by "buttering them up" through flattery and other forms of interpersonal artifice. He may also supplement his day-to-day dealing with officials by occasionally dispensing gifts (such as free passes to professional sports events) and supplying drinks at nearby bars in after-hour gatherings.

One measure of the degree of cooperativeness of court officials is whether they will comply with the bondsman's request to bring a case forward on a particular day's court calendar. This small but nonetheless significant service, which can be easily rendered by the court clerk, is a favor that the bondsman may seek in order to keep track of his cases or to accelerate release of a new customer for whom bail has just been posted. Without this assistance, the bondsman cannot "move" cases in court. Where such influence is available, however, the bondsman can sometimes negotiate convenient court dates, coordinate multiple appearances, and forestall issuance of bench warrants.

A more important form of assistance that the bondsman may wish to arrange is for certain of his customers to be released on recognizance, i.e., without being required to make financial bail. If a defendant is returned to jail because of new difficulties with the law before he has paid his debt to the bondsman, the bondsman's fee may be jeopardized. When this happens, the bondsman may face two unsatisfactory options: either lose the balance of the money owed by the defendant or assume a greater risk by posting another bail bond in hopes of collecting the fees owed on the original bond. If a judge or prosecutor can be persuaded to grant release without requirement of financial bail on the new charges, however, the need for deciding between the two options is eliminated.

By now it has become evident that the court clerk is a figure of major importance to the bondsman. In high-volume urban courts, there are many persons with this designation—one, in fact, for every separate court "part" or "department" to which each of the judges of a given court district is assigned. The administrative position of the court clerk makes him an object of continuous attention from other participants seeking information about or access to the court calendar. The resources he holds may be an important means for the bondsman's efforts to protect his investments. One bondsman stated:

"The court clerk is probably one of the most important people I have to deal with. He moves cases, he can get information to the judge, and he has control over various calendar matters. When he's not willing to help you out, he can make life very difficult. He knows he's important, and he acts like it."

Observations confirmed the value of cooperation from the court clerk for case management strategies employed by bondsmen. Two examples are given below:

A bondsman and a court clerk were chatting amiably during a recess in one of the Westville courtrooms. They kidded each other for a short time, each complaining about the "easy life" of the other. Then the court clerk asked the bondsman: "Hey, what about O'Hanlon? Isn't he your case? He didn't show this morning and I've got a bench warrant on him sitting on my desk right now. You'd better get in touch with Sheldon [an attorney] and have him call the judge for a continuance right away or that warrant is gonna be on its way."

On another occasion, a Westville bondsman was summoned to a nearby city by a prospective customer. After obtaining a verbal promise from the defendant's brother that the premium would be paid, the bondsman went to that city to post bail. When we arrived there at mid-morning, the bondsman's first contact was with the court clerk:

Al: You've got Mallen scheduled to come up this afternoon, don't you? (The clerk checked his records and nodded affirmatively.)

Al: Look this guy was picked up last night on plain drunk and he's still got a george heat on. I don't think he's fit to appear in anybody's court. He's still so stiff I swear I could smell it over the phone.

Clerk: Hmmm.

Al: I'm going over to the jail and take him out. How's about putting the guy on for tomorrow? He's gotta get himself cleaned up.

(After momentary hesitation, the clerk agreed.)

Clerk: Okay, I'll set him up for nine tomorrow.

As we walked to the jail, the bondsman told me that he had done a favor for the defendant. The postponement would give the defendant an extra day to sober up and would enable him to appear in court freshly shaved and wearing clean clothes. "Makes a much better impression on the judge if the guy looks decent." A short time later the defendant appeared at the jail booking desk. A middle-aged man, he had spent the night and most of the morning in jail. He was now completely sober, and although he presented a shabby appearance there seemed little doubt that he could have stood trial that afternoon. After posting bail, Al counseled the man: "Go home and get some rest, and then come back tomorrow morning at nine and put on your best manners. I don't think you've got anything to worry about. Judge Gardner is one of the best in the country."

In later conversation, the bondsman said that he regarded the man as "an alcoholic obviously beyond the point of being helped." He revealed that the reason for arranging postponement of the man's case was to increase the likelihood that the man would make his court appearance. "I've seen hundreds of cases like this guy—just simple drunks. In that condition, they're likely to wander off somewhere and fall asleep for a whole day. This way the guy doesn't have to worry about it. He can go home, sack out, and his chances of being able to make a court appearance in the morning are much better than if he has to hang around the court building for a couple of long, dry hours until his case is called."

Court "connections" are primarily useful to the bondsman for managing minor cases. One bondsman reported that a high proportion of his clientele consisted of persons arrested for traffic warrant violations. When asked about the business consequences of this fact, he replied:

"Great! [Laughter] What I mean by great is that these cases make up a lot of bread and butter in this business. But they're much more work than the big cases. Felony cases can't be moved around in the courts, but chicken-shit cases can. With traffic cases, you sometimes find yourself doing a lot of extra work in getting postponements and that kind of thing. You know, like when a guy is afraid he'll lose his job if he has to appear in court on a working day without permission from his boss."

This parallels the situation described above in which dispensation of legal advice appears to be confined to relatively trivial, although statistically frequent, criminal matters. Thus, minor cases provide a more reliable basis of income, higher returns on investments, and greater opportunity to exercise influence in the process of criminal justice.

BAIL ADMINISTRATION AND CONTROL OF ARRESTEES

Bail administration does not come to an abrupt end with the release of some defendants and the detention of others. On the contrary, it extends throughout the entire period between arrest and disposition. Official actions in this process have been described in several empirical studies (Foote, 1954, 1958). This section shows how the bondsman's decisions to post bail are linked to considerations of subsequent decisions by court officials. Through collaborative exercise of their respective discretionary powers, bondsmen and court officials exchange outcomes which strengthen legal control over arrested persons in the period before disposition.

Decisions to post bail

Compared with its importance for official decisions, the factor of offense appears to play a very minor role in the bondsman's assessment of defendants as possible customers. More serious crimes involve high bails, of course, and bondsmen have greater reason to be concerned over the possibility that defendants in these cases will "skip." At the same time, higher bails mean higher premiums. Some bondsmen believe that drug addicts and certain kinds of violent offenders tend to be less reliable than other criminals, and in such cases the bondsman may exercise special care in deciding to post bail. In general, however, bondsmen do not make categorical judgements about defendants based upon the offenses with which they are charged.

Similarly, bondsmen are not concerned about the possibility that released defendants might be re-arrested on new charges while at liberty. Bondsmen believe, just as do criminal justice officials, that chances of re-arrest may be quite high among certain classes of defendants, especially those accused of minor offenses like prostitution and shoplifting. Indeed, bondsmen share the view of many law enforcement and court officials that for some defendants, release on bail and return to "the streets" signals a period of intensified criminal activity in order to earn money to pay fees owed to bondsmen and attorneys. But bondsmen cannot afford to base their decisions on the probability of recidivism by released defendants. One bondsman revealed the tough-minded outlook required by his business:

"I don't care what any bondsmen's association says on this score. We don't care and we can't care about protecting society. We have means and methods of making these people pay, so we take the risks and the gambles. That's what we're in business for. There is almost nobody I won't take out, including people I'm certain will repeat their crimes."

The most important question is whether the defendant is likely to pay the premium for his bail. Ideally, full payment of the premium is demanded before the bondsman agrees to post bail. Depending on his assessment of the defendant's background, character, and financial capacity, however, the bondsman may decide to post bail on credit, i.e., to allow the defendant to pay the premium in installments. The financial qualifications of family members and friends may become an important consideration at this point. Surety companies seem to discourage installment agreements, but bondsmen generally operate on the assumption that it is better to extend credit broadly, accepting the risks of non-payment and partial payment that this method implies. Therefore, bondsmen usually have collection problems.

Bondsmen sometimes appear to make attempts at estimating the probability of defaults or "skips" by prospective customers before posting bonds, but not primarily because they entertain any special concern for the efficiency or integrity of court operations. The dominant question is rather the defendant's reliability as a paying customer. One bondsman said that he regarded the family life of defendants as being particularly important in this respect. "If a man is happily married and loves his kids, he's not going to leave town." Another bondsman attempted to sum up the problem by stating, "the good people are gonna cooperate and the bad people are gonna run." Later, however, he qualified this by explaining that he, like other bondsmen, looks into each defendant's criminal record, employment history, residence, and family situation before deciding to post bail. A third bondsman commented, "good actors have roots in the community."

Having determined that a defendant has the ability to pay the premium, however, the bondsman is extremely likely to accept the defendant as a customer. He may refuse to post bail on a defendant who already owes him a considerable amount of money for past services. Similarly, he will probably refuse to extend credit to a defendant whom he knows—either from his own past experience or occasionally on the advice of another bondsman—to be a "wise guy" or a "bad actor," i.e., a person likely to withhold payments or to go into hiding. Hesitancy on the bondsman's part is also likely when police records indicate outstanding warrants, for in such cases the defendant may be re-arrested and returned to custody before the bondsman has collected his fee. The police follow the business dealings of bondsmen with special interest and can sometimes use this knowledge to advantage when they wish to prevent particular defendants from gaining release.

Indemnification agreements

Of course, if he chooses to do so, the bondsman can insure himself against all losses from forfeited bonds by requiring each customer to complete a collateral agreement. To accomplish this, the defendant signs a collateral form or persuades another person to act as guarantor. This step would eliminate all uncertainty in client selection, since such an agreement guarantees complete indemnification of the surety for any losses he may incur. But bondsmen usually do not require indemnification contracts from their customers, for most criminal defendants are extremely poor and are unable to find guarantors to co-sign indemnification agreements on bail bonds posted for defendants. Although the guarantor may not fully understand the legal significance of his role,[6] he generally recognizes that he is being asked to pledge an amount of money or perhaps his property for the defendant's good conduct. The guarantor must place great trust in the defendant, which for most defendants narrows the field of potential guarantors to a small circle of persons.

It is difficult to determine the frequency with which bondsmen post bail unaccompanied by collateral agreements. No official figures are collected to indicate how often this happens, but some reasonable estimates can be made. During field interviews, bondsmen stated that they receive "hard" collateral—indemnification contracts backed up by specific assets such as bank accounts or property deeds—in 5 to 10 percent of their cases. These are probably cases involving more serious offenses and thus higher bail amounts. Estimates of the frequency of "hard" collateral were all within this range (see National Conference on Bail and Criminal Justice, 1965: 234). Similarly, another study of bail practices (Hoskins, 1968: 1141) concluded that "complete indemnification is seldom achieved" by bail bondsmen. However, in a fairly large proportion of cases, written promises of indemnification are obtained.

In these cases, the bondsman accepts from defendants or guarantors the pledge of such possessions as automobiles, jewelry, or household furnishings and appliances as collateral. Estimates

---

[6] "The guarantor who puts up collateral incurs several liabilities. A typical bail agreement contract between the surety company and the guarantor provides that the guarantor will pay the surety company the full amount of the bail bond immediately upon its forfeiture. The guarantor is also liable up to the full amount of the bail bond for the actual expenses which the surety incurs in securing the defendant's release and in recapturing him, if necessary, and if a bail forfeiture is not set aside, the guarantor's liability may extend to the expenses incurred in the attempted recapture in addition to the amount of the forfeiture. Finally, the surety may require the guarantor to pay as collateral upon demand the full amount of the bail bond whenever the surety deems such payment necessary for his self-protection, due to any material change in the risk he has assumed. The recording of the bail agreement constitutes a lien on the specified property of the guarantor in favor of the surety until the surety's liability has been completely exonerated" (Hoskins, 1968: 1140–1141).

by bondsmen of the frequency of such agreements ranged from 40 to 60 percent. The realizable market value of these items is often considerably less than the personal value they have for the guarantors who offer them. Thus it appears that most of the indemnification agreements obtained by bondsmen have relatively little value as collateral.

This impression is strengthened by bondsmen's reports concerning the difficulties of enforcing collateral agreements. "Unless you hold the collateral in your hand, it isn't worth anything," stated one bondsman. In five years of writing bail bonds, this informant claimed, three guarantors had reimbursed him for forfeited bonds without protesting. Another bondsman said that he had received voluntary compensation from a co-signor only once in fifteen years. Legal remedies are available to the bondsman, and when enforcement of collateral agreements becomes necessary the bondsman can turn to these. In many states, for example, co-signers are legally liable to pay costs incurred by bondsmen in attempting to recapture fugitive defendants up to the limit of the outstanding bond. Given the inevitable costs and uncertainties of litigation, however, bondsmen are more likely to resort to informal means of enforcing indemnification agreements with defendants and co-signers. The overriding purpose of indemnification agreements appears to be their presumed "psychological" value for protecting investments by underlining the obligations of defendants and co-signers to the bondsman.

In practice, therefore, whether to post bail on a defendant without obtaining collateral is the most important decision facing the bondsman. Because most defendants are unable to provide adequate collateral, the bondsman confronts this decision often. It is in exercising discretion not to impose "hard" collateral conditions on defendants and guarantors that the bondsman runs his largest risks and stands to make his highest profits. The bondsman must summon all of his business acumen and skill in "human relations" to make this decision. It is here that the bondsman's greatest impact on the justice system occurs, and it is here also that cooperative relations with court officials become most important.

Non-enforcement of bail forfeitures

The key factor in this aspect of bail bonding is the discretionary power of judges to exonerate outstanding bonds and to set aside bail forfeitures. When a bailed defendant fails to appear in court, the bondsman may have to forfeit the bail he has posted if he is unable to produce the defendant within the legal "grace" period (six months in the state where this study was done). Whether forfeiture is actually imposed is decided by the judge who presides in the case. Remission procedures, which permit this decision to be made, set out the conditions under which judges may authorize the return of forfeited bonds to sureties.[7]

The law gives judges wide latitude in these procedures, creating the suspicion that such decisions may sometimes reflect judicial improprieties. The opportunity for official misconduct would, of course, be present even if judges were not directly involved in approving requests for exoneration of forfeited bonds. But from another standpoint, the existence of these procedures is fortunate, for without them officials would be compelled to carry out a policy of strict and uniform enforcement of forfeited bail bonds. This would probably lead to a considerable increase in the number of persons unable to gain release on bail. Bondsmen ordinarily obtain complete indemnification on only a small percentage of all defendants for whom they post bonds, and insistence of bondsmen on full collateral would be a very likely adjustment to a policy of strict enforcement. Many defendants would thus fail to qualify for the services of bondsmen due to inability to raise collateral. This might be compounded by another effect of a policy of strict enforcement of bail forfeitures: such a policy quickly drives noncorporate sources of bail, including friends and relatives of defendants, out of the system (see Foote, 1954: 1060–1066).

Virtually every study of bail administration ever conducted has found that a large proportion of forfeitures are set aside by judges. This generous use of judicial discretion stems from one or more of several possible sources. As already suggested, one possibility is that forfeitures are routinely set aside because judges recognize the dependence of the court on the willingness of bondsmen to post bail for defendants who cannot provide full

---

[7] From the standpoint of legal theory, the need for some means to allow equitable relief of bail forfeitures can be justified on grounds that primary responsibility for assuring the defendant's return to court should be placed on the defendant rather than the bondsman. If it can be established legally that the surety has exercised reasonable diligence in trying to fulfill his promise to assure the defendant's appearance for trial, the surety should not be penalized for the defendant's irresponsibility or intentional failure to appear. For this reason, contemporary bail law contains several different procedures whereby sureties can secure remission of bail forfeitures. A detailed discussion of these issues is found in Hoskins, 1968: 1145–1150.

collateral. That bondsmen accept many defendants as customers without securing legally enforceable indemnification agreements not only increases the overall profitability of writing bail bonds, but it also enables large numbers of defendants to obtain release who would otherwise face pre-trial detention, thereby preventing intolerable pressures on detention facilities. The stake of the criminal justice system in the willingness of bail bondsmen to depart from norms of conservative business practice is considerable.

A second reason that judges so often exercise their power to remit bail forfeitures in favor of bondsmen is that they sometimes need reciprocity from bondsmen to prevent defendants from obtaining release. When court officials desire that a particular defendant not be released, they may pass the word on to local bondsmen (National Conference on Bail and Criminal Justice, 1966: 118). I learned of no such instance during my study, but it is fairly common knowledge that bondsmen in various cities were subject to severe pressures against writing bonds for persons arrested during civil rights protests during the last decade (Goldfarb, 1965: 84–85). Because bondsmen need the court's cooperation for a variety of reasons, they are unlikely to offend court officials by posting bail in such instances. In this way, judges can prevent release without actually denying bail or setting bail in an amount that the legally competent defendant might challenge as "excessive." The effective discretion exercised by court officials is therefore augmented by informal relationships with bondsmen.[8]

These relationships also help explain why it is that bondsmen ordinarily make no efforts to supervise defendants for whom they post bail. Bondsmen require only those defendants who owe money to make regular reports, and then the purpose is not to remind the defendant that his behavior is under scrutiny but to enable the bondsman to collect his fee. Even when a defendant fails to make a required court appearance, the bondsman is likely to make only minimal efforts to locate the defendant—for example, by placing a few telephone calls to persons whom the defen-

---

[8] Another explanation for the frequency with which forfeited bonds are remitted is that some judges may be rewarded financially by bondsmen and surety companies with contributions to election campaigns, political slush funds, and personal bank accounts. (Bail setting may also be affected by similar considerations.) It is true, as Chambliss (1971: 1156) has suggested, that discretion is always a "structural invitation to corruption." However, I found no evidence of improper influence on judges during my investigation, though it was rumored that insurance industry lobbyists were attempting to "buy" members of a state legislative committee looking into the problems of bail and poverty.

dant has named as references or by sending a telegram to an address given by the defendant. Only once during field observations did I learn of a case in which a bondsman was actively attempting to locate a defendant for reasons other than payment.

Despite the extensive protection afforded, bail bondsmen cannot place complete reliance on court officials to return all forfeited bonds. In some instances, particularly when large bail amounts are at stake, bondsmen may need to attempt to locate fugitive defendants. Bondsmen have extraordinary powers of arrest and extradition over bailed defendants who have fled.[9] No criminal justice official possesses the degree of legal authority over citizens that the bondsman holds and occasionally wields over his customers. Under powers vested in him by law, the bondsman can compel a defendant for whom he has posted bail to return with him to court at the point of a gun. The bondsman does not need to obtain a warrant for this purpose, and the defendant legally cannot offer resistance. The frequency with which bondsmen exercise their powers to retrieve fugitive defendants is not readily ascertainable and officials hold divergent views. Some law-enforcement officials claim that the most important service the bondsman renders to the state is in retrieving defendants who have absconded (Hoskins, 1968: 1144; National Conference on Bail and Criminal Justice, 1965: 237). But others assert that bondsmen rarely make special efforts to locate defaulting defendants for whom they have assumed bail obligations and that fugitive defendants are returned only when they later commit crimes for which they are re-arrested (U.S. Senate, 1964: 131). Of course, both of these views may be correct.

Even when bondsmen make use of their powers to capture and return fugitive defendants to court, they rarely engage directly in efforts to locate defendants. During field observations, several Westville bondsmen mentioned a legendary case in which one of their colleagues had spent considerable time and money "chasing

---

[9] These powers [were] described in a still authoritative 1872 U.S. Supreme Court opinion: "When bail is given, the principal is regarded as delivered to the custody of his sureties. Their dominion is a continuance of the original imprisonment. Whenever they choose to do so, they may seize him and deliver him up in their discharge; and if that cannot be done at once, they may imprison him until it can be done. They may exercise their rights in person or by an agent. They may pursue him into another state; may arrest him on the Sabbath; and, if necessary, may break and enter his house for that purpose. The seizure is not made by virtue of new process. None is needed. It is likened to the rearrest by the sheriff of an escaping prisoner" (*Taylor* v. *Taintor*, 83 U.S. 366, 371 [1872]).

a $14,000 skip all over the country" without result. But the more common practice involves indirect search operations whereby the bondsman seeks to purchase information about the location of a fugitive defendant for whom he is financially responsible. A Westville bondsman described one possibility:

"I have a case right now of a $1,100 skip. The guy is down in Valley City somewhere, I know that much. I've got a pimp down there working on it for me. There's no way anybody could find out that this pimp works for me, because he's cool and I'm cool. He's going to ask around to see if he can locate this guy. Then I'll go down there with another guy and we'll bring him back to Westville. It'll cost me about $150 to catch the guy, so I'll just about break even on this one." (The bondsman had already collected the $110 premium.)

Other bondsmen indicated that they contract with specialists— either professional detectives ("skip tracers") or underworld figures—to locate defaulting defendants. Such persons receive a certain proportion of the bail amount for information leading to successful capture of the defendant.

The bondsman's legal powers of arrest and extradition, like his discretion in posting bail, may occasionally be put to the advantage of criminal justice officials. Bondsmen "own" defendants for whom they post bail. Therefore, law-enforcement officials can informally borrow the bondsman's legal authority to avoid having to comply with expensive and cumbersome procedures necessary for interstate extradition of fugitive defendants. Under this arrangement, defendants who have been arrested in another state are turned over to bondsmen for return to face original charges in the state where they jumped bail. It is not known how widespread this practice is, but the use of bail bondsmen to circumvent formal extradition procedures is thought to be quite common in some states (see U.S. Senate, 1966: 23–24; Yale Law Journal, 1964).

SUMMARY AND DISCUSSION OF FINDINGS

The presence of bail bondsmen in American criminal courts rests upon the right of bail to which all persons accused of non-capital crimes are said to be entitled. The basis of this familiar legal concept is embedded in a tersely ambiguous clause of the United States Constitution. Most state constitutions and particularly those adopted after ratification of the U.S. Constitution, contain similar provisions. But the Eighth Amendment clause in question simply states that "Excessive bail shall not be required of defendants" in criminal cases. It says nothing about bail bondsmen, the surety companies which stand behind them, forfeitures of bail, and so on. These and other details of bail administration are spelled out in statutes and case law at both the federal and state levels (see Foote, 1965; Paulsen, 1966).

The bail system has come in for much criticism in the past decade and a half, mostly directed at the excessive reliance placed on money as a means of securing the presence of defendants for hearings and—on the rare occasions when they are held—trials. The problem, however, is not only that the bail system makes release before trial hinge on the defendant's financial situation. It is also that American law refuses to entrust officials with formal power to detain citizens who are only accused of crime.

Two comparative law scholars (Mueller and Le Poole-Griffiths, 1969: 23–4) highlight the problem in the following way:

Continental law has faced this issue with greater candor. Pre-trial detention, despite the probable guilt of the defendant, is always an exceptional measure and can be imposed only when . . . extremely high standards for issuance of a warrant can be met. But when, thus, the guilt of the perpetrator is highly probable, when the offense is major, when there is danger that he will flee, tamper with the evidence and repeat his offense, why then bother with an insurance contract insuring the defendant's next appearance? To release a suspect under those circumstances would be more than a gambler's folly, or the premium should have to be so high that nobody could meet it. Realizing this, continental law rarely insists on preliminary detention when we do, and, while nearly all codes have provisions on bail, there is rarely any occasion to apply them. When the risk of release is worth taking, release is ordered. Any other system is non-utilitarian and would only discriminate against the poor, a reason which led Sweden to abandon this institution.

In contrast, American law forbids criminal court officials from detaining a defendant who may appear dangerous or likely to flee if released. Our procedures, by defining pre-trial release decisions as questions of judicial and prosecutorial responsibility, are also unique in the extent to which they aim at excluding the police from such decisions (Goldfarb, 1965: 213). American law's institutionalized suspicion of official discretion[10] is apparent in the case of bail. Admittedly, the bail system fails to guarantee pre-trial freedom to every defendant claiming it as a right. But even if such claims often go unrecognized, it is clear that officials are not absolutely free to ignore them.

Bail bondsmen serve several functions in the criminal court system. First, they facilitate pre-trial release of large numbers of arrested persons. Of course, the defendant must pay for this "service." However, in deciding whether to post bail for a defendant's release, the only question in which the bondsman has any real interest is whether the defendant will pay the fee for what is in effect a loan of money. This means that monetary considerations override other concerns, such as the offense with which the defendant is charged, the likelihood of guilt, the probability of re-arrest, or even the risk of flight.

Bondsmen can afford to ignore these matters because of their intimate knowledge of court operations and the personalized relationships they cultivate with court officials. In large part, their work consists of drawing upon these resources to manage cases and protect investments. This is related to a second function performed by bondsmen, which is to help move defendants through the courts. Because their earnings depend directly upon the number of customers they handle, bondsmen gear their activities toward promoting rapid disposition of cases.

Third, bondsmen aid officials in dealing selectively with difficult cases. In one such arrangement, for example, the bondsman acts upon his legitimate business prerogatives by refusing to bond a certain defendant for pre-trial release, thereby tacitly carrying out official wishes. In another, the bondsman exercises his legal power of interstate extradition in order to help officials avoid the problems and expense of securing the return for prosecution of a fugitive defendant who has been apprehended in another state. Both of these arrangements work on the same principle. They require bondsmen to carry out informal and extra-legal directives issued by court officials. In turn, officials cooperate with bondsmen because of the organizational benefits that bondsmen confer on

---

[10] Cf. Lawrence Friedman's (1973: 504) observation that there is a "pervasive feature in American legal culture, horror of uncontrolled power. [The theory is] . . . that courts should be guided—ruled—by words of objective law, enacted by the people's representatives. . . ."

the legal system. Official reciprocity takes several forms, the most important of which is judicial non-enforcement of forfeited bail bonds.

The bail system, then, links the personal interests of bondsmen with the organizational requirements of criminal court operations. This linkage is accomplished by means of discretionary exchanges of outcomes which augment the effective authority of law enforcement and judicial personnel and which also take much of the risk out of bondsmen's business transactions. This system of interlocking obligations strengthens official control over arrested persons at the same time that it increases the profitability of selling bail bonds.

CONCLUSION

The last twenty years of appellate court rulings on criminal procedure have had profound effects on local court operations. For example, one articulate judge, viewing the scene from an intermediate appellate court, maintains that the cumulative impact on criminal courts has been literally devastating.[11]

The mood of alarm expressed by contemporary observers of American criminal courts can be more readily understood by recalling that at no time since the beginning of this century has anything but the roughest kind of justice been available for the majority of the cases in these courts. As the appellate judiciary over the last two decades has attempted to raise the standards of treatment accorded criminal defendants by local criminal justice officials, the resulting improvements have been slight by comparison with expectations for change which have been generated by these decisions.[12]

In addition to the tensions generated by the politics of local

---

[11] Fleming (1974: 6) sees the root of the problem in a misguided quest by members of his own profession for "perfect justice," which has led to an "overload of court machinery with retrials, rehearings, and collateral proceedings. . . ." The result is "an unworkable system unable to function, like the ostrich that has wings but can't fly, or like the beautiful mockup of the SST that never got off the ground."

[12] This statement is borne out quite forcefully by numerous studies in "impact" analysis by political scientists (see Wasby, 1970). However, these studies seem predisposed to come to this conclusion, because they are typically concerned with the effects of some particular decision rather than with the possibly cumulative effects of a line of decisions. See, e.g., the study by Ingraham (1974) and other works cited there.

justice, criminal courts now face a qualitatively different set of problems arising from the fact that their activities have been drawn into the politics of constitutional law.

In this vastly changed situation, the practical achievements of criminal court administration seem always to be lagging farther behind the evolving constitutional criteria of fair treatment. One should not imagine that this growing divergence has gone unrecognized by criminal justice officials or that it has caused them only minor inconveniences. In fact, as gaps between written law and official practice have widened, the exact role that trial courts are to play in the criminal justice system has become increasingly unclear.

Ambiguity is reflected in many ways. For instance, one innovation which has received great acclaim from judges and prosecutors in recent years is the idea that some individuals accused of crime can usefully be channeled away from the coercive context of court proceedings and toward the beneficent environment of informal "treatment" (Vorenberg and Vorenberg, 1973). In point of fact, every program based on the concept of "diversion" uses "the threat or possibility of conviction of a criminal offense to encourage an accused to do something," and the agreement thus obtained "may not be entirely voluntary, as the accused often agrees to participate in a diversion program only because he fears formal criminal prosecution" (National Advisory Commission, 1973: 27). There can be little doubt that the growing appeal of this concept among local criminal justice officials has an intimate and paradoxical connection with developments in constitutional law over the past two decades (Balch, 1974).

At the same time, a controversy has arisen over the question of whether and to what extent it falls to criminal courts to supervise the police in order to assure their compliance with changed procedural requirements (Milner, 1971). For it can be argued that the changes in police practices which have been mandated by appellate decisions over the last two decades are so sweeping, and the lack of any alternative enforcement mechanism so patent, as to presuppose a substantially new function for local level judicial officials. Many of these decisions, indeed, seem aimed precisely at extending the political doctrine of separation of powers, and the companion doctrine of judicial supremacy, to the administration of local criminal justice. The core assumption in nearly all of them has been that criminal courts must counter-balance the activities of police agencies in order to prevent mistreatment of citizens accused of crime. In this view, it becomes the responsibility of trial courts to monitor the actions of law-enforcement officials and, using the remedy of dismissal as a sanction, check any tendencies toward official lawlessness (LaFave and Remington, 1965).

The period between arrest and disposition has special importance in American criminal law, for it is during this period that defendants are supposed to begin taking advantage of the procedural protections to which appellate courts hold them entitled (Karlen, 1967: 135–166). In practice, however, relatively few defendants get any opportunity to do so. In most cases the period after arrest involves perfunctory official acknowledgment of the defendant's rights, followed by out-of-court negotiations aimed at rapid disposition. In lower criminal courts, the defendant's first appearance tends to be his only appearance (Mileski, 1971). The disposition process is somewhat less abbreviated in higher level trial courts, but the same tendency toward truncated procedure can be observed there (Blumberg, 1970).

The conception of the criminal court as a supervisor of police activities and the essentially hierarchical model of the criminal justice system implied in this conception have been criticized before (Bittner, 1970: 22–30; Feeley, 1973). The present article casts further doubt on these assumptions. It focuses on the stage of the criminal justice process that begins when law-enforcement functions give way, in principle at least, to judicial functions. The findings indicate that the business of court administration virtually merges with the enterprise of law enforcement at this period and strengthen the argument that the criminal court actually serves as an agency of law enforcement (Skolnick, 1969: 236–43). Thanks to the growing interest in criminal courts among social scientists, we now have some idea of why this merger takes place and how it affects the treatment of defendants. We are also coming to realize that the problems of criminal courts are both causes and effects of the chronic crisis in American criminal justice.

CASE

Taylor v. *Taintor,*
   1872   83 U.S. 366

REFERENCES

Ares, Charles and Herbert Sturz
1962 "Bail and the Indigent Accused," 8 *Crime and Delinquency* 12.

Balch, Robert W.
1974 "Deferred Prosecution: The Juvenilization of the Criminal Justice System," 38 *Federal Probation* 46.

Beeley, Arthur L.
1927 *The Bail System in Chicago*. Chicago: University of Chicago Press (reissued 1966).

Bittner, Egon
1970 *The Functions of the Police in Modern Society*. Washington, D.C.: U.S. Government Printing Office.

Blumberg, Abraham S.
1967 "The Practice of Law as a Confidence Game," 1 *Law & Society Review* 15.
1970 *Criminal Justice*. Chicago: Quadrangle Books.

Chambliss, William J.
1971 "Vice, Corruption, Bureaucracy, and Power,"
1971 *Wisconsin Law Review* 1150.

Cox, Archibald
1968 *The Warren Court*. Cambridge, Mass.: Harvard University Press.

Downie, Leonard
1971 *Justice Denied*. Baltimore: Penguin Books.

Feeley, Malcolm M.
1973 "Two Models of the Criminal Justice System: An Organization Perspective," 7 *Law & Society Review* 407.

Fleming, Macklin
1974 *The Price of Perfect Justice*. New York: Basic Books.

Foote, Caleb
1954 "Compelling Appearance in Court: Administration of Bail in Philadelphia," 102 *University of Pennsylvania Law Review* 1031.
1958 "A Study of the Administration of Bail in New York City," 106 *University of Pennsylvania Law Review* 693.
1965 "The Coming Constitutional Crisis in Bail," 113 *University of Pennsylvania Law Review* 959.

Freed, Daniel J. and Patricia M. Wald
1964 *Bail in the United States: 1964*. Washington, D.C.: National Conference on Bail and Criminal Justice.

Friedman, Lawrence M.
   1973   *A History of American Law*. New York: Simon and Schuster.

Goldfarb, Ronald
   1965   *Ransom: A Critique of the American Bail System*. New York: Harper and Row.

Hoskins, John
   1968   "Tinkering with the California Bail System," 56 *California Law Review* 1134.

Ingraham, Barton L.
   1974   "The Impact of Argersinger—One Year Later," 8 *Law & Society Review* 615.

Jackson, Donald Dale
   1975   *Judges*. New York: Atheneum.

James, Howard
   1971   *Crisis in the Courts*. New York: David McKay.

Karlen, Delmar
   1967   *Anglo-American Criminal Justice*. New York: Oxford University Press.

Lafave, Wayne R. and Frank J. Remington
   1965   "Controlling the Police: The Judge's Role in Making and Reviewing Law Enforcement Decisions," 63 *Michigan Law Review* 987.

Lefstein, N. et al.
   1969   "In Search of Juvenile Justice," 5 *Law & Society Review* 491.

Lemert, Edwin M.
   1970   *Social Action and Legal Change*. Chicago: Aldine.

Levin, Martin
   1972   "Urban Politics and Judicial Behavior," 1 *Journal of Legal Studies* 193.

Levy, Leonard W.
   1974   *Against the Law*. New York: Harper and Row.

Mather, Lynn M.
   1973   "Some Determinants of the Method of Case Disposition: Decision-Making by Public Defenders in Los Angeles," 8 *Law & Society Review* 187.

Mileski, Maureen
   1971   "Courtroom Encounters: An Observation Study of a Lower Criminal Court," 5 *Law & Society Review* 473.

Milner, Neal A.
  1971   *The Court and Local Law Enforcement*. Beverly Hills, Calif.: Sage Publications.

Moley, Raymond
  1930   *Our Criminal Courts*. New York: Minton, Balch and Company.

Mueller, Gerhard O. W. and Fre Le Poole-Griffiths
  1969   Used by permission of New York University Press from *Comparative Criminal Procedure,* by Gerhard O. W. Mueller and Fre Le Poole-Griffiths, © 1969 by New York University.

National Advisory Commission
  1973   National Advisory Commission on Criminal Justice Standards and Goals, *Report on Courts*. Washington, D.C.: U.S. Government Printing Office.

National Conference on Bail and Criminal Justice
  1965   *Proceedings and Interim Report*. Washington, D.C.

  1966   *Bail and Summons: 1965*. Washington, D.C.

Ohlin, Lloyd E. (ed.)
  1973   *Prisoners in America*. Englewood Cliffs, N.J.: Prentice-Hall.

Paulsen, Monrad
  1966   "Pre-Trial Release in the United States," 66 *Columbia Law Review* 109.

Pound, Roscoe
  1945   *Criminal Justice in America*. Cambridge, Mass.: Harvard University Press.

President's Commission
  1967   The President's Commission on Law Enforcement and Administration of Justice, *Task Force Report: Courts*. Washington, D.C.: U.S. Government Printing Office.

Rothman, David
  1972   "Of Prisons, Asylums, and Other Decaying Institutions," 26 *The Public Interest* 3.

Schubert, Glendon
  1970   *The Constitutional Polity*. Boston: Boston University Press.

Silverstein, Lee
  1966   "Bail in the State Courts—A Field Study and Report," 50 *Minnesota Law Review* 621.

Skolnick, Jerome H.
  1967   "Social Control in the Adversary System," 11 *Journal of Conflict Resolution* 52.

1969   *The Politics of Protest*. Washington, D.C.: U.S. Government Printing Office.

Suffet, Frederick
  1966   "Bail Setting: A Study of Courtroom Interaction," 12 *Crime and Delinquency* 318.

Sutherland, Edwin H. and Donald R. Cressey
  1970   *Principles of Criminology*. Philadelphia: J. B. Lippincott Company.

U.S. Senate
  1964   Hearings, Bills to Improve Federal Bail Procedures. 88th Cong., 2nd Sess.

  1966   Hearings, A Proposal to Modify Existing Procedures Governing the Interstate Rendition of Fugitive Bailees. 89th Cong., 2nd Sess.

Virtue, Maxine Boord
  1962   *Survey of Metropolitan Courts*. Ann Arbor: University of Michigan Press.

Vorenberg, Elizabeth W. and James Vorenberg
  1973   "Early Diversion from the Criminal Justice System," in Lloyd E. Ohlin (ed.), *Prisoners in America*. Englewood Cliffs, N.J.: Prentice-Hall.

Wasby, Stephen L.
  1970   *The Impact of the United States Supreme Court: Some Perspectives*. Homewood, Ill.: The Dorsey Press.

Wice, Paul
  1974   "Purveyors of Freedom: The Professional Bondsmen," 11 *Society* 34.

Wice, Paul and Rita James Simon
  1970   "Pretrial Release: A Survey of Alternative Practices," 34 *Federal Probation* 60.

Wood, Arthur L.
  1967   *Criminal Lawyer*. New Haven: College and University Press.

Yale Law Journal
  1961   "Bail: An Ancient Practice Reexamined," 70 *Yale Law Journal* 966.

  1964   "Bailbondsmen and the Fugitive Accused—The Need for Formal Removal Procedures," 73 *Yale Law Journal* 1098.

10

*Purveyors of freedom: The professional bondsmen**

Paul B. Wice

As President Lyndon Johnson signed the Bail Reform Act of 1966, he offered the following critical evaluation of the American bail system: "The defendant with means can afford to pay bail. He can afford to buy his freedom. But the poorer defendant cannot pay the price. He languishes in jail weeks, months, and perhaps even years before trial." Nearly two-thirds of those defendants who are fortunate enough to buy their freedom must rely upon bondsmen in order to raise the required bond. Who are these individuals whose profession allows them to have so critical a role in determining a defendant's pretrial freedom? In pursuit of an answer, bondsmen as well as knowledgeable public officials in ten cities were interviewed. Their answers supplied a major share of the information used here to construct a portrait of the bail bondsman and his profession.

Bondsmen have traditionally been pictured as heavyset, cigar-chomping, sinister individuals who are social parasites, living off the misfortune of others. They lurk in the courthouse corridors with only an alleyway or a phone booth for an office. Usually associated with the underworld, they are often one step ahead of the law and frequently discover that they require the services of bondsmen for themselves. Though many bondsmen may be respectable businessmen, this unflattering image still persists. In a recent survey conducted by the author, nearly 60 percent of the

---

* Reprinted from *Society*, vol. 11, no. 5 (July–August 1974), pp. 34–41.

public officials questioned thought it was necessary to reduce the power of the bondsmen.

However, the contemporary bondsman no longer fits this stereotyped image. Although one still would not easily confuse a corporate executive or a college professor with a typical bondsman, he has in recent years attempted to upgrade his image. His office has moved out of the alley and phone booth into quarters that are only a relative improvement. Typically, his office is located in one or two rooms adjacent to the courthouse. It is furnished with chairs that appear to be remnants from a deserted bus terminal. A single filing cabinet or a pile of cartons is used for storage. On top of an isolated desk is located a row of telephones, obscured by a moutainous collection of phone books from various cities. The floor is rugless and littered with cigarette butts and trash. This depressing habitat, however, does not occupy very much of the bondsman's time since he is usually to be found either at the courthouse or at his private residence. He may have an answering service or an assistant to take messages and contact him at his home.

The following two examples are to be found on either extreme of this typical bonding establishment. In Detroit, a pair of brothers operate a bonding company which is acknowledged to be the most successful in the city. Entering their spacious offices, one is greeted by a receptionist and directed to the waiting room which is furnished in tasteful Danish modern furniture. Thickly carpeted floors lead to the partners' pine-paneled offices. If he had not read the sign on the outer door, he would have thought he was entering the office of a successful lawyer or financier.

On the other extreme is the office of a bondsman interviewed in Baltimore, Maryland. His office is located on East Baltimore Street, referred to by local residents as the "block." It is a mecca for lonely men in search of thrills and illicit adventures. The bondsman's office is sandwiched between a burlesque house and a pornographic bookstore. The front of the office was unlit and filled with trash, broken chairs and empty boxes. The back wall contained a one-way mirror with the actual office located through a hidden door and behind a false front. Inside this second room the author found the bondsman surrounded by four of his cronies, engaged in a spirited game of cards. Cigar smoke and other acrid odors permeated the small, crowded room. The bondsman was sitting behind a desk with his feet propped up, majestically puffing on one of the four cigars that was polluting the limited air space in the cramped quarters.

These differences in physical environment are matched by the differences in character and conduct exhibited by the bondsmen. By examining the wide range of backgrounds from which these men evolved prior to entering the bonding business, one clearly sees the fallacy of the initial stereotype. Like most professions, the bondsmen were attracted to their vocation by a variety of motives, pressures and circumstances. The most common explanation offered for going into the bonding business was that their fathers had been in the business before them and they felt a family obligation to continue the operation. Two of the three bondsmen who "grew into" their fathers' occupation frankly stated their distaste for the business. They felt trapped into continuing in the profession because of financial necessity or familial obligations. The third bondsman, who inherited his family's business, engaged in the job only as a sideline, spending most of his time as a boxing commissioner for the state of Indiana. He is also a fight promoter and brought a heavyweight championship fight to his city.

Two bondsmen were influenced into going into the bonding business on the advice of policemen. Both were young and out of work, and were told that it was a "good hustle" supplying a regular source of income. One of these men came from a police family—his father had been police captain on the force and his brother had served as an officer.

Most of the bondsmen were drawn into the business at a fairly early age. All three bondsmen from Washington, D.C., commenced their bail-bonding experience in their early twenties. One had been a vacuum cleaner salesman earning decent wages before he was drawn into the bonding business. A second bondsman borrowed money from his father to help bail friends out of jail during prohibition. In the following months his friends, many of whom were lawyers, talked him into becoming a full-time bondsman. For the third Washington bondsman, the financial strain of temporary unemployment while attempting to earn money to pay for his last semester of college prompted his new career. The only work he could find at the time was a job with a bondsman. He never returned to college and soon went into business for himself.

The most interesting entrance into the bonding industry was by an Atlanta bondsman. The son of a wealthy insurance executive, he decided in high school that he wanted to "make it on his own." He moved into a boarding house and worked his way through high school, saving every cent he earned. By the time he entered college he was able to put a down payment on a small home for himself. He continued his conscientious working habits and by the time he finished college he was able to purchase additional pieces of real estate. Within ten years after his graduation, he was a wealthy man with numerous real estate holdings, a bowling alley and a chain of liquor stores. Becoming restless for some new endeavors, and confessing to increasing boredom with real estate transactions, he sought a new sideline to keep himself busy. The bail-bonding business at that time (1960) was monopolized by whites in Atlanta. The additional challenge of breaking the color line spurred his decision to enter the bonding business. Although it is only a sideline, since the large majority of his revenue still comes from his liquor stores and apartment houses, he spends most of his time working out of his bonding office, a small shack across the street from the county jail.

Since bondsmen are dependent on a predominantly black clientele, it is important to examine a racial breakdown of bondsmen. Seventeen percent of the bondsmen interviewed were black. This seems to mirror fairly well the estimated national percentage, although an accurate tabulation has never been made. The two black bondsmen in this sample, one from Washington, D.C., and the other from Atlanta, are the two best-educated bondsmen in the study's limited sample. They are also two of the most successful bondsmen in terms of professional prestige and financial security. The major distinction between the two men is their conflict in life-style, which is best exemplified by their contrasting manner of dress. The explanation for this difference is probably caused by their respective geographic locations. The man from Washington made what he believed was a needed attempt at bolstering the image of bondsmen by his mod style. He is easily recognized in the courthouse corridors by his flared pants and wide flowery ties. In contrast, the Atlanta bondsman dresses like a day laborer, wearing khaki work pants and a beat-up hat. He explains his carefully chosen, drab wardrobe by stating that in the South it is much easier for a black to deal with a white if he fits their sartorial stereotype and does not appear to be an "uppity nigra" even though he may be much wealthier than the whites he must deal with in the sheriff's department.

In this age of women's liberation an obvious question concerns the presence of bondswomen. Although none of the cities visited had a bondswoman, an Associated Press release revealed that one does operate out of Clearwater, Florida. Described as blonde and buxom—armed with chemical mace, leg irons, pink phones and hot pants—she is a prosperous bondswoman currently having custody of 1,900 clients who had written nearly $2 million worth of bonds in the first ten months of 1972. When asked why she entered the bail-bonding business, she was quoted as saying: "Because I thought it was a good place for a woman's touch. . . . I just thought this was a business where I could do some good."

The bondsmen interviewed for this study generally agreed that business has decreased in recent years. Blame was placed on bail-reform projects as well as increasing numbers of forfeitures. In Washington, D.C., the number of bonding companies has been cut in half, from ten to five, in the past six years. Six of the bondsmen interviewed were visibly distressed over the current financial condition and two of them were making plans to enter a new vocation within the year. Forced by economic pressures to resort to outside sources of income, several bonding companies are on the verge of economic collapse. The largest bonding enterprise studied, the United Bonding Insurance Company, based in Indianapolis with branches in 45 states, was recently liquidated by the Indiana Department of Insurance. An audit revealed that United had assets totaling $2,848,000 and liabilities of $4,144,000.

STATE AND LOCAL REGULATION

One of the most obvious and significant trends of the last decade reported by all bondsmen is the ever-increasing amount of state and local regulation of the bonding industry. A few states for the first time have enacted laws which impose certain entrance requirements on anyone wishing to become a bondsman. The most common requirement is that the bondsmen cannot have had a felony conviction or a past history of criminal activity. However, Michigan and California seem to be the only states where the entrance requirements are rigorously enforced.

An additional method of supervision is to periodically audit the bondsman's records or to compel him to requalify on a periodic basis for continued operation as a state- or city-authorized bonding company. In St. Louis bondsmen are required to submit their records each month and can be forced to discontinue bonding activities if the required corrections are not made. Outside the cities regulated by the strict California Insurance Commission, bondsmen experience very little regulation. Although other areas do have sufficient legislation to cover the regulation of bondsmen, the problem is in getting the responsible state and local officials to enforce this legislation. An Indianapolis bondsman, discussing the difficulties of adequate legislation, stated: "The present state rules are modeled after those of Florida, which are considered to be comprehensive and fair. Unfortunately the law is unenthusiastically enforced. With so many links in the chain of a bonding operation, the state has given 'loose reins' to the problem, deferring to the insurance companies who have historically been lax in controlling their agents." The only phase of implementation which the state has undertaken with any degree of regularity and rigor is the requirement that the state have $75,000 in escrow from each insurance company in order to cover forfeitures owed by their agents.

As noted in the Indianapolis example, bonding regulations are most often controlled at the state level by the insurance commissioner or comptroller. Individual cities have attempted to control the behavior of bondsmen by placing severe restrictions on when and where they are permitted in the courthouse. Bondsmen are usually allowed inside the courtroom only when they have a case coming up, and one of their clients will be failing to appear. They may visit potential clients at the detention facility only after they have been called by the defendant. The rationale behind these regulations is to eliminate opportunities for collusion and kickbacks between bondsmen and public officials. The problem of collusion has been greatly reduced in recent years, but this is due more to the inability of the financially strained bondsmen to pay kickbacks than to the elaborate reporting procedures that are so poorly enforced.

With all these rules and regulations governing the bail-bonding business, how does a bondsman obtain his clientele? The main problem is not with the multitude of seldom enforced rules, but rather with the intense competition among bondsmen for the best clients. To bondsmen, better clients mean those defendants who appear most likely to show up for their various court appearances with a minimum of supervision. As bail reform projects continue to release the best potential clients to appear on their own recognizance, the competition among bondsmen for the remaining defendants becomes even more intense. One amusing manifestation of this competition is the desire for each bondsman to be listed first in the telephone directory. The result is that in the Detroit listing, over 50 percent of the city's bonding companies begin with the letter "A." The assumption behind this maneuver is that when an inexperienced defendant turns to the yellow pages to select a bondsman he will naturally look at the first company listed. The intensity of this competition has also shown an ugly side which is all too frequently brought to the public's attention. One Atlanta defense attorney commented on this tarnished image by stating that bonding companies give the impression of engaging in corrupt activities designed to "screw each other out of business."

SOURCES AND SELECTION OF CLIENTELE

There are five major sources of clients for the bondsman. These five groups which call upon the bondsman for his services will be discussed in descending order according to the frequency of use. The first group is the defendant's family and friends. After a defendant is taken into custody, he is permitted one or two telephone calls and will invariably notify a relative or friend of his difficulty, requesting help in gaining his pretrial freedom. It will then be the relative or friend who will seek out a bondsman to help get the defendant out of jail. The second group is comprised of the defendants themselves. Particularly if a defendant has had prior experience in such situations, he will know how to directly contact a bondsman without bothering his family. He may have had a satisfactory previous relationship with a particular bondsman and prefer to renew that association. The third source is the defendant's lawyer. The bondsman often feels more confident in securing the defendant's appearance at court if he can work in conjunction with his lawyer. The fourth group is made up of court officials such as the court clerk or the bailiff. If both the bondsman and the clerk are "old-timers" a suggestion may be made to the bondsman as to a potential client. If the bondsman is amenable, the clerk or bailiff may contact the defendant and tell him to quickly call the bondsman who they believe will give him a fair deal. The police and custodial officers comprise the fifth group but their numbers are decreasing. Out of sheer helpfulness or with the thought of future favors in mind, some of these men may recommend specific bondsmen to the recently apprehended defendants. If the bondsmen discover that specific police officers and jailers are consistently referring clients in their direction, certain rewards are usually offered in gratitude. Aside from these five main sources of business, there is another group who may call upon the bondsman. They are the professional criminals who will have trusted friends notify a bondsman in the city where they intend to commit a crime, to be on the lookout for the defendant in case he slips up and is arrested. This procedure was revealed in an Atlanta interview but is engaged in on a national scale. It should be noted that all groups must initiate contact with the bondsman. The bondsman is unable to visit the defendant in his cell and therefore must wait to be notified by one of these groups.

Once a bondsman learns that a particular defendant wishes to use his services, he must decide whether he is willing to take a chance on him as a client. The bondsman must be an adroit judge of the defendant's future behavior, since he stands to lose a great deal of money if the defendant willfully forfeits. The common bonding fee of 10 percent means that the defendant pays the bondsman $100 on a $1,000 bond and if the defendant fails to show, the bondsman owes the court $1,000. With such grave financial stakes in the offing, bondsmen have formulated many criteria and guidelines to help them in this decision.

Little agreement was found among the bondsmen as to how they best ensure that they are selecting a reliable defendant. Most bondsmen admit that they use the same types of criteria utilized by bail-reform projects emphasizing the defendant's community ties and past criminal record. Bondsmen seek to supplement this basic information by going to the police or prosecutor's office in hope of ascertaining the strength of the state's case against the defendant. Most bondsmen discount information supplied by a prospective client since he is so involved in his own problems that he may be unable to objectively and honestly supply the necessary information. Therefore the bondsman commonly relies on discussions with the family or lawyer. One bondsman interviewed in Detroit disclosed that he will consult only with the family since they are the ones who must be trusted to make sure the defendant will appear in court.

Like most officials concerned with the administration of bail, the bondsman believes that the most important variable affecting the defendant's pretrial release is the nature of the crime of which he is charged. The categories of crimes which bondsmen classify as either poor risks or good risks are not based, however, on the seriousness of the offense but on the following collection of guidelines, premonitions and idiosyncrasies. Examining first the best risks, the bondsmen frequently listed any professional criminal as being the most reliable. These are experienced criminals who believe that their arrest is merely an occupational hazard. They have frequently employed the services of bondsmen and have worked out acceptable arrangements. The defendant knows that if he forfeits and causes the bondsman to lose money, word would be circulated and he would be unable to secure his pretrial release by any bondsman if he were to be arrested in the future, which is a possibility to be considered for a professional criminal. A second category of good risks is that of defendants arrested for crimes such as gambling, which is usually run by organized crime. In this case there will be a reliable source of money and the defendant's sponsoring organization will be a persuasive force in ensuring his return for trial. If the organization is interested in getting the defendant out of the jurisdiction, they will often cover the entire bond with the bondsman rather than pay the money directly to the court themselves.

Whom do bondsmen consider bad risks? One group which most bondsmen are reluctant to have as clients are first offenders. Their explanation is quite logical. They reason that first offenders have a greater fear of a possible prison sentence because they have never been imprisoned. Thus, there seems a greater possibility that they might panic as their court date approaches and, fearing the worst, run away. Another category of poor risks consists of those defendants categorized as recidivists whose crimes seem to carry the defendant into deeper trouble and eventually may force him to flee the city. Examples of these types of criminals are prostitutes and junkies. A Washington bondsman commented on the habits of both groups by stating: "Prostitutes and gypsies. They come into town for a while and get arrested. They get out on bond and they take off for another town. . . . The junkies are hazardous because even they don't know what they are going to do. The pushers are going to stay in town but you don't know about the users."

A third category of crimes that most bondsmen are apprehensive about are those involving guns or physical violence. Armed robbery was always mentioned as one of those violent crimes bondsmen try to avoid. Another seasoned Washington bondsman spoke out on why he steers away from armed robbers:

A guy that takes a gun and goes into a store or bank must have it in the back of his mind that he'll use it if he has to. Now if I bail him and can't produce him in court, I've got to get him. He didn't hesitate to pull a gun when he held you up and I make a good target, big as I am. Besides that, the bonds in these cases run high, making the potential losses greater. Taking someone who has gone to the gun just isn't worth the risk. Besides a guy charged with that kind of offense knows he may be going away for a long time and that increases the chances he'll skip.

The bondsmen have often been criticized for being very loose or irresponsible in their selection of clients. This criticism seems unjustified based on this study's observations. Most bondsmen are plagued by a potential clientele composed of less than ideal citizens. The bondsmen interviewed weren't anxious to empty the jails and write bonds for everyone. They are usually operating on shaky financial foundations and must exercise caution in order to avoid complete economic collapse. If they can be accused of anything, bondsmen can be chastised for turning down too many defendants and causing them to be detained in jail.

The amount a bondsman can charge a client is usually regulated by state statute. The customary amount is 10 percent of the total bond set. Because of the rising forfeiture rates and less desirable clientele, bondsmen have attempted to require additional collateral from the defendant or his family. This is usually a mortgage, a lien on property or a business. Several states prohibit this type of maneuver, but it is rarely enforced despite the fact that it is an extremely common practice among bondsmen. Another typical state ruling prohibits bondsmen from working on credit, but this, too, is rarely implemented.

The 10 percent fee which the bondsman charges represents his profit before operating expenses are deducted. After losses due to forfeitures and additional expenses and licensing fees are subtracted, the bondsman is left with less than half of the original figure. A Detroit bondsman frankly stated that if it were not for a few big bonds in the $20,000 to $30,000 range from professional criminals or members of organized crime rings, he would not be able to remain in business.

In a few jurisdictions bondsmen are permitted to write bonds on property. In Washington, D.C., a bondsman is allowed to write bonds on clients in the amount of three times the value of the property. Once the bondsman's limit is reached he cannot bail out anyone else.

SUPERVISING HIS CLIENTS

After the bondsman has decided to accept a defendant as a client, the crucial factor determining whether a forfeiture will occur is the degree of supervision which the bondsman exercises over the defendant—provided, of course, that the defendant has not initially made up his mind to skip town even before going to the bondsman. Although many bondsmen work long and hard at maintaining adequate contact with their clients, the majority seem to be lax and merely assume that the defendant will appear for trial. It is only when the defendant fails to appear that the typical bondsman springs into action and works through his network of informants and "skip tracers," modern-day bounty hunters, to retrieve the missing defendant.

The bondsman usually repeats the oral and written statements of the court notifying the defendant of the date of his next court appearance. For many bondsmen their contact with the defendant ends here, unless there is an attempt to forfeit. Among the procedures followed by the more conscientious bondsman are a series of phone calls, letters and visits to the defendant and his family. Several bondsmen sneer at such pampering and believe that if the defendants really require that much supervision, they should not have been accepted as clients in the first place. One bondsman in Washington who realized the necessity for this continuous supervision complained of the long hours required by such procedures: "You work from 8 to 5 at your office and then you have to run your people for the next day. Since many of them don't come home regularly, you have to go down to 14th and U streets or wherever they may be hanging out. It takes up to 18 hours a day."

The bondsman's caseload varies a great deal depending on the size of his operation. In the case of typical two- or three-man operations, it was estimated that they usually are working with about a hundred clients at a time. The size of the bonding company seems to have no effect on the degree of supervision, although the two largest companies appeared to have the most complete system of client supervision.

DEALING WITH FORFEITURES

The judgment of bondsmen concerning their clients is not infallible. The question of how many clients eventually forfeit is obscured by the poor record-keeping by both bondsmen and the state and local authorities. Only six of the cities visited were able to provide estimates of the forfeiture rate of bondsmen. The average forfeiture rate for these six cities was 5.7 percent with Detroit having the highest percentage (8 percent) and Philadelphia the lowest (4 percent). The national bond forfeiture rate has been estimated to be between 3 and 4 percent.

If the defendant is willfully avoiding his court appearance and cannot be located in a day or two, the bondsman must turn to his "skip tracers." These men work on commission of approximately 10 percent of the bond. They are usually armed and very often have prior criminal records. No state has actively sought to regulate these men who operate in the shadows of the criminal justice system.

The legal authority for allowing bondsmen to recall their clients from any jurisdiction in the country is a document called the "bail piece." The bail piece is similar to a contract between the bondsman and his client. The critical section of this contract is the stated agreement by the defendant that he is willing to waive his extradition rights and authorize the bondsman or his agent to retrieve him from wherever he has fled. The bondsman obtains the bail piece from the court after his client has jumped bail. This document, along with the bench warrant, is presented to the local police department in the place where the fugitive is recaptured. The bondsmen in most states are permitted official assistance from these local authorities in their efforts to recapture the fleeing defendant. The bondsmen often delegate their power to the skip tracer who is in possession of the bail piece and the bench warrant.

Some states have tried to impose restrictions on the more blatant offenses of bondsmen and skip tracers in their attempts at recapturing defendants in other jurisdictions. Unfortunately, most of their legislative endeavors are shortsighted, restricting only the questionable methods of out-of-state bondsmen who seek fugitives in their state. These restrictions do not extend to local bondsmen who go into other jurisdictions to recapture fugitives. Such a legislative defect was discussed in a *California Law Review* article which stated that "the state [California] encourages or at least condones the use of tactics by California bondsmen operating out of state which it would not tolerate if the bondsmen committed them within the state. While California authorities are not aware of incidents of physical or psychological abuse of California fugitives recaptured outside the state, other jurisdictions have reported incidents of such abuse."[1]

The abuses referred to in the previous quote, although infrequent, still occur too often. Two bondsmen from Atlanta, Georgia, were recently jailed in Memphis, Tennessee, as a result of their attempt to return a Memphis man to Georgia. They had vowed to return the man to Atlanta "dead or alive," and had been found threatening him with a pistol.

Despite the abundance of stories concerning the exploits of bondsmen recapturing fugitives, these tales appear to be greatly exaggerated. Bondsmen generally view the retrieval process as a very expensive proposition which is usually unsuccessful. As one bondsman related: "Going to get a bond jumper means paying for information to locate him, the cost of driving to wherever he is and back, meals and the $425 a day cost of hiring the gun, the man who'll guard the jumper on the return trip. A recent four-day trip to Akron cost $750."

One of the major improvements in the administration of bail is the recent willingness on the part of responsible state and local officials to collect from bondsmen all forfeitures in the full amount of the original bond. The significance of this improvement in collection enforcement is that it will compel bondsmen to keep closer contact with their clients so they will show up for trial. Bondsmen must be made to realize that they will be taking the risk of actually

---

[1] Copyright © 1968, California Law Review, Inc., reprinted by permission.

having to pay the forfeiture bond if their client flees. Judge Murphy of the District of Columbia's Court of General Sessions symbolizes this new attitude. He stated in an interview that "bondsmen have always been in a position where they just assumed nothing was going to happen to them. But I just don't have this clubhouse attitude about bondsmen."

The reader should be cautioned against being overly optimistic about overnight changes. There are still many cities where the bonds are not collected on a regular basis. In St. Louis, for example, records of the circuit court reveal that of the 318 forfeitures in felony cases in 1970, 304 were set aside. This tremendous number of unpaid forfeitures casts serious doubts on the manner in which these bonds are being collected.

The bondsmen are usually helped by the city if they have honestly attempted to recapture the fugitive. They are also provided aid in the form of extended periods of time in which to relocate their clients. This length of time varies from the 10–14 days for Detroit bondsmen to 180 days for bondsmen in San Francisco. The average time to return the defendant and pay the forfeiture, as in Atlanta and Baltimore, is 90 days. In nearly all cities studied, if the bondsman can convince the judge that the forfeiture was not his fault and that he diligently attempted to recapture the defendant, the judge will set aside all or part of the forfeiture amount due. In Atlanta, the district attorney's office offers a 25 percent discount on all forfeited bonds if it can be convinced that an effort was made to recapture the fugitive. A few cities employ a sliding scale where the sooner the bondsman can recapture the client, the less he will have to pay on the forfeited bond.

COLLUSION AND OTHER FORMS OF MISBEHAVIOR

As noted earlier, the sinister character commonly ascribed to bondsmen is largely a fictitious creation when compared to the behavior of the bondsmen who have been interviewed and observed at work. Most important, there is sufficient variation in their personalities and work habits so that it is impossible to construct a valid stereotyped image of the group. Nevertheless, it has been discovered that many bondsmen and their skip tracers still engage in illegal activities. In Indianapolis, for example, it has been found that one bondsman had his license revoked because of his numerous illegal extracurricular activities, while another of the city's bondsmen was arrested in July 1970 for theft and three counts of failure to file a bond affidavit.

An additional difficulty for bondsmen is the reputation of their clientele. The general public often indicts bondsmen by guilt through association. Unfortunately, bondsmen sometimes form business alliances with organized crime figures, which discredits the entire profession. Judge Moylan, Baltimore's former state attorney, commented that several bondsmen seem to be involved in every type of conspiracy and underworld activity in the city, with a special interest in gambling.

The most common complaint lodged against bondsmen by their clients was that they failed to return part of the 10-percent bonding fee when the case was quickly dismissed prior to trial. The decision not to prosecute is often made by the time of the preliminary hearing and means that the defendant may be paying several hundred dollars for only a week's freedom. A similar irritation is caused by the bondsman who changes his mind about bonding a client. The bondsman may go to the client's home and drag him back to jail, but fail to return the initial payment. This type of behavior may occur when the bondsman learns something new about the defendant or his case and decides that on the basis of this new information his client is no longer a desirable risk. It is presently unclear precisely what legal protections are offered to the bondsman's client from these practices.

Bondsmen do not function in a vacuum. Their interrelationships with officials and agencies involved in the administration of justice are essential to their livelihood. These relationships, however, have often led to alarmed cries of collusion and have been used as another example of the bondsman's illegal activities. It is impossible to arrive at an impartial and factual estimation of the amount of collusion actually taking place.

The most frequently named group to be accused of engaging in collusive activities with bondsmen are defense attorneys. In many of the cities included in the study, lawyers were alleged to have paid a 10 percent kickback to bondsmen who recommended them. In St. Louis one attorney went so far as to state that bondsmen have made several lawyers wealthy by referring cases to them. At least part of the blame can be placed upon the local bar associations that fail to control their members and permit these types of activities to continue.

A second group charged with conspiring with bondsmen are judges. An investigation in Philadelphia in 1964 revealed that certain judges were receiving money from bondsmen to set bail in all cases regardless of their seriousness, so they would have more potential clients. According to a defense attorney interviewed, this practice still persists, although to a lesser degree. He commented that a few judges will allow bondsmen to tell them how much they believe the defendant can afford. The bondsman may attempt to improve a working relationship with a judge by contributing to his campaign fund. The bondsmen of Detroit and St. Louis seem to be the most politically active in this respect. One bondsman in St. Louis is party chairman of a congressional district.

A third group accused of illegal dealings with bondsmen are the police. This illicit relationship supposedly begins with the arresting officer or someone in the stationhouse recommending a particular bondsman to the defendant. At the end of the month, the policeman can expect to receive a kickback from that bondsman, based upon the number of clients referred. It has been learned through interviews and many hours of observations in stationhouses, lockups and jails that this practice has sharply declined in the past five years, although it still continues sporadically. Two reasons are given for the abatement of a seemingly lucrative practice for both parties: the increasing supervision over the operations of bail-bonding companies by state and city agencies and the decreasing profit margin of bonding companies that have been forced to curtail expenditures such as kickback payments. These financial pressures have reduced their clientele and forced bondsmen to be more selective in whom they choose to represent.

The contemporary bondsman may still exert a great deal of influence over a defendant's pretrial freedom but he is a member of a dying profession. As bail-reform projects expand, operating expenses rise and state and local regulation increases, the bonding industry continues its steady decline. The bondsmen described in this article are neither glamorous nor sinister—they are simply fighting to survive. Many of them are not sympathetic characters and several engage in clearly unlawful practices, but until the traditional bail system is radically reformed, they will continue to be the one group offering an opportunity for pretrial freedom for most of the unfortunate individuals enmeshed in our nation's criminal justice system.

Chapter 6

The measurement of crime

The various methods of measuring crime include the use of police records, records of court proceedings, and records of correctional institutions. Insurance company records of claims made for property losses through theft and destruction provide an alternative avenue for gauging the frequency of some property crime. Anonymous questionnaires can be used to estimate the magnitude of criminal behavior in a given population, and interviews with samples of citizens can be used to determine whether, during a given year, they have been victims of any of a variety of crimes. The most widely used and most commonly accepted measures of the magnitude of crime are the frequencies found in police records, which are usually expressed in rates per 100,000 population in a given political jurisdiction. In this chapter these various measures of crime will be evaluated in terms of how accurately they report criminal behavior.

POLITICAL AND TECHNICAL PROBLEMS IN CRIME RECORDING

Police records

When crime rates are discussed, the source of information is usually the FBI Uniform Crime Reports. The Uniform Crime

Reports is an annual FBI publication which gives a detailed description of crime patterns in the United States for the year. For each state and every city over 10,000, it itemizes the frequency of all major types of crime reported to or discovered by the police. A separate reporting of all arrests is also included. The FBI also records information about juvenile misbehavior, including crimes committed by juveniles and two juvenile-status offenses, running away and curfew violations. The FBI Uniform Crime Reports distinguishes two types of offense categories—Part I and Part II crimes. Part I crimes, which are used to make up the highly publicized Crime Index, include only seven offenses. These are criminal homicide, forcible rape, robbery, aggravated assault, burglary, auto theft, and larceny-theft. Crimes are included in this count if they are reported to or in any other way known by the police. Part II crimes include all other offenses. Here the count is limited to cases in which suspects are apprehended and arrests made.

The crime rates published in the Uniform Crime Reports are based on the results of a questionnaire which all police departments are asked to complete annually. The FBI has no legal power to force departments to report, and some departments, especially the smaller ones in rural areas, do not report. Moreover, there is no provision for auditing department reports. Police recognize that the crime rates reported by the FBI may be used to rate their department's effectiveness. If they accurately report all crime, the high rates in their areas may convince some people that they are not doing a good job.

Police often attempt to persuade the public that they are doing a good job in controlling crime, but they also want to convey the message that crime is still a great threat. This apparently contradictory message of both decreases and increases in crime seems logically impossible, but it was achieved by the recent Justice Department claims that crime was increasing at a decreasing rate (Weis and Milakovich, 1974: 27). Government officials can argue, for example, that an 8 percent increase in crime in a given year actually represents a reduction as compared to a previous yearly increase of 10 percent, but this, of course, ignores the fact that smaller percentage increments are predictable as the base from which the increments are calculated increases. One problem with official police records is that the temptation to alter the figures may be very strong. If a police force has received anticrime funds to show a crime decrease, the pressure is very great to do just that. A politician running for reelection may feel the need to credit his leadership with similar reductions. Indeed, one could conclude that since arrest data reflect on *police* activities, a *police* organization like the FBI should not be collecting the data (Weis and Milakovich, 1974: 30).

In 1950 New York City reported crime figures to the FBI that seemed very low. The FBI typically accepts police department reports at face value, but in this instance the FBI did some checking, and it found that the number of property crimes reported by the police was approximately half the number reported to insurance companies (Bell, 1960: 152). In this case, it appears that the police department was not telling the whole story to the FBI to avoid the embarrassment that a high crime rate might cause to police officials. A more recent distortion of police records occurred in Washington, D.C. The political scientist David Seidman (*Time*, 1972: 55) found that "the police tend not even to record crime they believe they have little or no chance of solving." Moreover, the accounting firm of Ernst and Ernst audited the Washington, D.C., police records and found that more than 1,000 thefts of over $50 had been purposely downgraded to below $50. That made these thefts misdeameanors and dropped them from the roster of major crimes, which the department was committed to reducing.

In fairness, however, it should be mentioned that an effect of inflation and affluence is to increase the number of thefts of over $50, independent of any real increases in thefts. A $25 item stolen ten years ago may now be valued at over $50. Another consequence of prosperity has been an increase in burglary and theft insurance which requires the reporting of losses to the police as a condition for making an insurance claim (Biderman, 1966: 119–120). So a greater proportion of reported losses might also make it falsely appear that property crime is increasing. Perhaps as a result of these problems of political abuse and inflation, since 1973 the FBI has included all larcenies in its major crime index, not just those over $50, as was previously the case.

Among those urging the use of police data in the study of crime, some support the procedure of counting as crimes those events that the police saw or discovered to have been crimes, whereas others support the idea of using as data all events known to or reported to the police as crimes in order to avoid ignoring important information on crime (Sellin and Wolfgang, 1964). Wolfgang (1970: 308–309) observes that the problem of missing information is especially common for Part II crimes because most of these offenses never result in clearance by arrest and are therefore not recorded.

Although most Americans seem to have become accustomed to crime statistics reported from police records, the accuracy of police statistics varies with the type of crime. Some crimes, such as vice (gambling and prostitution) and price fixing, almost never become known to the police through reporting, either because there are no victims in the traditional sense or because those victimized do not know that they are victims. Such crimes must be discovered by the police through routine patrol, undercover work, or informants. This means that changes in the intensity of law enforcement activity and not changes in the amount of such crime may account for changes in the number of such offenses detected. The police are more often notified if the victims are harmed directly, as in assaults and theft. In such cases there is often someone, the victim or a friend or relative of the victim, who will call the police. Even when there is a victim in the traditional sense, however, a crime may not be reported to the police because of a belief that the police either cannot or will not do anything about it (Gould, 1971: 89).

Cicourel (1968) suggests that a very different picture of the extent and distribution of juvenile delinquency is obtained (1) by looking at official police records and (2) by looking at all cases known to the police. For one thing, the attitude of the youth is important in determing how his behavior will be initially interpreted by the police officer and how it will ultimately be reported in the official record. Moreover, middle- and upper-class children typically have the advantage of a conventional family unit that can show its concern, and this bodes well for the youth's future behavior in the officer's judgment. Both of these elements are important in determining whether the officer sees a particular behavior as serious. Such characteristics as a "bad attitude" or a "poor home environment" transform the juvenile into a person in need of formal disposition irrespective of the seriousness of the behavior in question. Even the repeated relatively violent acts of middle- and upper-class youths may be defined away as evidence of a natural phase of growing up in a troubled world, or at worst as evidence that the youths need professional and medical help. On the other hand, even minor crimes committed by children from racial and economic minorities, especially if the children are defiant, supply evidence to the police of the beginnings of a criminal career which must be nipped in the bud by some official action, such as incarceration. This shows how formal arrest records reflect both American racism and an interest in the protection of the affluent.

Other official crime statistics

Although at present there is considerable acceptance of the FBI's Uniform Crime Reports as a reflection of actual crime, there are some who believe that court records may have advantages over these police records. Among those urging the use of judicial statistics, some argue for a count of all cases coming before the courts, whereas others argue for reporting only convictions. For those who think of the Uniform Crime Reports as the only reasonable way of reporting crime, it will be instructive to learn that before World War I most countries used only judicial statistics and that the switch to police records has been made only in the last 40 years. One argument against the use of judicial records is that people are frequently accused of a number of crimes but are tried only for the most serious one. Thus the judicial records would exaggerate more serious crimes and minimize lesser crimes. It is also argued that the number of violators disclosed by judicial records does not reflect the number of law violations; one person may commit many crimes, or several persons may conspire to commit the same crime, and these differences do not balance each other out. On the other hand, some crime cannot be accurately counted until the personal responsibility of the suspect has been assessed in court and all the facts of the case have been presented and weighed as evidence. This, of course, argues for the use of judicial records (Sellin and Wolfgang, 1964).

Whether court or police statistics are used, changes in the number of arrests, trials, or sentences may not represent actual changes in the amount of crime but rather changes in the capacity of various elements of the criminal justice system. Increases or decreases in the number of police, judges, courtrooms, or bed spaces in correctional institutions will undoubtedly influence these statistics (Lejins, 1961).

Van Vechten (1942) has demonstrated that a loss of cases occurs at each stage in the criminal justice process, beginning with the crimes known to the police and continuing through arrests, prosecutions, convictions, and sentences. Sellin (1931: 335–336) has also argued that the adequacy of a crime index decreases as the distance increases between the criminal act and the statistical base (record keeping) in terms of the steps in the criminal justice process.

The value of a crime rate for index purposes decreases as the distance from the crime itself in terms of procedure increases. In other words, police statistics, particularly those of "crimes known to the police," are most likely to furnish a good basis for a crime index (Sellin, 1931: 346).

The records of a crime—from the time it becomes known to the police to its disposition by arrest, prosecution, conviction and commitment to a penal institution—represent successive steps in procedure. Crime rates based on these steps are all end results of a selective process into which enter the willingness to report a crime, the desire to record it, the ability on the part of the police to detect and arrest the criminal, the policy which guides the prosecutor in deciding whether to bring the offender to trial at all, or to trial on the crime charged, the desire on the part of the jury or the judge to convict, and, finally, the sentencing policy of the judge (Sellin, 1931: 341).

Sellin's argument holds that for a variety of reasons, including bargained-for guilty pleas for lesser charges, police records are of more value in reflecting the actual crime situation than are either court or institutional records. But it is also true that some innocent people are ultimately found not guilty in court, and in such cases court records are more adequate. Using Sellin's argument, the most *representative* measure of the crimes that actually occur is the crimes known to the police, including those not recorded by them, followed, in order, by measures of crimes recorded by the police, suspects charged, suspects tried, suspects convicted, and finally, convicted persons sentenced to a correctional institution. Unfortunately, the most representative measure—crimes known to the police—is least likely to provide an *accurate* count of the cases known to law enforcement officials at this level. Going into a police department and securing information about the total number of crimes known to the police, including those which for various reasons do not result in arrests, would be difficult, if not impossible, given the concern of the police for secrecy about their activities. On the other hand, officials willingly provide the most accurate counts on the least representative data of all, those obtainable from institutional records (Taft and England, 1964: 53). Any prison staff can quickly and accurately supply data on the number of persons it has in custody and the crimes for which they have been sentenced.

Interpretation of official crime records and the mass media

Even when argreement is reached on the use of a given crime index, its interpretation may be problematic. Common opinion holds that modern American cities are becoming more and more violent and dangerous. However, one study of a major American city shows that this assumption may be false and that it may be a result of considering only very recent trends in crime rates. Ferdinand (1967) indicates that in Boston the rate of minor crime as well as major violent crime had decreased over the preceding 100 years. The question is, how can crime be increasing in the United States if the crime rate is decreasing in major cities like Boston? Ferdinand suggests that this is happening because an increasing percentage of our population lives in cities, where, even though the crime rate is going down, it is still higher than the rural rate. The following table, based on an example from Ferdinand (1967: 99), demonstrates his point:

Population, 1870	*Urban and rural crime rates, 1870*	*Overall crime rate, 1870*
80% rural	40 per 1,000	52 per 1,000
20% urban	100 per 1,000	

Population, 1970	*Urban and rural crime rates, 1970*	*Overall crime rate, 1970*
10% rural	40 per 1,000	58 per 1,000
90% urban	60 per 1,000	

The argument is outlined below:

1. Crime rates in major cities have been decreasing.
2. Crime rates remain higher in major cities than in rural areas.
3. The proportion of the population living in cities has been rapidly increasing.

4. The overall nationwide crime rate has been going up.
5. The overall increase in the crime rate is due to massive population shifts to the cities, where the crime rate, though decreasing, is still higher than the rural crime rate.

Such research contradicts our current crisis orientation toward crime, especially in larger U.S. cities. Puttkammer (1953: 52–53) suggests that crime waves or crime crises are largely artificially created situations and that they often result from increased press activity and concern. Such intense press coverage may in turn generate more police activity, and this activity sends the arrest rates up. The rise in arrest rates has the circular effect of giving the media even more material regarding crime with which to further alarm the public.

Conklin (1975) observes that the feeling that a crime crisis exists is more likely to be generated by crime reporting in the mass media than by official crime rates. Crime reports in the mass media are more accessible and more easily understood than official crime rates, and therefore people's ideas about the gravity of the crime problem are more closely tied to mass media reports than to official reports. This, Conklin says, is especially true in the United States, whose newspapers have typically given more attention to sensationalist crime reporting than have the newspapers of other nations. The seemingly capricious nature of crime reporting in U.S. newspapers is reflected in a Colorado study (Davis, 1952) which found great variation in the amount of space devoted to crime stories in various Colorado newspapers, but found no relationship between local crime rates and the amount of crime news in the local newspapers. At times there was a negative relationship between official rates of crime and the amount of crime news. Conklin (1975: 24) suggests that the distorted nature of crime reporting is also reflected in the great variation in the space devoted to crime problems in competing daily newspapers in the same cities. Some newspapers devote relatively little space to crime, whereas others give the subject considerably more coverage.

The motivation for artificially created crime waves may appear to be a mystery to most Americans, especially those who believe in a truly independent watchdog press, such as that guaranteed by the First Amendment to the U.S. Constitution. However, as Sallach (1974) observes, most of the nation's mass media are not only owned by large corporations but require advertising from large corporations. Journalists' claims of independent news media which serve the public interests are largely a myth, since journalists rarely raise questions about the misdeeds of giant corporations. A public with an unquestioning conception of crime serves the interests of the giant corporations in their efforts to protect themselves from a potentially rebellious and demanding citizenry. It is in the interests of these corporations to control the public image of the amount, and especially the nature, of crime. The typical media message is that the nation faces a crime crisis involving purse snatching, burglary, and the Mafia, but usually nothing is said about the criminal activities of large corporations. (Also see Molotch and Lester, 1974: 104–105, for a discussion of media control by elites.)

Other crime measurement techniques

Given all these problems with the crime measurements provided by the mass media as well as by police records and other official data, it might be asked what alternatives are available. Two possibilities exist: victimization surveys and anonymous questionnaires. Victimization surveys involve interviewing a sample of people and asking them whether they or any other persons in their home have been victims of any of a series of crimes during the preceding year (Biderman, 1967; Ennis, 1967). In one survey (U.S. Department of Justice, 1974a), owners of businesses were also checked. Such surveys turn up many unreported crimes and imply a considerable undercounting of crime of all types in police records. Victims often do not report crimes because they believe that the police either cannot or will not do anything about their complaints. Victimization surveys are not without difficulties in interpretation, however. One difficulty involves failures to recall victimization, especially in the case of minor crimes and of incidents remote in time (Biderman et al., 1967). These problems of recall seem especially likely in high-crime areas, where victimization is a relatively frequent experience. Other limitations of such victimization data include an underreporting of crimes without victims, such as drug offenses, prostitution, and gambling, or of crimes in which the respondent-victim may have something to hide, as in the case of blackmail (U.S. Department of Justice, 1974b).

Through the years a number of studies have been conducted to determine how admitted criminal acts compare to those officially recorded. These studies have used anonymous questionnaires which were often given to student groups. The results of all such studies indicate that the image of criminal behavior as a typically lower-class problem is incorrect. In one study, all the college students questioned admitted that they had committed at least one crime (Porterfield, 1943). These admissions seemed to reflect the same types and seriousness of crimes as were found among youths brought before juvenile courts. Bloch and Flynn (1956: 11–14) found that 91 percent of middle-class college students admitted a wide variety of felony and/or misdemeanor offenses. Another such study in New York City found that 89 percent of the men sampled and 83 percent of the women sampled admitted committing some theft, and that 64 percent of the men and 29 percent of the women admitted to a felony, showing both the commonness of crime and its prevalence among various classes (Wallerstein and Wyle, 1947). A serious problem with such questionnaire information is that no ~~NOT~~ tests for truthfulness exist. Some respondents could well underre- ~~ACCUR~~ port or falsely claim law violations. However, these questionnaire studies, along with victimization surveys, indicate a considerable underreporting of crime in official records.

THE MEANING AND CONSTRUCTION OF CRIME RATES

Earlier we discussed the arbitrary nature of what is termed *crime*. The definition of crime varies not only across countries but across states as well. An act may be a felony in one state and a misdemeanor or not a crime at all in another, as with marijuana possession or homosexual relations between consenting adults. Moreover, the evidence required to prove the same type of crime may vary in different states. This makes the task of comparing crime rates across jurisdictions very difficult (Taft and England, 1964: 47). In addition, especially in youth crime, there is wide agreement that at least part of the increase can be accounted for by changing definitions of crime and delinquency. Acts which a century ago might have been called orneriness and handled informally with a good thrashing are now subject to official control mechanisms and called crime (Tetters and Matza, 1959).

As the youth in a country increase both in raw numbers and in their proportion to the total population, one would, of course, expect more youth crime. However, if crime rates are calculated on the basis of the number of crimes per 100,000 people committed in a given area during a specific period of time, as is usually the case, no controls can be made for changes in the proportion of youths in the society, and it may falsely appear that the rates of youth crime are increasing.

A murder rate of 5.0 would indicate that five murders were recorded for every 100,000 population in an area. This method of indicating the amount of crime in a given area has been accepted unquestioningly. The method assumes that all people in the area should be included in the calculations. However, it is by no means clear that this is the most accurate way of showing the propensity toward crime in a given area. We know, for example, that most crime is committed by males between ages 15 and 40, and therefore, perhaps only this group should be used as a base in calculating crime rates. In calculating abortion rates, perhaps only women of childbearing age should be included. Clearly, if a group of people cannot potentially be included in the numerator of the crime rate as either perpetrators or victims, then they should not be included in the denominator. Two-year-old children should not be included in the denominator in calculating rates of armed robberies since they can neither commit nor be victimized by such offenses. Moreover, it is not clear that the traditional method of calculating crime rates is meaningful to most citizens. Mayors of many large American metropolitan areas claim that their cities have lower crime rates than do many small towns, yet there is no evidence that people find this reassuring; people seem more concerned with the gross number of crimes than with crime rates. Obviously, if U.S. cities continue to grow, even if crime rates go down, as found by Ferdinand (1967), there will be more total crimes for newspapers and other media to report. According to Wolfgang (1970: 293), people are less interested in the rate of crime than in their perceived probability of being victims of crime. This probability may increase, not in accordance with actual crime rates, but as a result of changes in the total number of crimes reported.

Lemert (1951: 57–58) suggests that it is useful to think of crime waves in terms of what he calls the public's *tolerance quotient*. This is the ratio of actual criminal behavior to the public's tolerance of criminal behavior. If the public's tolerance is initially very low, then even slight changes in the amount of criminal behavior can generate a perceived crime wave. Two communities may have identical tolerance quotients if both the actual crime and the public's tolerance are greater in one community than in the other. The public's tolerance of crime in general or of specific types of crime can be measured by asking citizens to suggest appropriate criminal sanctions for various crimes and by asking them to rate the relative seriousness of a series of criminal offenses.

It has also been suggested that instead of comparing the occurrence of a specific crime to a total or specific population, the occurrence of a specific crime should be compared to the amount of opportunity for that type of crime in a given area (Boggs, 1965). Environmental opportunities for crime vary from neighborhood to neighborhood, depending on the activities which prevail in different sections of a city. The availability of such targets as safes, cash registers, dispensing machines, and people and their possessions are distributed differently across any city. Keeping such ideas in mind, in calculating rape the number of females might serve as a revised total population, and in calculating auto theft the amount of space for parking automobiles could be used as the base.

It is clear that the way in which crime rates are constructed represents an implicit theory about crime causation. If environmental measures are used as a crime rate denominator, the argument is that the amount of crime is somehow importantly related to opportunity for crime. This is in contrast to the usual assumption that crime is somehow importantly related to the size of the total population. Moreover, the fact that most crime rate reports, including the FBI's, include rates for various racial groups can easily be interpreted as a form of racism. Gilbert Geis' (1965) question is, if crime rates are reported for black Americans, why not for Baptists and Republicans? His point is that using racial distinctions in crime reporting, and not religious or political distinctions, reflect a form of racial prejudice and discrimination. Race and not religion is implicitly assumed to be important in crime causation.

In calculating the magnitude of the crime problem, one could consider, along with opportunity to commit crime, the amount of loss to victims or, alternatively, the damage crime causes to public confidence in, and respect for, law and order (Gould, 1971: 92–97). Although denominators based on such alternatives are not easy to construct, an example is possible. Using the number of registered motor vehicles rather than population as the denominator (opportunity to commit crime), auto theft shows a great decrease rather than an increase, as when population is used.

The problem with these alternative denominators is that they do not fit most Americans' concept of "crime," which is inseparable from the concept of the "criminal" as a class set apart from the rest of society. What is important to Americans is not how many crimes are committed per unit of property but how many criminals are loose in the society and whether the citizen's personal risk of being victimized has increased. Therefore, Americans understand per capita crime rates better than crime rates using property loss information.

[margin note: DATA NOT ＬＬ THIS!]

CONCLUSION

Of the various official records about crime, the most widely accepted and used are the police records in the FBI Uniform Crime Reports. Such records, however, have been shown to be beset with technical problems as well as with many potential distortions due to political pressures. Indeed, other sources of information about crime, such as victimization surveys and anonymous questionnaires, give a picture of the amount and distribution of crime very different from that contained in official records. Because there is no uniform set of criminal codes across the U.S. states and among nations, interstate or international comparisons of crime rates can be very misleading. Moreover, the official crime rates show little or nothing about the actual behavior from which they are constructed. Alternative methods of constructing crime rates are conceivable, and such methods might produce more representative reflections of the magnitude of criminal offenses.

The various measures of criminal behavior, however, can be evaluated not only in terms of their representativeness of such behavior but also in terms of their use in forming public policy decisions, their intrinsic human interest, and their use as a basis for law-and-order rhetoric and as a vehicle for judging the efficiency of the various elements of the criminal justice system. Official crime rates are routinely used to determine such matters of public policy as the allocation of federal and local funds for police departments and changes in criminal statutes. Increases in crime shown by official data are often followed by arguments for increasing police budgets and/or penalties in the criminal code. Such increases in crime rates, when paired with mass media hysteria, have impelled many Americans to abandon the cities and flee to what they see as the relative safety of the suburbs even though they have never personally experienced the direct threat of crime. Official crime rates are also useful as support for a get-tough, law-and-order rhetoric which many politicians find appealing to the frightened voter. These same rates are also sometimes used by politicians to assess the effectiveness of various elements of the criminal justice system. In fact, increases or decreases in the official crime rates usually tell very little about the effectiveness of law enforcement agencies, in part for the very reason that these agencies realize that such data will be used to evaluate them.

Most criminologists are well aware of the shortcomings of crime rates based on official data. Even so, after listing all the shortcomings, scholars typically proceed to use such data anyway, perhaps because they are the only data that are available (Matza, 1969). A survey of juvenile delinquency research indicated a heavy reliance on official sources (Galliher and McCartney, 1973), yet only in very rare cases do criminologists actually attempt a true intellectual defense of such data (Cohen, 1955: 42). However, if official crime records are recognized as arbitrary and as reflective of economic and racial discrimination, then their use as measures of criminal behavior is inexcusable. *How much less so when used as a basis for theory development ??*

REFERENCES

Bell, Daniel
    1960   *The End of Ideology.* Rev. ed. New York: Free Press.

Biderman, Albert D.
    1966   "Social Indicators and Goals," pp. 68–153 in Raymond A. Bauer, ed., *Social Indicators.* Cambridge, Mass.: MIT Press.
    1967   "Surveys of Population Samples for Estimating Crime Incidence," *Annals of The American Academy of Political and Social Science* 374(November): 16–33.

Biderman, Albert D., Louise A. Johnson, Jennie McIntyre, and Adrianne W. Weir
1967 *Report on a Pilot Study in the District of Columbia on Victimization and Attitudes toward Law Enforcement.* President's Commission on Law Enforcement and Administration of Justice, Field Surveys No. 1. Office of Law Enforcement Assistance, U.S. Department of Justice. Bureau of Social Science Research, Inc. Washington, D.C.: U.S. Government Printing Office.

Bloch, Herbert and Frank T. Flynn
1956 *Delinquency: The Juvenile Offender in America Today.* New York: Random House.

Boggs, Sarah L.
1965 "Urban Crime Patterns," *American Sociological Review* 30(December): 899–908.

Cicourel, Aaron V.
1968 *The Social Organization of Juvenile Justice.* New York: John Wiley and Sons.

Cohen, Albert K.
1955 *Delinquent Boys.* Glencoe, Ill.: Free Press.

Conklin, John E.
1975 *The Impact of Crime.* New York: Macmillan Publishing Co.

Davis, F. James
1952 "Crime News in Colorado Newspapers," *American Journal of Sociology* 57(January): 325–330.

Ennis, Philip H.
1967 *Criminal Victimization in the United States: A Report of a National Survey.* National Opinion Research Center, University of Chicago. Washington, D.C.: U.S. Government Printing Office.

Ferdinand, Theodore N.
1967 "The Criminal Patterns of Boston since 1849," *American Journal of Sociology* 73(July): 84–99.

Galliher, John F. and James L. McCartney
1973 "The Influence of Funding Agencies on Juvenile Delinquency Research," *Social Problems* 21(Summer): 77–90.

Geis, Gilbert
1965 "Statistics concerning Race and Crime," *Crime and Delinquency* 11(April): 142–150.

Gould, Leroy
1971 "Crime and Its Impact in an Affluent Society," pp. 81–118 in

Jack D. Douglas, ed., *Crime and Justice in American Society.* Indianapolis: Bobbs-Merrill Co.

Lejins, Peter P.
1961   "American Data on Juvenile Delinquency in an International Forum," *Federal Probation* 25(June): 18–21.

Lemert, Edwin M.
1951   *Social Pathology.* New York: McGraw-Hill Book Co.

Matza, David
1969   *Becoming Deviant.* Englewood Cliffs, N.J.: Prentice-Hall.

Molotch, Harvey and Marilyn Lester
1974   "News as Purposive Behavior: On the Strategic Use of Routine Events, Accidents, and Scandals," *American Sociological Review* 39(February): 101–112.

Porterfield, Austin L.
1943   "Delinquency and Its Outcome in Court and College," *American Journal of Sociology* 49(November): 199–208.

Puttkamer, Ernst W.
1953   *Administration of Criminal Law.* Chicago: University of Chicago Press.

Sallach, David L.
1974   "Class Domination and Ideological Hegemony," *Sociological Quarterly* 15(Winter): 38–50.

Sellin, Thorsten
1931   "The Basis of a Crime Index," *Journal of Criminal Law and Criminology* 22(September): 335–356.

Sellin, Thorsten and Marvin E. Wolfgang
1964   *The Measurement of Delinquency.* New York: John Wiley and Sons.

Taft, Donald R. and Ralph W. England
1964   *Criminology.* 4th ed. New York: Macmillan Co.

Tetters, Negley K. and David Matza
1959   "The Extent of Delinquency in the United States," *Journal of Negro Education* 28(Summer): 200–213.

Time
1972   "Street Crime: Who's Winning?" (October 23): 55–56, 58.

U.S. Department of Justice
1974a *Crime in the Nation's Five Largest Cities: National Crime Panel Surveys of Chicago, Detroit, Los Angeles, New York, and Philadelphia.* Law Enforcement Assistance Administration, National

Criminal Justice Information and Statistics Service. Washington, D.C.: U.S. Government Printing Office.

1974b *Crimes and Victims: A Report on the Dayton–San Jose Pilot Survey of Victimization.* Law Enforcement Assistance Administration, National Criminal Justice Information and Statistics Service. Washington, D.C.: U.S. Government Printing Office.

Van Vechten, Courtlandt C.
   1942   "Differential Criminal Case Mortality in Selected Jurisdictions," *American Sociological Review* 7(December): 833–839.

Wallerstein, James S. and Clement J. Wyle
   1947   "Our Law-abiding Law-breakers," *Probation* 25(April): 107–112, 118.

Weis, Kurt and Michael E. Milakovich
   1974   "Political Misuses of Crime Rates," *Society* 11(July–August): 27–33.

Wolfgang, Marvin E.
   1970   "Urban Crime," pp. 270–311 in James Q. Wilson, ed., *The Metropolitan Enigma.* Garden City, N.Y.: Anchor Books.

11

Politics and measures of success in the war on crime*

Michael E. Milakovich
and
Kurt Weis

Who is concerned about crime? Politicians, newspapers, and national magazines report surveys showing that the fear of crime is widespread and deep throughout America. Other sources, equally reliable, put this fear into perspective. A "personal fears" survey conducted by Gallup in 1971 showed that fear of crime ranked tenth and last after fears of ill health, war, unemployment, pollution, and drugs.[1] The fear of crime experienced by people living in high-crime areas must be differentiated from the concern about crime expressed by people in safer neighborhoods, who learn about crime from politicians and newspapers.

Furthermore, it is a clearly established anthropological principle that a discrepancy exists between "ideal" and "real" culture; that is, between verbally expressed values, sentiments, and attitudes on the one side and manifest behavior on the other. Research on attitudes toward crime and the relationship between expressed concern and avoidance behavior reinforces this long-standing methodological problem. In addition, questionnaire

* Reprinted from *Crime and Delinquency,* vol. 21, no. 1 (January 1975), pp. 1–10. An earlier draft of this article was presented at the Inter-American Congress of Criminology, November 19–26, 1972, in Caracas. Portions have appeared in "Political Misuses of Crime Rates," *Society,* July–August 1974; and "Who's Afraid of Crime?—Or: How to Finance a Decreasing Rate of Increase," in Sawyer F. Sylvester, Jr., and Edward Sagarin, eds., *Politics and Crime* (New York: Praeger, 1974).

[1] Alfred Cantril and C. W. Roll, *Hopes and Fears of the American People* (New York: Universe Books, 1971), pp. 19, 60.

items seeking individual evaluations of attitudes toward crime often reflect the researcher's political, social, economic, or moral bias. Certain investigators tend to have vested interest in the outcomes of particular studies. Frequently, to predict results before administration of the survey questionnaire, one need only look at the agency conducting the research, its method of funding, and the implicit values that are to be upheld.

In 1970 a Toronto survey team found that, for many, "concern with crime" was in part an artificial creation and that people were more concerned about crime in the abstract than about actually becoming a victim.[2] Therefore, it appears that crime is to some extent an imaginary problem, manufactured in the minds of many people.[3] Similarly, in their surveys for the President's Commission on Law Enforcement and Administration of Justice, the National Opinion Research Center and the Bureau of Social Science Research uniformly found that people feel safer in their own neighborhoods than in others, *even though* their own neighborhoods actually had a higher crime rate than surrounding areas. Another study of urban, suburban, and rural orientations toward crime control found that perspectives on violent crime varied according to where a person lives: central city residents, particularly blacks, and rural residents considered violent crime more likely than suburbanites.[4] In its conclusions, the President's Crime Commission also pointed to certain unreasonable aspects of people's stereotyped fear of crime; for example, individuals are more inclined to think of crime in moral rather than in social terms and fear most those crimes of violence which they are least likely to experience.[5] Fear of crime by a stranger persists despite volumes of research showing that violent crime occurs most frequently among friends and relatives and that, in many urban

[2] Malcolm Courtis, *Attitudes toward Crime and the Police in Toronto: A Report on Some Survey Findings* (Toronto: University of Toronto, Centre of Criminology, 1970), pp. 23, 24, 26. Similar data from a Baltimore survey are cited in Frank F. Furstenberg, "Public Reaction to Crime in the Streets," *American Scholar,* Autumn 1971, pp. 602–10.

[3] P. Macnaughton-Smith and M. Spencer, "First Steps in an Empirical Study of the Nature of Real and Imaginary Crime," paper presented at the VI International Congress on Criminology, Madrid, September 1970.

[4] Sarah L. Boggs, "Formal and Informal Crime Control: An Exploratory Study of Urban, Suburban, and Rural Orientations," *Sociological Quarterly,* Summer 1971, pp. 319–27.

[5] President's Commission on Law Enforcement and Administration of Justice, *The Challenge of Crime in a Free Society* (Washington, D.C.: U.S. Government Printing Office, 1967), pp. 49–52.

areas, one may be more endangered at night in his own home than in walking the streets.[6]

Accordingly, it is important to distinguish between the *problem* of crime and the *political issue* of crime. Persons living in high-crime areas fear crime for a simple reason: they *are* more likely to be victimized, and they may not always expect protection from the police. Persons living in relatively safe areas may also fear becoming victims of a crime, but their fear is based on the statements of public officials, candidates for public office, and newspaper articles that reinforce the political issue of crime.

Well-publicized concern about the problem of crime is often a prerequisite for a successful political campaign in which crime, either an all-out war or a brush-fire response to an increase or a promised decrease, is made a key issue. Politicians and police officials rather than actual or potential victims of crime are the ones who express frequent concern about rising crime, want to be on the winning side in the war against crime, and thus have a direct interest in controlling the measures used to indicate whether crime is increasing or decreasing. For this reason, the evaluation system used to measure the amount of criminal activity is both an important indicator of the social well-being of the nation and an invaluable tool for governments to assess the success of their criminal justice systems in deterring criminal activity. It is at this point—as evaluation becomes increasingly important in judging the federal government's war on crime—that politics directly affect measures of success.

TECHNIQUES USED BY POLICE TO MEASURE CRIME

Concern with crime is based on statistics which show that, for years, crime has been increasing, often at an alarming rate. From the time that police records were first kept, it seems, crime rates have been going up steadily. In 1895 Durkheim wrote that criminality in France had increased nearly 300 percent since the beginning of the nineteenth century, a conclusion drawn from crime statistics.[7] However, the logical possibility of an ever-increasing

---

[6] Norval Morris and Gordon Hawkins, *The Honest Politician's Guide to Crime Control* (Chicago: University of Chicago Press, 1970), p. 41.

[7] Emile Durkheim, *The Rules of Sociological Method* (New York: Free Press, 1964), p. 66.

crime wave is quite doubtful.[8] It is more correct to state that crime has always existed and to differentiate, as Daniel Bell does, between a crime wave and a "crime reporting wave."[9] A closer look at the system used to measure crime in the United States will show why this distinction is important.

Crime statistics are police statistics. We know, from victimization studies, that official police crime statistics mirror only a fraction of the actual amount of crime committed. "The actual amount of crime in the United States today is several times that reported in the UCR."[10] To appear in the FBI statistics and be counted as an "index" crime, an offense has to overcome certain bureaucratic hurdles. First, it has to be one of the crimes viewed by the FBI as indicators of national and regional crime trends: murder, forcible rape, robbery, aggravated assault, burglary, auto theft, and larceny of items worth $50 or more. Less than 10 percent of all persons arrested are charged with any of these seven crimes. Second, the crime has to become known to the police, either by reports from outside sources or by direct police detection. And third, this crime has to be booked by the police and reported to the FBI. Strangely enough, these obstacles are not easily overcome.

One explanation for the inaccuracy of FBI crime rates is that people quite frequently do not report to the police after being victimized. Reasons why some victims do or do not notify the police have been studied. Private requests to the police to institute criminal proceedings are often used to pursue personal conflicts rather than to enforce the law and thus result in almost a random selection of offenders. In this context, however, it is more important to realize that the amount of crime known to the police depends directly on the quality of the work they do and the confidence that citizens have in that work.

---

[8] Sometimes one wonders whether there was ever a significant increase in crime and when it might have occurred. The sentence, "The land is full of bloody crimes, and the city is full of violence," is not the lead in a recent Detroit newspaper story but the report of a crime wave in the Promised Land around 600 b.c., as recorded in Ezekiel 7:23. Consider the biblical origin of mankind: Adam, Eve, and Cain committed the worst offenses possible, and after Abel was killed, all survivors, or 75 percent of the first four human beings, had criminal records. In spite of all righteous claims to the opposite, this crime wave seems to have subsided.

[9] Daniel Bell, *The End of Ideology* (New York: Free Press, 1965), p. 153.

[10] President's Commission, op. cit. supra note 5, p. 21.

It is widely believed that one technique for increasing the rate of crimes detected and cleared by arrest is to improve or increase personnel and equipment. It is even more widely hoped that, because of the expected increase in efficiency, the public will gain more confidence in the job done by the police and will more fully inform them of crimes that previously were not reported. One of the reasons most frequently cited by victims for not notifying the police—"police could or would not be effective"—would then dwindle. Raising the quality of police work by awarding more money to increase manpower and improve equipment would, in the beginning, inevitably increase the amount of *reported* crime. However, if a *reduction* in reported crime has to be shown, the fastest way to reach this goal would be to decrease police manpower and lessen their effectiveness. If additional anticrime funds are to be spent on the police and if alleviation of public fears about crime is an objective, the temptation to modify crime reports in order to justify these expenditures may be irresistible.

Funding detection and apprehension programs might result only in recycling crime from one precinct to another but might lead to some actual decrease in crime. However, unless the relationship between crimes committed and crimes reported to the police is constant, or unless 100 percent of all crime is reported, increased expenditures for personnel or equipment will result in an inflated rate of reporting. This increase in the rate of reporting will antedate any decrease in crime committed.

There is no linear relationship between increasing expenditures for crime control and increasing effectiveness of prevention, detection, and apprehension. Beyond a certain point, costs will tend to increase without a comparable increase in crimes prevented. For example, doubling police manpower or the number of patrol cars (100 percent increase) might result in only a slight decrease in the actual amount of crime committed.

The results of a recent one-year study of the Kansas City Police Department raise questions about the effectiveness of increasing police patrols as a crime-control measure[11]: in precincts where police patrols were doubled, crime rates remained unchanged.

---

[11] The study was funded by the Police Foundation. Initial research findings were reported by David Burnham, "Police Study Challenges Value of Anti-Crime Patrols," *New York Times*, November 11, 1973.

While the Kansas City experiment needs to be supported by results from many other cities before conclusions are certain, it calls attention to a fact of critical importance: multiple measures of effectiveness are absent in many important aspects of urban service.[12]

In an article discussing the need for multiple indicators in measuring the output of public agencies, Elinor Ostrom states that the FBI reporting system has "too frequently been utilized as a single measure of the output of police agencies."[13] Ostrom and others have advocated the development of multiple indicators of the output of criminal justice agencies. These alternative measures of police performance might include (1) response time of police patrol cars, (2) the "clearance rate" of arrests, and (3) incidence of crime as reported by victims in sample surveys. Police departments should be encouraged to adopt multiple measures of performance to avoid the problems created by a single measure.

The last step in the crime-reporting system is the most critical. At present, the system depends entirely on the voluntary cooperation of local police officials with the FBI and does not have a provision for auditing the figures supplied by local departments. Even if there is a relatively constant relationship between the number of crimes committed and the number known to the police before submission of the figures to the FBI, the temptation (augmented by opportunity or necessity) to modify the figures may be oppressive. Here, objective evaluation is most susceptible to political influence. An official running for re-election may feel a need to keep crime rates down. In general, office holders may feel threatened by a "paper increase" in crime for which they are blameless and prefer a political situation in which they can laud a low crime rate, while office seekers prefer to lament a high rate. The actual number of crimes committed may go up because of an increase in population. The per capita rate of crimes may climb because the "baby boom" that took place after the latest World

---

[12] A comprehensive review and discussion of various alternative measures of police performance is contained in a paper by Roger Parks, "Complementary Measures of Police Performance: Citizen-Generated Appraisals and Police-Generated Data," delivered at a meeting of the American Political Science Association, New Orleans, La., September 1973.

[13] Elinor Ostrom, "The Need for Multiple Indicators in Measuring the Output of Public Agencies," *Policy Studies Journal,* Winter 1973, p. 87.

War made the 15–25 age group the fastest-growing group of the population—and it is also the most crime-prone group. Larceny of items worth $50 or more is bound to increase because of constant inflation. And if, in addition to this natural increase of crime, police do a good job of making inroads into the "dark figure" of hidden criminality, a completely honest reporting system may, indeed, have a politically suicidal effect on the reporters.

There are simple ways of limiting this "paper increase" of crime. The definition of a stolen car can be changed to eliminate cars found in less than twenty-four hours. Police officers can be encouraged to depreciate old articles before they decide whether the stolen item was worth more or less than $50. Other subtle ways of preventing the crime rate from "going through the roof" include questionable devaluations of larceny items or general downgrading of crimes.[14] Confession of an order not to "put in any burglaries for the rest of the month" may be expected from a police officer only after retirement.[15] A study of field encounters between police and complainants found that "the police officially disregard one-fourth of the felonies they handle in encounters with complainants," usually conforming with the preferences of the complainants for informal action.[16]

Consequently, police officials and law-enforcement statisticians, resenting reports by other departments that downgrade their own and make them look bad, advocate mandatory audits of all crime-reporting systems to reduce "shading." Bearing in mind that the FBI designed its Uniform Crime Reports as a statistical house organ of the police of the United States,[17] with statistics collected to document the police viewpoint, we not only should criticize the reports for lack of objectivity and neutrality but also should demand a new custodian of the data.[18]

In summary, police and FBI statistics do not tell us whether crime has actually increased or decreased.

---

[14] W. R. Morrissey, "Nixon Anti-Crime Plan Undermines Crime Statistics," *Justice Magazine*, June–July 1972, pp. 8 ff.

[15] Sophia M. Robison, "A Critical View of the Uniform Crime Reports," *Michigan Law Review*, April 1966, p. 1036.

[16] Donald J. Black, "Production of Crime Rates," *American Sociological Review*, August 1970, pp. 738 ff.

[17] Peter P. Lejins, "Uniform Crime Reports," *Michigan Law Review*, April 1966, p. 1011.

[18] Hans Zeisel, "The Future of Law Enforcement Statistics: A Summary View," in *Federal Statistics:* Report of the President's Commission, vol. 2, 1971, p. 542.

WHERE DOES THE FEDERAL MONEY GO?

Three groups have an interest in the reported rates of crime: Citizens, police, and politicians. As previously indicated, citizen concern, especially when built up through opinion surveys and the media, is more often spoken than real. Moreover, personal protective measures appear to be geared more to conviction and punishment of offenders than to the prevention of crime. In short, many citizens are more concerned about the political issue of crime than about the problem of crime.

Police concern is understandably more direct, although only 10 to 20 percent of police work is actually concerned with law enforcement and fighting crime. Although most police are more interested in fighting crime, the bulk of their work consists of order maintenance and social service.[19] Because they are generally judged by the FBI system of reporting crime, their primary interest is to merit the image of successful crime fighters. This value orientation is reinforced by internal promotional criteria and by absence of multiple measures of effectiveness. For example, in many departments, precinct captains are promoted solely on the basis of a reduced crime rate within their precincts. Police are often opposed to role redefinition that would orient them to "community service." Although community-service types of programs have been recommended by recent crime-control legislation and several national commissions for inclusion in state plans for criminal justice improvement, only a few have been established by police departments.

Police jealously guard the prerogative of fighting crime in their own way and resist interference by community-control organizations. Many lack enthusiasm for crisis intervention training and for services which, like youth service bureaus, lie beyond strict law enforcement. In evaluations of expenditures for crime control, federal agencies tend to define the role of the criminal justice system narrowly as law enforcement. California and New York were criticized in 1971 by auditors from the General Accounting Office for allocating "too much" (nearly 30 percent) of their state anticrime funds to projects dealing with the underlying causes of

---

[19] James Q. Wilson, *Varieties of Police Behavior* (Cambridge, Mass.: Harvard University Press, 1968), ch. 2.

crime.[20] In the same vein, on September 13, 1968, President Nixon stated: "I say that doubling the conviction rate in this country would do far more to cure crime in America than quadrupling the funds for Mr. Humphrey's war on poverty."[21]

For the police, then, successful crime-fighting does not mean social service, prevention of crime, or acceptance of citizen participation; rather, it is measured by self-reported arrests and clearance rates. To engage in their roles as crime fighters, police need crimes to be committed. Playing the cops-and-robbers game means apprehending criminals, not preventing crime.

This attitude is reinforced by the distribution of federal money made available to state and local criminal justice agencies through federal anticrime assistance programs. Under the LEAA program, block-grants are awarded to states according to population; most states, in turn, award grants according to crime rates, which are controlled by the police primarily to reflect the effectiveness of their work. Victimization research, however, might pose a threat to the police, especially if money were allocated according to its findings, which show that the number of crimes reported to survey interviewers is much greater than the number reported to the police.[22]

Although many states have produced impressive plans for the allocation of federal money according to the expressed needs of local criminal justice agencies, few have been able to put them into practice. Evidence from a three-year nation-wide study of anticrime programs suggests that the federal government does not

---

[20] Hearings, Subcommittee of the Committee on Government Operations, *Block-Grant Programs of the Law Enforcement Assistance Administration,* July 20–29, 1971 (Washington, D.C.: U.S. Government Printing Office, 1971), part 1, p. 129.

[21] Quoted in Arnold S. Trebach, "Nixon: Soft on Crime?" *Justice Magazine,* June–July 1972, p. 20.

[22] Limited experimentation with program evaluation on the basis of scientific surveys and victimization studies is being carried out, but it is still too early to judge its acceptability among police. One encouraging development has been the support given by the National Institute of Law Enforcement and Criminal Justice to a Pilot Cities Victimization Survey conducted by the U.S. Department of Commerce. The purpose of this project is to develop a baseline of data before the implementation of the High Impact Pilot Cities action program. For further description, see *3rd Annual Report of the Law Enforcement Assistance Administration* (Washington, D.C.: U.S. Government Printing Office, 1972), pp. 403–04. For initial results of the High Impact Study, see "8 Cities Show a Crime Disparity," *New York Times,* January 27, 1974. See also "Crime in the Nation's Five Largest Cities: National Crime Panel Surveys of Chicago, Detroit, Los Angeles, New York, and Philadelphia," Advance Report, U.S. Department of Justice, Law Enforcement Assistance Administration, Washington, D.C., April 1974.

know, and does not feel a responsibility to find out, where the money is going.[23] Under the block-grant concept, state governments have the major authority and responsibility for fighting the war on crime; yet, when asked in a 1972 survey to provide information on the amount of money spent (not planned), thirty-one states declined to respond.[24] In testimony before a 1971 Congressional investigating committee, LEAA administrators admitted that the agency did not know how states were spending federal money.[25]

Data received from five states responding to the 1972 survey show considerable difference between how federal grant funds were actually spent and how they were supposed to have been spent. (See Table 1.) Money was shifted from training, crime pre-

Table 1: Differences between planned and actual expenditures of crime-control funds in five states[a] by program categories, for fiscal 1970

Program category[b]	Planned allocation[c]	Percentage of total	Actual expenditure[d]	Percentage of total	Difference[e]
Upgrading training personnel	$ 4,000,000	24.8%	$ 2,600,000	15.2%	−9.6%
Juvenile delinquency	3,300,000	20.5	2,500,000	14.7	−5.8%
Crime prevention	2,000,000	12.4	1,000,000	5.9	−6.5%
Correction.....................	1,000,000	6.2	2,200,000	12.9	+6.7%
Court reform	800,000	5.0	1,200,000	7.0	+2.0%
Community relations	400,000	2.4	500,000	2.9	+0.5%
Research and development........	300,000	1.9	10,000	0.06	−1.8%
Organized crime	200,000	1.2	400,000	2.4	+1.2%
Apprehension and detection (equipment)	3,700,000	23.0	5,900,000	34.7	+11.7%
Riot control	400,000	2.4	700,000	4.1	+1.7%
Totals	$16,100,000	99.8%[f]	$17,010,000	99.8%[f]	

   [a] Indiana, Ohio, Missouri, Utah, and Wisconsin.

   [b] The ten categories correspond to the functions performed by major agencies in the criminal justice system. Grants for many of the categories may be awarded to police, courts, or correctional agencies as well as other interested groups and community organizations.

   [c] Source: *2nd Annual Report of the Law Enforcement Assistance Administration* (Washington, D.C., 1970), pp. 130–31.

   [d] Responses to mail survey, April 1972.

   [e] Between the amount planned and the amount actually spent. Of the 31 states included in the survey, 26 indicated they were free to re-allocate funds without LEAA approval and 4 others said LEAA must approve; only 1 did not allow re-allocations.

   [f] Does not equal 100 percent because of rounding.

---

[23] Michael E. Milakovich, "The War on Crime: Rhetoric, Reform, or Revenue Sharing?" University of Chicago Law School, Center for Studies in Criminal Justice, 1973.

[24] Id., ch. 10.

[25] Hearings, op. cit. supra note 20, part 2, p. 711, and correspondence with LEAA officials.

vention, and juvenile delinquency to additional apprehension and detection equipment for police departments. Although over 12 percent of the funds in five states was planned for crime prevention, less than 6 percent was spent on it; on the other hand, the 23 percent planned for apprehension and detection equipment grew to 35 percent of actual expenditure.[26]

The emerging trend is clear: local agencies are primarily interested in acquiring equipment for apprehension and detection of criminals, and state planning agencies have been unable to overcome local resistance to reform projects in training and prevention. Far from encouraging reform programs, LEAA money has been used to bolster traditional methods of law enforcement.

LEAA has been slow to fund experimental programs that might lead to changes in the FBI system of reporting crimes. Similarly, state criminal justice planning agencies have been reluctant to commission evaluative research on the effectiveness of LEAA-supported programs. And finally, both federal and state officials have ignored the consequences of police-dominated, federal anticrime programs. Public concern about crime has been manipulated for expansion of stockpiles in police armories.

POLITICS AND RATES OF REPORTED CRIME

In 1968 and again in 1972, President Nixon persuaded a majority of the American public that a "war on crime" was necessary because crime rates (police-controlled) were excessive and increasing. That war should have produced, at least initially, an increase in the number of reported crimes. Now, after an expenditure of $3-billion in tax funds, the public is again asked to believe that the war on crime is being won because the increase in the crime rate is decreasing. A promise to reduce crime helped elect a president in 1968 and re-elect him in 1972. It was, in effect, a promise to win the numbers game, and experience shows that this game can be won and the promise kept. In 1972, the increase in crime rates decreased by 4 percent, the first such drop in seventeen years.

Even the effectiveness of the Law Enforcement Assistance Administration is judged by an increase or decrease in the FBI crime index. Recently, LEAA was publicly criticized by Attorney General

---

[26] Milakovich, supra note 23, ch. 10.

William Saxbe, who noted that after six years of distributing federal funds, the agency had only recently set up a comprehensive way of measuring the effectiveness of its spending.[27] So long as the FBI index remains the primary means of assessing the performance of federal, state, and local police agencies, it is unlikely that LEAA program effectiveness can be validly assessed.

Police departments have a vested interest in not decreasing crime rates *too* much. Under the present system of judging police by only a single measure—the FBI Index—police are more likely to be penalized by a reduction in resources if the reported crime rate drops appreciably. If crime decreases somewhat, police are praised for successful work; if it decreases too much, the need for more law-enforcement personnel is less urgent—a situation to be avoided.

To summarize:

1. Citizens are concerned about crime, but many are responding to the political issue rather than the actual problem of crime.
2. Politicians and representatives of professional crime-fighting agencies, especially the police, are concerned about the problem *and* the issue.
3. The primary technique used for evaluating the effectiveness of federal anticrime programs is crime statistics.
4. These statistics, however, are self-serving measures of organizational effectiveness and a poor index of the true incidence of crime.
5. If improvement in the crime-*fighting* system is not accompanied by change in the crime-*reporting* system, the number of reported crimes should increase.
6. This paradoxical outcome, however, undermines public confidence in criminal justice agencies, threatens their resources, and increases public fear of crime.

Like all bureaucracies, criminal justice agencies can hardly be expected to implement policies that would diminish their importance; therefore, money appropriated to fight crime is allocated less to prevent crime than to detect and apprehend criminals after the crimes have been committed. As a result, it is impossible to ascertain whether additional funding of the Administration's "war

---

[27] *New York Times,* August 27, 1974, p. 14.

on crime" will result in a significant decrease in the amount of crime committed. Simply stated, an increase, decrease, or "decreasing rate of increase" in the FBI uniform crime rate can have many other explanations. Until a broader range of measures of effectiveness is available to criminal justice agencies, the political misuse of crime rates will continue.

12

The criminal patterns of Boston since 1849*

Theodore N. Ferdinand

There is a budding interest in the criminal patterns of other nations among American criminologists.[1] Different kinds of societies with different types of social organizations should, according to criminological theory, exhibit different patterns of criminality, and those who explore the criminality of other nations serve not only to broaden our knowledge of exotic forms of crime but also to confirm (or deny) our theoretical expectations regarding the relationship between social organization and crime. Both objectives, however, can be served not only by cross-cultural research but also by longitudinal studies of American communities. In tracing the criminal patterns of these communities as they assumed an urban, industrial character, it should be possible to identify the characteristic influences of a maturing urban social structure upon the criminal behavior of its population.

_____

* Reprinted from *American Journal of Sociology*, vol 73, no 1 (July 1967), pp. 84–99. A revised version of a paper presented at the AAAS meetings in Washington, D.C., on December 27, 1966. I am deeply grateful to Mrs. Jane Ferdinand and Mrs. Dorothy Fisher for the diligence with which they sought out and recorded the data upon which this paper is based. A word of thanks is also due to Professor Hans Mattick of the University of Chicago Law School who helped me improve this essay considerably, and to Professor Abraham Goldstein of the Yale University Law School who gave me some very valuable counsel on the peculiarities of the criminal code.

[1] See, in particular, Paul Tappan, *Comparative Survey of Juvenile Delinquency* (New York: United Nations, Department of Economic and Social Affairs, 1958); Tsung-yi Lin, "Two Types of Delinquent Youth in Chinese Society," in Marvin K. Opler (ed.), *Culture and Mental Health* (New York: Macmillan Co., 1959); Walter A. Lunden, *Statistics on Delinquents and Delinquency* (Springfield, Ill.: Charles C. Thomas, 1964); E. Jackson Bauer, "The Trend of Juvenile Offenders in the Netherlands and the United States," *Journal of Criminal Law, Criminology, and Police Science*, 55 (1964), 359–69.

In the United States, many of the best sites for such studies are found in New England where urban communities and institutions began to emerge in the seventeenth century, and where the history of their development through the eighteenth and nineteenth centuries has been carefully preserved both in the form of detailed anecdotal accounts of the times and as the official records of a variety of municipal agencies. As yet, few criminologists have utilized the archives of great metropolitan centers as a basis for studying criminal patterns of behavior, but such investigations are much more convenient and can yield just as much information about the criminal patterns of pre-industrial communities as cross-cultural studies.[2]

One of the reasons criminologists have failed to carry out such investigations may be a widespread suspicion that municipal records, both past and present, are too inaccurate to be usable. No one argues that the police and court records of any period are above suspicion, but the inadequacies of certain portions of these records are not adequate grounds for rejecting the entire archives of a city. Many of the biases in such data can be detected through internal analysis; moreover, the farther back in time one pursues these records, the more accurate and precise they tend to become. It is well known, for example, that the police of small, cohesive communities are considerably more effective in detecting and solving crime than the police of large, urban communities.[3] And even the largest cities in New England today were merely villages or small cities during most of the eighteenth and nineteenth centuries.

---

[2] For a recent longitudinal study of a major American city, see Elwin H. Powell, "Crime as a Function of Anomie," *Journal of Criminal Law, Criminology, and Police Science,* 57 (June 1966), 161–71. An early study of Boston's criminal patterns was performed by Sam Bass Warner, but he used court prosecutions from 1883 to 1932 as his basic data, not police arrest records (see his *Crime and Criminal Statistics in Boston* [Cambridge, Mass.: Harvard University Press, 1934]). In a related study, Leonard V. Harrison examined the arrest records of the Boston police from 1855 to 1932, and although he was concerned with only a few crimes, where his findings are comparable, they agree with my own (see his *Police Administration in Boston* [Cambridge, Mass.: Harvard University Press, 1934]). Robert Topitzer has undertaken an analysis of the criminal patterns of an early period in the history of an American city (see his *Court Proceedings in the Social Order of Boston, 1703–1732* [unpublished Master's thesis, Northeastern University, 1967]). And finally, A. H. Hobbs compared the criminal patterns of eighteenth-century Philadelphia with those found in 1937 (see his "Criminality in Philadelphia," *American Sociological Review,* 8 [1943], 198–202).

[3] The FBI has found that the police of small communities consistently solve a higher percentage of their more mild offenses than their metropolitan colleagues (see, e.g., *Uniform Crime Reports* [Washington, D.C.: Federal Bureau of Investigation, 1964], table 8, p. 95).

In addition, the attitude in New England toward crime was considerably more severe throughout much of its early history than it is today, suggesting that the vigilance and perseverance of the police were much stronger in the eighteenth and nineteenth centuries than they are now. Similarly, the records of New England courts in the eighteenth and nineteenth centuries are remarkable for the consistency with which they describe the apprehension and disposition of the simplest larcenies and the mildest of assaults.[4] If the frequency with which these simple crimes were set down in the court records is any indication of the diligence with which they were pursued, the police must have been vigilant indeed.

THE ARCHIVES OF THE BOSTON POLICE

The present study is based upon the arrest reports of the Boston police, which have been issued annually since 1849; and through them I shall examine the changing criminal patterns of Boston as it grew from a city of 136,000 in 1850 to a great metropolitan center in 1950 with a population of 801,000 in the central city.[5]

A longitudinal study of this type confronts a special difficulty. In addition to the actual changes in criminal activity that have occurred over the last century, the arrest trends also reflect changes in police practice as well as changes in the court's definition and interpretation of the criminal code. There is some risk, therefore, of confusing basic changes in criminal activity with more superficial changes in the manner in which the police and the courts have apprehended and dealt with crime over the years.

This risk, however, is more serious for certain kinds of crimes than for others. For example, it is unlikely that there has been a significant change over the last hundred years in the way in which murder has been defined or murderers apprehended. Similarly, forcible rape, robbery, and burglary are sufficiently serious as crimes to forestall drastic changes in their definitions or arresting practices. Minor crimes, on the other hand, may have been handled quite differently by the police of different eras. In the

---

[4] A preliminary analysis by the author of the records of the Boston Police Court for the year 1823 reveals many larcenies of less than fifty cents and a comparable number of assaults involving no more than throwing snowballs or spitting at an individual.

[5] Although the city of Boston had a population of 801,444 in 1950, a better measure of its metropolitan character is the population of its Standard Metropolitan Statistical Area, i.e., 2,410,372.

nineteenth century we have already seen that nearly every assault and larceny, no matter how slight, was dealt with in the same fashion as major crimes, that is, the offender was arrested and brought to court. Today, however, if the police in large urban centers were equally vigilant toward minor assaults and larcenies, the apparatus of justice would become completely inoperable. Other difficulties will be evident as we proceed with our analysis, but it must be remembered that all data contain comparable distortions and that these imperfections do not destroy the basic usefulness of our data. They simply make their interpretation somewhat more complex.

CODIFYING THE ARREST REPORTS

Since there was considerable variation in the classificatory systems used by the Boston police over the years, it was necessary, first, to reduce the arrest reports to a consistent and manageable form before beginning their analysis. The most general such schema available is that developed by the FBI in its annual reports of major crime.[6] Seven major classes of crime—(1) criminal homicide, including murder and non-negligent manslaughter; (2) forcible rape; (3) robbery; (4) aggravated assault; (5) burglary; (6) larceny of $50 or over; and (7) auto thefts—are utilized by the FBI in its crime index. For several reasons, however, it was not possible to adhere precisely to this method of classifying crime.

First, the Boston police did not consistently distinguish between negligent and non-negligent manslaughter through the years; hence, a single category—manslaughter—is utilized here which includes both types. Second, it was not possible to differentiate aggravated assault from simple assault with any consistency in the Boston police records; consequently, all assaults were included in the same category. Third, in analyzing the Boston data, it was not possible to distinguish consistently between larceny of $50 and over and larceny of less than $50, as the FBI does. Consequently, all larcenies were thrown into the same category, and a third departure from the FBI schema was the result. Finally, the Boston police did not begin reporting auto theft as a distinct category until 1927, and for this reason it is not included at all in this report.

---

[6] *Uniform Crime Reporting Handbook* (Washington, D.C.: Federal Bureau of Investigation, 1965), pp. 10–38.

Moreover, since auto thefts were not distinguished from other types of larcenies before 1927, any auto thefts that occurred prior to that year were included in the larceny totals. In all other respects, however, it was possible to conform to the schema developed by the FBI, that is, with regard to the crimes of forcible rape, robbery, and burglary.

Once the data of the original arrest reports had been coded in this fashion, the arrest rate for each crime was calculated by three-year periods to reduce the fluctuations that annual data generally show. Three times in the last century, however, the Boston Police Department was completely reorganized, and the arrest reports for these years changed so radically that they were incomparable with those of the others years. In 1854, for example, the police were consolidated with the watchmen and the constables, and the arrest report of that year covered only seven months. When the police department was reorganized again in 1879, the report covered only ten months, and again in 1885 the same thing happened. Thus, the reports for these three years were not comparable with the rest and could not be used. To compensate for these gaps in the data, therefore, it was necessary to use a five-year period in 1849–53, a four-year period in 1875–78, and a two-year period in 1883–84.

THE PATTERN OF MAJOR CRIMES IN BOSTON

The results of analyzing the original arrest reports in this fashion are presented in Figures 1 through 8. A glance at Figure 1 reveals that the aggregate crime rate in Boston has shown an almost uninterrupted decline from 1875–78 to the present era. The period immediately before the Civil War saw a high rate of major crime, but during and shortly after the Civil War, crime declined, only to rise to an all-time peak in 1875–78.[7] Since that time, the crime rate has declined steadily to a level about *one-third* that in 1875–78.

I shall have more to say about the trend in Boston's over-all

---

[7] The arrest reports of the years 1849–53 almost certainly underestimate the amount of crime in Boston because the police of that period shared the peace-keeping function with a force of constables in the daytime and watchmen at night. In all likelihood, the arrest reports of the police do not include arrests made by the constables or the watchmen during this period.

Figure 1: Rate of major crimes in Boston per 100,000 population, 1849–1951

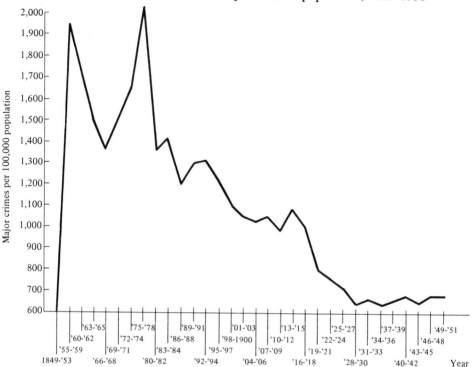

crime rate later, but for the present it should be noted that both the dramatic upturn following the Civil War and the steady decline from a peak around 1875–78 were also experienced by other American cities. Powell documents a rapid rise in serious crime in Buffalo shortly after the Civil War, and Rosenbaum cites several contemporary reports which suggest that there was a similar rise throughout the Northeast.[8] Powell shows also that the peak in serious crime established just after the Civil War in Buffalo was followed by a long decline to the present, broken only by rises in the early part of the twentieth century and in the 1930s.[9] And Willbach shows that Chicago and New York City also experienced a slow but steady decline in major crime rates in the first decades

---

[8] Powell, op. cit., p. 164; and Betty B. Rosenbaum, "The Relationship between War and Crime in the United States," *Journal of Criminal Law, Criminology, and Police Science,* 30 (1939–40), 726–29.

[9] Powell, op. cit.

of the twentieth century.[10] It would appear, then, that the long-term trend in major crime in Boston conforms to the pattern exhibited by several other American cities during the same period.

The reasons behind this long-term decline can only be guessed at without further information. The decline may mean, for example, that Bostonians have actually become less criminally inclined as the city grew into a metropolitan center, or it may mean that the city's courts and police have simply softened their approach to crime as the city developed.[11] An examination of the individual crimes described above should throw some light on this question, and, accordingly, let us begin with a consideration of the trend in the murder rate over the last one hundred years.

Figure 2 reveals that the rate of murders in Boston has declined steadily if erratically over the last century. The highest rate occurred in 1855–59, and the lowest rate was registered in 1937–39. Since murder is one of the more serious crimes, it is unlikely that this decline can be attributed to a decrease in police vigilance in dealing with murderers. Today, metropolitan police departments are every bit as effective in solving murders as small-town departments. Morever, it is difficult to relate the murder rate to specific events in the history of Boston. Neither great wars nor major depressions seem to have had any consistent effect upon the murder rate. During the Civil War the murder rate declined, but during the two world wars it increased slightly. Similarly, the depressions of 1873–78, 1893–98, 1919–21, and 1930–39 seem to have had no consistent influence. It would appear, therefore, that this steady decline reflects something more fundamental, that is, long-term shifts in the structure and organization of the city as it grew into a great metropolitan center.

The long-term trend of manslaughter, however, follows a quite different path. It is apparent from Figure 3 that the manslaughter rate in Boston remained relatively stable from 1849–53 to 1904–6.

---

[10] Harry Willbach, "The Trend of Crime in Chicago," *Journal of Criminal Law, Criminology, and Police Science*, 31 (1940–41), 726; and his "The Trend of Crime in New York City," ibid., 29 (1938), 72.

[11] It would appear that these changes do not simply represent fluctuations in the intensity of police coverage in Boston. From 1855–59 to 1866–68, there was a decline in the rate of major crime of 29.8 percent, while the number of policemen per 1,000 population was nearly stable at 1.63. Similarly, from 1866–68 to 1872–74, the rate of major crime increased by 21.1 percent while the number of policemen per 1,000 was increasing from 1.67 in 1867 to 1.83 in 1873 for an increase of only 9.6 percent (see Edward H. Savage, *Police Records and Recollections* [Boston: Jackson, Dale & Co., 1873], pp. 95, 98, and 104–6).

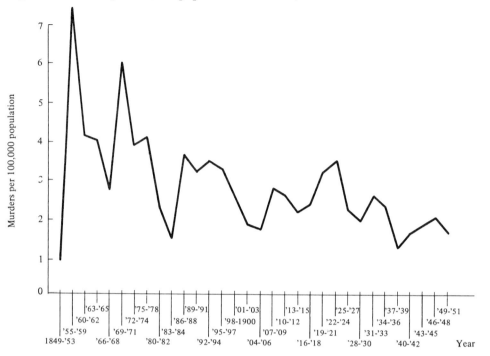

Figure 2: Murders per 100,000 population in Boston, 1849–1951

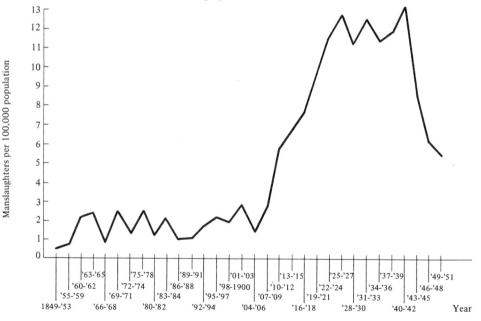

Figure 3: Manslaughters per 100,000 population in Boston, 1849–1951

In 1907–9, however, it began a sharp rise to a new plateau, roughly *six times* the level throughout the nineteenth century. This new plateau persisted for nearly twenty years, from 1916–18 to 1934–36, when the manslaughter rate began to sink again to a level midway between the high and low levels of the hundred-year period.

There is good reason to believe that these fluctuations reflect primarily the introduction of the automobile in Boston around the turn of the century.[12] We cannot account for them in terms of changes in the statutes governing manslaughter, since the criminal code of Massachusetts from 1901 to the present shows only a minor reduction in the minimum term of imprisonment from three years to two and one-half years. Moreover, there are no close relationships between the manslaughter rate and such specific events as wars or depressions. Since it seems hardly likely that the mountainous rise in the twentieth century can be explained entirely in terms of changes in the police attitude and practice toward manslaughter as a crime, the rise in manslaughter rates during the first third of the twentieth century probably reflects to a considerable degree the introduction of the automobile during this period.

It is more difficult, however, to explain the decline in manslaughter rates that began in 1934–36. Since this decline continued through the post–World War II period, it cannot be explained as a result of the decrease in cars on the road during the depression and World War II. Moreover, since the murder rate did not show a significant increase during this period, it is not likely that there was any tendency for the police to charge offenders with murder rather than manslaughter. It may be that the recent decline can be explained in terms of improved highways and an increasing skill and experience among the driving public, but before such a conclusion can be made with confidence, further information on this issue would be necessary.

The upward trend of forcible rape over the last century re-

---

[12] Warner noted the same peculiar pattern in manslaughters in Boston, and since he found that they paralleled prosecutions for motor-vehicle deaths, he concluded that the rise in manslaughters reflected primarily the growing use of autos in the Hub (cf. Warner op. cit., pp. 20–23). It is interesting to note, moreover, that from 1905 to 1920 the number of motor vehicles registered in the United States increased by a factor of 117.2, while in 1935 there were only 2.9 times as many motor vehicles registered as in 1920 (see Alfred D. Chandler, *Giant Enterprise: Ford, General Motors, and the Automobile Industry* [New York: Harcourt, Brace & World, 1964], p. 4).

quires a somewhat more complicated explanation.[13] Beginning with the simplest factors first, it can be seen from Figure 4 that major wars and severe depressions have been associated with a decline in the rate of forcible rape. The Civil War and World War

Figure 4: Forcible rapes per 100,000 population in Boston, 1849–1951

II were accompanied by minor declines in an otherwise upward tendency, and World War I saw a sharp drop in the rate, although the Spanish-American War was too short to have had any significant effect. The depressions of 1873–78, 1919–21, and 1930–39 all saw appreciable declines, with only the depression of 1893–98 showing an increase in rape. But even there the increase was slowed to some extent. Furthermore, it is clear from Figure 4 that the prosperous years of 1866–72, 1906–15, 1922–27, and 1940–51 witnessed sharp rises in the rate of forcible rape in Boston. Only

---

[13] In 1893, the age of consent in Massachusetts was advanced by statute from ten to sixteen. This means, in effect, that those who were performing sexual intercourse with females between the ages of eleven and sixteen with their consent were guilty of rape after 1893 but not before. Thus, from 1894 on, the rate of forcible rape was inflated to some degree by this statutory change. The continuing rise in the rate of this crime to the present day, however, *cannot* be a result of this single change.

during the prosperous years of 1880–92 did the rate fail to rise appreciably.[14]

The relationship between forcible rape and wartime is easily explained. As the proportion of physically able men in the community declines during wartime, the rate of forcible rape declines accordingly. The relationship between rape and the economic cycle, however, is somewhat more difficult to explain. It may be that economic depressions have a psychologically depressive effect such that the individual becomes interested more in preserving and consolidating what he already has than in initiating new and risky adventures. During prosperity, however, his inhibitions may relax to some extent, and the individual becomes somewhat more daring.

There are two other general patterns that are also noteworthy in Figure 4. There can be no mistaking the persistent upward tendency in the rate of forcible rape in Boston over the last century; the lowest rates are found at the beginning of the series, and the highest at the end. Moreover, there appears to be a distinct acceleration in the rise beginning about 1904–6. How might we interpret these two patterns?

The accelerated rise since 1904–6 coincides roughly with the introduction of the automobile and may reflect the influence of this invention upon sexual practices. Thus, as young couples found it easier to seclude themselves from the gaze of society, the incidence of every type of illicit sexual activity increased, including those based on force. The persistent upward tendency since the middle of the nineteenth century, however, may reflect a gradual expansion of the middle class in the social structure of Boston and the accompanying rise in the status of women. As a greater proportion of the population came to adhere to a middle-class style of life, the likelihood that a rape would be brought to the attention of the police and the offender arrested probably also increased. Even today, a middle-class girl is much more likely than a lower-class girl to complain to the authorities when she is molested by her escort. Thus, as far as forcible rape is concerned, it appears that

---

[14] It is impossible to test the relationship between this crime and the economic cycle in Boston with quantitative data, since there are no reliable long-term data on economic activity in Boston. Data for the United States as a whole do exist going back well into the nineteenth century, but the relevancy of these data to the economy of Boston is not close. Hence, relating them to longitudinal crime rates seems unwise.

such specific events as economic prosperity and peace have reinforced the general upward trend established by broad social structural changes and the introduction of the automobile among the
people of Boston.

With robberies, quite the opposite seems to have been the case.
A glance at Figure 5 shows that the long-term tendency in rob-

Figure 5: Robberies per 100,000 population in Boston, 1849–1951

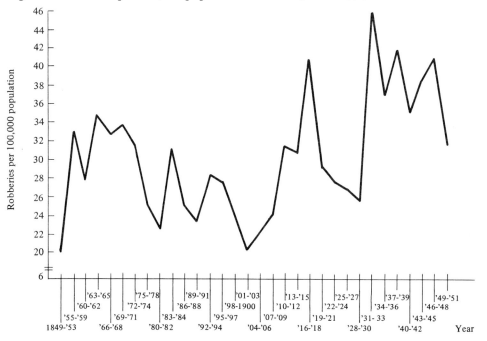

beries has been generally downward, with extraordinary events
superimposing dramatic increases on this downward trend from
time to time. Thus, the rate of robberies declined on average from
the Civil War to a low in 1901–3. World War I was accompanied by
a new high in 1916–18, and after a precipitous decline in the
1920s the Great Depression saw another new high in 1931–33.
The long-term decline set in again after this high, but World War
II in turn witnessed a reversal of the trend for several years.
Nevertheless, after the war, the general decline again reappeared.
Thus, it would seem that the social dislocations of wars and depressions have encouraged a high rate of robberies, whereas

broader, more enduring structural changes have contributed to a continuous erosion in the rate of robberies in Boston.

The same general pattern has also been found in Chicago and New York. Willbach's data over the twenty-year period indicate that both cities experienced their highest rate of robberies in 1931–33.[15]

Burglaries, according to Figure 6, have shown much the same

Figure 6: Burglaries per 100,000 population in Boston, 1849–1951

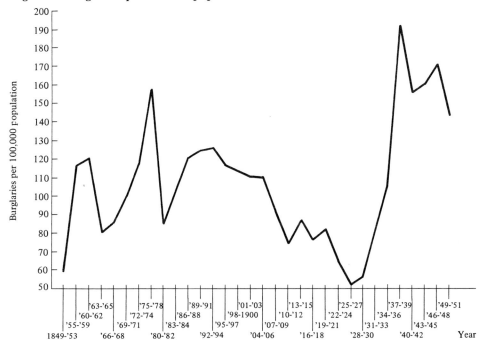

tendency as robberies. Superimposed upon a generally declining trend are several unusually high peaks that stem apparently from a series of extraordinary, nationally generated events. Severe depressions, for example, have been accompanied consistently by a high rate of burglary. The highest burglary rate for the entire time span was realized near the end of the Great Depression in 1937–39, and the second highest point occurred near the end of

---

[15] Willbach, "The Trend of Crime in Chicago," op. cit., p. 722; and his "The Trend of Crime in New York," op. cit., p. 69.

the severe depression of 1873–78. Unlike robberies, however, burglaries have not increased during wartime; indeed, the burglary rate in Boston has declined consistently during all three of the major wars in the last century.

The long-term trend of assaults in Boston, as revealed in Figure 7, exhibits an especially interesting pattern. It appears as if two

Figure 7: Assaults per 100,000 population in Boston, 1849–1951

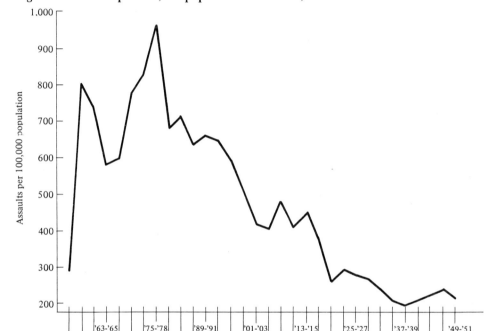

distinct curves with entirely different characteristics are joined in 1925, one stretching from 1855–59 to 1922–24 and the other running from 1925–27 to 1949–51. The first exhibits a marked responsiveness to such events as major wars and severe depressions, while the second shows very little sensitivity to either. The highest rate of assaults occurred during the depression of 1873–78, but the Great Depression had scarcely any effect. Similarly, the Civil War and World War I were accompanied by distinct drops in the rate of assaults in Boston, but World War II saw little

change. In other words, the rate of assaults in Boston seems to
have been especially responsive to conditions in the community
before 1925, whereas after that date even the most severe dislocations Boston has ever experienced produced little if any reaction.

This rather peculiar pattern probably reflects basic changes in
the manner in which the Boston police have dealt with assaults
over the last century. If during the nineteenth and early twentieth
centuries the police were especially persistent in pursuing those
who committed all kinds of assaults, the assault rate would have
been especially sensitive to changing conditions in the community.
Simple assault embraces a wide variety of acts and involves a relatively large portion of the population. Because it is diffused so
widely throughout the community, we might expect that a
momentous event, for example, a major war or a severe depression, would have a considerable impact upon the rate of this crime.
Moreover, in the early period when all assaults were being pursued diligently, simple assaults probably comprised the bulk of
offenses in this category. Consequently, in the nineteenth century
the over-all assault rate was responsive to the stream of historical
events in the community.

During the modern era, however, the police have been forced to
relax their vigilance toward minor crime, and accordingly, in recent years they have been making proportionately fewer arrests
for minor assault. In effect, this means that today aggravated assault is making a greater contribution to the over-all assault rate.
But if aggravated assault, like murder, is relatively insensitive to
the flow of events in the community, the responsiveness of the
assault rate to wars and depressions should be considerably less
today than it was in the nineteenth and early twentieth centuries,
as it is.

There is no basis upon which a direct evaluation of the diligence
of the Boston police in the nineteenth century might be made, but
I have already remarked on the thoroughness with which the
simplest assaults and larcenies were handled by the Boston Police
Court in the early part of the nineteenth century. If these practices
continued throughout the nineteenth century, it would seem that
a high proportion of those involved in assaults and larcenies were,
indeed, arrested during that period. By way of comparison, however, in the six-year period from 1960 to 1965, the Boston police
solved 56.6 percent of the aggravated assaults brought to their

attention, and of the larcenies reported, they solved only 42.7 percent.[16] These figures are roughly comparable with the experience of other metropolitan police departments, but they suggest that the nineteenth-century Boston police need not have had a very high arrest percentage to have created the kind of inconsistent pattern described above.

Coming back to the data at hand, it is clear from Figure 8 that

Figure 8: Larcenies per 100,000 population in Boston, 1849–1951

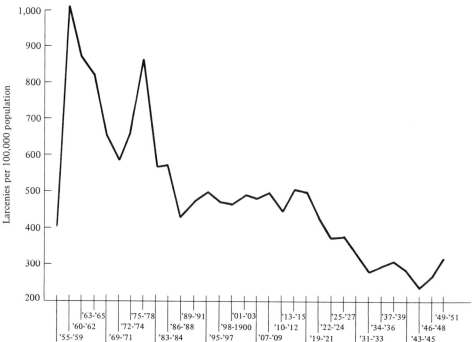

larcenies followed much the same pattern as assaults. Here again we find two distinct curves: first, an early one displaying a marked sensitivity to community events, followed by a curve showing little response at all. The only difference is that the shift from one type to the other seems to have occurred somewhat earlier, that is, by 1886–88. Thus, before 1886–88 the Civil War was accompanied by a dramatic drop from an all-time peak in 1855–59, which in

---

[16] *The Boston Sunday Globe,* May 8, 1966, p. A-3.

turn was followed by a sharp rise during the depression of 1873–78. After this early period of rather wide fluctuations, however, World Wars I and II produced only a slight decline, and the Great Depression of 1930–39 brought about only a minor increase in the rate of larcenies. This last is especially interesting in view of the fact that robberies and burglaries both established all-time peaks during the Great Depression. The conclusion that larcenies are not being diligently investigated and solved in the modern era seems inescapable.

AN INTERPRETATION OF BOSTON'S CRIMINAL PATTERN

In terms of this analysis, then, two broad types of factors seem to affect the criminal patterns of a community. On the one hand, we have those specific factors like wars and economic depressions that have a fleeting, though powerful effect upon the criminal patterns of a community; and, on the other, we have those secular factors like an expanding middle class that consist of gradual, enduring changes in the social structure and organization of the community. The latter occur so slowly that their impact in any one year is scarcely noticeable, but their cumulative effect through the years is likely to change fundamentally both the rate and the pattern of criminal activity in the community.

Among the specific factors, the economic cycle is perhaps most powerful. Robberies, burglaries, larcenies, and assaults have all shown an inverse relationship to the level of economic activity in the Hub during the last century, while forcible rape has varied directly with the economic fortunes of Boston.[17] Major wars seem to have had a depressive effect upon major crime in Boston; forcible rape, burglary, assault, and larceny all have declined rather consistently whenever Boston became involved in a major war. Only murder and manslaughter have shown little sensitivity to the influences of the economic cycle or wars.

Quite independent of these specific factors, several of the crimes examined here have shown tendencies that may well reflect basic,

---

[17] These results are generally consistent with those reported by Daniel Glaser and Kent Rice in their study, "Crime, Age, and Employment," *American Sociological Review,* 24, no. 5 (October 1959), 683. See also William F. Ogburn and Dorothy S. Thomas, "The Influence of the Business Cycle on Certain Social Conditions," *Journal of the American Statistical Association,* 18 (September 1922), 324–40.

secular shifts in the social structure of Boston. We have already mentioned the automobile as a factor in the rise in manslaughter and forcible rape, but there are several other social changes that must have had a profound effect upon the criminal patterns of Boston as it moved into the twentieth century.

First, the mechanisms of social control in a metropolis are much less personal and, therefore, much less effective in preventing deviancy of all kinds, and in a metropolis there is a much greater spirit of independence and personal freedom.[18] Second, the metropolis nearly always harbors a well-organized underworld in which a wide variety of criminal activities are pursued, including those involving the most serious kinds of crimes. These two changes alone would tend to produce increases in the rates of most crimes as a small city grew into a great metropolis, although it must be noted that few members of organized crime are ever arrested for their misdeeds.

Several other structural changes have probably influenced the crime rate in the opposite direction. Most American cities have grown in size primarily by assimilating large numbers of peoples who initially at least had little familiarity with urban manners and institutions. For example, Boston was inundated in the nineteenth century, first, by the starving yeomen of Ireland and, then, by the impoverished peasants of Sicily and southern Italy.[19] These immigrants were eventually assimilated by the city, but both the immigrants and the city suffered grievously in the process. There can be little doubt that the gradual adjustment of the descendants of the Irish and Italian immigrants to the urban patterns of Boston has resulted over the years in a gradual reduction in the city's crime rate.

And by the same token, the fact that the city, like most American communities, has enjoyed a gradually rising standard of living

---

[18] The best discussion of the relationship between mechanisms of social control and social organization is contained in Georg Simmel's "The Persistence of Social Groups," reprinted in Edgar F. Borgatta and Henry J. Meyer (eds.), *Sociological Theory* (New York: Alfred A. Knopf, Inc., 1959), pp. 373–75. Simmel also provides, perhaps, the deepest insight into the character of urban man (see his "The Metropolis and Mental Life," *Sociology of Georg Simmel* [New York: Free Press, 1950], pp. 409–24).

[19] Oscar Handlin reports that, in 1850, 35.0 percent of the Boston population was foreign born. In 1855 the figure was 37.9 percent, in 1865 it was 34.3 percent, and in 1880 it was still 31.6 percent (see his *Boston's Immigrants* [Cambridge, Mass.: Harvard University Press, 1959], pp. 243–44, 246, and 261). In 1960 the percentage of foreign born in Boston was 15.8 percent.

during nearly the entire period of this study must have had a significant effect upon its crime rate.[20] The rising standard of living of Bostonians was probably accompanied by a relative stabilization of their employment and ultimately of their community life as well. Hence crimes usually associated with economic distress and social disorganization have declined in proportion to other types of crime, while sexual crimes, which are probably more common among the higher economic classes, have increased to some extent.

Taking into account all types of structural change, then, we can see that there have been counterbalancing pressures on the crime rate as Boston grew from a small city into a large metropolis. The fact that the crime problem has declined on balance leads me to suspect that, in the long run, those forces tending to diminish crime in Boston have been more powerful, although of course, there is no way of evaluating this view more precisely with the data at hand. This issue can only be settled conclusively when, perhaps, twenty or thirty similar studies of other cities have been performed. At that point, the specific relationship between crime rates and single factors like social control and the broader relationships between social organization and criminal patterns can be more precisely determined.

SOME CONCLUSIONS

In conclusion, then, I have examined the criminal patterns of Boston over the long term, and the results suggest that the patterns of deviant behavior in the community as measured by police arrests depend basically upon three factors: the attitude and effectiveness of the police; the occurrence of momentary events in the community that have the effect of disturbing and dislocating the established social routines; and the occurrence of enduring changes in the structure of the community in response to qualitative changes in its function. The over-all effect of both the momentary events and the more enduring changes in Boston's structure has been to encourage an intermittent but persistent downward tendency in the rate of every major crime except forcible rape and manslaughter.

---

[20] See Bernard Barber, *Social Stratification* (New York: Harcourt, Brace & Co., 1957), chap. 16, for a careful discussion of the changing class structure in America.

This downward drift, of course, stands in stark contrast to the popular belief that crime is growing more rampant and more serious every year. This belief has been largely fostered by the annual reports issued by the FBI, where appalling increases in crime and delinquency are monotonously recorded. The FBI has been issuing these reports only since 1930, and as Figure 1 indicates, the crime rate in Boston has, indeed, risen slightly since then. But even if we assume that the *long-term trend* in Boston and other major metropolitan centers has been downward, we need not conclude that there is a basic contradiction between these data and the trends traced by the annual reports of the FBI. The migration pattern of this nation over the last one hundred years has been from areas of low crime rates, that is, rural areas and small towns, to areas of high crime rates, that is, large urban centers; and a chronic increase in the crime rate in the entire society is not inconsistent with a steady decrease in the crime rates of its large cities.[21]

---

[21] To illustrate the validity of this conclusion, consider the following hypothetical example. Suppose we have a society of 1,000,000 in which 80 percent of the population lives in villages where the crime rate is 40 per 1,000. The remaining 20 percent lives in urban areas where the crime rate is 100 per 1,000. The crime rate for such a society would be 52 per 1,000. Now suppose the village crime rate remains at 40 per 1,000, the urban crime rate *drops* to 60 per 1,000, and the percentage in urban areas rises to 90 percent of the total, which is still 1,000,000. The new crime rate for the society has risen to 58 per 1,000 even though the rate has fallen sharply in the cities.

Chapter 7

Real crime, other crime, and juvenile delinquency

Some behaviors very harmful to society are not officially designated as crime. Moreover, official definitions of crime tend to obscure the fact that behaviors not officially designated as crime may be equally harmful or more harmful. This chapter will discuss some behaviors officially designated as crime, including violent crime, drug offenses, organized crime, witchcraft, crimes of businessmen, rape, female crime, and juvenile delinquency, in an attempt to demonstrate that both the differences between crimes and noncrimes and the differences among crimes are constructed, socially defined, and dependent on human designations. The analysis will also show that official designations reflect the interests of some segments of society more than they reflect the interests of other segments.

Social definition of actors and their acts. If we compare white-collar crime with organized crime, it becomes clear that the social definition or stigma attached to the actors is much more important in determining how others respond to them than the actors' behavior per se. We can start this comparison by considering two men—one an alleged Mafia chieftain and the other a top executive of an American corporation. Even if a businessman is involved in price fixing, black marketing, or other corporate crime, the public may not be outraged, for generally the businessman is accorded great respect in our society. Sutherland

(1949: 46–51) observes that this respect for businessmen exists among the legislators responsible for drafting criminal laws and among the general public, in part because the mass media are controlled by business interests and usually describe these interests in the most favorable light. He also recognizes, however, that legislators' respect for businessmen is supplemented by a measure of fear that corporate moneys will be used to unseat them should they pass legislation contrary to business interests. On the other hand, even if an alleged Mafia figure is in a legitimate business, many law enforcement officials feel that he should be harassed and pursued. Robert Kennedy (1960), a former attorney general of the United States, lamented the fact that Mafia figures were increasingly going into legitimate businesses and were therefore becoming harder to apprehend. At times they gain footholds in such operations by force and extortion, but it is acknowledged that entry is often gained merely by investments (Woetzel, 1963). Organized crime, we are told, may attempt to establish control over a labor union or a business by means of force, intimidation, bribery, or extortion. It is said that in some cases this makes it possible for a business operating under the protection of organized crime to undersell competitors by producing goods more cheaply. It is also said that the expenses of such businesses may be lower because the labor union cooperates with the employers and will not protect the employees against low pay and bad working conditions. Those alleged to be involved in organized crime are also charged with having embezzled funds from organizations in which they have gained positions of influence. The weakness of such arguments is that, even if they are true, embezzlement and bribery have undoubtedly also been committed by businessmen whose names are not linked to the Mafia.

How the actors actually carry out their activities—whether they do or do not offer a good product or service at a fair price—is of no concern in determining the public definition. Even if business executives make a demonstrably unsafe product, as have the auto manufacturers, they are not widely condemned, whereas Mafia figures will be publicly condemned even if they offer a good product at a fair price. The black-marketing businessman selling impure products, though condemned, does not appear to be feared and hated as much by most citizens as an alleged Mafia figure selling reasonably good and clean pizza. These curious societal

Chart 1: Social definitions of actors and their acts

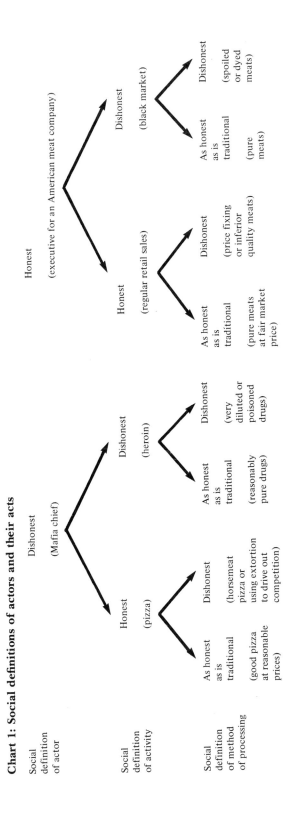

Social
definition
of actor

Honest
(executive for an American meat company)

Dishonest
(Mafia chief)

Social
definition
of activity

Honest
(pizza)

Dishonest
(heroin)

Honest
(regular retail sales)

Dishonest
(black market)

Social
definition
of method
of processing

As honest
as is
traditional

(good pizza
at reasonable
prices)

Dishonest

(horsemeat
pizza or
using extortion
to drive out
competition)

As honest
as is
traditional

(reasonably
pure drugs)

Dishonest

(very
diluted or
poisoned
drugs)

As honest
as is
traditional

(pure meats
at fair market
price)

Dishonest

(price fixing
or inferior
quality meats)

As honest
as is
traditional

(pure
meats)

Dishonest

(spoiled
or dyed
meats)

reactions will become clearer in the following discussions of organized crime and the crimes of businessmen.

REAL CRIME

Violent crime

Although it may be conceded that some crime is a result of arbitrary definitions, for example, victimless offenses such as gambling and prostitution, some crime strikes us as real because we can empathize with the injury to the victim. The victim of an armed robber is really robbed and may be dead. Nevertheless, death at the hands of another person is not necessarily defined as murder. Former President Richard Nixon ordered the bombing of thousands of Asians and was reelected to a second term as president. The number of civilians killed by U.S. police is six times as great as the number of police killed in the line of duty (Robin, 1963). Yet police are still largely defined as defenders of law and social order. As mentioned earlier, *violence* is typically seen as a product of those outside government even when it is recognized that representatives of government *kill* and *injure*.

Wolfgang and Ferracuti (1967) developed the notion that a subculture of violence exists among lower-class people and used that notion to explain assaultive behavior among poor whites and ghetto blacks. This emphasis on lower-class violence ignores the evidence of personal aggression committed by more affluent persons and by the government. A survey conducted by Stark and McEvoy (1970) found, for example, that a higher percentage of middle-class than of lower-class persons had physically assaulted another person. This finding is contrary to police statistics showing more violence among the poor. Stark and McEvoy suggest that the affluent are underrepresented in arrest data because they can rely on private sources, such as marriage counselors, to settle disputes, whereas the poor must often rely on the police. Also the middle classes typically have greater privacy in their disputes, whereas the quarrels of the poor often take place in bars, on sidewalks, or in crowded apartments and are therefore more likely to become known to the police.

The lack of predictability in the definition of killing and assault has been systematically investigated by Blumenthal et al. (1972).

In a survey of American men, they found no relationship between gross destruction of property or injury to people and the percentage calling such acts violence. A higher percentage of their respondents defined the burning of a draft card as violence than the percentage who defined beating of students or the shooting of looters by police as violence. Thus, even on a supposedly concrete issue, such as the definition of *violence,* there is no necessary relationship between the dictionary definition—the exertion of physical force to injure or abuse (Webster, 1956)—and human perceptions. In a survey of Baltimore citizens, Rossi et al. (1974) found that selling marijuana was generally considered as serious as beating up a policeman and much more serious than knowingly selling defective used cars as completely safe. Although defective used cars, unlike marijuana, have a proven potential for destruction, selling such cars was defined as less serious than selling marijuana.

Moreover, public and official definitions of real crime can shift drastically. "To mention a more modern example, the abrupt and rapid changes in the lawmaking power structure at the time of the Hungarian revolution in 1956 resulted in criminals becoming heroes and then again criminals, and law-abiding citizens turning into criminals and then again into conformists—all within eight days" (Schafer, 1974: 33).

It may well be that if the Axis powers rather than the Allies had won World War II, instead of the Nuremberg trials, there might have been Washington trials to sentence Generals MacArthur and Eisenhower for war crimes, and President Truman for genocide in ordering atomic bombings of Japan. Had this happened, it is also likely that American-born children would be learning different definitions of these men and their acts.

Drugs and drug abuse

If we were to question a sample of American adults, most of them would probably agree that drugs include such things as barbiturates, penicillin, morphine, heroin, LSD, and marijuana. They would probably place coffee, alcohol, and tobacco in quite a different category. These respondents might also indicate that all ingested drugs have a physiological impact on the body. On that basis, however, coffee, alcohol, and tobacco would have to be included among drugs. The wary respondent might then reply that these are not drugs because they are not as harmful as "real" drugs. One might point to the thousands of auto deaths caused by drinking and to the deaths from lung cancer and heart disease that have been linked to cigarette smoking, but probably to no avail. The respondent might then reply that real drugs are more addictive than the others, even though in this regard marijuana seems no different from coffee, cigarettes, or alcohol. The commonsense perception of drugs includes marijuana but not martinis, even if this perception cannot be empirically defended. Goode (1972: 18) has correctly observed that "the concept 'drug' is a cultural artifact, a social fabrication. *A drug is something that has been arbitrarily defined by certain segments of society as a drug.*"

Substances called drugs do not share pharmacological traits setting them apart from nondrugs. If the category "drugs" is an artificial construct, then the category "drug abuse" is also artificial. Clearly, what is considered "abuse" is also a cultural artifact with no basis in chemical fact. Alcoholism or the three-pack-a-day cigarette habit is not drug abuse, of course, because alcohol and cigarettes are not usually considered drugs. But even within the category of real drugs, some use is considered abuse, but some, even massive use, is not. Most Americans probably consider any consumption of marijuana and—especially—heroin as drug abuse. However, the use of morphine administered by a physician before an operation is considered appropriate, whereas the sale of the same amount of morphine by a street pusher is regarded as drug abuse. The common addiction of affluent adults to barbiturates is not typically seen as drug abuse either, again perhaps because it is a legal addiction, whereas addiction to heroin is not. Thus the addiction itself is not the central problem. Rather, legality becomes the important commonplace referent for the definition of drug abuse. The logic seems to be that specific drug use would not be illegal if there were not something wrong with it.

Organized crime[1]

Another type of crime that is seen as real and threatening by Americans is the Mafia, or organized crime. If the flood of government reports, newspaper articles, books, and movies involving American organized crime is any indication of citizen awareness,

---

[1] Most of the section on organized crime appeared earlier. See Galliher and Cain (1974).

then surely Americans are currently very conscious of this phenomenon. Numerous popular books on the subject, both fiction and nonfiction, have been published in recent years. Several have been made into movies, and one, *The Godfather,* broke all box-office records. Although there is some variation from source to source, the central image is that of a multibillion-dollar-a-year conspiracy of Sicilian origin called either the Mafia or Cosa Nostra, in which a code of secrecy (called Omerta) is enforced, if necessary, by violence. This conspiracy is purportedly international in scope, yet organized around 24 families in America's largest urban areas. It is thought to be involved in a large share of the illegal gambling and narcotics trafficking in this country and to have infiltrated and corrupted legitimate business. This view of American organized crime is supported by the research of the eminent criminologist Donald R. Cressey (1967: 25–60; 1969), who collected information on organized crime in his role as a consultant to the President's Commission on Law Enforcement and Administration of Justice. Cressey (1969: x) observes:

Upon being invited to work for the Commission, I was not at all sure that a nationwide organization of criminals exists. . . . I changed my mind. I am certain that no rational man could read the evidence that I have read and still come to the conclusion that an organization variously called "the Mafia," "Cosa Nostra," and "the syndicate" does not exist. . . . [The] Deputy Director of the President's Commission invited law-enforcement and investigative agencies to submit reports on organized crime to the Commission. A summer spent reading these materials, exploring other confidential materials, and interviewing knowledgeable policemen and investigators convinced me.

There are a few journalists and other writers who have questioned this dominant image of organized crime. For example, a novel by Jimmy Breslin (1969) characterizes a Mafia family in New York City as being in disarray and poverty, and engaged in continual conflict with other Mafia families. A similar picture of internal decay and internecine conflict emerges from Gay Talese's (1971) study of the Bonannos, one of the better-known New York City families. Using government wiretap evidence which was presented in court, Murray Kempton (1969) demonstrates that the members of a New Jersey *Mafia* family, were involved, not in multimillion-dollar drug shipments or nationwide gambling syndicates, but in crimes netting no more than a few hundred dollars. This family had difficulty in paying the rent and sometimes found legitimate occupations more lucrative than crime. Kempton's revelations are especially convincing if one accepts the government's traditional argument that one of the few methods of learning the truth about organized crime is through such wiretap information.

A few sociologists have also challenged the folklore on organized crime, suggesting that sufficient evidence is not available to prove the existence of a national or international conspiracy (Bell, 1960: 138–150; Hawkins, 1969; Horton and Leslie, 1960: 138–139; Albini, 1971). Hawkins observes that, given the assumption of a code of secrecy, no counterevidence is possible, since witness denials of an international conspiracy only substantiate the effectiveness of the code. Moreover, he contends that the contemporary view of the Mafia is based largely on Joseph Valachi's testimony, which is both uncorroborated and ridden with internal contradictions. It is credible only because Americans need to find a scapegoat on which to saddle the blame for our current problems with crime.

Nevertheless, social scientists have been much less active than journalists in collecting information about organized crime. Perhaps this is true because, as Polsky (1967: 117–149) suggests, social scientists mistakenly believe that such research is impossible. Polsky does admit that criminologists collecting information about organized crime may face some problems, such as being subjected to criminal charges for withholding information on criminal activity from the police, but he indicates that criminology textbook writers invariably give the false impression that to conduct such research one must pass as a criminal or even engage in a crime as the only means of gaining cooperation. However, in the 1920s John Landesco (1968: xiv–xv) conducted a pioneering study of organized crime in Chicago which involved "not only the collection of newspaper and other printed sources but, in the tradition of Chicago sociology, the development of extensive contacts with criminal groups in the city." More recently, Ianni (1972) conducted a study of a Mafia family, relying mainly on participant observation supplemented by interviews with key informants. Another contemporary study, by Chambliss (1971), used interviews with those involved in organized vice or its control. Albini (1971) has also recently used such interviews along with a variety of existing records in his study of organized crime. None of these studies mentions the problems often alleged to exist by criminology textbook writers, nor have these studies uncovered any evidence of a national conspiracy. But such social science research on organized crime is not common. Albini (1971: 8) observes:

There is no question that much of the material written in the area of organized crime thus far is not scholarly in nature, all too frequently falling into the medium of the journalistic and sensation-oriented style of writing where documentation of sources is either at a minimum or completely absent. Too often these writings are value-laden resulting in outright distortion of fact and, in many cases, the creation of utter nonsense.

The lack of "scholarly" material and the dominance of "journalistic and sensation-oriented" writing present a dilemma to the social scientist writing a criminology text. The choice apparently is either to ignore the topic of organized crime or to use the available sources with all their obvious limitations. The question, then, is, what types of materials have criminologists who have written descriptions of organized crime used to support their contentions?

The answer is that there is a heavy reliance among criminologists on journalistic and especially official government documents, and in particular on the Kefauver Senate Committee hearings of the early 1950s. But as Moore (1974: 75) suggests of the Kefauver Committee hearings:

What has rarely been appreciated is that congressional committees were better dramatists than investigators, that the limited staff and training available, the political atmosphere in which committees worked, and the necessity of arriving at solutions rather than in-depth understanding of problems severely curtailed the amount of serious research a committee could pursue. . . . Investigating committees do little real investigating, but rather, they dramatize a particular perspective on a problem and place the prestige of a Senate body behind the chosen point of view.

This dependence on journalistic and official documents to understand the nature of organized crime is at least partially a consequence of the limitations of traditional social science research techniques. As Polsky (1967: 117–149) observes, criminologists have typically assumed that field research on professional criminals is impossible. Assuming the code of secrecy, the usual sociological techniques of data collection through interviews, questionnaires, or participant observation seem irrelevant or even dangerous. Moreover, the morality or ethics guiding most social science research would hamper the study of any such secret society. The American Sociological Association Code of Ethics, for example, appears to compel the researcher to secure voluntary subject cooperation and prohibits releasing information about subjects against their will (*American Sociologist,* 1968: 316–318; Galliher, 1973).

There are, however, some limitations in analyzing citations to documents such as referred to here. Citations to a document may be used for more than one purpose; sometimes a piece is cited not to indicate a source of relevant information but rather to point out the weaknesses or even absurdity of the document. For a complete analysis of the effect of these citation-use patterns, one must also observe the conclusions reached in these discussions of organized crime. It then appears that though there are differences in style and in the amount of support for the folklore about organized crime, none of these conclusions directly challenges the image of organized crime found in government reports. This reliance on official documents is not really dissimilar from the well-known dependence of criminologists on official arrest records in their other areas of study (Matza, 1969: 94–100). Matza illustrates how criminologists typically acknowledge the limitations of arrest records yet still use them in their research, bemoaning the fact that no alternatives are available. Undoubtedly, this same reasoning helps explain the widespread use of Senate hearings as a basic source of data on organized crime.

Since in their analysis of organized crime social scientists have largely limited themselves to secondary sources of data, particularly government documents, they could not be expected to give an independent check or challenge to such sources. There are two troublesome aspects to reliance on such sources, one empirical, the other political. In arriving at conclusions and statements of fact, the journalist or political investigator is not bound by the canons of scientific investigation, as is the social scientist. Jacobs (1970: 348–350) has observed that the journalist's need to produce exciting copy rapidly requires a sacrifice of the careful accumulation and sifting of information characteristic of scientific investigation. Moreover, Hawkins (1969: 26–28) suggests that in political hearings it is not clear what would constitute counterevidence against the existence of the Mafia, and without the possibility of such nonconfirming information, there can be no real tests of the issue.

The largely unchecked folklore regarding organized crime provided an important rationale for the provision in the Omnibus Crime Control and Safe Streets Act (1968: 14) for court use of wiretap information. The bill reads: "Organized criminals make extensive use of wire and oral communications in their criminal activities. The interception of such communications to obtain evidence of the commission of crimes or to prevent their commission is an indispensable aid to law enforcement and the administration of justice."

Such an alteration in constitutional guarantees would not be sensible and could not be justified in combating local criminal gangs, about whose existence there is of course no dispute, but can be defended, if at all, only on the assumption that organized crime is operated by a massive, well-integrated, interstate conspiracy. Cressey's (1969: x) research as a consultant to an official crime commission, using reports from law enforcement agencies, predictably convinced him of the government's claims of organized crime's massive proportions and certain threat. Because of organized crime's allegedly gigantic scale, he (1969: 323–324) concludes that it cannot be effectively controlled by using traditional law enforcement techniques. As a possible solution, he suggests that government agencies might attempt to control organized crime by means of a treaty much like those entered into with foreign enemy states (Cressey, 1969: 324): "It is highly unlikely, but not inconceivable, that Cosa Nostra would agree to give up its political involvements and its illegal operation of legitimate businesses, which in combination threaten to undermine the whole nation, if it could be assured that it will be permitted to keep the profits, after payment of taxes, on bet-taking." Obviously such an extreme proposal could only seem credible to those accepting the image of a large-scale conspiracy.

One need only go back to the McCarthy era in the early 50s, or to the relocation and internment of Japanese-Americans after the bombing of Pearl Harbor, to recognize that extreme measures are easily justified when people believe they are facing a widespread conspiratorial threat. Unfortunately, authors of criminology textbooks have purveyed the common belief in the conspiratorial threat posed by organized crime, usually without indicating the limitations of their sources. Mythology and folklore can, of course, have varying degrees of basis in fact; therefore, more empirical studies are needed, such as those called for by Polsky and executed by Landesco, Ianni, Chambliss, and Albini. Since it has become official policy that a national conspiracy of organized crime exists, social scientists claiming an interest and expertise in the study of crime have a special responsibility to discover the true nature of this phenomenon. The international Mafia, so much a part of our common discourse, may be in fact no more than an image created largely by government propaganda.

Summary

Our point in this discussion of violence, drug abuse, and organized crime is that even where victims obviously exist, the constructed and class-based nature of what is classified as crime can still be demonstrated. Loss of life, destruction of property, or drug addition cannot account for public definitions of crime as well as can the exercise of the class interests of societal elites. The widespread definitions of violence, drug abuse, and organized crime can all be demonstrated to serve the ends of specific elite, class, and ·powerful interest groups—violence does not include deaths associated with structural defects of automobiles; drug abuse does not include barbiturate addiction; and organized crime does not include large U.S. corporations, but rather involves 24 Mafia families. As Reasons (1974: 230) has observed: "Our interest and concern with the 'organized underworld' has directed our attention away from the 'organized upperworld.'"

OTHER CRIME

Some crimes do not have the shocking reality of armed robbery or homicide and therefore may be easier to conceive of as products of cultural labeling. There is a compelling reality to armed robbery, the Mafia, or drug abuse, whereas for other types of behavior the artificial or created quality of what is called crime is more readily understood. Perhaps it is easier to demonstrate the arbitrary and capricious nature of human judgment by looking at another time and place.

Witchcraft

We can easily see the crime of witchcraft as a historical curiosity, reflecting the superstitions of an earlier and more naive period. Witchcraft (Currie, 1968) could be proven in 15th century Europe without proving any actual or observable behavior. It came to be defined as a thought crime—making a pact with the devil or putting a hex on someone. Earlier, in the 13th century, the Catholic church took the position that the belief in witchcraft was an illusion. But by the 15th century, attitudes had changed. No lesser men than John Calvin and Martin Luther, for example, believed in witchcraft.

Since no one had ever been seen making a pact with the devil, ordinary sources of evidence were worthless. Indeed, ordinary people were thought to be unable to see the devil. In most cases of witchcraft, direct proof was impossible to come by, so a premium was placed on securing confessions through torture. Since such confessions included the revealing of other witches, a steady flow of witches was assured. Confessions were publicly read at executions and distributed to the populace at large. This justified the trials to the public and helped reinforce the reality of witchcraft itself. The increasing numbers of witches mentioned in confessions frightened the populace and legitimated even more stringent suppression.

If the accused witch had a good reputation in the community, he or she was clearly a witch, for according to stereotype, witches sought to be well-thought-of as a disguise. If the accused was not well-though-of, this was also understandable, since no rational person would approve of witches. Stubbornness in refusing to confess was considered a sure sign of alliance with the devil, who was known to demand silence from witches—no negative evidence was possible.

In England the response to witchcraft took place within a framework of effective limitations on the power of the state. English citizens, unlike their counterparts on the Continent, had explicit rights of due process. Also, the property of suspected witches was not confiscated in England, as on the Continent, so English officials did not have the same vested interest in the discovery and conviction of witches. There was less torture in England, and confessions were rare. On the Continent, by contrast, court officials, including executioners, torturers, and judges of witches, were paid high wages supported by confiscated property. It is not accidental, therefore, that on the Continent most witches were people of wealth and property, whereas in England they were usually poorer and much fewer in number (Currie, 1968).

Thus in continental Europe, a form of deviance was nurtured by the confiscation of property and maintained largely through the efforts of a self-sustaining bureaucratic organization dedicated to its discovery and punishment. When confiscation was outlawed, this form of deviance ceased to be recognized. Witchcraft is an extreme case, in the sense that it is an invented form of deviance whose definition lacks roots in concrete behavior. By their nature, systems of repressive control tend to foster the growth of officially created deviance and an organizational structure which is oriented to self-perpetuation.

The parallels between the "real" Mafia and fictitious witchcraft are not difficult to discover. As witchcraft is a pact with the devil which only the devil can know of, the pact of the Mafia is with other insiders and known only to them. In both cases no direct empirical evidence of the crime is possible. Therefore, as with witchcraft, confessions are the only evidence of the Mafia—mainly the confession of Joe Valachi. Also, as with witchcraft, no negative evidence is possible to disprove the existence of the Mafia since denials only reflect the code of secrecy (Hawkins, 1969). As witches were blamed for assorted problems, today the Mafia is blamed for a wide assortment of crimes. As with witchcraft, reports of massive organized crime have alarmed the public and elected officials, and consequently the law has been altered to allow police to use more extreme measures in fighting organized crime, including more liberalized use of secret wiretaps (Harris, 1969). The inputs to the witch courts were property, and the inputs to the modern police agencies are larger public appropriations.

The crime of communism

Just as the artificial nature of witchcraft is apparent today, most contemporary Americans probably also recognize the outrageousness of the accusations associated with the communism panic of the early 1950s. Senator Joseph R. McCarthy, a Wisconsin Republican, accused numerous Americans of criminal conspiracy with Communists. His special skill at propaganda triggered a nationwide panic. McCarthy's accusations of treason were directed especially at the government officials in the State Department and the Army, and numerous careers were destroyed by his groundless charges (Cook, 1971; Watkins, 1969). Just as the Kefauver Senate hearings captured the public's interest in organized crime, the McCarthy Senate hearings on Communists in government generated a national paranoia about Communists. Neither Kefauver nor McCarthy, of course, was concerned with evenhanded, objective fact-gathering and analysis. Ultimately, the outrageous accusations of McCarthy so antagonized the Senate that it formally moved to condemn him, and thereafter he was ignored. Yet this episode offers a contemporary example of the way in which powerful government figures, with access to the mass media, can create public designations of crime to suit their personal interests.

Crimes of businessmen

The economic crimes committed by businessmen in the course of their work are usually referred to as *white-collar crimes* (Sutherland, 1949). Generally, such crimes do not seem to arouse Americans much more than witchcraft currently does. Sutherland documented the myriad crimes committed by America's largest corporations, including such offenses as price fixing, tax evasion, misrepresentation in advertising, and unfair labor practices, such as the coercion and intimidation of those attempting to organize unions. There is no evidence that the public is outraged by the crimes of businessmen even when there is proof of the nature and extent of such crimes.

Rossi et al. (1974) found that traditional crimes, such as robbery and rape, are seen as more serious than white-collar crimes. In a survey of citizens in Baltimore, where respondents ranked a list of offenses according to their seriousness, selling marijuana was seen as more serious than such white-collar crimes as "manufacturing and selling autos known to be dangerously defective," "knowingly selling defective used cars as completely safe," "a public official accepting bribes in return for favors," and "fixing prices" (Rossi et al., 1974: 228–229). In fact, price fixing was considered to be among the least serious of the crimes ranked, approximately equivalent in seriousness to "shoplifting a book in a bookstore" or "repeated refusal to obey parents."

In a survey of public reaction to violations of pure food laws by businessmen, such as selling contaminated foods, Newman (1957) also found little public outrage. He found that "respondents viewed food adulteration [by large corporations] as more comparable to serious traffic violations than to burglary" (Newman, 1957: 231).

As indicated above, Reasons (1974: 230) suggests one possible explanation for public indifference to the crimes of businessmen:

Our interest and concern with the "organized underworld" has directed our attention away from the "organized upperworld." While the terms "organized crime," "mafia," and "Cosa Nostra" conjure up images of insidious, ruthless, sly, machine-gun-toting gangsters who are a major threat to our national viability, we fail to recognize that "they" merely represent the tip of the iceberg, [with so-called legitimate corporations reaping the biggest benefits from crime.]

Geis (1973) suggests that the low public awareness of and concern about white-collar crime is a result of the fact that the injuries and costs of most corporate crimes, such as price fixing, are highly diffused and widely scattered, making the effects almost imperceptible compared to the larger sums stolen from each victim by burglars. Air and water pollution assaults victims in a slow and subtle fashion, though it is no less damaging than street muggings.

To increase public awareness of white-collar crime, Geis (1973) suggests some alternatives. One is for the FBI to include white-collar offenses in its reports, as, in fact, was done originally. Geis also recommends the infiltration of corporations suspected of crimes by police agents trained in undercover work, much as other criminal operations are infiltrated. The cost would be minimal, since agents would, of course, be paid a salary by the corporations and because corporation fines would help pay informer fees.

Black marketing

The possibility of committing this type of crime emerged during World War II (Clinard, 1952). Laws were passed making it a criminal violation to charge more than a specified price for nearly all commodities, and for the first time in American history there was compulsory rationing of goods by the government.

Those involved in black-marketing operations had generally

not been involved in previous criminal practices. They were simply the businessmen who were in the line of supply. Before the passage of the price-fixing law they were usually not considered to be violating any statutes, when they charged what the market would bear but when they continued their old practices after the passage of the law, they were in violation of a statute. Only one in ten of the businessmen known to have been involved in the black market had a previous record. The infrequency of a previous record, along with the high social class standing of many black marketers, may help explain why there were only a small number of prosecutions for price violations. The absence of a previous record made conviction or imprisonment more difficult, and this may have discouraged prosecutors from taking official action.

Some of the behavior engaged in by black marketers, such as representing a product to be of a higher quality than it really was, was illegal before the establishment of wartime price controls. But a great deal of the black marketers' behavior was legal before controls or if not strictly legal, such as bribes to secure contracts, it was at least overlooked in peacetime. Finally, even if new laws had not been enacted, the war gave businessmen greater opportunities to engage in law violation because there was a greater scarcity and a greater competition for the goods the businessmen controlled, and it was therefore easier for them to exploit their customers.

Clinard (1952) claims that an effort was made by the government to convince the American public that the black marketers were dangerous criminals who were jeopardizing the national interest. However, this government effort was not completely successful, perhaps for at least two reasons. (1) It requires abstract reasoning to understand the harm done by the crimes of black marketers. For example, diverting gasoline and tires from the war effort and selling them at high cost causes inflation that weakens the economy. Armed robberies and rapes are easier to understand. (2) As indicated above, much black marketing was simply traditional business behavior that was abruptly made illegal, and public sentiment toward such behavior did not change as quickly as did the law.

Embezzlement and price fixing

Because of the early and well-known work by Cressey (1953), most of the information criminologists have relied on in discussing white-collar crimes and white-collar criminals has come from a study of the embezzler. However, the generalizations arrived at by studying the embezzler do not hold for other types of white-collar crime. Violations of antitrust laws, for example, present a different set of circumstances than does embezzlement. Not only are the offenders from a different socioeconomic class, but the techniques and justifications for carrying out the crimes are different. Cressey indicates that the white-collar crime of embezzlement arises from a situation in which previously honest white-collar workers find that they have a problem involving money, such as gambling debts, which they are ashamed to share with others. Such individuals also realize that they can solve the problem by taking their employers' money temporarily, as a loan. They justify the act to themselves by telling themselves that they are really not stealing since they intend to pay back the money. Perhaps because of their high status, embezzlers find it difficult to perceive themselves as criminals.

The information we have about price fixers leads us to believe that the description of embezzlement does not supply an adequate picture of price fixing (Geis, 1967). Price fixing does not appear to be an individual solution to an individual money problem. Rather, it is a group solution to a group money problem. The individuals involved do not commit the crime because of personal need or gain, but claim that it is merely part of their job. Corporations would like to know in advance, for example, what share of government contracts they will receive in a given year. This makes future budgeting, hiring, and plant expansion less risky. If they know which and how many contracts they will be awarded, then their probability of spending money on plant expansion or training new employees when neither is needed is very small. Price fixing, then, may serve to maximize corporate profits.

Price fixing, like embezzlement, is usually done with secrecy, but unlike embezzlement, a group of people know about it. Also unlike embezzlement, no guilt feelings attach to this activity. Embezzlers are humiliated and mortified when their defalcations are made public because they have violated their own code of behavior—not so price fixers.

The case of the electric companies' price fixing in 1961 was the focus of considerable attention. The defendants, executives of several large U.S. corporations, did not contest the charges of the government, which avoided a public trial. This case was unusual in that seven of the defendants were given jail sentences. In cases of this kind, fines are usually levied against the company and its employees, with the company usually paying the employees' fines.

Originally, General Electric's position was that the behavior of its employees was not harmful, since even with price fixing its products were a bargain. The defendants justified what they had done on the ground that it was just part of their job. They recognized that their behavior was technically illegal but argued that it served the worthwhile purpose of stabilizing prices. They distinguished between illegal and immoral acts. There was general admission that their behavior had been illegal, but they still felt that it could not be characterized as immoral.

Being publicly labeled a price fixer was not a ground for dismissal from Westinghouse, and the imprisoned price fixers whose corporations did fire them were quickly hired by other companies after their release from jail (Geis, 1967). This indicates that no stigma or public outrage was attached to the price fixers' behavior. An embezzling bank teller will not be hired in any position of trust again. But for some high-level executives, not honesty but the ability to be flexible with the law seems to be a prime occupational requirement. This comparison clearly indicates how elite class interests operate, yet the character of those operations would not usually be disclosed by the commonly used example of embezzlement.

Ghetto merchants

If the government and the general public are victimized by much white-collar crime, we might predict even greater victimization in the black ghettos, where the victims are the least powerful citizens.

Consumption may be even more important for low-income people than for those in higher classes since the former have no prospect of upward occupational mobility, and only through consumption can they share in the success which is the American dream (Caplovitz, 1967). This emphasis on consumption makes such people easy victims for scheming businessmen. They are exceedingly easy to sell goods to. Yet these people cannot buy with cash and usually have unstable jobs, making them poor credit risks.

States limit the amount that can be legally charged for credit, but ghetto merchants often cover their risks by not letting the customer even know the interest being charged, and only giving the customer a payment card. This, of course, also violates the law. Although interest is regulated by law, the price of merchants' goods is not. In addition to charging predictably high prices, ghetto merchants carry low-quality goods. Both their pricing practices and the low quality of their goods give ghetto merchants some protection which they feel is necessary because of their risky credit business.

In fact, at times the actual price of a product is misrepresented (Caplovitz, 1967). Caplovitz describes a case in which a salesman told a customer that the price of a television set was $250. The customer signed a contract to buy the set on time payments and later got a contract in the mail specifying a $300 purchase price. In another case, a woman bought a lamp for $29 from a door-to-door salesman, making an initial deposit. A week later the salesman came back to her home and told her that the price had gone up. She could not pay the extra amount, so he took the lamp back and did not return the deposit.

According to Caplovitz (1967), ghetto merchants sometimes use false advertising of a special sale when no such goods exist at the advertised prices and then try to sell something more expensive to the people they lure into their stores in this way. Also, the goods these merchants sell are sometimes misrepresented. A man bought what he believed was a new television set, but it lasted only a short time. A television repairman informed him that it was a reconditioned set in a new cabinet.

The bill collection practices of ghetto merchants are also often illegal. Yet there is no evidence that law enforcement officials or the general public views the ghetto merchant as a lawless predator. One illustration Caplovitz (1967) uses is that of the forced repossession of the lamp. In another instance, two police officials came to a man's apartment to collect the money he owed on lamps, then physically assaulted him and took all the money in his wallet. When the low-income consumer fails to make payments, merchants can use the law to protect their rights and sometimes even use the police to achieve what are not their legal rights, as in strong-arm collections. When a merchant fails to back up a promise or guarantee, however, the low-income consumer is powerless because of ignorance of his legal rights and because of laws which favor merchants, such as a lack of government controls on the price and quality of goods (Caplovitz, 1967). Like many other crimes of businessmen, this behavior is usually not discussed as crime either by the press or by professional criminologists.

Assigning blame

It is a mistake, however, to blame only corporation vice presidents or retail merchants for their illegal practices, since at times they are forced into these practices by more powerful elites which control an entire market. As an example, Farberman's (1975: 438–439) research demonstrates "how one elite, namely, automobile manufacturers, creates a 'criminogenic market structure' by imposing upon their new car dealers a pricing policy which requires high volume and low per unit profit." High volume is in the manufacturer's interest because it permits the economies of large-scale production, that is, reducing the cost of producing each automobile. However, this high-volume, low-profit pattern forces dealers into fraudulent service operations in order to survive financially. Such practices include "billing for repairs not actually done, replacing parts unnecessarily, and using rebuilt parts but charging for new parts" (Farberman, 1975: 455; see also Leonard and Weber, 1970).

Since pressures are exerted on new car dealers to sell cars quickly, their used car managers in turn have many cars to sell and often make sales to wholesalers on the basis of personal bribes. Used car wholesalers can obtain the funds they need for such bribes by engaging in "short-sales" (Farberman, 1975: 442–445), that is, accepting cash for part of the purchase price and recording a lower selling price. Not reporting the full price of the sale to the state gives the customer a sales tax break and gives the wholesaler some unrecorded cash to use in paying bribes for cars from used car managers. All this illegal behavior is generated by the elite manufacturers' demands that retailers purchase large numbers of their new autos.

Chambliss (1971) provides an example of pressure applied by powerful interests to force local businessmen to participate in crime. He reports that the new owner of a restaurant was pressured by gamblers to allow an illegal bookmaking operation to continue in his business. The gamblers argued that this was the only way the restaurant could operate at a profit. Moreover, so many laws controlled the operation of the business that the owner was constantly in violation of some statute. This made him vulnerable to harassment by city officials, and, indeed, because he refused to participate in bookmaking, he was harassed by city police as well as city health and fire inspectors, showing the complicity of local political officials in gambling. Ultimately, the restaurant owner was forced to sell the business back to the previous owner at a considerable loss.

Rape

Brownmiller (1975) presents convincing evidence that rape is often not perceived as really violent by male social scientists, historians, journalists, or police. Since these groups, for the most part, do not take this crime any more seriously than they take witchcraft or white-collar crime, rape is seldom reported or studied. A common assumption is that good women do not get raped: "A woman with her dress up can run faster than a man with his pants down." The conventional wisdom, supported by Freudian psychiatry, is that if the truth were known, women who are raped really enjoy it and secretly desire to be raped. Therefore, Brownmiller contends, when a woman is raped, it is often held to be at least partly the victim's fault, for wearing sexy clothing, or staying out late at night, or going to dangerous places alone. In other words, taking adequate precautions against rape involves living like a cloistered nun. Unlike victims of robbery and assault, victims of rape are legally required to prove that they resisted.

One might assume that such thinking exists only in the most conventional and politically conservative elements of society, yet Brownmiller (1975) shows that even those considering themselves liberals do not usually consider rape to be a serious problem and only become concerned with this crime when white women's accusations of rape lead to the execution or lynching of black males. Here again, mistrust of the raped female is revealed. In fact, Brownmiller indicates that black radicals, such as Eldridge Cleaver, view the rape of white women as an appropriate revolutionary act against the white man's property—woman. The punishment of rapists has been most severe where such punishment has reflected a need to protect the white man's property—in this case, white women against black males—and in such instances the person seen as most wronged by rape has usually been a man, the father or the husband, rather than the female victim.

Female crime

With only a few exceptions, the misbehavior of females has not been a subject of writing and research by students of crime.[2] Most major positivist orientations are explicitly or implicitly limited to the study of the criminal behavior of male offenders, and female criminality is usually treated even less seriously than are white-collar crimes. *This inattention seems to reflect the idea that female misbehavior is not really crime in the same sense as offenses committed by males.* Scholarly inattention to the study of female offenders and female offenses mirrors a societal lack of concern for female criminality (Adler, 1975). Unlike male crime, female crime does not seem to demand attention by striking fear into the hearts of observers. Except in unusual cases, even women convicted of assault or homicide are not really feared. Moreover, the lack of concern with female crime is reflected in the character of prisons for women.

Since the crimes of women are usually taken less seriously than the crimes of men, women's prisons are typically minimum security; the possible escape of female prisoners is not of great concern (Additon, 1951; Adler, 1975). But because women are not feared, the accommodations, recreational facilities, and vocational training programs of these institutions are ignored without anyone feeling a great risk (Barnes and Tetters, 1959: 414; Simon, 1975: 82–83; Adler, 1975). Where vocational training programs are available for women prisoners, they offer much less variety than do such programs for male prisoners, and they are usually limited to occupations that fit the female stereotype, such as cosmetologist and nurse's aide.

The typical view that women commit mainly sex-linked crime is not supported by self-reported behavior. Such reports give a picture of female crimes of the same variety as is found among men (Chesney-Lind, 1973, 1974). Yet females charged with nonsexual offenses are usually subjected to gynecological examinations to

---

[2] Some of the best known of these exceptions are Davis (1961), Lombroso (1903), Pollak (1950), and Thomas (1927).

determine whether they have venereal disease, and younger, single females are examined to determine whether they have ever had sexual relations. The sexualization of nonsexual offenses reflects the assumption that females accused of any type of crime are also promiscuous, and supports the view that criminal definitions are imposed and artificial.

According to stereotype, women are thought to present a genuine crime problem only with regard to sex-linked offenses. If criminologists do discuss female criminality, they usually focus on prostitution. Since prostitution takes two participants—most often a man and a woman—it is noteworthy that men are absent from both scholarly discussions of prostitution and from arrest records for this offense. Roby (1969) discusses an unsuccessful attempt in New York to hold the patrons of prostitutes to be as criminally responsible as the prostitutes themselves. Such a law passed the state legislature but was not enforced, in part because of concerns about the possible arrest and embarrassment of the prostitutes' businessmen-customers. This example again shows the operation of powerful class interests.

Summary

Such behaviors as contemporary witchcraft, price fixing, and crimes committed by or against females are not usually seriously considered as crimes because they are not felt to pose a genuine threat to the community. Since such behaviors are not taken seriously, the public definitions of these crimes can easily be used to demonstrate the operation of specific biases and class interests.

JUVENILE DELINQUENCY

Definitions of delinquency—Old and new, at home and abroad

Juvenile delinquency is also easy to recognize as a cultural creation, given the great variation in this designation across different times and places. Not all nations have the same concept of juvenile delinquency (Lejins, 1961). The concept of juvenile delinquency, assumes the concept of adolescence, a transitional stage between childhood and adult status, and not all societies have this stage (Cavan and Cavan, 1968). In cultures where individuals pass directly from childhood to adult status, the notion of juvenile delinquency cannot develop. Moreover, in many countries which recognize the existence of juvenile delinquency, it includes *only* criminal code offenses committed by persons below a certain age (Lejins, 1961).

Under traditional English common law the concept of juvenile delinquency did not exist:

Children under the age of seven were presumed incapable of committing a crime, whereas "on the attainment of fourteen years of age, the criminal actions of infants are subject to the same modes of construction as those of the rest of society." Children between the ages of seven and fourteen were also presumed to be "destitute of criminal design," a presumption which could be rebutted by the prosecution if "guilty knowledge" was clearly and unambiguously demonstrated. The burden of proof was on the prosecution and any doubt had to operate in favor of the defendant (Platt, 1969: 188).

Youths were either considered capable of having criminal intent and subject to the criminal law or were exempt. However, no special law was applicable to them.

In the contemporary United States, however, we have a greatly altered and much broader conception of juvenile misdeeds which are alleged to require state intervention. Although there is considerable variation from state to state, the following list of violations reflects the broad range of prohibited behaviors found in laws applying to the behavior of U.S. juveniles (Rubin, 1949: 2).

Violates any law or ordinance
Immoral or indecent conduct
Immoral conduct around school
Engages in illegal occupation
(Knowingly) associates with vicious or immoral persons
Grows up in idleness or crime
(Knowingly) enters, visits house of ill repute
Patronizes, visits policy shop or gaming place
Patronizes saloon or dram house where intoxicating liquor is sold
Patronizes public poolroom or bucket shops
Wanders in streets at night, not on lawful business (curfew)
(Habitually) wanders about railroad yards or tracks
Jumps train or enters car or engine without authority

Habitually truant from school
Incorrigible
(Habitually) uses vile, obscene, or vulgar language (in public place)
Absents self from home without consent
Loiters, sleeps in alleys
Refuses to obey parent, guardian
Uses intoxicating liquors
Is found in place for which adult may be punished
Deports self so as to injure self or others
Smokes cigarettes (around public place)
In occupation or situation dangerous to self or others
Begs or receives alms (or in street for purpose of)

The outlandish *breadth* of these prohibitions found in the various juvenile codes is readily apparent. They cover behaviors ranging from violation of the law to public smoking and swearing. Moreover, many of the prohibitions seem too *vague* to be fairly implemented. It is not clear how incorrigibility is to be defined or what qualifies as vulgar language, growing up in idleness, or indecent conduct. Finally, the language of some of these prohibitions, as well as many of the regulations themselves, reflect an *archaic* and *dated* quality. The definitions of *dram house* or *bucket shops* are undoubtedly unknown to most contemporary Americans, and public smoking by juveniles hardly generates public outrage in contemporary America.

The juvenile codes of all 50 states cover what are often referred to as "status offenses," or conduct that is illegal only because of the culprit's age. As can be seen in the list above, such illegal misconduct includes incorrigibility, immorality, idling, and being beyond reasonable parental control or otherwise in need of supervision. Moreover, cases involving dependent children without homes are also usually processed by juvenile courts.

Minimum age limitations are infrequent in juvenile codes, and the maximum age of persons covered by a state's juvenile code varies from 15 to 18 (Levin and Sarri, 1974: 13). The age qualification sometimes refers to age at the time of the offense, but under some statutes only age at the date of apprehension and detention is relevant (Levin and Sarri, 1974: 14). In most states, the authority of the juvenile court can be waived so that juveniles above a given age can be tried as adults for major felonies when there is a public outcry for retribution. Some states require that the juvenile court make this judgment, and some empower the prosecutor to do so (Levin and Sarri, 1974: 17).

Thus the picture we have of contemporary juvenile codes in the United States is one of broad and exceedingly vague statutes that vary from state to state. Included in this variation are differences in juvenile age limits. Moreover, the authorities are often free to waive the use of the juvenile court and to try juveniles as adults. This means that juveniles often get the worst of both worlds— vague laws describing wide liability for minor misdeeds combined with the prospect of losing their juvenile status if more serious charges are involved and law enforcement authorities believe that in this way the juveniles will be dealt with even more punitively than is possible under juvenile law.

All of this shows not only that the definition of juvenile delinquency is broad and unclear but, as might be expected, that the operation of the juvenile court is also ambiguous, with the juvenile deprived of some of the constitutional rights of due process afforded other citizens. The question is, How did this unhappy state of affairs come about?

The invention of delinquency

A century ago, the notion of juvenile delinquency was unknown. Young people accused of serious crime typically were either considered old enough to be held responsible or released outright (Platt, 1969). Truancy and swearing were either ignored or handled informally, usually by a sound thrashing. The first U.S. juvenile court provided for by law was established in Illinois in 1899. That court became a model for similar courts in other states. By 1917 all but three states had juvenile courts.

These courts were established largely through the efforts of a cadre of middle-class women whom Platt (1969) calls the child savers. These women were uniformly disenchanted with the city, and believed wayward youth should be institutionalized in rural areas away from saloons and gangs. The child savers advocated not only reform in the treatment of young people but also the parental discipline of the nuclear family, agricultural life, and the assimilation of immigrants. Although these women viewed themselves as humanitarians, they brought attention to and, in fact, invented a new recognized category of youthful misbehavior.

Platt observes:

Although the child savers were responsible for minor reforms in jails and reformatories, they were most active and successful in extending governmental control over a whole range of youthful activities that had been previously ignored or dealt with informally. . . . The child savers were prohibitionists in a general sense who believed that social progress depended on efficient law enforcement, strict supervision of children's leisure and recreation, and the regulation of illicit pleasures. Their efforts were directed at rescuing children from institutions and situations [such as] (theaters, dance halls, saloons, etc.) (Platt, 1969: 99).

Ideally, the child savers wanted to intervene in the lives of "pre-delinquent" children and maintain control over them until they were immunized against "delinquency" (Platt, 1969: 107).

It was not by accident that the behavior selected for penalizing by the child savers—drinking, begging, roaming the streets, frequenting dance-halls and movies, fighting, sexuality, staying out late at night, and incorrigibility—was primarily attributable to the children of lower-class migrant and immigrant families (Platt, 1969: 139).

True to the child savers' goals, the original juvenile court statutes enabled the courts to investigate a wide variety of youthful needs and misbehavior—no legal distinctions differentiated the delinquent from the dependent.

Statutory definitions of "delinquency" included (1) acts that would be criminal if committed by adults, (2) acts that violated county, town or municipal ordinances, and (3) violations of vaguely defined catchalls—such as "vicious or immoral behavior," "incorrigibility," "truancy," "profane or indecent language," "growing up in idleness," "living with any vicious or disreputable person" (Platt, 1969: 138).

The juvenile court's control mission is reflected in the fact that its staff consisted primarily of police and truant officers. In the early years of the juvenile court, most delinquency cases involved charges of "crimes without victims," such as disorderly behavior, immorality, vagrancy, truancy, and incorrigibility (Platt, 1969: 140). Yet the juvenile court was also prepared to process crimes against people and property. Moreover, contrary to a provision in the act setting up the juvenile court, its establishment did little to improve the lot of incarcerated children, who continued to be imprisoned with adults in county and city jails (Platt, 1969: 146).

Summary

Juvenile delinquency is so all-inclusive a concept as to be almost without boundaries or definition. Moreover, it includes behavior which is punishable only when committed by those below a given age. Both of these qualities emphasize the association of age and power in determining what behavior is included under the heading of juvenile delinquency.

CONCLUSION

In this chapter real or traditional crime, such as personal assault, was distinguished from other, more subtle forms of crime which have not evoked such widespread outrage. Examples of the latter include price fixing and the practices of ghetto merchants. Contrary to popular opinion, both real crime and such other forms are classifications imposed by societal elites on specific human behaviors. Even intentional killing is not necessarily murder. The discriminatory nature of cultural definitions of human behavior is well illustrated in what has been defined as juvenile delinquency. Social scientists studying crime often feel that they are at their liberal muckraking best when they describe the illegal policies of electric company vice presidents or auto dealers. Yet it has been demonstrated that even such criminal behavior of affluent business people is often necessitated by elites who control the economic situation in which those guilty of that behavior must survive.

Most important for this analysis is the conclusion that the distinctions between crime and noncrime and between serious and other crime work to the advantage of powerful segments of American society, such as businessmen, and to the disadvantage of the poor and racial minorities. Designating certain behavior as juvenile delinquency seriously erodes the freedom of another U.S. minority—the young. In the definition of both crime and juvenile delinquency, the definition of the actor seems of more consequence than the objective characteristics of his or her actions.

REFERENCES

Additon, Henrietta
  1951   "Women's Institutions," pp. 297–309 in Paul Tappan, ed., *Contemporary Correction*. New York: McGraw-Hill Book Co.

Adler, Freda
  1975 *Sisters in Crime: The Rise of the New Female Criminal.* New York: McGraw-Hill Book Co.

Albini, Joseph L.
  1971 *The American Mafia: Genesis of a Legend.* New York: Appleton-Century-Crofts. (Current copyright held by Irvington Publishers, Inc. N.Y.)

American Sociologist
  1968 "Toward a Code of Ethics for Sociologists," 3(November): 316–318.

Barnes, Harry E. and Negley K. Tetters
  1959 *New Horizons in Criminology.* 3d ed. Englewood Cliffs, N.J.: Prentice-Hall.

Bell, Daniel
  1960 *The End of Ideology.* Rev. ed. New York: Free Press.

Blumenthal, Monica D., Robert L. Kahn, Frank M. Andrews, and Kendra B. Head
  1972 *Justifying Violence: Attitudes of American Men.* Ann Arbor: Institute for Social Research, University of Michigan.

Breslin, Jimmy
  1969 *The Gang That Couldn't Shoot Straight.* New York: Viking Press.

Brownmiller, Susan
  1975 *Against Our Will: Men, Women, and Rape.* New York: Simon and Schuster.

Caplovitz, David
  1967 *The Poor Pay More.* New York: Free Press.

Cavan, Ruth S. and Jordan T. Cavan
  1968 *Delinquency and Crime: Cross-Cultural Perspectives.* Philadelphia: J. B. Lippincott Co.

Chambliss, W. J.
  1971 "Vice, Corruption, Bureaucracy, and Power," *Wisconsin Law Review,* 1150–1173.

Chesney-Lind, Meda
  1973 "Judicial Enforcement of the Female Sex Role: The Family Court and the Female Delinquent," *Issues in Criminology* 8(Fall): 51–69.

  1974 "Juvenile Delinquency: The Sexualization of Female Crime," *Psychology Today* 8(July): 43, 45–46.

Clinard, Marshall B.
1952   *The Black Market: A Study of White Collar Crime.* New York: Rinehart and Co.

Cook, Fred J.
1971   *The Nightmare Decade.* New York: Random House.

Cressey, Donald R.
1953   *Other People's Money: A Study in the Social Psychology of Embezzlement.* Glencoe, Ill.: Free Press.
1967   "The Functions and Structure of Criminal Syndicates," *Task Force Report: Organized Crime,* Appendix A. President's Commission on Law Enforcement and Administration of Justice. Washington, D.C.: U.S. Government Printing Office.
1969   *Theft of the Nation.* New York: Harper and Row, Publishers.

Currie, Elliott P.
1968   "Crimes without Criminals: Witchcraft and Its Control in Renaissance Europe," *Law and Society Review* 3(August): 7–32.

Davis, Kingsley
1961   "Prostitution," pp. 262–288 in Robert K. Merton and Robert A. Nisbet, eds., *Contemporary Social Problems.* New York: Harcourt, Brace and World.

Farberman, Harvey A.
1975   "A Criminogenic Market Structure; The Automobile Industry," *Sociological Quarterly* 16(Autumn): 438–457.

Galliher, John F.
1973   "The Protection of Human Subjects: A Reexamination of the Professional Code of Ethics," *American Sociologist* 8(August): 93–100.

Galliher, John F. and James A. Cain
1974   "Citation Support for the Mafia Myth in Criminology Textbooks," *American Sociologist* 9(May): 68–74.

Geis, Gilbert
1967   "White Collar Crime: The Heavy Electrical Equipment Antitrust Cases of 1961," pp. 139–151 in Marshall B. Clinard and Richard Quinney, eds., *Criminal Behavior Systems: A Typology.* New York: Holt, Rinehart and Winston.
1973   "Deterring Corporate Crime," pp. 182–197 in Ralph Nader and Mark J. Green, eds., *Corporate Power in America.* New York: Grossman Publishers.

Goode, Erich
1972   *Drugs in American Society.* New York: Alfred A. Knopf.

Harris, Richard
1969   *The Fear of Crime.* New York: Praeger Publishers.

Hawkins, G.
1969   "God and the Mafia," *Public Interest* 14(Winter): 24–51.

Horton, Paul B. and Gerald R. Leslie
1960   *The Sociology of Social Problems.* 2d ed. New York: Appleton-Century-Crofts.

Ianni, Francis A. J.
1972   *A Family Business: Kinship and Social Control in Organized Crime.* New York: Russell Sage Foundation.

Jacobs, R. H.
1970   "The Journalistic and Sociological Enterprises as Ideal Types," *American Sociologist* 5(November): 348–350.

Kempton, Murray
1969   "Crime Does Not Pay," *New York Review of Books* 13(September 11): 5, 6, 8, 10.

Kennedy, Robert F.
1960   *The Enemy Within.* New York: Harper and Row, Publishers.

Landesco, John
1968   *Organized Crime in Chicago.* Chicago: University of Chicago Press.

Lejins, Peter P.
1961   "American Data on Juvenile Delinquency in an International Forum," *Federal Probation* 25(June): 18–21.

Leonard, William N. and Marvin Glenn Weber
1970   "Automakers and Dealers: A Study of Criminogenic Market Forces," *Law and Society Review* 4(February): 407–424.

Levin, Mark M. and Rosemary C. Sarri
1974   *Juvenile Delinquency: A Comparative Analysis of Legal Codes in the United States.* National Assessment of Juvenile Corrections. University of Michigan, Ann Arbor.

Lombroso, Cesare
1903   *The Female Offender.* 1920 translation. New York: Appleton-Century-Crofts.

Matza, David
1969   *Becoming Deviant.* Englewood Cliffs, N.J.: Prentice-Hall.

Moore, William H.
1974   *The Kefauver Committee and the Politics of Crime, 1950–1952.* Columbia: University of Missouri Press.

Newman, Donald J.
   1957   "Public Attitudes toward a Form of White-Collar Crime," *Social Problems* 4(January): 228–232.

Omnibus Crime Control and Safe Streets Act of 1968
   1968   Public Law 90-351, 90th Congress, H.R. 5037 (June 19).

Platt, Anthony M.
   1969   *The Child Savers: The Invention of Delinquency.* Chicago: University of Chicago Press.

Pollak, Otto
   1950   *The Criminality of Women.* Philadelphia: University of Pennsylvania Press.

Polsky, Ned
   1967   *Hustlers, Beats, and Others.* Chicago: Aldine Publishing Co.

Reasons, Charles E.
   1974   *The Criminologist: Crime and the Criminal.* Pacific Palisades, Calif.: Goodyear Publishing Co.

Robin, Gerald D.
   1963   "Justifiable Homicide by Police Officers," *Journal of Criminal Law, Criminology, and Police Science* 54(June): 222–231.

Roby, Pamela A.
   1969   "Politics and Criminal Law: Revision of the New York State Penal Law on Prostitution," *Social Problems* 17(Summer): 83–109.

Rossi, Peter H., Christine E. Bose, and Richard E. Berk
   1974   "The Seriousness of Crimes: Normative Structure and Individual Differences," *American Sociological Review* 39(April): 224–237.

Rubin, Sol
   1949   "The Legal Character of Juvenile Delinquency," *Annals of the American Academy of Political and Social Science* 261(January): 1–8.

Schafer, Stephen
   1974   *The Political Criminal: The Problem of Morality and Crime.* New York: Free Press.

Simon, Rita James
   1975   *Women and Crime.* Lexington, Mass.: Lexington Books.

Stark, Rodney and James McEvoy III
   1970   "Middle-Class Violence," *Psychology Today* 4(November): 52–54, 110–112.

Sutherland, Edwin H.
    1949   *White Collar Crime.* New York: Holt, Rinehart and Winston.
Talese, Gay
    1971   *Honor Thy Father.* New York: World Publishing Co.
Thomas, W. I.
    1927   *The Unadjusted Girl.* Boston: Little, Brown, and Company.
Watkins, Arthur V.
    1969   *Enough Rope.* Englewood Cliffs, N.J.: Prentice-Hall.
Webster's New World Dictionary of the American Language
    1956   Cleveland: World Publishing Co.
Woetzel, Robert K.
    1963   "An Overview of Organized Crime: Mores versus Morality,"
            Annals of the American Academy of Political and Social Science
            347(May): 1–11.
Wolfgang, Marvin E. and Franco Ferracuti
    1967   *The Subculture of Violence: Towards an Integrated Theory in
            Criminology.* London: Social Science Paperbacks.

13

Vice, corruption, bureaucracy, and power*

William J. Chambliss

INTRODUCTION

At the turn of the century Lincoln Steffens made a career and helped elect a president by exposing corruption in American cities.[1] In more recent years the task of exposure has fallen into the generally less daring hands of social scientists who, unlike their journalistic predecessors, have gathered their information from police departments, attorney generals' offices, and grand jury records.[2] Unfortunately, this difference in source of information has probably distorted the descriptions of organized crime and may well have led to premature acceptance of the Justice Department's long-espoused view regarding the existence of a national criminal organization.[3] It almost certainly has led to an over-emphasis on the *criminal* in organized crime and a corresponding de-emphasis on *corruption* as an institutionalized component of America's

Author's note: I am grateful to W. G. O. Carson, Terence Morris, Paul Rock, Charles Michener, Patrick Douglas, Donald Cressey, and Robert Seidman for helpful comments on earlier versions of this paper.

* Reprinted from *Wisconsin Law Review*, no. 4 (1971), pp. 1150–73.

[1] L. Steffens, *The Shame of the Cities* (1904). See *The Autobiography of Lincoln Steffens* (1931).

[2] D. Cressey, *Theft of the Nation* (1969); Gardiner, "Wincanton: The Politics of Corruption," Appendix B of *The President's Commission on Law Enforcement and Administration of Justice, Task Force Report; Organized Crime* (1967); in W. Chambliss, *Crime and the Legal Process* 103 (1969).

[3] The view of organized crime as controlled by a national syndicate appears in D. Cressey, supra note 2. For a criticism of this view see N. Morris & G. Hawkins, *The Honest Politician's Guide to Crime Control* (1970).

legal-political system.[4] Concomitantly, it has obscured perception of the degree to which the structure of America's law and politics creates and perpetuates syndicates that supply the vices in our major cities.

Getting into the bowels of the city, rather than just the records and IBM cards of the bureaucracies, brings the role of corruption into sharp relief. Organized crime becomes not something that exists outside law and government but is instead a creation of them, or perhaps more accurately, a hidden but nonetheless integral part of the governmental structure. The people most likely to be exposed by public inquiries (whether conducted by the FBI, a grand jury, or the Internal Revenue Service) may officially be outside of government, but the cabal of which they are a part is organized around, run by, and created in the interests of economic, legal, and political elites.

Study of Rainfall West (a pseudonym), the focus of this analysis of the relationship between vice and the political and economic system, dramatically illustrates the interdependency. The cabal that manages the vices is composed of important businessmen, law enforcement officers, political leaders, and a member of a major trade union. Working for, and with, this cabal of respectable community members is a staff which coordinates the daily activities of prostitution, gambling, bookmaking, the sale and distribution of drugs, and other vices. Representatives from each of these groups, comprising the political and economic power centers of the community, meet regularly to distribute profits, discuss problems, and make the necessary organizational and policy decisions essential to the maintenance of a profitable, trouble-free business.

Data collection

The data reported in this paper were gathered over a period of seven years, from 1962 to 1969. Most came from interviews with

---

[4] Most recent examples of this are D. Cressey, supra note 2; N. Morris & G. Hawkins, supra note 3; King, "Wild Shots in the War on Crime," 20 *J. Pub. Law* 85 (1971); Lynch & Phillips, "Organized Crime-Violence and Corruption," 20 *J. Pub. Law* 59 (1971); McKeon, "The Incursion by Organized Crime into Legitimate Business," 20 *J. Pub. Law* 117 (1971); Schelling, "What Is the Business of Organized Crime?" 20 *J. Pub. Law* 71 (1971); Thrower, "Symposium: Organized Crime, Introduction," 20 *J. Pub. Law* 33 (1971); Tyler, "Sociodynamics of Organized Crime," 20 *J. Pub. Law* 41 (1971). For a discussion of the importance of studying corruption see W. Chambliss, supra note 2, at 89; W. Chambliss & R. Seidman, *Law, Order, and Power* (1971); McKitvick, "The Study of Corruption," 72 *Pol. Sci. Q.* 502 (1957).

persons who were members of either the vice syndicate, law enforcement agencies, or both. The interviews ranged in intensity from casual conversations to extended interviewing, complete with tape recording, at frequent intervals over the full seven years of the study. In addition, I participated in many, though not all, of the vices that comprise the cornerstone upon which corruption of the law enforcement agencies is laid.

There is, of course, considerable latitude for discretion on my part as to what I believe ultimately characterizes the situation. Obviously not everyone told the same story, nor did I give equal credibility to all information acquired. The story that does emerge, however, most closely coincides with my own observations and with otherwise inexplicable facts. I am confident that the data are accurate, valid, and reliable; but this cannot be demonstrated by pointing to unbiased sampling, objective measures, and the like for, alas, in this type of research such procedures are impossible.

The setting: Rainfall West

Rainfall West is practically indistinguishable from any other city of a million population. The conspicuous bulk of the population—the middle class—shares with its contemporaries everywhere a smug complacency and a firm belief in the intrinsic worth of the area and the city. Their particular smugness may be exaggerated due to relative freedom from the urban blight that is so often the fate of larger cities and to the fact that Rainfall West's natural surroundings attract tourists, thereby providing the citizenry with confirmation of their faith that this is, indeed, a "chosen land!"[5]

However, an invisible, although fairly large minority of the population, do not believe they live in the promised land. These are the inhabitants of the slums and ghettos that make up the center of the city. Camouflaging the discontent of the center are urban renewal programs which ring the slums with brick buildings and skyscrapers. But satisfaction is illusory; it requires only a slight effort to get past this brick and mortar and into the not-so-

---

[5] Thinking of one's own residence as a "chosen land" need not of course be connected with any objectively verifiable evidence. A small Indian farm town where the standard of living is scarcely ever above the poverty level has painted signs on sidewalks which read "Isn't God good to Indians?" Any outside observer knowing something of the hardships and disadvantages that derive from living in this town might well answer an unequivocal no. Most members of this community nevertheless answer affirmatively.

enthusiastic city center—a marked contrast to the wildly bubbling civic center located less than a mile away. Despite the ease of access, few of those living in the suburbs and working in the area surrounding the slums take the time to go where the action is. Those who do go for specific reasons: to bet on a football game, to find a prostitute, to see a dirty movie, or to obtain a personal loan that would be unavailable from conventional financial institutions.

BUREAUCRATIC CORRUPTION AND ORGANIZED CRIME: A STUDY IN SYMBIOSIS

Laws prohibiting gambling, prostitution, pornography, drug use, and high interest rates on personal loans are laws about which there is a conspicuous lack of consensus. Even persons who agree that such behavior is improper and should be controlled by law disagree on the proper legal response. Should persons found guilty of committing such acts be imprisoned, or counseled? Reflecting this dissension, large groups of people, some with considerable political power, insist on their right to enjoy the pleasures of vice without interference from the law.

In Rainfall West, those involved in providing gambling and other vices enjoy pointing out that their services are profitable because of the demand for them by members of the respectable community. Prostitutes work in apartments which are on the fringes of the lower-class area of the city, rather than in the heart of the slums, precisely because they must maintain an appearance of ecological respectability so that their clients will not feel contaminated by poverty. While professional pride may stimulate exaggeration on the part of the prostitutes, their verbal reports are always to the effect that "all" of their clients are "very important people." My own observations of the comings and goings in several apartment houses where prostitutes work generally verified the girls' claims. Of some fifty persons seen going to prostitutes' rooms in apartment houses, only one was dressed in anything less casual than a business suit.

Observations of panorama—pornographic films shown in the back rooms of restaurants and game rooms—also confirmed the impression that the principal users of vice are middle and upper class clientele. During several weeks of observations, over 70 percent of the consumers of these pornographic vignettes were well-

dressed, single-minded visitors to the slums, who came for fifteen or twenty minutes of viewing and left as inconspicuously as
possible. The remaining 30 percent were poorly dressed, older
men who lived in the area.

Information on gambling and bookmaking in the permanently
established or floating games is less readily available. Bookmakers
report that the bulk of their "real business" comes from "doctors,
lawyers, and dentists" in the city:

It's the big boys—your professionals—who do the betting down here. Of
course, they don't come down themselves; they either send someone or
they call up. Most of them call up, 'cause I know them or they know Mr.
_____ [one of the key figures in the gambling operation.]

Q. How 'bout the guys who walk off the street and bet?

A. Yeh; well, they're important. They do place bets and they sit around
    here and wait for the results. But that's mostly small stuff. I'd be
    out of business if I had to depend on them guys.

The poker and card games held throughout the city are of two
types: (1) the small, daily game that caters almost exclusively to
local residents of the area or working-class men who drop in for a
hand or two while they are driving their delivery route or on their
lunch hour; (2) and the action game which takes place twenty-four
hours a day, and is located in more obscure places such as a suite
in a downtown hotel. Like the prostitutes, these games are located
on the edges of the lower-class areas. The action games are the
playground of well-dressed men who were by manner, finances,
and dress clearly well-to-do businessmen.

Then, of course, there are the games, movies, and gambling
nights at private clubs—country clubs, Elks, Lions, and Masons
clubs—where gambling is a mainstay. Gambling nights at the different clubs vary in frequency. The largest and most exclusive
country club in Rainfall West has a funtime once a month at which
one can find every conceivable variety of gambling and a limited,
but fairly sophisticated, selection of pornography. Although admission is presumably limited to members of the club, it is relatively easy to gain entrance simply by joining with a temporary
membership, paying a two dollar fee at the door. Other clubs, such
as the local fraternal organizations, have pinball machines present
at all times; some also provide slot machines. Many of these clubs
have ongoing poker and other gambling card games, run by

people who work for the crime cabal. In all of these cases, the vices cater exclusively to middle and upper class clients.

Not all the business and professional men in Rainfall West partake of the vices. Indeed, some of the leading citizens sincerely oppose the presence of vice in their city. Even larger [numbers] of the middle and working classes are adamant in their opposition to vice of all kinds. On occasion, they make their views forcefully known to the politicians and law enforcement officers, thus requiring these public officials to express their own opposition and appear to be snuffing out vice by enforcing the law.

The law enforcement system is thus placed squarely in the middle of two essentially conflicting demands. On the one hand, their job obligates them to enforce the law, albeit with discretion; at the same time, considerable disagreement rages over whether or not some acts should be subject to legal sanction. This conflict is heightened by the fact that some influential persons in the community insist that all laws be rigorously enforced while others demand that some laws not be enforced, at least not against themselves.

Faced with such a dilemma and such an ambivalent situation, the law enforcers do what any well-managed bureaucracy would do under similar circumstances—they follow the line of least resistance. Using the discretion inherent in their positions, they resolve the problem by establishing procedures which minimize organizational strains and which provide the greatest promise of rewards for the organization and the individuals involved. Typically, this means that law enforcers adopt a tolerance policy toward the vices, selectively enforcing these laws only when it is to their advantage to do so. Since the persons demanding enforcement are generally middle-class persons who rarely venture into the less prosperous sections of the city, the enforcers can control visibility and minimize complaints by merely regulating the ecological location of the vices. Limiting the visibility of such activity as sexual deviance, gambling, and prostitution appeases those persons who demand the enforcement of applicable laws. At the same time, since controlling visibility does not eliminate access for persons sufficiently interested to ferret out the tolerated vice areas, those demanding such services are also satisfied.

This policy is also advantageous because it renders the legal system capable of exercising considerable control over potential sources of real trouble. For example, since gambling and prostitution are profitable, competition among persons desiring to provide these services is likely. Understandably, this competition is prone to become violent. If the legal system cannot control those running these vices, competing groups may well go to war to obtain dominance over the rackets. If, however, the legal system cooperates with one group, there will be a sufficient concentration of power to avoid these uprisings. Similarly, prostitution can be kept clean if the law enforcers cooperate with the prostitutes; the law can thus minimize the chance, for instance, that a prostitute will steal money from a customer. In this and many other ways, the law enforcement system maximizes its visible effectiveness by creating and supporting a shadow government that manages the vices.

Initially this may require bringing in people from other cities to help set up the necessary organizational structure. Or it may mean recruiting and training local talent or simply coopting, coercing, or purchasing the knowledge and skills of entrepreneurs who are at the moment engaged in vice operations. When made, this move often involves considerable strain, since some of those brought in may be uncooperative. Whatever the particulars, the ultimate result is the same: a syndicate emerges—composed of politicians, law enforcers, and citizens—capable of supplying and controlling the vices in the city. The most efficient cabal is invariably one that contains representatives of all the leading centers of power. Businessmen must be involved because of their political influence and their ability to control the mass media. This prerequisite is illustrated by the case of a fledgling magazine which published an article intimating that several leading politicians were corrupt. Immediately major advertisers canceled their advertisements in the magazine. One large chain store refused to sell that issue of the magazine in any of its stores. And when one of the leading cabal members was accused of accepting bribes, a number of the community's most prominent businessmen sponsored a large advertisement declaring their unfailing support for and confidence in the integrity of this "outstanding public servant."

The cabal must also have the cooperation of businessmen in procuring the loans which enable them individually and collectively to purchase legitimate businesses, as well as to expand the vice enterprises. A member of the banking community is therefore a considerable asset. In Rainfall West the vice president of one of the local banks (who was an investigator for a federal law enforcement agency before he entered banking) is a willing and knowledgeable participant in business relations with cabal members. He not only serves on the board of directors of a loan agency controlled by the cabal, but also advises cabal members on how to keep their earnings a secret. Further he sometimes serves as a go-between, passing investment tips from the cabal on to other businessmen in the community. In this way the cabal serves the economic interests of businessmen indirectly as well as directly.

The political influence of the cabal is more directly obtained. Huge, tax-free profits make it possible for the cabal to generously support political candidates of its choice. Often the cabal assists both candidates in an election, thus assuring itself of influence regardless of who wins. While usually there is a favorite, ultracooperative candidate who receives the greater proportion of the contributions, everyone is likely to receive something.

THE BUREAUCRACY

Contrary to the prevailing myth that universal rules govern bureaucracies, the fact is that in day-to-day operations rules can and must—be selectively applied. As a consequence, some degree of corruption is not merely a possibility, but rather is a virtual certainty which is built into the very structure of bureaucratic organizations.

The starting point for understanding this structural invitation to corruption is the observation that application of all the rules and procedures comprising the foundation of an organization inevitably admits of a high degree of discretion. Rules can only specify what should be done when the actions being considered fall clearly into unambiguously specifiable categories, about which there can be no reasonable grounds of disagreement or conflicting interpretation. But such categories are a virtual impossibility, given the inherently ambiguous nature of language. Instead, most events fall within the penumbra of the bureaucratic rules where the discretion of office-holders must hold sway.

Since discretionary decisionmaking is recognized as inevitable in effect, all bureaucratic decisions become subject to the discretionary will of the office-holder. Moreover, if one has a reason to look, vagueness and ambiguity can be found in any rule, no matter how carefully stipulated. And if ambiguity and vagueness are not sufficient to justify particularistic criteria being applied, contradictory rules or implications of rules can be readily located which have the same effect of justifying the decisions which, for whatever reason the office-holder wishes, can be used to enforce his position. Finally, since organizations characteristically develop their own set of common practices which take on the status of rules (whether written or unwritten), the entire process of applying rules becomes totally dependent on the discretion of the office-holder. The bureaucracy thus has its own set of precedents which can be invoked in cases where the articulated rules do not provide precisely the decision desired by the office-holder.

Ultimately, the office-holder has license to apply rules derived from a practically bottomless set of choices. Individual self-interest then depends on one's ability to ingratiate himself to office-holders at all levels in order to ensure that the rules most useful to him are applied. The bureaucracy therefore is not a rational institution with universal standards, but is instead, irrational and particularistic. It is a type of organization in which the organization's reason for being is displaced by a set of goals that often conflict with the organization's presumed purposes. This is precisely the consequence of the organizational response to the dilemma created by laws prohibiting the vices. Hence, the bureaucratic nature of law enforcement and political organization makes possible the corruption of the legal-political bureaucracy.

In the case of Rainfall West the goal of maintaining a smooth functioning organization takes precedence over all other institutional goals. Where conflict arises between the long-range goals of the law and the short-range goal of sustaining the organization, the former lose out, even at the expense of undermining the socially agreed-upon purposes for which the organization presumably exists.

Yet, the law-enforcement agency's tendency to follow the line of least resistance of maintaining organizational goals in the face of conflicting demands necessarily embodies a choice as to whose demands will be followed. For bureaucracies are not equally susceptible to all interests in the society. They do not fear the castigation, interference, and disruptive potential of the alcoholics on skid row or the cafe-owners in the slums. In fact, some residents of the black ghetto in Rainfall West and of other lower-class areas of the city have been campaigning for years to rid their communities of the gambling casinos, whorehouses, pornography stalls, and bookmaking operations. But these pleas fall on deaf ears. The letters they write and the committees they form receive no publicity and create no stir in the smoothly functioning organizations that occupy the political and legal offices of the city. On the other hand, when the president of a large corporation in the city objected to the "slanderous lies" being spread about one of the leading members of the crime cabal in Rainfall West, the magazine carrying the "lies" was removed from newstand sale, and the editors lost many of their most profitable advertisers. Similarly, when any question of the honesty or integrity of policemen, prosecuting attorneys, or judges involved in the cabal is raised publicly, it is either squelched before aired (the editor of the leading daily newspaper in Rainfall West is a long-time friend of one of the cabal's leading members) or it arouses the denial of influential members of the banking community (especially those bankers whose institutions loan money to cabal members), as well as leading politicians, law enforcement officers, and the like.

In short, bureaucracies are susceptible to differential influence, according to the economic and political power of the groups attempting to exert influence. Since every facet of politics and the mass media is subject to reprisals by cabal members and friends, exposition of the ongoing relationship between the cabal and the most powerful economic groups in the city is practically impossible.

The fact that the bureaucrats must listen to the economic elites of the city and not the have-nots is then one important element that stimulates the growth and maintenance of a crime cabal. But the links between the elites and the cabal are more than merely spiritual. The economic elite of the city does not simply play golf with the political and legal elite. There are in fact significant economic ties between the two groups.

The most obvious nexus is manifested by the campaign contributions from the economic elite to the political and legal elites. We need not dwell on this observation here; it has been well documented in innumerable other studies.[6] However, what is not well

---

[6] See generally W. Domhoff, *Who Rules America?* (1969); Overa, *Presidential Campaign Funds* (1946); J. Shannon, *Money and Politics* (1959); Overa, *Money in Elections* (1932); Bernstein, "Private Wealth and Public Office: The High Cost of Campaigning," 22 *The Nation* 77 (1966).

recognized is that the crime cabal is itself an important source of economic revenue for the economic elite. In at least one instance, the leading bankers and industrialists of the city were part of a multi-million dollar stock swindle engineered and manipulated by the crime cabal with the assistance of confidence-men from another state. This entire case was shrouded in such secrecy that eastern newspapers were calling people at the University of Rainfall West to find out why news about the scandal was not forthcoming from local wire services. When the scandal was finally exposed, the fact that industrialists and cabal members heavily financed the operation (and correspondingly reaped the profits) was conveniently ignored in the newspapers and the courts; the evil-doers were limited to the outsiders who were in reality the front men for the entire confidence operation.

In a broader sense, key members of the economic elite in the community are also members of the cabal. While the day-to-day, week-to-week operations of the cabal are determined by the criminal-political-legal elite, the economic elite benefits mightily from the cabal. Not surprisingly, any threat to the cabal is quickly squelched by the economic elite under the name of "concerned citizens," which indeed they are.

The crime cabal is thus an inevitable outgrowth of the political economy of American cities. The ruling elites from every sphere benefit economically and socially from the presence of a smoothly running cabal. Law enforcement and government bureaucracies function best when a cabal is part of the governmental structure. And the general public is satisfied when control of the vices gives an appearance of respectability, but a reality of availability.

VICE IN RAINFALL WEST

The vices available in Rainfall West are varied and tantalizing. Gambling ranges from bookmaking (at practically every street corner in the center of the city) to open poker games, bingo parlors, off-track betting, casinos, roulette and dice games (concentrated in a few locations and also floating out into the suburban country clubs and fraternal organizations), and innumerable two and five dollar stud-poker games scattered liberally throughout the city.

The most conspicuous card games take place from about ten in the morning—varying slightly from one fun house to the next—until midnight. A number of other twenty-four hour games run constantly. In the more public games, the limit ranges from one to five dollars for each bet; in the more select twenty-four hours a day games, there is a pot limit or no limit rule. These games are reported to have betting as high as twenty and thirty thousand dollars. I saw a bet made and called for a thousand dollars in one of these games. During this game, the highest stakes game I witnessed in the six years of the study, the police lieutenant in charge of the vice squad was called in to supervise the game—not, need I add, to break up the game or make any arrests, but only to insure against violence.

Prostitution covers the usual range of ethnic group, age, shape, and size of female. It is found in houses with madams *à la* the New Orleans stereotype, on the street through pimps, or in suburban apartment buildings and hotels. Prices range from five dollars for a short time with a streetwalker to two hundred dollars for a night with a lady who has her own apartment (which she usually shares with her boyfriend who is discreetly gone during business operations).

High interest loans are easy to arrange through stores that advertise, "your signature is worth $5,000." It is really worth considerably more; it may in fact be worth your life. The interest rates vary from a low of 20 percent for three months to as high as 100 percent for varying periods. Repayment is demanded not through the courts, but through the help of "The Gaspipe Gang," who call on recalcitrant debtors and use physical force to bring about payment. "Interest only" repayment is the most popular alternative practiced by borrowers and is preferred by the loan sharks as well. The longer repayment can be prolonged, the more advantageous the loan is to the agent.

Pinball machines are readily available throughout the city, most of them paying off in cash.

The gambling, prostitution, drug distribution, pornography, and usury which flourish in the lower-class center of the city do so with the compliance, encouragement, and cooperation of the major political and law enforcement officials in the city. There is in fact a symbiotic relationship between the law enforcement-political organizations of the city and a group of *local,* as distinct from national, men who control the distribution of vices.

CORRUPTION IN RAINFALL WEST

In the spring of 19— a businessman whom I shall call Mr. Van Meter sold his restaurant and began looking for a new investment when he noticed an advertisement in the paper which read: "Excellent investment opportunity for someone with $30,000 cash to purchase the good will and equipment of a long established restaurant in down town area. . . ." After making the necessary inquiries, inspecting the business, and evaluating its potential, Mr. Van Meter purchased it. In addition to the restaurant, the business consisted of a card room which was legally licensed by the city, operating under a publicly acknowledged tolerance policy which allowed card games, including poker, to be played. These games were limited by the tolerance policy to a maximum one dollar limit for each bet.

Thus, Mr. Van Meter had purchased a restaurant with a built-in criminal enterprise. It was never clear whether he was, at the time of purchasing the business, fully aware of the criminal nature of the card room. Certainly the official tolerance policy was bound to create confusion over the illegality of gambling in the licensed card rooms. The full extent to which this purchase involved Mr. Van Meter in illegal activities crystallized immediately upon purchase of the property.[7]

[W]e had just completed taking the inventory of [the restaurant]. I was then handed the $60,000 keys of the premises by Mr. Bataglia, and he approached me and said, "Up until now, I have never discussed with you the fact that we run a bookmaking operation here, and that we did not sell this to you; however if you wish to have this operation continue here, you must place another $5,000 to us, and we will count you in. Now, if you do not buy it, we will put out this bookmaking operation, and you will go broke." "In other words," Mr. Bataglia continued, "we will use you, and you need us." I told Mr. Bataglia that I did not come to this town to bookmake or to operate any form of rackets, and I assumed that I had purchased a legitimate business. Mr. Bataglia said, "You have purchased a legitimate business; however, you must have the bookmaking operation in order to survive." I promptly kicked him out of the place.

The question of how "legitimate" the business Mr. Van Meter had purchased was is not so simple as he thought. It was, to be

---

[7] All quotations are from taped interviews. The names of persons and places are fictitious.

sure, a licensed operation; there was a license to operate the restaurant, a license to operate the card room attached to the restaurant, and a license to operate the cigar stand (where much of the bookmaking operation had taken place before Mr. Van Meter purchased the place). These licenses, although providing a "legitimate business," also had the effect of making the owner of the business constantly in violation of the law, for the laws were so constructed that no one could possibly operate a "legitimate" business "legally." Thus, anyone operating the business was vulnerable to constant harassment and even closure by the authorities if he failed to cooperate with law enforcement personnel.

The card room attached to the business was the most flagrant example of a legitimate enterprise that was necessarily run illegally. The city of Rainfall West had adopted by ordinance a tolerance policy toward gambling. This tolerance policy consisted of permitting card rooms, which were then licensed by the city, pinball machines that paid off money to winners, and panorama shows. The city ordinance allowed a maximum one dollar bet at the card table in rooms such as those in Mr. Van Meter's restaurant.

This ordinance was in clear and open violation of state law. The State Attorney General had publicly stated that the tolerance policy of the city was illegal and that the only policy for the state was that all gambling was illegal. Despite these rulings from higher state officials, the tolerance policy continued and flourished in the city, although it did so illegally.

This general illegality of the card room was not, however, easily enforceable against any one person running a card room without enforcement against all persons running card rooms. There were, however, wrinkles in the tolerance policy ordinance which made it possible discriminately to close down one card room without being forced to take action against all of them. This was accomplished in part by the limit of one dollar on a bet. The card room was allowed to take a certain percentage of the pot from each game, but the number of people playing and the amount of percentage permitted did not allow one to make a profit if the table limit remained at one dollar. Furthermore, since most people gambling wanted to bet more, they would not patronize a card room that insisted on the one dollar limit. Mr. Van Meter, like all other card room operators, allowed a two to five dollar limit. The ordinance was written in such a way that, in reality, everyone would be in violation of it. It was therefore possible for the police to harass or close down whatever card rooms they chose at their own discretion.

The health and fire regulations of the city were also written in such a way that no one could comply with all the ordinances. It was impossible to serve meals and still avoid violation of the health standards required. Thus, when the health or fire department chose to enforce the rules, they could do so selectively against whatever business they chose.

The same set of circumstances governed the cabaret licenses in the city. The city ordinances required that every cabaret have a restaurant attached; the restaurant, the ordinance stated, had to comprise at least 75 percent of the total floor space of the cabaret and restaurant combined. Since there was a much higher demand for cabarets than restaurants in the central section of the city, this meant that cabaret owners were bound by law to have restaurants attached, some of which would necessarily lose money. Moreover, these restaurants had to be extremely large in order to constitute 75 percent of the total floor space. For a one hundred square foot cabaret, an attached three hundred square foot restaurant was required. The cabaret owner's burden was further increased by an ordinance governing the use of entertainers in the cabaret, requiring that any entertainer be at least twenty-five feet from the nearest customer during her act. Plainly, the cabaret had to be absolutely gigantic to accommodate any customers after a twenty-five foot buffer zone encircled the entertainer. Combined with the requirement that this now very large cabaret had to have attached to it a restaurant three times as large, the regulatory scheme simply made it impossible to run a cabaret legally.

The effect of such ordinances was to give the police and the prosecuting attorney complete discretion in choosing who should operate gambling rooms, cabarets, and restaurants. This discretion was used to force pay offs to the police and cooperation with the criminal syndicate.

Mr. Van Meter discovered the pay off system fairly early in his venture:

I found shortages that were occurring in the bar, and asked an employee to explain them, which he did, in this manner: "The money is saved to pay the 'juice' of the place." I asked him what was the "juice." He said in this city you must "pay to stay." Mr. Davis said, "You pay for the beat-man [from the police department] $250 per month. That takes care of the various shifts, and you must pay the upper brass, also $200 each month. A beat-man collects around the first of each month, and another man collects for the upper brass. You get the privilege to stay in business." That is true; however, you must remember that it is not what they will do for you, but what they will do *to* you, if you don't make these payoffs as are ordered. "If I refuse, what then?" I asked. "The *least* that could happen to you is you will lose your business."

During the next three months, Mr. Van Meter made the payoffs required. He refused, however, to allow the bookmaking operation back into the building or to hire persons to run the card room and bar whom members of the organized crime syndicate and the police recommended to him for the job. He also fired one employee who he found was taking bets while tending bar.

In August of the same year, a man whom Mr. Van Meter had known prior to buying the restaurant met him in his office:

Mr. Danielski met with me in my office and he came prepared to offer me $500 per month—in cash deductions—of my remaining balance of the contract owing against [the restaurant] if I would give him the bookmaking operation, and he would guarantee me another $800 a month more business. He warned that if he wanted to give my establishment trouble, he would go to a certain faction of the police department; if he wanted me open, he would go to another faction. "So do some thinking on the subject, and I will be in on Monday for your answer." Monday, I gave Mr. Danielski his answer. The answer was no.

In June of 19—, a man by the name of Joe Link, who I found later was a second-string gang member of Mr. Bataglia's, made application to me to operate my card room. I did give him the opportunity to operate the card room because I had known him some twenty years ago when he was attending the same high school that I was. After I had refused the offer of Mr. Danielski, Mr. Joe Link had received orders from Mr. Danielski and Mr. Bataglia to run my customers out and in any way he could, cripple my operation to bring me to terms. I terminated Mr. Link on November 6, 19—, and shortly after, after I had removed Mr. Link, Police Officer Herb C. conferred with me in my office, and Officer Herb C. said that I had better re-appoint Mr. Link in my card room; that his superiors were not happy with me. If I did not return Mr. Link to his former position, then it would be necessary to clear anyone that I wanted to replace Mr. Link with. Officer C. felt that no one else would be acceptable. He further stated I had better make a decision soon, because he would not allow the card room to run without an approved boss. I informed Officer C. that I would employ anyone I chose in my card room or in any other department. Officer C. said, "Mr. Van Meter, you, I think, do not realize how powerful a force you will be fighting or how deep in City Hall this reaches. Even I am not let know all the bosses or where the money goes." I did not return Mr. Link, as I was ordered by Officer C., and I did select my own card room bosses.

On November 7, 19—, I received a phone call stating that I soon would have a visitor who was going to shoot me between the eyes if I did not comply with the demands to return Mr. Link to his former position.

The crime cabal in Rainfall West (including police officers, politicians, and members of the organized criminal syndicate), like the criminal law which underpins it, relies on the threat of coercion to maintain order. That threat, however, is not an empty one. Although Mr. Van Meter was not "shot between the eyes" as threatened, others who defied the cabal were less fortunate. Although it has never been established that any of the suspicious deaths that have taken place involving members of the crime cabal were murder, the evidence, nonetheless, points rather strongly in that direction. Eric Tandlin, former county auditor for Rainfall West, is but one of thirteen similar cases which occurred from 1955 to 1969.

Tandlin had been county auditor for seventeen years. He kept his nose clean, did the bidding of the right politicians, and received a special gift every Christmas for his cooperation. In the course of doing business with the politicians and criminals, he also developed extensive knowledge of the operations. Suddenly, without warning or expectation on his part, Eric was not supported by his party, for re-election as auditor, losing the nomination to the brother-in-law of the chief of police. It was a shock from which Eric did not soon recover. He began drinking heavily and frequenting the gambling houses; he also began talking a great deal. One Friday evening, he made friends with a reporter who promised to put him in touch with someone from the attorney general's office. Saturday night at 6:30, just as the card rooms were being prepared for the evening, word spread through the grapevine along First Street that Eric had been done in: "Danielski took Eric for a walk down by the bay."

The Sunday morning paper carried a small front page story:

Eric Tandlin aged forty-seven was found drowned in back bay yesterday at around 5:00 p.m. The Coroner's office listed the cause of death as possible suicide. Friends said Mr. Tandlin who had been county auditor for many years until his defeat in the primaries last fall had been despondent over his failure to be re-elected.

The coroner, who was the brother-in-law of the chief of police, described the probable cause of death as "suicide." The people of Miriam Street knew better. They also knew that this was a warning not to talk to reporters, sociologists, or anyone else "nosing around." In the last few years the cabal has been responsible for the deaths of several of its members. Drowning is a favorite method of eliminating troublemakers, because it is difficult to ascertain whether or not the person fell from a boat by accident, was held under water by someone else, or committed suicide.[8] L.S., who was in charge of a portion of the pinball operations, but who came into disfavor with the cabal, was found drowned at the edge of a lake near his home. J.B., an assistant police chief who had been a minor member of the cabal for years, drowned while on a fishing trip aboard one of the yachts owned by a leading member of the cabal. In both instances the coroner, who was the brother-in-law of one of the leading cabal members, diagnosed the deaths as "accidental drownings." Over the years, he has often made that diagnosis when cabal members or workers in the organization have met with misfortune.

Other deaths have been arranged in more traditional ways. At least one man, for example, was shot in an argument in a bar. The offender was tried before a judge who has consistently shown great compassion for any crimes committed by members of the cabal (although he has compensated for this leniency with cabal members by being unusually harsh in cases against blacks who appear before him), and the case was dismissed for lack of evidence.

However, murder is not the preferred method of handling uncooperative people. Far better, in the strategy of the crime cabal, is the time-honored technique of blackmail and cooptation. The easiest and safest tactic is to purchase the individual for a reasonable amount, as was attempted with Mr. Van Meter. If this fails, then some form of blackmail or relatively minor coercion may be in order.

---

[8] According to one informant: "Murder is the easiest crime of all to get away with. There are 101 ways to commit murder that are guaranteed to let you get away with it." He might have added that this was especially true when the coroner, the prosecuting attorney, and key police officials were cooperating with the murderers.

For instance, Sheriff McCallister was strongly supported by the cabal in his bid for office. Campaign contributions were generously provided since McCallister was running against a local lawyer who was familiar with the goings-on of the cabal and had vowed to attack its operations. McCallister won the election—cabal candidates almost never lose local elections—but underwent a dramatic change-of-heart shortly thereafter. He announced in no uncertain terms that he would not permit the operation of gambling houses in the county, although he did not intend to do anything about the operations within the city limits since that was not his jurisdiction. Nevertheless, the county, he insisted, would be kept clean.

The cabal was as annoyed as it was surprised. The county operations were only a small portion of the total enterprise, but they were nonetheless important, and no one wanted to give up the territory. Further, the prospect of closing down the lay-off center operating in the county was no small matter. The center is crucial to the entire enterprise, because it is here that the results of horse races and other sports events come directly to the bookmakers. The center also enables the cabal to protect itself against potential bankruptcy. When the betting is particularly heavy in one direction, bets are laid off by wiring Las Vegas where the national betting pattern always takes care of local variations. Clearly, something had to be done about McCallister.

No man is entirely pure, and McCallister was less pure than many. He had two major weaknesses: gambling and young girls. One weekend shortly after he took office a good friend of his asked if he would like to go to Las Vegas for the weekend. He jumped at the opportunity. While the weekend went well in some respects, McCallister was unlucky at cards. When he flew back to Rainfall West Sunday night, he left $14,000 worth of IOUs in Las Vegas.

Monday morning one of the cabal chiefs visited McCallister in his office. The conversation went like this:

Say, Mac, I understand you was down in Vegas over the weekend.
Yeah.
Hear you lost a little bit at the tables, Mac.
Uuh-huh.
Well the boys wanted me to tell you not to worry about those pieces of paper you left. We got them back for you.

I don't. . . .

Also, Mac, we thought you might like to have a momento of your trip; so we brought you these pictures. . . .

The "momentos" were pictures of McCallister in a hotel room with several young girls. Thereafter things in the county returned to normal.

Lest one think the cabal exploitative, it should be noted that McCallister was not kept in line by the threat of exposure alone. He was, in fact, subsequently placed on the payroll in the amount of $1,000 a month. When his term as sheriff was over, an appointment was arranged for him to the state parole board. He was thus able to continue serving the cabal in a variety of ways for the rest of his life. Cooperation paid off much better than would have exposure.

Threats from outside the organization are more rare than are threats from within. Nevertheless, they occur and must be dealt with in the best possible way. Since no set strategy exists, each incident is handled in its own way. During Robert Kennedy's days as attorney general, the federal attorney for the state began a campaign to rid the state of the members of the cabal. People who held political office were generally immune, but some of the higher-ups in the operational section of the cabal were indicted. Ultimately five members of the cabal, including a high ranking member of the local Teamsters' Union, were sentenced to prison. The entire affair was scandalous; politicians whose lives depended on the cabal fought the nasty business with all their power. They were able to protect the major leaders of the cabal and to avert exposure of the cabal politicians. However, some blood ran, and it was a sad day for the five sentenced to prison terms. Yet the organization remained intact and, indeed, the five men who went to prison continued to receive their full share of profits from the cabal enterprises. Corruption continued unabated, and the net effect on organized crime in the state was nil.

One reason that Mr. Van Meter was not "shot between the eyes" was that, although not fully cooperative, he was nonetheless paying in to the cabal $450 a month in "juice." Eventually he cut down on these payments. When this happened Mr. Van Meter became a serious problem for the cabal, and something more than mere threats was necessary:

No extortion was paid by me directly to them, but it involved a third party. Some time shortly after the first of each month, the sum of $250 was paid to [the above-mentioned] Officer C., which he presumably divided up with other patrolmen on the beat. Two hundred dollars each month was given to [another bagman] for what the boys termed as "It was going to the upper braid." The $200 per month was paid each month from June 19— with payment of $200 being made in January 19—. After that I refused to make further payments. . . . After some wrangling back and forth, I just told them that I would not pay any more. They said, "Well, we will take $100 per month on a temporary basis. I paid $100 per month for the next twelve months. Early the next year I had planned to cut off all payments to the patrolmen. . . . About the 8th of July the explosion occurred. Police officers Merrill and Lynch conducted a scare program; jerked patrons off stools, ran others out of my establishment; Patrolman Lynch ordered my card room floorman into the rest room; and ordered my card room closed. When my floorman came out of the rest room, he left white and shaking and never to be seen in the city again.

Following this incident, Mr. Van Meter met with his attorney, the chief of police, and a former mayor. Although the meeting was cordial, he was told they could do nothing unless he could produce affidavits substantiating his claims. He did so, but quickly became enmeshed in requests and demands for more affidavits, while the prosecuting attorney's office resisted cooperating.

The refusal of cooperation from the prosecuting attorney was not surprising. What Mr. Van Meter did not realize was that the prosecuting attorney was the key political figure behind the corruption of the legal and political machinery. He was also the political boss of the county and had great influence on state politics, coming as he did from the most populous area of the state. Over the years his influence had been used to place men in key positions throughout the various government bureaucracies, including the police department, the judiciary, the city council, and relevant governmental agencies such as the tax office and the licensing bureau.

There was, however, a shift in emphasis for a short time in the cabal's dealings with Mr. Van Meter. They offered to buy his business at the price he had paid for it. But when he refused, the pace of harassment increased. Longshoremen came into his restaurant and started fights. Police stood around the card room day and night observing. City health officials would come to inspect the cooking area during mealtimes, thereby delaying the food being served to customers; the fire department made frequent visits to inspect fire precautions. On several occasions, Mr. Van Meter was cited for violating health and safety standards.

Finally, he was called to the city council to answer an adverse police report stating that he allowed drunks and brawling in his establishment. At the hearing, he was warned that he would lose all of his licenses if a drunk were ever again found in his restaurant.

During the next six months, the pressure on Mr. Van Meter continued at an ever-increasing rate. Longshoremen came into the restaurant and card room and picked fights with customers, employees, and Mr. Van Meter himself. The health department chose five o'clock in the evening several days running to inspect the health facilities of the establishment. The fire inspector came at the lunch hour to inspect the fire equipment, writing up every minor defect detectable. Toward the end of Mr. Van Meter's attempt to fight the combine of the government, the police force, and the criminal syndicate, he received innumerable threats to his life. Bricks and stones were thrown through the windows of his building. Ultimately, he sold his business back to the man from whom he had purchased it at a loss of $30,000 and left the city.

The affair caused considerable consternation among the legal-political-criminal cabal which controlled and profited from the rackets in Rainfall West. In the "good old days" the problem would have been quickly solved, one informant remarked, "by a bullet through the fat slob's head." But ready resort to murder as a solution to problems was clearly frowned upon by the powers that operated organized crime in Rainfall West. Although the syndicate had been responsible for many murders over the past ten years, these murders were limited to troublesome persons *within* the syndicate. As nearly as could be determined, no outsider had been murdered for a number of years.

Overall the gambling, bookmaking, pinball, and usury operations grossed at least $25,000,000 a year in the city alone. It was literally the case that drunks were arrested on the street for public intoxication while gamblers made thousands of dollars and policemen accepted bribes five feet away.

Payoffs, bribes, and associated corruption were not limited

solely to illegal activities. To obtain a license for tow-truck operations one had to pay $10,000 to the licensing bureau; a license for
a taxi franchise cost $15,000. In addition, taxi drivers who sold
bootleg liquor (standard brand liquors sold after hours or on Sunday) or who would steer customers to prostitutes or gambling
places, paid the beat policeman and the sergeant of the vice squad.
Tow-truck operators also paid the policeman who called the company when an accident occurred.

As one informant commented:

When I would go out on a call from a policeman I would always carry
matchbooks with three dollars tucked behind the covers. I would hand
this to the cops when I came to the scene of the accident.
Q. Did every policeman accept these bribes?
A. No. Once in a while you would run into a cop who would say he
wasn't interested. But that was rare. Almost all of them would take
it.

Most of the cabarets, topless bars, and taverns were owned
either directly or indirectly by members of the organized crime
syndicate. Thus, the syndicate not only controlled the gambling
enterprises, but also "legitimate" businesses associated with night
life as well. In addition, several of the hotels and restaurants were
also owned by the syndicate. Ownership of these establishments
was disguised in several ways, such as placing them formally in the
name of a corporation with a board of directors who were really
front-men for the syndicate or placing them in the names of relatives of syndicate members. It should further be underlined that
the official ownership by the syndicate must be interpreted to
mean by all of the members who were in the political and legal
bureaucracies and simultaneously members of the syndicate, as
well as those who were solely involved in the day-to-day operations
of the vice syndicate.

The governing board of the syndicate consisted of seven men,
four of whom held high positions in the government and three of
whom were responsible for the operation of the various enterprises. The profits were split among these seven men. We are *not*
then talking about a syndicate that paid off officials, but about a
syndicate that is part and parcel of the government, although not
subject to election.

CONCLUSION

There is abundant data indicating that what is true in Rainfall West is true in virtually every city in the United States and has been true since at least the early 1900s. Writing at the turn of the century, Lincoln Steffens observed that "the spirit of graft and of lawlessness is the American spirit." He went on to describe the results of his inquiries:

in the very first study—St. Louis—the startling truth lay bare that corruption was not merely political; it was financial, commercial, social; the ramifications of boodle were so complex, various and far-reaching, that our mind could hardly grasp them. . . . St. Louis exemplified boodle; Minneapolis Police graft; Pittsburgh a political and industrial machine; Philadelphia general civil corruption. . . .[9]

In 1931, after completing an inquiry into the police, the National Commission on Law Observance and Enforcement concluded:

Nearly all of the large cities suffer from an alliance between politicians and criminals. For example, Los Angeles was controlled by a few gamblers for a number of years. San Francisco suffered similarly some years ago and at one period in its history was so completely dominated by the gamblers that three prominent gamblers who were in control of the politics of the city and who quarrelled about the appointment of the police chief settled their quarrel by shaking dice to determine who would name the chief for the first two years, who for the second two years, and who for the third.

Recently the gamblers were driven out of Detroit by the commissioner. These gamblers were strong enough politically to oust this commissioner from office despite the fact that he was recognized by police chiefs as one of the strongest and ablest police executives in America. For a number of years Kansas City, Mo., was controlled by a vice ring and no interference with their enterprises was tolerated. Chicago, *despite its unenviable reputation,* is but one of numerous cities where the people have frequently been betrayed by their elected officials.[10]

Frank Tannenbaum once noted:

It is clear from the evidence at hand—that a considerable measure of the crime in the community is made possible and perhaps inevitable by the

---

[9] See L. Steffens, *The Shame of the Cities* 151 (1904).

[10] Garrett & Monroe, "Police Conditions in the United States," 14 *National Commission on Law Observance and Enforcement Report on Police* 45 (1931).

peculiar connection that exists between the political organizations of our large cities and the criminal activities of various gangs that are permitted and even encouraged to operate.[11]

Similarly, the Kefauver Commission summarized the results of its extensive investigation into organized crime in 1951:

1. There is a nationwide crime syndicate known as the Mafia, whose tentacles are found in many large cities. It has international ramifications which appear most clearly in connection with the narcotics traffic.
2. Its leaders are usually found in control of the most lucrative rackets in their cities.
3. There are indications of centralized direction and control of these rackets, but leadership appears to be in a group rather than in a single individual.[12]

And in 1969, Donald R. Cressey, using data gathered from the attorney general of the United States and local crime commissions, capsulized the state of organized crime in the United States:

In the United States, criminals have managed to put together an organization which is at once a nationwide illicit cartel and a nationwide confederation. This organization is dedicated to amassing millions of dollars by means of extortion, and from usury, the illicit sale of lottery tickets, chances on the outcome of horse races and athletic events, narcotics and untaxed liquor.[13]

The frequency of major scandals linking organized criminals with leading political and legal figures suggests the same general conclusion. Detroit, Chicago, Denver, Reading, Pennsylvania, Columbus and Cleveland, Ohio, Miami, New York, Boston, and a horde of other cities have been scandalized and cleansed innumerable times.[14] Yet organized crime persists and, in fact, thrives. Despite periodic forays, exposures, and reform movements prompted by journalists, sociologists, and politicians, organized crime has become an institution in the United States and in many other parts of the world as well.[15]

---

[11] F. Tannenbaum, *Crime and the Community* 128 (1938).

[12] *President's Commission on Law Enforcement and Administration of Justice, The Challenge of Crime in a Free Society* 7 (1967).

[13] D. Cressey, supra note 2. For a discussion of similar phenomena in Great Britain see N. Lucas, *Britain's Gangland* (1969). See also D. Bell, *The End of Ideology* (1960).

[14] Wilson, "The Police and Their Problems: A Theory," 12 *Pub. Policy* 189 (1963).

[15] See McMullen, "A Theory of Corruption," 9 *Soc. Rev.* 181 (1961).

Once established, the effect of a syndicate on the entire legal and political system is profound. Maintenance of order in such an organization requires the use of extra-legal procedures since, obviously, the law cannot always be relied on to serve the interests of the crime cabal. The law can harass uncooperative people; it can even be used to send persons to prison on real or faked charges. But to make discipline and obedience certain, it is often necessary to enforce the rules of the syndicate in extra-legal ways. To avoid detection of these procedures, the police, prosecuting attorney's office, and judiciary must be organized in ways that make them incapable of discovering events that the cabal does not want disclosed. In actual practice, policemen, prosecutors, and judges who are *not* members of the cabal must not be in a position to investigate those things that the syndicate does not want investigated. The military chain of command of the police is, of course, well-suited to such a purpose. So, in fact, is the availability of such subtle but nonetheless important sanctions as relegating uncooperative policemen to undesirable positions in the department. Conversely, cooperative policemen are rewarded with promotions, prestigious positions on the force, and of course a piece of the action.

Another consequence is widespread acceptance of petty graft. The matchbox fee for accident officers is but one illustration. Free meals and cigarettes, bottles of whiskey at Christmas, and the like are practically universal in the police department. Television sets, cases of expensive whiskey, and on occasion new automobiles or inside information on investments are commonplace in the prosecuting attorney's office.

Significantly, the symbiotic relationship between organized crime and the legal system not only negates the law enforcement function of the law vis-à-vis these types of crimes but actually increases crime in a number of ways. Perhaps most important, gradual commitment to maintaining the secrecy of the relationship in turn necessitates the commission of crimes other than those involved in the vices per se. At times, it becomes necessary to intimidate through physical punishment and even to murder recalcitrant members of the syndicate. Calculating the extent of such activities is risky business. From 1955 to 1969 in Rainfall West, a conservative estimate of the number of persons killed by the syndicate is fifteen. However, estimates range as high as "hundreds."

Although such information is impossible to verify in a manner that creates confidence, it is virtually certain that some murders have been perpetrated by the syndicate in order to protect the secrecy of its operations. It is also certain that the local law enforcement officials, politicians and businessmen involved with the syndicate have cooperated in these murders.

The location of the vices in the ghettos and slums of the city may well contribute to a host of other types of criminality as well. The disdain which ghetto residents have for the law and law enforcers is likely derived from more than simply their own experiences with injustice and police harassment. Their day-to-day observations that criminal syndicates operate openly and freely in their areas with complete immunity from punishment, while persons standing on a corner or playing cards in an apartment are subject to arrest, cannot help but affect their perception of the legal system. We do not know that such observations undermine respect for and willingness to comply with the law, but that conclusion would not seem unreasonable.

It is no accident that whenever the presence of vice and organizations that provide the vices is exposed to public view by politicians, exposure is always couched in terms of organized crime. The question of corruption is conveniently left in the shadows. Similarly, it is no accident that organized crime is inevitably seen as consisting of an organization of criminals with names like Valachi, Genovese, and Joe Bonanno. Yet the data from the study of Rainfall West, as well as that of earlier studies of vice, make it abundantly clear that this analysis is fundamentally misleading.

I have argued, and I think the data demonstrate quite convincingly, that the people who run the organizations which supply the vices in American cities are members of the business, political, and law enforcement communities—not simply members of a criminal society. Furthermore, it is also clear from this study that corruption of political-legal organizations is a critical part of the lifeblood of the crime cabal. The study of organized crime is thus a misnomer; the study should consider corruption, bureaucracy, and power. By relying on governmental agencies for their information on vice and the rackets, social scientists and lawyers have inadvertently contributed to the miscasting of the issue in terms that are descriptively biased and theoretically sterile. Further, they have been diverted from sociologically interesting and important issues raised by the persistence of crime cabals. As a consequence, the real significance of the existence of syndicates has been overlooked; for instead of seeing these social entities as intimately tied to, and in symbiosis with, the legal and political bureaucracies of the state, they have emphasized the criminality of only a portion of those involved. Such a view contributes little to our knowledge of crime and even less to attempts at crime control.

14

A criminogenic market structure: The automobile industry*

Harvey A. Farberman

Sociologists have come under attack for ignoring the role powerful elites play in controlling society's central master institutions by establishing political and economic policies which set the structural conditions that cause other (lower level) people to commit crimes[1] (Gouldner, 1968, 1970; Quinney, 1970; Liazos, 1972; Taylor et al., 1974). My aim here is to suggest how one elite, namely, automobile manufacturers, creates a "criminogenic market structure"[2] by imposing upon their new car dealers a pricing

Author's note: I presented working notes for this paper at the Minnesota Symposium on Symbolic Interaction in June 1974, and at the annual meetings of the American Sociological Association in August 1974. I wish to thank Herbert Blumer, Norman K. Denzin, Erich Goode, Peter M. Hall, David R. Maines, Carolyn and Martin Needleman, Harold Orbach, and Gregory P. Stone for helpful comments.

* Reprinted from *The Sociological Quarterly* 16 (Autumn 1975), pp. 438–457.

[1] Typical explanations for this neglect include the observation that sociologists of deviance often work out of a symbolic interactionist perspective, and that this perspective has an ideological-theoretical bias which offers tacit support to power elites (Thio, 1973); that it has a philosophical-methodological bias which focuses attention on the passive, powerless individual and thus cannot conceptualize transcendent, unobservable, active groups (Schervish, 1973); and, finally, that it tends toward a grounded-emergent rather than a logico-theroretic style of theory construction and thus is vulnerable to the unequal power distribution embodied in everyday life and, consequently, has a conservative bias (Huber, 1973). For a reply to some of these points, see Stone et al. (1974).

[2] I borrow the term "criminogenic market" from Leonard and Weber (1970), who contend that the most useful conceptual approach to occupational crime is to see it as a *direct consequence of legally established market structure*. In the present study, by "criminogenic market structure" I mean the deliberate and lawful enactment of policies by those who manage economically concentrated and vertically integrated corporations and/or industries which coerce lower level (dependent) participants into unlawful acts. Those who set the conditions which cause others to commit unlawful acts remain nonculpable, while those

431

policy which requires high volume and low per unit profit. While this strategy gives the *manufacturer* increased total net aggregate profit (by achieving economies of scale and by minimizing direct competition among oligopolist "rivals"), it places the new car dealer in a financial squeeze by forcing him to constantly free-up and continuously recycle capital into fixed margin new car inventory. This squeeze sets in motion a downward spiral of illegal activities which (1) inclines the new car dealer to engage in compensatory profit taking through fraudulent service operations, (2) under certain conditions, generates a "kickback" system which enables used car managers of new car dealerships to exact graft from independent used car wholesalers, and (3) forces the independent used car wholesalers into illegal "short-sales" in order to generate unrecorded cash for kickback payments. I shall present the evidence which provides the grounding for this model as I came upon it in the research process. What follows, then, is a natural history which reconstructs the stages of my investigation.[3]

THE BASE SITE

My principal research site was a medium-sized used car wholesale operation located in an eastern metropolitan area.[4]

---

who perform under these conditions remain eminently culpable. A micro illustration suggestive of this approach was played out in the heavy electric industry where the U.S. government was able to show that a cartel existed among corporations which resulted in a price-fixing conspiracy. Nevertheless, the actual corporate officials who were indicted and convicted came from the second and third echelon of the corporate hierarchy and, upon exposure, were legally and morally disavowed by the first level echelon. Division heads and vice presidents were censured and repudiated by presidents and directors for contravening corporate policy. Those indicted and convicted, however, never for a moment thought of themselves as contravening corporate policy, nor of having done anything but what was expected of them—their jobs (Smith, 1961). Although this case describes activity *within* a corporation, I wish to extrapolate it to an entire industry. Thus, at the pinnacle of the economically concentrated auto industry sit four groups of manufacturers who control 92 percent of the new car market and who, on the distribution side of the industry, set economic conditions which control approximately 31,000 franchised new car dealers, approximately 4,000 used car wholesalers, and approximately 65,000 "independent" used car retailers. Despite the fact that those on the top cause the conditions which compel others into untoward patterns of action, they do not reap the public's wrath. At the same time that new car and used car dealers consistently trail far behind every other occupational grouping in terms of public esteem, there never has been a presidential administration—beginning with Franklin Roosevelt—without an automobile *manufacturing executive* in a cabinet or subcabinet position!

[3] For a discussion of this presentation format see H. Becker (1970: 37).

[4] For a breezy, journalistic description of the used car wholesaling scene see Levine (1968: 26–29). For sociological insight into various levels of the auto industry see: Brown (1973) for independent used car retailing; Vanderwicken (1972) for franchised new car dealing; and Robbins (1971) for manufacturing.

There are approximately 40 other wholesale operations in this area,[5] the top three of which sell between 6,000 and 8,000 cars per year.[6] My base operation, which sold 1,501 cars in 1971 and 2,124 in 1972,[7] carried a 125-car wholesale inventory and a repair shop at one location and a 25-car retail inventory at another location. There were 16 employees altogether, including three partners (an older one who runs the office and two younger ones who function as buyers), three additional buyers (who also sell wholesale when not on the road), a retail manager, a retail salesman, two shop workers, a bookkeeper, and two-to-five drivers. The firm also retains the services of a lawyer and an accountant.[8]

Entry into my principal research site and later into other operations was relatively easy, for during my high school and college days I had made pin money selling used cars on a lot owned by the older partner. Later I came across two old acquaintances from high school days who hustled cars when I did; one is now a new car agency general sales manager, and the other a partner in a "family-owned" new car dealership.

Although I was always more an observer than a participant, I increasingly was expected to answer phone calls, take messages, move cars around the wholesale lot, and deliver cars as part of a "caravan" with the regular drivers.[9] Eventually, I gained access to

---

[5] This figure derives from enumeration by wholesalers themselves. I was forced to rely on this source for three reasons. First, the appropriate State Departments of Motor Vehicles informed me that their statistical information does not distinguish between new and used and wholesale and retail dealers. Nevertheless, they intend to introduce such breakdowns within the next few years. Second, the *U.S. Bureau of the Census, County Business Patterns, 1970* places fundamentally different *kinds* of wholesale automobile establishments into the same reporting category. Thus, wholesale body and fender shops, junk yards, auction sales, free-lance wholesalers, and regular wholesalers appear in the same category. Moreover, the census also includes businesses that are legally chartered in a state but not actually doing business there. Consequently, for my purposes the census was not helpful. Third, the various county Yellow Pages phone books in which used car wholesalers advertise did not allow me to distinguish "cut-book" wholesalers, who free lance and work out of their home addresses, from regular wholesalers, who have substantial business premises, a staff of employees, and sizeable inventories.

[6] This figure also comes from wholesalers themselves.

[7] I compiled these figures from the dealers' "Police Book." For each car in stock, dealers must enter 23 items of descriptive information. Detectives from the Motor Vehicle squad routinely inspect this book.

[8] Subsequent to the completion of my study, three more operations were opened: a retail lot with a 30-car capacity, a wholesale lot with a 40-car capacity, and a 12-stall body and fender shop. Each of these operations was situated on land or in buildings purchased by the corporation. The staff also increased with the addition of three more buyers, two retail salesmen, seven body and fender men, one mechanic, and a pool of part-time drivers which fluctuates from three to ten on any given day.

[9] For a discussion of the ratio of observation to participation see Gold (1958: 217–233).

all files. At about the same time the firm offered me a gasoline credit card, reimbursement for my private telephone bill, maintenance work on my own car, and drivers to pick me up at the airport when I returned from out-of-town trips. I did not decline the maintenance work or the airport service;[10] however, I did break off field appearances—but maintained social contact—when the firm adopted one of my opinions as the basis for its expansion policy, and it became clear that my role as an investigator had somehow given way to that of an advisor or consultant.

From December 1971 to August 1973, I spent an average of one day a week including evenings and weekends at my principal site, on the road, and at the homes of or out socializing with various members of my base organization and their families. Sometimes, though, I would hang around the lot for two or three consecutive days in order to get some sense of the continuity and rhythm of the operation. I always carried a notebook and, when necessary, made entries in full view of all present. I also tape-recorded extensive in-depth interviews with the consent of participants, but only when I knew more or less what I wanted information about, thus not abusing the privilege. These "formal" interviews allowed me to nail down—for the record—what I had observed, participated in, or been told during the course of everyday activity or conversation over the course of nearly two years. The insight and information gleaned from these informal conversations were the basis for the "formal" interviews, the first of which I held during the sixth month of my field appearances.

SERENDIPITY

I should note here that I did not start out to study a criminogenic market structure. Rather, I wanted to follow up on a

---

[10] During one of these trips, I parked my car—a small 1965 Buick Special—on the wholesale lot. As a gag, and in addition to whatever prudential motives may have been involved, the firm sold my car and with the proceeds put me into a large 1970 Oldsmobile. The firm, at considerable expense to itself, and, in the words of one of the partners, "felt that a Professor, who you also call Doctor, should drive around in a better car." At one and the same time the "gag" shows deference to my status, takes liberty with my property (albeit improves it), and coerces me into a more conventional status appearance. This gambit smacks of something approaching a hazing ritual. It is fun, yet it prepares the initiate for further entree into the club by manipulating him into club conventions. I imagine field workers often run this sort of gamut before they gain entrance into the secret place. Unhappily, these experiences usually remain unrecorded.

speculative hypothesis which grew out of some previous research on low income consumers (Farberman, 1968; Farberman and Weinstein, 1970). As a result of the latter study in particular, I had hypothesized that low income consumers strengthened their bargaining position vis-à-vis high status or expert sales or service people by changing the normative ground of the transaction from universalism to particularism, and thereby were able to coerce the expert other to respond as a concerned friend rather than as a mercenary stranger. Consequently, I began the present investigation to see if I could discover if people who bought used cars employed (wittingly or unwittingly) a set of bargaining tactics. I therefore observed over 50 transactions between retail customers and used car salesmen and, indeed, have been able to identify several bargaining tactics, associate them with distinct types of customers, and provide a theoretical interpretation.[11]

My interest in the systemic nature of occupational crime developed without my realizing it for sometimes, while I wrote up notes in the office after watching a sales transaction, I would vaguely overhear or observe the sales manager and customer "write-up" the deal. I began to notice that occasionally the customer would make out a check *as well as* hand over some cash. This was accompanied by the customer's saying how "taxes were killing the little man" and "if you didn't watch out, the Governor would bleed you to death." Out of simple curiosity I began *deliberately to observe* the "write-ups"—something I had originally paid no attention to since I thought the transaction was actually over after the bargain had been made and the salesman had "closed" the deal. It was at the "write-up," however, that a new research problem emerged, because what I had witnessed—and what, in fact, led me off in a new direction—was an instance of "selling short," or "a short-sale," an illegal act which constitutes the first link in a chain of activity that goes back to Detroit.[12] In the section which follows, I will describe (*a*) what a "short-sale" is; (*b*) how it benefits and

---

[11] See my forthcoming article "Coming-to-Terms: The Reconciliation of Divergent Meanings and Values in the Sale of Used Cars."

[12] Although my initial research problem situated me so that I luckily tripped over and recognized a new problem, the new problem actually links to the old problem so that my understanding of the dynamics of customer/salesman interaction is enlarged by my understanding of the systemic dynamics of "short sales." In fact, deliberate—as opposed to accidental—problem transformation may be integral to the methodology of contextual, vertical analysis.

costs both the retail customer and the dealer; and (c) why the dealer feels compelled to engage in it.

THE SHORT-SALE

A "short-sale" begins to develop when a retail customer observes the sales manager compute and add on to the selling price of the car the state sales tax—a hefty 8 percent. Often, the customer expresses some resentment at the tax bite and asks if there is any way to eliminate or reduce it. The sales manager responds in a sympathetic fashion and allies himself with the customer in a scheme to "cut down on the Governor's share of the deal" by suggesting that the customer might make out a check for less than the actual selling price of the car. In turn, the manager will make out a bill of sale for the lesser amount. The customer then will pay the difference between the *recorded* selling price and the *actual* selling price in cash. A car which normally costs $2,000 would carry an additional 8 percent (or $160) state sales tax, thus actually costing the customer $2,160. If a bill of sale which records the selling price as $1,500 is made out, however, then at 8 percent the taxes would be $120, for an apparent total of $1,620. Although the customer still pays $2,000 for the car ($1,500 by check and $500 in cash), he "saves" $40 in taxes.

Almost as important as saving the $40 is the obvious delight the customer typically takes at finally discovering himself in a situation where he can "even the odds," "give the big guys what for," and "make sure the little guy gets his two cents too." The attitude and mood which washes through the short-sale suggests a welcome, if minor, triumph in the back-stepping of everyday life. As an observer witnessing this "petty" collusion between little Davids against remote Goliath, I had a rather difficult time identifying it pursuant to the criminal code—as a conspiracy to defraud the government through tax evasion. Obviously, the meaning, value, and sentiment attached to the act by at least one of the participants (the customer) is totally incongruous with the meaning, value, and sentiment attached to it by the criminal code. Thus does a minor victory in everyday life co-exist in the same act with a punishable transgression of law. The victory is often more symbolic than material, however, since, if the customer at any future time has an accident or theft, his insurance company, in part, will initiate compensation calculations based on the selling price recorded in the bill of sale—a sum which understates the actual price paid.

But, if the customer derives both a small material savings and a large measure of delight, what does the dealer derive? For one thing, a lot of money; more precisely, a lot of *unrecorded* cash. At the moment the customer "saves" $40 in taxes the dealer gains $500 in cash. The "short-sale" to the customer allows the dealer to "steal-from-the-top." In any given year an accumulation of these short-sales can total to tens of thousands of dollars. In an effort to determine if "stealing-from-the-top" was anything other than rank venality, I questioned one of the partners in my principal site.

Q: You've just said that it's [stealing-from-the-top] O.K. for the customer but bad for you. I don't understand that. Jeez, look at the money!

A: Yeah, sure, but who the hell wants to live with any of the retail customers? You see what goes on. They don't know shit about a car. They look at the interior, turn on the radio, check the odometer, kick the tire, push the windshield wiper button, turn on the air conditioner, open up the trunk, look at the paint. What the fuck has any of that got to do with the *condition* of the car? I mean, the way the fucker runs. If I put money into all this crap, I can't put it into improving the mechanical condition. Three weeks later the fucking car falls apart and they're on my ass to fix it. Then I got to live with them. They drive me off the wall. Then that broad down [at] the consumer affairs office wants to know why I don't give the customer a fair shake. Shit, why the hell don't she educate the customers? It would make things a lot easier.

Q: Listen, if they're such a pain, why do you put up with them?

A: What do you mean?

Q: I don't know what I mean, but there is usually a bottom line and it's usually money!

A: Well, if you mean that they bail me out every now and then, sure.

Q: What do you mean?

A: Well, you know those creeps [buyers] I got on the road buying for me, you know what their philosophy is? "If you don't buy, you don't earn." They pay big numbers; what do they care; it's my money. If they get in too high on a package [group of cars] or a piece [one car], and I can't blow [wholesale] it out, then I look for a retail shot [sale]. But that means I can't turn over my money quickly, I got to lay with it out on the lot and hope some yo-yo [retail customer] comes along.

Believe me, it's a pain in the ass. This whole business is in and out, in and out. Anything that slows the turnover costs money.

Q: O.K., so retail customers generally are a pain, but you put up with them because they bail you out on bad buys, but that still doesn't get to it. What about those retail sales that are "short-sales," that's where the bread is. That's what I'm trying to get at.

A: All right, listen: A wholesaler runs a big grocery store; if it's not on the shelves, you can't buy it. Without cars to sell, I can't sell cars. Look, we make enough legit, but you can't pay graft by check. Those bums get you coming and going.

Q: What bums?

A: You ever wanta meet a crook, go see a used car manager [of a new car dealership]. They clip a quarter [$25], a half [$50], a yard [$100], maybe more [on each car]. Put a package together and take it out [buy it from them] and they'll zing you for a week's pay. They steal their bosses blind.

Q: So, you have to pay them to get cars. You mean something under the table?

A: Yeah, the "vig."

Q: The what?

A: The grease, the commission, the kickback. How I'm gonna stay in business with no cars? You tell me.

Q: Incidentally, how many of your retail sales do you figure are "short"?

A: Maybe 70–75 percent. I can't be sure.[13]

---

[13] Since the operation in question is primarily a *wholesale* not a retail house, the proportion of retail sales typically do not exceed 25 percent of total sales. Of these, however, about 75 percent are "short sales." Thus, of 2,124 total sales, 398 are short. At a minimum of $100 stolen from the top per short-sale, approximately $39,000 is generated in unrecorded cash. Used car *wholesalers* may well engage in retail selling for cash and, therefore, are clearly different from used and new car retailers who avoid cash sales in favor of "credit" or "installment" sales. This latter point was vividly disclosed at a hearing before California's Corporations Commissioner when Sears, Roebuck and Company requested a license to make low cost automobile loans *directly* to customers, thus by-passing dealers. Direct loans, in effect, would turn consumers into cash customers. This the dealers emphatically did not want as the following testimony reveals:

Q: . . . Do you want to sell cars for cash?
A: I do not want to sell them for cash if I can avoid it.
Q: You would not want to sell the cars you do for a cash price, then?
A: No, sir.
Q: Does this mean that you are not really in the business of selling automobiles?
A: It does not mean that at all.
Q: But you don't want to sell automobiles for cash?
A: It means that I want to sell cars for the most profit that I can per car. Finance reserve

Q: Tell me, do you ever wind up with more than you need for the kickbacks?

A: Sure, am I gonna lie to you? So I put a little away [in safety deposit boxes]. You think I'm the only one? But if it's buried, you can't use it. Better it should be in the business; I could use it—besides, who needs the aggravation?

Q: Are you ever able to get it [buried money] back into the business?

A: Yeah.

Q: How?

A: Aw, you know.

Apparently, the dealer's reasons for engaging in "short-sales" include, but are not confined to, rank venality. After all, most, but not all, of the unrecorded money is passed along in the form of "kickbacks"; only the residual excess actually finds its way directly into his own hands, and even this excess must be buried or occasionally laundered.[14] The principal reason the dealer engages in short-sales is to come up with kickback cash in order to keep his sources of supply open, and this imperative is more than enough to keep him involved with "short-sales," even though it means he has to deal with retail customers—the very bane of his existence.

The antagonism the dealer holds toward the retail customer is incredibly intense and appears to have two sources. First, it stems from the dealer's apparent inability to sell the customer what the dealer considers to be the *essential* element of a car—namely, its *mechanical condition*. Instead, he is compelled to sell what to him is

---

[dealer's share of the carrying charges] and insurance commissions are part of the profit derived from selling a car on time.

Moreover, these dealers have no qualms about extending credit to poor risk customers; the car always can be repossessed and resold (quoted in Macaulay, 1966: 186).

[14] *"Burying money"* means putting it in a safety deposit box. Ironically, this money becomes a source of long-term anxiety instead of long-term security. First, it remains a concrete symbol of criminality and is at odds with the dealer's self-image. Second, it also always is the target of potential investigatory disclosure although known instances of such activity are virtually unheard of. Third, the dealer resents the accumulation of "idle" cash and is frustrated by his inability to "turn it over" easily and make it productive. *Laundering* occurs in tight money situations when capital *must* be made available. It invokes a symbiotic relationship between the dealer and a "bookie." The bookie is hired on as a "commissioned agent" of the dealership. The dealer "pays" him a weekly salary using a legitimate business check; in return, the bookie gives the dealer an equal amount in cash. The dealer provides the bookie with a W2 form and the bookie declares and pays taxes on this "income." The dealer then "declares" the income brought in by the bookie. Since this income derives from nonexistent buying or selling it is subtly apportioned and spread over actual transactions. The dealer also periodically writes a letter to the bookie's probation officer testifying to the bookie's reliable and gainful contribution to the business.

nonessential—*physical appearance*. If he is to improve the car's physical appearance, then he must skimp on improving its mechanical condition. This, in the long run, works to his own disadvantage since he must "live with the customer" and, in some measure, make good on repairs affecting mechanical condition. Put another way, the wholesaler's *conceptualization* of the car and the retail customer's *conceptualization* of the car do not overlap. Where the wholesaler wishes to sell such *unobservables* as a good transmission, a tight front end, a solid chassis, and an engine without knocks in it, the typical retail customer wishes to buy such *observables* as a nice paint job, a clean interior, etc. The wholesaler and the retail customer basically have a hard time "coming-to-terms," that is, abstracting out of the vehicle the same set of concrete elements to invest with meaning and value. The vehicle literally *means* different things to each of them and the establishment of a shared meaning which is *mutually* valued is extremely problematic.[15]

The second source of the dealer's antagonism stems from his overwhelming dependence on these ignorant customers. This dependence heightens dramatically when the dealer's own professional "house" buyers make bad buys; that is, pay too high a "number," or price, for the car, which makes it impossible for the car to be quickly rewholesaled. If the car is in basically sound mechanical condition, it will be "shaped" out in hopes of "bailing out" through a "retail shot." Though a bad buy can be redeemed through a retail sale, this route of redemption bodes ill for the house buyer since it reflects on his competence. It bodes ill for the dealer as well since he must tie up money, men, and space waiting for a fickle retail customer to get everyone off the hook. Thus, the dealer's antagonism toward the retail customer stems from his own dependence, for short-sales and bail-outs, on ignorant yo-yo's who don't know anything about cars. The dealer's redemption, then, lies in the hands of "idiot saviors," an unhappy situation at best.

KICKBACKS AND SUPPLY

In any event, based on what I had seen, heard, and been told, I concluded that the wholesale used car dealer engaged in "short-sales" principally to insure his supply of used cars. Since this con-

---

[15] See my already cited forthcoming article for an elaboration of this.

clusion was derived exclusively from observation and interview, I wanted to check it out against the dealer's inventory files. In the following section, I seek evidence of two things: (*a*) that the predominant source of the wholesaler's inventory, in fact, is the used car department of new car agencies; and (*b*) that used car managers in new car agencies universally receive kickbacks.

Accordingly, I classified all vehicles in my base site for the years 1971 and 1972 by their source of origin. Table 1 indicates that, of the 1,501 vehicles bought in 1971, 1,134 or 75.5 percent came from used car departments of new car dealers; of the 2,124 bought in 1972, 1,472 or 69.3 percent came from the same source. These figures corroborate the used car wholesaler's overwhelming dependence on the used car department of the new car agency for supply. They also suggest that there may well be a decreasing supply in the number of used cars available on the market altogether. From 1971 to 1972 there was a 6.2 percent decrease (75.5 to 69.3) in the proportion of cars from used car departments of new car dealers even though the number of new car agencies dealt with increased from 72 to 94.[16]

Given an overall paucity of used cars on the market, it would seem that used car managers of new car agencies are in a perfect

---

[16] These figures are consistent with national trend figures provided to me by Thomas C. Webb, research assistant, National Automobile Dealers Association (personal communication, March 11, 1974). Estimations of the number of used cars sold "on" and "off" the market in 1960 and 1973 indicate that, of the 20.7 million used cars sold in 1960, 14.9 million or 71.6 percent were sold "on" the market, whereas of the 31.4 million used cars sold in 1973, 18.7 million or 59.6 percent were sold "on" the market. Thus, there was a net decrease of 12.0 percent. A possible explanation for the decreasing supply of used cars on the market may be the consequence of an already established social-economic trend toward the multiple car family. Whereas a decade ago only 15 percent of the total population owned more than one car, today 30 percent do. Indeed, one out of every three families whose head of household is between the ages of 35–44 owns two cars and one out of ten whose head of household is between 45–54 owns three cars (MVMA, 1974: 38–39). What this probably means is that cars are *handed down* from husband to wife to children and literally "run-into-the-ground." In other words, we may well be seeing the reemergence of "second-hand" cars. Cars change hands but outside the commercial nexus, i.e., "off-the-market." An additional factor which may be contributing to this trend is declining public confidence in auto dealers. Not too long ago a poster showed a picture of former President Nixon with a caption which asked, "Would you buy a used car from this man?" The credibility of the new and used car dealer apparently has never been lower. Confirmation of this comes from several different polls which seek to determine the public image of new and used car dealers compared to other occupational groups. Auto dealers uniformly trail way behind others in terms of the trust they inspire in the buying public (Leonard and Weber, 1970). Still another compatible and contemporary factor is the deteriorating condition of our national economy where the combination of rising prices and decreasing purchasing power inhibit overall consumer demand and thus retard new car sales and accompanying trade-ins.

Table 1: Units* within, and vehicles generated by, various sources of supply

		1971		1972	
Source of supply		*Units*	*Vehicles*	*Units*	*Vehicles*
1.	Used car departments of new car agencies	72	1,134	94	1,472
2.	Rental, lease, or fleet companies	9	145	18	104
3.	Off-the-street customers......................	116	116	172	172
4.	Dealers' auctions	2	38	1	38
5.	Body and fender shops	6	35	6	105
6.	Retail used car dealers	11	27	17	193
7.	Wholesale used car dealers	3	6	4	40
		219	1,501	312	2,124

* The generic term "units" encompasses "establishments" as in categories 1–2 and 4–7, and customers as in category 3.
Source: Dealer's Police Books.

position to exact tribute from the independent used car wholesaler whose major source of supply is in their hand. I thus proceeded to check out the universality of kickbacks. I classified all inventory by the *specific* new car agency it came from, and then asked the older partner of my base operation to indicate at which agencies kickbacks were paid. As shown in column 4 of Table 2, kickbacks

Table 2: Kickbacks by vehicle, agency, and franchise

	No. of agencies		No. of vehicles		Kickback agencies		No. of kickback vehicles	
Franchise	*1971*	*1972*	*1971*	*1972*	*1971*	*1972*	*1971*	*1972*
Giant Motors	35	51	571	976	7	7	304	614
Fore	10	16	159	209	—	—	—	—
Crisis	15	16	256	191	—	—	—	—
U.S.	1	2	1	5	—	—	—	—
Foreign	8	6	143	62	—	—	—	—
Unknown	3	3	4	29	—	—	—	—
	72	94	1,134	1,472	7	7	304	614

were paid on 304 (out of 1,134) vehicles in 1971 and on 614 (out of 1,472) vehicles in 1972. Moreover, column 3—much to my surprise—shows that *all* of these cars come from only *seven* (7) agencies in both 1971 and 1972 and each of these agencies carried a Giant Motors franchise. Note, however, that these seven constitute only a small proportion of the total number of GM agencies dealt with, which is 35 in 1971 and 51 in 1972. Moreover, only 10 percent of *all* agencies in 1971 and less than 7 percent in 1972 required kickbacks. Nevertheless, in 1971 these agencies did, in fact, provide nearly 27 percent of all supply coming from used car departments of new car agencies and 20 percent of total supply. Similarly, in 1972 they provided 56 percent of supply from used car departments and 31 percent of all supply.

A closer examination of these seven GM agencies, however, discloses some common characteristics. First, an inspection of their zip codes and street addresses reveals that all seven are located in the same high density, urban area. Second, a rank ordering of all new car agencies by the number of cars they supply, as shown in Table 3, reveals that these seven are the top supply sources and, by

Table 3: Number of dealerships by number of vehicles supplied—1972

Number of dealerships	*Number of vehicles supplied*
2	100+
1	75+
4	50+
8	25+
79	1+

agreement among house buyers, are large agencies. Third, the remaining eight agencies among the top 15 supply sources all are located in suburban areas and are described by house buyers as medium sized.

With this information in hand, I again questioned the older partner of my base operation.

Q: Listen, didn't you know that you only paid kickbacks at large, urban GM agencies? Why did you guys give me the impression that you paid kickbacks to *all* used car managers?

A: Really?

Q: Really, what!?

A: Really, you thought we paid off all the managers? Well, I guess these are the big houses for us—it seems like a lot. I'll tell ya, the hicks are O.K. They don't know from conniving. The city is full of crooks.

A: Really? Don't you think it has anything to do with these particular agencies, maybe the way they're set up or maybe with GM? After all, the other manufacturers have agencies there too.

A: No, it's a freak thing! It just means that seven crooks work at these places.

Q: Aw, come on. I don't believe that.

A: Listen, you're barking up the wrong tree if you think it has anything to do with GM.

Q: But why only at GM? and why only at GM agencies in the city?

A: Look, there's more GM agencies than [Fore] and [Crisis]. GM sells more cars, they get more trade-ins, they have solid used cars operations. These crooks go where the action is. They're good used car men, they get the best jobs. But they're crooks. I'm telling you, believe me!

Q: But if they're crooks, and you know it, why don't their bosses know it?

A: Look, the bosses aren't stupid. They know what's going on. If the used car man pushes the cars out, and turns over capital, and doesn't beat the boss too bad—they're happy.

Q: I guess I must be thick, I'm still not convinced.

A: All right. The boss is busy running the new car operation. He brings in a sharp used car man and bankrolls him. The used car man pays rent to the boss for the premises and splits profits with him depending on the deal they work out. OK? The used car man takes the trade-ins, he keeps the good stuff and wholesales the bad. He wholesales me an off-model, say, for two grand. He tells his boss, the car brought $1,875. I send a check for $1,875, and grease him a buck and a quarter. At $1,875, he still made a legitimate fifty or a hundred on the car—the boss gets half of that. As long as the used car man doesn't get too greedy, there's no problem. The boss takes a short profit but frees up his capital. Believe me, that's crucial, especially if he's paying one percent a month interest on his bankroll to begin with.

Q: So, what you're saying, is that the best agencies are in the city, that they're GM, that GM dealers know their used car men are beating them, but that they don't get uptight as long as they make something and can free-up their capital.

A: Yeah.

Q: Listen, you've got a point, but isn't there another way to look at this? Isn't it possible that the boss does more than just tolerate being ripped off a little by his used car man? Isn't it possible that he's working with the used car man and beating his own business? In other words, he's splitting the kickbacks or something like that?

A: Look, anything's possible, but all I know is that the used car managers are a bunch of crooks. The bosses, I can't say; as for [Giant Motors], forget it, they're a legit concern.

Q: Maybe you're right, but it sure would make sense if the bosses [GM dealers] did both—you know, turn over money and beat their own business. Hell, you do it and you're the boss, why shouldn't they?

A: Well, I have to. I don't know about them. Just don't go off half-cocked. Be careful before you lean on anybody.

This interview material has two intriguing aspects. Despite the dealer's strenuous insistence that kickbacks are the artifact of corrupt and venal individual used car managers, there is also the suggstion that such venality can take place precisely because large, urban GM agencies sell a lot of cars and therefore have an abundance of trade-ins, the best of which are recycled back into the agencies' used car retail line while the surplus is wholesaled out. The power to determine how this surplus is dispersed into the wholesale market places the used car managers of the involved agencies in the position to demand and receive "kickbacks." Moreover, the new car dealer himself, who is under pressure to free-up capital in order to avoid paying excess interest on money borrowed to purchase new car inventory, may have an incentive to "look-the-other-way," and perhaps even split "kickbacks" as long as his used car manager keeps moving cars and freeing capital.

THE FINANCIAL SQUEEZE

In the section which follows, I seek to check out (*a*) the existence of a financial squeeze on dealers, and (*b*) whether this squeeze inclines dealers to tolerate or even participate in kickbacks. By way of checking these points, I contemplated interviewing some people in the "kickback" agencies. The more I thought about how to guide myself in such interviews, the more I realized I was facing an interesting dilemma. I wanted to do the interviews precisely because I had discovered that the agencies were paid kickbacks by the wholesalers. Yet, in each case the kickback was being paid specifically to the manager of the used car department of the agency and I was not sure if the manager was acting on his own or was acting with the knowledge of his principal. If he was acting on his own, and I disclosed this, I might then put him in jeopardy. If he was acting with the knowledge of his principal, it was certain I would have an unreliable interview since in these cases I did not have personal bonds strong enough to insure truthful responses. Since I did not wish to deceive or jeopardize any of the respondents, and since I did not feel I could be truthful—as no doubt I would have had to disclose just how I had discovered the "kickback" arrangement, and thus transgress the trust that I had established with the wholesalers and run the risk of jeopardizing their ongoing business relationships with the new car dealers—I developed another approach. I decided to interview GM dealers in "nonkickback" agencies and try to elicit information which would allow me to pinpoint the key differences between kickback and non-kickback agencies, thereby nailing down an interpretation of the "kickback" phenomenon.

I managed to arrange interviews with three different dealers. The following quoted interview lasted five hours, was granted on the basis of a personal tie, and therefore is most reliable and valid. In addition, the elicited material is highly representative of the other interviews. The general thrust of my questioning was first to ask the dealer to talk about issues which are problematic in the running of his own business, and then to comment on the "kickback" phenomenon at the urban agencies. I was interested mainly in knowing if the pressure to turn over capital and avoid interest payments would encourage a dealer to "look-the-other-way" on "kickbacks" or even split them.

Q: How long have you been a dealer?

A: A dealer? About 20 years. About five or six years after [I finished] college, my dad and I went in as partners. It's mine now.

Q: Have you enjoyed it?

A: Well, it's been good to me for a goodly number of years, but frankly, during these past three to four years the business has changed markedly. It's a tougher, tighter business. I'm more tied down to it now than ever before. I can't be as active in the community as I would like. You know, that's important to me.

Q: Why is that the case? Is the business expanding?

A: Not really, well it depends on how you measure it. I work harder, have a larger sales and service staff than ever, I've expanded the facilities twice and refurbished the fixtures and touched up several times, and yes, I'm selling more new cars than before, but is the business expanding? Well, I suppose, yes, but not the way I'd like it to.

Q: Could you elaborate on that?

A: Well, the point is—and I know this will sound anomalous, well, maybe not to you—but I wish I could ease off on the number of new cars and pick up somewhere else, maybe on used cars.

Q: Why is that?

A: It boils down to investment-return ratios. The factory [manufacturer] has us on a very narrow per unit profit margin [on new car sales]. But if I had the money and the cars, I could use my capital more effectively in used cars.[17]

Q: In other words, GM establishes how much profit you can make on each new car you sell?

A: Just about. And more than that, they more or less determine how much [new car] inventory I have to carry, and the composition of that inventory.

Q: So, you have to take what they give you—even if you don't want or need it. How do you pay for the inventory?

A: I borrow money at prevailing interest rates to finance the inventory. And, sometimes it gets tight. Believe me, if I am unable to sell off that inventory relatively quickly, I'm pressed. I have got to keep that money turning or that interest begins to pinch.

Q: Is it fair to say that you compensate for narrow margins on new cars by making wider margins on used cars?

A: Not really, not in practice, at least not out here [in the suburbs]. Used cars, good used cars, are hard to come by. I imagine the city dealers have an easier time getting trade-ins. We get a lot of repeat customers, but I don't believe they trade up. They just buy new cars. Actually, we tend to pick up additional revenue from our service repair operation. I'm not particularly proud about it, but there is a lot of skimping going on. It's quite complicated. The factory has a terrible attitude toward service repair generally, and the [mechanics] union is overly demanding and inflexible. It's rather demoralizing and, frankly, I'm looking out for myself, too.

Q: Could you expand on that?

A: I prefer you not press me on that.

Q: If you had a choice, how would you prefer to set up your operation?

A: Well, if I had a choice—which I don't—I would rather have a low volume, high margin operation. I could get by with smaller facilities, a smaller staff, put less time into the business, and not constantly face the money squeeze.

---

[17] Leonard and Weber (1970: 4) estimate that a dealer can make a gross profit margin of $400 on a $2,000 used car but only $150–200 on a $3,200 new car. Indeed the new car dealers I interviewed all indicated a desire to be able to sell more used cars.

Q: Do you think the really large city dealers would prefer the same kind of alternative?

A: I guess so, but it's hard to say. Their situation is somewhat different from mine.

Q: In what way?

A: Well, first of all, some of them, especially if they're located in [megalopolis] have even less control over their operation than I do. Some of them really run factory stores. That is, GM directly owns or controls the agency. Those outfits are really high volume houses. I don't see how they can make a go of it. The factory really absorbs the costs.[18]

Q: You did say that they probably had strong used car operations or, at least, had a lot of trade-ins. Do you think that helps?

A: Possibly.

Q: Do you think a really sharp used car man could do well in that kind of operation?

A: Well, he would do well in any operation in which he had used cars to work with.

Q: He could both retail and wholesale?

A: Oh, yes, if he had the cars to work with.

Q: Is it likely, in the wholesale end, he could demand and receive "kickbacks" from wholesalers?

A: Well, it's been known to happen. You know, those wholesalers, they're always willing to accommodate a friend. But it would only pay them to do that in relatively large operations where they could anticipate a fairly steady flow of cars.

Q: So, it would certainly make sense for them to accommodate friends in large, high volume, urban GM agencies?

A: Sure.

Q: Do you suppose the used car managers split kickbacks with their bosses?

A: Well, it's possible, but more than likely, the boss is more interested in moving those cars out quickly any way he can, so he can turn over that money and place it back into new car inventory.

---

[18] According to White (1971), Detroit manufacturers generally avoid owning their own retail outlets or "factory" stores since a network of financially independent but exclusively franchised dealers helps to spread the risk of doing business, defrays cost, and provides local management with entrepreneurial incentive. Edwards (1965) also suggests that a franchise dealer system establishes local identity for products as well as provides facilities which handle trade-ins and repairs. Nevertheless, as a matter of prestige and because no individual dealer can afford the extremely high cost of land in this particular megalopolis, manufacturers usually own retail outlets directly.

Although this material does not permit any educated guess as to whether the dealers might split kickbacks with their used car managers, it does provide some assurance that new car dealers are under pressure to sell off cars relatively quickly in order to turn over capital and thus reduce interest payments. This pressure may be enough of a stimulus to, at least, incline the dealer to "look-the-other-way" if and when his used car man partakes in graft. As long as the used car man doesn't become too greedy and cut into the boss's pocket, his activity will be tolerated. Of course, we may still speculate, but not conclude, that if a "boss" is merely managing or only controlling a minimal share in a new car agency which is principally owned directly by GM, he may be inclined to collude with his used car manager against "his own" agency. In any event, it is safe to presume that dealers feel under constant pressure to continuously recycle capital back into new car inventory and to get out from under interest payments. Corroboration of this comes from Vanderwicken (1972: 128) who did a financial analysis of a medium-sized Fore agency located in a suburb of Cleveland, Ohio, and reported that:

The average car is in inventory thirty days before it is sold. Quick turnover is important to a dealer, the instant a car leaves the factory, he is billed for it and must begin paying interest on it. This interest is one of [the dealer's] biggest single expenses.

Additional support also comes from Fendell (1975: 11) who asked a New Jersey [Fore] dealer how he was coping with decreasing consumer demand and received the following response:

I'm making deals I lose money on just to get the interest costs off my back. Those cars sit out there, costing me money every second. [Fore] has been paid in full for them a long time ago.

The dealer went on to say that his interest rates run between 10.25 percent and 11 percent per year.

MANUFACTURERS' PRICING POLICY

The constant and unremitting emphasis on new car inventory and the capital squeeze it places dealers in apparently is no accident. To the contrary, it is the calculated outcome of the manufacturers' pricing policy. According to Stewart Macaulay (1966: 8), manufacturers and dealers enter into relationships for the mutual goal of making profit; however, their strategies for making that profit may differ.

For example, a . . . dealer might be able to make a hundred dollars profit on the sale of one car or a ten dollar profit on each sale of ten cars. . . . [it makes a great deal of difference to the manufacturer] because in one case it sells only one car while in the other it sells ten. . . . It must sell many units of all the various models it makes. . . .

This imperative to sell *many* cars stems from the manufacturer's effort to achieve economies of scale, that is, savings in production and other costs as a result of massive, integrated, and coordinated plant organization. George Romney, when President of American Motors, testified before a Senate Judiciary Subcommittee on Antitrust and Monopoly and reported that:

A company that can build between 180,000 and 220,000 cars a year on a one-shift basis can make a very good profit and not take a back seat to anyone in the industry in production efficiency. On a two-shift basis, annual production of 360,000 to 440,000 cars will achieve additional small economies . . . (quoted in Lanzillotti, 1968: 266).

An economist, Joe S. Bain (quoted in Edwards, 1966: 162), estimates that an even higher minimal production volume is needed for savings.

In general, 300,000 units per annum is a low estimate of what is needed for productive efficiency in any one line.

Thus, in order to cut costs to a minimum, the manufacturers—as in days gone by—must continue to engage in mass production,[19] which leads to mass distribution and the need for a dealer network into which the manufacturer can pump massive doses of new cars in a *controlled* fashion. According to economist Lawrence J. White (1971: 139), this translates into a "forcing model," which may be defined as "the requirement that the retailer sell a specified number of units as a condition of holding his franchise."[20] In effect, this allows the manufacturer to manipulate dealer inven-

---

[19] In principle, much the same strategy was used in the early 1900s when Henry Ford introduced mass production techniques and reduced the price of the Model "T" from $950 in 1909 to under $300 in the early 1920s and, as a result, boosted sales from 12,000 to two million and captured 50 percent of the market (Lanzillotti, 1968). Rothchild (1973) undoubtedly is correct when she observes that the auto industry continues to rely on ancient and probably obsolete formulas.

[20] For a further mathematical articulation of this model, see Pashigan (1961: 33–34; 52–56) and White (1971: 137–145).

tories in a way that serves the oligopolist interests of an economically concentrated industry. Oligopolist "rivals" recognize their interdependence and avoid direct competition. Placing new dealerships in each other's territory would only call forth counter placements which, rather than expanding total auto sales, would perhaps cut into one's own already established dealerships. Thus,

it would be better to concentrate on lowering the [profit] margins of existing dealers, which could only be met by equal actions . . . by one's rivals and which . . . has the effect of expanding the overall demand for the product (White, 1971: 142.)

All the manufacturer need do then to reduce per unit margins, which increases total net aggregate profit for the manufacturer, is to increase dealer inventory volume. This puts pressure on the dealer to free-up capital from alternative investment possibilities such as used cars or to borrow capital at prevailing interest rates. Either way, the dealer faces a financial squeeze and has a powerful incentive to sell off his inventory as quickly as possible, which industry trend statistics bear out. Despite the fact that new car dealers can achieve more efficient investment-return ratios from used car inventory—that is, if it is available—the ratio of new to used car sales from 1958 to 1972 per franchised new car dealer reflects an increasing preoccupation with new car sales. Examination of Table 4, column 3, indicates that over the last decade and a

Table 4: Cars sold per franchised new car dealer—1958–1972

Year	New	Used	Ratio used to new
1958	125	221	1.77
1959	168	272	1.62
1960	191	285	1.49
1961	175	271	1.55
1962	208	302	1.45
1963	225	317	1.41
1964	239	311	1.30
1965	283	354	1.25
1966	285	336	1.18
1967	269	328	1.22
1968	302	326	1.08
1969	309	389	1.26
1970	281	292	1.00
1971	331	—	—
1972	354	275	0.81

Source: Compiled from *The Franchised New Car and Truck Dealer Story,* Washington, D.C. (National Automobile Dealers Association, 1973), p. 32, and *Automobile Facts and Figures* (Detroit: Automobile Manufacturers Association, 1971), p. 33.

half new car dealers have been forced away from used cars and into new cars. In 1958, the ratio of used to new car sales was 1.77, but [it] steadily declined until it reached 1.00 in 1970. And after 1970 it actually reversed itself so that in 1972 it was .81.[21]

This pressure to slant one's operation overwhelmingly in the direction of new car sales places the dealer in a tight margin operation. Vanderwicken (1972: 121) observes that ". . . most people have a vastly exaggerated notion of a car dealer's profits. . . . the average car dealer earns less than 1 percent on his volume, a minuscule margin far below that of most other retailers." He also provides a breakdown for the Ford agency he studied. Thus, on a car that the customer paid the dealer $3,337, the dealer paid the manufacturer $3,025.00. The dealer's gross margin was therefore $312 or 9 percent. (Average gross margin for retailers in other industries runs between 20–25 percent). Nevertheless, of this $312 the dealer paid $90 in salesman's commission, $43 in wages and salaries, $30 in advertising, $28 in interest, $27 miscellaneous, $24 in taxes, $22 in rent and maintenance, $16 in preparation and pre-delivery work, $9 in free customer service, and $7 in employee benefits—giving him a net profit of $16 per unit. As the boss of the Ford agency remarked, "Our low margins reflect the manufacturer's constant clamor for volume. . . . the manufacturer sure as hell gets his . . ." (Vanderwicken, 1972: 124).[22]

Should the dealer seek to protest this situation because it locks his time, effort, and money exclusively into fixed margin new car sales, he finds himself under subtle coercion. Quick delivery from

---

[21] Interestingly enough, the decreasing ratio of used to new car sales more or less parallels the increasing market penetration of foreign auto makers. In 1963 foreign auto makers held 6.0 percent of the American market; that percentage increased to 14.6 percent by 1972. And the very year the ratio of used to new car sales declined to 1:00 or parity, in 1970, GM lost nearly 7.1 percent of its previous market share (NADA, 1973: 5). Put another way, increasing market penetration by foreign firms may have placed greater pressure on American auto makers to push harder on new car sales. One plausible way to accomplish this would be to require the dealer distribution network to put still more capital into new car inventory thus enabling the manufacturer to increase the volume of sales and thereby hold its market share. There is another compatible interpretation for the dramatic and unprecedented 7.1 percent market loss sustained by GM in a one year period. This interpretation is held widely by dealers themselves, namely, that GM was attempting to prevent rumored anti-trust action by the Justice Department and was inclined to show itself under competitive siege. In the following year, 1971, GM recouped all but 1.6 percent of its previous loss and has held subsequently at about 45.4 percent of the total market.

[22] The per unit net of $16 does not reflect per unit revenue from financing or insurance which can boost that figure by 200 percent. Little wonder retail dealers want to avoid cash customers.

the factory becomes problematic and so does a substantial supply of "hot" models (Macaulay, 1966: 173). Moreover, unfavorable sales comparison with "factory" stores, which sell cars below average retail price, raises questions of effective management (Leonard and Weber, 1970: 416). And should such subtle coercion fail to reach home, there is always the threat of franchise termination—a threat which cannot be dismissed as idle given the elimination of over 3,300 dealerships between 1961 when there were 33,500 and 1970 when there were 30,200[23] (NADA, 1973: 30). If a franchise is cancelled, it is unlikely that another manufacturer will step in and offer a new franchise or that a new dealer will offer to buy one's premises, equipment, stock, and reputation. Consequently, new car dealers apparently accommodate to this "forcing" procedure and avoid direct reaction. Nevertheless, it appears that they do undertake a form of indirect reaction.

DEALER REACTION

An expert witness who testified before the Senate Judiciary Subcommittee on Antitrust and Monopoly in December 1968 reported on a series of "rackets" which dealers perpetrate on the public in order to supplement their short new car profits. These "rackets" include charging for labor time not actually expended, billing for repairs not actually done, replacing parts unnecessarily, and using rebuilt parts but charging for new parts (Leonard and Weber, 1970). In addition to fleecing customers, they also attempt to retaliate against manufacturers whom they accuse of having a hypocritical attitude on service work. Virginia Knauer (Sheppard, 1972: 14), special assistant to the President for consumer affairs, reports that complaints about auto service repair lead the list of all complaints. According to Knauer, local car dealers themselves complain that the manufacturers simply do not care about service repairs because if they did, they would adequately compensate dealers for pre-delivery inspection and for warranty work and they certainly would not set up—as one of the Big Three did—a

---

[23] It is difficult to know what percentage of these 3,300 was the result of attrition, voluntary termination, bankruptcy, or direct and indirect franchise cancellation. It is probably safe to assume, however, that the existing network of franchises reflects manufacturers' preferences relative to location and pricing strategy.

regional competition in which prizes were awarded to regions that *underspent* their warranty budgets (Leonard and Weber, 1970). Indeed, the resentment held by the dealers toward the factory on the issue of service work, as well as the manner and magnitude of retribution engaged in by the dealers against the factory, has been of such proportion that one manufacturer, General Motors, recently fired its entire Chevrolet Eastern Zone office, which has jurisdiction over no less than 60 Chevrolet dealers, for colluding with those dealers against the factory, in the cause of more just compensation for dealer's service work (Farber, 1975).

It would seem, then, that the forcing of fixed margin new car inventory works to the manufacturer's advantage by increasing total net aggregate profit without risking direct competition. This high volume low per unit profit strategy, however, precipitates a criminogenic market structure. It forces new car dealers to free-up money by minimizing their investment in more profitable used car inventory as well as by borrowing capital at prevailing interest rates. The pressure of interest payments provides a powerful incentive for the dealer to move his inventory quickly. The need to turn money over and the comparatively narrow margins available to the dealer on new car sales alone precipitate several lines of illegal activity: First, it forces dealers to compensate for short new car profit margins by submitting fraudulent warrantee statements to the manufacturers, often with the collusion of the manufacturers' own representatives. Second, it forces dealers to engage in service repair rackets which milk the public of untold sums of money. Third, it permits the development of a kickback system, especially in large volume dealerships, whereby independent used car wholesalers are constrained to pay graft for supply. Fourth, the wholesalers, in turn, in order to generate unrecorded cash, collude with retail customers in "short-sales." Fifth, to the extent that short-sales spawn excess cash, the wholesaler is drawn into burying and laundering money. In sum, a limited number of oligopolist manufacturers who sit at the pinnacle of an economically concentrated industry can establish economic policy which creates a market structure that causes lower level dependent industry participants to engage in patterns of illegal activity. Thus, criminal activity, in this instance, is a direct consequence of legally established market structure.

REFERENCES

Becker, Howard S.
1970 *Sociological Work: Method and Substance*. Chicago: Aldine Publishing Company.

Brown, Joy
1973 *The Used Car Game: A Sociology of the Bargain*. Lexington, Mass.: Lexington Books.

Edwards, Charles E.
1965 *Dynamics of the United States Automobile Industry*. Columbia: University of Southern Carolina Press.

Farber, M. A.
1975 "Chevrolet, citing 'policy violations,' ousts most zone aids here." *New York Times,* Sunday, January 12, section L.

Farberman, Harvey A.
1968 "A Study of Perzonalization in Low Income Consumer Interactions and Its Relationship to Identification with Residential Community." Unpublished Ph.D. thesis, Department of Sociology, University of Minnesota.

Farberman, H. A., and E. A. Weinstein
1970 "Personalization in lower class consumer interaction." *Social Problems* 17 (Spring): 449–457.

Fendell, B.
1975 "Dealers struggle for survival." *New York Times,* Sunday, February 2, section A.

Gouldner, Alvin
1970 *The Coming Crisis of Western Sociology*. New York: Basic Books.
1968 "The sociologist as partisan: Sociology and the welfare state." *American Sociologist* 3 (May): 103–116.

Huber, Joan
1973 "Symbolic interaction as a pragmatic perspective: The bias of emergent theory." *American Sociological Review* 38 (April): 274–284.

Lanzillotti, Robert F.
1971 "The automobile industry." Pp. 256–301 in W. Adams (ed.), *The Structure of American Industry,* 4th edition. New York: Macmillan Company.

Leonard, W. N., and N. G. Weber
1970 "Automakers and dealers: A study of criminogenic market forces." *Law and Society Review* 4 (February): 407–424.

Levine, L.
1968   "Jerome Avenue." *Motor Trend* 20 (December): 26–29.

Liazos, A.
1972   "The poverty of the sociology of deviance: Nuts, sluts, and preverts." *Social Problems* 20 (Summer): 103–120.

Macaulay, Stewart
1966   *Law and the Balance of Power: The Automobile Manufacturers and Their Dealers*. New York: Russell Sage Foundation.

Motor Vehicle Manufacturing Association
1972   1972 *Automobile Facts and Figures*. Detroit: MVMA.

National Automobile Dealers Association
1973   *The Franchised New Car and Truck Dealer Story*. Washington, D.C.: NADA, table 6, p. 30.

Pashigan, Bedros P.
1961   *The Distribution of Automobiles: An Economic Analysis of the Franchise System*. Englewood Cliffs, N.J.: Prentice-Hall.

Quinney, Richard
1970   *The Social Reality of Crime*. Boston: Little, Brown and Company.

Robbins, Harold
1971   *The Betsy*. New York: Trident Press.

Rothchild, Emma
1973   *Paradise Lost: The Decline of the Auto-Industrial Age*. New York: Random House.

Schervish, P. G.
1973   "The labeling perspective: Its bias and potential in the study of political deviance." *American Sociologist* 8 (May): 47–57.

Sheppard, Jeffrey M.
1972   *New York Times*, Sunday, November 5, section A.

Smith, R. A.
1961   "The incredible electrical conspiracy." Parts 1 and 2, *Fortune* (April –May).

Stone, G. P., D. Maines, H. A. Farberman, G. I. Stone, and N. K. Denzin
1974   "On methodology and craftsmanship in the criticism of sociological perspectives." *American Sociological Review* 39 (June): 456–463.

Taylor, I., P. Walton, and J. Young
1974   "Advances towards a critical criminology." *Theory and Society* 1 (Winter): 441–476.

Thio, A.
  1973   "Class bias in the sociology of deviance." *American Sociologist* 8 (February): 1–12.

Vanderwicken, Peter
  1972   "How Sam Marshall makes out with his 'deal.' " *Fortune* 86 (December): 121–130.

White, Lawrence J.
  1971   *The Automobile Industry since 1945*. Cambridge: Harvard University Press.

Chapter 8

The control and prevention of crime

THE CONTROL OF CRIME THROUGH PUNISHMENT

The view that the current crime crisis in the United States can be controlled by punishment is widely accepted by Americans. Some argue that our prisons have been turned into country clubs for criminals and that the police have been handcuffed by the Supreme Court, which has been excessively concerned about equality and citizens' constitutional rights. The argument continues that if, as a society, we really get tough with criminals through longer sentences, and if we show less concern about suspects' constitutional rights, a sense of safety now lacking can be restored to American cities.

Basically, this argument suggests that punishment can be used as *deterrence*. Implicit in this argument is Bentham's (1823) notion that people are pleasure-seeking, pain-avoiding creatures. Recently, after a long dormancy, a new interest in deterrence has developed. The dormancy is understandable, given the long history of positivism in criminology. If the positivist belief that people are forced to commit crime is accepted, then studying deterrent techniques becomes a fruitless activity (von Hirsch, 1976: 37). According to Bentham, however, crime can be controlled if the penalties are no greater, but also no smaller, than necessary to deter the individual offender in the future. This is sometimes referred to as primary deterrence. Bentham's rationale for punishment implies taking stronger measures against poor law violators because their poverty gives them stronger motives to commit crimes. The price-fixing business executive need only be fired from his job to deter similar offenses in the future, whereas the knife- and pistol-wielding poor must be imprisoned to deter a repetition of their offenses (von Hirsch, 1976: 147). At times a person is punished to make an example of him and thus help restrain potential law violators. This is called secondary deterrence. Secondary deterrence is often criticized as unjust because it requires the infliction of pain on some individuals for the benefit of others (Grupp, 1971). However, primary deterrence has also been characterized as unjust. Morris (1974b), for example, suggests that it is unjust to imprison a person for long periods because of his alleged future dangerousness, since this is punishment in advance of criminal behavior.

Incarceration because of alleged future dangerousness is also unjust because, as Morris (1974a) recognizes, the concept dangerousness is vague and imprecise. Consequently, attempting to incarcerate individuals who would commit future dangerous or violent acts could result in the mistaken incarceration of a large number of individuals who would not commit such acts if released. Indeed, Morris reviews research which indicates that therapists are unable to make accurate predictions of future dangerousness. Since it is not possible to predict such future behavior accurately, many who would not have committed dangerous acts if released are held in prison longer because their sentences have been influenced by such incorrect predictions (von Hirsch, 1976: 21). But even if accurate predictions of future dangerous behavior were possible, the problem of injustice would remain (von Hirsch, 1976: 125).

Aside from these moral problems in using punishment as deterrence, it has been demonstrated, contrary to the rantings of some U.S. politicians, that merely increasing the penalties prescribed in the criminal statutes will not effect an increase in obedience to law. Recent research comparing different political jurisdictions has found that the severity of punishment for specific types of crimes is not usually associated with lower rates of these offenses (Gibbs, 1968; Tittle, 1969), though certainty of punishment is associated with lower crime rates and therefore does appear to have some deterrent effect. Earlier, in our discussion of the Nebraska marijuana law (Galliher et al., 1974) and property crimes in England (Hall, 1952), we showed that prescribed penalties have been reduced rather than increased to increase the likelihood that the law would be enforced. In both instances the prescribed penalties were so severe that judges, prosecutors, and juries, often allowed law violators to escape any punishment. The consequences of the 1955 Connecticut crackdown on speeders can be understood in the same terms. The prescribed penalties were increased dramatically, but there was also a sharp rise in the percentage of speeding violators judged not guilty (Campbell and Ross, 1968).

At times the punishment of law violators may even encourage some people to violate the law. One study indicates that some people claimed that they had begun minor falsifications of their tax returns after hearing that others had been convicted of tax evasion. These respondents said that the convictions, which involved blatant violators, had inadvertently made them aware of safe or moderate offenses, which they then committed (Schwartz and Skolnick, 1962).

It is sometimes suggested that punishing a law violator will in some way be good for him, that it will *rehabilitate* him or be therapeutic for him by teaching him a new respect for the law and the rights of other people (Grupp, 1971). Such an argument may seem sound when the analogy of the punishment of a child by a parent is used, but it is widely recognized that American prisons do not teach new respect for the law and the rights of others (American Friends, 1971). Long-term isolation from family and friends in decaying and barren institutions, combined with the brutal treatment commonly received from guards and other prisoners, can hardly be character-building.

Punishment justified as *retribution* is much easier to defend on logical grounds, even if not on moral grounds. Punishment produces the pain which citizens believe the criminal deserves. It is sometimes argued that it is desirable to provide for an orderly collective expression of society's disapproval of criminal acts. Indeed, as noted earlier, Durkheim (1933: 70–110) argued that a certain amount of crime is functional for a society because when the society responds by punishing the guilty party, this response increases the identification with the norms of the society among all its members. Punishment of deviance reaffirms and clarifies the normative boundaries of the group. When certain behavior is punished, people see clearly that this behavior is outside the acceptable limits. In fact, it has been argued that one function of crime waves and the consequent punishment of deviance in society is that these can give meaning to a group when it needs it most, at the time of a group identity crisis (Erikson, 1966). Moreover, without such punishment of law violators, the law-abiding citizens in a society would become indignant and ultimately demoralized. They would see people who apparently suffer no ill effects and perhaps even prosper while violating the law, leading lives that seem to compare favorably with their own humdrum conventional existence.

The moral indignation associated with punishment as retribution may be seen in 17th century England among the lower middle-class businessmen who accepted puritanical rules for living (Ranulf, 1964). These people were interested in worldly success, but they saw this as something that should be obtained only by great self-discipline. They could, however, see that the lower classes and the nobility were enjoying life more than they did. Many of these people did not suffer for their revelry, as the middle class's puritanical religion suggested would follow. The members of the nobility imposed no discipline on themselves but still managed to get along well, and even the lower classes appeared reasonably happy in their debauchery. Members of the middle class felt that their rewards for denying themselves worldly pleasures were inadequate, and that others who were living it up still had more than they did. This created strain for the middle class. It was important to the middle class that these people should be punished, and during this period very brutal punishments for law violators emerged at the urging of middle-class merchant groups.

This violent reaction to the transgressions of others served to protect the value system of the middle class. Through severe punishments the middle class reassured itself of the worthlessness of these law violators. Convicts were punished publicly and held up to public ridicule to emphasize that people who lived as they did were degraded even if they were successful; and in this way the middle class could still stand out as God's elect even if it was not as wealthy as the nobility. This need for vicious punishment would not have occurred if success had been distributed solely on the basis of morality, but it was not, so another means was required to dramatize the middle class's adherence to a godly way of life.

The influence of affluence, power, and class interests is clearly evident in this example of middle-class moral indignation.

Another interpretation of the class origins of punishment is that of Rusche and Kirchheimer (1939), who observe that specific forms of punishment are associated with given stages of economic development. In support of their argument, they provide numerous examples. They assert that generally conditions in prisons are determined by the living standard of the lowest classes of free people; the living standard of prisoners' must be lower, or else prisons are no threat. Rusche and Kirchheimer also trace the development of punishment through the Middle Ages.

Penance and fines were the preferred methods of punishment in the early Middle Ages. They were gradually replaced during the later Middle Ages by a harsh system of corporal and capital punishment which, in its turn, gave way to imprisonment about the seventeenth century (Rusche and Kirchheimer, 1939: 8).

Initially, the lot of the workers was quite good, but in the later Middle Ages conditions deteriorated and

the inability of lower-class evildoers to pay fines in money led to the substitution of corporal punishment in their case (Rusche and Kirchheimer, 1939: 9).

In practice, it [the fine] was reserved for the rich, whereas corporal punishment became the punishment of the poor (Rusche and Kirchheimer, 1939: 17).

The constant increase in crime among the ranks of the poverty-stricken proletariat, especially in the big towns, made it necessary for the ruling classes to search for new methods which would make the administration of criminal law more effective (Rusche and Kirchheimer, 1939: 14).

The creation of a law effective in combating offenses against property was one of the chief preoccupations of the rising urban bourgeoisie (Rusche and Kirchheimer, 1939: 15).

The poorer the masses became, the harsher the punishments in order to deter them from crime (Rusche and Kirchheimer, 1939: 18).

At this time mutilation became quite common (Rusche and Kirchheimer, 1939: 19).

The whole system of punishment in the later Middle Ages makes it quite clear that there was no shortage of labor (Rusche and Kirchheimer, 1939: 20).

In short, the inability of the poor to pay fines led to corporal punishment for them, and the brutal system of punishment in the later Middle Ages reflected a plentiful labor supply. The working masses were expendable as far as the elites were concerned. The transition to a capitalist economy in 14th and 15th century Europe led to the development of harsh criminal punishments directed at the lower classes because of the continuing increases in crime among this increasingly poverty-stricken group which found no place in the emerging capitalist society. The punishment imposed was determined not by the crime committed but by the economic status of the criminal, and it was harsher if the culprit was poor.

However, when a labor shortage developed in the 17th century, poor convicted criminals were no longer executed or mutilated but were put to work in prisons to help ease the shortage. Moreover, in the early 19th century, when there was a great demand for labor due to rapid economic development, the type of prison organization known as the Auburn system (first used in Auburn, New York), came to be preferred over the Pennsylvania system, developed by the Philadelphia Quakers. The Auburn system allowed the use of inmates in prison factories, whereas the Pennsylvania system required the total solitary confinement of all inmates. The development of machine production made solitary handwork in prisons uneconomical. The transportation of convicted criminals and the use of convicts in galley servitude also reflect the need for labor in specific historical situations. This analysis of patterns of punishment demonstrates that convicted criminals have been used in various ways for the benefit of economic elites.

CONTROL OF CRIME THROUGH REHABILITATION

Rothman (1971) demonstrates that in 19th century America the belief grew that convicted criminals could be rehabilitated by incarceration in prisons. During the Colonial period in the 18th century this optimism about the reformative potential of incarcerating criminals did not exist. Colonial Americans believed crime to be an inevitable part of social life which should be dealt with mainly by fines and whippings. Offenders were to be coerced rather than rehabilitated.

Those who advocated incarceration for rehabilitation held that if convicted criminals were incarcerated and subjected to the proper routine, they could be turned away from a life of crime. This stress on an orderly routine stemmed from the concern of 19th century policymakers that due to increasing social and geographic mobility, American people were less aware of their place than they had been in the more stable Colonial society. Presumably a stint in a well-organized prison could help restore knowledge of one's proper place in society.

This faith in rehabilitation has been bolstered in the 20th century by the development of the behavioral and social sciences, whose practitioners typically support this same view of human behavior. Currently the typical liberal position on crime and its control is that convicted criminals should not be punished for their crimes, but should be treated and rehabilitated so that they can lead law-abiding and useful lives after their release from prison. At first glance, this may sound both humanitarian and enlightened, but the argument is not without its problems.

The incompatibility between rehabilitation and criminal justice

One problem with attempting to treat or rehabilitate accused criminals is that there are some importance differences in the approaches to deviance by legal justice and mental health (Aubert, 1965). Legal justice is achieved by disregarding many features characteristic of the actor. It involves responding to a specific act with a specific type of reaction. However, the whole personality is relevant to the psychiatric mental health approach.

Psychiatry attempts to be applied science, whereas legal practice does not. Obviously the diagnosis and treatment of criminals cannot become an applied science as long as the jury has the last word in these matters and as long as the judge plays such an important role. Although we do not object to having nonmedical people, such as the judge and jury, contribute to legal practice, we would consider it absurd for them to deal with health problems.

Also, the practice of law is public in the sense that its decisions and procedures are in principle open to scrutiny by anyone who is affected or interested. On the other hand, medicine and psychology are secret in that the processes involved in their diagnostic and therapeutic decisions are rarely revealed to the parties involved and are almost never revealed to the public (Aubert, 1965).

Moreover, the nature of the responsibility to the public is different for criminal justice than for mental health. If a court makes a correct description of the facts of a case and chooses the proper legal response, it is free from blame for any consequences that may develop as a result of its action. How the court's decision affects the offender or other people concerned is not usually the judge's responsibility. The judge is not supposed to think predominantly in such utilitarian terms—he is bound by the law. Whereas the applied scientist is responsible for the future consequences of his decisions, the lawyer and, especially, the judge are free from such responsibility, provided that their decisions are in line with past decisions, or precedents. One role is oriented and responsible to the past, whereas the other is oriented and responsible to the future (Aubert, 1965).

However, despite the incompatible orientations of mental health and criminal justice, in the United States the criminal justice system is sometimes used to provide what are essentially medical and social services. There are three results of attempting this unworkable combination (Allen, 1964: 3–11): (1) the medical and social services are not effectively delivered by the justice system; (2) personnel and money of the justice system are diverted from the services which could be effectively offered; and (3) the agencies of criminal justice are sometimes corrupted and demoralized.

The ineffective delivery of social services is reflected in the handling of the crime of vagrancy, which is usually associated with alcoholism. The continual legal processing of vagrant alcoholics is a legal reaction to a problem of medical need. It is easy to demonstrate that repeated arrests and convictions of vagrant alcoholics do not effectively deal with the problem. Obviously such arrests and convictions divert the time of police officers and judges from other law enforcement activities. Finally, at times the combination of social-medical services and criminal justice leads to the corruption of law enforcement agencies, since in such cases there is sometimes no complainant, making it easy for the police to be bought off, as in the enforcement of the laws prohibiting homosexual relations between consenting adults or the illegal sale of narcotics to drug addicts.

Social workers, psychologists, psychiatrists, and sociologists generally agree that a progressive legal structure pays little attention to the crime alleged, but instead focuses attention on the needs of the defendant. Rather than take the old neoclassical position of making the punishment fit the crime, they argue for making the state's reaction fit the needs of the individual. However, this position overlooks the possibility that before we can know an individual's problems we must first know the nature of his or her acts. After all, some persons mistakenly convicted of crimes have been subjected to many years of unnecessary rehabilitation. The problem is that the concern with rehabilitation has encouraged procedural laxity and irregularity, since its emphasis on the individual's needs results in a lessened concern with the exact facts of a case.

Troy Duster (1970) notes society's inconsistent attitude regarding the relationship between crime and mental disease. The criminal is often seen as responsible for his acts, yet at the same time as mentally ill and in need of therapy, for most serious crime is commonly considered the work of madmen. "One must be mentally healthy in order to commit a crime, but the commission of a crime reflects an unhealthy mental state" (Duster, 1970: 227). The way this inconsistency is usually resolved is to consider the accused criminal to be mentally responsible during arrest, trial, and conviction. Just prior to the trial, the defense attorney and the prosecutor usually attempt to bargain with the accused, assuming that he is a rational person. Once incarcerated, the convicted becomes defined as mentally ill and therefore in need of a prison rehabilitation program.

The myth of rehabilitation

What seems to be an increasing amount of talk and writing by professional social scientists, journalists, and government officials about the rehabilitation of criminals serves to perpetuate the fiction that something called rehabilitation is taking place in American prisons. One initial indication that this talk is public relations fantasy work may be found in the personnel breakdown and budgets of most correctional institutions. Typically no more than 5 percent of the budgets are spent directly on therapists and other social scientists who could participate in a therapy program. One interesting practice to support the fiction of rehabilitation is a name change in many institutions. Prisons become training centers, and reformatories become youth camps. All this helps foster the myth at no added cost and with no organizational change.

Social science knowledge

This discussion of the myth of rehabilitation or therapy programs, however, should not be construed as a suggestion that well-funded and fully implemented programs are a panacea for crime control. There is considerable evidence that in California, the state which has made the greatest efforts to develop and maintain a well-financed therapy program, the program has had little or no effect on the target population (Mitford, 1973). There is considerable evidence that social scientists, including psychiatrists, do not have sufficient information to develop a useful rehabilitation program even when funds are made available. The evidence indicates that the type of institution, the type of therapy program, the type of staff, and the length of sentence appear to have no impact on recidivism rates (Martinson, 1974; Bailey, 1966; Wilkins, 1969: 78). Community-based treatment, such as confining convicted criminals in halfway houses at night and allowing them to work by day in the community, is more humane and less costly, but is no more effective in altering recidivism rates (von Hirsch, 1976: 15).

Other evidence exists that there is insufficient information to implement rehabilitation programs. A recent study found that psychiatrists could not distinguish between a group of pseudopatients acting normally and other hospital patients (Rosenhan, 1973). This inability to distinguish real patients from pseudopatients raises doubts about whether the medical model of crime control is a viable alternative to models which assume the essential rationality of actors, even those which assume that they act from the basest of motives.

The sexual psychopath laws, whose passage and content have been greatly influenced by psychiatrists, are a good example of the lack of information about mental disease (Sutherland, 1950). Tappan (1960: 411) shows that

by statutory definition in a number of the states, sexual psychopaths are individuals who are neither insane nor feeble-minded but who lack the capacity to control their sexual impulses. . . .

Since the concept of psychopathy is so variously defined by the specialists, it is not surprising to discover a wide disparity in the definitions that have been formulated in these statutes. The states obviously look to quite different qualities as evidence of dangerous sexual psychopathy (Tappan, 1960: 412).

Indeed, there is no agreement as to the syndromes or aberrations that justify special treatment. The statutes generally specify that those found to qualify as sexual psychopaths are subject to indefinite civil commitment to a state mental hospital.

Hospital personnel responsible for alleged sexual psychopaths committed to them by the courts discover a wide range of psychological types, including many people with no recognizable psychological problem (Tappan, 1960: 412–413).

Psychopathology is defined in the statutes by such terminology as "impulsiveness of behavior," "lack of customary standards of good judgment," "emotional instability," or "inability to control impulses" (Tappan, 1960: 413).

It is argued by some psychiatrists that these laws do not accurately describe the psychological characteristics of those charged with sex offenses (Tappan, 1960: 413).

Indeed, the extreme has been reached recently by Alan Harrington (1972: 45–46), who puts almost everyone into the psychopath category:

We are now confronted by a band of psychopaths . . . in their various ways evil and sometimes beneficent, headlong and magical, louts and schemers, children unrestrained and charged with energy . . . drunkards and forgers, addicts, flower children, Mafia loan shark battering his victim who can't pay up, charming actor who makes crippled little boys and girls laugh, charming orator, murderer, the prophet who makes us love life again, gentle, nomadic guitarist, hustling politician, hustling judge, writers and preachers coming back with a vengeance to visit retribution on the middle classes that rejected them, whore and pimp, cop on the take, chanters filling the multitudes with joy, prancing Adonis of rock concerts, the saint who lies down in front of tractors, and student rebel, icily dominating Nobel Prize winner stealing credit from laboratory assistants, the businessman who then steals the scientist's perception, turning it into millions . . . all, all doing their thing, which is the psychopathic commandment.

As a consequence of this confusion of definitions, very often social scientists mistake what Hartung (1966: 177) calls their upper-class conception of what the average upper-class person is, for a scientific definition of mental health. For the most part, persons are judged to be mentally ill because their behavior fails to measure up to middle- or upper-class values. The angry outbursts of ghetto blacks, for example, are defined by most whites, including white psychiatrists, as evidence of *irrational* rage and psychological *maladjustment*. A small percentage of lower-class people classified as mentally ill can be identified as such by other lower-class people, as, for example, a man who claims he is Napoleon and acts accordingly. But much of what is called mental illness may simply be lower-class behavior that those in higher social classes define as pathological. This would help explain why researchers find so much of what is defined as serious mental illness and hospitalization among the poor (Hollingshead and Redlich, 1958). Also, it should not be surprising that Linsky (1970) found that the ratio of involuntary to voluntary admissions to mental hospitals was highest among nonwhites and persons with the least education.

It is sometimes claimed that individuals are civilly committed because they are dangerous, even if only to themselves, yet some types of dangerous behavior are ignored, and some are even rewarded, such as race-car driving and the behavior of trapeze artists, astronauts, and Green Berets (Szasz, 1968: 45–46). Moreover, much of the behavior that is most dangerous to society may reflect a normal adaptation to conditions of life that the courts cannot control (Allen, 1964: 52). Rehabilitation in such instances is a farce; the court hears such cases for one reason only—because of the threat to the community, not in order to rehabilitate or change the defendants, since the community conditions which are the source of the defendants' problems cannot be changed by the court. People are committed not because of dangerousness but because their criminal behavior is annoying to someone in the community. However, the results of anonymous questionnaires show that most middle-class Americans have committed crimes; yet these seldom result in commitment.

What, then, is meant when people discuss adjustment and rehabilitation for those convicted of crime and then incarcerated? Are they referring to an attempt to help the individual adjust better to his social environment both in the prison and in society? If so, one problem is that adjustment to the artificial environment of the prison may impede rather than facilitate adjustment to free society, where the individual must assume many responsibilities which are absent from the controlled atmosphere of the prison. Aside from this problem, what if, as is very common, the prisoner's home is in a decaying black ghetto where poverty is rampant and children die of lead poisoning from paint and from the bites of rats as large as small dogs? Does adjustment mean helping the "client" learn to live with the rats and like it? Is not, in fact, the human response to such conditions hatred and aggression? It reflects an obscene professionalism when social scientists recommend that their clients adjust to conditions which they themselves would find unendurable.

Types of rehabilitation programs

Several types of contemporary rehabilitation programs which aim at the control of criminal behavior will be discussed to demonstrate the coercive and often obscene nature of such ideas.

Behavior modification. One attractive fad in rehabilitation is behavior modification. Although there are different types of behavior modification, the basic idea is the use of rewards to reinforce desired behavior and/or the use of punishment to extinguish unwanted behavior.

A psychologist, James V. McConnell (1970: 74), boasts:

I believe that the day has come when we can combine sensory deprivation with drugs, hypnosis and astute manipulation of reward and punishment to gain almost absolute control over an individual's behavior. It should be possible then to achieve a very rapid and highly effective type of positive brainwashing that would allow us to make dramatic changes in a person's behavior and personality. I foresee the day when we could convert the worst criminal into a decent, respectable citizen in a matter of a few months—or perhaps even less time than that.

We'd assume that a felony was clear evidence that the criminal had somehow acquired [a] full-blown social neurosis and needed to be cured, not punished. We'd send him to a rehabilitation center where he'd undergo positive brainwashing until we were quite sure he had become a law-abiding citizen who would not again commit an antisocial act. We'd probably have to restructure his entire personality (emphasis ours) (McConnell, 1970: 74).

McConnell's assumption that all crime is somehow related to mental illness is speculative at best and ignores the issue of the law violator's rights, denying him even the integrity of his own personality.

Some attempts at behavior modification in rehabilitation programs use positive reinforcement or rewards, such as special privileges in the institution for conforming behavior (Schwitzgebel, 1971). One example of the use of rewards for conforming behavior is the "token economy" program often employed in institutions for juveniles. The idea is that a juvenile who enters the institution receives no privileges—is not allowed to go to movies or eat desserts, and has only the barest essentials in his room—until, by obeying the institutional rules, the youth earns credits with which to buy such privileges (see, for example, Schwitzgebel, 1971: 7–8). Although such programs using positive reinforcement are not frightening, the bizarre degree of control claimed by McConnell does lend itself to abuses. These abuses are of special concern because of McConnell's questionable assumptions regarding crime and mental illness, which spawned or at least legitimated such programs. "At the Iowa Security Medical Facility, inmates who lie or swear are injected with apomorphine, a drug that sets them vomiting uncontrollably for from 15 minutes to an hour" (Sage, 1974: 17).

Another drug, Anectine, which induces sensations of suffocation and drowning, has been used at California's maximum security institution at Vacaville in an attempt to associate the drug with and extinguish violent behavior. As could be expected, this drug causes great anxiety among subjects (Mitford, 1973: 127–128).

Such cases are more than curious anomalies. They are natural outgrowths of the total lack of respect for the individual and for human dignity that provides the philosophic foundation for behavior modification.

Reality therapy. Another psychiatric idea for the rehabilitation of prisoners is the relatively new Reality Therapy, developed by William Glasser, which has rapidly caught on in state after state as the approved vehicle for rehabilitation programs. The basic tenets of Reality Therapy are outlined below (Glasser, 1965: 6).

In their unsuccessful effort to fulfill their needs, no matter what behavior they choose, all patients have a common characteristic: *they all deny the reality of the world around them.* . . . . Therapy will be successful when they are able to give up denying the world and recognize that reality not only exists but that they must fulfill their needs within its framework.

The therapist must teach the patient better ways to fulfill his needs within the confines of reality (Glasser, 1965: 21).

In other words, Reality Therapy is an effort to help patients adjust to their situation or station in life, no matter how lowly and debased it is. Furthermore, unlike conventional Freudian therapy, Reality Therapy lays great stress on abiding by social values and morals. Instead of attempting to reduce concern and anxiety, as does Freudian therapy, it seeks to increase patients' concern regarding the violation of societal norms. Obviously, such an approach is extremely supportive of obedience to the status quo, and it wrongly assumes either that there is a value consensus or that the ethics of powerful groups are more reasonable than the ethics of other groups in American society.

In this view, the therapist's problem is to help patients act "responsibly." *Correcting the patients' behavior and not their attitudes is the goal of Reality Therapy.* People violate the law, according to Glasser, because they are irresponsible, not because they are angry or bored. In other words, what should be impressed upon the law violator is that his violation is entirely his own fault.

After having sanctified obedience to law, Glasser (1965: 23) concedes, using Thoreau as an example, that some responsible people do not conform to society's rules. And at times, according to Glasser, to be responsible one must violate the laws of society (1965: 14): "In Nazi Germany, a responsible man, by our definition, would have been placed in a concentration camp." Yet almost immediately he swings back and encourages docility in the face of American racism and American poverty (Glasser, 1965: 32):

We never encourage hostility or acting out irresponsible impulses, for that only compounds the problem. We never condemn society. If a Negro, for example, feels limited by the white society, he must still take a responsible course of action.

In other words, responsible Germans violated the law, whereas responsible Americans must obey the law.

Responsibility, a concept basic to Reality Therapy, is here defined as the ability to fulfill one's needs, and to do so *in a way that does not deprive others of the ability to fulfill their needs* (Glasser, 1965: 13).

The clear implication is that legal rights could be substituted for needs. The "responsible" person never violates the legal rights of others. Responsible action includes only behavior within the legal boundaries of the society, for "usually the law is psychiatrically right . . . because human beings with human needs have made the law according to their needs" (Glasser, 1965: 57). What is known about the social origins of law and pressure from special interest groups makes Glasser's optimism seem terribly naive. Even so, Glasser (1965: 9) wavers again in admitting that some people, such as blacks in the South, cannot meet their needs because of environmental, not psychiatric, problems.

Since the boundary between environmental and psychological problems is not defined and seems subject to personal whim, Reality Therapy appears to be no more than intellectually empty moralizing, and the term *irresponsible behavior* appears to be no more than name-calling or labeling. Small wonder that this approach to adjustment is so popular among law enforcement officials charged with the control and rehabilitation of prison inmates, usually without adequate income, information, or personnel.

Uses of the rehabilitation myth

Szasz suggests that the myth of rehabilitation may be useful to a group interested in coercion and political power. "The redefinition of moral values as health values will now appear in a new light. If people believe that health values justify coercion, but that moral and political values do not, those who wish to coerce others will tend to enlarge the category of health values at the expense of the category of moral values" (Szasz, 1968: 5–6).

The rehabilitation ideal or myth has led to longer sentences, for if individuals are civilly committed to a mental hospital, there is no date of mandatory release, and each commitment is potentially a life sentence. Completely indeterminate prison sentences, for example, one year to life, and indeterminate-range prison sentences, such as 1–5 or 5–15 years, have a similar effect. The logic is that if the criminally committed are sick and need rehabilitation, then the prison serves the same purpose as a hospital. The argument continues that it is difficult to know exactly how long the cure will take, so an indeterminate sentence is usually acceptable to those supporting rehabilitation programs. Instead of the old-fashioned punitive system of two years of incarceration as punishment for auto theft, now, with the blessing of many social scientists (von Hirsch, 1976: 27), the convicted criminal is given 1–10 years in the same institution. In the minds of the general public, legislators, and judges, the 1–10-year sentence may be defined in terms of an average rather than its potential maximum. However, indeterminate-type sentences, in fact, result in longer periods of imprisonment since parole board members are more conservative than is usually imagined (Rubin, 1961). Contrary to popular opinion, indeterminate sentences are not necessary for early release on parole; even states with sentences specifying a definite term to be served have early-release provisions.

Another problem in indeterminate sentencing is that such sentencing helps a prison staff maintain a reign of terror. Prisoners recognize that the only way they can possibly hope for an early release is to bow to every staff whim, since a bad recommendation can scuttle their parole chances (Mitford, 1973). After serving the minimum term of a sentence, the prisoner typically has at least a right to an annual review of his case for possible parole. Many prisoners, however, do not insist on such hearings because they regard them as shams which only raise false hopes of release. The prospect is very tantalizing and tortuous for the prisoner—being potentially very close to freedom yet still facing the prospect of serving many more years.

The Soviet Union has raised the use of the medical model for political coercion to a high art (see Stone, 1972; Medvedev and Medvedev, 1971). The Soviet logic seems to be that anyone not liking the existing political regime is insane, since life in that Soviet socialist country is obviously a paradise for the masses.

Traditional versus democratic treatment alternatives

Traditional assumptions of rehabilitation programs.[1] Much of the original concern for the rehabilitation of prison inmates came from groups of religious people who believed that through evangelism and isolation they could change the felon and perhaps save his soul. Given this historical emphasis on the individual soul, we should not be surprised that most contemporary practical and theoretical approaches to the rehabilitation of prison inmates have usually focused on the individual personality as the object in need

---

[1] The following paragraphs concerning rehabilitation are taken from Galliher (1971).

of change (Cressey, 1955: 116–117, 1965: 87–88). Cressey attributes this emphasis on the individual personality to the sociologists' neglect of rehabilitation theory; by this neglect, they have left the field to psychiatrists. He also suggests that such an orientation to the rehabilitation of prison inmates is of little practical value, since it is impossible to recruit even the minimum number of professional therapists needed into correctional work (1965: 88).

It has also often been implicitly assumed by many of those involved in correctional research (perhaps as an outgrowth of the religious underpinnings) that an *overall* or *general* change in the individual personality structure may be required to insure against recidivism (Cressey, 1955, 1965; Ohlin, 1956: 29–32; Sykes, 1956). Among many of these same students of correction, however, there is wide agreement that the harsh environment of the prison is an unlikely place to implement any reformation of the prisoner (Sykes, 1956; Barnes, 1965; Cressey, 1960; Clemmer, 1950), and this helps account for the popularity of Reality Therapy, which attempts less than total reformation of people's attitudes. Since most contemporary prisons are not only oppressive and antiquated but also fail to provide adequate professional treatment services, it is obvious that the prison is no place to attempt major alterations in the attitudes and orientation of the prisoners.

Recently there seems to have been some movement away from the individualist psychiatric position and toward awareness of the role of the group in the development and support of attitudes and behavior. Consequently, there has been a similar shift toward the use of techniques which attempt to modify the orientation of the group in which the prisoner is involved.[2] However, even though these techniques work through the social group, the ultimate goal is still usually to implement a *basic change in the orientation of the individual.* It is still often assumed that the successful culmination of these treatment techniques is the subject's rejection of criminal motives and his acceptance of new, noncriminal motives. By treating groups rather than individuals, these techniques minimize the problem of insufficient professional staff. However, since these group techniques share the essential goals of the psychiatric ap-

---

[2] For a discussion of these group-related techniques, see McCorkle (1952), Conrad (1967: 236–248), Weeks (1958), and Fenton et al., (1967).

proach, they also share the problem of an unsuitable treatment environment.

Traditional parole practices. Again, probably because much of the original concern for the rehabilitation of convicted prisoners came from religious groups, the supervision of convicts after their release from prison has traditionally been very stodgy and decidedly moralistic. Many states have insisted that parolees abstain from alcoholic beverages and extramarital cohabitation, keep regular hours, have regular employment, and not marry without permission (Arluke, 1956). All these requirements seem designed to force the parolee to live a circumspect rural middle-class way of life. This is especially inappropriate for the rehabilitation of urban lower-class prisoners, who make up the majority of most prison populations. Some parole officers claim, however, that these rules are not usually enforced but that they are useful in revoking paroles when it is believed but cannot be proved that a parolee has committed another crime. The injustice of this is obvious.

The compulsive concern for rigidly conventional behavior as evidence of rehabilitation is, predictably, also reflected in attempts at occupational guidance and training. Anything less than an honest day's work, usually measured in terms of physical labor, is not considered wholly desirable for the rehabilitation of the inmate. Not only his leisure-time pursuits but also his work choice must stand the test of puritanical moral guidelines that even many generally law-abiding citizens would be hard put to satisfy. Apparently we have traditionally demanded that the released prisoner lead an even more exemplary life than do most other citizens. It is curious that we should demand greater conformity from those alleged to be least able to conform.

We are forced to recognize that the psychiatric personality-reformation approach to rehabilitation is both incomplete and unworkable with the existing resources. Newer group-related techniques, though avoiding some of the manpower problems of the psychiatric approach, are still usually oriented to the same impossible goals. Moreover, it is also apparent that the demands made upon parolees are equally unworkable and unreasonable. If current correctional practices are not useful, then we might ask what sociology has to offer in their place.

Anomie theory and rehabilitation. To provide a sociological and noncoercive alternative to existing correctional practice and theory, it is first necessary to have some idea of current sociological notions about the causes of deviance. Modern anomie theory as formulated by Merton (1957, chapters 4, 5) has enjoyed wide popularity among sociologists as an explanation of deviant behavior. In contrast to psychiatric explanations, anomie theory emphasizes social structural variables in explaining the etiology of deviant behavior. Anomie theory holds that deviance is a consequence of discrepancies between culturally prescribed goals and the socially approved means available to achieve those goals. Some people are in relatively unfavorable competitive positions vis-à-vis legitimate means for goal attainment. Consequently, these people experience frustration and strain and are motivated to resort to deviant or illegitimate means.

If anomie theory is accepted as a reasonable explanation of the social etiology of deviant behavior, then it seems logical to consult it when attempting to modify such behavior. Perhaps anomie theory can offer useful and heretofore untapped leads in efforts to rehabilitate the offender. From this point of view giving prisoners vocational training in conventional occupations, such as carpentry and plumbing, can be seen as opening legitimate avenues for success. However, such programs are effective only among inmates who assume a conventional orientation and reject the notion allegedly prevalent among prisoners that "only fools work" (Sykes and Messinger, 1960: 11). Quite obviously, carpentry skills are of little value to the individual who rejects their use in possible future employment.

Training in social manipulation—A democratic alternative. Other useful training, however, can be offered in the prison—training that does not necessarily assume a conventional orientation. This seems to be true of the Dale Carnegie "human relations" courses taught in some state and federal prisons and reformatories. One fundamental goal of such programs is to train the inmate in the known techniques of social manipulation. The student in such a course is taught how to control other people by means of consciously effected and skillfully convincing role playing (Carnegie, 1936). The acquisition of these skills appears to open up (1) new legal avenues for achieving success, (2) new illegal avenues, and (3) new avenues that are neither strictly legal nor clearly illegal.[3]

---

[3] For a discussion of the opening up and closing off of legitimate and illegitimate opportunities as alternative responses to deviance, see Cohen (1965: 9–12).

In such courses inmate-students are sometimes taught techniques for manipulating social situations that might arise during interviews for employment. They practice skills useful in handling the responses of employers who are suspicious and leery of ex-convicts. Such techniques may be useful in securing an initial opportunity in many different types of legitimate employment that might otherwise be closed to the individual because of his criminal record. More specifically, expertise in social manipulation obviously supplies some of the requisite skills for legitimate careers in sales and public relations. This illustrates how possession of these skills opens noncriminal means of achievement which do not generally conflict with the nonconventional belief that only fools work, since prisoners, most of whom have lower-class backgrounds, would probably define work as involving physical labor. Also, conventional sales work may not require a basic change in orientation among inmates who are cynical and predatory in their relations with others. The individual can usually perform adequately in legal sales work without necessarily changing this attitude. Like Reality Therapy, training in social manipulation requires no changes in attitudes but only alterations in activities.

New illegal avenues for achievement might also be opened as a result of training in social manipulation. As Sutherland (1937: 21) has noted, professional thieves, including successful con men, are generally not recruited from the slums, since slum dwellers usually lack the social skills required for such activities. As a consequence of training in social manipulation, however, the lower-class inmate-student may acquire the necessary finesse for manipulating people to obtain illegal goals without resorting to physically aggressive behavior. Artfully executed confidence games and swindles can be accomplished with the individual's new knowledge of human relations (Maurer, 1940). Some would argue that these illegal avenues for achievement have the distinct advantage of involving less likelihood of criminal prosecution than would physically aggressive crimes. The likelihood of detection is lessened because victims of confidence games are either too embarrassed by their own gullibility or too deeply involved in the crime itself to complain to the police. An example of such involvement is the person who, believing that he has been given a tip through illegal sources on the outcome of a horse race, then bets a large sum of money, only to find that both the tip and the bet were frauds. Even if the offender is prosecuted, the punishment is likely to be lighter than that for physically aggressive crime.

Finally, new avenues for achievement are opened that are neither strictly legal nor clearly illegal. Such behavior may be proscribed by statute, that is, it is technically illegal, yet seldom or never actually prosecuted. Certain business practices, perhaps best exemplified in the used car enterprise which misrepresents the goods it sells, fall into this category. In more general terms, the ability to use social manipulation techniques allows the individual to take advantage of the fact that in our achievement-oriented society there is a large gap between strictly legal and clearly illegal practices in money matters and business transactions. The kind of behavior that falls between business practices that are considered morally exemplary and those that are clearly proscribed by law is characterized by normative confusion and ambivalence (Sutherland, 1949: 45–51; Aubert, 1952). This ambivalence is reflected in the public admiration for the salesman who could "sell an icebox to an Eskimo" even though the intent of such a sale is obviously exploitative. The traditional laissez-faire orientation to business practices, and the caveat emptor admonition (let the buyer beware), furnish other evidence of the relative lack of normative control of business affairs. The caveat emptor admonition appears to warn the buyer to be on his guard because fair and honest treatment is not guaranteed by the normative structure. As a matter of fact, a case can be made for the argument that in an achievement-oriented acquisitive society like ours, the wide gap between the strictly legal and the illegal in business transactions allows individuals more freedom in their attempts to meet the culturally prescribed demands for success.

The training of prisoners in social manipulation should in most cases be supplemented by instruction in language skills. The required pleasant and conventional facade can be projected only if the student commands a passing middle-class knowledge of word meaning, pronunciation, and sentence structure. Undoubtedly, some prisoners will be unable to develop these skills, and others will do so only with great effort. Such training in social manipulation does not coerce prisoners and is designed to help equalize opportunities between the rich and the poor. Clearly, this proposal does not envisage the best of all possible worlds, but attempts to bring greater equality to a society thoroughly based on human exploitation.

Setting up the rehabilitation program

We are not suggesting that prison or parole authorities openly advocate that inmates resort to nonviolent illegal means of achievement. This would not be tolerated by the public. Rather, it seems that the staff should endorse role-playing skills for use only in strictly legal enterprises. Those inmates who are not conventionally oriented are likely to discover for themselves the potential use of such skills in illegal activities.[4]

The programs should be fairly easy to implement in most areas. Unlike industrial production in prisons or industrial training and apprenticeship programs, which are often opposed by labor and manufacturing groups because they feel that such programs unfairly compete with their economic interests, training in social manipulation meets with no similar outside opposition. In some cases, initial opposition to such programs may come from political and correctional officials. Those involved in the development of these programs can argue that this approach to the rehabilitation of prison inmates would benefit not only the prisoner but also society. Since these programs give an ex-prisoner more alternative opportunities to achieve success, the likelihood that he will choose an illegal solution is probably diminished. Even if acquisition of these manipulatory techniques does not deter an individual from future criminal violations, the likelihood that he will resort to aggressive violations of the law seems to be diminished since other illegal avenues of goal attainment are available to him. The person now possesses skills in socially manipulating others and can use those skills in criminal activities. According to Sutherland (1937: 43), professional thieves who are skilled in social manipulation do not find it necessary to resort to physical aggression in following their illegal careers.

The suggestion is for more flexible rehabilitation programs not demanding a display of basic attitude alterations among the unconventionally oriented. Such programs would include courses in human relations. They would demand less moral rectitude in the occupational choice of the parolees when the facts indicate that this could help them lead a less dangerous, less bothersome, and perhaps even more law-abiding life. If our current attempts to

---

[4] In one reformatory, the inmate-clerk responsible for the administration of the program confided that some men were initially motivated to participate in the Dale Carnegie course by the stated desire to become good confidence men.

rehabilitate prison inmates are judged to be less than a complete success, one possible reason may be that we have been attempting in a feeble manner to implement more change among inmates than is reasonable or fair.

Not all offenders, however, commit crimes because of a lack of access to legitimate opportunities for income. Those who have committed sex offenses do not usually have this problem. Yet even for this group, the same principle of opening new opportunities without imposing any moral judgments is applicable and has been used. "At Atascadero State Mental Hospital in California, homosexual child molesters are trained to cruise in gay bars so they will not have to resort to children . . . ; heterosexual child molesters are taught to pick up women at parties; and rapists are coached in sex techniques to improve their relationships with their wives" (Sage, 1974: 16) (copyright © 1974 *Human Behavior* Magazine. Reprinted by permission).

CONSTITUTIONAL CHANGE TO CONTROL CRIME

Constitutional change is yet another method of attempting to control crime. In 1968 the U.S. Congress, in near-hysteria over the series of political assassinations, riots, and demonstrations that occurred earlier in the 1960s, passed the Omnibus Crime Control Bill and Safe Streets Act (Harris, 1968). The act specifically provided that information obtained from clandestine police wiretaps could be used as evidence in court in cases involving national security and organized crime, contrary to the Fifth Amendment's protection against self-incrimination and the Fourth Amendment's limitations on legal police searches. Earlier, we discussed the fear generated by the Mafia myth. That fear also lent support to this constitutional change.

LEGALIZATION AND DECRIMINALIZATION

Legalization and decriminalization are the most efficient methods for eliminating a crime problem, and, applied to much behavior now classed as criminal, would pose no threat to society. Decriminalization, unlike legalization, might control the activity through civil fines rather than arrests, which is sometimes suggested as an approach to prostitution. Decriminalization might involve medical treatment rather than arrests, as is often recommended in dealing with alcoholism. Homosexual relations between consenting adults could also be decriminalized, with no increased physical threat to the community. Legalization, on the other hand, occurred when prohibition was repealed. Americans who were routinely committing alcohol-related offenses could now legally continue their sale and distribution of alcohol. Similar changes in our nation's vice laws are sometimes recommended in this context. Prostitution could be legalized, as has been done in some parts of Nevada. The same applies to gambling, which has been legalized in some forms in Nevada and New York.

Alfred Lindesmith (1965) has urged the adoption of the British system in the control of drug addiction. This system decriminalizes drug addiction by enabling addicts in Great Britain to obtain drugs legally and maintain their habit at a small cost through prescriptions from physicians. This not only legalizes what is, in fact, a physical state (addiction), but reduces other crimes as well. It is estimated that many property crimes are committed by addicts who steal to obtain the vast amounts of money required to support their addiction (Schur, 1965: 140). The only reason addiction is so expensive is that since the drugs are illegal, the risk in selling them is high, forcing the price up. If the drugs could be obtained from physicians, the price would plummet, forcing most clandestine drug dealers out of business. This happened to many bootleggers when prohibition was repealed.

Since decriminalization forces clandestine dealers out of business, we could anticipate their opposition to such legal changes, as well as opposition from narcotics control agencies whose existence and need for being are also threatened by such changes (Schur, 1965). Opposition also sometimes comes from moral conservatives, such as fundamentalist Protestant groups. Concerted opposition from such diverse groups has made legalization very difficult to achieve. Yet such an approach to crime control seems especially well suited to victimless offenses, such as prostitution, gambling, and drug use. A similar decriminalization is in order for the handling of lower-class alcoholics, now usually prosecuted for vagrancy.

CRIME PREVENTION

The idea of preventing crime from occurring rather than merely punishing the offender sounds very attractive at first glance. It is only when specific proposals for preventing crime are put forward that we see how frightening this idea can, in fact, be. The four methods of controlling crime, that is, punishment, rehabilitation, constitutional change, and legalization, are also ways of approaching prevention.

Punishment before trial of those considered crime prone may seem ridiculous, yet that was suggested in 1969 by the Nixon Administration (Graham, 1969). It was called preventive detention and would have involved denying bail to those awaiting trial if the judge felt that there was a likelihood of their continuing to commit crimes. Rehabilitation might also be used in crime prevention. When certain personality characteristics are linked to crime, as they are by some researchers, these findings suggest that it would be useful if such personality traits were spotted in schoolchildren so that they can be given special help, perhaps special medication, before they get into trouble with the law. Constitutional change might involve giving the police and courts greater freedom to arrest and incarcerate those considered most predisposed to crime. Legalization or decriminalization of certain behaviors would, of course, prevent the labeling as criminal of those predisposed to such acts. Homosexuals and drug addicts would obviously benefit from the change.

At times political liberals urge social reforms, such as slum clearance and equalization of opportunities, with the promise that taking such steps would prevent crime. Such promises were made in the 1960s, as Moynihan (1969) has observed, yet no decreases in crime occurred. The problem is that bad living conditions and lack of educational and occupational opportunity are not the only causes of crime because, as evidence from anonymous questionnaires and the White House Watergate tapes indicates, all types of crime occur in all social classes. When even the leaders of the nation are implicated in burglaries, it is time to reconsider the importance of slums as a direct cause of crime. Such social changes as slum clearance must be justified in their own right as morally compelling without the empty promise that they will prevent crime.

CONCLUSION

The various justifications for the punishment of crime are readily recognized and easy to understand. Ironically, the alternative of treatment or rehabilitation has even greater potential for repression than punishment, mainly because its coercive nature is not usually recognized. Political conservatives often deride the notion of rehabilitation as senseless sentimentality and argue instead for swift and sure punishment of convicted criminals as a means of controlling crime. The late J. Edgar Hoover (1958: 1–2), the longtime head of the FBI, aptly represented the conservative position. However, political liberals typically support programs labeled as rehabilitation and oppose punishment. They see punishment as heartless as well as ineffective in controlling crime and argue that treatment is morally and intellectually superior. This continuing dialogue, and especially the liberals' claims that rehabilitation is an effective and humane method of crime control, seems to have diverted public attention from the coercive characteristics of rehabilitation programs.

The only just rehabilitation alternatives are those which attempt to open up new opportunities to those convicted of crime. Legalization is another noncoercive solution to crime control. It seems especially useful in cases of crimes without victims, such as prostitution, gambling, drug use, and vagrancy. Recently, Americans and their elected representatives have been so cowed and frightened by the specter of crime that they have allowed a major constitutional alteration to be enacted under the banner of crime control.

This book has made no attempt to present a value-free approach to crime and its control. As stated at the outset in Chapter 1, the explicit ethical orientation of our approach maintains that all people deserve equal chances for personal freedom and physical survival. If one accepts that orientation, then laws which represent only the needs of elites or powerful interest groups are patently unjust. The same conclusion is reached when we consider the unequal treatment that the poor receive in their dealings with the police and the courts. Moreover, such an ethical position allows no excuses for the use of official government crime statistics as reflective of actual criminal behavior and leads to the conclusion that in U.S. society crime is for the most part a result of discriminatory and elitist definitions.

REFERENCES

Allen, Francis A.
   1964   *The Borderland of Criminal Justice: Essays in Law and Criminology.* Chicago: University of Chicago Press.

American Friends Service Committee
1971   *Struggle for Justice.* New York: Hill and Wang.

Arluke, Nat R.
1956   "A Summary of Parole Rules," *National Probation and Parole Association Journal* 2(January): 6–13.

Aubert, Vilhelm
1952   "White-Collar Crime and Social Structure," *American Journal of Sociology* 58(November): 263–271.
1965   *The Hidden Society.* Totowa, N.J.: Bedminster Press.

Bailey, Walter C.
1966   "Correctional Outcome: An Evaluation of 100 Reports," *Journal of Criminal Law, Criminology, and Police Science* 57(June): 153–160.

Barnes, Harry E.
1965   "The Contemporary Prison: A Menace to Inmate Rehabilitation and the Repression of Crime," *Key Issues* 2: 11–23.

Bentham, Jeremy
1823   *An Introduction to the Principles of Morals and Legislation.* Reprinted 1948. New York: Hafner Publishing Co.

Campbell, Donald T. and H. Laurence Ross
1968   "The Connecticut Crackdown on Speeding: Time-Series Data in Quasi-Experimental Analysis," *Law and Society Review* 3(August): 33–53.

Carnegie, Dale
1936   *How to Win Friends and Influence People.* New York: Simon and Schuster.

Clemmer, Donald
1950   "Observations on Imprisonment as a Source of Criminality," *Journal of Criminal Law and Criminology* 41(September–October): 311–319.

Cohen, Albert K.
1965   "The Sociology of the Deviant Act: Anomie Theory and Beyond," *American Sociological Review* 30(February): 5–14.

Conrad, John P.
1967   *Crime and Its Correction.* Berkeley: University of California Press.

Cressey, Donald R.
1955   "Changing Criminals: The Application of the Theory of Differential Association," *American Journal of Sociology* 61(September): 116–120.

1960   "Limitations on Organization of Treatment in the Modern Prison," pp. 78–110 in *Theoretical Studies in Social Organization of the Prison,* Pamphlet No. 15, Social Science Research Council, New York.

1965   "Theoretical Foundations for Using Criminals in the Rehabilitation of Criminals," *Key Issues* 2: 87–101.

Durkheim, Emile
1933   *The Division of Labor in Society.* George Simpson, trans. Glencoe, Ill.: Free Press.

Duster, Troy
1970   *The Legislation of Morality: Law, Drugs, and Moral Judgment.* New York, Free Press.

Erikson, Kai T.
1966   *Wayward Puritans: A Study in the Sociology of Deviance.* New York: John Wiley and Sons.

Fenton, Norman, Ernest G. Reimer, and Harry A. Wilmer, eds.
1967   *The Correctional Community.* Berkeley: University of California Press.

Galliher, John F.
1971   "Training in Social Manipulation as a Rehabilitative Technique," *Crime and Delinquency* 17(October): 431–436.

Galliher, John F., James L. McCartney, and Barbara Baum
1974   "Nebraska's Marijuana Law: A Case of Unexpected Legislative Innovation," *Law and Society Review* 8(Spring): 441–455.

Gibbs, Jack P.
1968   "Crime, Punishment, and Deterrence," *Southwestern Social Science Quarterly* 48(March): 515–530.

Glasser, William
1965   *Reality Therapy: A New Approach to Psychiatry.* New York: Harper and Row, Publishers.

Graham, Fred P.
1969   "Preventive Detention Studied as Method of Curbing Crime," *St. Louis Post Dispatch,* (January 30): 1, 4.

Grupp, Stanley E., ed.
1971   *Theories of Punishment.* Bloomington: Indiana University Press.

Hall, Jerome
1952   *Theft, Law, and Society.* 2d ed. Indianapolis: Bobbs-Merrill Co.

Harrington, Alan
1972   *Psychopaths.* New York: Simon and Schuster.

Harris, Richard
  1968 *The Fear of Crime.* New York: Praeger Publishers.

Hartung, Frank E.
  1966 *Crime, Law, and Society.* Detroit: Wayne State University Press.

Hollingshead, August B. and Frederick B. Redlich
  1958 *Social Class and Mental Illness: A Community Study.* New York: John Wiley and Sons.

Hoover, J. Edgar
  1958 "Statement of Director J. Edgar Hoover," *FBI Law Enforcement Bulletin* 27 (November): 1–2.

Lindesmith, Alfred R.
  1965 *The Addict and the Law.* Bloomington: Indiana University Press.

Linsky, Arnold S.
  1970 "Who Shall Be Excluded?: The Influence of Personal Attributes in Community Reaction to the Mentally Ill," *Social Psychiatry* 5(July): 166–171.

Martinson, Robert
  1974 "What Works—Questions and Answers about Prison Reform," *Public Interest* (Spring): 22–54.

Maurer, David W.
  1940 *The Big Con.* New York: Bobbs-Merrill Co.

McConnell, James V.
  1970 "Criminals Can Be Brainwashed—Now," *Psychology Today* 3(April): 14, 16, 18, 74.

McCorkle, Lloyd W.
  1952 "Group Therapy in the Treatment of Offenders," *Federal Probation* 16(December): 22–27.

Medvedev, Zhores A. and Roy A. Medvedev
  1971 *A Question of Madness.* New York: Alfred A. Knopf.

Merton, Robert K.
  1957 *Social Theory and Social Structure.* Rev. ed. Glencoe, Ill.: Free Press.

Mitford, Jessica
  1973 *Kind and Usual Punishment: The Prison Business.* New York: Alfred A. Knopf.

Morris, Norval
  1974a *The Future of Imprisonment.* Chicago: University of Chicago Press.
  1974b "The Future of Imprisonment: Toward a Punitive Philosophy," *Michigan Law Review* 72(May): 1161–1180.

Moynihan, Daniel P.
1969   *Maximum Feasible Misunderstanding.* New York: Free Press.

Ohlin, Lloyd E.
1956   *Sociology and the Field of Corrections.* New York: Russell Sage Foundation.

Ranulf, Svend
1964   *Moral Indignation and Middle Class Psychology.* New York: Schocken Books.

Rosenhan, D. L.
1973   "On Being Sane in Insane Places," *Science* 179(January 19): 250–258.

Rothman, David J.
1971   *The Discovery of the Asylum: Social Order and Disorder in the New Republic.* Boston: Little, Brown and Co.

Rubin, Sol
1961   *Crime and Juvenile Delinquency.* New York: Oceana Publications.

Rusche, Georg and Otto Kirchheimer
1939   *Punishment and Social Structure.* New York: Columbia University Press.

Sage, Wayne
1974   "Crime and the Clockwork Lemon," *Human Behavior* 3(September): 16–25.

Schur, Edwin M.
1965   *Crimes without Victims.* Englewood Cliffs, N.J.: Prentice-Hall.

Schwartz, Richard D. and Jerome H. Skolnick
1962   "Two Studies of Legal Stigma," *Social Problems* 10(Fall): 133–142.

Schwitzgebel, Ralph K.
1971   *Development and Legal Regulation of Coercive Behavior Modification Techniques with Offenders.* Chevy Chase, Md.: National Institute of Mental Health, Center for Studies of Crime and Delinquency, Public Health Service Publication No. 2067.

Stone, I. F.
1972   "Betrayal by Psychiatry," *New York Review of Books* 18(February 10): 7–8, 10, 12, 14.

Sutherland, Edwin H.
1937   Ed., *The Professional Thief, by a Professional Thief.* Chicago: University of Chicago Press.
1949   *White Collar Crime.* New York: Dryden Press.
1950   "The Diffusion of Sexual Psychopath Laws," *American Journal of Sociology* 56(September): 142–148.

Sykes, Gresham M.
  1956 "The Corruption of Authority and Rehabilitation," *Social Forces* 34(March): 257–262.

Sykes, Gresham M. and Sheldon L. Messinger
  1960 "The Inmate Social System," pp. 5–19 in *Theoretical Studies in Social Organization of the Prison*, Pamphlet No. 15, Social Science Research Council, New York.

Szasz, Thomas S.
  1968 *Law, Liberty, and Psychiatry.* New York: Collier Books.

Tappan, Paul W.
  1960 *Crime, Justice, and Correction.* New York: McGraw-Hill Book Co.

Tittle, Charles R.
  1969 "Crime Rates and Legal Sanctions," *Social Problems* 16(Spring): 409–423.

von Hirsch, Andrew
  1976 *Doing Justice: The Choice of Punishments.* New York: Hill and Wang.

Weeks, H. Ashley
  1958 *Youthful Offenders at Highfields.* Ann Arbor: University of Michigan Press.

Wilkins, Leslie T.
  1969 *Evaluation of Penal Measures.* New York: Random House.

15

*Two studies of legal stigma**

Richard D. Schwartz
and
Jerome H. Skolnick

Legal thinking has moved increasingly toward a sociologically meaningful view of the legal system. Sanctions, in particular, have come to be regarded in functional terms.[1] In criminal law, for instance, sanctions are said to be designed to prevent recidivism by rehabilitating, restraining, or executing the offender. They are also said to be intended to deter others from the performance of similar acts and, sometimes, to provide a channel for the expression of retaliatory motives. In such civil actions as tort or contract, monetary awards may be intended as retributive and deterrent, as in the use of punitive damages, or may be regarded as a *quid pro quo* to compensate the plaintiff for his wrongful loss.

While these goals comprise an integral part of the rationale of law, little is known about the extent to which they are fulfilled in practice. Lawmen do not as a rule make such studies, because their traditions and techniques are not designed for a systematic examination of the operation of the legal system in action, especially outside the courtroom. Thus, when extra-legal

* Reprinted from *Social Problems*, vol. 10, no. 2 (Fall 1962), pp. 133–43. Revised version of paper read at the annual meeting of the American Sociological Association, August 1960. This paper draws upon materials prepared by students of the Law and Behavioral Science Division of the Yale Law School. We wish to acknowledge the contributions of Michael Meltzner, who assisted in the experiment, and especially those of Dr. Robert Wyckoff, who surveyed medical practitioners. We are indebted to Donald T. Campbell and Hanan Selvin for valuable comments and suggestions.

[1] Legal sanctions are defined as changes in life conditions imposed through court action.

consequences—e.g., the social stigma of a prison sentence—are taken into account at all, it is through the discretionary actions of police, prosecutor, judge, and jury. Systematic information on a variety of unanticipated outcomes, those which benefit the accused as well as those which hurt him, might help to inform these decision makers and perhaps lead to changes in substantive law as well. The present paper is an attempt to study the consequences of stigma associated with legal accusation.

From a sociological viewpoint, there are several types of indirect consequences of legal sanctions which can be distinguished. These include differential deterrence, effects on the sanctionee's associates, and variations in the degree of deprivation which sanction imposes on the recipient himself.

First, the imposition of sanction, while intended as a matter of overt policy to deter the public at large, probably will vary in its effectiveness as a deterrent, depending upon the extent to which potential offenders perceive themselves as similar to the sanctionee. Such "differential deterrence" would occur if white-collar anti-trust violators were restrained by the conviction of General Electric executives, but not by invocation of the Sherman Act against union leaders.

The imposition of a sanction may even provide an unintended incentive to violate the law. A study of factors affecting compliance with federal income tax laws provides some evidence of this effect.[2] Some respondents reported that they began to cheat on their tax returns only *after* convictions for tax evasion had been obtained against others in their jurisdiction. They explained this surprising behavior by noting that the prosecutions had always been conducted against blatant violators and not against the kind of moderate offenders which they then became. These respondents were, therefore, unintentionally educated to the possibility of supposedly "safe" violations.

Second, deprivations or benefits may accrue to non-sanctioned individuals by virtue of the web of affiliations that join them to the defendant. The wife and family of a convicted man may, for instance, suffer from his arrest as much as the man himself. On the

---

[2] Richard D. Schwartz, "The Effectiveness of Legal Controls: Factors in the Reporting of Minor Items of Income on Federal Income Tax Returns." Paper presented at the annual meeting of the American Sociological Association, Chicago, 1959.

other hand, they may be relieved by his absence if the family relationship has been an unhappy one. Similarly, whole groups of persons may be affected by sanctions to an individual, as when discriminatory practices increase because of a highly publicized crime attributed to a member of a given minority group.

Finally, the social position of the defendant himself will serve to aggravate or alleviate the effects of any given sanction. Although all three indirect consequences may be interrelated, it is the third with which this paper will be primarily concerned.

FINDINGS

The subjects studied to examine the effects of legal accusation on occupational positions represented two extremes: lower-class unskilled workers charged with assault, and medical doctors accused of malpractice. The first project lent itself to a field experiment, while the second required a survey design. Because of differences in method and substance, the studies cannot be used as formal controls for each other. Taken together, however, they do suggest that the indirect effects of sanctions can be powerful, that they can produce unintended harm or unexpected benefit, and that the results are related to officially unemphasized aspects of the social context in which the sanctions are administered. Accordingly, the two studies will be discussed together, as bearing on one another. Strictly speaking, however, each can, and properly should, stand alone as a separate examination of the unanticipated consequences of legal sanctions.

Study I: The effects of a criminal court record on the employment opportunities of unskilled workers

In the field experiment, four employment folders were prepared, the same in all respects except for the criminal court record of the applicant. In all of the folders he was described as a 32-year-old single male of unspecified race, with a high school training in mechanical trades, and a record of successive short-term jobs as a kitchen helper, maintenance worker, and handyman. These characteristics are roughly typical of applicants for unskilled hotel jobs in the Catskill resort area of New York State where employment opportunities were tested.[3]

The four folders differed only in the applicant's reported record of criminal court involvement. The first folder indicated that the applicant had been convicted and sentenced for assault; the second, that he had been tried for assault and acquitted; the third, also tried for assault and acquitted, but with a letter from the judge certifying the finding of not guilty and reaffirming the legal presumption of innocence. The fourth folder made no mention of any criminal record.

A sample of 100 employers was utilized. Each employer was assigned to one of four "treatment" groups.[4] To each employer only one folder was shown; this folder was one of the four kinds mentioned above, the selection of the folder being determined by the treatment group to which the potential employer was assigned. The employer was asked whether he could "use" the man described in the folder. To preserve the reality of the situation and make it a true field experiment, employers were never given any indication that they were participating in an experiment. So far as they knew, a legitimate offer to work was being made in each showing of the folder by the "employment agent."

The experiment was designed to determine what employers would do in fact if confronted with an employment applicant with a criminal record. The questionnaire approach used in earlier studies[5] seemed ill-adapted to the problem, since respondents confronted with hypothetical situations might be particularly prone to answer in what they considered a socially acceptable manner. The second alternative—studying job opportunities of individuals who had been involved with the law—would have made it very difficult to find comparable groups of applicants and potential em-

---

[3] The generality of these results remains to be determined. The effects of criminal involvement in the Catskill area are probably diminished, however, by the temporary nature of employment, the generally poor qualifications of the work force, and the excess of demand over supply of unskilled labor there. Accordingly, the employment differences among the four treatment groups found in this study are likely, if anything, to be *smaller* than would be expected in industries and areas where workers are more carefully selected.

[4] Employers were not approached in pre-selected random order, due to a misunderstanding of instructions on the part of the law student who carried out the experiment during a three and one-half week period. Because of this flaw in the experimental procedure, the results should be treated with appropriate caution. Thus, chi-squared analysis may not properly be utilized. (For those used to this measure, $P < .05$ for Table 1.)

[5] Sol Rubin, *Crime and Juvenile Delinquency*, New York: Oceana, 1958, pp. 151–56.

ployers. For these reasons, the field experiment reported here was utilized.

Some deception was involved in the study. The "employment agent"—the same individual in all 100 cases—was in fact a law student who was working in the Catskills during the summer of 1959 as an insurance adjuster. In representing himself as being both an adjuster and an employment agent, he was assuming a combination of roles which is not uncommon there. The adjuster role gave him an opportunity to introduce a single application for employment casually and naturally. To the extent that the experiment worked, however, it was inevitable that some employers should be led to believe that they had immediate prospects of filling a job opening. In those instances where an offer to hire was made, the "agent" called a few hours later to say that the applicant had taken another job. The field experimenter attempted in such instances to locate a satisfactory replacement by contacting an employment agency in the area. Because this procedure was used and since the jobs involved were of relatively minor consequence, we believe that the deception caused little economic harm.

As mentioned, each treatment group of 25 employers was approached with one type of folder. Responses were dichotomized: those who expressed a willingness to consider the applicant in any way were termed positive; those who made no response or who explicitly refused to consider the candidate were termed negative. Our results consist of comparisons between positive and negative responses, thus defined, for the treatment groups.

Of the 25 employers shown the "no record" folder, nine gave positive responses. Subject to reservations arising from chance variations in sampling, we take this as indicative of the "ceiling" of jobs available for this kind of applicant under the given field conditions. Positive responses by these employers may be compared with those in the other treatment groups to obtain an indication of job opportunities lost because of the various legal records.

Of the 25 employers approached with the "convict" folder, only one expressed interest in the applicant. This is a rather graphic indication of the effect which a criminal record may have on job opportunities. Care must be exercised, of course, in generalizing the conclusions to other settings. In this context, however, the criminal record made a major difference.

From a theoretical point of view, the finding leads toward the conclusion that conviction constitutes a powerful form of "status degradation"[6] which continues to operate after the time when, according to the generalized theory of justice underlying punishment in our society, the individual's "debt" has been paid. A record of conviction produces a durable if not permanent loss of status. For purposes of effective social control, this state of affairs may heighten the deterrent effect of conviction—though that remains to be established. Any such contribution to social control, however, must be balanced against the barriers imposed upon rehabilitation of the convict. If the ex-prisoner finds difficulty in securing menial kinds of legitimate work, further crime may become an increasingly attractive alternative.[7]

Another important finding of this study concerns the small number of positive responses elicited by the "accused but acquitted" applicant. Of the 25 employers approached with this folder, three offered jobs. Thus, the individual accused but acquitted of assault has almost as much trouble finding even an unskilled job as the one who was not only accused of the same offense, but also convicted.

From a theoretical point of view, this result indicates that permanent lowering of status is not limited to those explicitly singled out by being convicted of a crime. As an ideal outcome of American justice, criminal procedure is supposed to distinguish between the "guilty" and those who have been acquitted. Legally controlled consequences which follow the judgment are consistent with this purpose. Thus, the "guilty" are subject to fine and imprisonment, while those who are acquitted are immune from these sanctions. But deprivations may be imposed on the acquitted, both before and after victory in court. Before trial, legal rules either permit or

---

[6] Harold Garfinkel, "Conditions of Successful Degradation Ceremonies," *American Journal of Sociology,* 61 (March 1956), pp. 420–24.

[7] Severe negative effects of conviction on employment opportunities have been noted by Sol Rubin, *Crime and Juvenile Delinquency,* New York: Oceana, 1958. A further source of employment difficulty is inherent in licensing statutes and security regulations which sometimes preclude convicts from being employed in their pre-conviction occupation or even in the trades which they may have acquired during imprisonment. These effects may, however, be counteracted by bonding arrangements, prison associations, and publicity programs aimed at increasing confidence in, and sympathy for, ex-convicts. See also, B. F. McSally, "Finding Jobs for Released Offenders," *Federal Probation,* 24 (June 1960), pp. 12–17; Harold D. Lasswell and Richard C. Donnelly, "The Continuing Debate over Responsibility: An Introduction to Isolating the Condemnation Sanction," *Yale Law Journal,* 68 (April 1959), pp. 869–99; Johannes Andeneas, "General Prevention—Illusion or Reality?", *J. Criminal Law,* 43 (July–August 1952), pp. 176–98.

require arrest and detention. The suspect may be faced with the expense of an attorney and a bail bond if he is to mitigate these limitations on his privacy and freedom. In addition, some pre-trial deprivations are imposed without formal legal permission. These may include coercive questioning, use of violence, and stigmatization. And, as this study indicates, some deprivations not under the direct control of the legal process may develop or persist after an official decision of acquittal has been made.

Thus two legal principles conflict in practice. On the one hand, "a man is innocent until proven guilty." On the other, the accused is systematically treated as guilty under the administration of criminal law until a functionary or official body—police, magistrate, prosecuting attorney, or trial judge or jury—decides that he is entitled to be free. Even then, the results of treating him as guilty persist and may lead to serious consequences.

The conflict could be eased by measures aimed at reducing the deprivations imposed on the accused, before and after acquittal. Some legal attention has been focused on pre-trial deprivations. The provision of bail and counsel, the availability of habeas corpus, limitations on the admissability of coerced confessions, and civil actions for false arrest are examples of measures aimed at protecting the rights of the accused before trial. Although these are often limited in effectiveness, especially for individuals of lower socioeconomic status, they at least represent some concern with implementing the presumption of innocence at the pre-trial stage.

By contrast, the courts have done little toward alleviating the post-acquittal consequences of legal accusation. One effort along these lines has been employed in the federal courts, however. Where an individual has been accused and exonerated of a crime, he may petition the federal courts for a "Certificate of Innocence" certifying this fact.[8] Possession of such a document might be expected to alleviate post-acquittal deprivations.

Some indication of the effectiveness of such a measure is found in the responses of the final treatment group. Their folder, it will be recalled, contained information on the accusation and acquittal of the applicant, but also included a letter from a judge addressed "To whom it may concern" certifying the applicant's acquittal and reminding the reader of the presumption of innocence. Such a

---

[8] 28 United States Code, Secs. 1495, 2513.

letter might have had a boomerang effect, by reemphasizing the legal involvement of the applicant. It was important, therefore, to determine empirically whether such a communication would improve or harm the chances of employment. Our findings indicate that it increased employment opportunities, since the letter folder elicited six positive responses. Even though this fell short of the nine responses to the "no record" folder, it doubled the number for the "accused but acquitted" and created a significantly greater number of job offers than those elicited by the convicted record. This suggests that the procedure merits consideration as a means of offsetting the occupational loss resulting from accusation. It should be noted, however, that repeated use of this device might reduce its effectiveness.

The results of the experiment are summarized in Table 1. The

Table 1: Effect of four types of legal folder on job opportunities (in percent)

	No record	Acquitted with letter	Acquitted without letter	Convicted	Total
	(N = 25)	(N = 25)	(N = 25)	(N = 25)	(N = 100)
Positive response	36	24	12	4	19
Negative response	64	76	88	96	81
Total	100	100	100	100	100

differences in outcome found there indicate that various types of legal records are systematically related to job opportunities. It seems fair to infer also that the trend of job losses corresponds with the apparent punitive intent of the authorities. Where the man is convicted, that intent is presumably greatest. It is less where he is accused but acquitted and still less where the court makes an effort to emphasize the absence of a finding of guilt. Nevertheless, where the difference in punitive intent is ideally greatest, between conviction and acquittal, the difference in occupational harm is very slight. A similar blurring of this distinction shows up in a different way in the next study.

Study II: The effects on defendants of suits for medical malpractice

As indicated earlier, the second study differed from the first in a number of ways: method of research, social class of accused, relationship between the accused and his "employer," social support available to accused, type of offense and its possible relevance to occupational adequacy. Because the two studies differ in so many ways, the reader is again cautioned to avoid thinking of them as providing a rigorous comparative examination. They are presented together only to demonstrate that legal accusation can produce unanticipated deprivations, as in the case of Study I, or unanticipated benefits, as in the research now to be presented. In the discussion to follow, some of the possible reasons for the different outcomes will be suggested.

The extra-legal effects of a malpractice suit were studied by obtaining the records of Connecticut's leading carrier of malpractice insurance. According to these records, a total of 69 doctors in the State had been sued in 64 suits during the post–World War II period covered by the study, September 1945, to September 1959.[9] Some suits were instituted against more than one doctor, and four physicians had been sued twice. Of the total of 69 physicians, 58 were questioned. Interviews were conducted with the approval of the Connecticut Medical Association by Robert Wyckoff, whose extraordinary qualifications for the work included possession of both the M.D. and LL.B. degrees. Dr. Wyckoff was able to secure detailed response to his inquiries from all doctors contacted.

Twenty of the respondents were questioned by personal interview, 28 by telephone, and the remainder by mail. Forty-three of those reached practiced principally in cities, 11 in suburbs, and 4 in rural areas. Seventeen were engaged in general practice and 41 were specialists. The sample proved comparable to the doctors in the State as a whole in age, experience, and professional qualifications.[10] The range was from the lowest professional stratum to chiefs of staff and services in the State's most highly regarded hospitals.

Of the 57 malpractice cases reported, doctors clearly won 38; 19 of these were dropped by the plaintiff and an equal number were won in court by the defendant doctor. Of the remaining 19 suits, 11 were settled out of court for a nominal amount, four for ap-

---

[9] A spot check of one county revealed that the Company's records covered every malpractice suit tried in the courts of that county during this period.

[10] No relationship was found between any of these characteristics and the legal or extra-legal consequences of the lawsuit.

proximately the amount the plaintiff claimed and four resulted in judgment for the plaintiff in court.

The malpractice survey did not reveal widespread occupational harm to the physicians involved. Of the 58 respondents, 52 reported no negative effects of the suit on their practice, and 5 of the remaining 6, all specialists, reported that their practice *improved* after the suit. The heaviest loser in court (a radiologist) reported the largest gain. He commented, "I guess all the doctors in town felt sorry for me because new patients started coming in from doctors who had not sent me patients previously." Only one doctor reported adverse consequences to his practice. A winner in court, this man suffered physical and emotional stress symptoms which hampered his later effectiveness in surgical work. The temporary drop in his practice appears to have been produced by neurotic symptoms and is therefore only indirectly traceable to the malpractice suit. Seventeen other doctors reported varying degrees of personal dissatisfaction and anxiety during and after the suit, but none of them reported impairment of practice. No significant relationship was found between outcome of the suit and expressed dissatisfaction.

A protective institutional environment helps to explain these results. No cases were found in which a doctor's hospital privileges were reduced following the suit. Neither was any physician unable later to obtain malpractice insurance, although a handful found it necessary to pay higher rates. The State Licensing Commission, which is headed by a doctor, did not intervene in any instance. Local medical societies generally investigated charges through their ethics and grievance committees, but where they took any action, it was almost always to recommend or assist in legal defense against the suit.

DISCUSSION

Accusation has different outcomes for unskilled workers and doctors in the two studies. How may these be explained? First, they might be nothing more than artifacts of research method. In the field experiment, it was possible to see behavior directly, i.e., to determine how employers act when confronted with what appears to them to be a realistic opportunity to hire. Responses are therefore not distorted by the memory of the respondent. By contrast, the memory of the doctors might have been consciously or unconsciously shaped by the wish to create the impression that the public had not taken seriously the accusation leveled against them. The motive for such a distortion might be either to protect the respondent's self-esteem or to preserve an image of public acceptance in the eyes of the interviewer, the profession, and the public. Efforts of the interviewer to assure his subjects of anonymity—intended to offset these effects—may have succeeded or may, on the contrary, have accentuated an awareness of the danger. A related type of distortion might have stemmed from a desire by doctors to affect public attitudes toward malpractice. Two conflicting motives might have been expected to enter here. The doctor might have tended to exaggerate the harm caused by an accusation, especially if followed by acquittal, in order to turn public opinion toward legal policies which would limit malpractice liability. On the other hand, he might tend to underplay extra-legal harm caused by a legally insufficient accusation in order to discourage potential plaintiffs from instituting suits aimed at securing remunerative settlements and/or revenge for grievances. Whether these diverse motives operated to distort doctors' reports and, if so, which of them produced the greater degree of distortion is a matter for speculation. It is only suggested here that the interview method is more subject to certain types of distortion than the direct behavioral observations of the field experiment.

Even if such distortion did not occur, the results may be attributable to differences in research design. In the field experiment, a direct comparison is made between the occupational position of an accused and an identical individual not accused at a single point in time. In the medical study, effects were inferred through retrospective judgment, although checks on actual income would have no doubt confirmed these judgments. Granted that income had increased, many other explanations are available to account for it. An improvement in practice after a malpractice suit may have resulted from factors extraneous to the suit. The passage of time in the community and increased experience may have led to a larger practice and may even have masked negative effects of the suit. There may have been a general increase in practice for the kinds of doctors involved in these suits, even greater for doctors not sued than for doctors in the sample. Whether interviews with a control sample could have yielded sufficiently precise data to rule out these possibilities is problematic. Unfortunately, the resources available for the study did not enable such data to be obtained.

A third difference in the two designs may affect the results. In the field experiment, full information concerning the legal record is provided to all of the relevant decision makers, i.e., the employers. In the medical study, by contrast, the results depend on decisions of actual patients to consult a given doctor. It may be assumed that such decisions are often based on imperfect information, some patients knowing little or nothing about the malpractice suit. To ascertain how much information employers usually have concerning the legal record of the employee and then supply that amount would have been a desirable refinement, but a difficult one. The alternative approach would involve turning the medical study into an experiment in which full information concerning malpractice (e.g., liable, accused but acquitted, no record of accusation) was supplied to potential patients. This would have permitted a comparison of the effects of legal accusation in two instances where information concerning the accusation is constant. To carry out such an experiment in a field situation would require an unlikely degree of cooperation, for instance by a medical clinic which might ask patients to choose their doctor on the basis of information given them. It is difficult to conceive of an experiment along these lines which would be both realistic enough to be valid and harmless enough to be ethical.

If we assume, however, that these methodological problems do not invalidate the basic finding, how may it be explained? Why would unskilled workers accused but acquitted of assault have great difficulty getting jobs, while doctors accused of malpractice—whether acquitted or not—are left unharmed or more sought after than before?

First, the charge of criminal assault carries with it the legal allegation and the popular connotation of intent to harm. Malpractice, on the other hand, implies negligence or failure to exercise reasonable care. Even though actual physical harm may be greater in malpractice, the element of intent suggests that the man accused of assault would be more likely to repeat his attempt and to find the mark. However, it is dubious that this fine distinction could be drawn by the lay public.

Perhaps more important, all doctors and particularly specialists may be immune from the effects of a malpractice suit because their services are in short supply.[11] By contrast, the unskilled worker is one of many and therefore likely to be passed over in favor of someone with a "cleaner" record.

Moreover, high occupational status, such as is demonstrably enjoyed by doctors,[12] probably tends to insulate the doctor from imputations of incompetence. In general, professionals are assumed to possess uniformly high ability, to be oriented toward community service, and to enforce adequate standards within their own organization.[13] Doctors in particular receive deference, just because they are doctors, not only from the population as a whole but even from fellow professionals.[14]

Finally, individual doctors appear to be protected from the effects of accusation by the sympathetic and powerful support they receive from fellow members of the occupation, a factor absent in the case of unskilled, unorganized laborers.[15] The medical society provides advice on handling malpractice actions, for instance, and referrals by other doctors sometimes increase as a consequence of the sympathy felt for the malpractice suit victim. Such assistance is further evidence that the professional operates as "a community within a community,"[16] shielding its members from controls exercised by formal authorities in the larger society.

In order to isolate these factors, additional studies are needed. It would be interesting to know, for instance, whether high occupational status would protect a doctor acquitted of a charge of

---

[11] See Eliot Freidson, "Client Control and Medical Practice," *American Journal of Sociology*, 65 (January 1960), pp. 374–82. Freidson's point is that general practitioners are more subject to client control than specialists are. Our findings emphasize the importance of professional as compared to client control, and professional protection against a particular form of client control, extending through both branches of the medical profession. However, what holds for malpractice situations may not be true of routine medical practice.

[12] National Opinion Research Center, "Jobs and Occupations: A Popular Evaluation," *Opinion News*, 9 (September 1947), pp. 3–13. More recent studies in several countries tend to confirm the high status of the physician. See Alex Inkeles, "Industrial Man: The Relation of Status to Experience, Perception, and Value," *American Journal of Sociology*, 66 (July 1960), pp. 1–31.

[13] Talcott Parsons, *The Social System*, Glencoe: The Free Press, 1951, pp. 454–73; and Everett C. Hughes, *Men and their Work*, Glencoe: The Free Press, 1958.

[14] Alvin Zander, Arthur R. Cohen, and Ezra Stotland, *Role Relations in the Mental Health Professions*, Ann Arbor: Institute for Social Research, 1957.

[15] Unions sometimes act to protect the seniority rights of members who, discharged from their jobs upon arrest, seek re-employment following their acquittal.

[16] See William J. Goode, "Community within a Community: The Professions," *American Sociological Review*, 22 (April 1957), pp. 194–200.

assault. Information on this question is sparse. Actual instances of assaults by doctors are probably very rare. When and if they do occur, it seems unlikely that they would lead to publicity and prosecution, since police and prosecutor discretion might usually be employed to quash charges before they are publicized. In the rare instances in which they come to public attention, such accusations appear to produce a marked effect because of the assumption that the pressing of charges, despite the status of the defendant, indicates probable guilt. Nevertheless, instances may be found in which even the accusation of first degree murder followed by acquittal appears to have left the doctor professionally unscathed.[17] Similarly, as a test of the group protection hypothesis, one might investigate the effect of an acquittal for assault on working men who are union members. The analogy would be particularly instructive where the union plays an important part in employment decisions, for instance in industries which make use of a union hiring hall.

In the absence of studies which isolate the effect of such factors, our findings cannot readily be generalized. It is tempting to suggest after an initial look at the results that social class differences provide the explanation. But subsequent analysis and research might well reveal significant intra-class variations, depending on the distribution of other operative factors. A lower-class person with a scarce specialty and a protective occupational group who is acquitted of a lightly regarded offense might benefit from the accusation. Nevertheless, class in general seems to correlate with the relevant factors to such an extent that in reality the law regularly works to the disadvantage of the already more disadvantaged classes.

CONCLUSION

Legal accusation imposes a variety of consequences, depending on the nature of the accusation and the characteristics of the accused. Deprivations occur, even though not officially intended, in the case of unskilled workers who have been acquitted of assault

---

[17] For instance, the acquittal of Dr. John Bodkin Adams after a sensational murder trial, in which he was accused of deliberately killing several elderly women patients to inherit their estates, was followed by his quiet return to medical practice. *New York Times,* November 24, 1961, p. 28, col. 7. Whether the British regard acquittals as more exonerative than Americans is uncertain.

charges. On the other hand, malpractice actions—even when resulting in a judgment against the doctor—are not usually followed by negative consequences and sometimes have a favorable effect on the professional position of the defendant. These differences in outcome suggest two conclusions: one, the need for more explicit clarification of legal goals; two, the importance of examining the attitudes and social structure of the community outside the courtroom if the legal process is to hit intended targets, while avoiding innocent bystanders. Greater precision in communicating goals and in appraising consequences of present practices should help to make the legal process an increasingly equitable and effective instrument of social control.

16

*The Connecticut crackdown on speeding: Time-series data in quasi-experimental analysis**

Donald T. Campbell

and

H. Laurence Ross

Social research frequently encounters the task of evaluating change produced in nonrandomly selected groups by events which are beyond the researcher's control. The social scientist must verify that there has in fact been a change, and that the indicated event is its cause. Illustrations are manifold: a state terminates capital punishment, and proponents of this type of punishment predict an increase in the murder rate; a school is integrated, and supporters of the reform expect to find an increase in the positive self-evaluation of Negro pupils; a natural disaster occurs in a community, and altruistic behavior is expected to increase. Because in these situations the investigator has no control over the assignment of individuals or groups to "experimental" and "control" situations, the logic of the classical exper-

Authors' Note: The preparation of this paper has been supported in part by the National Science Foundation (Grant GS 1309x), the U.S. Office of Education (Project C-998, Contract 3-20-001), the U.S. Bureau of Public Roads (CPR 11-5981), the National Institutes of Health, the U.S. Public Health Service (RG-5359), and the Automotive Safety Foundation (as an aspect of Experimental Case Studies of Traffic Accidents conducted at Northwestern University). A brief version of it appears as H. L. Ross & D. T. Campbell, "The Connecticut Speed Crackdown: A Study of the Effects of Legal Change," in *Perspectives on the Social Order: Readings in Sociology* 30–35 (2d ed. H. L. Ross ed. 1968).

* Reprinted from *Law & Society Review*, vol. 3, no. 1 (August 1968), pp. 33–53.

iment must be reexamined in a search for optimal interpretative procedures.

This paper introduces, in the context of a problem in applied sociology and the sociology of law, a mode of analysis designed to deal with a common class of situations in which research must proceed without the benefit of experimental control. The general methodology expounded here is termed "quasi-experimental analysis." The specific mode of analysis is the "interrupted time-series design." Perhaps its fundamental credo is that lack of control and lack of randomization are damaging to inferences of cause and effect only to the extent that a systematic consideration of alternative explanations reveals some that are plausible. More complete explications of quasi-experimental analysis have appeared elsewhere;[1] this paper will merely illustrate its use in a situation where a series of observations has been recorded for periods of time both prior and subsequent to the experience of the specific event to be studied. Such data are quite commonly available, yet they are seldom fully utilized and investigators often confine themselves unnecessarily to much less satisfactory methodologies. The 1955 crackdown on speeding in the State of Connecticut furnishes an apt example of the potentialities of such quasi-experimental analysis.

A PROGRAM FOR REDUCING HIGHWAY FATALITIES

In 1955, 324 people were killed in automobile accidents on the highways of Connecticut. Deaths by motor vehicle accidents had reached a record high for the decade of the fifties as the usually hazardous Christmas holidays approached. Two days before Christmas, Governor Abraham Ribicoff of Connecticut initiated an unparalleled attempt to control traffic deaths by law enforcement, and announced his crackdown on speeders in that state.

---

[1] E.g., D. T. Campbell & J. S. Stanley, "Experimental and Quasi-Experimental Designs for Research on Teaching," in *Handbook of Research on Teaching* 171–246 (N. L. Gage ed. 1963), reprinted as *Experimental and Quasi-Experimental Designs for Research* (1963); D. T. Campbell, "From Description to Experimentation: Interpreting Trends as Quasi-Experiments," in *Problems in Measuring Change* (C. W. Harris ed. 1963): D. T. Campbell & K. N. Clayton, "Avoiding Regression Effects in Panel Studies of Communication Impact," in *Studies in Public Communication* 99–118 (Dept. of Sociology, University of Chicago, No. 3, 1961), reprinted in Bobbs-Merrill Reprints in Sociology as S-353. For an application of this type of analysis to legal impact, see R. Lempert, "Strategies of Research Design in the Legal Impact Study," 1 *L. & Soc'y Rev.* 111 (1966).

Ribicoff believed, along with many safety specialists, that excess speed was the most common contributing factor in traffic deaths, and that control of speed would result in diminished fatalities. He believed that previous efforts to control speeding under the usual court procedures and by the existing "point system" had been inadequate. In a study of three months' records of the police court in Hartford, it was noted that no more than half the persons originally charged with speeding were so prosecuted, the charge often being diminished to a less serious one. Ribicoff wanted to initiate a program with reliable procedures and strong sanctions as a means to control speeding and thus to reduce traffic deaths.

On December 23, 1955, Governor Ribicoff announced that in the future all persons convicted of speeding would have their licenses suspended for thirty days on the first offense. A second violation was to mean a sixty-day suspension, and a third conviction for speeding would result in indefinite suspension of the driver's license, subject to a hearing after ninety days.

The decree was put into force through the Governor's power of appointment over local judges. Under Connecticut practice, the Motor Vehicle Department was suspending licenses on the recommendation of police court judges. The judges were appointed by the Governor, who threatened loss of reappointment in 1957 to judges who appeared lax in the conviction of speeders, or who did not recommend suspension of licenses to the Motor Vehicle Department.

In the first three months of 1956, license suspensions for speeding numbered 2,855, an increase of almost 2,700 over the corresponding period in 1955. There were ten fewer fatalities, and 765 fewer arrests for speeding. The Governor was reported "encouraged" by the drop in violations and in fatalities. The press quoted him as saying, "This is positive proof that operators are not only driving slower, but are driving better."

By late May, deaths had declined from 122 in 1955 to 107 in 1956. Suspensions for speeding numbered 4,559, as against 209 in 1955. Speeding arrests had dropped 53 percent. The Governor received a telegram of commendation for the program from the National Safety Council.

At the end of June there were twenty-two fewer fatalities than in the first six months of 1955, representing a 15 percent reduction. Suspensions for speeding in the first six months of the year had risen from 231 to 5,398, and arrests had declined from 4,377 to 2,735. Ribicoff announced:

Connecticut has succeeded in stopping the upward surge in highway deaths, and in the first six months of this year, contrary to the national trend, we have saved lives. Fewer people died on the highways this year than in the same period last year, in Connecticut. We did it by enforcing the law, something the safety experts said couldn't be done because the people wouldn't be behind it.

In July, a new State Police program, using unmarked police cars and making extensive use of radar, was inaugurated. The police issued a report stating that 2 percent of the cars observed by radar on July 4 were found to be speeding; at a later date, it was claimed that no speeders were found among 53,000 cars similarly observed.

In the late summer, however, Connecticut experienced a very high number of traffic fatalities. By the beginning of September, 194 people had been killed, a number almost equal to the 195 of the comparable period in the previous year. The accident "epidemic" was embarrassing to the authorities, who retreated to defending the speeding crackdown on the grounds (*a*) that the fatality rate remained low in comparison with the national trend, which showed a 7 percent increase; (*b*) that exposure to accidents in the State had increased by 100 million vehicle miles without an increase in deaths; and (*c*) that the total accident rate had risen, thereby lowering the proportion of fatal accidents to total accidents.

Fatalities were fewer in the fall of 1956, and by the end of the year Connecticut could count 284 deaths in traffic as against 324 in 1955. The Governor stated, "With the saving of forty lives in 1956, a reduction of 12.3 percent from the 1955 motor vehicle death toll, we can say the program is definitely worthwhile."

The crackdown on speeding is still in effect in Connecticut, although it is no longer the subject of newsworthy comment. It was not entirely a political asset for the Democratic Governor. From the start, there were problems with neighboring states, which originate a substantial share of Connecticut traffic, and which at first refused to suspend licenses of drivers convicted of speeding in Connecticut. More important, many powerful individuals and groups within Connecticut resented the direct effects of the crackdown. Members of the Republican Party wanted the program "tempered with justice." The Teamsters sponsored a bill to eliminate compulsory license suspension on a first offense, and other legislation granting restricted driving permits for "hardship" cases was introduced. These efforts were not successful in officially moderating the crackdown policy.

The people of Connecticut and their officials are paying what in many instances appears to be a high price for the continuation of the crackdown on speeding. Few will feel the price is too high if it can be shown that as many as forty lives per year are being saved. However, the question must be raised as to whether the results claimed for the program in 1956 are valid in the light of both formerly and more recently available statistics on highway fatalities.

QUASI-EXPERIMENTAL ANALYSIS

Before-and-after measures

Traffic fatalities in Connecticut for 1956, compared with 1955, are presented in Figure 1. These are the data upon which Governor Ribicoff relied in claiming success for the crackdown on speeding. Skillfully presented, such results can look impressive, but can also be fundamentally misleading.

We can speak of the evidence presented in Figure 1 as a quasi-experiment: there is a "pretest" (the 1955 figures), an "experimental treatment" (the crackdown), and a "posttest" (the 1956 figures). A substantial change is noted which one would like to ascribe to the "experimental treatment." In quasi-experimental analysis this interpretation is held to be legitimate, provided consideration is given to plausible rival explanations of the differences, with supplementary analyses being added to eliminate these where possible. In the language of quasi-experimental analysis, the data of Figure 1 constitute a One-Group Pretest-Posttest Design. This design fails to control for the six common threats to the validity of experiments specified below:

1. *History.* This term denotes specific events, other than the experimental treatment, occurring between the pretest and posttest, which might account for the change. It furnishes a "rival hypothesis" to the experimental hypothesis, a competing explana-

Figure 1: Connecticut traffic fatalities, 1955–1956

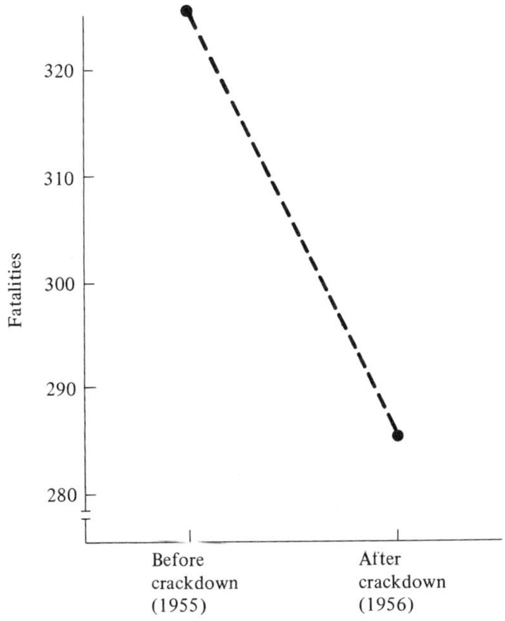

tion of the before-to-after change that must be eliminated as implausible, by one means or another, before full credence can be given to the experimental hypothesis. For instance, 1956 might have been a particularly dry year, with fewer accidents due to rain and snow, or there might have been a dramatic improvement of the safety features on the 1956-model cars. In fact, neither of these is a particularly plausible rival hypothesis in this instance, and we have not encountered more likely ones, so this potential weakness may not be crucial here.

2. *Maturation.* This term originates in studies of individuals, where it refers to regular changes correlated with the passage of time, such as growing older, more tired, more sophisticated, etc. It is distinguished from history in referring to processes, rather than to discrete events. Thus, one could classify here the general long-term trend toward a reduction in automobile mileage death rates, presumably due to better roads, increased efficacy of medical care, etc. The better designs discussed below provide evidence concerning this trend in Connecticut in previous years, and in other states for the same year.

3. *Testing.* A change may occur as a result of the pretest, even without the experimental treatment. In the present instance, the assessment of the traffic death rate for 1955 constitutes the pretest. In this case it is conceivable that the measurement and publicizing of the traffic death rate for 1955 could change driver caution in 1956.

4. *Instrumentation.* This term refers to a shifting of the measuring instrument independent of any change in the phenomenon measured. In the use of public records for time-series data, a shift in the government agency recording the fatality statistics could account for such a shift. For example, suicide statistics increased a dramatic 20 percent in Prussia between 1882 and 1883, when record keeping was transferred from the local police to the national civil service.[2] Similarly, Orlando Wilson's reforms of the police system in Chicago led to dramatic increases in rates for most crimes, due presumably to more complete reporting.[3] In earlier versions of the present study, the death rate per hundred million vehicle miles is computed by using the number of gallons of gasoline sold in the state to estimate the number of miles driven. The latter figure is obtained by multiplying the former by an empirically-derived constant. A decrease in the actual miles obtained per gallon, as through engines of larger horsepower or driving at higher speeds could masquerade as a lower mileage death rate through inflating the estimate of miles driven. Conversely, if the crackdown actually reduced driving speeds, this would increase the miles-per-gallon actually obtained, leading to an underestimate of mileage driven in the postcrackdown period, and consequently an overestimate of the fatalty rate.

5. *Instability.*[4] A ubiquitous plausible rival hypothesis is that the change observed is due to the instability of the measures involved. Were Figure 1 to show fatality rates for a single township, with the

---

[2] Cited in C. Selltiz, M. Jahoda, M. Deutsch, & S. W. Cook, *Research Methods in Social Relations* 323 (1959).

[3] J. Sween & D. T. Campbell, A Study of the Effect of Proximally Autocorrelated Error on Tests of Significance for the Interrupted Time Series Quasi-Experimental Design 31–32, Figs. 11 & 12 (mimeographed Research Report, Department of Psychology, Northwestern University, 1965). These figures also will appear in D. T. Campbell, "Reforms as Experiments," *Am. Psychologist* (to be submitted).

[4] Instability has not been singled out as a specific threat to validity in previous discussions of quasi-experimental design, although the discussion of tests of significance in such situations has implied it. Tests of significance obviously do not provide "proof" relevant to the many other sources of invalidity, but they are relevant to this one plausible rival hypothesis even where randomization has not been used.

same 12.3 percent drop, we would be totally unimpressed, so unstable would we expect such rates to be. In general, as is made explicit in the models for tests of significance, the smaller the population base, the greater the instability. In the uncontrolled field situation sample size is only one of many sources of instability. Much instability may be due to large numbers of change-producing events of the type which, taken individually, we have called history.

6. *Regression.* Where a group has been selected for treatment just because of its extreme performance on the pretest, and if the pretest and posttest are imperfectly correlated, as they almost always are, it follows that on the average the posttest will be less extreme than the pretest. This regression is a tautological restatement of the imperfect correlation between pretest and posttest, as it relates to pretest scores selected for their extremity. The r of the correlation coefficient actually stands for the percentage of regression toward the mean. An analogous regression problem exists for time-series correlations.

Selection for extremity (and resultant retest regression) can be seen as plausibly operating here in two ways: (*a*) of all states in 1955, this treatment was most likely to be applied to one with an exceptionally high traffic casualty rate; (*b*) for Connecticut, the most likely time in which a crackdown would be applied would be following a year in which traffic fatalities were exceptionally high.

In the true experiment, the treatment is applied randomly, without relation to the prior state of the dependent variable: the correlation between pretest scores and exposure to treatment is zero. Likewise, in the most interpretable of quasi-experiments, the treatment is applied without systematic relationship to the prior status of the group. Thus, an analysis of the effects of a tornado or an earthquake can be made with confidence that the pretreatment values did not cause the tornado or the earthquake. Not so here: the high 1955 rates can plausibly be argued to have caused the treatment. That 1956 was less extreme would then be expected because of regression.[5]

---

[5] This issue is extremely complex. In ordinary correlation, the regression is technically toward the mean of the second variable, not to the mean of the selection variable, if these means differ. In time-series, the regression is toward the general trend-line, which may of course be upward or downward or unchanging. A more expanded analysis of the regression problem in correlation across persons is contained in Campbell & Clayton (1961) and in Campbell & Stanley (1963), both supra note 1.

Interrupted times-series analysis

Figure 2 plots traffic fatalities for five years before and four years after the crackdown. This mode of quasi-experimental

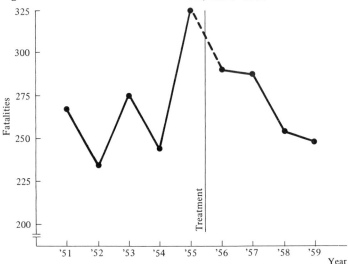

Figure 2: Connecticut traffic fatalities, 1951–1959

analysis has been labeled "Interrupted Time-Series" to distinguish it from the time-series analysis of economics. In the latter, the exogenous variable to which cause is imputed is a continuously present variable, occurring in different degrees. In the Interrupted Time-Series, the "causal" variable is examined as an event or change occurring at a single time, specified independently of inspection of the data.

The Interrupted Time-Series design represents a use of the more extensive data which are often available even when only before-and-after measures are reported. Some potential outcomes of such a time-series analysis greatly reduce the plausibility of certain threats to validity. If the preexposure series shows but minor point-to-point fluctuations and no trend anticipating a big transtreatment shift, then maturation may not be plausible, for in most instances the plausible maturation hypothesis would have predicted shifts of the same order as the transtreatment shift in each of the pretreatment stages. Reasonable models of the testing effect would have the same implications. (In our instance, this would be on condition that the annual fatality rates had been given equal publicity.) The outcome in Figure 2 is not of this readily interpretable sort, although the trend is perhaps generally upward prior to the treatment, and steadily downward subsequently.

Judgments of the plausibility of instrumentation effects must be based upon other than time-series data. However, notice should be taken here of a frequent unfortunate confounding: the administrative reform which is meant to produce a social change very frequently is accompanied by a coincident reform of the record keeping, ruling out valid inferences as to effects. The Chicago police reform cited above is a case in point. In the present instance, we have found no evidence of a change in record keeping or index computing of the type that would produce a pseudo-effect.

The likelihood of regression, or of selection for "treatment" on a basis tending to introduce regression, is supported by inspection of the time-series data. The largest change of any year is not the one after the crackdown, but is instead the upswing in the series occurring in 1954–55, just prior to the crackdown. In terms of crude fatality rates, 1955 is strikingly the highest point reached. It thus seems plausible that the high figure of 1955 caused the crackdown, and hence it seems much less likely that the crackdown caused the low figure of 1956, for such a drop would have been predicted on regression grounds in any case.

The graphic presentation of the precrackdown years provides evidence of the general instability of the accidental death rate measure, against which the 1955–56 shift can be compared. This instability makes the "treatment effect" of Figure 1 now look more trivial. Had the drop following the treatment been the largest shift in the time series, the hypothesis of effect would have been much more plausible. Instead, shifts that large are relatively frequent. The 1955–56 drop is less than half the magnitude of the 1954–55 gain, and the 1953 gain also exceeds it. It is the largest drop of the series, but it exceeds the drops of 1952, 1954, and 1958 by trivial amounts. Thus the unexplained instabilities of the series are of such a magnitude as to make the 1955–56 drop understandable as more of the same. On the other hand, it is noteworthy that after the crackdown, there are no year-to-year gains, and in this respect, the character of the time-series has changed. The plausibility of the hypothesis that instability accounts for the effect can be judged by visual inspection of the graphed figures, or by qualitative discussion, but in addition it is this one threat to validity which can be evaluated by tests of significance. These will be discussed later, and they do find some evidence of change exceeding that which the pretreatment instability would lead one to expect.

Multiple time-series

In many situations, time-series involving but a single experimental unit will be all that are available. In these situations, analyses on the above model are a great improvement over the usual before-and-after study. However, it is in the spirit of quasi-experimental analysis to make use of *all* available data that could help to rule out or confirm any plausible rival hypothesis. In a

Figure 3: Connecticut and control states traffic fatalities, 1951–1959 (per 100,000 population)

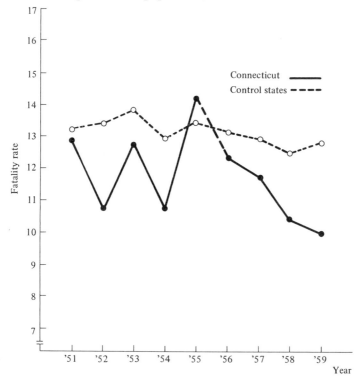

setting such as this, no randomly assigned control group is available. But in quasi-experimentation, even a non-equivalent control group is helpful. It provides the only control for history (for those extraneous change agents that would be expected to affect both the experimental and control group), and assists in controlling maturation, testing, and instrumentation. For Connecticut, it was judged that a pool of adjacent and similar states—New York, New Jersey, Rhode Island, and Massachusetts—provided a meaningful comparison. Figure 3 plots the death rates for the control states alongside Connecticut, all data being expressed on a per 100,000 population base to bring the figures into proximity. The control data are much smoother, due to the much larger base, i.e., the canceling out of chance deviations in the annual figures for particular states.

While in general these data confirm the single time-series analysis, the differences between Connecticut and the control states show a pattern supporting the hypothesis that the crackdown made a difference. In the pretest years, Connecticut's rate is parallel or rising relative to the control, exceeding it in 1955. In the posttest years, Connecticut's rate drops faster than does the control, steadily increasing the gap. While the regression argument applies to the high point of 1955 and to the subsequent departure in 1956, it does not plausibly explain the steadily increasing gap in 1957, 1958, and 1959.

Figure 4 shows the comparison states individually. Note that four of the five show an upard swing in 1955, Connecticut having the largest. Note that all five show a downward trend in 1956. Rhode Island is most similar to Connecticut in both the 1955 upswing and 1956 downswing, actually exceeding Connecticut in the latter—in a striking argument against the hypothesis of a crackdown effect. However, the trend in 1957, 1958, and 1959 is steadily upward in Rhode Island, steadily downward in Connecticut, supporting the concept of effect.

The list of plausible rival hypotheses should include factors disguising experimental effects as well as factors producing pseudo-effects. Thus, to the list should be added *diffusion*, the tendency for the experimental effect to modify not only the experimental group, but also the control group. Thus the crackdown on speeding in Connecticut might well have reduced traffic speed and fatalities in neighboring states. Dodd reports such an effect in his

Figure 4: Traffic fatalities for Connecticut, New York, New Jersey, Rhode Island, and Massachusetts (per 100,000 persons)

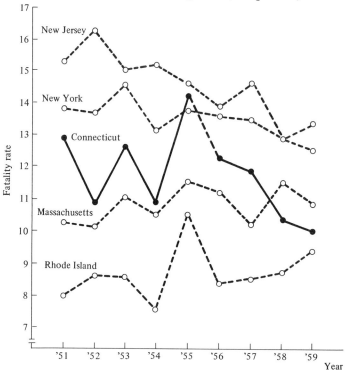

classic experiment on community hygiene in Syria.[6] The comparison of posttreatment levels of Connecticut and the neighboring states might thus be invalid, or at least underestimate the effects. Conceivably one might for this reason prefer the single time-series analysis to the multiple time-series one. If highly similar remote states were available, these would make better controls, but for matters of either weather or culture, adjacency and similarity are apt to be strongly associated.

Tests of significance

Our position in regard to tests of significance is an intermediate one. On the one hand, we would agree that they are overly hon-

---

[6] S. C. Dodd, *A Controlled Experiment on Rural Hygiene in Syria* (1934).

ored and are often mistaken as protecting against all of the threats to valid interpretation, when in fact they are only relevant to one—to instability. On the other hand, they are often useful in ruling out that one threat and should be used for that purpose. They are appropriate even where randomization has not been used because even there it is a relevant threat to validity to be able to argue that even had these data been assigned at random, differences this large would be frequent.[7]

The simplest tests conceptually are those testing for a difference in slope or intercept between pretreatment and posttreatment observations. As applied here these assume linearity and independence of error. It has been shown that the "proximally autocorrelated" error typical of natural situations (in which adjacent points in time share more error than non-adjacent ones) biases the usual tests in the direction of finding too many significant differences.[8] Unaffected by this bias is a t-test by Mood which compares a single posttreatment point with a value extrapolated from the pretreatment series.[9] None of these approached any interesting level of significance.

Glass[10] has introduced into the social sciences a more sophisticated statistical approach, based upon the work of Box and Tiao.[11] This has the advantages of realistically assuming the interdependence of adjacent points and estimating a weighting parameter thereof, of avoiding the assumption of linearity (at least in a simple or direct manner), and of weighting more heavily the observa-

---

[7] D. T. Campbell, "Quasi-Experimental Design," in 5 *Int'l Encyc. Soc. Sci.* 259 (Sills ed. 1968).

[8] J. Sween & D. T. Campbell, supra note 3. The tests thus biased include tests of slope and intercept provided by H. M. Walker & J. Lev, *Statistical Inference* 390–95, 399–400 (1953). Note that this invalidates the discussion of tests of significance in Campbell, "From Description to Experimentation," supra note 1, at 220–30. The "Clayton test" presented there was found in the Monte Carlo simulation by Sween & Campbell to have additional errors leading it to be too optimistic.

[9] A. M. Mood, *Introduction to the Theory of Statistics* 297–98 (1950).

[10] G. V. Glass, "Analysis of Data on the Connecticut Speeding Crackdown as a Time-Series Quasi-Experiment," 3 *L. & Soc'y Rev,* 55–76 (1968); T. O. Maguire & G. V. Glass, "A Program for the Analysis of Certain Time-Series Quasi-Experiments," 27 *Educational and Psychological Measurement* 743–50 (1967); G. V. Glass, G. C. Tiao, & T. O. Maguire, "Analysis of Data on the 1900 Revision of German Divorce Laws as a Time-Series Quasi-Experiment," 3 *L. & Soc'y Rev.* (1969) (in press).

[11] G. E. P. Box & G. C. Tiao, "A Change in Level of a Non-Stationary Time Series," 52 *Biometrika* 181–92 (1965); G. E. P. Box, "Bayesian Approaches to Some Bothersome Problems in Data Analysis" in *Improving Experimental Design and Statistical Analysis* (J. C. Stanley ed. 1967).

tions closer to the point of treatment. A number of assumptions about the nature of the data must be made, such as the absence of cycles, but these can be examined from the data. Applying this test to monthly data, he finds a drop in fatalities not quite reaching the P < .10 level of significance. Using a monthly difference between Connecticut's rate and that of the pool of the four control states, still less of a significant effect is found. In what he regards as the most powerful analysis available, he computes an effect parameter for each of the four comparison states and compares the effect parameter of Connecticut with this. Connecticut shows more effect, with a significance level somewhere between P < .05 and P < .07, with a one-tailed test. . . .

Thus on the graphic evidence of steadily dropping fatality rates, and on these marginal statistical grounds, there may be an effect. This effect, it must be restated, could be due to the crackdown, or could be due to the regression effect. (Regression effects can of course produce "statistically significant" results.)

Supplementary analyses

In this section, we will present data that will further illustrate time-series analysis and, substantively, both indicate that the crackdown was put into effect and that it had some unanticipated and, to the policymakers, probably undesired consequences.

Figure 5 presents evidence that the crackdown was put into effect, as indicated by a great increase in suspensions of licenses for speeding. Unfortunately, we have not been able to get control state data for this and the following variables, but the single state time-series is quite convincing in itself. We regard it as confirming the appropriateness of the statistical tests that they indicate significant differences. The single-point-extrapolation t is 4.33 with 4 degrees of freedom, where 3.75 is significant at the P < .02 level.

Figure 6 plots the percentage which speeding violations constitute of all traffic violations. This shows a decline, due presumably to greater conformity to speed limits, although it is possible that policemen and prosecutors were more willing, in the light of severe sanctions for speeding, to overlook minor infractions or to charge them as something else. While the graphic portrayal of declining speeding violations is convincing of a genuine effect, the

Figure 5: Suspensions of licenses for speeding, as percent of all suspensions

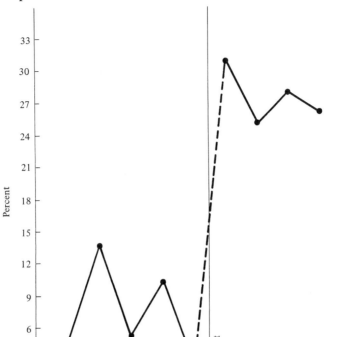

statistical tests are not so emphatic. The single-point-extrapolation *t* is 2.66 with 4 degrees of freedom, not reaching the P < .05 level of 2.78.

From Figure 5 and the reports cited in the first section of this paper it is clear that a real change in enforcement behavior resulted. It seems likely that the proportion of drivers exceeding the speed limits on Connecticut highways actually decreased. However, over and above these desired effects there are signs of unforeseen and unwanted reactions. Figure 7 concerns persons whose licenses were further suspended because they were convicted of driving with a suspended license, expressed as a percentage of all suspensions. This jumps from an almost consistent zero

Figure 6: Speeding violations, as percent of all traffic violations

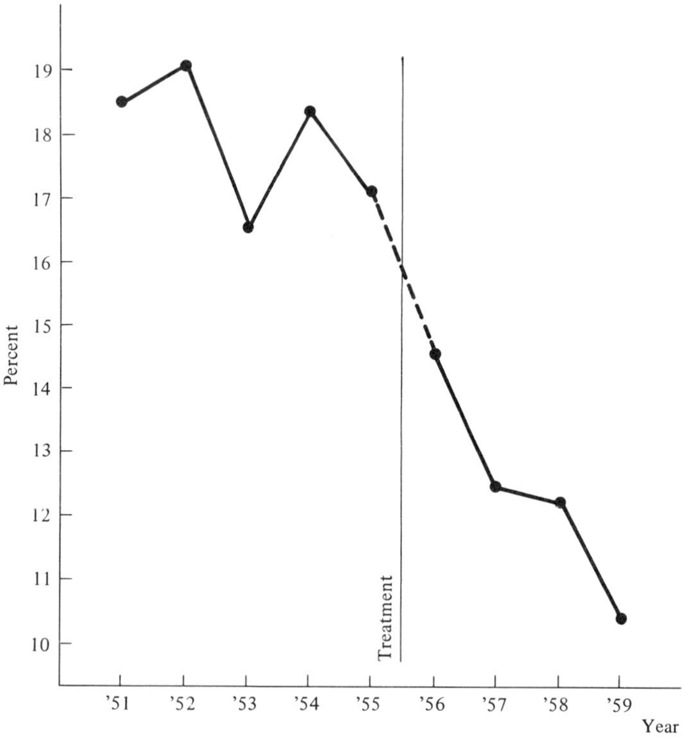

to some 4 to 6 percent. Tests of significance confirm the effect. The single-point-extrapolation t reaches an incredible 130.75, due to the very small error term which the negligible variance of the pretest scores produces. (While one feels uneasy with a practically zero variance, the consistent pretest zero does genuinely make the later values unlikely.) Our interpretation of this phenomenon is that automobile transportation has become a virtual necessity for many residents of the diffusely settled megalopolitan region that includes Connecticut, and these people are willing to risk very severe sanctions in order to continue daily routines that involve driving. Since they are willing to drive with a suspended license, suspension does not have the desired restrictive effect on this group of drivers, which is probably much larger than the number apprehended and appearing in these statistics would indicate. Alternatively, of course, the increase could result, in whole or part, from more vigorous efforts at enforcement both in the crackdown

Figure 7: Arrested while driving with a suspended license, as percent of suspensions

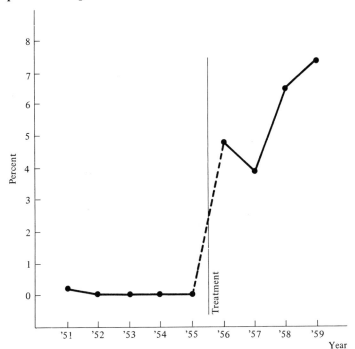

itself and in special efforts at inspection comprising a follow-up of the crackdown effort.

Figure 8 shows a reaction on the part of the legal system. Even with fewer speeding violations reaching the courts (Figure 6), the courts were more lenient in their handling of these cases as expressed by the proportion of not guilty decisions. Tests of significance are borderline. The single-point-extrapolation t is 2.42, which with but 4 degrees of freedom fails to reach significance at the $P < .05$ level, for which 2.78 would be required. Larger proportions of not guilty judgments could be the result of more cases getting to court because of tightening of precourt standards, more generous handling by judges and prosecutors, or more vigorous defenses by the accused because more is at stake. The two effects shown in Figures 7 and 8 indicate a vitiation of the punitive effects of the crackdown in operation in a society where dependence on automobile transportation is acknowledged.

Figure 8: Percent of speeding violations judged not guilty

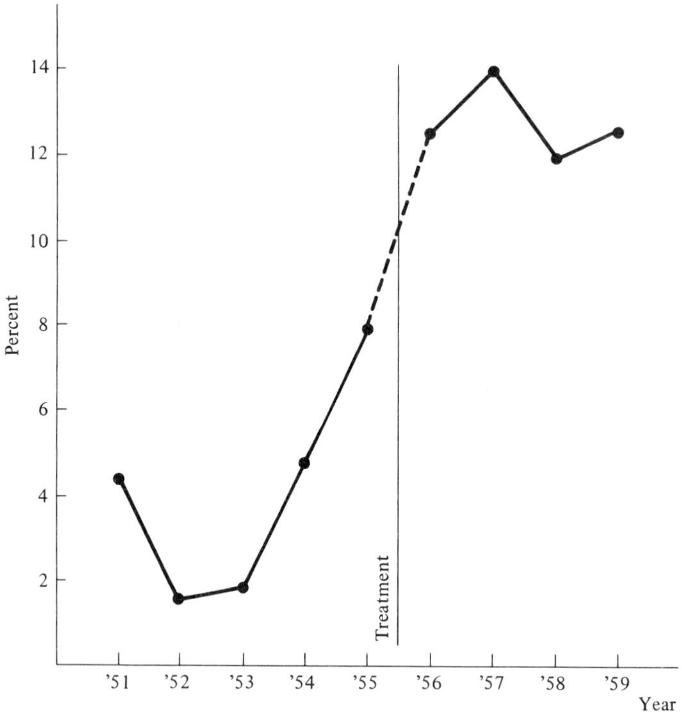

CONCLUSION

On the substantive side, the analysis has demonstrated that the Connecticut crackdown on speeding was a substantial enforcement effort, although some of its most punitive aspects were mitigated in practice. As to fatalities, we find a sustained trend toward reduction, but no unequivocal proof that they were due to the crackdown. The likelihood that the very high prior rate instigated the crackdown seriously complicates the inference.

We have, however, learned something about the response of the legal system to a reform bearing a harsh penal sanction. The courts, and probably also the police, are apparently unwilling to invoke penalties that might seem severe and unfamiliar in context. Moreover, the force of such penalties as are inflicted is vitiated by the willingness of the public to evade them. As in the case of white-collar crime, the effective punishment varies with the criminal.[12]

More important, we believe, than the specific findings of the study is the methodology here explored. While the social scientist cannot as a rule experiment on a societal scale, societal "experimentation" or abrupt focused social change is continually going on, initiated by government, business, natural forces, etc. The social scientist adds to his tools for understanding the social system when he attends to these events and documents their effects in as thorough a fashion as is possible. Insofar as correlational approaches differ from experimental analysis, it adds depth to the social scientist's work when he examines the fit of an experimental interpretation with full attention to the uncontrolled competing hypotheses.

The methodology for such quasi-experimental analysis has a long but unsystematic history, and offers much room for development. It should be remembered that not only are the raw materials shaped by the tools, but in the long run the tools are shaped by the materials upon which they work. We should not passively accept a methodology as a revealed truth, but rather should test it in use with our materials. Methodology has in fact an empirical history and its constituents have the status of empirical discoveries. The classical control group experiment is not typical of the physical sciences, but instead emerged from psychological laboratory research, and is peculiar to the social sciences and their problems.[13] Medical research has the placebo control group, and neurophysiology the sham operation control, as achievements of specific research traditions, not as logical dispensations from the philosophy of science or mathematical statistics. So too the methods for quasi-experimentation in settings like the present will emerge from an iteration of effort and criticism, in which many approaches will be rejected.

A final note on the treatment of uncontrolled variables is in order. On the one extreme there is that attitude often unwittingly inculcated in courses on experimental design, which looks askance

---

[12] The classic reference is E. H. Sutherland, *White Collar Crime* (1959). See also II. L. Ross, "Traffic Law Violation: A Folk Crime," 8 *Social Problems* 231–41 (1961).

[13] E. G. Boring, "The Nature and History of Experimental Control," 67 *Am. J. Psychology* 573–89 (1954).

at all efforts to make inferences where some variables have been left uncontrolled or where randomization has not taken place. In contrast, the quasi-experimental approach takes a radically different posture: any experiment is valid until proven invalid. The only invalidation comes from plausible rival explanations of the specific outcome. Regression effects and test-retest effects are such in many settings. An absence of randomization may in some specific way plausibly explain the obtained results. But unless one can specify such a hypothesis and the direction of its effects, it should not be regarded as invalidating. Subsequent consideration may uncover plausible rival hypotheses which have been overlooked, but such transitory validity is often the fate of laboratory experiments too.

At the other extreme is the naive attribution of cause which blithely fails to consider any explanations other than the author's favorite candidate. Such an orientation is likewise opposed. The quasi-experimentalist is obliged to search out and consider the available plausible rival hypotheses with all the vigilance at his command. While our coverage in this regard has been incomplete, we hope that we have at least illustrated such an approach.

Author index

527

Subject index